*Explorations in
Semantic Parallelism*

Explorations in Semantic Parallelism

James J. Fox

PRESS

Published by ANU Press
The Australian National University
Canberra ACT 0200, Australia
Email: anupress@anu.edu.au
This title is also available online at http://press.anu.edu.au

---

National Library of Australia Cataloguing-in-Publication entry

Author: Fox, James J, 1940 - author.

Title: Explorations in semantic parallelism / James J. Fox.

ISBN: 9781922144690 (paperback) 9781925021066 (ebook)

Subjects: Semantics. Parallelism (Linguistics)

Dewey Number: 401.43

All rights reserved. No part of this publication may be reproduced, stored in a retrieval system or transmitted in any form or by any means, electronic, mechanical, photocopying or otherwise, without the prior permission of the publisher.

Cover design by Nic Welbourn and layout by ANU Press

This edition © 2014 ANU Press

Contents

Acknowledgments.........................vii

Dedication............................xi

Comparative Issues

1. Introduction........................3
2. Roman Jakobson and the comparative study of parallelism...19
3. Trajectories in the continuing study of parallelism........41
4. Semantic parallelism in Rotenese ritual language.........91
5. 'Our ancestors spoke in pairs'..................129
6. On binary categories and primary symbols...........149
7. Category and complement....................181
8. Exploring oral formulaic language................201

The Traditional Oral Canon

9. Genealogies of the Sun and Moon................219
10. Manu Kama's road, Tepa Nilu's path..............229
11. Genealogy and topogeny....................265
12. Blood-red millet: An origin narrative..............277
13. Admonitions of the ancestors: Giving voice
    to the deceased........................283
14. To the aroma of the name: The celebration of a ritual
    of rock and tree........................295

The Christian Oral Canon

15. The appropriation of Biblical knowledge in the creation
    of new narratives of origin..................317
16. Adam and Eve on the island of Rote..............343
17. The Rotenese sermon as a linguistic performance.......355
18. Present and future research..................365
Bibliography............................387
Appendix: Petrus Malesi's Recitation Of 'The Coming Of Rice'. 419
Index..............................433

Acknowledgments

This volume in the ANU Press's Summations series comprises a collection of my published papers on parallelism to which I have added an introduction and a conclusion. I have also added a couple of papers intended to extend the scope of the presentation of my research on parallelism.

The preparation of this volume has given me the opportunity to make minor corrections and changes to each of my previously published articles. I have also slightly altered some of the introductions to these papers to give them an overall coherence in this context.

These papers follow developments in my research on parallelism and I am grateful to the publishers of the original articles for their permission to reprint them.

I wish to acknowledge my debt to the organisations and presses that originally hosted these publications. Specifically, I express my thanks to the following.

The Koninklijk Instituut voor Taal-, Land en Volkenkunde for permission to publish the following three papers

- 1971 'Semantic parallelism in Rotinese ritual language' in *Bijdragen tot de Taal-, Land- en Volkenkunde* 127:215–55.
- 1989 'To the aroma of the name: the celebration of a Rotinese ritual of rock and tree' in *Bijdragen tot de Taal-, Land- en Volkenkunde* 145:520–38.
- 2003 'Admonitions of the ancestors: giving voice to the deceased in Rotinese mortuary rituals', in P. J. M. Nas, G. Persoon and R. Jaffe (eds) *Framing Indonesian Realities: Essays in symbolic anthropology in honour of Reimar Schefold*, pp. 15–26. Leiden: KITLV Press.

Cambridge University Press for permission to publish the following two papers

- 1974 '"Our ancestors spoke in pairs": Rotinese views of language, dialect and code' in R. Bauman and J. Sherzer (eds) *Explorations in the Ethnography of Speaking*, pp. 65–85. Cambridge: Cambridge University Press.
- 1988 '"Manu Kama's road, Tepa Nilu's path": theme, narrative and formula in Rotinese ritual language' in J. J. Fox (ed.) *To Speak in Pairs: Essays on the ritual languages of eastern Indonesia*, pp. 161–201. Cambridge: Cambridge University Press.

Pacific Linguistics at The Australian National University for permission to publish the following two papers

- 1982 'The Rotinese Chotbah as a linguistic performance', in A. Halim, L. Carrington and S. A. Wurm (eds) *Accent on Variety*, Papers from the Third

International Conference on Linguistics Vol. 3, pp. 311–18. Canberra: Pacific Linguistics.

- 2010 'Exploring oral formulaic language: a five poet analysis' in J. Bowden and N. P. Himmelman (eds) *A Journey through Austronesian and Papuan Linguistics and Cultural Space*. Canberra: Pacific Linguistics.

The Association of Social Anthropologists of the Commonwealth for permission to publish the following paper

- 1975 'On binary categories and primary symbols: some Rotinese perspectives', in R. Willis (ed.) *The Interpretation of Symbolism*, ASA Studies 2, pp. 99–132. London: Malaby Press.

Southeast Asia Program Publications at Cornell University for permission to publish the following paper that appeared in the journal Indonesia

- 1983 'Adam and Eve on the island of Roti: a conflation of oral and written traditions' in *Indonesia* 36:15–23.

University of Michigan Press for permission to publish the following paper

- 1989 'Category and complement: binary ideologies and the organization of dualism in eastern Indonesia', in D. Maybury-Lewis and U. Almagor (eds) *The Attraction of Opposites: Thought and society in a dualistic mode*, pp. 33–56. Ann Arbor: University of Michigan Press.

A version of the paper entitled 'Blood-red millet: an origin narrative' was originally published in German as follows

- 2008 'Blutrote Hirse. Eine locale Ursprungserzählung von der Insel Roti', in V. Gottowik, H. Jebens and E. Platte (eds) *Zwischen Aneignung und Verfremdung: Ethnologische Gratwanderung*, pp. 401–9. Frankfurt: Campus.

I express my gratitude to Peter de Ridder and the Peter de Ridder Press, which appears to have ceased publishing in 1986, for the following paper

- 1977 'Roman Jakobson and the comparative study of parallelism', in C. H. van Schooneveld and D. Armstrong (eds) *Roman Jakobson: Echoes of his scholarship*, pp. 59–90. Lisse: Peter de Ridder Press.

I also express my gratitude to the Assosiasi Antropologi Indonesia for the following paper

- 1997 'Genealogies of the sun and moon: interpreting the canon of Rotinese ritual chants', in E. K. M. Masinambow (ed.) *Koentjaraningrat dan Antropologi di Indonesia*, pp. 321–30. Jakarta: Assosiasi Antropologi Indonesia/Yayasan Obor.

Over the years, many individuals have supported me in my research on parallelism. In the endnotes to my various papers, I specifically thank those who gave me advice and comment at the time. Here I want to thank those who have been involved in helping me put together this volume and assisting me in my current research on parallelism. First and foremost, I thank my wife, Irmgard, who has been with me from the time of our first fieldwork and, over the years, has read and reread all my writings, and corrected and advised me on my work. I would also like to thank all of the Rotenese poets whom I have known and recorded over many decades but I would like to extend special thanks to Esau Pono, my oldest living colleague on Rote, whom I first came to know in 1965 and with whom I have continued to work until the present. He is a close friend and collaborator with whom I share many memories. I would also like to thank three individuals who have joined me in my most recent research efforts. The first of these is the late Dr Tom Therik, who helped organise the first three gatherings of poets on Bali; Dr Lintje Pellu, who joined the second gathering of poets and has organised and joined all the subsequent poet gatherings; and Dr David Butterworth, who worked as my research assistant and joined our third gathering. In addition, I would like to thank Jennifer Sheehan of the Cartography Unit in the College of Asia and the Pacific for all of the charts and diagrams she has produced for this volume.

For the record, these charts, diagrams and figures are all of my creation; the translations from the Rotenese are my personal attempts to convey the beauty of Rotenese poetry while still retaining its parallel structure; and the photographs of Rote in this volume are from my extensive archive of photographs dating back to 1965. The film clip of the poet, Peu Malesi, included in this volume was taken by Tim Asch during our joint film expedition to Rote in 1977. I was responsible for sound recording.

Dedication

'Old Meno', Stefanus Adulanu, my first and foremost teacher on Rote

Comparative Issues

1. Introduction

Since 1965, when I first began to record and attempt to understand the ritual poetry of the Rotenese, the study of semantic parallelism has been a major focus of my research. My chief concern has been with the semantics of canonical parallelism. In my view, the study of parallelism and particularly the study of canonical parallelism is no minor subject but is, in fact, a matter of central theoretical importance for both anthropology and linguistics. To introduce this collection of papers, let me begin by offering some explanation of the importance I attach to research on this topic.

Parallelism as a focus for research

Parallelism describes the common tendency to resort to the pairing of words and phrases to provide emphasis, authority or significance to an expression of ideas. It is a common, frequently used rhetorical device in many forms of elevated speech. It is also a recurrent feature of poetic discourse—what the linguist Roman Jakobson has called the 'poetic artifice…of recurrent returns', or, in a similar vein, what the poet Gerald Manley Hopkins referred to as 'the repeated figure' in poetry. Examples of such parallelism are numerous and can be encountered daily. Winston Churchill's speech to the Commons on 4 June 1940 is a ringing example of the use of parallelism. I have intentionally arranged this passage to highlight its rhetorical pairings:

> We shall not flag nor fail.
>
> We shall go on to the end.
>
> We shall fight in France
>
> and on the seas and oceans;
>
> We shall fight with growing confidence and growing strength
>
> in the air…
>
> We shall fight on beaches,
>
> landing grounds,
>
> in fields,
>
> in streets and on the hills.

Canonical parallelism is something different: a linguistic phenomenon that is more specific and more circumscribed but for that reason, theoretically more engaging. Canonical parallelism draws on the tendency involved in the common use of recurrent, parallel phrasing but it defines what terms and phrases may form pairs. This culturally defined, more obligatory aspect of parallelism constitutes what I refer to as 'canonical parallelism'.

In 1753 Robert Lowth adopted the term 'parallelism' (or in Latin, *parallelismus membrorum*) to describe the linguistic phenomenon that he encountered in his research on Hebrew poetry: 'a certain equality, resemblance, or parallelism between members of each period...as if fitted to each other by a kind of rule or measure.' Thus the term parallelism was originally used to designate a regulated correspondence of terms and phrases. In time, however, this usage of the term widened and its technical sense became eroded, requiring further specification. Roman Jakobson introduced the idea of a 'canonic parallelism' and I have appropriated this usage in my research. His designation of this phenomenon, pointing to both its prevalence and its pertinence, is clear:

> Those poetic patterns where certain similarities between successive verbal sequences are compulsory or enjoy a high preference appear to be widespread in the languages of the world, and they are particularly gratifying both for the study of poetic language and for linguistic analysis in general. Such traditional types of canonic parallelism offer us an insight into the various forms of relationship among different aspects of language. (Jakobson 1966:399)

The first identification of parallelism as a distinct means of poetic composition was made in relation to Hebrew poetry, and this Biblical insight gave impetus to a growing recognition of the occurrence of parallelism and its significance in oral poetic compositions throughout the world. Parallelism occurs in widely diverse oral poetic traditions, from Finno-Ugric and Mongolian to Chinese and Vietnamese, as well as in numerous Dravidian, Austronesian and Amerindian languages, with particularly elaborate forms in Mayan languages. Historically, however, the Hebrew traditions of parallelism, which have now been linked to similar traditions in Canaanite poetry, were the starting point for the study of parallelism. These traditions form part of a more ancient tradition that extends back to beginnings in Sumer when the first known forms of ritual poetry were committed to writing.

Some of the oldest existing examples of canonical parallelism can be found on cuneiform tablets that date to at least 1750 BC. Samuel Noah Kramer spent much of his life deciphering these cuneiform materials and was one of the leading authorities on the use of parallelism in the traditions of the Middle East (Kramer 1979.. In an effort to convey the beauty of these often fragmented texts, he recruited the poet Diana Wolkstein to assist him to translate a set of the ritual texts relating to the goddess Inanna. The following short specimen, an example of this collaboration, describes the beginnings of time before the planting of the sacred Huluppu tree from which both the throne and the marriage bed of Inanna were carved. Its parallelism is evident:

In the first days, in the very first days,

In the first nights, in the very first nights,

In the first years, in the very first years,

In the first days when everything needed was brought into being,

In the first days when everything needed was properly nourished,

When bread was baked in the shrines of the land,

And bread was tasted in the homes of the land,

When heaven had moved away from earth,

And earth had separated from heaven

And the name of man was fixed...[1]

These lines—and the great corpus of similar compositions from which they come—establish the existence of parallelism as a means of poetic diction that stands at the beginnings of human literature.

In terms of understanding this parallelism, the breakthrough in scholarship came with the recognition that the composition of parallel lines and phrases—Lowth's correspondence of 'words to words'—was based on a repertoire of fixed word pairs and, with the discovery at Ras Shamra in 1928 of a cuneiform library of Ugaritic texts, that many of the parallel terms in Hebrew were shared by the Canaanite poetic tradition. This gave rise to an extensive scholarship.[2]

Although for the most part confined within the defined bounds of its own scholarship, there is hardly a linguistic observation within this Biblical research that does not relate to the wider body of comparative research on traditions of parallelism throughout the world. It is this comparative dimension that is critical.

---

1 This brief illustrative passage is taken from DianaWolkstein and Samuel Noah Kramer's *Inanna, Queen of Heaven and Earth: Her stories and hymns from Sumer* (1983:4,). Kramer made an earlier translation of these lines, which appeared in his *From the Poetry of Sumer* (1979:23). The two translations are similar and both provide a strong sense of the parallelism in Sumerian poetry.
2 See Mitchell Dahood's summary account of the history of this scholarship (Dahood and Penar 1972) and his monumental efforts (1975, 1981) to add yet more Ugaritic–Hebrew 'parallel pairs' to his extensive, if not exhaustive, annotated list of shared terms.

For this reason, the first paper I have included in this volume is an extended comparative examination of the studies of parallelism and of the major textual sources of parallel poetry. This chapter, 'Roman Jakobson and the comparative study of parallelism', which I have substantially updated, was originally written in recognition of the work of the linguist Roman Jakobson, who had a continuing interest in the study of parallelism throughout his lifetime and who wrote profoundly and influentially about parallelism as a linguistic phenomenon.

The Jakobson bequest

I began my own research on parallelism through the personal promptings of Roman Jakobson whom I met soon after I took up a position in the Department of Anthropology at Harvard University in 1969. I had already gathered an extensive corpus of Rotenese ritual chants during fieldwork on the island of Rote in 1965–66. Having completed my doctoral dissertation at Oxford—a thesis concerned mainly with the social organisation of the Rotenese of the domain of Termanu—I was beginning to turn my attention to translating and interpreting some of the chants within this corpus.

The first chant I translated, analysed and published was one of the most beautiful compositions I had recorded. This chant, entitled *Dela Koli ma Seko Bunak*, was recited by the oldest poet in Termanu, Stefanus Adulanu, who was both teacher and mentor in my study of Rotenese ritual language. My translation and analysis were published in 1971 as 'Semantic parallelism in Rotinese ritual language' (Chapter 3 in this volume).[3] Citing Jakobson's 'Grammatical parallelism and its Russian facet' as my starting point, I also attempted in this paper to set out the comparative evidence for the use of canonical parallelism, particularly among other Indonesian populations. My principal goal for the paper was to set out as clearly as possible a single, relatively long ritual language text to illustrate the workings of Rotenese parallelism.

At a personal level, the paper allowed me to show Jakobson just what I was working on and to provide some basis for our subsequent discussions. During my time at Harvard, I would meet with him at his invitation and invariably at his home, which was a short walk from my office in William James Hall. For the most part, Jakobson would talk and I would listen. The same was true when we had lunch

---

3 Over several hundred years there have been many different spellings given to the island that I refer to in this volume as 'Rote'. Whereas Dutch sources frequently referred to the island as 'Rotti', the most common designation on English maps at the time of my first fieldwork was 'Roti'. I adopted this designation and used it for most of my publications; however, the official Indonesian designation for the island established its name as 'Rote' and I therefore followed suit, using 'Rote' in later publications. It is perhaps relevant to add that in the central domain of Termanu and in various other dialect areas, there is no initial 'r'. Hence, as I explain in my discussion of ritual placenames, in Termanu the most common name for Rote is *Lote do Kale*.

together and were joined by his wife, Krystyna Pomorska-Jakobson. Jakobson seemed to want to prime me with references to the work of other linguists that would assist me in my own research and would always try to situate his references to particular studies within a personal context. There was no doubt that for him parallelism was a central concern. He referred to the study of parallelism as 'the double door' linking linguistics and anthropology.

At the time that I wrote my first paper on Rotenese parallelism, I was one of the supervisors of Gary Gossen's PhD thesis on Chamula oral traditions, research that was eventually published in 1974 as *Chamulas in the World of the Sun*. Gossen's work gave me an initial glimpse into the rich parallel traditions of the Maya and set me off in search of other linguistic traditions of parallelism. These comparative efforts eventuated in my paper 'Roman Jakobson and the comparative study of parallelism', which was published in 1977 with 33 other contributions in a tribute volume entitled *Roman Jakobson: Echoes of his scholarship*. Chapter 2 in the present volume is based on that original paper, but since that paper was written more than 30 years ago, I have felt it necessary to expand upon it and update references to new sources that I have subsequently discovered and other work that has appeared in the continuing study of parallelism.

By the time my tribute to Jakobson appeared, I had moved to The Australian National University to take up a position as Professorial Fellow in the Department of Anthropology in the then Research School of Pacific Studies. Jakobson kept in touch by regularly sending me copies of his latest reprints. In response to my paper, he sent me a reprint, 'A few remarks on Peirce, pathfinder in the science of language' (1977), on which he wrote: 'To James J. Fox with thanks for the convincing parallel to my Parallelism, Roman Jakobson.'

Jakobson's selection of this particular reprint with its focus on the work of Charles Sanders Peirce was, in my view, intended to send me a message. He was already familiar with the beginnings of my analysis of Rotenese ritual language and my use of the concept of a 'dyadic set', which could be specified by the simple notation (a,b), to refer to paired terms. Hence, I took his selection of quotes from Peirce in the reprint—'[a] *dyad* consists of two *subjects* brought into oneness' or 'there is an element of twoness in every set'—as explicit encouragement of my efforts of analysis since such notions also underline my understanding of a dyadic set.

Parallelism figured prominently in the framework Jakobson created in his study of language and poetics. His recourse, in *Fundamentals of Language* (Jakobson and Halle 1956), to the use of opposition to articulate this framework resulted in his formulation of two contrasting aspects of language: a bipolar structure consisting of metaphoric and metonymic poles of discourse. A contiguous sequential arrangement of elements defines the metonymic pole, whereas a selective articulation of elements defines the metaphoric pole. The one relies on contiguity and results in syntactic relations among elements; the other relies on similarity and results in semantic relations among elements. It is precisely in this context that Jakobson made a particularly cogent argument for the significance of parallelism:

> In verbal art the interaction of these elements is especially pronounced. Rich material for the study of this relationship is to be found in verse patterns which require a compulsory parallelism between adjacent lines, for example in Biblical poetry or in the West Finnic and, to some extent, the Russian oral traditions. This provides an objective criterion of what in a given speech community acts as a correspondence. (Jakobson and Halle 1956:77)

This understanding of metaphor as semantic selection could be considered a departure point in my research, but from the beginnings of my 'explorations' of parallelism, I have been interested in investigating the connectivity of semantic elements. As such, the dyadic set can rarely be considered on its own; its particular terms or elements have invariably to be considered as part of a larger network of relationships.

There are other aspects of canonical parallelism that also require great attention. One of the major goals of my research has been to provide a comprehensive study of one still-living tradition of canonical parallelism.

Arrangement of the volume

The papers that comprise this volume were written over a period of more than 40 years. They chart the development of my understanding of parallelism in general and the Rotenese tradition of parallelism in particular.

This volume is divided into three sections. The first section is made up of eight chapters that deal with general issues of parallelism. These chapters include this introduction, an initial survey of the literature on parallelism, which I wrote as a tribute to Roman Jakobson, and another chapter that attempts to update this earlier survey with an extended examination of recent research on the comparative study of parallelism. The remaining chapters in this section focus on the specific traditions of canonical parallelism among the Rotenese of eastern Indonesia.

Each of these chapters is a distinct exploration of Rotenese parallelism, developing a variety of analytic perspectives and situating the use of this parallelism within its social, linguistic and historical context. In particular, Chapter 4, 5 and 6 were foundational for my understanding of Rotenese parallelism. They were all written in the 1970s as early research efforts. Chapter 4 was intended to present and to analyse a complete Rotenese composition, setting out as clearly as possible the main characteristics of Rotenese 'ritual language' as compositions in strict canonical parallelism Chapter 5 was written for a symposium on the ethnography of speaking. In it, I was particularly interested to examine the use of ritual language in relation to ordinary Rotenese discourse and to the use of Malay (and eventually Indonesian), which was adopted as a register for elite communication on Rote from the early eighteenth century. Chapter 6 was written in an attempt to define a symbolic core to the Rotenese ritual canon.

Although each of these papers covers different general aspects of Rotenese parallelism, these paper engage, in varying degrees, in similar modes of analysis, examining, in particular, the relational character of Rotenese parallel semantics and the use of networks as a means of comprehending these relationships. These papers also hint at the use of dialects in ritual language, a subject that became more important in my later work.

By contrast, Chapters 7 and 8 are concerned with other aspects of parallelism. Chapter 7 was written for a symposium on 'dual organisation'. In the chapter, I am particularly concerned to distinguish parallelism as a linguistic phenomenon from other forms of dual structures that are dependent on the analogical ordering of categories. Parallelism can be a resource for the symbolic construction of a variety of dual structures. Its use, however, is selective and should not be confused with these forms of dualism. Finally Chapter 8, written and eventually published in 2010, deals with the use of 'formulaic' expressions in Rotenese ritual language. In it, I examine a few of the formulae used by five different poets in composing some 18 or so lines all excerpted from single chant *Suti Solo do Bina Bane,* which I first began recording in 1965. Although this paper is merely illustrative of the use of such formulae, it could only have been written after extended examination of numerous compositions over many decades.

The second section of this volume goes on to examine the traditional Rotenese oral canon, knowledge of which can only be conveyed in ritual language. This is a rich canon that has taken many years to compile and fathom and has involved numerous return visits to Rote since 1965. Although I have recorded ritual language compositions from all of the main dialect areas of Rote, over the years, I have concentrated on an in-depth recording of the ritual language of the speech community of Termanu. Most of the traditional oral canon cited in this volume comes from this single speech community and reflects my growing personal involvement in the social life of that domain. Based in Termanu at the centre of the island, however, I have been able to look both east and west in my research.

The five chapters that comprise this second section provide a glimpse—but only a glimpse—of what was once regarded as most venerated of Rotenese ancestral knowledge. Much of this knowledge has to do with mythic relations between the Sun and Moon and the Lords of the Sea. Chapter 9 was written as an attempt to sort out some the genealogical relationships among these heavenly ancestral figures as means of ordering the different parts of the Rotenese canon of origin chants. Chapter 10 examines the oldest recorded specimen of ritual language, a text originally recorded by the Dutch linguist, J.C.G. Jonker, probably in the late nineteenth century and published without translation in 1911. In translating and commenting on this beautiful composition, I have tried to identify some of recurring themes that dominate Rotenese conceptions of human life. Chapter 11 examines a particular origin chant that recounts the coming of the seeds of rice and millet to the island and their dissemination throughout the fields of the domains. Just as persons, so, too, places on Rote are given dual names in ritual recitations. Each part of the island of Rote—its many domains, individual fields and gardens, and its innumerable significant sites—possesses at least one and sometimes a succession of dyadic ritual names. In Chapter 11, I introduce the ideas of 'topogeny' as an ordered recitation of place names that serves, as does the ordered succession of names in a genealogy, to provide a narrative structure. Not only is the use of topogeny a common feature in Rotenese ritual language compositions, it is also a common compositional feature in other traditions of parallelism. Chapter 12 offers a brief examination of another chant that recounts the origin of a specific variety of millet.

Mortuary chants form a large component of the traditional Rotenese canon. Chapter 13 provides an example of a mortuary chant of particular interest in that the deceased is given voice at his own funeral to admonish the living before departing for the land of the dead. Chapter 14 is an account of the mortuary rituals that I sponsored for the 'Head of the Earth'—Stefanus Adulanu, known as 'Old Meno'—who was my teacher and collaborator in my initial efforts to learn ritual language in 1965–66. The Chapter examines the importance of the final mortuary memorials of 'rock and tree' erected to notable individuals and discusses the significance that Rotenese accord to the 'aroma' of the name that lives on in memory long after death.

The third section of this volume looks at how, under the influence of Christianity, another sacred canon has been created and is now, appropriately, expressed in ritual language. A crucial factor in Rote's history was the adoption of Christianity by various domain rulers in the early eighteenth century. The adoption of Christianity was closely linked to the use of Malay and particularly to the use of the Malay Bible. This led to the early establishment of local domain schools, creating a Malay-speaking, educated elite on the island and more widely in the Timor area. Malay, in various forms, became an accepted speech register on the island—the only speech register that was considered, for at least 150 years, as the proper vehicle for writing and the only appropriate vehicle for preaching the Scriptures.

This situation began to change towards the end of the nineteenth century. Increasingly, in the twentieth century, parallel compositions in ritual language became the vehicle for Biblical knowledge among a new cohort of local Rotenese preachers. Three chapters in section three give some idea of these changes. Chapter 15 discusses the historical creation of this new Christian oral canon and the appropriation of Biblical knowledge for its creation.

The degree to which individual recitations conform to Biblical foundations varies. At present, there are many compositions in ritual language that merge traditional and Biblical forms of knowledge. Chapter 16 provides an example of one such recitation that in its retelling of the story of Adam and Eve purports to recount the origin of death. Finally Chapter 17 gives an example of the use of parallelism in a Rotenese sermon. As knowledge of the traditional oral canon declines, the use of ritual language is becoming ever more important for the performance of Christian ceremonies.

In 2006, I embarked on a renewed effort to understand 'Rotenese ritual language' more systematically across the entire island. Instead of attempting to ferret out particular Rotenese ritual-language specialists in their local settings, I began by inviting poets from different dialect areas to Bali for week-long recording sessions. I relied on a few leading poets to select other poets whom they knew either personally or by reputation. Bali was strategically chosen as a gathering point specifically to remove, or at least lessen, the various cultural requirements that restrict local recitation. For the poets, the plane trip ('above the clouds') to the 'Land of Bali and the Water of the Gods' (*Bali Dae//Dewata Oe*) provided a separation from Rote that was liberating. Together in a group, with poets from other parts of Rote, most of the poets who came to Bali were intent on demonstrating their domain's special linguistic heritage.

To date, I have held eight recording sessions on Bali between 2006 and 2013 involving 27 different Rotenese poets from 10 separate domains on the island. The initial objective of the project, which continues, was to gather as wide and as rich a corpus of ritual compositions as possible from the full spectrum of Rotenese cultural traditions among the different domains and from as many distinct dialects as was possible. The past several years have been perhaps the most fruitful period of research on Rotenese parallelism.

The last chapter in this volume discusses this research in some detail. It serves therefore not so much as a conclusion to this volume as a kind of on-going discussion of current and future research directions for the comparative study of semantic parallelism.

Explorations in Semantic Parallelism

Theme and idiom in the two oral canons

The distinction that I make between a traditional oral canon and a Christian oral canon points to an emerging difference in the nature of ritual language compositions and, more significantly, a difference in a general regard for foundational knowledge in Rotenese culture. These changes reflect the Rotenese conversion to Christianity but more importantly the assimilation and appropriation of Christian ideas within Rotenese culture. They also reflect a change in language usage: a switch from an exclusive reliance on Malay as the vehicle for Christian preaching to a greater use of Rotenese in combination with Malay. I examine these historical changes in Chapter 16.

Although these distinct canons are intended to convey different sources of knowledge, the idioms and cultural concerns of the two canons remain much the same. Thus, for example, the two canons are deeply concerned with origins: the beginnings of things and their consequences. In the traditional canon, the most important recitations constitute a special set of origin narratives, whereas in the Christian canon, the most frequent recitations involve the retelling of Genesis. Both Chapter 15 and Chapter 16 give examples of these retellings.

Similarly, in both canons there is a great emphasis on speaking—a continued internal dialogue among the actors of the narratives. In the traditional canon, the Sun and Moon direct their children, their sons argue with the Lords of Ocean and Sea, the birds of the air and creatures of the depths oppose, object and dispute with their interlocutors, spiders and stick-insects announce their creative actions, and in the funeral chants, the dead are given leave to instruct and admonish the living. In the Christian canon, God speaks His creation into being; He speaks to Adam while Eve speaks with the serpent. Speaking, for the Rotenese, is the indispensable feature of sociability. Both canons reflect this cultural obsession.

Throughout both canons, there is also a continuing reliance on a botanic idiom to describe human development and personal interrelations. Botanic icons—a host of different plants and trees, each with its particular characteristics—are used as images for growth and differentiation, for the spread of knowledge and for the paths of life. The world may be metaphorically represented as a great banyan tree with branches leading in different directions; trees whose branches scrape together provide a prime image of social interaction; in rituals, boys are likened to banana and sugar cane; women to coconut and areca nut. Similarly, in the Christian canon, the establishment of Christianity is seen as the planting of a new tree, and its spread, like the spread of rice and millet recounted in the traditional canon, involves its dissemination and successful cultivation in new fields.

Another feature of both canons is the narrative recurrence of the journey. Chant characters move through an identifiable landscape and their journeys are significant. These journeys are undertaken in the search for companionship or for a spouse, for wisdom and special knowledge or simply for a resting place in Heaven or in the realm of the dead. Journeys proceed through a succession of named places whose exegesis is often vital to an understanding of the quest. Many Rotenese ritual-language narratives follow a structure of ordered locations or more explicitly recount an ordered succession of placenames—what I call a 'topogeny' that has similar significance to the personal succession of names in a genealogy. For the Rotenese, life is a journey and their rituals proclaim this view.

A more specific image but one that is central to this world view is the idea of the 'orphan and widow', which I discuss in Chapter 10. Virtually all the mortuary-ritual recitations of the traditional canon involve this image in concrete terms, but underlying the specifics of mourning and separation is the more general understanding that death, as the fate of all humanity, is the one journey that is common to everyone and thus the denominator that reduces everyone to the same status. This view—that everyone is an orphan and a widow—is enunciated in both the traditional canon and the Christian canon.

Personal engagement

There is also a deeply personal dimension to this research. The essays in this volume represent research that was begun in the 1960s and has continued to the present. This research has involved a continuing personal engagement with master poets whose oral compositions I have been able to record and discuss in my attempts to translate and comprehend them. This personal engagement has figured prominently in my work and is clearly articulated in the chapters that make up this volume. Most of these poets I consider as friends. Some have been my closest friends on Rote.

Chapter 4 for example, contains a composition entitled *Dela Koli ma Seko Bunak* by the poet Stefanus Adulanu, who was known simply as Old Meno (Meno Tua) at the time of my first fieldwork. In 1965–66, Old Meno took me under his wing and became my principal teacher of ritual language. Elsewhere I have written at length about my involvement with Old Meno. Here it is perhaps enough to quote some of my earlier comments on the way he coaxed and guided me to an understanding of ritual language:

> [Old Meno] became for me my most profound mentor. He had a way of teaching which I found at first frustrating but I soon came to realize that it was—and is—the most essential way to teach. Meno would 'guide' me to an understanding but never make explicit what he was guiding me toward. Thus it was always up to me to make connections and come to my own understanding. Much of our time together involved circling an

understanding and only when he felt that I had achieved some degree of comprehension could we move on further...Learning from Meno was one of the most valuable experiences of my life. (Fox 1992:109)

Old Meno died before my first return visit to Rote so I was only able to record him in 1965–66, yet in my corpus, Old Meno's compositions are among the finest and most significant pieces I have recorded. Many of them are origin narratives that were, at the time I recorded him, considered ritually circumscribed and inherently powerful. On one occasion, Old Meno told me explicitly that he had left out a key passage from a narrative but he also made it clear to me what that passage revealed. The composition *Dela Koli ma Seko Bunak* is in fact linked to the restricted corpus of origin narratives. When Old Meno recited this chant, he left out its origin dimensions and instead presented it as a mortuary chant. Years later, another chanter, Seu Ba'i, who had actually heard Old Meno recite this chant for me, revealed that it was in fact the chant that recounted the origin of two prominent rocky outcrops, Sua Lai ma Batu Hun, that are considered defining natural icons of the domain of Termanu. Seu Ba'i gave me his version and I have subsequently recorded yet another version of this chant.

In addition to Seu Ba'i, Peu Malesi was another Termanu poet from whom I recorded a great deal of material. In 1965, he was the first poet who dared to provide me with my first recording of the origin of fire and cooking, excerpts of which are included in Chapter 6. On my second long stay on Rote, in 1972–73, he visited the house where I stayed at Ufa Len so frequently that he became my regular companion and drinking partner.

Peu Malesi had great versatility in his compositions. Chapter 11 contains his narrative of the origin of rice and millet together with his extended topogeny of the spread of these seeds throughout Rote; Chapter 15 contains his account of the origin of death, a version of Adam and Eve in a Rotenese setting. Importantly as well, towards the end of my second visit, Peu Malesi took a prominent role in the performance of the mortuary ceremonies that I sponsored in honour of Old Meno. In 1977 and again in 1978, when I visited Rote with the filmmaker Tim Asch, we were able to film him chanting. He appears in both films that we made: *The Water of Words* (1983) and *Spear and Sword* (1988). Although Peu Malesi had great abilities, he was unable to replace Old Meno as a teacher. Peu Malesi could recite at great length but could not provide any kind of reflective exegesis on his own compositions. Often I would work with him to transcribe one of his chants. Invariably he would refer to the voice on the tape recorder as an externalised third person. His response to most of my questions was to recite another (often similar) passage.

During my first fieldwork on Rote, I spent time in Oe Handi in the domain of Thie, living briefly in the house of the oldest and most renowned poet in that domain, N. D. Pah, who was known as Guru Pah. His first question to me when I arrived at his house was why it had taken so long for me to come to see him. The origin chants that he recited for me were as revelatory as those that I had recorded from Old Meno and Peu Malesi. These chants and subsequent chants that I recorded in Thie also provided me with another perspective on the 'traditional oral canon' as I have described it: basically, that this canon may once have constituted a more coherent repertoire of recitations recounting relations between the Sun and the Moon and the shark and crocodile as Lords of the Sea. What I was encountering in my fieldwork were separate fragments of a large whole. This is an idea that I develop in Chapter 9, 'Genealogies of the Sun and Moon', and it underlies my continuing efforts to gather chants across dialect areas of the island.

Yet another poet of considerable ability whom I was able to record in 1965–66 was Stefanus Amalo, who was almost the same age as Old Meno. I was able to visit him only once in Pua Mata, where he lived, but he came to visit me in Ufa Len. One evening, close to midnight, he suddenly arrived and told me he wished me to record his recitation. This recitation, *Pau Balo ma Bola Lungi*, came to roughly 390 lines. I have since recorded other versions of this chant but none that compares in length or beauty with this first version.

The person who became my closest friend on Rote and eventually my most reliable ritual-language commentator was Esau Pono, whom I hardly knew in 1965–66. At that time, he was a young man, only a few years older than me, and was involved in a difficult dispute over the payment of bride-wealth to marry a woman from a clan that was based in Sosadale near Ufa Len. Six years later, by the time of my second visit, he had begun to gain a reputation as a local preacher and I turned to him for his help to provide the Christian component to the traditional ceremonies that I held in Old Meno's honour. On subsequent visits, we became good friends. Thus, as part of our film work in Termanu, Tim Asch filmed 'Pak Pono', as he was known, conducting a Sunday service in the local church near Ufa Len. Afterwards, we invited him to Canberra to help with transcriptions and translations.

In the years that have followed, I have kept in close contact with Pak Pono. During this time, he has become Termanu's most respected ritual chanter. In terms of knowledge, fluency and versatility, he is without a rival within the domain and is well known among the chanters of the island. Therefore when I embarked on my project to record poets from all the dialect areas of Rote, I recruited Pak Pono to join me in my effort and he has continued to participate in each subsequent recording session, helping also to select and invite other notable chanters. In the process, I have been able to record from him two separate recitations of the chant *Suti Solo do Bina Bane*, but more importantly still, I have relied upon his deep knowledge of his language and traditions. Like Old Meno, he is able to reflect and comment on his own compositions and those of others.

Figure 1.1: Esau Pono, poet and preacher, my oldest friend and collaborator on Rote

As part of new research on the dialects of Rote, I have come to know at least another dozen master poets. Among these poets, there is one who stands out. This is Ande Ruy from the domain of Ringgou. At present, 'Pak Ande' is the most able poet and performer on Rote and is generally recognised as such. Pak Ande is a born showman: he sings, he drums, he plays the Rotenese *sasandu* and he is an exceptionally fluent chanter in a variety of modes. As a consequence, he is frequently called upon for official cultural performances.

Pak Ande and Pak Pono, to whom he defers, have participated in all the recording sessions I have held. Pak Ande has provided me with a torrent of material, which I have struggled to understand because of the density of its metaphors and allusions and because it is in a dialect that I find most difficult to comprehend. Even Pak Pono has admitted to me that he, too, has difficulty at times in understanding Pak Ande. The second of the Genesis recitations in Chapter 16 is a good example of a Pak Ande composition. In many ways, Pak Ande is like Peu Malesi. The exegesis that he offers of his recitations often involves more recitation.

All Rotenese chants are bound in ritual. They are dense revelations that require a degree of exegesis (and possible paraphrase) to make them intelligible. When I began recording these chants, particularly the origin narratives, they were considered as restricted knowledge. For that reason, I have hesitated to publish in full my main corpus of origin narratives. Chapter 6 in this volume provides a selection of passages from the narrative of the origins of fire and of cooking with appropriate commentary, but not the whole of the narrative. Similarly, I have published passages from the narrative of the origin of weaving in the paper 'Figure shark and pattern crocodile' (1980), and various passages from the narrative of the house in a paper, 'Memories of ridgepoles and crossbeams' (Fox 1993).

Over the past 45 years or more, the restrictions on Rotenese chant revelations that once applied have gradually lifted. I have discussed this issue with many poets, including both Pak Pono and Pak Ande, and all of these poets have assured me that it would now be appropriate to publish my corpus of origin narratives, particularly the long versions of the chants that I recorded in 1965–66. This represents yet another project that I have before me. As I see it, there remains much to be done before I can feel satisfied in having presented the full richness of Rotenese ritual language.

A note on the transcription of Rotenese

As I explain in this volume, Rotenese rulers established local Malay-based schools in their different domains beginning early in the second quarter of the seventeenth century. Until nearly the end of the nineteenth century, all writing was confined to Malay; however, this began to change in the twentieth century, as the Rotenese—particularly schoolteachers (known as 'Malay Masters')—began writing their own language. For this purpose, they relied on the same Latin script used for Malay. Various attempts were made to modify this script, but in the end, the same script used for Malay was used for Rotenese. This was not a perfect solution because Rotenese dialects have sets of long vowels as well as short vowels (e, o, u, i), but it was adequate for communication and did not jeopardise understanding. Except for a few words, the contrast between long and short vowels does not produce phonemic distinctions. Moreover, there are regular patterns to the use of these long and short vowels. Thus, for example, the second (and third) vowels in a sequence of similar vowels (as in partial reduplication) are lengthened: dedéak, kokólak, lulúnú, titítík. The transcription of Rotenese used in this volume follows common Rotenese usage.

2. Roman Jakobson and the comparative study of parallelism[1]

For most of his career, Roman Jakobson was concerned with the linguistic study of parallelism. It is particularly noteworthy, therefore, to discern the firm foundations of this lifelong research in some of the youthful assertions of his earliest writings on poetry. In 1919, in an essay on the new Russian poetry, Jakobson enunciated certain of these fundamental insights in a series of clear, almost aphoristic, assertions:

> Poetic language consists of an elementary operation: the bringing together of two elements...The semantic variants of this operation are: parallelism, comparison (a particular instance of parallelism), metamorphosis (parallelism projected in time), metaphor (parallelism reduced to a point)...The euphonic variants of this process of juxtaposition are: rhyme, assonance, and alliteration (or repetition). (Jakobson 1973:21)

Decades later, on discovering similar insights in the writings of the poet G. M. Hopkins, Jakobson felt compelled to insist on their importance (Jakobson 1960:368; 1966:399; 1968:602). In 1966, for example, he began the introduction to a major article devoted to the discussion of parallelism with the following statement:

> When approaching the linguistic problem of grammatical parallelism one is irresistibly impelled to quote again and again the pathbreaking study written exactly one hundred years ago by the juvenile Gerard Manley Hopkins: 'The artificial part of poetry, perhaps we shall be right to say all artifice, reduces itself to the principle of parallelism, ranging from technical so-called Parallelisms of Hebrew poetry and the antiphons of Church music to the intricacy of Greek or Italian or English verse.' (Jakobson 1966:399)

Between the assertion and the rediscovery of his insights in Hopkins, there can be found in the various writings of Roman Jakobson innumerable comments

---

[1] This chapter was first published in 1977 as 'Roman Jakobson and the comparative study of parallelism', in C. H. van Schooneveld and D. Armstrong (eds), *Roman Jakobson: Echoes of his scholarship*, Peter de Ridder Press, Lisse, pp. 59–90. The research for part of the original paper was supported by a National Institute of Mental Health (NIMH) grant (MH-20, 659). In surveying the literature on parallelism, I am indebted to a host of scholars who, in response to earlier papers of mine, have referred me to further instances of canonical parallelism: R. Burling, W. Davenport, M. Edmonson, P. Friedrich, G. Gossen, K. Hale, R. Jakobson, E. Leach, F. Lehman, R. Needham, H. Phillips, G. Sankoff, I. Sherzer and P. Voorhoeve. For the references in Polish, Russian and Finnish, I have had to rely on secondary sources and summaries.

on parallelism. These cover his specific research on Russian epic poetry, theoretical remarks on poetic language, detailed analyses of individual poetic creations and comparative statements on the significance of parallelism in oral literature. In this chapter, I propose to examine some of Jakobson's ideas on parallelism and to outline the influence they have had in directing linguists, anthropologists and students of folklore towards an understanding of the phenomenon of parallelism.

Parallelism has two aspects and the use of the term 'parallelism' varies in relation to these aspects. In its first sense, parallelism is an ever-present aspect of poetic language. According to Jakobson (1966:399), 'on every level of language the essence of poetic artifice consists of recurrent returns', just as in Hopkins' definition verse is 'spoken sound having a repeated figure' (Hopkins 1959:267). Parallelism, in this sense, is an extension of the binary principle of opposition to the phonemic, syntactic and semantic levels of expression. Rather than some form of deviation, poetic language is the most manifest and complex expression of binary opposition.

Parallelism, in its other aspect, refers to the specific manifestations of this binary principle as a strict, consistent and pervasive means of composition in the traditional oral poetry of a wide variety of peoples of the world. Parallelism is promoted to a canon 'where certain similarities between successive verbal sequences are compulsory or enjoy a high preference' (Jakobson 1966:399). Jakobson has described this form of parallelism as 'compulsory' or 'canonical' parallelism—what Hopkins referred to as 'the technical so-called Parallelisms of Hebrew poetry'. The study of parallelism, as indeed the initial terminology for its study, derives primarily from the recognition of canonical parallelism in specific oral traditions. Jakobson's contributions to the study of parallelism have been to draw together the separate, and at times isolated, linguistic studies of these phenomena, to call attention repeatedly to their comparative significance and to suggest directions for further research.

The comparative study of canonical parallelism

The term 'parallelism' dates back to the eighteenth century and derives from the studies of Robert Lowth. In 1753, in a series of lectures delivered as professor of Hebrew poetry in the University of Oxford, Lowth made what was, at the time, the remarkable observation that one of the major principles of composition in much of the Old Testament was a carefully contrived pairing of line, phrase and verse. In his nineteenth lecture, Lowth first expounded this view:

> The poetic conformation of the sentences, which has been so often alluded to as characteristic of the Hebrew poetry, consists chiefly in a certain equality, resemblance, or parallelism between the members of each period; so that in two lines (or members of the same period) things

for the most part shall answer to things, and words, to words, as if fitted to each other by a kind of rule or measure. This parallelism has much variety and graduations. (Lowth 1753:157)

Later, in his 'Preliminary Dissertation' on a new translation of Isaiah, published in 1778, Lowth set forth, in a more explicit fashion, a terminology for what he called *'parallelismus membrorum'*:

The correspondence of one verse or line with another, I call parallelism. When a proposition is delivered, and a second is subjoined to it, or drawn under it, equivalent, or contrasted with it in sense, or similar to it in the form of grammatical construction, these I call parallel lines; and the words or phrases, answering one to another in the corresponding lines, parallel terms. (Lowth 1778:IX)

The impact of Lowth's research was immediate and profound. It inspired the writing of English poetry in a Hebrew vein (see Jakobson 1966:400) and influenced J. G. Herder in his *Vom Geist der ebräischen Poesie* (1782). Lowth's writings were soon translated and went through numerous editions. Lowth himself was made Lord Bishop of London in 1777 and, in 1783, was offered the position of Archbishop of Canterbury, which he refused.

More importantly, Lowth's research gave rise to a voluminous scholarship. Since Lowth's early observations, scholars have continued to examine the 'repetitive parallelism' of Hebrew poetry. G. B. Gray's *The Forms of Hebrew Poetry* (1915), devoted in large part to a 'restatement' of Lowth's study, carried this research into the twentieth century; L. I. Newman and W. Popper's tripartite *Studies in Biblical Parallelism* (1918–23) marked its further advance; while the 1928 discovery, at Ras Shamra, of Canaanite or Ugaritic texts led a host of recent scholars to examine, in meticulous detail, the extent to which Lowth's 'parallel terms' constitute, in the ancient oral traditions of Syria and Palestine, a standardised body of fixed word pairs by means of which verse forms were composed. An annotated bibliography on Hebrew poetry since Gray, including references to the work of such scholars as Albright, Cross, Dahood, Driver, Gevirtz, Ginsburg, Gordon and Rin on Ugaritic parallels with Hebrew, can be found in D. N. Freedman's 'Prolegomenon' to the reprinted edition of Gray (Freedman 1972:VII–LIII). Newman's introduction to his monograph *Parallelism in Amos* provides a valuable survey of a wide range of near Eastern traditions of parallelism—ancient Egyptian, Sumerian, Babylonian, Assyrian and Arabic—as well as a discussion of the diminished use of parallelism in the New Testament, and in rabbinical, medieval and modern Hebrew literature.[2]

Lowth's research began to have another major effect on scholarship, however, in the nineteenth century as various linguists, literary scholars and, not

---

2 Newman, 'Parallelism in Amos', in Newman and Popper (1918–23:57–135).

infrequently, missionary Bible translators encountered similar traditions of oral composition in widely scattered areas of the world. The sheer accumulation of these diverse studies has created a rich comparative literature.

One of the earliest of these comparative observations of parallelism is in an essay by J. F. Davis, 'On the poetry of the Chinese' (1830). Citing Lowth, Davis contended that constructive parallelism, the equivalent of what Lowth termed 'synthetic parallelism', was the 'most common species of parallelism in Chinese'. He went on to write:

> It pervades their poetry universally, forms its chief characteristic feature, and is the source of a great deal of its artificial beauty...The constructional parallelism of sentences extends to prose composition, and is very frequent in what is called *wun-chang*, or fine writing, which is measured prose, though written line by line, like poetry. (Davis 1830:414–15)

Davis's often quoted remarks[3] initiated a long tradition of Sinological studies on parallelism (see Schlegel 1896; Tchang Tcheng-Ming 1937; Boodberg 1954–55a, 1954–55b, 1954–55c; Hightower 1959; Shih 1959:190–4; T'sou 1968). Certain features of Chinese, first observed by Davis—namely, 'the exact equality in the number of words which form each line of a poetic couplet, and the almost total absence of recurring particles' (Davis 1830:417)—provide a basis for a sustained and elaborate parallelism. This linguistic predisposition is enhanced in written Chinese and has frequently been remarked on by other writers in connection with the occurrence of parallelism.[4] Manifestations of parallelism in Chinese have been noted in a variety of forms: in the earliest of written documents (Granet 1919), in popular poetry (Jablonski 1935), in proverbs (Scarborough 1875; Smith 1902:48–62), in love songs (Clementi 1904), in *thefu* or 'rhyme-prose' of the Han period (Watson 1971) and in the later literary style *p'ien-wen*, known as 'parallel prose' (Hightower 1966:38–41). The modular design of Chinese verse, coupled with the possibility of concurrent oppositional parallelism between level and deflected tones, is itself the subject of an incisive paper by Jakobson (1969).

Granet was convinced that parallelism arose in China as a direct reflection of ancient Chinese society and of a division of the world according to the categories of Yin and Yang. This duality found expression, on ritual occasions, in poetic recitations carried on by alternating choruses of young men and women. As one of the appendices to his study of the festivals and songs of ancient China, Granet (1919:278–301) included a considerable number of 'ethnographic notes' on love dialogues and poetic choruses in different areas of China, Tibet and Japan and among different groups (Thai, Miao, Lolo, among others) on the mainland of South-East Asia. Although Granet's evidence was meagre and not altogether

---

3   See Newman, 'Parallelism in Amos', in ibid., p. 69; Jakobson (1966:401).
4   See Hervey-Saint-Denys (1862:LXIV–LXVII) for essentially the same statement.

convincing, his intellectual stimulation led to further studies of parallelism. The Polish Sinologist W. Jablonski was inspired by Granet in his study of parallelism in Chinese popular poetry (Jablonski 1935), as was Nguyen Van Huyen, even more directly, in his doctoral dissertation, *Les chants alternés des garçons et des filles en Annam* (1933). This superb study deserves special note for the range of its coverage, beginning with the music of Vietnamese chants, the semantic structure of its common word pairs, its verse forms, means of improvisation and the thematic development of chants.

Vietnamese, of all the languages of mainland South-East Asia, has the greatest similarities with Chinese in its tradition of parallelism. Nguyen Dinh Hoà (1955:237), who has undertaken a linguistic examination of this parallelism, has observed:

> A characteristic feature of Vietnamese literary utterances is parallelism, which is found not only in verse but also in prose. This parallel structure requires the use of two phrases, or 'two sentences, that go together like two horses in front of a cart.' The nature of the parallelism may reside in the content and/or the form. Parallelism of form or structure is the minimum, however.

Chinese influence on Vietnamese parallel poetry is evident in what is considered Vietnam's great literary classic, the *Tryuen Thuy Kieu*, Nguyen Du's long narrative poem written at the beginning of the nineteenth century (see Huynh Sanh Thong 1973).

While Chinese influences are unmistakable in Vietnamese, it is also apparent that the various populations of South-East Asia have their own indigenous traditions of canonical parallelism. Among the first to recognise this parallelism was the missionary linguist O. Hanson (1906:XX), who noted that the 'most marked characteristic' of Katchin religious language was '*parallelismus membrorum*, or the attempt to unfold the same thought in two parallel members of the same verse or stanza'. Although these indigenous traditions have not been as well studied as in the case of the Vietnamese, anthropologists have pointed to the existence of these traditions among the Garo, Shan, Burmese and Thai.[5] One of the most intriguing aspects of this study of parallelism concerns the use, in diverse languages of the area, of what are referred to variously as 'binomes', 'doublets' or 'reduplicative formations'. These offer a ready-made lexical resource for the construction of parallel statements.[6] As Emeneau (1951:76) has stressed, 'any attempt at elevation of style, even in the most casual conversation, has as one of its marks a multiplication of pairs of verbs'.

---

[5] For the evidence of the prevalence of parallelism in Burmese and in Garo, I have relied on personal communications from F. Lehman and R. Burling.
[6] Emeneau (1951:159 ff.) on Vietnamese; Bernot and Pemaungtin (1966) on Burmese.

Canonical parallelism is evident in the oral traditions of numerous Austronesian or Malayo–Polynesian-speaking peoples. In some cases, it is the pervasive idiom for all formal public speaking, chanting or singing. In other cases, it has become a more restricted form of speech reserved for sacred utterances or for summoning spirits, and has occasionally become a prerogative of a priestly class. Again, it was a missionary linguist, A. Hardeland, who, in 1858, described this feature of Dayak 'spirit language' (Basa Sangiang): *'Der Charakter der basa Sangiang ist poetisch, voll Sinnbilder. Die Form ähnelt der Hebräischen Dichtersprache hinsichtlich des Rhythmus und kurzen parallelen Glieder'* (1858:5).

Another missionary linguist, J. Sibree (1880:148), made a similar observation about Malagasy: 'in the more formal Malagasy speeches the parts of every sentence are regularly balanced in construction, forming a kind of rhythm very closely resembling the parallelism of Hebrew poetry.'[7]

The present writer has briefly surveyed the major collections of parallel texts among the Austronesian peoples (see Fox 1971:217–19). These include Paulhan's collection of Merina verse from Madagascar; the Rhade epic, *La Chanson de Damsan*, from the mountains of south-central Vietnam studied by Sabatier; Steinhart's large corpus of Nias texts; Dunselman's publications on the Kendayan and Mualang Dayak and Schärer's two volumes on the Ngaju Dayak; van der Veen's collection of Sa'dan Toraja chants from the Celebes; a corpus of Rotenese texts with translations (Fox 1972); and, as an example from the Pacific region, the *Kumulipo*, the Hawaiian creation chant edited and translated by Beckwith. The islands of eastern Indonesia are an area where the canons of this oral poetry are vitally maintained and where studies of these traditions are continuing.

In this same general region of the world, Hale (1971) has studied a special form of parallelism used in the rituals of the Walbiri of Australia; the French scholar L Berthe (1972) prepared a large collection of texts, mostly in parallel verse, from the Papuan-speaking Bunaq of Timor; while Sankoff (1977) has examined the parallel poetry of the Buang of Papua New Guinea. These scattered studies indicate that there is much more to be done in this linguistically complex region.

A great deal of research is also needed in the investigation of parallelism in the oral poetry of Dravidian languages. Publication of ritual texts, such as those of Rosner (1961:77–113) from the Sadars of Jashpur, Madhya Pradesh, are clear evidence of its importance, while Kailasapathy's (1968:170 ff. 46) discussion of oral verse-making in Tamil heroic poetry is also indicative. Only Emeneau, however, in a series of studies, has attentively examined such a tradition of 'formulaically fixed pairs of song units' from among the Todas (see Kailasapathy

---

7 The reliance on parallelism in the work of Dutch Bible translators is discussed in van der Veen (1952:211–40) and in Onvlee (1953:16–23).

1968:170 ff. 46). As Emeneau (1937:560) has aptly phrased it, 'if we combine the Hebrew parallelism and the use of stereotyped phraseology of the epics or the Vedas, and push the combination to its furthest point, we have Toda poetry'.

Jakobson has already admirably surveyed the principal literature on parallelism among the peoples of the Ural–Altaic area (Jakobson 1966:403–5). Studies of Finnish oral poetry offer the classic case. The *Kalevala* is probably the most frequently cited example of parallel poetry after that of the Old Testament. Wolfgang Steinitz's (1934) major monograph, *Der Parallelismus in der finnisch–karelischen Volksdichtung*, traced the development of these studies. Before Lowth, the similarities between Finnish and Biblical verse were noted by Cajanus (1697), Juslenius (1728) and Porthan (1766. Marmier's (1842:96) passing observation on parallelism in Finnish was among the first occasions in which Lowth's terminology was adopted explicitly to characterise these verse forms. Ahlqvist's (1863) dissertation, Steinitz's (1934) pioneering study and his further research on Ostyak (1939–41), followed by Austerlitz's (1958) monograph on Ostyak and Vogul folk poetry, have all advanced this study and have made this group of languages a field in which parallel poetry has been examined most carefully. Furthermore, Steinitz (1934:4–14), Lotz (1954) and Austerlitz (1958:125) suggest a wider spread for this poetic tradition.

In the epic poetry of the Mongolians, parallelism was first remarked on by H. C. von der Gabelentz (1837:22): '*Das unerlässlichste Erforderniss scheint bei allen der Parallelismus der Glieder zu sein, der sich oft durch Wiederkehr derselben Endungen* (Reim) *oder derselben Worte* (Refrain) *kund giebt.*' This research begun by von der Gabelentz has been carried forward particularly by N. Poppe (1955; 1958:195–228). The major research on parallelism among Turkic languages has been that of Kowalski (1921) and Schirmunski (1965). In Lotz's (1954:374) words, 'parallelism is a common phenomenon in Uralic and Altaic folk poetry'.

Parallelism in Indo-European languages presents a less determinate case. In his three-part study, *Rig-Veda Repetitions*, M. Bloomfield (1916:5) drew attention to the 'catenary structure' of the Vedic texts and considered this to be 'analogous to so-called parallelism in Hebrew poetry'. In a long, discursive monograph, 'Stylistic repetition in the Veda', J. Gonda (1959) has similarly compared Hebrew parallelism with the 'balanced structures and symmetrical word groups' that make up the '*carmen* style' of the Vedas. Indeed, he contends that 'these parallel pairs of cola are of considerable frequency, not only in the Veda and the Avesta, but also in conservative ancient poetry of other [Indo-European] peoples, especially in the Dainos of the Lithuanians, and the Old-Norse Edda' (Gonda 1959:55).

Despite this contention, it is difficult to determine all that Gonda intends by his comprehensive concept of a *carmen* style. In some instances, this includes simple repetition, anaphoric phrasing or the recurrence of set formulae. Since, however, in Bloomfield's estimation, one-fifth of the *Rig-Veda* consists of repeated *padas*, this cannot be a form of parallelism. Nor does the frequent occurrence of 'twin formulae' or '*Zwillings-formeln*' (Meyer 1889; Salomon 1919), 'polar expressions' (Kemmer 1903; Lloyd 1966) or, in more recent parlance, (irreversible) 'binomials' (Malkiel 1959:73; Jakobson 1966:405)—common throughout Indo-European languages—constitute, by themselves, the evidence of a tradition of pervasive canonical parallelism. Parallelism of various sorts is unquestionably an important feature of certain Indo-European poetic traditions, but often its occurrence is optional, sporadic or at times subordinate to the requirements of rhyme, alliteration, assonance and a variety of complex metrical rules.

According to Jakobson, 'the only living oral tradition in the Indo-European world which uses grammatical parallelism as its basic mode of concatenating successive verses is the Russian folk poetry, both songs and recitatives' (1966:405).[8] In other Slavic languages, parallelism possesses varying degrees of importance (see Peukert 1961), but among none of these is parallelism as consistent a principle of composition as in Russian. This parallelism and its comparative significance, as Jakobson indicated, were noted anonymously in a Petersburg periodical in 1842 and later picked up by Šafranov (1878–79:199–205) in his study of Russian folk songs. In this connection, Jakobson (1966:407–22) has analysed in detail the complex metrical and grammatical parallelism in 21 lines of an eighteenth-century Russian song of grief.

Although in many Indo-European poetic traditions parallelism does not have the status of an oral canon, it is an inseparable aspect of poetic language; less transparent, perhaps, than in pervasive parallelism, it is nonetheless of considerable importance. Chiasmus and antimetabole, for example, are literary glosses for particular syntactic manifestations of this principle. In his study *Repetition and Parallelism in English Verse*, C. A. Smith (1894) has shown by judicious selection of verses from various periods of English literature the importance of this fundamental 'technique of poetry'. Given the special attention that Jakobson has devoted to the poetry of Edgar Allan Poe, it is worth noting that Smith, too, ranks Poe as one of the masters of parallelism in English:

And all my days are trances,

And all my nightly dreams

Are where thy dark eye glances

And where thy footstep gleams,—

In what ethereal dances,

By what eternal streams. (Poe: 'To One in Paradise')

---

[8] See Peukert (1961), whom Jakobson cites for his discussion of parallelism in Serbo-Croatian and Macedonian lyric songs.

Such a stanza illustrates a parallelism of sound and sense in which, following Poe's precept, 'the sound must seem an echo of the sense' (see Jakobson 1960:371–3). Smith notes also Poe's influence on his passionate admirer, the poet Baudelaire. It is therefore not unreasonable to see certain poets within a tradition as more susceptible than others to certain forms of structural construction. Certainly, Blake, Poe and Baudelaire—to name only three poets whose work Jakobson has scrutinised—all possess an almost diaphanous symmetry akin to the traditions of canonical parallel poetry.

In English literature there are, however, at least two instances of pervasive parallel poetry written in a conscious attempt to imitate canonical parallelism; the first was directly inspired by Lowth. The poet Christopher Smart, a contemporary of Lowth's, was his great admirer and regarded his lectures on Hebrew poetry as 'one of the best performances that has been published for a century' (Dearnley 1968:138). In his work, Smart is often considered a precursor to Blake and is perhaps best known for his impassioned religious poem *A Song of David*, reputedly first scrawled in charcoal on the walls of the madhouse in which he was confined. During one of his confinements, he also wrote a long, cryptic and highly idiosyncratic parallel poem, *Jubilate Agno*. Since the manuscript of this poem was discovered only in 1939, it has had little influence in English literature and it has served scholars mainly in piecing together the peculiarities of Smart's life and the genesis of his other poetry:

> For I this day made over my inheritance to my mother
>
> in consideration of her infirmities.
>
> For I this day made over my inheritance to my mother
>
> in consideration of her age.
>
> For I this day made over my inheritance to my mother
>
> in consideration of her poverty. (Smart: 'Jubilate Agno')

The appearance of another long parallel poem, in the nineteenth century, caused a far greater stir. This was Henry Wadsworth Longfellow's *The Song of Hiawatha*, published in 1855. Three years earlier, Schiefner had translated the *Kalevala* into German and Howitt had made an English translation of it. Longfellow's critics seized on this fact and accused him of gross plagiarism, to which he replied that he had been inspired equally by American Indian poetry and Finnish poetry. Although few critics grasped this point, it was clear that Longfellow, influenced by Schoolcraft's (1839) *Algic Researches*, was conscious of the common structural principle in both these poetic traditions. On 7 December 1885, the German poet Ferdinand Freiligrath wrote to Longfellow from London:

> Of course William Howitt is right; and your trochaic metre is taken from the Finns, not from the Spanish...The characteristic feature which shows that you have fetched the metre from the Finns, is the *parallelism* adopted so skillfully vb vand so gracefully in *Hiawatha*. I wonder that just this decisive circumstance is overlooked by all the combatants. It settles the question at once.

On receiving this letter, Longfellow noted in his *Journal* on 11 January 1856:

> A letter from Freiligrath, and a short article by him on the metre of *Hiawatha*, which is making some discussion in the English papers. He puts the matter right at once. But he does not seem aware that the parallelism, or *repetition*, is as much the characteristic of Indian as of Finnish song. (Longfellow 1893:298–303)

Other nineteenth-century scholars shared Longfellow's intimations about American Indian poetry. The vocabulary of *Hiawatha*—its initial allusion, for example, to Indian legends and traditions 'with their frequent repetitions and their wild reverberations'—had its effect. D. G. Brinton, who, after Schoolcraft, was one of the earliest American pioneers in the study of American Indian literature, accepted 'repetition' as the basis of his theory of poetry. Not unlike Hopkins, he argued: 'All metres, all rhythm, all forms of alliteration and assonance are but varied applications of the principle of harmonious repetition.' According to Brinton, American Indian poetry consisted in repetition in its simplest expression.

> The same verse may be repeated over and over again; or the wording of the verses may be changed but each may be accompanied by a burden of refrain, which is repeated by the singer or the chorus. These are the two fundamental characteristics of aboriginal poetry and are found everywhere on the American continent. (Brinton 1887–89:18–19)

Boas (1927:314) provides an important link in this distinctive American tradition of studying parallelism. In his discussion of literature in *Primitive Art*, he notes that 'in poetry repetitions of identical formal units are frequent'. Citing a variety of examples of parallelism in Indian poetry, but concentrating on Kwakiutl verse, Boas extends his discussion as follows:

> Exact observations show that rhythmic complexity is quite common. Regular rhythms consist of from two to seven parts, and much longer groupings occur without recognizable regularity of rhythmic structure. Their repetition in a series of verse proves that they are fixed units... Stress is most frequently given by repetition...Emphasis is also given by an accumulation of synonyms. Alternate terms are often used in this manner and in the original they often have an added rhythmical value on account of the homology of their form. (Boas 1927:16–19)

Reichard was the only one of the Boas students in American Indian linguistics to pursue this study of parallelism. Her monograph *Prayer: The compulsive word* (1944) develops a notation and a schematic system for analysing the elaborate 'forms of rhythmic repetition' evident in Navaho chants. Her research, however, does not seem to have stimulated further comparative studies of parallelism.

Although careful and extensive work on North American Indian poetry remains to be done, a considerable amount of research has already been done on various poetic traditions of Middle America, where Brinton saw the greatest flowering of poetic canons. Garibay (1953), in his monumental study of Nahnatl literature, lists parallelism as the first principle of Mayan poetry, and his entire two volumes abound in illustrative materials. Thompson (1950:61–3) had already recognised this as the principle of the ancient literature and Leon-Portilla (1969:76) further underscored this in his book *Pre-Columbian Literature of Mexico*: 'Anyone who reads indigenous poetry cannot fail to notice the repetition of ideas and the expression of sentiment in parallel form.' The recognition of this principle has also led to the retranslation of old texts. Edmonson (1970:14–23; 1971) completed a superb retranslation of the *Popul Vuh* of the Quiche Maya, demonstrating that this long parallel poem was based on a formal canon of traditional lexical pairs.

Several Harvard-trained anthropologists have begun to study this canonical parallelism in the oral traditions of the modern Maya. Bricker has examined this 'couplet poetry' among the Zinacantecos of highland Chiapas and has considered further historical usages in the Yucatan Peninsula (Bricker 1974). Gossen (1974a, 1974b) has studied these 'metaphoric couplets' within the context of Tzotzil Maya speech genres. A number of undergraduates in the Department of Anthropology at Harvard have produced theses on the parallel language of Mayan prayer as it is used in various contexts: Boster (1973) on prayer in the curing practices of the K'ekchi Maya of British Honduras (Belize), Siskel (1974) on Tzotzil curing in Chamula and Field (1975) on Tzotzil prayer in general.

These studies of parallelism are not, however, confined to the Maya. Drawing from Steinitz and Jakobson, F. W. Kramer (1970) has devoted most of his monograph *Literature Among the Cuna Indians* to an examination of parallelism in Cuna poetry and this has, in turn, prompted further illuminating studies of these important materials (Sherzer and Sherzer 1972; Sherzer 1974a, 1974b).

Issues and problems in the study of parallelism

The extent of the literature and the frequency with which canonical parallelism has been cited in different oral traditions suggest it is a phenomenon of near universal significance. This very literature, however, raises doubts and suspicions. It is apparent that nineteenth-century scholars, in particular, shared enough of a common cultural background to be made aware of a resemblance between Hebrew poetry and the poetry of other oral traditions that they encountered. And they had available to them, as a ready label, the term 'parallelism'. Yet a phenomenon so widely noted and so little understood warrants initial scholarly caution. When one assesses the extent to which this phenomenon has been the subject of rigorous research, a reasonable conclusion is that studies of parallelism are in their infancy. What constitutes a tradition of 'pervasive canonical parallelism' is understood only vaguely and the differences in the complexity of these traditions are all too apparent. Furthermore, the partial incomparability of both present and previous research cannot be ignored. The predominant studies on parallelism in Hebrew and Canaanite, and in Chinese and Vietnamese, have involved literary sources. In Hebrew, parallelism has often been used as a tool in disputed areas of textual reconstruction. The parallelism in the oral traditions of the Finno-Ugric, Turkic and Mongolian peoples has long been studied, yet among these many studies, only two monographs stand out for their detail and thoroughness: that of Steinitz (1934) and that of Austerlitz (1958). In contrast, basic research in Central America and in Indonesia is in its early stages. In several respects, this work holds promise. Older textual materials abound while much of the present research is directed to the study of current traditions of oral poetry. These researchers share, to a certain extent, a common theoretical framework influenced by Jakobson; they are aware of one another's present endeavours and are interested in the possibilities of comparison within their own regions and more broadly. Above all, a great deal of attention is being given to the social context of oral production (see Bricker 1974; Fox 1974; Sherzer 1974a).

Unresolved questions predominate at all stages of research. In the literature, syntactic and semantic parallelism are often distinguished although they are just as often intimately related. In his use of the term 'grammatical parallelism', Jakobson attempts to encompass both. For example, Kunene's (1971) discussion of the pattern of what he calls 'oblique' and 'cross-line' parallelism in the oral poetry of the Basotho raises fundamental questions about the syntactic positioning of semantically parallel elements. If the pattern that Kunene describes is widespread in Bantu poetry and is to be included within an understanding of parallelism, a new range of distinctions is needed for comparative purposes.

Similarly, the occurrence or non-occurrence of canonical parallelism within different language families raises various questions. Within the Austronesian-language family, canonical parallelism is so widely evident that the lack of this tradition in any particular group is not of general significance. There is enough evidence to make clear how, for example, among some small Borneo groups among whom parallel poetry had become the exclusive religious 'language' of a native priestly class, the rapid and wholesale conversion of the group led to the virtual disappearance of parallelism in a generation or two. On the other hand, it is of problematic significance that among Indo-European speakers only Russian and possibly certain other Slavic peoples should possess a living folk tradition based on grammatical parallelism (Jakobson 1966:405 ff.).

Questions relating to the role of parallelism in the development of various poetic traditions are also of major importance. Schirmunski, for example, has sketched the rough outlines of a possible developmental sequence for Turkic and Finno-Ugric verse. The sequence begins with simple repetition and proceeds toward a formal parallelism based on syntactically paired elements. This syntactical arrangement of verse develops further metrical relations by means of rhyme and alliteration until eventually syllable counting becomes 'a dominant metrical principle' and end-rhyme becomes 'obligatory'. At this point, both alliteration and parallelism diminish. Thus Schirmunski (1965:40–1) concludes that parallelism, as a stylistic device, is often suppressed 'under the outside influence of more developed metrical forms'.

Although this may appear to be a plausible outline of what has occurred in the Turkic and Finno-Ugric traditions, it would be unwarranted to regard this construction as the only possible course of development for other traditions. It seems to imply a primitiveness to parallelism that allows its survival only until it comes into contact with more advanced forms of poetry. The persistence, therefore, of parallelism either as the hallmark of certain folk traditions or as accepted literary style would seem to belie this assumption. Rhyme, for instance, which has often been considered as the phonemic equivalent of syntactic parallelism, does not occur universally in all parallel poetic traditions. Or it may persist in conjunction with parallel poetry as a mark of a distinct form of poetic diction. It is also evident that where set metrical forms or other strict canons come to define what constitutes genuine 'poetry', parallel verse, rather than disappearing, may be displaced and may assume the status of a semi-poetry: either an 'unmetrical poetry' or a 'parallel and/or rhymed prose'. This would seem to be the case in both Arabic[9] and in Chinese (Hightower 1966:2–41). So much remains to be investigated in this regard, however, that secure generalisations are still unlikely.

Another problem in studies of parallelism has concerned attempts to define the precise nature of and semantic criteria for word pairs in parallel verse. This concern began, in fact, with Lowth, who distinguished three sorts of pairs: 1) synonymous pairs, 2) antithetic pairs, and 3) synthetic or constructive pairs. As a result, many writers, in adducing evidence for the existence of parallelism, have been content merely to list examples of Lowth's typology. In some instances, this typology has led to disputes about whether a particular tradition of parallelism was indeed similar to that of Hebrew. Davis, for example, in his

---

9   Newman, 'Parallelism in Amos', in Newman and Popper (1918–23:95–109).

early article on Chinese poetry, maintained that constructive parallelism was the 'most common species of parallelism in Chinese'. In contrast, Liu (1962:146–7) has argued that Chinese poetry is unlike Hebrew poetry because it is based primarily on antithesis rather than on synonymy.

Unfortunately, this broad level of typologising offers insufficient understanding of the complexity of semantic relations in even the simplest traditions of canonical parallelism. Perfect synonymy in language is an illusion. The choice of similar words in parallel lines is intended to have a 'stereophonic' effect. 'Parallelistic juxtaposition', as Boodberg (1954–55b:17) has illuminatingly argued, gives us 'the satisfaction of experiencing the build-up step-by-step, first viewing the panorama presented by the poet from one syntactical angle, then from another, and fully savoring the stereoscopic after sensation or afterimage'. Thus an analysis that reduces lexical congruence to identity misrepresents the essential features of the language of this poetry. Similarly, as Hale (1971:481–2) has made clear, a tradition of parallelism based primarily on a principle of antonymy, such as *tjiliwiri* or 'upside-down Walbiri', used only in the context of Australian Aboriginal ritual, cannot be reduced exclusively to this single principle. Many of the fundamental oppositions in *tjiliwiri* turn out to be what Lowth would have called 'synthetic' pairs. In every tradition of parallelism, these synthetic pairs are what present the most interest for an analysis simply because they defy simplistic categorisation based on synonymy or antonymy. A further and perhaps more serious criticism of this typologising of word pairs is that this procedure generally assigns each pair to a specific category without examining the possibility of systematic connections among lexical elements in different paired relations.

The sobering conclusion to be drawn from a survey of issues and problems in the study of parallelism is that while many studies are suggestive and promising, much research adequate to deal with the richness of this verbal art remains to be done. In this connection, it is useful to consider some of the directions Jakobson has proposed for the study of parallelism.

Levels of complexity in traditions of parallelism

In *Fundamentals of Language* (Jakobson and Halle 1956), Jakobson called for an examination of parallelism in the context of his discussion of the metaphorical and metonymical poles of language: the interrelation of selection and combination or of similarity and contiguity. In this connection, he wrote:

> In verbal art the interaction of these two elements is especially pronounced. Rich material for the study of this relationship is to be found in verse patterns which require a compulsory parallelism

between adjacent lines, for example in Biblical poetry or in the West Finnic and, to some extent, the Russian oral traditions. This provides an objective criterion of what in the given speech community acts as a correspondence. (Jakobson and Halle 1956:77)

In the 'Poetry of grammar and grammar of poetry',[10] Jakobson (1968:600) repeated this statement: 'Parallelistic systems of verbal art give us a direct insight into the speakers' own conception of the grammatical equivalencies.' Once again, in his major article 'Grammatical parallelism and its Russian facet', Jakobson re-emphasised the importance of parallelism for an understanding of these linguistic equivalencies or correspondences:

> Such traditional types of canonical parallelism offer us an insight into the various forms of relationship among the different aspects of language and answer the pertinent question: what kindred grammatical or phonological categories may function as equivalent within the given pattern? We can infer that such categories share a common denominator in the linguistic code of the respective speech community. (Jakobson 1966:399)

Instead of a ready-made typology or a hasty assignment of word pairs to a limited set of formal categories, Jakobson has urged a decidedly more open exploration of the pairing of elements in corresponding sequences. The essential feature of this pairing—whether it is based on supposed synonymy, antonymy or 'synthetic' determinations—is that it involves simultaneously identification and differentiation. In this sense, parallelism is distinguished from repetition, which involves identification alone. In any parallel composition, the relation of parallelism to repetition must be considered carefully, but these two principles should not be confused. As Jakobson (1966:423) has phrased it: 'Any form of parallelism is an apportionment of invariants and variables. The stricter the distribution of the former, the greater the discernibility and effectiveness of the variations.'

On a comparative basis, there would appear to be a range of complexity in parallel traditions. One could almost construct a scale of these different traditions on the basis of the relation of parallelism to repetition or, as Jakobson has suggested, of variance to invariance. Selections from various traditions can be used to illustrate a possible range. Near one end of this scale, there is the parallelism of the Cuna of Panama. Dina and Joel Sherzer have written with great clarity on this precise issue in Cuna verbal art. By a careful textual examination of a hunting chant known as *bisep ikar* taken from Kramer (1970:51), they have been able to detail these relations. The following is the translation of the Cuna text accompanied by a simple notation that is intended to specify the repetitions and parallels (Sherzer and Sherzer 1972:190–2):

---

10 Published in various versions between 1960 and 1968—for example, in *Lingua*, vol. 21 (1968), pp. 597–609.

The bisep plant, in the golden box, begins to be born	a b (c_1 x_1)
The bisep plant, in the golden box, is being born	a b (c_1 x_2)
The bisep plant, in the golden box, begins to move	a b (c_2 x_1)
The bisep plant, in the golden box, is moving	a b (c_2 x_2)
The bisep plant, in the golden box, begins to tremble	a b (c_3 x_1)
The bisep plant, in the golden box, is trembling	a b (c_3 x_2)
The bisep plant, in the golden box, begins to swing	a b (c_4 x_1)
The bisep plant, in the golden box, is swinging	a b (c_4 x_2)
The bisep plant, in the golden box, begins to rise and fall	a b (c_5 x_1)
The bisep plant, in the golden box, is rising and falling	a b (c_5 x_2)
The bisep plant, in the golden box, begins to sound	a b (c_6 x_1)
The bisep plant, in the golden box, is sounding	a b (c_6 x_2)
The bisep plant in the golden box, is making a noise	a b (c_7 x_2)

As the Sherzers indicate, this short text comprises: 1) 13 repetitions of the same two elements, 'a, b'; 2) the coupled repetition of seven parallel verb stems, '$c_1 \ldots c_7$'; and 3) six repetitions of syntactically parallel verbal suffixes, 'x_1, x_2'. (Further repetition not evident in the notation involves the recurrence of the same verb stem, *makke*, in parallel verbs c_2 through c_7.) For an understanding of Cuna conceptions of equivalence, it is particularly interesting to note that the seven parallel verbs equate semantic features of birth, movement and sound.[11] Also of interest is the fact that the text ends with a so-called 'orphan line' whose parallel, in this case, is clearly implied but left unstated. Among the Cuna, lengthy chants are a sign of verbal art and of a performer's ability. The steady succession of gradually changing semantic elements provides a means of extending these linguistic performances.

In the Tzotzil Maya oral traditions studied by Gossen (1974a), parallelism is the mark of ancient narratives and of a ritual language that the Chamula Maya refer to as the 'language for rendering holy'. This ritual language is used in songs, prayers and chants performed individually or collectively. Parallel verse is in couplet form and generally each line of a couplet comprises the same repeated verse frame, which involves the change of a single parallel term per line. An example of this most common form of parallelism is the following excerpt from a long curing chant (Gossen 1974a:211–12):

I seek you in this petition	a b c1
I seek you in this cure, my Lord	a b c2 x
For the payment lies at your feet	d e f1
For the payment lies before your hands...	d e f2

---

[11] The equation of these features is particularly relevant to the discussion of transition and percussion begun by Needham (1967:606–14).

A change of parallel terms usually occurs in an initial or final position within the verse frame but may, on occasion, occur at some intermediate location.[12] With one semantic change of parallel terms in each couplet, these Chamula chants can also become lengthy performances. From the point of view of the performer, there is an almost unremitting regularity to the composition of prayers and chants.

Parallel songs, on the other hand, are interesting in that, as Gossen points out, they are as 'redundant' as the music that accompanies them. Like certain set melodies, these short songs are repeated over and over again and can be used as 'fillers' at various rituals. Instead of being composed for the particular occasion, they are remembered and retained. When, however, one looks at the structure of 'The Song of the Jaguar' quoted by Gossen (1974a:221–22), its composition appears to be slightly more varied than most prayers (the notation is according to Tzotzil syntax):

Jaguar Animal of heaven,	$a^1 b^1$
Jaguar Animal of earth.	$a^1 b^2$
Patron of heaven,	$a^2 b^1$
Patron of earth.	$a^2 b^2$
Your legs are lame, Jaguar Animal,	$c^1 d^1 a^1$
Your legs are long, Jaguar Animal.	$C^2 d^1 a^1$
Your whiskers are spiny, Jaguar Animal,	$C^3 d^2 a^1$
Your whiskers are long, Jaguar Animal.	$C^2 d^2 a^1$
Get up, father,	$e^1 f^1$
Get up, mother.	$e^1 f^2$
Stand up, father,	$e^2 f^1$
Stand up, mother.	$e^2 f^2$
Rise up, father,	$e^3 f^1$
Rise up, mother.	$e^3 f^2$

This simple song comprises six parallel sets, four of which (a, b, d, f) are dyadic and two of which (c, e) are triadic. The recurrence of a^1 in successive couplets may be considered the only extended repetition in the song, although in fact all dyadic sets are repeated at least twice.

In his study *Ob-Ugric Metrics*, Austerlitz (1958:45 ff.) provides a complete typology of all permissible forms of parallel lines for his entire corpus of Ostyak and Vogul folk poetry. Shorter verbal lines and segments can also be parallel, but Austerlitz deals with these separately. Unlike Tzotzil couplet poetry, parallel lines in this tradition are not always contiguous, although they are hardly ever more than six lines apart. As in Tzotzil, parallel lines involving one parallel word are common. These occur most frequently initially or internally in a line

---

12   See Field (1975) for a detailed dissension of these possibilities.

but rarely as a final element. Equally common, however, are parallel lines with two parallel terms. The most general pattern of occurrence of two parallel terms is conjointly in an internal position or disjointedly in initial and final positions. What is most interesting is Austerlitz's (1958:46) observation that 'generally there are no lines with more parallel words than two'. Viewed exclusively in terms of a scale of complexity of parallelism, Ostyak and Vogul poetry would seem to mark an advance on Tzotzil. Yet this poetry, too, sets an evident upper limit on its use of parallelism.

In the poetry of the Rotenese of eastern Indonesia studied by this author (see Bibliography, this volume), there is an even greater reliance on the use of parallelism. This usage is typical of the folk traditions of numerous peoples of Indonesia, in which parallelism is the defining feature of poetry. In the composition of Rotenese poetry, the overwhelmingly most common poetic form is the couplet, but the lines of couplets may often be interlaced rather than adjacent. The number of parallel terms per line varies from one to four. Three, however, is by far the most common number of parallel terms that can occur in a line. Since Rotenese is a relatively uninflected language and since inflection is further reduced in poetry, most parallel terms consist of semantic elements. The following provides a brief example of this poetry. For the sake of simplicity, the notation omits connectives that link alternating lines (Fox 1971:236):

All the great ones	a1 b
All you superior ones	a2 b
Do remember this	c (x1 d1)
Do bear this in mind	c (x2 d2)
Orphans are the froth of cooking palm syrup	e1 f1 g1
And widows are the heads of palm stalks	e2 f2 g2
Palm froth spills over twice	f1 g1 h1 j1
The spill you gather for them	j1 j1 k
And a palm stalk's head droops thrice	f2 g2 h2 i2
The drooping head you grasp for them	i2 j2 k
Leaving orphans still intact	e1 i m1
And leaving widows still in order	e2 i m2
Intact like a thick wood	m1 n1 o1
Intact for a long time	m1 p1 q1
And in order like a dense forest	m2 n2 o2
Ordered for an age.	m2 p2 q2

This poem is composed of 14 dyadic sets, 13 of which (a, d, e, f, g, h, i, j, m, n, o, p, q) are semantic pairs and one of which (x) is a verbal prefix. In addition to connectives, there are only four repeated forms (b, c, k, l). One couplet consists of a single set of parallel terms; another has four. Two couplets have two sets each while four couplets have three parallel sets each.

Certainly, some of the Chinese poetry or 'parallel prose' described by Hightower (1959) is more complex in its parallelism than Indonesian parallel poetry, especially since Chinese canons often require, in addition to semantic parallelism, a further tonal parallelism (see Jakobson 1969). The question to be asked, however, is whether the use of more than four parallel terms per line or four sets per couplet marks some kind of dividing line between oral and written literary composition.

Criteria for defining 'canonical parallelism'

The complexity of a system of parallelism relates directly to an understanding of its use in a tradition of canonical parallelism. Since parallelism is of common occurrence and since this occurrence need not involve a formal set of canons that affects the selection of parallel elements, it becomes necessary to specify what constitutes 'a tradition of canonical parallelism'.

According to Jakobson (1966:399), such a tradition is implied 'where certain similarities between successive verbal sequences are compulsory or enjoy a high preference'. Recurrent parallel patterning can, without a doubt, be found in the varied poetry of individuals who have no recourse to specific oral canons, but if one accepts the idea that canonical parallelism provides 'an objective criterion of what in a given speech community acts as a correspondence' (Jakobson and Halle 1956:77) then a very careful examination of the nature of this pairing is required.[13]

One of the most frequently encountered statements in the published literature on parallelism is the mention of prescribed word pairs. The knowledge of these is said to be essential to proper composition in a particular oral tradition. In describing the parallelism in Toda songs, for example, Emeneau provides a clear statement in this regard:

> The most striking feature of the structure of the songs is that each phrase or sentence can occur only in a parallel phrase or sentence, so that the song as a whole falls into couplets...A further peculiarity, almost a corollary of the first, is that the pairs of units used in making up the couplets are rigidly prescribed by convention. (Emeneau 1937:545)

Similarly, Gevirtz (1963) discusses these 'conventionally fixed pairs of words' in his study of Hebrew poetry. For the Hebrew poet, these fixed pairs formed

---

13 From a generative point of view, Kiparsky (1974:240) has suggested that a difference between 'loose' parallelism and strict canonical parallelism can be its point of transformational derivation from some deep structure: 'The tighter the constraints on the abstract pattern, the stricter the parallelism tends to be, and the closer it holds to surface structure.'

the 'essentials of his craft' (Gevirtz 1963:11). Moreover, one of the major results of the discovery of the corpus of Ugaritic texts has been the recognition of a common poetic tradition:

> [P]airs of parallel terms occurring in both Ugaritic and Hebrew poetry number more than sixty. These form the foundations for the theory of a traditional poetic diction common to Syro-Palestinian literatures.
>
> Since Hebrew poetry contains many more than these sixty-odd pairs of fixed parallels and since extant Syro-Palestinian literature is limited, it follows that if a pair of words found in parallel relationship in the Bible can be shown to have been a fixed, or relatively fixed, pair for the Old Testament poets—even if the pair has not yet made its appearance in Ugaritic or any other 'Canaanite' literature—it must nevertheless represent an element of the same, or a similar, literary tradition. (Gevirtz 1963:8)

Although in his study of Ostyak and Vogul parallel poetry Austerlitz (1958:50-1) states that he is not concerned primarily with 'a semantic characterization' of parallel words, he nevertheless provides 'a list of the most common parallel words' from his central corpus. More intriguingly, Edmonson (1970:14) reports that the anonymous Franciscan dictionary prepared in 1787 on Quiche Maya is almost entirely composed of 'couplet entries'.

The simple listing of word pairs—however extensive these lists are—is insufficient to specify the conventions involved in the proper pairing of terms. Such lists, by focusing exclusively on individual word pairs, may actually disguise more complex interrelations that occur among elements that happen to pair. What is needed is a more comprehensive view of the semantics of a particular poetic tradition.

Research under way on Rotenese poetry is intended to provide one such view of the semantic resources and conventions of a tradition of canonical parallelism. Since this research requires the detailed analysis of a large corpus of poetry of a single speech community, present results reflect only the preliminary views of a continuing research project (see Fox 1975). To date, 25 lengthy chants that comprise approximately 5000 lines of verse have been translated (Fox 1972). These chants derive from the Rotenese dialect area of Termanu and Ba'a. An equally large number of recorded chants from this same area remain to be translated as well as a further sizeable corpus of texts from the dialect area of Thie. The research is, therefore, in its early stages. On the basis of the translated corpus, however, a dictionary for Rotenese poetry has been compiled that contains slightly more than 1000 word pairs (Fox 1972).[14] From this dictionary

---

14 This dictionary has also been computerised to facilitate future analysis.

there emerges some idea of what is obligatory and what involves choice in the selection of word pairs. There appears to be, roughly speaking, three levels of word pairing.

Of the 1400 separate semantic elements recorded in the present dictionary, a significant number of elements are limited in their pairing to a single dyadic set, which has no links with any other set. The existence of such a large number of fixed, obligatory word pairs indicates that there is a great deal of specific information that must be mastered to attain a thorough competence in this art form. This would also support the frequently stated Rotenese contention that it is only as one grows old that true mastery of the language is possible. Without detailed knowledge—knowledge of the necessary and unique pairing of specific species of named trees, fish and insects, of particular cultural objects or, for example, of certain emotionally expressive verbs—an individual poet does not have this true mastery. With knowledge of only some of these sets, he can, however, begin to express himself. Since any mistake in these pairs is immediately detectable and—among Rotenese—quickly challenged, an aspiring poet must have a firm command of a good number of these unique pairs before he begins to compose. He can, however, grow in the further knowledge of these as his art improves.

Although word pairs or dyadic sets are essential to the composition of all Rotenese poetry, the significant feature of this poetic language is that many semantic elements may occur in more than one word pair or dyadic set. Any element may have a range of elements with which it forms a set and these elements, in turn, may pair with still other elements creating a network of interlinkages. Thus an element, A, may pair with elements B, C and D; B may pair as well with E and F; and C with G, H and so on to form a network: 'A…N'.

Another significant portion of the present dictionary consists of elements that have a range of linkages greater than one but rarely more than four. In other words, rather than forming unique dyadic sets, these semantic elements may pair with a few other elements to form limited semantic fields varying in size from networks of three elements to networks of perhaps 25 elements. With these pairings, the range of the poet's options is still constrained but the very fact that these options are available in the creation of the poetry is sufficient to dispel any illusion about the mechanical nature of composition (Jousse 1925).

The remaining third of the present dictionary forms a single large, complexly interrelated network. It is likely, as the dictionary expands, that this network will continue to be enlarged and joined by many of the smaller networks that are presently evident. The organisation of this large network has yet to be fully determined. It already includes virtually all elements that have a range of permissible pair linkages greater than four, but it also includes numerous elements that have a limited number of linkages. There are certain elements that may pair with as many as 10 or more other elements to form acceptable sets. Many of these 'polysemic' elements form pairs with each other and there are some indications that these polysemic elements serve to organise elements with fewer linkages in a kind of semantic hierarchy (see Fox 1974:77–9; 1975:11–21).

From the point of view of the oral poet, speaking in pairs involves more than a routine process of combination. Certain of the pairs he uses are conventionally fixed, but the majority is based on a differing range of selection. In any learning process, knowledge of the more polysemic elements and of the range of their pairings would seem to be essential. Understanding some of the complexity of this oral composition is therefore one of the aims of the Rotenese study.[15]

Concluding remarks: Parallelism and the study of symbolic systems

Jakobson (1973:485) has noted that 'the linguistic study of poetry has a double door'. It leads to the study of the relations and functions of verbal signs as well as to the study of these same signs as vehicles of cultural expression. In this regard, the use of parallelism clearly indicates a marked form of speaking. In addition to its common formal aspects, it is impossible not to be struck by the recurrent use of parallelism for special, specific purposes: in scriptures, in the utterance of sacred words, in the preservation of ancient traditions, in ritual relations, in curing, shamans' journeys and in other communications with spirits. The study of parallelism leads immediately to the study of myth and ritual. Recent studies of myth and ritual, many of which also reflect the seminal influence of Jakobson, suggest that an understanding of the formal properties of parallelism can be of the utmost importance. The foremost question of this research concerns the relationship of the phenomenon of parallelism to the prevalent construction of systems of dual symbolic classification throughout the world (Needham 1973). Parallelism, however pervasive, does not constitute a dual symbolic classification. Such schemata are characterised by the analogical ordering of dyadic elements according to some extra-linguistic criterion of asymmetry. The study of pervasive parallelism can, however, provide some understanding of how linguistic phenomena are culturally transformed and elaborated.

---

15 Another of the aims of this Rotenese study is to lay the groundwork for further comparisons. Elizabeth Traube of the Department of Anthropology at Harvard University has conducted linguistic fieldwork for more than two years among the Mambai-speaking peoples of East Timor. The Mambai possess a rich and varied oral literature, including an elaborate tradition of canonical parallelism, which should serve as material for comparison with Rotenese.

3. Trajectories in the continuing study of parallelism

Introduction

When my paper 'Roman Jakobson and the comparative study of parallelism' was published in 1977, I imagined—or perhaps, it would be better to say, I hoped—that Jakobson's influence and his persuasive argument for the critical importance of parallelism in understanding poetic language would prompt an explosion in the study of parallelism at a wider comparative level. Yet no such explosion occurred.

Instead, since 1977, there has been a steady development in the study of parallelism occasionally marked by new materials and flashes of analytic insight. This development has occurred, for the most part, in a number of separate intellectual silos defined in terms of particular language groups with relatively little reference to other comparative linguistic traditions of parallelism. A program for the study of parallelism as a 'near-universal' (as Jakobson phrased it) has barely begun. In my own work over the past decade, I have to recognise that I, too, have concentrated my attention primarily on the comparative occurrence of canonical parallelism within the Austronesian language family.

For this volume, I feel that it is appropriate to update my 1977 paper: 1) to highlight important developments in the study of parallelism, particularly canonical parallelism; 2) to document the continuing recognition of new traditions of canonical parallelism; and, in the process, perhaps 3) to venture comparative comment on parallelism as a general but situated linguistic phenomenon. It is the contention of this chapter that there is a host of similar semiotic processes evident in the use of parallelism in distinct traditions throughout the world but it is only when one examines the range of these traditions that it becomes possible to glimpse these similar semiotic processes. I offer this summary excursion as an addendum to my original paper and as a prelude to my own research included in this volume. Given my concern in attempting to recognise similarities across different traditions, I will be strategically selective in my comparative examination and commentary but will try to be more inclusive in citing references to recent work within the field and to issues that relate to my own research on parallelism.

Biblical scholarship: The Hebrew and Ugaritic traditions

No area of study has produced a greater volume of research touching on parallelism than that of Biblical studies. Yet despite the fact that the comparative study of parallelism was initially given impetus by Robert Lowth's researches, the extensive and erudite study of Biblical parallelism remains largely a self-referencing field and only rarely draws upon, or contributes to, a wider global discussion. Nevertheless, the study of Biblical parallelism offers considerable value for comparative consideration.

In this regard, there has been a succession of publications since 1977 that require consideration. The first of these is James J. Kugel's *The Idea of Biblical Poetry: Parallelism and its history* (1981); the second is Wilfred G. E. Watson's *Classical Hebrew Poetry: A guide to its techniques* (1984), which includes a particularly useful chapter on parallelism; and the third is Adele Berlin's *The Dynamics of Biblical Parallelism* (1985), which is the most significant and relevant of recent studies. Two other volumes that take a specific, detailed look at parallelism are also worth including in this list: Robert Alter's *The Art of Biblical Poetry* (1985:1-28) and David L. Petersen and Kent Richards' *Interpreting Hebrew Poetry* (1992: 21-35).

Kugel's volume is a work of considered, conventional Biblical scholarship. His focus is on what he calls the 'parallelistic line', which he defines as the 'basic feature' of the Hebrew poetic tradition for the expression of songs, sayings, proverbs, laws, laments, blessings and prayers. The parallelistic line consists of two brief clauses, separated by a pause with the second clause associated with, linked to, or corresponding with the first clause. The connection between these two clauses can correspond closely in syntactic structure and semantics but can also be loosely associated with the first clause. In Kugel's assessment, the 'majority of parallelisms in the Bible fall between such extremes…complete correspondence is relatively rare' (Kugel 1981:2–3). Kugel cites Jakobson's 1966 paper on parallelism, but is concerned mainly but only briefly with comparative considerations of Semitic parallelism.

Drawing upon a considerable range of scholarly research, Watson's volume provides a more incisive discussion of parallelism and its occurrence in the Hebrew, Ugaritic and Akkadian traditions of poetic composition. His discussion covers a range of general issues in parallelism as well as others that are specific to Semitic parallelism. Thus, for example, he calls attention to the common occurrence of 'gender-matched parallelism' in both Hebrew and Ugaritic. This form of parallelism was first identified by Umberto Cassuto in his study *The Goddess Anath: Canaanite epics of the patriarchal age* (1971), and was subsequently shown to be a recurrent feature in Hebrew compositions as well. A number of studies have been done on this form of parallelism (Berlin 1979; Watson 1980).

Watson gives various examples of this 'gender-matched parallelism'.

From Isaiah (49, 22):

> They shall bring your sons in their embrace (m.),
>
> and your daughters shall be carried on their shoulders (f.).

From Jeremiah (48, 37):

> On every pair of hands (f.), a slash (f.),
>
> On every pair of hips (m.), sackcloth (m.).

From Ugaritic poetry:

> Scarcely had his word (m.) issued from his mouth (m.),
>
> From his lips (f.), his word (f.).

And from Akkadian:

> In the city the young girl's song (m.) is altered
>
> In the city the young man's tune (f.) is altered.

Watson also compares 'number parallelism' in Hebrew and Ugaritic—a subject first broached by Ginsberg and discussed extensively by Gevirtz (1963:15–24, 29–30). In Hebrew, only some of the numbers from 1 to 7 can pair with their successor digit, thus: (x//x+1); 7//8 is of frequent occurrence but 8//9 is not used.

From the Psalms (62, 12):

> Once hath God spoken,
>
> Twice have I heard this.

From Proverbs (30, 15):

> Three things are never satisfied,
>
> Four never say: 'Enough'.

From Proverbs (6, 16):

> Six things doth YHWH hate,

And seven are his disgust.

From Ecclesiastes (11, 2):

Give a portion to seven,

And also to eight.

The pair 7//8 can be multiplied by 10 or more often by 11 to indicate larger quantities: 70//80 or 77//88. A variation on this combination is 'sevenfold//seventy-seven'.

From Genesis (4, 24):

For sevenfold is Cain avenged

but Lamech, seventy and seven!

The Hebrew tradition also uses the pair: thousand//ten thousand.

From I Samuel (18, 8):

They have given to David ten-thousands

And to me have they given the thousands.

The Ugaritic tradition uses virtually the same number pairs, similar multiplication by 11 and combines one thousand with ten thousand.

Let bread be baked in the fifth

Food for a sixth month.

Seven years may Baal fail

Eight, the Rider of the Clouds.

Sixty-six cities did he seize

Seventy-seven towns.

He took a thousand pitchers of wine

Ten thousand he mixed in his mixture.

Akkadian, by contrast, makes less use of number parallelism and most occurrences of this parallelism are in incantations. Watson notes the existence of number parallelism in Phoenician and Aramaic, but makes no reference to similar forms of parallelism in other non-Semitic traditions. Such number parallelism is common in other traditions of parallelism and thus offers a specific point of comparison.

Much of Watson's discussion of parallelism is taken up with a consideration of what he calls 'parallel word pairs'. This is the term he prefers to a plethora of other terms in the Biblical literature—'standing pairs', 'fixed pairs', 'A-B pairs' or 'parallel pairs'—used to identify the canonical semantic pairs.

The critical focus on these pairs began with the discovery in 1928–29 of the repository of Ugaritic texts at Ras Shamra in northern Syria and the decipherment of these texts, written, as they were, in a distinctive alphabetic script using cuneiform. Ginsberg (1935) was the first to note these pairs, which he called 'standing pairs'. He described them as 'certain fixed pairs of synonyms that recur repeatedly, as a rule in the same order' (1936). Others followed Ginsberg's lead, most notably Gevirtz in his seminal study *Patterns in the Early Poetry of Israel* (1963). Recognition of these pairs and their compilation has itself become a substantial undertaking. Michel Dahood has made the most prominent contribution to this task. Initially in 'The grammar of the Psalter' (1970), written with Tadeusz Penar, Dahood compiled an extensive list of Hebrew/Ugaritic parallel word pairs that occur specifically in the Psalms; he then went on to publish three further compilations (Dahood and Penar 1972; Dahood 1975, 1981), bringing to 449 his count of parallel pairs.

In this connection, Watson notes the use of rare terms that combine with more commonly recognised terms. Thus, in an A-B pair, one term, the A word, whose occurrence is relatively common, can combine with other 'rare and esoteric words'. An understanding of these esoteric words derives from their relation to their more common partnered terms. Also implied in this is the possibility that any particular term can form a pair with a number of other terms. This opens up the possibility of analysis that goes beyond the listing of fixed word pairs. The combination of two terms—one common and the other, in some way, unusual—is of frequent occurrence in other traditions of semantic parallelism; in some cases, the 'rare' term may originate from another dialect or even from another language.

Watson also discusses the use of chiasmus—the reversal or inversion of word order in consecutive verses—as a common device for poetic composition in Hebrew (1984:201–13). It was Dahood, however, who had earlier linked this compositional technique to the use of synonymous pairs. Basing his argument on a host of examples taken from Job, Dahood argued that 'when the poet uses the chiastic word order, the synonymy of the parallel members tends to be stricter than when the order is not chiastic' (1974:120). A couple of examples may serve to illustrate this feature in Hebrew poetry.

From Job (28:2):

> Iron is taken from ore,
>
> And from smelt rock, bronze.

From Job (32:14):

> I shall not marshal against him your arguments,
>
> And with your words I shall not rebut him.

In his discussion, Watson also considers what might be called the 'oral hypothesis' adopted by Biblical scholars to explain the variability in the use of fixed word pairs in different parts of the Bible. He considers in particular a paper by Perry B. Yoder, 'A-B pairs and oral composition in Hebrew poetry' (1971), which articulates this position—a position that can in fact be traced back to Ginsberg and Gevirtz.

For Yoder, the 'stock of word pairs was not the work of any individual poet... but it was the poetic inheritance of each generation of poets' (1971:472). The use of this inheritance varies considerably in different passages of the Bible. Yoder cites Psalm 54 as an example of the 'high-density' use of such pairs. Watson, in his translation, italicises those word pairs on which the psalm is constructed: name//might, save//defend, hear//give ear, prayer//words of my mouth, foreigners//vicious men, risen up against me//seek my life, helper//supporter, evil recoil//destroy, sacrifice//praise your name, enemies//foes.

Psalm 54:

> O God, by your *name save* me
>
> and by your *might defend* me
>
> O God, *hear* my *prayer*
>
> *give ear* to the *words of my mouth*
>
> For
>
> *foreigners* have *risen up against me*
>
> *vicious men seek my life*;
>
> See!
>
> God is my *helper*
>
> the Lord really is the *supporter* of my life

Making *evil recoil* on my slanderers

In truth, he really *destroyed* them

For generosity I will *sacrifice* to you

I will *praise your name*, Yahweh, for it is good.

For

from all my *enemies* he rescued me

and my eyes gloated over my *foes*.

Yoder regards 'the technique of parallelistic composition by the use of traditional word pairs as a technique developed by oral poetic traditions to meet the needs of oral poets' (1971:483). Invoking the work of Milman Parry on oral formulaic expressions in Homer, Yoder then goes on to argue that for poets in the Ugaritic–Hebrew tradition the use of fixed pairs was equivalent to the use of formulaic expressions in the Homeric tradition. Since there is a great deal of variation in the 'density' of the use of fixed pairs, particularly in the Bible, it follows, as Yoder indicates, that wherever this density is high, the text reflects a strong oral poetic influence.

Yoder's analysis is essentially an extended supportive restatement of Gevirtz's early argument that 'the poets of Syria and Palestine had at their command a body of conventionally fixed pairs of words upon which they might freely draw in the construction of their literary compositions' (1963:38).[1]

Watson also enumerates and briefly summarises the varieties of forms of parallelism that occur in Hebrew and Ugaritic compositions: staircase parallelism, synonymous-sequential parallelism, noun–verb parallelism, and vertical parallelism. One of the useful aspects of Watson's summary discussion of research on parallelism within the Semitic field is his inclusion of short, relevant bibliographies for each of the topics he discusses.

One of the most valuable studies of Biblical parallelism to be published to date is Adele Berlin's *The Dynamics of Biblical Parallelism* (1985). Berlin takes her cue from Lowth—not by arguing over his specific claims but rather in recognising, as she writes, that Lowth 'was right about the essence of parallelism: it is a *correspondence of one thing with another*' (1985:2). More significantly, Berlin explicitly adopts Jakobson's perspective on poetic language as her framework of analysis—quoting Jakobson's famous dictum that 'the poetic function

---

[1] For other scholars who have contributed to this position, see Boling (1960); Whallon (1963); and, for a contrary position, see Culley (1967:117 ff.), who argues the importance of formulaic expressions but does not regard fixed pairs as the equivalent of these other formulaic elements.

projects the principle of equivalence from the axis of selection into the axis of combination'. She describes this pronouncement as 'piercingly insightful and maddeningly general' (1985:7), but she carefully elaborates and develops on Jakobson's ideas, drawing on the exegeses on these ideas by Linda Waugh (1980). Her stated goal 'is to present an overarching, integrated and linguistically based description of biblical parallelism' (1985:29).

Berlin refers to my 1977 paper on the comparative study of parallelism but her primary interest is in a thoroughgoing analysis of the Hebrew tradition of poetry, and much of her book is taken up in a dialogue with a variety of other Biblical scholars—in particular, Kugel—who have adopted differing conceptions of the parallelism and its significance. She divides her study into sections on the examination of: 1) grammatical, 2) lexical-semantic, and 3) phonological parallelism, and each of these sections is further subdivided into varieties of parallelism. Thus, for example, gender parallelism, noun/pronoun parallelism, or contrasts in person, number or case are separately discussed and illustrated under the rubric of grammatical parallelism. Berlin also examines what she calls positive–negative parallelism: pairings in which a corresponding line or phrase is just the 'negative transformation' of the previous line or phrase:

From Proverbs (6, 20):

> Guard, my son, the commandment of your father
>
> And do not forsake the teaching of your mother.

From Deuteronomy (9, 7):

> Remember, do not forget.

Berlin's discussion of lexical-semantic parallelism leads to a partial but not particularly successful attempt to explain the specific pairing of words by different linguistic rules such as marking or minimal contrast. She concludes her study with a valuable consideration of the 'expectation' and 'effect' of parallelism. The book, as a whole, is a remarkably rich work of detailed Biblical scholarship written in a new key within the discipline. As such, its conclusion is worth quoting:

> Parallelism, then, consists of a network of equivalences and/or contrasts involving many aspects and levels of language. Moreover by means of these linguistic equivalences and contrasts, parallelism calls attention to itself and to the message which it bears. Parallelism embodies the poetic function, and the poetic function heightens the focus on the message. (Berlin 1985:141)

The earliest evidence of parallelism: The Sumerian tradition

Since 1875, Sumerian studies have been engaged in piecing together the scattered fragments of cuneiform tablets stored in museums and other repositories around the world in an effort to restore the diverse literary creations of Sumer. No-one has contributed more to this immense effort and to the translation of works of great importance than Samuel Noah Kramer. His book *From the Poetry of Sumer* (1979) is a landmark study that provides a glimpse into this poetic tradition, much of it characterised by pervasive parallelism.

Despite evident parallelism, the fragmentary nature of these cuneiform texts often leaves the interpretation of their mythic meaning of many passages uncertain. One of these fragmentary poems that describes a fecund world impregnated after a great flood—a fragment that Kramer specifically labelled as 'perplexing, problematic and enigmatic' (1979: 30)—nonetheless provides a good illustration of this complex Sumerian parallelism:

> The old man instructed, the old man exhorted
>
> After the rain had poured down, after it had demolished walls;
>
> After hailstones and firebrands had poured down,
>
> After man had confronted man defiantly,
>
> After there had been copulation—he had also copulated.
>
> After there had been kissing—he had also kissed,
>
> After the rain had said: 'I will pour down,'
>
> After it had said: 'I will demolish walls,'
>
> After the Flood had said: 'I will sweep everything away,'
>
> Heaven impregnated, Earth gave birth,
>
> Gave birth to the *numun*-plant, also,
>
> Earth gave birth, Heaven impregnated,
>
> Gave birth to the *numun*-plant, also,
>
> Its luxuriant reeds kindled fires. (Kramer 1979:32)

Some years after the publication of *From the Poetry of Sumer*, Kramer began a productive collaboration with the poet and folklorist Diane Wolkstein.

Together they produced a volume, *Inanna: Queen of Heaven and Earth* (1983), which draws together an extensive assemblage of ritual compositions regarding the goddess Inanna and puts these retranslated pieces together in a coherent fashion. While Kramer and Wolkstein each contributed separate background essays, the translation is a joint effort. The result is a work of exceptional scholarship lifted to a literary plane. Virtually every passage in the volume is expressed in parallelism.

Some of the most remarkable poetic passages in *Inanna: Queen of Heaven and Earth* can be found in the dialogue between between Inanna and her lover and consort, Dumuzi, the shepherd. The parallelism in these passages is as explicit as it is erotic and multiple metaphors it produces reflect Sumerian ritual concerns with fertility and fecundity. The following are excerpts of dialogue from the Courtship of Inanna and Dumuzi:

Inanna spoke:

"What I tell you

Let the singer weave into song.

What I tell you,

Let it flow from ear to mouth,

Let it pass from old to young:

My vulva, the horn

The Boat of Heaven,

Is full of eagerness for the young moon

My untilled land lies fallow.

As for me, Inanna

Who will plow my vulva?

Who will plow my high field?

Who will plow my wet ground?

Dumuzi spoke:

"Great Lady, the king will plow your vulva.

I, Dumuzi the King, will plow your vulva."

Inanna sang:

"Make your milk sweet and thick, my bridegroom.

My shepherd, I will drink your fresh milk.

Wild bull, Dumuzi, make your milk sweet and thick.

I will drink your fresh milk.

Let the milk of the goat flow in my sheepfold.

Fill my holy churn with honey cheese.

Lord Dumuzi, I will drink your fresh milk."

Dumuzi spoke:

"My sister, I would go with you to my garden.

Inanna, I would go with you to my garden.

I would go with you to my orchard.

I would go with you to my apple tree.

There I would plant the sweet, honey-covered seed."

Inanna called for the bed:

"Let the bed that rejoices the heart be prepared!

Let the bed that sweetens the loins be prepared!

Let the bed of kingship be prepared!

Let the bed of queenship be prepared!

Let the royal bed be prepared!"

(Wolkstein and Kramer 1983: 36-42)

Parallelism in Sumerian poetry relies as often on triplet sets as on dyadic sets and often these triplet sets consist of a succession of an initial general term followed by more specific terms: garden, orchard, apple tree.

As a student of Stanley Kramer, Adele Berlin's first major publication was a monograph on a critical Sumerian text: *Enmerkar and Ensuhkešdanna: A Sumerian narrative poem*. This narrative poem, made up of 282 lines, features a contest between the ruler of Uruk and the ruler of the Aratta over the right to marry the goddess Inanna. For this study, Berlin identified the cuneiform tablets from which she constructs her text and then provided a transliteration and translation of her constructed text with an extensive critical commentary.

She devoted considerable attention to the use of parallelism throughout the text. She refers to the succession of parallel terms, as in the triplet sets noted by Wolkstein, a 'progression' of parallel terms in successive linesand provides examples of this kind of parallel progression:

> Like a wild donkey of Sakan, he runs over the mountains
>
> Like a large powerful donkey, he races
>
> A slender donkey, eager to run, he rushes forth.
>
> (Berlin 1979:lines 45–7)

Such parallel enumeration can continue for many lines.

Berlin's interest is in the varied uses of parallelism in composition, rather than identifying recurrent formulae or particular fixed pairs. In the current state of textual reconstruction, emphasis continues to focus on the scholarly construction and expansion of the corpus of Sumerian poetry. This corpus may not yet be at a stage at which it is feasible to identify the full range of recurrent semantic pairs.

Thorkild Jacobsen is another distinguished scholar of Sumerian culture. His book, *The Harps That Once...: Sumerian poetry in translation* (1987) is a rich compendium of Sumerian ritual and poetic texts with valuable annotations and commentary. In his collection of texts, many in parallelism, is a ritual text that is believed to date from the time of the restoration of the Sumerian capital of Ur after the fall of the Third Dynasty and the sacking of Ur around 2004 BC. This cuneiform text is a harp-lament for the destruction of Ur but is thought to have been used in a ritual for the restoration of Ur around 1940 BC. The entire lament consists of 413 lines, almost all in strict parallelism. It is a formulaic composition that progresses by the ordered recitation of the names of particular gods or goddess and of the specific sites of the temples dedicated to them. As such, it is almost certainly the earliest example of what I describe in Chapter 11 of this volume as a 'topogeny'—an ordered recitation of successive place names, the spatial equivalent to the ordered recitation of personal names in a genealogy. Although not confined to traditions of parallelism, the recitation of topogenies is a common feature of many traditions of parallelism throughout the world.

This Sumerian topogeny is a recitation of abandonment. The invasion by the Elamites is likened to a storm that forces a shepherd to abandon his byre and sheepfold. The storm strikes one Sumerian city after another and destroys its temple, forcing the god or goddess of that city to abandon it. The topogeny is thus an ordered recitation of the cities of Sumer, the main temple in each city and the gods who held sway in those temples. The 'Lament for Ur' begins with the following stanza and continues in steady succession with only slight alteration to the same formula:

His byre he was abandoning,

and his sheepfold, to the winds

the herder was abandoning his byre

and his sheepfold, to the winds,

the lord of all lands was abandoning it

and his sheepfold to the wind,

at the temple close, Enlil was abandoning Nippur

and his sheepfold to the wind,

his consort Ninlil was abandoning it

and her sheepfold, to the winds

at their dwelling house, Ninlil was abandoning Kiur

and its sheepfold, to the winds. (Jakobsen 1987:447–74)

This formula is repeated to produce an ordered progress—a procession—of gods and goddess, each of whom abandons their city and temple. At its conclusion, the text launches into yet another long topogeny based on another formula that proceeds systematically through the cities and temples of Sumer, again linking a city, its temple and its god or goddess. A brief excerpt from this second topogeny gives a sense of the beauty of its reiterative parallelism:

Brickwork of Ur, bitter is the wail

the wail is set up for you!

Ekishnugal, bitter is the wail,

the wail is set up for you!

Temple close Agrunkug, bitter is the wail

the wail is set up for you!

The evidence of parallelism in early Egyptian

Parallelism is also evident in early ritual compositions in Egypt. Writing of Egyptian literature, Miriam Lichtheim identifies three literary styles, one of which she designates as an 'intermediate style' between prose and poetry:

> The intermediate style...is characterized by symmetrically structured sentences. It was employed exclusively in direct speech. Hence I call it 'symmetrically structured speech,' or, the 'orational style'...In Egyptian as in biblical literature, the principle [sic] device that activates the orational style is the *parallelism of members*. (Lichtheim 1973:11)

One of the oldest examples of this orational style comes from hieroglyphics on the walls of the sarcophagus chambers adjoining rooms and corridors of Unas, the last king of the Fifth Dynasty of the Old Kingdom, dating from approximately 2300 BC. Known as the Pyramid texts, this corpus of incantations was intended to direct the passage of the deceased king to join the sun-god, Re, and to promote his transformation.

The parallelism in utterances 273–4 of these Pyramid texts, which give expression to Unas' transformation, provides a striking example of the early orational style in Egyptian:

> Sky rains, stars darken
>
> The vaults quiver, earth's bones tremble,
>
> The planets stand still
>
> At seeing Unas rise as power,
>
> A god who lives on his fathers
>
> Who feeds on his mothers...
>
> He has encompassed the two skies,
>
> He has circled the two shores;
>
> Unas is the great power who overpowers the powers,
>
> Unas is the divine hawk, the greatest hawk of hawks,
>
> Whom he finds on his way he devours whole.
>
> Unas's place is before all the nobles in lightland,
>
> Unas is god, oldest of the old,

Thousands serve him, hundreds offer to him,

Great-Power rank was given him by Orion, father of gods.

Unas has risen again in heaven,

He is crowned as lord of lightland. (Lichtheim 1973:36–8)

The wider Chinese and South-East Asian traditions of parallelism

The role of parallelism and the specific extent of semantic parallelism in early Chinese writing remain sources of speculation. Following in the footsteps of Marcel Granet, who emphasised the insistent binary nature of Chinese traditions, Léon Vandermeersch has argued that the earliest forms of Chinese divination that derived its answers through an interrogation of a symbolic delineation of the turtle's carapace provided the prototype for literary parallelism (1989). More substantially relevant is C. K. Wang's examination in *The Bell and the Drum* (1974) of the 'stock phrases' utilised as 'conventions of composition' in the creation of the *Shih Ching, The Book of Odes*. In his paper on parallel structures in the canon of Chinese poetry, David J. Liu has argued that 'for the ancient Chinese, the concept of parallelism was implicit in the very structure of the universe, manifesting itself in an all pervasive complementary bi-polarity'. He goes on to note that 'one of the earliest bodies of writing, the *I Ching* ("Book of Changes"), compiled circa 1100 BC, contains oracular statements in parallel couplets' (1983:642).

A similar pervasive parallelism marks the verses of the *Yuandao*, the Chinese treatise on the Dao that forms a crucial component of the *Huainanzi*, an early Han dynasty compendium of knowledge written in the second century BC around the year 139 BC. The treatise presents the Dao as the 'oneness of all things', and the complementary dualism that endows the Dao pervades the parallel language in which it is described.

The opening lines of the *Yuandao* exhibit parallelism both between lines and within lines:

It [the Dao] shelters the heavens and supports the earth

Extends beyond the four points of the compass

And opens up the eight points of the compass.

It is high beyond reach

And deep beyond reckoning

It envelops the cosmos

And gives to the yet formless.

Flowing from its source it becomes a gushing spring

What was empty slowly becomes full;

First turbid and then surging forward,

What was murky slowly becomes clear. (Lau and Ames 1998:1)

The sixth-century literary commentator Liu Hsieh (456–522), in his grand survey of Chinese literature, now translated as *The Literary Mind and the Carving of Dragons* (Shih1959), concludes his discussion of the importance of linguistic parallelism in Chinese poetry with an instructive *tsan* in parallel form from the *Li-Chi, The Book of Rites*:

A body requires its limbs to be in pairs

A phrase, once forged, must have its counterpart.

With the left hand one lifts; and one holds with the right,

To attain both the essence and the flavor,

Parallelism gleams and dazzles like flowers which are entwined,

Reflecting without distortion like a calm mirror,

It flows in two streams, smooth as jade

Giving rhythm as do the pendant jewels. (Shih 1959:194)

Also intriguingly pertinent to a discussion of parallelism is Hua Wu's assertion that the seventeenth-century literary critic Jin Shengtan, in his critical discourse on *The Water Margins*, recognised parallelism as fundamental to all composition. As Hua Wua claims: 'for Jin Shengtan, parallelism is the basic principle underlying the role of all writing, including that of *The Water Margin*' (1988:172). When examined more specifically, this supposed parallelism is itself, in Jin Shengtan's analysis, based on a set of abstract principles: 1) repetition (*chongfu*), 2) synonymous substitution (*jiaohu ercheng*), 3) contrast (*jinshu duisheng*), 4) gradation (*chuanje erchu*), and 5) contiguity (*chengu pinfa*)—all of which are prototypically exemplified in *The Analytics of Confucius* (1988:171).

R. A. Stern, in his discussion of ancient Tibetan poetry (1972:252-259), compares modes of expression in this poetry to that of the alternating songs of ancient

China found in the *Shih cheng*. He asserts that the *"principle of parallelism is so strong that same sentence is often uttered, once with a descriptive expression, once with a corresponding name"*. He gives as an example of this in the following lines:

Of the enemy, he cut out the heart;

of the wild yak Karwa, he cut out the heart;

For the kinsman, he achieved vengeance;

for the brother Yikyi Dangcham,

he achieved vengeance.

Stern (1972:253)

Parallelism occurs in a great variety of forms, often with each limb separated by a caesura *ni, which Stern translates as 'yes'*:

With a wide mouth, yes, grass he eats,

with a wide neck, yes, water drinks.

Stern (1972:254)

Many of these forms of parallelism have carried on into contemporary Tibetan ritual traditions.

Of notable interest in this regard is the occurrence of 'binary ritual language expressions' among various Tibeto-Burman tribal groups in the central and eastern Himalayas. Nicholas Allen was the first to call attention to this form of parallelism (1978). Since then, Martin Gaenszle and his research colleagues have documented the occurrence of 'binominals'—the term they give to 'expressions of paired words'—in the ritual speech of other related groups now living in Nepal (Gaenszle et al 2005; 2011). There is evidence of traditions of parallelism as well among the Tibeto-Burman speakers of Nocte, Tangsa and Singpho and among a variety of Tai speakers in Upper Assam and in Arunachal Pradesh in India (see Morey nd). Similarily Anthony Walker has documented the use of parallelism among the Lahu Nyi or Red Lahu, a Tibeto-Burman-speaking hill tribe living in southwestern Yunnan, western Laos and northern Thailand (1972).

Of considerable relevance also to the study of canonical parallelism is the work of David Holm. In his research among the Donglan Bouyei Zhuang, a Tai-speaking population in the north-western highlands of Guangxi, he came upon manuscripts of indeterminate age written in Chinese script for the performance of key rituals: texts for buffalo sacrifice, for funerals and for summoning the souls of the dead (Holm 2001, 2003, 2004). The salient feature of all these texts is a pervasive parallelism. Holm has translated and published these texts with valuable notes and commentary on their background and context. A short excerpt recounting the beginnings of creation taken from an early segment of the text (lines 46–63) for the buffalo sacrifice gives an indication of this parallelism:

> In the beginning the world was suddenly dark and suddenly light
>
> All at once it was suddenly heaven and suddenly earth.
>
> No one yet knew of night nor evening
>
> They knew not of short nor long,
>
> They knew neither crosswise nor straight ahead…
>
> The Emperor had not yet been created
>
> Family Property had not yet been established
>
> Not yet had everything under the sky been created
>
> Not yet had everything on earth been created
>
> Not yet had the moon and the sun been established
>
> The great spirit in the sky looked down from above,
>
> The Sky gods made a decision on high.
>
> They made a Seal and issued it,
>
> Then they sent down a certain King Pangu
>
> The sky then opened into two halves,
>
> The sky then transformed itself into two paths.
>
> It formed a road for him to descend,
>
> It formed a path for him to come on. (Holm 2003:108)

Holm notes that

> while the texts are written artefacts, transmitted by copying, they show signs of oral composition. On the other hand, the fact that they were written down helped make them ritually powerful, given the pervasiveness of Buddhist and Taoist notions of the efficacy of texts and the enormous prestige of the Chinese script. (2003:36)

It is certainly evident from the texts themselves that they were meant to be recited. Holm describes the ritual masters (*boumo*) who take it in turn to recite these scriptural texts and includes a CV with recitations in his 2003 and 2004 publications. An illustrative example of the ritual speaking voice occurs in many places in the texts, as, for example, in the buffalo sacrifice:

'Whittle a pair of chopsticks from *nanmu* wood

While I speak of the times before

Whittle an arrow of Tree of Heaven wood,

While I talk about times before,

While I speak of those fabled times,

While I tell you the story of the Emperor's Inheritance.' (Holm 2003:108)

Holm calls particular attention to linguistic borrowings that occur in the creation of synonymous pairings: 'A particularly interesting feature of the parallelism is the way in which indigenous Zhuang concepts are frequently brought into parallel relation with terms borrowed from the Han' (2003:36). This is the same phenomenon that Watson and other Biblical scholars discuss under the rubric of 'rare and esoteric words', especially when they cannot identify the origin of an esoteric word. The composition of pairs based on strategic borrowing across distinct dialects and different languages can be considered a fundamental feature of many—perhaps most—complex systems of semantic parallelism (see Fox 1974:80–1; Chapter 4, in this volume). It extends comprehension and communication beyond single speech communities especially in areas of linguistic diversity.

Since 1977, a variety of studies of the oral literatures of the highland populations of mainland South-East Asia has shed new light on less well-known traditions of parallelism. Frank Proschan (1984, 1989, 1992 has written on parallelism in the verbal arts of the Khmhu as has Håkan Lundström (see Lundström and Tayanin 2006; Lundström 2010), while Jacques Lemoine (1972) and Jean Mottin (1980) have noted the importance of parallelism in various poetic genre among the Hmong. (Kenneth White (1983) has provided an English translation of a Hmong Kr'ua Ke mortuary chant that Lemoine recorded.) Both Proschan and Mottin point to the use of parallelism in 'love songs'—a speech genre identified by Granet in his *Festivals and Songs of Ancient China* (1919) as prone to the use of alternating parallel expressions. However, the use of parallelism in mortuary and ancestral propitiation is also wide spread.

The traditions of parallelism among the languages of Middle America

One of the most intellectually exuberant areas for the study of parallelism in the past several decades has been that of Middle America. The developments have coincided with the decipherment of the Mayan glyphs (see Coe 1992), and the addition of a new historical dimension has given impetus to the study of the diverse oral traditions of parallelism in the region. Reflecting on the decipherment of the glyphs, Floyd Lounsbury has signalled the importance of parallelism in the process:

> And a native literary convention, the 'poetic couplet,' grounded in an oral tradition that is still very much alive today and that in ancient times was carried over even into the unwieldy medium of hieroglyphic inscriptions, also serves to bring out equivalences. Passages which are in this form present parallel strophes, 'rhyming' (so to speak) in meaning rather than sound, and conveying their message twice but in different phrasings. It was the recognition of this device that led to the discovery of the equivalence between some of the diverse forms of 'birth glyphs'. (Lounsbury 1989:233)

Adding to this historical dimension for the study of parallelism has been a renewed attention to colonial manuscripts, many of which were written in parallelism, as well as considerable oral repertoire reflecting the Mayan past. In addition to his invaluable translation of the *Popul Vuh* (1971) based on a manuscript written between 1550 and 1555 by a Mayan noble of Quiche, Munro Edmonson has gone on to translate the *Book of Chilam Balam* (2008). Denis Tedlock has done his own translation of the *Popul Vuh* (1985;Revised: 1996) as well as a translation of the *Rabinal Achi* (2003), the remarkable Mayan dialogue and dance drama first recorded in 1856, but performed locally from the sixteenth century to the present. Similarly, Gary Gossen, whose work has focused on parallelism among the Tzotzil Maya, has edited and translated in parallel verse form a collection of some 74 separate Tzotzil tales, spanning four cycles of creation, destruction and restoration, to create a single vast 'epic' (2002). Gossen's work is reminiscent of Elias Lönnrot's nineteenth-century efforts in the creation of the *Kalevala*, compiled from various sources to become one of the longest continuous compositions in parallelism in world literature.

The opening verses of Edmonson's translation of the *Popul Vuh* provide an illustration of Mayan parallel composition that often interpolates triplet semantic sets in the midst of a string of dyadic semantic sets:

> This is the root of the former word
>
> Here is Quiche by name

Here we shall write then,

We shall start out then,

The former words The beginnings

And the taproots

Of everything done in Quiche town,

The tribe of the Quiche people.

So this is what we shall collect then,

The decipherment,

The clarification,

And the explanation

Of the mysteries

And the illumination

By the Former

And Shaper;

Bearer

And Engenderer are their names,

Hunter Possum

And Hunter Coyote

Great White Pig

And Coati,

Majesty

And Quetzal Serpent,

The Heart of the Lake

And Heart of the Sea,

Green Plate Spirit

And Blue Bowl Spirit.

(Edmonson 1971: 3)

Explorations in Semantic Parallelism

One can compare this semantic parallelism with the parallelism in the final soliloquy by the warrior Cawek in Tedlock's translation of the *Rabinal Achi*:

'Alas, then, Sky!

Alas, then, Earth!

If I am truly dead

if I am lost

at the navel of the sky

navel of the earth

then I shall resemble

that squirrel

that bird

that died on the branch of a tree

in the flower of a tree

while searching

for his meals

his morsels

here at the navel of the sky

here at the navel of the earth.

You then, Eagle

you then, Jaguar

Come now!

Do your duty

Do your work.

Do it now with your teeth

your claws.

But you certainly won't stand my hair on end

In the blink of an eye

because

I am truly brave

coming as I do

from my mountain

my valley.

May Sky and Earth be with you too

Little Eagle, little Jaguar.' (Tedlock 2003:121–2)

In a paper on the semantics of Mayan parallelism, Edmonson examines the 'associational chains' among 42 pairs that occur in the first 94 lines of the *Popul Vuh*, arranging these sets on a continuum between the universal and the particular. Some, such as, for example, word//name, root//tree, heaven//earth, mother//father, he classifies as 'universal'; others, such as plant//root, tribe//town, lake//sea, bowl//plate, he classifies as 'widespread'; while others, such as white//book, white//tribe, tree//know, heart//breath, possum//coyote and pig//coati, he describes as 'particular'. The universal categories, he views, as grounded in 'general human experience'; the widespread categories are 'contingent upon experiences common to many, but not all cultures', while the particular categories are 'found only in Middle America, some of them perhaps only among the Quiche Maya of the sixteenth century' (1973:239).

For Edmonson, the 'exotic associations' equating 'white' with 'book' and 'tribe' are of special interest, revealing metaphors central to Quiche religion. 'The particularistic semantics of the Popul Vuh suggests that details of expression in that work are significantly conditioned by ideas peculiar to the Quiche Maya and organized around their special view of cornfarming, hunting, priesthood and parenthood' (1973:242).

Tedlock has taken a different approach to the *Popul Vuh*. Working with a native speaker of Quiche, Andrés Xiloj, who was also a ritual specialist, Tedlock offers a reading—or rather a 'hearing'—of the *Popul Vuh* as if it were recited in a contemporary ceremonial setting. He is interested, importantly, in the 'movement' of the text/recitation: 'the vertical movement of verse and the horizontal movement of prose' (1987:151). Here he disagrees, as in his translation (1985), with Edmonson's attempt to render the whole of the work in couplet verse.

Although the pervasive parallel semantics of the text is retained, its flow, which involves a semantic inventory of occupations, takes on a different form:

Fulfill your names—

Hunahpu Possum

> Hunahpu Coyote
>
> bearer twice over, begetter twice over,
>
> great peccary, great tapir,
>
> lapidary, jeweller, sawyer, carpenter,
>
> maker of green plates,
>
> maker of green bowls,
>
> incense maker, master craftsman,
>
> grandmother of day, grandmother of light.
>
> (Tedlock 1987:153–4)

Tedlock also points to the importance (noted already by Hymes 1980) of the role of 'framesetting' terms that indicate the beginnings of a poetic phrase. He emphasises the importance not just of parallel couplets but also of parallel triplets, arguing that these triplets, which are also common in contemporary ritual discourse, 'often occur at or near the beginning or end of a series of couplets' (Tedlock 1987:159). He gives this example from the *Popul Vuh*:

> Now it still ripples,
>
> now it still murmurs
>
> ripples,
>
> it still sighs,
>
> it still hums,
>
> and it is empty
>
> under the sky. (Tedlock 1987:158)

Whether these are all genuine semantic triplets and thus composed of three separate elements, or simply 'performative' triplets and thus single expressions of a recognised doublet, is an empirical question that probably requires more systemic analysis. Nevertheless, as in his other work, Tedlock's performance-oriented perspective provides useful insights into the composition and use of parallelism.

One of the most important recent studies on Maya parallelism is the PhD thesis by Kerry Hull, 'Verbal art and performance in Ch'orti' and Maya hieroglyphic writing' (2003). In this thesis, Hull provides an extensive documentation of

Ch'orti' Mayan ritual language, locating this speech among the oral narrative genres in Ch'orti' and linking its poetic expressions and rhetorical devices to similar features in Mayan hieroglyphic writing.

More recently still, together with Michael Carrasco, Hull has put together and edited a remarkable collection of 17 papers on Mayan ethno-poetics entitled *Parallel Worlds: Genre, discourse, and poetics in contemporary, colonial and classical Maya literature* (2012). This is a volume that includes virtually all of the leading researchers in the field with an exceptional range of expertise on poetics and parallelism in historical sources and contemporary usage. As such, it deserves particular consideration.

In the introduction to his paper in *Parallel Worlds*, Hull expounds on the importance of parallelism and its pervasiveness in formal speaking among the Maya:

> The preferred vehicle for literary expression among all modern Mayan languages is paralleled discourse. Quite simply, parallelism defines poetic or ornate discourse in the minds of the Maya themselves. Within its seemingly strict confines, the Maya are able to elaborate profoundly complex cultural knowledge by means of associative connections. Exploiting these relationships, be they complementary, contrastive or otherwise, Maya poetics operate at times outside the boundaries of the line, usually only showing their true literary qualities when in juxtaposition…in modern Maya languages, a general adage applies: the more form the discourse, the more parallel structures appear…It is undoubtedly on ritual and formal speech occasions where the full flowering of parallel structures can be found among the Maya…Both knowing which word combinations are acceptable and understanding the metaphorical extensions that often accompany such groupings are crucial elements in one's communicative competence in many Maya societies. (2012:74–5)

In his paper, Hull examines a dozen of what he calls 'diphrastic kennings': the pairing of two distinct elements to produce another, more abstract concept. The term 'diphrastic' is borrowed from Ángel Maria Garibay, who was the first to use the term '*difrassimos*', to describe such parallel terms in Nahuatl literature (1953:112). Among the list of these diphrastic kennings are pairs or dyadic sets that Edmonson might have classified as universal—sky//earth, male//female, stone//wood, green//yellow—and others that he would have regarded as more particular: bread//water, flint//shield and throne//mat. Hull traces each of these pairs from their use in Mayan hieroglyphs through their appearance in colonial Mayan writings to their continuing use among different present-day Mayan groups.

Hull's intention is to demonstrate the 'poetic tenacity' of these pairings but his analysis shows much more. Thus, for the pair sky//earth, the linkage of these elements is retained in whatever language is used to expressed the concept: *cham//kab* in the inscriptions in the Palenque Palace, *kaj//ulew* in the *Rabinal Achi*, *can//cabal* among the Yuketekan Maya, or even borrowed Spanish terms, *syelo//mundo*, as used as among Ch'orti' healers. There is persistence of a semantic category that utilises different lexical elements for its expression.

Parallel Worlds is a significant publication and indispensable for the study of Mayan parallelism. While a number of papers offer a dense analysis of the historical underpinnings and complex mythology expressed in the inscriptions of the classic period and of post-classic codices, other papers focus on the poetics of Mayan ritual language.

Michael Carrasco considers the 'high poetic value' of the 'rhetoric of political propaganda' incised on the Temple of Inscriptions at Palaque, whose construction dates from between 678 and 690. The parallelism of the inscriptions on behalf of K'inich Janaab Pakal, the Divine Palenque Lord, is stunning, even if the full significance of these assertions may be obscure:

His second stone-seating

[was] 12 Ajaw 8 Keh

the Eleventh K'atun

The face-of-the-sky Maize God had become lord

the face of the jewel tree had sprouted

the face of the 'Five origins' tree had sprouted.

The heavenly bundle of jade

the earthly bundle of jade;

the necklace,

the earspool...

(Carrasco: 2012:136)

Lloyd Anderson notes the importance of 'coupleting' to the decipherment and translation of Mayan inscriptions: 'After coupleting was recognized as common in Mayan discourse, both spoken and written, this feature claimed enormous attention' (2012:175). He also argues, however, for the importance of the syntactic placement of temporal markers and the arrangement of text as critical for a full understanding. Similarly, in his contribution to the volume, Tedlock looks at Mayan glyphs in inscriptions and vase painting as 'graphic poetry' whose arrangement is critical to the message conveyed.

Examining a Ch'orti' manuscript of the colonial period, Danny Law looks at the various borrowings from Spanish that combine with an appropriation of native terms to incorporate new Christian concepts in mixed-language couplets. Thus, for example, in addressing the Christian God, the couplet 'mother-father' (*na'//mi*) is combined with the Spanish *Dios* and the Ch'orti' term for 'lord' (*ahaw*):

natz'et ka-na' ka-mi	You (sing) are our Mother, our Father
natz'et hun-te'tak Dios, noh-noh ahaw	You are the one God, big, big Lord. (Law 2012:280)

The creation of new concepts through the recombination of existing dyads is a hallmark of traditions of parallelism and is commonly noted in the comparative literature on parallelism. The ritual engagement with Christianity and assimilation of Christian ideas in parallel compositions among the Maya provide a particularly rich field for comparison with other traditions of parallelism that have had a similar religious engagement, as, for example, among the Rotenese (see Chapters 15, 16 and 17, in this volume).

Luis Enrique Sam Colop presents a superb and subtle reconsideration of the poetics of the *Popul Vuh*, giving his own interpretation of the compositional ordering of its lines with accompanying illustrative translation of its opening lines. The translation is arranged to highlight parallels in couplets, triplets and quatrains:

This is the root of the Ancient Word of this place called K'iche

Here we will write

we will implant the Ancient Word,

the beginnings

and the source of everything done in the town of K'iche

the nation of the K'iche people

Thus, we will take up the teaching

the clarification and

the account of what has been hidden

of what has been revealed

by the Maker

Modeler

Bearer

Begetter...

(Colop 2012:302)

Threading his way between Edmondson and Tedlock, Colop concludes with highly specific observations on the compositional structure of the *Popul Vuh*:

> [V]erbal art in K'iche Mayan is organized in parallel lines. Parallelism, however, does not mean contiguity of two lines only...In couplets, the modifier is generally dropped in the second line, and in triplets it is dropped more frequently in the second of the three lines. In quatrains it is the last verse that generally breaks the paradigm to move the discourse into prose. Thus Maya texts integrate both verse and prose without one excluding the other. (2012:307)

Following Colop, Allen Christenson examines chiasmus as a poetic device used by the K'iche in the colonial period. Charles Hofling also looks at chiasmus in connection with the use of parallelism repetition in a comparison of the narrative styles of two different Mayan groups: the Mopan and the Itzaj. In a region where the possibilities of comparisons in the use of parallelism among different Mayan groups is considerable, Hofling's paper is the only one to consider, if only briefly, similarities and differences in performative styles. In fact, with the exception of several references in the paper by Colop and in another paper by Auore Bequenlin and Alain Breton, there is little comparative focus beyond the region and little recognition or acknowledgment of similar linguistic processes, such as chiasmus, in other traditions of parallelism. The quality and depth of research on Maya parallelism are, however, encouraging. This is particularly the case where native Mayan-language speakers take up this research. Hilaria Cruz de Abeles' linguistic examination of Chatino oratory (2009) is a well-nuanced example of this kind of research.

The study of parallelism in Nahuatl, Kuna, Quechua and Navajo

The study of parallelism in Middle America is by no means confined to Mayan research. Some of the earliest research on parallelism began with Garibay (1953), and this research continues to the present. In his presidential address to the annual meeting of the Linguistic Society of America, William Bright took the opportunity to examine the parallelism of a classical Nahuatl text dating from 1524. This text, *Coloquios y doctrina Cristiana*, edited with a translation, commentary and facsimile of the original manuscript by Miquel Leon-Portilla (1986), is a record preserved by Father Bernardino de Sahugun of a theological disputation between a group of Aztec priests and their spiritual counterparts, a dozen Franciscan friars. From the language used in this disquisition, this encounter was conducted in high formality.

Although the Aztecs acknowledged the death of their gods and the rightness of Christianity, they pleaded for the preservation of their ritual way of life. The text, which Bright quotes at length, reveals some remarkable aspects of semantic parallelism of this period. Within less than a decade of the overturn of their world in 1519, the Aztecs had already begun to fashion new forms of semantic parallelism to communicate their situation: either by using traditional pairs to designate new referents or by creating new dyads with constituent elements of previous dyadss. Thus, for example, Christ is referred to as 'He who is Night//who is Wind' (*in youalli//in ehecatl*); the Bible is 'His book// His writing, the word of heaven (lit. 'the heaven-word)//the divine word (the god-word)'. The Aztecs thus were able to converse in new theological terms using a formal language that had previously been reserved for their own sacred mysteries. This process of refashioning ritual languages to incorporate Christian concepts occurred at all levels of society throughout Middle America and was probably one of the reasons such parallelism has remained as a spoken heritage to the present.

In the Americas, the study of parallelism is not confined to areas of Nahuatl or Mayan languages. Joel Sherzer, whose earlier research highlighted the importance of parallelism among the Kuna (1972, 1974), has gone on to situate these forms of speaking in two notable studies: *Kuna Ways of Speaking: An ethnographic perspective* (1983) and *Verbal Art in San Blas* (1990). Bruce Mannheim, who has written on parallelism in various contexts (1986, 1987), has intriguingly examined the use of parallelism in a document, *El primer nueva corónica i buen gobierno*, written by Felipe Guaman Poma de Ayala in 1615 (1986). This document, in Quechua and Spanish, purports to describe the festival of the Inka in Cuzco at which the Inka sang to a tethered llama draped in a red mantle in thanksgiving for a successful harvest. As Mannheim explains, '"[s]emantic couplets" are a peculiarly Quechua poetic device in which two otherwise morphologically and syntactically identical lines are bound together by the alternation of two semantically related word stems' (1986:52).

Of particular interest is Mannheim's examination of various of these semantic couplets: 'tears' (*weqe*) pair with 'raindrops' (*para*), 'woven shawl' (*lliklla*) pairs with 'skirt' (*aqsu*), 'to carry' (*apay*) pairs with 'to guide' (*pusay*), 'to look at' (*rikuy*) pairs with 'to watch'. Most interesting, however, is his discussion of the synonymous pairing of two terms for 'water', *unu* and *yaku*: *unu*, the word for 'water' in the Cuzco area, and *yaku*, the word for 'water' from the Ayachuco dialect of southern Peruvian Quechua. Mannheim's discussion thus documents the use of dialect terms in the creation of a particular pairing—a phenomenon often alluded to in other traditions of parallelism but rarely so clearly examined.

Another area with a significant focus on parallelism is the study of Navajo poetry and ritual.

Building on the work of Gladys Reichard, particularly her monograph *Prayer: The compulsive word* (1944), various researchers (Witherspoon 1977; Gill 1980; Webster 2008) have examined the poetics of Navajo curing rituals. In this regard, Margaret Field and Taft Blackhorse have called attention to the role of 'metonymy' in Navajo prayer (2002). The most common feature of Navajo curing is the combination of repetition and parallelism: the reiterative use of a single compositional frame in which a succession of ordered semantic elements is inserted. Field and Blackhorse provide a simple example of this compositional sequence:

> I will be healthy,
>
> Wind will be beneath my feet,
>
> Wind will be beneath my legs,
>
> Wind will be beneath my body,
>
> Wind will be beneath my mind,
>
> Wind will be beneath my voice.
>
> (Field and Blackhorse 2002:124)

This is a compositional feature that Navajo shares with other traditions of parallelism, as, for example, the Kuna. (An example of this sequential mode of composition among the Kuna was discussed in my 1977 paper; see Chapter 2, in this volume.) The important semantic aspect of this Navajo example of parallelism is the ordered relationship among enumerated elements of the person: feet, legs, body, mind, voice. In Field and Blackhorse's terminology, this sequential relationship is designated as 'metonymy'; for Gill (1980:41), these terms are part of a 'catalogue' that depends on the particular curing ceremony that is conducted; for Paul Friedrich, these terms form an inventory of contiguity-based tropes (1991). For the Navajo, there is a directionality to this ordering of terms that is conceptualised as 'upward-moving'. Ritual requires a specifically ordered sequence as in the naming of the four directions—east, south, west and north—in a clockwise order.

The semantic relations among these 'equivalent' units are part of a yet wider semiotic process whereby a sequence of terms and their succession can follow a more extended path. This process involves a combination of parallelism and repetition. Sherzer, for example, writes of the 'Kuna passion for listing people, within frames provided by literary formulas and parallel lines and verses, mapped on to a narrative'. He goes on to argue that the 'use of lists in order to generate forms of discourse is so widespread in the world that it clearly constitutes a universal principle of oral discourse, of course as an instance of the most general universal principle, repetition' (1990:48–9).

This mode of discourse can result in extended genealogical lists, but it can also frequently follow an ordered sequence of places—what I have described as as a 'topogeny' (see Fox 1997:8–17; and in this volume, Chapter 11). There are common features to all such parallel recitations: the use of a set frame—often requiring one substitution, or possibly two, per line—combined with an ordered secession of terms: personal names, placenames, special categories or colours, sequential actions, and a variety of fixed inventories. In all such sequences, attention is focused on the set relationship among the successive elements of the sequence—the significance of a particular cultural metonymy.

Finnish and Ural-Altaic studies in parallelism

In recognising similarities between Finnish and Hebrew oral composition, early Finnish scholarship can be credited with initiating the comparative study of parallelism. E. Cajanus's Åbo dissertation, 'Linguarum ebraeae et finnicae convenientia', published in Lund in 1697, and Daniel Juslenius's *Oratorio de convenientia lingua Fennicae cum Hebraea et Graeca*, published in Stockholm in 1728, both predate the work of Bishop Lowth, while Henricus Gabriel Porthan's *Dissertationis de Poesi Fennica*, published in Åbo in 1766—the most explicit of these studies in its examination of Finnish parallelism—was carried out independently of Lowth.

> Elias Lönnrot's compilation of oral recitations—possibly from as many as a dozen different singers—took shape over several decades in the nineteenth century to become the present *Kalevala*. An initial version of these recitations, known as the *Old Kalevala*, was published in two volumes in 1835–36; the present expanded version, the standard version, appeared in 1849. This compilation became Finland's national epic and perhaps the best-known narrative composition in parallelism. Although there have been many translations of the *Kalevala* into English, Francis Peabody Magoun's translation (Lönnrot 1963), though in prose, provides an exceptional glimpse into one of the world's

literary classics. The singer's voice in the opening lines of the *Kalevala* is reminiscent of the composer of the *Popul Vuh*, whose intention was also to reveal: It is my desire, it is my wish

to set out to sing, to begin to recite,

to let a song of our clan glide on, to sing a family lay.

The words are melting in my mouth, utterances dropping out,

coming to my tongue, being scattered about on my teeth.

(Magoun translation of Lönnrot 1963:3)

Wolfgang Steinitz's *Der Parallelismus in der finnisch-karelischen Volksdichtung* (1934) set the basis for future research on Finnish-Karelian parallelism that has continued to the present. Based on research with one particular Karelian singer, Steinitz's monograph is a model of linguistic analysis that gives particular attention to the semantics of canonical composition. Much of the current research on parallelism is published in Finnish and is therefore less accessible to a wider readership. A key survey document in English on recent research is the volume *Song Beyond the Kalevala: Transformations of oral poetry*, edited by Anna-Leena Siikala and Sinikka Vakimo (1994). This is a useful compilation of papers on a variety of issues in *Kalevala* scholarship. With the exception of Pertti Anttonen's paper, 'Ethnopoetic analysis and Finnish oral verse', the scholarship in this volume, however, is less concerned with semantic parallelism and more with other distinctive features of the Finnic oral tradition, in particular, its metrical structure and its consistent use of alliteration. Frog and Eila Stepanova identify this combination of poetic features: 'The strichic trochaic tetrameter characterized by alliteration and mutual equivalence in parallel lines, called "Kalevala metre" in Finnish and *regivärrs* in Estonian, is found among Finns, Karelians, Ingrians, Votes and Estonians' (2011:204). Pentti Leino (1986) provides an excellent introduction to this metrical system; Janika Oras (2012) has added a further dimension to these studies by examining how musical patterning is interwoven with verse parallelism in the Estonian runo songs known as *regilaul*. Among various publications, given Berlin's examination of negative parallelism in Hebrew, it is also pertinent to cite the work of Felix Oinas, 'Negative parallelism in Karelian-Finnish folklore (1976). Oinas' *Studies in Finnish Folklore: Homage to the Kalevala* (1985) is also concerned with Kalevala parallelism.

Steinitz extended his study of Finno-Ugric parallelism by further research in Russia on Khanty (or Ostyak) and published his results in a two-volume work, *Ostjakische Volksdichtung und Erzählungen aus zwei Dialekten*, which first appeared in 1939–41but has since been reprinted with a foreword by Roman Jakobson in 1975–76 and expanded to four volumes. Continuing in this line of research, Brigitte Schulze has written a dissertation on semantic parallelism in Khanty, 'Der Wordparallelismus als Stilmittel der ostjakischen Volksdichtung' (1982). To honour Steinitz on his eightieth birthday, Ewald Lang and Gert Sauer published a volume, *Parallelsimus und Etymologie* (1987). In this volume, Lang puts forward his argument for parallelism as a 'universal principle of overall structural composition' (1987).

Parallelism in Australian and New Guinea languages

There are various indications of the use of parallelism in Australian and New Guinea languages. The most important contribution to the study of parallelism in Australia is T. G. H. Strehlow's masterly examination of Aranda songs, *Songs of Central Australia* (1971). As the son of a missionary, Strehlow was raised among the Aranda and had a native speaker's knowledge of the language. He was also acquainted with the literature on Hebrew parallelism. His work among the Aranda was the first study to examine the varied use of parallelism in ritual compositions and it remains the most extensive analysis of parallelism in any Aboriginal language. Strehlow's summary description makes clear the different levels at which this parallelism operates:

> [I]n a native song words and word-weaving receive as much attention as the rhythms and tonal patterns which accompany them…the Aranda couplets (or quatrains) tend to consist of two individual lines which, musically and rhythmically, stand in a complementary relation to each other: the second line of a couplet is either identical in rhythm and construction with the first, or it balances the first line antithetically and rounds off the couplet by a contrasting rhythm of its own. The relation of parallelism and antithesis also characterizes the language of the songs. As a general rule each couplet, like a Hebrew psalm verse, falls into two halves: the second half either reiterates or restates, in slightly different words, a subject already expressed by the first half, or it introduces a new thought or statement, thereby advancing or completing the subject that has been expressed in the first half. (1971:109–10)

As an example of this 'word-weaving' parallelism, Strehlow cites the five-couplet lines of a song in which the ancestor Ankōṭa gives voice to his performance in a sacred ceremony:

> I am red like a burning fire;
>
> I am covered with glowing red down.
>
> I am red like a burning fire;

> I am gleaming red, glistening with ochre.
>
> I am red like a burning fire;
>
> Red is the hollow in which I am lying.
>
> I am red like the heart of a fire
>
> Red is the hollow in which I am lying.
>
> A tjurunga is standing upon my head
>
> Red is the hollow in which I am lying. (1971:110)

In Strehlow's view, this poetry is simple but effective.

Myfany Turpin, who has done more recent research on Aranda song, confirms Strehlow's analysis of the structure of these songs. Following Linda Barwick (1989:18), she designates this basic dual prosodic structure of Aranda songs as consisting of 'text-line pairs' (TLP) composed of two nearly identical 'text-lines' for the insertion of lexical elements (2007:103). While concentrating on the melodic and rhythmic structure of these songs, Turpin defers to Strehlow's work for analysis of their semantic complexity.

A number of researchers have taken up Paul Friedrich's idea of 'polytropy' in their analysis of parallelism in Aboriginal song. In his analysis of Murriny Patha songs, Michael Walsh cites the use of parallelism (and repetition) as an instance of Friedrich's 'formal macrotrope' (2010:126–7). Similarly, Peter Toner enumerates a range of compositional features in Yolngu songs—repetition, synonymic repetition, synonymic parallelism and formulaic parallelism—as different kinds of 'formal tropes' (2001:145–6). As an example of synonymic and formulaic parallelism, he provides the text of a song known as 'jewfish' (*makani*) that would appear to be a kind of topogeny—an ordered recitation of placenames. In this case, the places named are the beaches that were created by an ancestral jewfish as it swam past them. A few lines of this song provide an idea of its structure:

> [J]ewfish/jewfish/jewfish/jewfish
>
> gone/my/[beach] of Buburru
>
> gone/my/[beach] of Gumbula
>
> gone/my/[beach] of Nawurapu
>
> getting closer/over there/[beach] of Aluwarra
>
> getting closer/over there/[beach] of Amadhadhiltj

getting closer/over there/[beach] of Nyinybini

gone/my/[beach] of Aluwarra

gone/my/[beach] of Marrurru. (Toner 2001:145–7)

Elsewhere Toner discusses 'the prolonged inventory of places named' in other songs as an instance of Friedrich's 'contiguity tropes' (2001:152).

Overall it would appear that though parallelism does occur in Australian Aboriginal compositions, particularly songs, such parallelism is not a pervasive or canonical feature of such compositions as is the case in other traditions of parallelism.

The use of parallelism is also reported in various New Guinea languages. Documented examples of parallelism are to be found in spells and in some song poems among the Foi (Weiner 1991), in the narrative genre known as *Tom Yaya Kange* among the Ku Wara in Highland New Guinea (Rumsey 2001, 2002, 2010) and in the poetic song traditions of the Ambonwari in East Sepik (Telban 2008).

In one of his papers on Ku Wara parallelism, Alan Rumsey gives examples of what he describes as 'pairing compounds': two nouns combined in sequence followed by a suffix that marks them as a pair. These pairs, as Rumsey notes, carry a meaning that encompasses more than their parts. Thus the pair 'marsupial-bird' connotes 'hunted animals of the forest'; the pair 'pig-dog' can be used to refer to all 'domestic animals' but can also connote 'people with uncontrolled appetites'; while the pair 'sugarcane-banana' carries a connotation of 'snack food' (2002:278–80). A particularly interesting pair is the combination '(Catholic) mass-(Lutheran)prayer/invocation', which together is used to refer to Christianity. The semantics that Rumsey describes for such compounds is in fact a critical feature of innumerable dyadic sets in different traditions of canonical parallelism. Of further interest from a regional perspective is the occurrence of specific pairing compounds such as 'yam-taro' and 'sugarcane-banana', which are among the most widespread canonical pairs that occur in traditions of parallelism throughout much of eastern Indonesia. These pairs are generally used as botanic icons for persons (see Fox 1971:242–4; 1988:23; 1992; see also Nakagawa 1988:233).

Similarly, in his study of the Melpa of Mount Hagen, the German missionary ethnographer Hermann Strauss has emphasised the fundamental importance of pairing compounds—what he refers to as 'a concept of complementation': 'Complementation to form a pair-unit is a very central feature of the religion and culture of the *Mbowamb* [Melpa]' (1990:12). Certainly the texts that he has included in his ethnography give evidence of parallelism but not of an extensive or elaborated tradition as such.

In New Guinea, as in Australia, it would appear that the use of parallelism is definitely a feature of oral composition but this feature does not appear to have been developed to the same level of elaboration, as occurs, for example, throughout much of the Austronesian-speaking world.

The study of parallelism in Austronesian languages

The use of parallelism occurs across the whole of the Austronesian-language family. As a speech form, parallelism is, as elsewhere, a feature of elevated discourse and is invariably used as a vehicle for ritual communication and as a means of preserving sacred knowledge. The use of parallelism was a living tradition in many areas of the Austronesian-speaking world until recently and this traditional use continues particularly in the islands of eastern Indonesia.

Nowhere, however, does there exist the historical depth for the study of parallelism that exists in Middle America. The oldest existing texts in parallelism date from the middle of the nineteenth century. The Bible translator A. Hardeland, in his *Versuch einer Grammatik der Dajackschen Sprache* (1858), was the first to note the Hebraic parallels in Dayak 'spirit language' (Basa Sangiang), but he provided only a single illustration of this 'spirit language' with translation and commentary; however, the posthumous publication of the Swiss missionary H. Schärer's two-volume compilation of texts in Basa Sangiang, *Der Totenkult der Ngadju Dajak in Süd-Borneo* (1966), advances Hardeland's initial work by providing a substantial corpus for study. This corpus on the Ngaju has been further extended by the substantial work of Sri Kuhnt-Saptodewo (1993, 1999).

Other large compilations of ritual-language texts are those assembled by D. Dunselman (1949, 1950, 1954, 1955, 1959, 1961) from the Kendayan and Mualang Dayak of West Borneo; by H. Lagemann (1893, 1906) and W. L. Steinhart (1934, 1937, 1938, 1950, 1954) from Nias; by W. Dunnebier (1938, 1953) from Bolaang Mongondow; by H. van der Veen (1929, 1950, 1965, 1966) and by Dana Rappoport (2013) from the Sa'dan Toraja; and by P. Middelkoop (1949) from the Atoni Pah Meto of West Timor and by A. Quack (1981, 1985), D. Schröder and A. Quack (1979), with a more recent collection of ritual texts by Josiane Cauquelin (2008), for the Puyuma of Taiwan. Another recent study of a priestly language—that of the transvestite *bissu* priests of the Bugis of South Sulawesi—is Gilbert Hamonic's *Le Langage des Dieux* (1987), which includes a considerable number of prayers in parallelism. Most of these collections of texts, with accompanying translations and commentary, were produced by their various authors primarily for the purposes of cultural exegesis.

H. van der Veen's monograph *The Merok Feast of the Sa'dan-Toradja* (1965) provides a good illustration. The main Merok feast chant, which takes the form of a journey, consists of more than 790 double-lines filled with paired metaphoric images in an array of successive formulaic frames. It has many of the features that one encounters in other traditions of parallelism: admonitions, ritual directives, inventories and topogenies. An example of this is the inventory for the spiritual journey that it sets forth. This semantic inventory is repeatedly framed in the double-lines: 'As sustenance for the journey//as provisions on the way' (*ammi pokinallo ilalan//ammi pokokong dilambanan*):

> As sustenance for the journey, take the three-eared rice
>
> As provisions on the way, take the cut one, branched in three...
>
> As sustenance for the journey, take the gold kris of great size
>
> As provisions on the way, take the piece of beadwork, with cords hanging low...
>
> As sustenance for the journey, take an auspicious dream
>
> As provisions on the way, take a pregnant nocturnal vision. (van der Veen 1965:37–9)

After the long recitation of these provisions, the chant sets forth the path that should be followed, using another simple dyadic frame that combines 'path' and 'way' (*lalan//lambanan*):

> Then shalt thou take the rainbow as thy path
>
> Thou shalt make thy way along the arch of the sky. (van der Veen 1965:39–40)

The longest section of this chant, which runs for more than 140 double-lines, is a topogeny that invokes and then invites the gods from all directions and from all of the Toraja territory and beyond, named and ordered in dyadic form:

> The God of the *Leatung* region,
>
> the Lord of the district of *Mangkaranga*
>
> The God of the Patua' region
>
> the Lord of the district of Mila'.
>
> (van der Veen 1965:42–61)

The recitation of this invitation to the gods among the Toraja—a requirement in many ritual performances—is similar in function and form to the extended Zhuang invitation to their gods and spirits recorded by Holm (2003:60–9).

Lexicons of ritual language

Hardeland's concern with parallelism was primarily philological. He thus attempted to distinguish different classes of vocabulary (1858:4–5): 1) slightly altered Dayak words; 2) Malay words, also slightly altered; and 3) special words, whose meaning and form were confined exclusively to use in the 'spirit language'. His dictionary (1859) includes some 900 of these Basa Sangiang words. M. Baier (see Baier et al 1987) continued this work of more than a century by publishing a dictionary of Basa Sangiang based on materials from both Hardeland and Schärer.

Following Hardeland, B. F. Matthes (1872) noted the use of similar sorts of lexical items in the parallel language of the transvestite priests of the Bugis, as did the missionary linguist N. Adriani, who wrote a brief comparative paper in Dutch on 'Indonesian priest languages' (1920, reprinted 1932:III, pp. 1–21) and another similar paper in German on 'magic speech' (1926, reprinted 1932:III, pp. 167–75).

The concern with the constituent origin of the lexicon of these ritual languages has continued to interest researchers to the present. In his study of Dusun 'sacred language', Evans (1953:495–6) distinguished five classes of words that made up this register: 1) 'ordinary Dusun words'; 2) 'special but easily recognizable forms of ordinary words—poetic forms—derived from ordinary Dusun'; 3) 'words not usually current in the village...but found in other villages, near or far away'; 4) 'loan words from Malay'; and 5) 'words used, as far as known, only in the "sacred language", for which derivations are not obtainable'.

Writing of the Timugon Murut priestesses (*babalian*) whose ritual curing performances require a strict pairing of all ritual utterances, D. J. Prentice gives particular attention to the origin of the lexicon of these utterances. In such performances, which can last for days, the principal priestess utters the first line to which her acolyte, who accompanies her, responds with the second. Prentice describes the first line of each couplet as 'couched in a style of language which has much in common with the poetic style normally used in non-ritual singing', whereas the 'response' (*taam*) is 'couched in a special ritual language' (1981:130–1). Prentice identifies various sources for such response words: 1) 'a small number of cases where the ritual substitute is a synonym that already exists in the normal language...numerals may also be reckoned as belonging to this category since a numeral "X" is replaced in the *taam* by the numeral "X + 1"'; 2) 'more frequently, the *taam*-word exists in normal Timugon, but with a different (sometimes even contradictory) meaning'; 3) '*taam*-words which exist in normal language, but in a different form (i.e. a derivative rather than as a base, or *vice versa*)'; 4) 'a very large number of ritual terms...known only from cognates in some other Murut dialect or in another language'; and, finally, as in the case with Evans' analysis of Dusun, 5) 'a number of substitute words for which no connections are known, either in Timugon or in any other dialect or language' (1981:133–5).

The rules for the pairing of terms combined with the required use of special terms in the make-up of many pairs are evidence that these ritual languages are not simply the elevated pairing of ordinary speech but rather are special registers that invariably require a considerable learning process.

Parallelism in Austronesian speech genres

At the same time that in the nineteenth century some missionary linguists were focusing attention on priestly registers among the Austronesians, other missionaries had begun to recognise the more general nature and widespread use of parallel compositions. Thus, for example, in 1880, writing of Malagasy, the British missionary James Sibree noted: 'It is most pleasant therefore to listen to a native orator, especially as in the more formal Malagasy speeches the parts of every sentence are regularly balanced in construction, form a kind of rhythm very closely resembling the parallelism of Hebrew poetry' (1880:148).

As a special register for oratory, prayer, poetry or song, such formal socially elevated composition is not necessarily confined to a specific class of practitioners and is therefore more likely to be used in a variety of settings. Whereas in the case of 'priestly registers' identification is generally couched in relation to particular performers or religious performances, oratorical registers (based on similar modes of composition but often with a less obscure lexicon) are generally discussed in terms of different speech genres or literary productions. Often, however, oral poets in Austronesian societies are regarded as 'spirit-enlightened' figures whose roles are similar to, and often overlap with, that of priests, priestesses or shamans. Based on his research among the Berawan of Sarawak, Peter Metcalf has published a collection of prayers in parallelism by which, for example, individuals instruct sacrificial animals to convey their words to specific deities (1989, 1994). In a different context, Margaret Florey has studied the preservation of a local genre of 'incantations' among the Alune of Seram in Central Maluku, who are undergoing rapid social and linguistic changes (Florey 1998; Florey and Wolff 1998).

The literature on these various poetic registers is diverse. Thus, for example, L. Sabatier has published the text of a major 'epic' in pervasive parallelism for the Rhade (1933); in his commentary on the Salasilah of Koetai (1956), W. Kern has commented on the comparative significance of parallelism in Malay *penglipur-lara* tales, Middle Malay *anday-anday* and Minangkabau *kaba* (1956); and Nigel Phillips has produced an exemplary study of *Sijobang*, the sung narrative poetry of West Sumatra (1981). For the Philippines, H. J. Wigglesworth has emphasised the role of parallelism as a rhetorical device in Manobo narrative discourse (1980); as has Nicole Revel among the Palawan (2013). J. P. B. de Josselin de Jong has written a critical study of eastern Indonesian poetry (1941). Timo Kaartinen has examined the parallelism of a song tradition among the displaced 'Bandanese' in the Kei Islands (1998) and Aone van Engelenhoven has provided a preliminary study of the parallelism of 'royal speech' and 'song speech' among the people of Leti in the southern Moluccas (1997). His article includes the translation of a parallel text first recorded in 1846. Similarly, Gillian Sankoff has analysed parallelism in poetry of the Buang, an Austronesian-speaking population of Papua New Guinea (1977). The *Kumulipo*, the long Hawaiian narrative chant translated by Martha Beckwith (1951), provides an excellent example of similar forms of extended literary parallelism. While most of these compositions are in strict canonical parallelism, others show parallelism in varying degrees. The Iban, for example, whose ritual traditions have been particularly well documented by Benedict Sandin (1977), James Masing (1997) and Clifford Sather (2001), use parallelism to a lesser extent than other Borneo populations such as the Kendayan or Berawan.

The prominence of parallelism in societies on the islands of Sumba, Flores and Timor has meant that most ethnographic accounts of these populations discuss the use of parallelism in social and ritual contexts. This is particularly true of the island of Sumba with its closely related yet distinct groups: Danielle Geirnaert-Martin (1992), for example, examines the use of parallelism in the Paddu rituals of Laboya; Janet Hoskins (1993) the parallel language of the calendric rituals of Kodi; Webb Keane (1997) considers the whole rhetoric of performance and representation among the Anakalang; while Joel Kuipers has written two important studies (1990, 1998) on Weyewa ritual speech. Although the Weyewa tradition appears to lack an extended narrative genre like some found on neighbouring islands, the use of ritual speech extends to a variety of what Kuipers refers to as political, religious and personal genres of speech. Kuipers (1998:37) identifies no less than 19 such genres. He also addresses the question of ongoing changes in the use of ritual speech styles, noting the marginalisation of an aggressive performance genre expressing the anger of politically powerful figures in favour of nostalgic laments and school-sanctioned children's performances (1998). Adding to this array of studies on parallelism in Sumba, Elvira Rothe, in an unpublished dissertation for Ludwig Maximilian University in Munich (2004), has produced a remarkably detailed linguistic examination of the Poddu rituals of Loli.

The same is true for Flores and Timor. The ethnographies by Philipus Tule for the Keo of central Flores (2004) and by Karl-Heinz Kohl for the Belogili of eastern Flores rely on compositions in parallel language in their expositions. Tule's ethnography, which focuses on a mixed Catholic–Muslim population, includes prayers in parallelism both for the ordination of a priest and for the safe journey of someone going on the Haj. Kohl's ethnography records the rituals of the rice cycle. Three as yet unpublished PhD theses—the first by Michael Vischer (1992) focusing on the island of Palué, the second by Penelope Graham (1991) on the community of Lewotala in eastern Flores, near the Belogili, and the third by David Butterworth (2008) on the Krowe community in central eastern Flores—provide further detailed ethnographic evidence of the use of parallelism in Flores.For Timor, the use of parallelism with critical attention to the cultural significance of key semantic pairs forms the basis of the ethnographies by Andrew McWilliam on the Atoni Pah Meto (2002), by G. Tom Therik on the southern Tetun at their ritual centre in Wehali (2004), and by Elizabeth Traube on the Mambai (1986), while Gregor Neonbasu's ethnography (2011) is organised specifically around the oral traditions of the Atoni of Biboki. Herbert Jardner's monograph *Die Kuan-Fatu-Chronik* (1999) records and examines parallelism in the narratives of the Atoni of Amanuban. The unpublished PhD thesis by Benjamin de Araujo Corte-Real (1999) on the verbal arts of the Mambai offers a further important contribution to the study of parallelism in Timor.

Of particular comparative significance is the publication of a substantial collection of Bunaq texts collected by Louis Berthe (1972). The Bunaq are a non–Austronesian-language group situated in—indeed surrounded by—Austronesian-speaking populations. Historically, the Bunaq have been drawn into the ritual spheres of neighbouring Kemak and Tetun and their parallelism reflects this historical involvement. In their sacred texts, numerous Bunaq canonical pairs combine Bunaq and Tetun/Kemak terms, thus bridging language families by coupling lexical elements of Austronesian and non-Austronesian. Engelenhoven (2010) has documented the use of parallel discourse among the Fataluku, another non-Austronesian language group at the eastern end of Timor-Leste, comparing its specific pairs with those of other neighbouring Austronesian-languages groups within the region.

An ethnographically focused comparison of the ritual languages of eastern Indonesia can be found in the volume edited by Fox, *To Speak in Pairs: Essays on the ritual languages of eastern Indonesia* (1988). This volume consists of 10 studies of different ritual languages on Sumba, Flores, Rote and Sulawesi. The collection as a whole provides an indication of the diversity of social contexts in which these registers continue to be used in societies of eastern Indonesia: for divination and spirit communication, prayers and sacrificial invocations, bride-wealth negotiations, ordeals, mortuary ceremonies, complex origin-cycle rituals, and a variety of other critical oratorical contexts. Several authors focus on the ritual-language traditions of different groups in west Sumba: Janet Hoskins examines the formal etiquette of communication with spirits in Kodi; David Mitchell explicates the metaphoric couplets in oratory among Wanukaka speakers; Brigitte Renard-Clamagirand focuses on the speech used in a ceremony for 'banishing transgression'; and Joel Kuipers examines the pattern of prayer among the Weyewa. Gregory Forth contrasts the invocatory and oratorical speeches in Rindi in eastern Sumba. For Flores, Eriko Aoki provides a detailed examination of a sequence of divination and ordeal to discover stolen objects among Lio speakers; Satoshi Nakagawa considers the formal idioms of marriage among Endeh speakers; while Douglas Lewis examines the performance of a narrative history in Tana Ai. Fox examines the formulaic structure of a long mortuary chant on Rote and Charles Zerner and Toby Volkman consider the language of one ritual in a complex cycle of Toraja ceremonies.

The prominence of the ritual voice

While each of the papers in *To Speak in Pairs* examines a distinct tradition of parallelism in a different speech community, there is an underlying commonality to all of these traditions in eastern Indonesia. In addition to the broad similarity of many shared semantic pairs, there occurs in ritual speech throughout the region what might be called a distinct 'ritual voice'. The chanter, poet or speaker takes on and merges with the *persona* or *personae* of the performance and personally directs the ritual message. Several examples may illustrate the variety of modes of this ritual voice.

The words of Mo'an Robertus Rapa of clan Ipir in Wai Brama, as quoted by Douglas Lewis (1988:271), give an indication of one form of ritual voice—the proud ritual voice:

> I am clan Ipir, the great ebony tree
>
> I am exalted like the large birds of the mountains
>
> The domain of Wai Brama and Wolobola
>
> Raja as far as Balénatar
>
> Speaking to the sky and earth
>
> Addressing the sun and moon.

In contrast with this ritual voice, there is the ritual voice—the humble ritual voice—in the 'deference' mode of speaking described by Janet Hoskins (1988:54–5) among the Kodi:

> Only we are left, spiders with no livers
>
> Only we are left, snails with no thoughts...
>
> There is no one here to tell us the many long myths

There is no one here to teach us more of our customs

I am alone like a child holding the net for a discus toy

I am alone like a child grasping the rope on a spinning top.

This is the voice that even the most respected Kodi chanters adopt in pleading with the ancestral 'spirits of the inside' to whom they are indeed children.

Among the Atoni of Timor, knowledgeable ritual speakers take on the *persona* of their clan embodied in the clan name: the *kanaf*. The history of the clan can thus be recited as a journey of the name—a dense personal topogeny that moves through a specific landscape. The narrative of the difficult 'path' of the Nabuasa clan, as recounted by Andrew McWilliam (2007:107; see 2002:80), gives an idea of this ritual voice:

As a great man,

one who kicks the land and

one who kicks the water

travelling past

the slippery bamboo and

the swollen stream

Amsam Noetasi

Monam Saibet.

Not staying long

not remaining [but]

turning back

returning from

The rising moon,

The rising day.

A ritual voice can also be so specifically engaged in the details of a ceremony that it is almost incomprehensible without careful exegesis of the speaker's intention and the context of his speaking. Joel Kuipers has examined a sequence of ceremonies among the Weyewa (1990:115–16)—a placation ritual that followed an earlier divination ritual by the speaker and specialist Mbani Mata. He was acting on behalf of someone, Malo Dunga, who, it was determined, had failed to carry out the promises of his ancestors, Mbili and Koni. Excerpts from this ritual that make reference to Malo Dunga as 'cucumber flower'//'gourd fruit' and the problem that Mbani Mata has uncovered by 'cutting the tree to its base'//'searching for water to its source' provide a glimpse of the complex involvement of a ritual voice:

> You cucumber flower offspring there
>
> you gourd fruit descendant there
>
> he arrived at shadow of the house eaves
>
> he arrived at the porch
>
> and if I cut the tree
>
> to its base
>
> and if I search the water
>
> to its source
>
> don't hide the source of red ants
>
> don't hide the fish in a bamboo jar…
>
> I say to you right now…
>
> to help us listen to Mother's voice
>
> to help us listen to Father's voice…
>
> do not deviate from the path
>
> do not raise your sword at me.

As Kuipers explains, a speaker may change names—and thus *personae*—many times in the course of a single ritual.

The ritual voice may be revelatory but it may also be intentionally obscure—a voice that struggles to express ancient mysteries that can not be fully comprehended. Thus, among the Mambai of Timor-Leste, the Ritual Lord who combines the conjoined attributes of male and female is conceived of as a new born infant. As Elizabeth Traube explains, this representation figures prominently in ritual oratory: 'Drawing on images of birth, performers liken themselves to babies who have just emerged from womb:

> My brow is soft
>
> My navel is bloody

There is oil over my brow

There is blood over my eyes.

My ears are still full

My head is still whole,

I show with the mouth

I reveal with the eyes.

(Traube 1986: 105)

In these and other contexts, the ritual voice is that of the speaker transformed, no longer a mere individual, but rather a collective instrument of formal annunciation and communication whose formal language is culturally established, semantically ordered and recognisably meaningful.

Comments on the comparative use of parallelism

This survey of directions and diversions in the comparative study of parallelism serves several purposes. It demonstrates the prevalence and pertinence of parallelism as a linguistic phenomenon. It also indicates its considerable persistence as an oral tradition as well as its continuance as a literary tradition. It is also notable that parallelism emerged in ritual compositions at the beginnings of so many traditions of early writing—in Sumer, in Egypt, in China and also among the Maya. The library unearthed at Ras Shamra contained cuneiform texts that linked the Ugaritic tradition of parallelism to the Akkadian and ultimately Sumerian traditions. Research has similarly shown the persistence of Mayan traditions of parallelism—even the persistence of fixed pairs—from the Palenque inscriptions to present-day Mayan ritual performances. Chinese, it could be argued, has also maintained a continuous tradition of parallel composition.

Although most of the research on parallelism has been carried out largely independently on different language traditions, it is evident that there are similarities in many of the features that define parallelism as a linguistic phenomenon. There are also striking gradations in the use of parallelism in composition. These gradations are evident between different traditions as well as within particular traditions. In their simplest forms, parallel compositions may consist of a repeated formulaic frame with a succession of single semantic substitutions. In other traditions, linked parallel lines may consist of three, or possibly even four, semantic pairs. The most elaborate of these traditions are generally based on culturally specific requirements for (or at least the expectation of) the canonical pairing of semantic elements.

Parallelism is invariably an elevated speech register; in many traditions, the greater the emphasis on parallelism and the set pairing of words and phrases, the more elevated is the level of speaking and the greater is the significance of the message this speaking is intended to convey. Parallelism is thus a device of ritual and high oratory but also a device for the preservation of sacred knowledge.

Parallelism can occur at many levels and there is a great variety of modes of composition both oral and literary. The semantics of parallelism is, however, paramount and offers the widest scope for research. There is nothing either simple or mechanistic about this semantics. The pairing of terms is more than the sum of its individual elements. In Jakobson's framework, the metaphoric axis of similarity is projected onto the metonymic axis of continuity. Although this describes the formal process of pairing, the process of pairing creates new meanings.

The link between two words produces a metaphoric connection that may have multiple meanings and interpretations. In this semantic relationship, the complementarity of elements at the literal level enunciates a further interpretative level. As Hull notes, 'older brother'///'younger brother' can refer more widely to 'all men'; 'mother'///'father' to a complex set of relations of nurture or superiority. Among the Rotenese, when 'elder brother'///'younger brother' are paired, their referent is specifically to '(male) members of the same clan'; when 'mother'///'father' are paired, the sense, as among the Maya, is that of nurture and superiority, but the referent is often specifically to a ruler or government official.

Or, for example, where in this translation of the *Popul Vuh*, Edmonson gives a literal rendering to the couplet 'green plate'///'blue bowl', Sam Colop in his translation interprets this pair in its fuller metaphoric sense as 'green earth'///'blue sky'. Among the Weyewa, 'cucumber flower'///'gourd fruit' is a botanic metaphor for a 'descendant' or 'offspring', and as Joel Kuipers explains, the recurrent pair 'horse'///'dog' or the even more expressive parallel phrase 'horse with a standing tail'///'dog with a black tongue', while striking in itself, is in fact intended as a reference to the orator or narrator of a composition, allowing him to insert his presence within his composition.

Underlying all such pairings is the notion of the 'canonical': 'fixed word pairs', 'conventional couplets', 'diaphrastic kenning', 'dyadic sets'—however they are identified, the interpretable semantic stock of pairs recognised by a particular speech community. The range of these pairs and their relationship to one another are fundamental to the understanding of any tradition of parallelism. To date, Dahood's 'Ras Shamra Parallels'—a listing with commentary of shared

Ugaritic and Hebrew pairs—is the most extensive compilation of such canonical elements. My own, as yet unpublished, dictionary of Rotenese dyadic language has at present more than 1750 such pairs and, as it continues to expand, may well run to more than 2500 pairs.

Another recurrent observation made of traditions of complex canonical parallelism is their utilisation of what in the literature on Hebrew parallelism are referred to as 'rare and esoteric words'. The sharing of pairs between Ugaritic and Hebrew is an aspect of this linguistic phenomenon. It indicates the historical inheritance and preservation of a common semantic tradition but it is also an indication of a readiness to borrow from other linguistic sources. In the Middle East, the shared inheritance of semantic sets evident in Hebrew may well extend to the earlier Akkadian/Sumerian traditions of parallels whereas a similar sharing of semantic couplets in the Mayan region extends from the earliest inscriptions to the present. The borrowing of new terms from other languages and the recombination of existing terms to create new semantic concepts are equally fundamental to the continuing development of traditions of parallelism. Together, all of this is evidence of the development of traditions of elaborate semantic parallelism in areas of linguistic diversity and indeed the exploitation of linguistic diversity to create an increasingly rich repertoire of pairings.

Seen from the perspective of a single speech community, the tendency has been to consider this use of 'external' linguistic resources as an impediment to normal intelligibility—the creation of specialised, exotic, priestly registers. In situations of multiple language use, however, and of dialect diversity, parallel languages can actually promote communication—especially ritual communication—across linguistic boundaries. My own research on the island of Rote with its chain of dialects gives evidence of this 'inter-dialect' aspect of its ritual language. To appreciate this 'dialect concatenation', it is essential to examine the function of a tradition of parallelism from beyond the confines of a single speech community and instead to consider it from the perspective of the multiple speech communities that have a share in it.

In the literature on parallelism, considerable attention is given to varied forms of composition: the arrangement of lines, couplet, triplet and quatrain-structures, chiasmus, negative pairs, internal pairing or the ordering of inventories. This important focus on the varieties of dual structures that occur at the surface level of composition does not, however, give attention to the possible semantic networking of the terms that compose these dyadic structures. In traditions of canonical parallelism, many of the lexical terms that form particular pairs also occur in other pairings. There is thus more to the study of parallelism than the identification and listing of specific pairs or couplets.

Key terms may link with other terms and can, in this way, be embedded within complex semantic networks. These networks are themselves of interest in understanding the ideas of a particular culture. Thus, for example, in Chapter 5 in this volume, I examine the semantic network formed by verbs for 'speaking' in Rotenese, and in Chapter 6, I consider the network of the key terms—or primary symbols—in Rotenese ritual language defined as those terms that have the greatest linkages among themselves and with other terms in ritual language.

In my 'Introduction' to the volume *To Speak in Pairs*, I also compared the semantic 'embeddedness' of terms for 'earth, land, ground, country' in Rindi, a dialect of east Sumbanese, with those for the same term in Rotenese (1988:25–6). In Rindi, this term is *tana* and in Rotenese, it is *dae*. In his paper for the volume (1988:129–60), Gregory Forth listed the various terms that paired with *tana*, and I did the same for the term for *dae* in Rotenese.

Rindi	Gloss	*Rotenese*	Gloss
tana//ai	tree, wood	dae//ai	tree, wood
//wai	water	//oe	water
//watu	stone	//batu	stone
//awangu	sky	//lai(n)	sky
//rumba	grass	//tua	lontar palm
//luku	river	//dale	inside
//pindu	gate	//de'a	outside
//paraingu	domain	//dulu	east

This simple illustration indicates that Rindi and Rote share a common set of ritual associations that link 'earth', 'water', 'stone' and 'tree'. For both there also exists a contrastive association between 'earth' and 'sky'. For the east Sumbanese, other associations of 'earth' or 'land' are with 'grass' and 'river' whereas among the Rotenese there is an association of 'earth' with the 'lontar palm', a primary source of livelihood. In Rotenese, the term *dae* can function as a directional indicator meaning 'below', and through this sense, it links to other directional terms such as 'inside', 'outside' and 'east'. In contrast, in Rindi, the further association of *tana* is with 'gate' and 'domain'. Although this illustration provides only an initial set of linkages for these terms, it shows how formal comparison might be made between different systems of meaning. Both terms form part of yet larger semantic networks and these networks can be examined either in terms of the 'embedding' of particular elements or in terms of their larger overall structures. Chapter 6 in this volume provides another perspective on the embedding of *dae* as a primary ritual symbol. Using the evidence of the linkages among parallel terms, it is certainly possible to imagine comparisons among the different cultural traditions of eastern Indonesia but it is also possible to conceive of comparisons, for example, between eastern Indonesia and the Mayan region—both areas of still vital traditions of parallelism.

This survey makes clear that parallelism is no simple phenomenon. In its many manifestations, it varies considerably in its semantic complexity and in the varieties of its performative expression. What is most evident from this survey is that parallelism is not always immediately evident. What constitute culturally defined notions of equivalence, opposition or complementary—in Robert Lowth's phrase, the 'correspondences…answering to one another'—can only be interpreted from within particular traditions. Criteria for categories of gendered opposition, positive-negative pairings, rules of tonal complementarity and of alliteration, metrical congruence and the reversals defined by chiasmus define the nature of particular traditions of parallelism.

The semantic complexity of such traditions of parallelism range from a successive iteration of particular terms, often comprising a set repertoire of related items, through a plethora of culturally specific registers that use a variety of semantic pairings to yet more elaborate systems of canonical parallelism hedged with ritual injunctions that demand adherence.

A great deal of the literature on parallelism documents traditions that have ceased to exist as oral traditions—that are now literary objects of analysis that may, at best, hint at earlier stages of their composition. However, in parts of the world, particularly in Middle America and Southeast Asia, there still exist living oral traditions of parallel composition—some of considerable complexity and vitality. Although these traditions are under threat, they remain a special area for continuing research.

This survey of recent research on parallelism has the purpose of providing a prelude to the study on a single, still active performative tradition of canonical parallelism—that of the Rotenese of eastern Indonesia.

4. Semantic parallelism in Rotenese ritual language[1]

My objective here is: 1) to discuss the semantics of Rotenese ritual language; 2) to offer an exemplary text with translation and analysis; and 3) to consider some directions in the study of this language form.[2] Rotenese ritual language is a form of oral poetry characterised by the required coupling of virtually all semantic elements. The language is formal, formulaic and parallelistic. Semantic elements comprise prescribed dyadic sets; these sets are structured in formulaic phrases; and, as a result, composition generally consists in the production of parallel poetic lines. While simple in structure, elements of this language are of sufficient number, variety and complexity to allow considerable scope for stylistic elaboration but little scope—if any at all—for individual improvisation. Knowledge of these ritual forms is essential to an understanding of Rotenese social classification. Any recitation of ritual language requires a ceremonial context. A minimal ceremonial context, for the Rotenese, involves the giving of native lontar gin ('the water of words') to one's guest. A practice, among elders and especially among chanters on visits to each other, is to recite short *bini* at each other between successive rounds of gin. These minor contests often end in excited incoherence. Some ancestral figures, I was told, as they grew older, abandoned ordinary language entirely and spoke only in ritual language.

Parallelism and its Indonesian occurrence

This linguistic phenomenon, which Roman Jakobson (1966:403) has aptly described as 'canonical, pervasive parallelism', is of widespread, general comparative significance. Robert Lowth, who in publications on ancient Hebrew poetry between 1753 and 1779 first articulated the concept of *parallelismus membrorum*, distinguished between 'parallel lines', the parallelism of conjoined verses and 'parallel terms', 'the words of phrases, answering one to another in the corresponding lines' (Lowth 1778:ix). Since Lowth's early observations, Biblical scholarship has painstakingly examined the 'repetitive parallelism' of Hebrew poetry and, in tracing its relation to Ugaritic and Canaanite forms, has demonstrated that Lowth's 'parallel terms' constitute, in the Semitic oral

---
1   This chapter was first published in 1971 as 'Semantic parallelism in Rotenese ritual language', *Bijdragen tot de Taal-, Land- en Volkenkunde*, vol. 127, pp. 215–55.
2   The research on which the original paper was based was supported by a Public Health Service fellowship (MH-23, 148) and grant (MH-10, 161) from the National Institute of Mental Health and was conducted in Indonesia (1965–66) under the auspices of what is now Lembaga Ilmu Pengatahuan Indonesia. I am particularly indebted to Dr Rodney Needham for his direction of my research on Rote and to Stefanus Adulanu of clan Meno in Termanu for his supervision of my instruction in ritual language.

traditions of Syria and Palestine, a standardised body of conventionally fixed word pairs by means of which verse forms were composed (Newman and Popper 1918–23; Gevirtz 1963).

The study of parallelism, originally inspired by these Hebraic parallels, has become a subject of research among the oral literatures of the world. Major studies have been made on the languages of the Ural-Altaic area, particularly on Finnish-Karelian folk poetry, and on the epics and songs of the Turkic and Mongolian peoples; on Chinese 'parallel prose'; on Russian and other Slavic folk traditions; and on the 'polar-expressions' in ancient Greek literature.[3] Emeneau (1966) published an article on 'formulaically fixed pairs of song units' among the Toda, which suggested parallelism may be of wider occurrence within the Dravidian language group.[4] Parallelism was also evidently characteristic of ancient Maya poetry (Thompson 1950:61–3) and is preserved in the oral traditions of the modern Maya (Gossen 1970:315–61).

This sheer accumulation of studies on parallelism, in its varied metric, syntactic and semantic appearances, seems, at times, to reduce the phenomenon to nothing more than a device of stylistic repetition, an ornate redundancy (cf. Gonda 1959), whereas what certain facets of 'compulsory' semantic parallelism offer is a means to formal research on the 'metaphoric correspondences' of particular speech communities (Jakobson and Halle 1956:76–82). The parallelism prevalent—often in priestly or esoteric speech forms—among many of the Indonesian peoples provides an extensive field for comparative research on this form of binate semantics.

The Bible translator Hardeland, in his *Versuch einer Grammatik der Dajackschen Sprache* (1858:5), was the first to note the Hebraic parallels in Dajak 'spirit language' (Basa Sangiang): '*Der Charakter der basa Sangiang ist poetisch, voll Sinnbilder. Die Form ähnelt der Hebräischen Dichtersprache hinsichtlich des Rythmus und der kurzen parallelen Glieder.*' As an illustration of this language, Hardeland included as an appendix to his grammar a long text with translation and commentary. The text was, in some ways, a curiosity since it consisted of a running German translation with Dajak words inserted, singly or in pairs, above their appropriate German equivalents, making it difficult, if not impossible,

---

3 Jakobson, in his article 'Grammatical parallelism and its Russian facet' (1966), presents a short discussion of the development of the study of parallelism. Chief among the numerous studies he cites are the following—for the Ural-Altaic area: Steinitz (1934); Lotz (1954); Schirmunski (1965); Poppe (1958). For Chinese: Schlegel (1896); Tchang Tcheng-Ming (1937); Hightower (1959). To these can be added Granet's (1919) more sociologically oriented study *Fêtes et Chansons Anciennes de la Chine*, which contains an appendix with some 20 further citations on similar antiphonal poetic styles throughout East Asia. An important study on ancient Greek literature is Kemmer (1903), and, from a different viewpoint, Lloyd (1966). Newman in part one of his *Studies in Biblical Parallelism* (in Newman and Popper 1918–23) discusses some of the evidence for parallelism in Egyptian, Babylonian and Arabic.
4 Ritual texts such as those of Rosner (1961) from the Sadars of Jashpur, Madhya Pradesh, would clearly seem to substantiate this suggestion.

for anyone unacquainted with Dajak to construct the verse parallels. The posthumous publication of Schärer's two-volume *Der Totenkult der Ngadju Dajak in Süd-Borneo* (1966), however, provided an enormous corpus of texts in Dajak Basa Sangiang. Had Schärer completed his intended five volumes with its promised lexicon, his research would have been a unique monument in the study of parallelism.

Parallel language forms are not confined to this one area of Borneo. Of considerable importance also, from the Mualang and Kendajan Dajak groups, are the ritual and cosmological texts published by Dunselman (1949, 1950a, 1950b, 1954, 1955, 1959a, 1959b, 1961). Evans, in his study of the Tempasuk Dusun (1953), made a short analysis of Dusun sacred language and provided several exemplary texts in this language. And, over many years, Harrison and Sandin have recorded numerous Iban chants, many of which give evidence of a traditional parallelism (cf. Harrison 1966).

Of special importance, because it drives from a people outside the immediate Indonesian area who yet pertain to the Indonesian language group, is the magnificent Rhade epic, in parallel verse, 'La Chanson de Damsan', translated by Sabatier (1933).

An outstanding collection of rigorously parallel ritual verses originates from Nias and the Batu Islands. The collection includes a 'hero epic' and a selection of verses from women's ceremonies, by Lagemann (1893, 1906), some translated but unexplicated texts by the dictionary compiler Sundermann (1905), and two long 'priestly litanies' and some 40 'songs', most of which vary in length from 200–400 verse couplets each (with Dutch translations and copious philological and ethnographic commentary) by Steinhart (1934, 1937a, 1937b, 1938, 1950, 1954). As Lagemann first observed (1906:341): '*Die Form dieser älteren Ueberlieferungen ist eine poetische, und zeigt durchweg einen Parallelismus der Verse, wobei es weniger auf den Reim als auf einen gewissen Rythmus ankommt.*'

Another area remarkable for its parallel ritual verse is the Celebes. Adriani, despite the fact that neither he nor Kruyt published any long ritual texts,[5] noted in several important articles (1932a, 1932b, 1932c) that the prayers and invocations of the Bare'e Toradja *tadu* priestesses were highly formulaic: 'Almost always they are parallel' (1932a:205). His analyses, however, concentrated on the sound changes, word exchanges, ellipses, archaisms and borrowings that

---

[5] Van der Tuuk (1864–67:v–vi), in his classification of Batak speech forms, mentioned differing forms of 'ornamented' speech for mourning, divination and cosmological instruction by *datu* priests. Similarly, Matthes (1872) produced a meticulous—near-model—study of the certain Bissu rituals of the Buginese. As Adriani (1932b:6) has observed, however, neither of these men published extensive texts in these special languages. What remains puzzling is why Adriani, who was acquainted with Toradja sacred language and who, in addition, recognised the importance of the study of this speech form, did not record a corpus of his own.

distinguished elements in this language form from those in ordinary language. To these transformations, he attributed an 'animistic magic' that made this ritual language central to Toradja life.

Dunnebier, in his linguistic work on Bolaang Mongondow (1938, 1953), has provided some short examples of parallel verse from the northern area of Celebes but the finest collection from the Celebes is van der Veen's excellent and well-annotated Sa'dan Toradja texts (1929, 1950, 1965, 1966), which, together with his *Tae'-Nederlandsch woordenboek met register Nederlandsch-Tae* (1940), provide excellent specimens of Toradja ritual verse and the means for their thorough study. As he noted also, in all these texts, 'two lines of a strophe are linked by parallelism, i.e. more or less the same content being expressed in both lines though with different words' (van der Veen 1966:17). What is most strikingly apparent in these verses—as with those of Nias—is their thoroughgoing, consistent binate semantics.

In eastern Indonesia, parallelism has been evidenced in several publications (cf. Arndt 1933; Onvlee 1934; de Josselin de Jong 1941; Vroklage 1952). The only large, critical corpus of parallel verse is, however, the collection of funeral chants translated by Middelkoop in 'Een Studie van het Timoreesche Doodenritueel' (1949).[6] For Rotenese,[7] the linguist Jonker published a single text in parallel verse, *Ana-Ma Manu Kama ma Falu-Ina Tepa Nilu*, a funeral chant for orphans, widows or strangers. Jonker added this chant, together with a paraphrase in ordinary language, to his collection of Rotenese folktales (1911:97–102) to provide 'an example of the poetic style' that he characterised as marked by 'sustained parallelism' (1911:130). He admitted the chant was obscure and he therefore limited himself to translating only the paraphrase and adding notes to various words in the chant itself. These notes, although sometimes incorrect, seem to indicate that Jonker had partially grasped the organising principles of Rotenese semantic parallelism. This present analysis may therefore, I hope, be regarded as a continuation of his investigations on Rotenese.

---

6 These texts are extraordinary in one respect: they are translated and annotated by a man whom many Atoni regard as a practised master of their ritual language. As some Atoni point out, one of the chief reasons for the rapid spread of Christianity on Timor was Dr Middelkoop's adaptation of Atoni ritual language in his Bible translations and hymnal. (For a discussion of the problems of translation raised by native Sumbanese verse and Hebrew parallels, see Onvlee 1953:16–23; Lambooij 1932:139–44.)

7 Van de Wetering (1925) has recorded a number of parallel verse excerpts from the marriage rituals of the Rotenese. One of these (1925:640–1), a 12-line excerpt from the marriage ceremonies of Thie in southern Rote, so pleased my own chief instructor in ritual languages, S. Adulanu, when he heard me read it that he made me recite it to him repeatedly until he had committed it to memory.

Ritual language and the speech forms of the Rotenese

The Rotenese pride themselves on being an articulate, contentious, talkative people. The skilful manipulation of their language in all its facets is highly prized and their *dede'ak* ('language, speech, dialect litigation') can be classified into a variety of subtly interrelated speech forms, each distinguished by some intersection of specific criteria—those of subject, style, context or usage. Thus, for example, 'mockery speech' (*a'ali-o'olek*), usually marked by two individuals' repartee from what is, in effect, a relatively circumscribed set of short, insulting phrases, differs as much from 'ordinary conversation' (*kokolak*) as a more conventional folk genre such as 'riddles' (*neneuk*) differs from 'tales' (*tutuik*) or that subset of tales which, when linked to specific genealogies, are regarded as 'true tales' (*tutui-tete'ek*) and serve as charters for political practice (Fox 1971). What these various speech forms do is signal different standardised social contexts, each with separate conditions and expectations for the use of semantic elements. The study of these speech forms could approximate an ethnography of Rotenese social life.

Ritual language is confined to two speech forms in Rotenese: *bini* ('poems, chants') and *sosodak* ('song'). Although the Rotenese frequently speak of ritual language as if it were a separate language—'the language of the ancestors', with its own unique vocabulary and rules of utterance—it might more accurately be described as a poetic style characteristic of the *bini*. All *bini* are, by native definition, in ritual language, but not all songs. Songs in ritual language are precisely those whose verses might be equally well recited as *bini*. The distinction is one in the manner of performance. Short *bini* may be either recited or sung (*soda*), while long *bini* are chanted (*helo*) publicly at ceremonial gatherings. This distinction, however, is by no means rigid. In ritual language, the verbs *soda* and *helo* form a single dyadic set.

Ritual language ought to be used on all formal occasions when individuals or groups come together.[8] There exist, therefore, standard *bini* for greeting strangers, for bidding farewell, for making requests to superiors, for all the crucial states of courtship, for initiating or facilitating bride-wealth negotiations, for the installation of a lord, at haircutting rituals for house-building ceremonies, at the annual *hus* feasts when these feasts were still held, for weddings and particularly for funerals. Although used at ceremonies, ritual language is not primarily a

---

8   The use of Indonesian, especially an oratorical or Biblical style of Indonesian, by young schoolteachers and some native preachers as an equivalent of ritual language at ceremonies has tended, in recent times, to restrict the use of ritual language. The issue is not, however, clear-cut. Many native Christian preachers have adopted ritual-language forms and some are outspoken exponents of its use. Furthermore, some ceremonies involve the use of Indonesian for Christian phases of the ritual and Rotenese for traditional phases.

religious language. Unlike 'special' languages in other areas of Indonesia, it is not a vehicle for communication with the spirits who should properly be addressed in the speech form (*-seseo*) nor is it a vehicle for the preservation of ancestral histories that are told in ordinary language in the form of *tutui-tete'ek*. Ritual language is simply the language of formal social or ceremonial interaction.

It is for funerals—the most complex rituals of Rotenese ceremonial life—that the repertoire of *bini* is most elaborated. These *bini* are either chanted in praise of the deceased or danced to in a circle-dance with a leader and surrounding chorus.[9] The repertoire seems intended to delimit all possible categories of deceased persons. With the exception of those who have died a violent, inauspicious death, there are particular funeral *bini* for nobles or for commoners, for young noblemen, for rich commoners, for someone who has died from a lingering illness, for a girl who has died as a virgin ('unripe'), for a widow or for an orphan, for an eldest child, or for a child who has died shortly after birth. These funeral *bini* have a general format. The deceased is compared with a chant character and then the stereotyped genealogy and life course of this chant character are told. In most instances, the chants explain the reasons for and circumstances of the chant character's death; in some instances, the chant character describes his illness or admonishes his descendants; and most chants conclude with the mourning and funeral of the chant character.

Since ritual language is desired in all formal interaction, it is not the exclusive preserve of any class or priesthood. Some women demonstrate almost as much knowledge of ritual language as men and their active use of this language is often called upon especially at various stages of the marriage ceremonies. Although youth are not socially expected to betray a serious interest in ritual affairs, many—in spite of their own disclaimers—show a surprising knowledge of proper dyadic sets and have usually memorised some short *bini* and songs. Participation in the circle-dance with its antiphony between leader and chorus is an effective means of social instruction.

There are, however, individuals who are popularly regarded as master poets or composers of *bini*. These are the 'chanters' (*manahelo*). They are usually male elders, personally jealous of their abilities and privately disparaging of their rivals' knowledge. Since the title *manahelo* is not conferred but is the popular

---

9   The circle-dance or 'round-dance' is reported for many areas of eastern Indonesia. A good, short description of an evening of Rotenese dancing observed in Oenale in 1908 can be found in Lekkerkerker (1910). Lekkerkerker described the rivalry between chanters who took their place at the centre of the circle and the repetition of the changer's verses by the chorus of surrounding dancers. He indicated, however, that women began the dance and were later joined by men. In all the round-dances I observed or participated in, in Termanu and in Ba'a, men and women danced together from the start. Since Granet, for one, has claimed to have discovered the origin of parallelism in the customary antiphonal rivalry of festival choruses, I should emphasise that however appealing this hypothesis is, the round-dance is an important but by no means exclusive context for the use of ritual language.

attribute of a fluid consensus, it is impossible to number the chanters on the island.[10] To judge from the folktales, lords used formerly to challenge each other by sponsoring rival chant contests between their domains, and, to some extent, any ceremonial gathering can erupt into a competitive performance between *manahelo*.

Any recitation of ritual language requires a ceremonial context. A minimal ceremonial context, for the Rotenese, involves the giving of native lontar gin ('the water of words') to one's guest. A practice, among elders and especially among chanters on visits to each other, is to recite short bini at each other between successive rounds of gin. These minor contests often end in excited incoherence. Some ancestral figures, I was told, as they grew older, abandoned ordinary language entirely and spoke only in ritual language.

Introduction to the text

The text[11] for analysis is a funeral chant from the domain of Termanu for a first child, of a noble family, who dies about the age of three months. The child is likened to Dela Kolik and Seko Bunak and the chant recounts the following events: 1) the marriage of the woman Pinga Pasa and So'e Leli to the man Kolik Faenama and Bunak Tunulama; 2) the onset of Pinga Pasa and So'e Leli's pregnancy and her various cravings, which culminate in the theft of an egg from the eagle and hawk Tetema Taoama and Balapua Loniama; 3) the birth of Dela Kolik and Seko Bunak and his swift abduction by the eagle and hawk; 4) Pinga Pasa and So'e Leli's pursuit of the eagle and hawk, first towards

---

10   I recorded, in the domain of Termanu, long ritual texts from seven acknowledged *manahelo*, one of whom was a woman. I met, heard perform or was told about several other *manahelo*. I would estimate, for Termanu in the mid-1960s, with its population of just less than 5800 people, that there were approximately 15 recognised chanters in the domain. On the other hand, I gathered shorter *bini* from numerous individuals and many of these people within their own village area might, at times, be praised as *manahelo*. Although not yet capable of long composition, many of these individuals would also be described as *hataholi ma-lelak* ('people who know').

11   The way in which I came to be given this text should be explained. Sometime after I had settled in Termanu, I was visited by the chanter A. Patola. Some men from my village area chided him by claiming that there was no chant he could tell me that I did not already know. In the situation, I was unable to intervene. He left but returned, unannounced, late one night several weeks afterwards and recited for me a chant about the eagle and hawk (*tetema*//*balapua*). With the help of J. Pello, I was able to transcribe this chant from my tape and, in search of a translation and exegesis, I visited my principal instructor in ritual language, Stefanus Adulanu. He was a lively man, well over seventy, and, at the time, a younger chanter, a man of about fifty, Eli Pellando, was spending much of his time with him in a relationship that might be characterised as a further 'apprenticeship'. Both chanters criticised A. Patola's version of the chant and, rather than providing me with help in understanding it, they offered to give me the 'correct' version. Several days later, they presented me with the chant I publish here. Although Stefanus Adulanu assumed—as was his due—the credit for this version, it is almost certainly the joint composition of the two chanters. Furthermore, the chant has, in fact, been 'influenced' by A. Patola's version, which, though it rambles and then ends abruptly, is in excellent ritual language. A comparison of the two chants could offer some insight into variation and composition among chanters.

eastern Rote (as is implied by the use of certain proper names) and then to the westernmost domain of the island, Delha; 5) the flight of the eagle and hawk seaward, then upwards to the Sun and Moon, thus ending the possibility of further pursuit; and finally 6) the return of the eagle and hawk and the gathering and burial of Dela Kolik and Seko Bunak's remains. The chant suggests that the primary disposal of the corpse was once left to carrion birds and that a secondary burial was performed thereafter on the bones of the deceased. Although similar practices have been reported for some neighbouring islands, there is no evidence for such burials from the ethnography of Rote's recent past nor did the chanters who provided exegesis to the text remark on this possibility. Primary tree burial of this sort is, however, alluded to in other chants where it is formulaically referred to as *fua beuk//ndae kak* ('to burden the beuk tree// to drape the kak tree').[12] The present chant is now performed at a funeral ceremony for the interment of the entire corpse.

An initially confusing feature of all ritual-language texts is the freedom of alternation between singular and plural forms. Several eminent chanters insisted that singular and plural were irrelevant in ritual language. One chanter advocated a convention, which he did not consistently follow in his own performances, of always coupling a single pronoun with a plural pronoun, or a 'we-inclusive pronoun' with a 'we-exclusive pronoun', thereby transforming Rotenese pronominals into distinct dyadic sets. The reason for the variation of singular and plural is that all personal names, all placenames, all objects, actions and events are dyadic while their reference, as in the case of elaborately allegorical funeral chants, is often to a singular individual and event. Therefore, rather than claim that a dyadic set is either a unity or merely the union of its elements, the chanters commit themselves to the view that it can be both.

Some chanters insist that whereas anything can be 'translated' into ritual language, ritual language itself cannot be 'translated'. By this they do not mean that ritual language is unintelligible or meaningless. Rather, it is simply that they can take specimens of Indonesian (the medium of which they conceive of translation) and cast them into ritual verse, but Indonesian—as it is known on Rote—possesses none of the conventions of ritual language. Dyadic sets are haphazardly formed and thus lose their standard yet particular 'metaphorical' qualities. The following translation, therefore, is as literal as is possible to demonstrate the chant's pervasive parallelism.

---

12 Ritual language preserves many references to practices that have long since ceased. The hunting with bow and blowpipe, often mentioned in the chants, has waned to a mere child's game since the introduction of firearms in the seventeenth century.

The text: *Dela Kolik ma Seko Bunak*

Lae:	They say:
1. *Soku-la Pinga Pasa*	They carry Pinga Pasa
2. *Ma ifa-la So'e Leli.*	And they lift So'e Leli.
3. *De ana sao Kolik Faenama*	She marries Kolik Faenama
4. *Ma tu Bunak Tunulama.*	And weds Bunak Tunulama.
5. *De tein-na da'a-fai*	Her womb enlarges
6. *Ma su'u-na nggeo-lena.*	And her breasts darken.
7. *Boe-te ana ma-siu dodoki*	Her tongue craves for odd bits
8. *Ma metu-ape u'una.*	And her mouth waters for assorted things.
9. *De ma-siu bote aten*	The tongue craves goat's liver
10. *Ma metu-ape tena ban.*	And the mouth waters for buffalo's lung.
11. *De ala dodo bote-la leu*	They slaughter goats
12. *Ma pa'u tena-la leu*	And stab buffalo
13. *De ho'i-la bote aten*	They take the goat's liver
14. *Ma ho'i-la tena ban.*	And take the buffalo's lung.
15. *De dode se'ok no hade*	They cook and mingle rice
16. *De hade lutu bui-nggeo*	Black-tipped grains of rice
17. *Ma hopo balik no tua*	And dissolve and mix lontar sugar
18. *De tua batu meni-oek.*	White rock lontar sugar.
19. *De na'a te bei boe ma-siu*	She eats but still the tongue craves
20. *Ma ninu te bei boe metu-ape.*	And she drinks but still the mouth waters.
21. *De ma-siu fani-ana*	The tongue craves bees' larvae
22. *Ma Metu-ape bupu-ana.*	And the mouth waters for wasps' larvae.
23. *De leni fani-ana mai*	They bring bees' larvae
24. *Ma leni bupu-ana mai.*	And they bring wasps' larvae.
25. *De ala dode se'ok no hade*	They cook and mingle rice
26. *Fo hade lutu bui-nggeo*	Black-tipped grains of rice
27. *Ma Hopo se'ok no tua*	And dissolve and mingle lontar sugar
28. *Fo tua batu meni-oek.*	White rock lontar sugar.
29. *Te-hu na'a bei ma-siu*	She eats and the tongue still craves
30. *Ma ninu bei metu-ape.*	And she drinks and the mouth still waters.
31. *Boe-te ma-siu bia keak*	The tongue craves chunks of turtle [meat]
32. *Ma metu-ape lola liuk.*	And the mouth waters for strips of sea cow [flesh].
33. *De touk Kolik Faenama*	The man Kolik Faenama
34. *Ma ta'ek Bunak Tunulama*	And the boy Bunak Tunulama
35. *Ana ule sini tua-na*	He winds a lontar bundle
36. *Ma tata pele nanamo*	And splits a nanamo torch
37. *De neu pele lelelu kea*	He goes around to torch-light fish for turtle
38. *Ma neu loti teteo luik.*	And goes about to search for sea cow.

39. De leni bia keak mai	They bring chunks of turtle [meat]
40. Ma leni lola liuk mai.	And bring strips of sea cow [flesh].
41. De na'a te-hu bei ma-siu	She eats but still the tongue craves
42. Ma ninu te bei metu-ape.	And she drinks but still the mouth waters.
43. De ma-siu tema tolo	The tongue craves a hawk's egg[A]
44. Ma metu-ape pua ana	And the mouth waters for an eagle's child
45. Fo Tetema Taoama nai nitas-sa lain	Tetema Taoama on top of the nitas tree[B]
46. Fo Taoama Dulu nitan	Taoama Dulu's nitas tree
47. Ma Balapua Loniama nai delas-sa lain	And Balapua Loniama on top of the delas tree
48. Fo Loniama Langa delan.	Loniama Langa's delas tree.
49. De ana lino tolo nai lai	He spies an egg above
50. Ma ana mete ana nai lai	And sees a child above
51. Te-hu masa-keni kakodek	But the tree is as slick as a kakodek tree
52. Ma manga-moi lalanok	And as slippery as a lalanok tree
53. De ela lima tekek bai dei	It needs the hands of a lizard
54. Ma ela kala kodek bai dei	And needs the chest of a monkey
55. Fo dei laba kae-nala lain	To mount and climb upward
56. Ma tinga hene-nala lain.	And to step and ascend upward.
57. De ala dodo doak lon	They think carefully
58. Ma ala ndanda sota lon.	And they ponder deeply.
59. Besak-ka lada hade ma-modon-na	Now with tasty new ripening rice
60. Ma lole tua oe-bun-na	And with good freshly tapped lontar juice
61. Ala solo neu teke ei-ku'u telu	They buy a three-toed lizard
62. Ma upa neu lafo ma-nisi duak	And hire a two-toothed mouse
63. Besak-ka kae-nala nitas lain	And now climb the nitas tree
64. Ma hene-nala delas lain.	And mount the delas tree.
65. Boe-te ana tete tetema ein	He cuts the hawk's leg
66. Ma nggute balapua lidan.	And snips the eagle's wing.
67. De tetema na-lai	The hawk flees
68. Ma balapua tolomu.	And the eagle escapes.
69. Besak-ka neni tetema tolon	Now he brings the hawk's egg
70. Ma neni balapua anan.	And brings the eagle's child.
71. De fe Pinga Pasa na'a	He gives Pinga Pasa to eat
72. Ma fe So'e Leli ninu boe.	And gives So'e Leli to drink.
73. Ma ta ma-siu	And the tongue no longer craves
74. Do metu-ape sok.	Or the mouth ceases to water.
75. Besak-ka tein-na nama-sela	Now her womb grows larger
76. Ma su'un-na nama-tua.	And her breasts grow bigger.
77. De ana nggeo-lena	They enlarge

78. Ma ana da'a-fai.	And they darken.
79. De bongi-na popi-koak	She gives birth to 'a cock's tail feathers' [a male child].
80. Ma lae-na lano-manuk.	And she bears 'a rooster's plume' [a man child].
81. De loke lae Dela Kolik	They call him Dela Kolik
82. Ma hule lae Seko Bunak.	And they name him Seko Bunak.
83. Faik esa manunin	On one definite day
84. Ma ledok dua mateben	And at a second certain dawn
85. Boe-te inan-na Pinga Pasa	His mother, Pinga Pasa,
86. Ma te'on-na So'e Leli	And his aunt, So'e Leli,
87. Iifak Dela Kolik	Carries Dela Kolik out
88. Neme uma tisa-tetetin	From under the thatch of the house
89. Ma koko'ok Seko Bunak	And cradles Seko Bunak
90. Neme lo hedahu-hohonan.	Away from the ladder of the home.
91. Boe-te Tetema Taoama	Tetema Taoama
92. Nafa-ndele lololo	Continually remembers
93. Ma Balapua Loniama	And Balapua Loniama
94. Nasa-neda ndanda	Constantly recalls
95. Neu tolon-na bai	Her egg again
96. Ma neu anan-na boe.	And also her child.
97. Boe-te ana la memeli mai	She flies down quickly
98. Ma tena mese-mese mai	And sweeps down rapidly
99. De lau neni Dela Kolik	Seizes and carries off Dela Kolik
100. Ma tenga neni Seko Bunak	And grasps and carries off Seko Bunak
101. Leo nitas-sa lain	Toward the top of a nitas tree
102. Fo Sepe Ama-Li nitau	Sepe Ama-Li's nitas tree
103. Ma neu delas-sa lain	And to the top of a delas tree
104. Fo Timu Tongo-Batu delan.	Timu Tongo-Batu's delas tree.
105. De ana mamaman leo mafok	She chews it like half-ripe fruit
106. Ma mumumun leo latuk.	And sucks it like a ripe plant.
107. Boe-te inak-ka Pinga Pasa	The woman Pinga Pasa
108. Ma fetok-ka So'e Leli	And the girl So'e Leli
109. Ana sue totoko tenen	She strikes her ribs in anguish
110. Ma ana lai babako paun.	And she beats her thighs in distress.
111. De neu tunga balapua	She goes to follow the eagle
112. Ma neu sanga tetema	And she goes to seek the hawk
113. Fo ela no falik Dela Kolik	To bring back Dela Kolik
114. Ma no tulek Seko Bunak.	And to return Seko Bunak.
115. De neu nitan ma neu ndan	She goes to see him and goes to meet him
116. Nai Sepe Ama-Li nitan lain	High in Depe Ama-Li's nitas tree

117.	Ma nai Timu Tongo-Batu delan lain.	And high in Timu Tongo-Batu's delas tree.
118.	Boe-te inak-ka Pinga Pasa	The woman Pinga Pasa
119.	Ma te'on-na So'e Leli	And his aunt, So'e Leli,
120.	Boke ein neu nitas	Kicks her foot against the nitas tree
121.	Ma bapa lima neu delas,	And slaps her hand against the delas tree,
122.	Fo ela Dela Kolik, ana tuda	That Dela Kolik, he might fall
123.	Ma Seko Bunak, ana monu.	And Seko Bunak, he might drop.
124.	Boe-te tetema na-hala	Then the hawk answers
125.	Ma bapaputa na-fada, nae:	And the eagle speaks, saying:
126.	'O sue anam leo bek,	'Just as you love your child
127.	Na au sue anang leo ndiak	So I love my child
128.	Ma o lai tolom leo bek,	And just as you cherish your egg
129.	Na au lai tolong leo ndiak boe.	So I love my egg also.
130.	De o mu'a au-anang-nga so	You have eaten my child
131.	De besak-ia au u'a o-anam-ma	Now I eat your child
132.	Ma o minu au-tolong-nga so	And you have drunk my egg
133.	De au inu o-tolom-ma bai.'	So I drink your egg also.'
134.	Boe-te tetema la seluk	Then the hawk flies once more
135.	Ma balapua lapu bai.	And the eagle takes wing again.
136.	De neu Taoama Dulu nitan	She goes to Taoama Dulu's nitas tree
137.	Ma neu Loniama Langa delan	And goes to Loniama Lang's delas tree
138.	Ka neni Dela Kolik	Chewing, while carrying, Seko Bunak
139.	Ma mumu neni Seko Bunak.	And sucking, while carrying, Seko Bunak.
140.	De ala boe tungan	They go to follow her
141.	Ma leu sangan.	And they go to seek her
144.	De leu ndukun ma losan.	They reach her and approach her.
145.	Boe-te tetema lapu seluk	The hawk takes wing once more
146.	Ma balapua la bai.	And the eagle flies again.
147.	De neu Loma-Loma Langa nitan	She goes to Loma-Loma Langa's nitas tree
148.	Ma Pele-Pele Dulu delan.	And Pele-Pele Dulu's delas tree
149.	Te inak-ka Pinga Pasa	The mother, Pinga Pasa,
150.	Ma te'ok-ka So'e Leli	And the aunt, So'e Leli,
151.	Bei boe neu tungan	Still she goes on following her
152.	Ma neu sangan.	And goes on seeking her.
153.	De losan ma ndukun.	She approaches her and reaches her.
154.	Boe-te tetema lapu seluk	But the hawk takes wing once more
155.	Ma balapua la seluk	And the eagle flies once more
156.	Kaka'ak Dela Kolik	Continuously chewing Dela Kolik
157.	Ma mumumuk Seko Bunak.	And continuously sucking Seko Bunak.
158.	De la Ana Iko neu	She flies to Ana Iko [Delha]

159. Ma lapu Dela Muli neu.	And takes wing to Dela Muli [Delha].
160. Leo ndia te Pinga Pasa boe tungan	So Pinga Pasa also follows her
161. Ma So'e Leli boe sangan.	And So'e Leli also seeks her.
162. De neu losa Dela Muli	She goes toward Dela Muli
163. Ma neu nduku ana Iko.	And goes until Ana Iko.
164. Te tetema to poïn	But the hawk does not loose him
165. Ma balapua ta nggalin.	And the eagle does not scatter him
166. De tetema la seluk	The hawk flies once more
167. Ma balapua lapu bai.	And the eagle takes wing again.
168. De leo sain posin-na neu	Toward the sea's sandy edge
169. Ma liun unun-na neu.	And toward the ocean's rocky reef.
170. Te boe neu tungan	She also goes to follow her
171. Ma boe neu sangan.	And she also goes to seek her.
172. De neu posi maka-mu mekon	She goes to the edge resounding like a gong
173. Ma unu ma-li labun-na.	And the reef rumbling like a drum.
174. Boe-te tetema la seluk	But the hawk flies once more
175. Ma balapua lapu bai.	And the eagle takes wing again.
176. De neu liun sasalin	She goes toward the overflowing ocean
177. Ma neu sain loloen.	And toward the receding sea.
178. Boe-te inak-ka Pinga Pasa	The mother, Pinga Pasa,
179. Ma te'on-na So'e Leli	And his aunt, So'e Leli,
180. Ta neu lena li	Cannot wade the waves
181. Ma ta neu ladi nafa.	And cannot cross the swell.
182. De ana falik leo una mai	She returns to the house
183. Ma tulek leo lo mai.	And goes back to the home.
184. De ana lu mata	She lets drop tears from the eyes
185. Ma pinu idu	And mucus from the nose
186. Nai uma ma lo	In the house and home
187. Tunga faik ma nou ledok.	Each day and every dawn [sun].
188. Te-hu nai liun sasalin	But on the overflowing ocean
189. Ma nai sain loloen-na	And on the receding sea
190. Ai ta nai ndia	There is no stick
191. Ma batu ta nai na.	Nor is there stone.
192. De tetema ta saë	The hawk does not perch
193. Ma balapua ta lu'u	And the eagle does not brood
194. Fo ana kaka Dela Kolik	So she may chew Dela Kolik
195. Ma ana mumumu Seko Bunak.	And she may suck Seko Bunak.
196. Boe-te ana la leo lain neu	So she flies to the heavens
197. Ma lapu leo poin neu	And takes wing to the zenith
198. De neu losa bulan nitan	And goes to the Moon's nitas

199.	*Ma neu nduku ledo delan.*	And goes to the Sun's delas.
200.	*Besak-ka ana lino ba'e*	Now she rests on a branch
201.	*Ma sa'e ndanak.*	And perches on a limb.
202.	*De ana kukuta Dela Kolik*	She continues to munch Dela Kolik
203.	*Ma mumumu Seko Bunak.*	And continues to suck Seko Bunak.
204.	*De na,a na-mada man*	She eats to dry her tongue
205.	*Ma ninu na-meti apen-na*	And drinks to slake her thirst
206.	*De henu tein-na boe*	To fill her stomach
207.	*Ma sofe nutun-na boe*	And to satisfy her gizzard
208.	*De ela kada dui manun*	Leaving only chicken bones
209.	*Ma ela kada kalu kapan.*	And leaving only buffalo sinews.
210.	*De ana lino na-helen*	She rests gripping him
211.	*Ma Luü na-nepen*	And broods holding him
212.	*Nai bulan nitan lain*	On top of the Moon's nitas
213.	*Ma ledo delan-na lain.*	And on top of the Sun's delas.
214.	*Faik esa manunin*	One definite day
215.	*Ma ledo dua mateben*	And a second certain dawn
216.	*Besak-ka Tetema Taoama*	Now Tetema Taoama
217.	*Ma Balapua Loniama a*	And Balapua Loniama
218.	*Nafa-ndele dae-bafok*	Remembers the Earth
219.	*Ma nasa-neda batu-poin.*	And recalls the world.
220.	*De ana la falik*	She returns flying
221.	*Ma ana lapu tulek.*	And she wings her way back.
222.	*Besak-ka la neni dui manun*	She flies carrying chicken bones
223.	*Ma lapu neni kalu kapan*	And wings her way carrying buffalo sinews
224.	*Fo Dela Kolik duin*	The bones of Dela Kolik
225.	*Ma Seko Bunak kalun.*	And the sinews of Seko Bunak.
226.	*De ana mai Sua Lai tolek mafon*	She comes to Sua Lai's dark shadow
227.	*Ma Batu Hun modok sa'on.*	And to Batu Hun's green shade.
228.	*Besak-ka tetema tapa henin*	Now the hawk throws him away
229.	*Ma balapua tu'u henin.*	And the eagle casts him away.
230.	*Boe-ma inak-ka Pinga Pasa*	The mother, Pinga Pasa,
231.	*Ma te'on-na So'e Leli neu*	And his aunt, Soë Leli,
232.	*De tenga do hele nenin.*	Takes or picks him, carrying him.
233.	*De la-toi dui manun*	They bury the chicken bones
234.	*Ma laka-dofu kalu kapan.*	And they cover with earth the buffalo sinews.

Note A: A classification of Rotenese birds remains to be worked out. The principal criteria for native classification seem to be, in order of importance, size and colour markings, feeding and nesting habits, and cry or song. The same Linnaean species in different developmental phases may be classified under separate terms while several different Linnaean species may be included under the same term. Both balapua (pua) and tetema (tema) included a number of subcategories: balapua langa fula, balapua nggeok, tema nggelak, tema ndiik and also selu or selu kolo. The balapua langa fula ('white-headed balapua') can, however, be identified as the 'white-headed sea eagle' or 'brahminy kite', Haliastur Indus (intermedius), in its adult phase.

Note B: The delas tree is the Indonesian dedap (*Erythina* spp.) and the nitas tree is the Indonesian kelumpang (*Sterculia foetida*).

In this analysis,[13] the distinction is developed between the expression of dyadic sets in parallel verse and the underlying semantic organisation of the elements of these sets. I discuss the relation of dyadic expressions to ordinary language forms, their arrangement in lines of verse and their formation in complex expressions and formulaic chains. I then consider, more briefly, some directions for research suggested by the preparation, in its initial stages, of a dictionary of ritual language. These concern the combinatorial possibilities and potential range of elements of sets and the means for specifying an element as a locus of semantic relations.

Dyadic sets and ordinary language

The only explicit native rule concerning the *bini* is that words must 'form dyads'. This is usually phrased in Rotenese using the verb *laka-dudua*, formed from the root *dua* ('two'). In Indonesian, the rule is commonly paraphrased by statements that words must 'be paired' (*berpasang*) or that the ancestors were always 'balancing or comparing' (*membanding*). The consistent application of this rule is evident in the chant.

Omitting proper names and complex sets, the chant *Dela Kolik ma Seko Bunak* (*DK//SB*) comprises just under 120 dyadic sets. (A list of these sets with simple glosses is appended to this chapter.) In general, nouns (*ana//tolo*: 'child'//'egg'; *ate//ba*: 'liver'//'lungs'), verbs (*bapa//boke*: 'to slap with the hand'//'to stamp with the foot'; *bongi//lae*: 'to give birth'//'to bear'), adjectives (*beu//modo*: 'new'//'ripening green'; *-keni//-moi*: 'slippery'//'smooth') and adverbs (*doa-//sota-*: 'carefully'//'painstakingly'; *lololo//ndanda*: 'constantly'//'continually') all form dyadic sets. However, a precise, predetermined syntactic specification of these elements of speech presents considerable difficulty.

In ordinary language, root elements, usually with the aid of prefixed or suffixed morphemes, can take on an array of syntactic forms. In ritual language, these

---

13 This analysis is of the semantics of ritual language and leaves undiscussed important problems of metrics. This is not intended to neglect or slight this fundamental aspect of ritual language. Metric constraints do not, to my mind, directly affect the semantics of ritual language but they have important bearings on what, from an exclusively semantic viewpoint, appear to be 'optional' morphological variants.

morphemes can often be dispensed with entirely.[14] Hence: 1) the membership of an element in a particular dyadic set, and 2) the context established by the word order of a line, serve to define an element's use and its possible semantic significance. Judgments on a word's use, however, based on its use in ordinary language, can be misleading since ritual language derives much of its 'poetic character' from systematic deviation from ordinary language usage. The following examples are intended to illustrate aspects of this relationship of ritual language to ordinary language. These examples do not constitute a systematic presentation but have been chosen to cover a variety of relationships that can be discussed by reference to *Dela Kolik ma Seko Bunak*.

In lines 31 and 32, 39 and 40, *bia*//*lola* form a dyadic set. Context as well as native exegesis establish these elements as nouns with the meaning 'chunks or pieces'//'strips' (of meat). In ordinary language (cf. Jonker 1908:48), *bia* serves as a verb meaning 'to cut or chop into small pieces': *ana bia naka-lulutuk pa-a* ('he cuts the meat into chunks'). A piece of chopped meat is *pa bibiak*, but the shortened form, *biak*, meaning 'piece' of meat, can also occur: *ana ke pa-a neu biak dua* ('he cuts the meat into two pieces'). In ordinary language (cf. Jonker 1908:322), *lola* takes the partially reduplicated form, *lolola*, and as a verb means 'to cut into slices or long strips': *ana lolola pa* ('he cuts the meat into strips'). *Lolola* can be used in an adjectival sense, as in the expression, *pa lololak* ('meat cut into strips'), but no shortened adjectival form, *lola(k)**, occurs nor is the word used as a noun. In ritual language, however, *lola* takes its form by analogy with *bia* and both serve as nouns, representing the results of their respective verbal actions.

31. *Boe-te ma-siu bia keak*	The tongue craves chunks of turtle
32. *Ma metu-ape lola liuk.*	The mouth waters for strips of sea cow.

The formation of one element by means of analogy with its paired member is a characteristic process in the creation of numerous dyadic sets.

A somewhat different example occurs in lines 35 through 38:

35. *Ana ule sini tua-na*	He winds a lontar bundle
36. *Ma tata pele nanamo*	And splits a nanamo torch
37. *De neu pele lelelu kea*	He goes around to torch-light fish for turtle
38. *Ma neu loti teteo luik.*	And goes about to search for sea cow.

The crucial element is *pele*. In ordinary language, *pele* may refer to: 1) the dried leaves used to make a torch, 2) the torch itself, and 3), as a verb, the act of

---

14 I avoid any claim that ritual language is simply a morphologically 'bare' form of ordinary language. Though superficially suggestive, the claim would then have to ignore certain verbal and adverbial stylised reduplications, which are characteristic only of ritual language.

hunting or fishing by torch-light. In lines 35 and 36, *pele* forms a set with *sini*, 'bundles of dried leaves' (usually used for thatching a roof). The significance of the set and its use as a noun are clear, but immediately after these lines, *pele* forms a set with *loti*, a verb that in ordinary language means 'to look for something by torch-light'. The significance of this set and its use as a verb are also clear. The polysemy of *pele* in ordinary language is resolved into separate dyadic sets of ritual language.

In ritual language, the numbers combine to form dyadic sets. In *Dela Kolik ma Seko Bunak*, there are two such sets: *esa//dua* ('one'//'two') and *dua//telu* ('two'//'three'). An odd number occurs with an even number and their combination might be expressed by the formula: $X//X + 1$. This rule excludes use of the numbers five (*lima*) and six (*ne*). The set *lima//ne* does occur in ritual language but never in a context in which its significance could possibly be numeric. This is because *lima*, in ordinary language, has two meanings: 'five' and 'hand'. Thus in ritual language, *lima* may also form a set with *ei* ('foot'), as in lines 121 and 122:

| 121. Boke ein neu nitas | [She] kicks her foot against the nitas tree |
| 122. Bapa lima neu delas | And slaps her hand against the delas tree |

Wherever *lima//ne* occur, *lima* is always used to mean 'hand' or 'other hand'. Hence in ritual language, the polysemy of *lima* is suppressed in the very form that might best express it.

It is evident from the preceding examples that one element of a set may be used to clarify the form and the meaning of its pair.[15] In ritual language, there exists a class of sets, one of whose elements does not occur in the ordinary spoken language of that particular speech community. (In the case of *Dela Kolik ma Seko Buna,* this would be the dialect community of the domain of Termanu.) Some examples of these sets in are: 1) *sao//tu* ('to marry'//'to wed'); 2) *bongi//lae* ('to give birth'//'to bear [a child]'); 3) *fali//tule* ('to return'//'to turn back'); 4) *bote//tena* ('goat'//'buffalo [small//large, female animal]').

The initial elements of the first three sets, *sao*, *bongi* and *fali*, are common ordinary-language verbs while the second elements of these sets, *tu*, *lae* and *tule*, neither occur nor appear to be related to any forms in ordinary language. Most native commentators, therefore, argue on formal grounds that set membership and context make it apparent that the unknown element must be interpreted in terms of its known pair. Some commentators, however, suggested conceivable

---

15 For many sets, it could be analytically useful to distinguish between a dominant element that tends to establish the meaning or form for the set and a dependent element whose meaning or form can be interpreted only by reference to its paired element.

ordinary-language forms to which unknown elements might be related. (*Tu*, it was remarked, might be related to *-tu*, 'to sit'.) That some of these suggestions were implausible, even to those who made them, ought not obscure the fact that the Rotenese assume that ritual language elements derive from ordinary language. Elements, or some portion of these elements, however obscure, are not regarded as some special 'secret' vocabulary. Furthermore, unknown or unrelated elements decrease in number as knowledge of ordinary language and of the rules for the derivation of ritual elements increases.[16]

The set *bote//tena* offers further problems in exegesis. According to Jonker (1908:620), *tena* is a classifier for young, female animals and can apply to any animal, whether buffalo or chicken. Native commentators insisted (to me) that *tena* could apply only to large, female livestock (horses or water buffalo) and, in the context of sacrifice, this could mean only a water buffalo (*kapa*); while *bote*, for which there seemed to be no ordinary-language form, designated smaller livestock, especially the goat (*bii-hik*) and the sheep (*bii-lopo*). The assuredness with which these commentators provided their exegesis was probably based on the fact that *bote//tena* occurred in other chants in a more complex form: *bote bi'ik//tena kapak*. Here again, it is set membership that resolves any obscurity of meaning.

Analytically, there is another class of sets, whose member elements are synonymous dialect variants. The dialect situation on Rote is complex. On phonetic grounds, Jonker (1913) recognised nine dialect groupings on the island. Rote's 18 domains vie among each other to possess distinguishing speech characteristics. It is regarded as appropriate that each domain has its own 'language' (*dede'ak*). In addition, the Rotenese divide their island conceptually into two named territorial divisions: an eastern division, Lamak-anan, and a western division, Henak-anan. The natively recognised dividing line for these divisions cuts through the middle of the expansionist domain of Termanu. These divisions are said to be distinguished by a variety of supposed characteristics, one of which is a broad difference in key dialect words. Certain ritual-language sets utilise, and consequently correspond with, this bipartite dialect division. These sets combine an element from the eastern division with an element from the western division. In ritual language, for example, the dyadic set for 'man' is *hataholi//daehena* (*dahena*). *Hataholi* is 'man' in Termanu and in western Rote; *daehena* (*dahena*) is 'man' in most domains of eastern Rote. Examples of these kinds of sets in *Dela Kolik ma Seko Bunak* are *henu//sofe* and *li//nafa*; *henu* is 'to be full, sufficient, satisfied' in Termanu and in eastern Rote, but is replaced with *sofe* throughout most of western Rote. *Li* is 'wave, waves (of the sea)' in Termanu

---

16   It is possible that many of the sets with an element unrelated to some form in ordinary language would be clarified if the dialect variations of ordinary language were better known. In fact, it seems difficult to distinguish in all cases between sets with an 'unknown' element and sets composed of dialect variants.

and western Rote, while *nafa* takes its place in areas of eastern Rote. Although Termanu may or may not be the most strategic area for the recognition of sets of this kind, it should be noted that these sets, composed of dialect variants, are those about which ordinary Rotenese (and not just the chanters) readily offer exegesis, labelling elements as either eastern or western terms. Dialect difference is a subject of common awareness and ritual language exploits this knowledge.[17]

On the basis of these preceding examples, it is possible to make a number of comments on the general nature of ritual language. First, ritual language is a developed and elaborated speech form and its dyadic sets are astonishingly rich, varied vehicles of expression. Its occurrence cannot be attributed to some simple reiterative mentality. Second, all dyadic sets are formulaic in the sense that each set is a traditionally fixed unit. It is from the stock of these units that the *bini* are composed. Although it is impossible to demonstrate this by recourse to just one text, it is possible to assert that all the sets in *Dela Kolik ma Seko Bunak* recur in other texts. They are neither unique nor confined to this single chant. Third, ritual language is 'poetic' and 'metaphoric' but its metaphors are systematically ordered and constrained by their dyadic structure. The ambiguity in the use of elements in ritual language is often less than the use of those same elements in ordinary language. Fourth, the semantic study of any language raises problems of polysemy, homonymy and synonymy. What ritual language provides is a highly formalised native reflection on ordinary language. Ritual language can suggest a means of resolving problems in the semantics of ordinary language.

---

17   In this study of Dusun 'sacred language', Evans (1953:495–6) distinguished five classes of words that made up this sacred language: 1) 'ordinary Dusun words'; 2) 'special but easily recognizable forms of ordinary words—poetic forms—derived from ordinary Dusun words'; 3) 'words not usually current in the village… but found in other villages, near or far away'; 4) 'loan words from Malay'; and 5) 'words used, as far as known, only in the sacred languages, for which derivations are not obtainable'. This classification resembles that of Hardeland (1858:4–5). He distinguished: 1) ordinary or slightly altered Dajak words; 2) Malay words, also slightly altered; and 3) special words, whose meaning or form confined them to sacred language. Hardeland, however, used the term Basa Sangiang to refer to the sacred language as a whole and to its distinctive, special words, which made up only a part of its total vocabulary. In his dictionary (1859), Hardeland included about 900 of these Basa Sangiang words. Schärer (1966:8), using Hardeland's textual material, discovered that ordinary Dajak words of Hardeland's time had come to be regarded, within 100 years and in the areas where Schärer worked, as special Basa Sangiang terms. (This observation does not necessarily imply that the vocabulary of Basa Sangiang as a whole had changed radically—in fact, Schärer makes several statements to suggest that it had not—but rather that, as changes occurred in the ordinary language and culture of the Ngadju groups, the relationship of Basa Sangiang to ordinary language had altered.) It appears that what Schärer intended to include as the conclusion to his fourth volume was a word list of special Basa Sangiang terms. Two points ought to be emphasised. First, the philological concern with the origin of particular words in these Indonesian sacred languages tends to obscure their essential dyadic structure. Schärer (1966:6) indicated that his principal means of translating obscure words was by reference to their parallel elements. In this way, he was able to 'translate' all but five words of his enormous corpus. Second, judgments on the origin of particular words (whether as altered or ancient ordinary words, dialect or Malay loan words, or special terms) are fraught with difficulty and can never be made certain. Working with a number of chanters from different dialect areas and many elders, it is possible to obtain some explanation of nearly all elements of ritual language. This does not, however, always make clear the origins of these elements.

Finally, it seems that dyadic sets are not simply systematically derived from related elements in ordinary speech, but are systematically related among themselves. This area of investigations offers promising possibilities.

Dyadic sets and parallel verse

Whereas the Rotenese are emphatic about the need for the pairing of elements in ritual language, they do not formulate explicit rules themselves about the arrangement of these pairs into poetic lines of verses. Consequently, any assessment of poetic form must be based on observed regularities in the texts. First, it is apparent that dual structure does not encompass all words. There exist a limited number of recurrent elements that do not form dyadic sets. The single text *Dela Kolik ma Seko Bunak* contains a high proportion of all such unpaired forms. They can be classed as follows: 1) connectives such as *ma* ('and'), *de* ('or'), *te* (*te-hu*) ('but'), *de, boe, boe-ma, boe-te*, which, if translated at all, can be glossed by 'and', 'then' or 'also'; 2) pronouns, such as *au, o, ana, ala* ('I', 'you', 'he, she, it', 'they'); 3) inflected 'prepositions' (Jonker's term) such as *nai//lai* (third-person singular/plural) ('to be at, on, upon'), *no//lo* ('to be with'), *neni//leni* ('to bring with'), *neu//leu* ('to go toward'); and 4) invariable, uninflected elements, such as *be* ('what'), *bei* ('still'), *leo* ('to, toward'), *kada* ('always, still') and the exclamation *na*. (A fuller list of these elements is also appended to this chapter.) For some elements, dyadic sets are optional. *Boe*, when used as a 'filler' in the middle and especially at the end of a line, may form a set with *bai* ('again'). The demonstrative pronoun *ndia* ('there') may form a set with the demonstrative *na* ('there'), but this is variable within the same chant and even within successive lines. The verb *fe* ('to give') rarely forms a dyadic set, nor does the negative *ta(k)*. Whether or not these elements form dyadic sets is, to judge from discussion with chanters, a matter of individual style. The chanter's goal is not to produce a monotony of parallel forms in successive lines.

In composition, the overwhelmingly most apparent poetic form is the distich or couplet. Nearly the whole of *Dela Kolik ma Seko Bunak* consists of either consecutive or alternative parallel lines. Using a, a¹, b and b¹ to designate lines (and not elements of sets), these two forms may be illustrated as follows:

a	1. *Soku-la Pinga Pasa*	They carry Pinga Pasa
a¹	2. *Ma ifa-la So'e Leli*	And they lift So'e Leli
b	3. *De ana sao Kolik Faenama*	She marries Kolik Faenama
b¹	4. *Ma tu Bunak Tunulama.*	And weds Buna Tunulama.
a	15. *De dode se'ok no hade*	They cook and mingle rice
b	16. *De hade lutu buinggeo*	Black-tipped grains of rice
a¹	17. *Ma hopo balik no tua*	And dissolve and mix lontar sugar
b¹	18. *De tua batu meni-oek.*	White rock lontar sugar.

Elements that form dyadic sets should, in parallel lines, correspond exactly in position and, as far as possible, in morphological structure. An element that does not form a dyadic set may, in the second of two parallel lines, be omitted and its sense is understood. (In lines 3 and 4, the pronoun *ana*, 'she', is not repeated. Other instances of this tendency can be seen in the text in lines 11/12, 25/26, 35/36, 55/56.)

The only potential exception to the rule of position in *Dela Kolik ma Seko Bunak* is the dyadic expression *ma-sui//metu-ape*. The expression is composed of two dyadic sets. *Ma//ape* ('tongue'//'saliva') form a set, as do *siu//metu*. *Siu* is the verb 'to crave' (said of a pregnant woman), but *metu* corresponds with no recognisable ordinary-language verb and, according to the chanters, has the meaning 'to salivate or crave' only in the expression *metu-ape*. Hence, while *ma//ape* may occur on its own (as in lines 204 and 206), *siu//metu* may not. Since *ma-siu//metu-ape* is an unalterable expression, *ma* and *ape* do not violate the positional rule on the arrangement of dyadic elements in parallel lines. The poetic play on this expression and its component set are used with great effectiveness in *Dela Kolik ma Seko Bunak*. The eagle and hawk's devouring of the child revenges the cravings of Pinga Pasa and So'e Leli. Lines 19/20:

19. De na'a te bei boe ma-siu	She [Pinga Pasa] eats but still the tongue craves
20. Ma ninu te bei boe metu-ape	She [So'e Leli] drinks but still the mouth waters

are answered by lines 204/205:

204. De na'a na-mada man	She [the eagle] eats to dry her tongue
205. De ninu na-meti apen-na	She [the hawk] drinks to slake her thirst

The rule on the parallelism of morphological structures does not necessarily include number. Although singular forms usually parallel each other as do plural forms, singular forms may occasionally and acceptably combine with plural forms. Morphological parallelism can be illustrated best by the reduplication of verbs. (In general, the partial reduplication of verbs, with or without prefix, indicates an intensified, repetitive or continuing action.) *Ka* (*kaka*)//*mumu* ('to chew'//'to suck') form a dyadic set. The set is first used in unreduplicated form (lines 138/139) and thereafter in reduplicated form (lines 156/157, 194/195):

138. Ka neni Dela Kolik	Chewing (while carrying) Dela Kolik
139. Ma mumu neni Seko Bunak.	And sucking (while carrying) Seko Bunak.
156. Kaka'ak Dela Kolik	Continuously chewing Dela Kolik
157. Ma mumumuk Seko Bunak.	Continuously sucking Seko Bunak.

Any element whose pair is expressed in reduplicated form must be similarly reduplicated. This rule extends to adverbs, although, unlike verbs, partial reduplication may parallel total reduplication. In lines 97/98, for example, the set *meli//mese* ('quickly'//'rapidly') is expressed as *memeli//mese-mese*.

The rule of morphological parallelism is of considerable importance given the processes by which ritual language dispenses with standard morphological forms of ordinary language and develops it own elaborate forms. In lines 92/94 and 218/219, the set *neda//ndele* ('to remember'//'to recall') is expressed as *nasa-neda//nafa-ndele*. Each element of this expression would pass as an acceptable ordinary-language usage. In other chants, however, *neda//ndele* is expressed more emphatically as:

| *De neda masa-nenedak* | Recall, do continually recall |
| *Ma ndele mafa-ndendelek* | And remember, do continually remember |

Such a distinctively styled expression can occur only in ritual language. The length of a parallel line and the number of its constituent dyadic elements are rigidly fixed. Disregarding elements that do not pair, the maximum number of dyadic elements of any line of *Dela Kolik ma Seko Bunak* is four:

a   b   c   d

a^1 b^1 c^1 d^1

An example of this is:

| b^1 | *Ala solo neu teke ei-ku'u telu* | They hire a two-toothed mouse |
| b^2 | *Ma up neu lafo ma-nisi duak* | They buy a three-toed lizard |

The majority of lines in *Dela Kolik ma Seko Bunak* have either two or three elements:

a   b   a   b   c

or

a^1 b^1 a^1 b^1 c^1

Several examples of three-element lines have already been quoted (lines 1–4, 15–18, 204–5). Examples of two-element lines are:

11. *De ala dodo bote-la leu*	They slaughter goats
12. *Ma pa'u tena-la leu*	And stab buffalo
67. *De tetema na-lai*	The hawk flees
68. *Ma balapua tolomu*	And the eagle escapes

There also occur, in *Dela Kolik ma Seko Bunak*, several single lines that have no parallel. Some of these lines are:

153. De losan ma ndukun	She approaches her and reaches her
186. Nai uma ma lo	In the house and home
187. Tunga faik ma nou ledok	Each day and every dawn [sun]
232. De tenga do hele nenin	Takes or picks him, carrying him

These lines are neither incomplete nor incorrect, stray forms. Rather each is composed of one or more dyadic sets, which makes it complete and entire in itself. The form of these lines is either: a a^1 or a b a^1 b^1. The fact that these single lines are acceptable demonstrates that parallel line structure is not primary in Rotenese; it is the product of composition in terms of dyadic sets.

Dyadic sets and complex expressions

To this point, discussion has centred on the formulaic features of dyadic sets as traditionally fixed units of expression. One of the further features of these simple dyadic sets is that they are neutral, unordered pairs.[18] Although chanters tend to establish patterns for themselves in their compositions, it is largely irrelevant which element of a set occurs first or second in a single line or in parallel lines. For example, the verbs of the set *la//lapu* may be interchanged:

145. Boe-te tetema lapu seluk	The hawk takes wing once more
146. Ma balapua la bai.	And the eagle flies again.
174. Boe-te tetema la seluk	The hawk flies again
175. Ma balapua lapu bai.	And the eagle takes wing again.

Dyadic sets may also combine in more complex sequences. These expressions may vary from double dyadic expressions to longer formulaic chains. In complex expressions, the combination of sets and the ordering of elements within them are constrained and, depending on the type of expression, these follow recognisable patterns.

A double dyadic expression involves the combination of two simple dyadic sets. It is possible to distinguish three types of these expressions: 1) unrestricted expressions whose component sets are freely separable and whose significance is not altered in separation; 2) restricted idiomatic sets whose significance is

---

18 A possible exception to this statement is the expression of ritual numbers. A lower number seems always to precede a higher number in expression.

dependent on a unique combination of sets and whose meaning cannot be derived by analysis of its components; and 3) names whose component sets have their own rules of ordering.

An example of an unrestricted double dyadic expression in *Dela Kolik ma Seko Bunak* is the following:

> 55. *Fo dei laba kae nala lain*   To mount and climb upward
> 56. *Ma tinga hene nala lain.*   And to step and ascend upward.

The components of this expression are *laba//tinga* ('to climb [a tree using a back-strap]'//'to step [up a tree, using carved niches]') and *kae//hene* ('to ascend [in short steps]'//'to mount' [often used in the sense of increase]). Each of these sets may be used separately (as, for example, *kae//hene*, in lines 63/64), but commonly they occur as a complex unit. Another example of this type of expression is *tona ofa//balu pau*, which is composed of two dyadic sets, each of whose elements is another name for a kind of boat or watercraft. The way in which the verbs 'to bite', 'to chew', 'to suck' and 'to munch' occur in *Dela Kolik ma Seko Bunak* suggests that *kaka mamma//kukuta mumumu* might also be a double dyadic expression.

Examples of idiomatic double dyadic expressions are: *da'a-fai//nggeo-lena* ('to enlarge' [said of the womb]//'to darken' [said of the breasts]); *ma-siu//metu-ape* ('to crave with the tongue'//'to salivate'); *bui-nggeo(k)//meni-oe(k)* ('black-tipped'//'white sugared'); *popi-koak//lano-manuk* ('a cock's tail feathers'//'a rooster's plume'), the ritual expression for a male child (the equivalent expression for a female child is *ke-fetok//tai-inak*); and *dae-bafok//batu-poik*, the ritual expression for the Earth (literally, 'the Earth's mouth or valley'//'the rock's points'). These double expressions must be considered as wholes since any literal analysis of their dyadic components renders them incomprehensible. Furthermore, a rearrangement of the elements of these components (such as *da'a-lena//nggeo-fai**, *popi-manuk//lano-koak**, *dae-poik//batu-bafok** or *bui-oek//meni-nggeok**), although strictly correct by rule of the ordering of simple dyadic sets, is unacceptable in ritual language.

Names form by far the largest class of double dyadic expressions. Personal names always assume this form, while placenames usually assume it. Rotenese names are complex and most individuals have a minimum of three distinct names accorded them by several interrelated naming procedures. Naming in ritual language resembles the system of Rotenese 'genealogical naming'. Ordinary genealogical names are binomials and, provided bride-wealth is paid, a person receives the first element of his father's binomial as the second element of his personal binomial. (The first element of a person's binomial is—or was once—determined by divination from a large selection of former ancestral names.) The difference between ordinary names and ritual-language names is that, in ordinary naming, a person has a single binomial while, in ritual language, a chant character has two binomials or, in other words, a double dyadic name. Another feature of ritual naming not found in ordinary genealogical naming is the frequent use of placename dyadic sets as components of personal names. Ritual names therefore often suggestively locate as well as distinguish a chant character.

Features of ritual naming are well illustrated in *Dela Kolik ma Seko Bunak*. To begin with, the set *Buna//Koli* (in the name Buna Tunulama//Koli Faenama) is the ritual name for the domain of Termanu or Pada. *Pasa//Leli* (in the name Pinga Pasa//Soë Leli) is the ritual name for an area on the northern coast of Termanu (including the present village area of Leli)[19] near two conspicuous coastal rock formations, known in ritual and ordinary language as Batu Hun//Sua Lain. The set *Dulu//Langa* ('East'//'Head', in the name Loniama Langa//Taoama Dulu) and the set *Sepe//Timu* ('Pink, the colour of the dawn'//'East, the direction of the island of Timor', in the name Sepe Ami-Li//Timu Tongo-Batu) indicate that the pursuit of the eagle and hawk, which begins in Termanu, turns first towards the eastern end of the island and then moves towards Rote's westernmost domain, Delha, known in ritual language as Ana Ikio//Dela Muli. (The set *Muli//Iko*, 'West'//'Tail', which matches *Dulu//Langa*, is indicative of the Rotenese cosmological conception of their island as a creature, a crocodile, with its head in the east and its tail in the west.) In *Dela Kolik ma Seko Bunak*, the context in which action occurs is clearly implied by the names used in the chant.

A man from Termanu therefore, Buna Tunulama//Koli Faenama, marries a girl from Leli, Pinga Pasa//Soë Leli (native exegesis supplied the further information that Pinga Pasa//Soë Leli is the child of Pasa Bobio//Leli Kekeo). Their child receives the first elements of his father's binomials and is named Dela Koli//Seko Buna. By this same system, the eagle and hawk (*balapua//tetema*) is named Balapua Loniama//Tetema Taoama and is the child of Loniama Langa//Taoama Dulu. Although no native commentator mentioned this obvious fact, it was clear from the rules of the naming system that another character in the chant, Loma-Loma Langa//Pele-Pele Dulu, was the sibling of Loniama Langa//Taoama Dulu.

The importance of ritual names and the lengths to which these names are elaborated cannot be overemphasised. Whole chants (those on the origin of rice and millet and on weaving) consist lately of what seems to be a boring recitation of names. Each of the 18 domains of Rote has several ritual names and each domain, in turn, is subdivided into numerous ritually named areas.

---

19   Historically, it is interesting to note that Pasa//Leli was formerly (in the seventeenth century) a separate domain, which eventually became incorporated within Termanu (Fox 1971).

Explorations in Semantic Parallelism

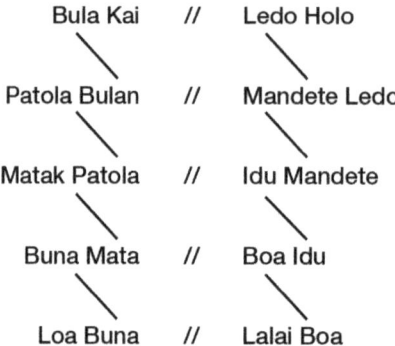

Figure 4.1: A genealogical succession of dual ritual names

One reason for this concern with names is that the chanters are the genealogists of the Rotenese, especially the noble Rotenese. The sharpest criticism in any chanter's collection of deprecating remarks about his rivals is that the man confuses names. In some chants, a succession of marriages and births is recited before the birth of the main chant character. The following six-generation, double-dyadic genealogy gives some idea of the length of this elaboration in ritual naming:

In the genealogy, the simple dyadic sets (*Bula*//*Ledo*, 'Moon'//'Sun'; *Patola*//*Mandete*, the names of two 'noble' cloth motifs; *Mata*//*Idu*, 'eye'//'nose'; *Buna*//*Boa*, 'flower'//'fruit') are regularly ordered and systematically transmitted. In the analysis of ritual language, what is significant about naming is that it forms a highly important subsystem within the language with its own rules, formulae and constraints on the combination of simple dyadic sets.[20]

Rotenese ritual language is formulaic at yet another level. Simple dyadic sets are fixed units; double dyadic expressions further constrain the ordering of simple dyads. In addition, however, there occur certain lines that vary so little from chant to chant that they can be interpreted only as standardised formulaic chains. These formulaic chains are particularly important in beginning and ending chants and in indicating new, important episodes or new stages of events within chants. The simplest example of this in *Dela Kolik ma Seko Bunak* is the three-set chain that occurs in lines 83/84 and again in lines 214/215 and, at each point, announces a further development in the narration:

83/214. Faik esa manunin	On one definite day
84/215. Ma ledo dua mateben.	And at a second certain dawn [sun].

---

20 Names will make up a separate subsection in the dictionary of ritual language. While many elements of names are intelligible and occur also as elements outside the naming system, many elements are obscure and become the subject of multiple, speculative exegeses on the part of the Rotenese.

4. Semantic parallelism in Rotenese ritual language

To introduce the main chant character, many funeral chants begin with the marriage of the character's mother, her pregnancy and the eventual birth of the main character. Some chants elaborate this through several generations (that is, the marriage of the grandmother, her pregnancy, the birth of the father, the marriage of the mother and father, the mother's pregnancy, the birth of the main character, and so on). These genealogical introductions constitute a necessary but highly standardised format in many funeral chants. The formulaic chains of lines 5/6 or lines 75/76 appear, in other chants, as part of formats of this kind.

5. De tein-na da'a-fai	Her womb enlarges
6. Ma suü-na nggeo-lena	Her breasts darken
75. Besak-ka tein-na nama-sela	Now her womb grows larger
76. Ma su'un-na nama-tua.	Now her breasts grow bigger.

Similarly, because a mother's cravings are regarded as indicators of an unborn child's character, the repeated lines about Pinga Pasa and So'e Leli's desire for various foods are also formulaic chains. What differs from chant to chant is the food that is craved.

Most interesting of all, from the point of view of composition, are those formulaic chains that relate the marriage and birth of specific chant characters. In each of these lines, there occurs the name of a new chant character. Nearly always, these chains consist of three sets, one set of which is a verb and two sets of which are components of proper names. To illustrate the formulaic pattern of genealogical introductions, the following six lines are rendered in an alphabetical notation that may be applied to express correctly any genealogical introduction. The fact is, however, that this notation expresses only one format of which there can be several variations.[21] The lines are:

1. Ala soku-la Pinga Pasa	They carry Pinga Pasa
2. Ma ifa-la So'e Leli	And they lift So'e Leli
3. De ana sao Kolik Faenama	[Then] she marries Kolik Faenama
4. Ma tu Bunak Tunulama	And she weds Bunak Tunulama
5. De ana bongi-na Dela Kolik	[Then] she gives birth to Dela Kolik
6. Ma lae-na Seko Bunak	And she bears Seko Bunak

(IC	P	a^1	$N[i^1$	$j^1]$
SC	(P)	a^2	$N[i^2$	$j^2]$
IC	P	b^1	$N[k^2$	$l^1]$

---

21 Variations that might be inserted—one after the first and the other after the second line—are:
Fo Pasa Boboi anan Pasa Boboi's child
Fo Leli Kekeo anan Leli Kekeo's child

SC	(P	b²	N[k²	l²]
IC	P	c¹	N[m¹	k¹]
SC	(P)	c²	N[m²	k²]

The notations are: 'C' is a connective; 'IC' is an initial connective such as *de*, *boe-ma*, *besak-ka*, and so on; 'SC' is a subsequent connective, either *do* or *ma*; '( )' indicates that the element is optional, with the understanding that, in theory, any element that is not part of a dyadic set is potentially optional; 'P' is a pronoun and may be either singular or plural; 'a¹'//'a²', in this genealogical introduction, stands for *soku*//*ifa*. The suffixed morphemes *-la* or *–nala*, which, in ordinary language, involve singular/plural, subject/object agreement, are variable and optional in ritual language and are, for the moment, not considered in the notation; the same is true of the suffixed morpheme for *bongi*//*lae*; 'b¹'//'b²' stands for *tu*//*sao*; 'c¹'//'c²' stands for *bongi*//*lae*. It makes no difference which element of a set occurs first. A complex of double dyadic sets is indicated by '[ ]'; the 'N' preceding these brackets indicates that the elements enclosed are names. The letters 'i', 'j', 'k', 'l', 'm', and so on stand for any dyadic sets in the naming system. The formulation in this notation would be as follows:

Research directions in the study of ritual language

A further crucial aspect of the analysis of ritual language relates not to the expression of dyadic sets in parallel lines but to the organisation of elements in dyadic sets. An element is not restricted to inclusion in only one dyadic set. In fact, it is common for an element to form dyadic sets with more than one element. The combinatorial possibilities of any element vary and these constitute its range. Included in an element's range are all those other elements (and only those elements) with which it forms dyadic sets. Its full range may be expressed by the number of all sets with which it combines.[22]

A dictionary of ritual language, including all the sets of the naming system, could consist of several thousand dyadic sets. The 120-some sets of *Dela Kolik ma Seko Bunak* are therefore hardly sufficient to do more than illustrate the limited ranges of selected elements. The simplest illustration is that of the numbers 'one' (*esa*), 'two' (*dua*), 'three' (*telu*) and 'four' (*ha*). *Esa* has a range of one; it forms a set only with *dua*. *Dua*, however, has a range of two, since it may form sets with *esa* and *telu*. *Telu*, in turn, also has a range of two, since it

---

22 A possible means of dealing with those elements, such as *bei*, *boe* and *ndia*, which may optionally form dyadic sets, would be to allow the combination of an element with itself to be included in its range.

may form sets with *dua* and *ha*. *Ha*, however, is confined to a range of one; it forms a set only with *telu*, since *lima* (as the numeral 'five') is not included in the number system of ritual language.

Elements vary considerably in range. Certain elements have highly restricted (sometimes 'unique') ranges while other elements have wide (potentially 'open') ranges. Names for animals, for example, in certain sets that are central to Rotenese cosmology, appear to be highly restricted. (It is possible that their occurrence in sets of the naming system belies this appearance.) The elements, therefore, of sets such as *foe//iu* ('shark'//'crocodile'), *kea//luik* ('turtle'//'sea cow'), *koa//nggia* ('honeybird'//'parrot') have a narrow range while animal names such as *kapa* ('water buffalo'), *manu* ('chicken') and *kode* ('monkey') have a much wider combinatorial range.

The study of the combinatorial range of elements in dyadic sets also provides a formal means of tracing the (systematic) interrelation of sets and their elements. In *Dela Kolik ma Seko Bunak*, *batu* ('rock, stone') has a range of three. It forms sets with *dae* ('earth, ground'), *ai* ('wooden stick, tree') and with *lutu* ('pebble, grain, granule'). In ritual language, each of these elements, in turn, forms sets with other elements. *Dae* forms a set with *lai(n)* ('sky, heaven'), which in turn forms a set with *poi(n)* ('point, heights'); *dae* also forms a set with *oe* ('water, liquid'), which in turn forms a set with *tasi* ('sea'). *Ai* combines with *na'u* ('grass, straw, tinder') and *lutu* with *dea* ('stone, seawall'). An illustration of the simple network of semantic elements linked to *batu* would be the following:

Figure 4.2: Semantic elements linked to *batu*

In this way, it is possible to construct networks of related elements based solely on the criterion of their occurrence in dyadic sets. Every element in ritual language can thereby be specified as a location or a node in a particular network of semantic relations.

Conclusions: Dyadic language and dual cosmologies

In Indonesian mythological studies, scholars have focused attention on coordinate systems of complementary dualism. Wherever these systems are most impressively evidenced (Nias, Ngadju, Toradja, Sumba, Timor and the islands of eastern Indonesia), their means of expression is an elaborate tradition of pervasive parallelism. Of enormous importance is research into the relationship of these dual cosmologies to their medium of expression in dyadic language.

Some descriptions of the religious and cosmological systems of the Indonesian peoples rely on the analysis of a select number of important complementary dual oppositions. For example, Rotenese ritual language includes, among its dyadic sets, such familiar dual oppositions as:

sun//moon   right//left

sky//earth   male//female

land//water   elder//younger

east//west   red//green

odd number//even number

An even longer selection of such oppositions would, however, hardly do justice to the parallelism of ritual language. To do this would require a list of all dyadic sets—a column of several thousand units. Furthermore, an emphasis on a limited number of these sets renders rigid and static what is, in fact, a flexible system of symbolic classification. Dual elements need not be confined to a single form of complementary opposition. Their range, though always constrained, can add appreciably to their symbolic potential. Contrarily, a parallelism, however pervasive, does not on its own constitute a dual cosmology. A dual cosmology is characterised not by the simple pairing of elements but by the analogical ordering of elements within pairs according to some criterion of asymmetry. The rules of parallelism provide no such criterion. Dyadic sets are essentially neutral pairs; one element in a set is not 'superior' to another element and either element may precede the other in expression. Extra linguistic evaluations are required to transform the elements of dyadic sets into the elements of a dual cosmology.

Rotenese annunciate such evaluations, some of which are explicitly, almost syllogistically, formulated. The following two aphorisms provide some idea of the native criteria by means of which elements of sets may be ordered analogically. For the set *dae//lain* ('earth'//'heaven') there is this aphorism: *Lain loa dae, dae loa lain, tehu Manetua nai lain, de lain loa lena dae* ('Heaven is as broad as the Earth, Earth is as broad as Heaven, but the Great Lord is in Heaven, therefore Heaven is broader than Earth'). For the set *dulu//mulik* ('east'//'west') there is this aphorism: *Dulu nalu muli, tehu ledo neme dulu mai, de dulu ba'u lena muli* ('The east is as long as the west, but the Sun comes from the east, therefore the east is much greater than the west'). Using similar aphorisms based on the native concept of 'greater than' (*lena*), it is possible to construct the ordered directional coordinates of Rotenese cosmology. These provide a basis for a further ordering of other sets and the systematic foundation for a dual cosmology. Not all sets, however, can be linked to these directional coordinates. For some sets, other criteria are invoked and for many sets—perhaps a majority—there appear to be no clear criteria for ordering. Hence, whereas linguistic parallelism can offer the underlying basis for dual cosmology, not all elements of this language need necessarily be taken up and ordered within this framework.

Robert Lowth, in the first study on parallelism, distinguished three sorts of parallels: 1) synonymous parallels, 2) antithetic parallels, and 3) synthetic parallels. It might be possible to further subdivide Lowth's antithetic parallels into complementaries, contraries and contradictories. The overwhelming majority of parallels in Rotenese are, however, 'synthetic'. They reflect the correspondence of elements recognised by a specific speech community, its stock of prescribed social 'metaphors'. What is important in ritual language is neither the form, which is dyadic, nor the content of compositions, which may vary, but the overall and highly detailed view of the world communicated by the structure of thousands of dyadic sets.

Appendix 4.1

Simple dyadic sets

1. *ana//tolo*, child//egg.

2. *ape//ma*, spittle//tongue.

3. *ate//ba*, liver//lungs.

4. *ba'e//ndana*, branch//limb.

5. *bafo//poi*, mouth, valley//tip, peak.

6. *bako (babaco)//toko (totoko)*, to clap//to slap.

7. *balapua (pua)//tetema (tema)*, eagle//hawk.

8. *bai//boe*, again//also.

9. *bai//seluk*, again//once more.

10. *bali//se'o*, to blend//to mix.

11. *bapa//boke*, to slap//to stamp.

12. *batu//ai*, stone//stick.

13. *batu//dae*, stone//earth.

14. *batu//lutu*, stone//grain, pebble.

15. *beu//modo*, new//green.

16. *bia//lola*, to cut into chunks//to slice into strips.

17. *bongi//lae*, to give birth//to bear (a child).

18. *bote//tena*, female goat//female water buffalo.

19. *bula//ledo*, moon//sun.

20. *bupu//fani*, wasp//bee.

21. *dela//nita*, delas tree (*Erythina spp.*)//nitas tree (*Sterculia foetida*).

22. *do(dodo)//nda (ndanda)*, to think//to ponder.

23. *doa-//sota-*, carefully//painstakingly.

24. *dode//hopo*, to cook (rice)//to mix (lontar syrup).

25. *dodo//pau*, to cut the throat//to stab.

26. *doki (dodoki)//una (uüna)*, all sorts (of things)//all kinds (of things).

27. *-dofu//-toi*, to fill with earth//to bury.

28. *dua//esa*, two//one.

29. *dua//telu,* two//three.

30. *dui//kalu*, bone//sinew.

31. *dulu//langa*, east//head.

32. *ei//lida*, foot//wing.

33. *ei//lima*, foot//hand.

34. *ei-ku'u//nisi*, toe//tooth.

35. *-fada//-hala*, to speak//to say.

36. *fai//ledo*, day//sun.

37. *fali//tule*, to return//to turn back.

38. *feto//ina*, girl//woman.

39. *hade//tua-oe*, uncooked rice//lontar juice.

40. *head-hu//tisa*, ladder//roof thatch (of a house).
41. *hele//tenga*, to pick up//to grasp.
42. *-hele//-nepe*, to hold tight//to make firm.
43. *hene//kae*, to mount//to ascend.
44. *henu//sofe*, to be full//to be sufficient.
45. *hona (hohona)//teni (teteni or titini)*, foot of ladder//edge of roof.
46. *ho'i//(la'e)*, to take//to touch.
47. *hule//noke*, to ask//to call.
48. *hu//lai*, trunk, origin//top.
49. *ifa (iifa)//ko'o (koko'o)*, to cradle in the lap//to carry in the arms.
50. *idu//mata*, nose//eye.
51. *iko//muli*, tail//west.
52. *ka (kaka)//kuta (kukuta)*, to bite//to munch.
53. *ka//mumu*, to bite//to suck.
54. *kakodek//lalano*, kakodek tree//lalano tree.
55. *kapa//manu*, water buffalo//chicken.
56. *kea//luik*, turtle//sea cow.
57. *-keni//-moi*, slippery//smooth.
58. *koa//manu*, cock's tail feather//chicken, cock.
59. *kode//teke*, monkey//gecko, lizard.
60. *kuta//mumu*, to munch//to suck.
61. *la//lapu*, to fly//to take wing.
62. *laba//tinga*, to climb//to step.
63. *labu//meko*, drum//gong.
64. *lada//lole*, tasty//good, pleasing.
65. *ladi//lena*, to cross//to wade through.

66. *lafo//teke*, mouse//gecko, lizard.
67. *lai//sue*, to love//to like.
68. *lain//poin*, heaven, heights//top, peaks.
69. *lai//tolomu*, to flee//to run away.
70. *lali//soku*, to move//to leave, to lift.
71. *lano//popi*, feather plume//lontar-leaf garland.
72. *latu//mafo*, ripe//half-ripe.
73. *la'u//tenga*, to seize in flight//to grasp.
74. *lelu (lelelu)//teo (teteo)*, to glance//to look around.
75. *li//nafa*, wave//wave, swell.
76. *-li//-mu*, to sound (of drum or gong)//to resonate, hum.
77. *lima//kala*, hand//chest.
78. *lino//luü*, to rest//to brood (of birds), to settle.
79. *lino//mete*, to spy//to watch.
80. *lino//sae*, to rest//to sit (of birds).
81. *liun//sain*, sea//ocean.
82. *lo//uma*, house// house.
83. *loe (loloe)//sali (sasali)*, receding//overflowing.
84. *lolo (lololo)//nda (ndanda)*, constantly//continually.
85. *losa//nduku*, toward//up to.
86. *loti//pele*, to search by torch-light//to fish by torch-light.
87. *lu//pinu*, tears//mucus, snot.
88. *-mada//-meti*, to dry//to ebb.
89. *mafo//sa'o*, shade//shadow.
90. *mama (mamama)//mumu (mumumu)*, to chew//to suck.
91. *meli (memeli)//mesi (mesimesi)*, quickly//rapidly.

92. *modo//tole*, green//dark.

93. *monu//tuda*, to fall//to drop.

94. *na//ndia*, that there//there.

95. *naä//ninu*, to eat//to drink.

96. *nanamo//tua*, nanamo plant//lontar palm.

97. *-neda//-ndele*, to remember//to recall.

98. *(n)ita//nda*, to see//to meet.

99. *noü//tunga*, each//every.

100. *nutu//tei*, gizzard//stomach.

101. *nggalia//po'i*, to scatter//to set loose.

102. *nggute//tete*, to snip//to cut.

103. *pau (pu)//tene*, thigh//ribs.

104. *pele//sini*, palm-leaf torch//dried leaves.

105. *pinga//so'e*, plate//coconut-shell dish.

106. *posi//unu*, shore's edge//reef.

107. *sa'e//tai*, to sit (of birds)//to grip, hold on.

108. *sanga//tunga*, to seek//to follow.

109. *sao//tu*, to marry//to wed.

110. *-sela//-tua*, to be large//to be big.

111. *sepe//timu*, dawn red//east.

112. *solo//upa*, to pay//to hire.

113. *su'u//tei*, breast//stomach.

114. *ta'e//tou*, boy//man.

115. *tapa//tu'u*, to throw//to cast.

116. *tata//ule*, to split, chop//to wind.

117. *tebe//(n)uni*, true//certain.

Complex dyadic expressions

Unrestricted expressions

118. *laba kae//tinga hene*, to climb, ascend//to step, mount.

Restricted expressions

119. *batu-poik//dae-bafok*, earth//world.

120. *bui-nggeo//meni-oe*, black-tipped//white-sugared.

121. *da'a-fai//nggeo-lena*, to enlarge (of the womb)//to darken (of the breasts).

122. *lano-manu//popi-koa*, male child//boy child.

123. *ma-siu//metu-ape*, to crave with the tongue//to salivate.

Personal names

124. Balapua Loniama//Tetema Taoama.

125. Buna Tunulama//Koli Faenama.

126. Dela Koli//Seko Buna.

127. Loma-Loma Langa//Pele-Pele Dulu.

128. Loniama Langa//Taoama Dulu.

129. Pinga Pasa//Soë Leli.

130. Sepe Ama-Li//Timu Tongo-Batu.

Placenames

131. Ana Iko//Dela Muli, domain of Delha.

132. Batu Hun//Sua Lain, twin rock formations in Termanu.

Connectives, pronouns, prepositionals and invariable elements

Connectives

1. *besak-ka* (*besak-ia*), now.
2. *boe* (*boe-ma, boe-te*), then, and, but, also.
3. *de*, then.
4. *do*, or.
5. *fo*, that (indicator of an appositional phrase).
6. *ma*, and.
7. *te* (*te-hu*), but.

Pronouns

8. *ala*, they.
9. *ana*, he, she, it.
10. *au*, I.
11. *o*, you.

Prepositionals (third-person singular/plural forms only)

12. *nae//lae*, to speak to.
13. *nai//lai*, to be at, on, upon.
14. *neme//leme*, to come from.
15. *neni//leni*, to bring with.
16. *neu//leu*, to go toward.
17. *no//lo*, to be with.

Invariable elements

18. *be*, what.
19. *bei*, still.

20. *dei*, well, so, first (emphatic particle).
21. *ela* (*fo-ela*), so that.
22. *fe*, to give.
23. *kada*, always, still.
24. *leo*, to, toward.
25. *mai*, to come.
26. *na*, exclamation.
27. *ta*, no, not.
28. *so(k)*, finished (indicator of past action).

5. 'Our ancestors spoke in pairs'[1]

For a Rotenese the pleasure of life is talk—not simply an idle chatter that passes time, but the more formal taking of sides in endless dispute, argument and repartee or the rivalling of one another in eloquent and balanced phrases on ceremonial occasions. Speeches, sermons and rhetorical statements are a delight. In this class society, however, with hierarchies of order, there are notable constraints on speech. In gatherings, nobles speak more than commoners, men more than women, elders more than juniors; yet commoners, women and youth, when given the opportunity as they invariably are, display the same prodigious verbal prowess. Lack of talk is an indication of distress. Rotenese repeatedly explain that if their 'hearts' are confused or dejected, they keep silent. Contrarily, to be involved with someone requires active verbal encounter and this often leads to a form of litigation that is conducted more, it would seem, for the sake of argument than for any possible gain.

Three hundred years of Dutch records for the island provide an apt chronicle of this attitude toward speaking. The Dutch East India Company's annual reports for Timor in the eighteenth century are crammed with accounts of the shifting squabbles of related Rotenese rulers. By the twentieth century, the colonial service had informally established Rote as a testing ground. If a young administrator could weather the storms of the litigious Rotenese, he was due for promotion. The Rotenese, in turn, obliged the Dutch by reviving all old litigation to welcome each incoming administrator. Even occasional visitors to the island were struck by these Rotenese qualities. In 1891, the naturalist Herman ten Kate, on a tour of the islands of eastern Indonesia, briefly visited Rote and observed:

> Nearly everywhere we went on Rote, there was a dispute over this or that. The native, to wit the Rotenese, can ramble on over trivia like an old Dutch granny. I believe that his loquaciousness is partially to blame for this, for each dispute naturally provides abundant material for talk. (ten Kate 1894:221)

I was fortunate to arrive on Rote late at night and thus did not become involved in dispute until early the next morning.

An ethnography of speaking on an island where speech takes so many complex forms is a daunting undertaking. Here, my concern is to discuss certain views Rotenese hold of themselves, of their language and of their dialects. My

---

1 This chapter first appeared in 1974 in Richard Bauman and Joel Scherzer (eds), *Explorations in the Ethnography of Speaking*, Cambridge University Press, Cambridge, pp. 65–85.

object, however, is to focus these conceptions on the examination of a single, island-wide form of speaking, a code used mainly in situations of formal interaction. This ritual language is an oral poetry based on a binate semantics that requires the coupling of fixed elements in the production of phrase and verse. It is a particular instance of the phenomenon of canonical parallelism whose extensive distribution among the oral traditions of the world has only begun to be surveyed. That this phenomenon should occur in the traditions of such diverse languages as Cuna, Finnish, Hebrew, Mongolian, Quiche, Rotenese and Toda and can be found among the languages of the Ural-Altaic area, in Dravidian areas of India, through most of South-East Asia, in Austronesian languages from Madagascar to Hawai'i, and in Mayan languages compels critical attention. The first task, in comprehending the role of this ritual language, is to sketch the general language situation and to examine the various forms of speaking that obtain on the island.

Rotenese: The general language situation

The island of Rote lies off the south-western tip of the island of Timor in eastern Indonesia. It is a small island, the southernmost of the Indonesian archipelago. In length, it measures 80 km and, at its widest point, it is no more than 25 km across.

The Rotenese made early adaptations to the arrival of the Portuguese and the Dutch in eastern Indonesia: their rulers accepted alliances, contracts of trade and Christianity. By the middle of the eighteenth century, they were already supporting their own local schools. After an initial period of sporadic localised opposition, the Rotenese managed to avoid major interference in their island affairs by deft token compliance with the Dutch and, in comparison with other peoples of eastern Indonesia, they seem to have taken maximum advantage of the colonial situation. Rote was an area of indirect rule; but, with a subsistence economy dependent on the tapping of lontar palms, the island was never drawn into the colonial cultivation system. In a region of increasing aridity, this palm-centred economy affords the Rotenese distinct economic advantage over neighbouring peoples whose swidden agriculture has reached its limits. By the early 1970s, there were more than 100 000 Rotenese: approximately 70 000 on Rote itself and more than 30 000 on Timor and other islands of eastern Indonesia. Migration from Rote, begun and fostered during the colonial period, continues to the present. The Rotenese are a proud, assertive and energetic people. They neither model themselves on nor are they assimilating to any other local group in the area.

Apart from language, dress is a distinctive mark of Rotenese identity. Their attire is unique in Indonesia. Everyday dress—particularly of Rotenese men—is strikingly unlike that of any other people in eastern Indonesia. Instead of a head-cloth, men wear a broad sombrero-like palm hat. Their traditional tie-dyed cloths combine native design motifs with *patola* patterns taken from Gujarati cloths imported, as elite trade goods, by the Dutch East India Company in the eighteenth century. Except when working, a Rotenese man wears one of these cloths folded and draped over his shoulder. Together, cloths and hats as ideal visible badges are worn as a conscious mark of differentiation. To the outsider, this is a badge of identity.

Language is another marker of identity. *Dede'ak*, the Rotenese word for 'language' or 'speech', has multiple levels of specification. It can refer to 'Rotenese' (Dede'a Rote or Dede'a Lote) or to any dialect of Rotenese: *dede'a Pada* ('dialect of Pada') or *dede'a Oepao* ('dialect of Oepao'). Without a qualifying term, *dede'ak* can refer to any organised coherent speech: 'a court case', 'a dispute', 'some specific news' or a 'piece of recent information'. At this level, *dede'ak* emphasises what is current, is still in process and is personal. It is closely related to *kokolak or* ('talk' or 'conversation'), but distinguished from other forms of organised speaking such as *tutuik* ('tales'), *tutui-tete'ek* ('true tales or history'), *neneuk* ('riddles'), *namahehelek ma babalak* ('beliefs and consequences'), *lakandandak meis* ('dream interpretations'), *a'ali-o'olek* (a highly standardised form of 'mockery') and *bini* (the designation for all compositions in parallel verse, since all of these relate to some past event or follow a fixed 'ancestral' pattern). At one level, *dede'ak* comprises all forms of speaking; at another, it contrasts ordinary speech with other forms of more formal speaking. (The distinction resembles that between English 'speech' and 'a speech'.) The use of *dede'ak*, or any other form of speaking, is not simply situation specific but situation creative. Litigants in a court case are involved in *dede'ak*; lords and elders, in comment and in rendering judgment, invoke *bini*. Bride-wealth negotiations require *bini*; if these overtures are successful, details in the negotiation can be worked out in *dede'ak*. A change in speaking can indicate a subtle change of phase in a continuous speech event.

Dede'a Lote is the language of Rote. It is identified with Rote and is said to be spoken by all Rotenese throughout the island. Interestingly, it is not credited with qualities that make its speakers uniquely human. Dede'a Lote is contrasted with other known languages of the area: Dede'a Ndao ('Ndaonese'), Dede'a Helok ('Helong') or Dede'a Malai ('Malay or Indonesian'). To its speakers, even those who have migrated to other islands, it is a distinct and delimitable language. The situation is, however, more complex.

To the west of Rote is the tiny island of Ndao; to the east, the slightly larger island of Semau. On both of these islands live separate ethnic groups of 2000 or more people conscious of their gradual linguistic, cultural and economic assimilation by the Rotenese. For the Ndaonese, the situation is of long standing (Fox 1972). Since the 1720s, Ndao has been treated as one of the semi-autonomous political domains of Rote. The Ndaonese economy, like that of Rote, is dependent on palm utilisation. The Ndaonese, however, have the special distinction that all men of the island are goldsmiths and silversmiths who, during each dry season, leave their island to fashion jewellery for the people of the Timor area. Ndaonese have migrated to Rote for centuries. In every domain of Rote, there is one clan said to be of 'Ndaonese origin' and, to this clan, new immigrants can readily assimilate. Recently—in the past two generations—Ndaonese have adopted Rotenese hats and the design motifs of western Rotenese cloths. Women have begun to leave the island in large numbers to sell finished cloths or to take orders for the weaving of new cloths. Ndaonese is of the Bima-Sumba subfamily of languages; Rotenese is of the Timor-Ambon grouping of languages. Most Ndaonese are polyglots, having spent long periods on neighbouring islands; virtually all Ndaonese men are, at least, bilingual in Rotenese and Ndaonese and an increasing number of women are becoming similarly bilingual. The assimilation is gradual, increasing but also selective. Rotenese parallel songs, for which there are said to be no Ndaonese equivalents, seem to have already been completely adopted. There are, therefore, fluent Rotenese speakers who dress much like Rotenese but who retain their own language and separate homeland. Many of these speakers, when they cease their special occupation, abandon their language entirely and become full Rotenese.

For Helong speakers of Semau and of a single remaining coastal village near Kupang on Timor, the situation is somewhat different (Fox 1972). Helong is a language related to Rotenese, but recent contact between speakers of these languages has occurred only in the past 100 years. The Helong, under pressure from the Timorese, accompanied their ruler to Semau some time before 1815—the time of the first wave of Rotenese migration to Timor. From Timor, Rotenese later began to settle on Semau. The result is that the Helong, with a precarious swidden economy, have been swamped by Rotenese. Lacking a viable and separate means of livelihood and in close contact with Rotenese, many Helong have adopted Rotenese ways and are bilingual in Rotenese and their own language.

The other language with which Rotenese speakers have long been in contact is Malay. Unlike Ndaonese or Helong, Malay, in some form, is understood by a majority of Rotenese. Not long after 1660, Rotenese rulers began an annual exchange of letters with the Dutch East India Company's Governor-General in Batavia. This correspondence and other dealings with the company's representatives were carried out initially through Malay-speaking scribes and interpreters located in Kupang on Timor. In 1679, the Dutch General Missives report that one young Rotenese ruler was even transported to Kupang for the express purpose of learning Malay (Coolhaas 1971:338). By 1710, the first company interpreter was stationed on Rote; in 1729, the first Rotenese ruler converted to Christianity; and by 1735, the first Malay-speaking schoolmaster from Ambon had arrived on the island. Within a generation (by 1753), there were six local schools, maintained by Rotenese rulers, and Rotenese had begun to replace company-appointed teachers from other islands. From the beginning, Malay was a 'literary language' linked with Christianity. Knowledge of Malay was necessary to read the Bible and to carry on official correspondence with the Dutch.

Malay also became the language of the heterogeneous settlement of peoples that grouped around the company's fort, Concordia, at Kupang. Eventually, Rotenese predominated in this settlement and in the surrounding area. Over 300 years, this language of Kupang, known as Basa Kupang (Bahasa Kupang) became a distinct dialect of colloquial Malay with unmistakable Rotenese influences. Many Rotenese who live on Timor regard it as their own peculiar and special form of speaking. It is never the language of official business or, on Rote, the language of home or village, but, like other local variants of Malay, it is a language of the 'marketplace', spoken in town when dealing with friends and acquaintances. Later, with the increasing use of Malay in the colonial administration, with its adoption as the official language of the nation and with its use in all the schools, Rotenese were introduced to a new standard form of Malay, the official language of national unity and identity: modern Indonesian (Bahasa Indonesia).

These three varieties of Malay ('Biblical' Malay, Basa Kupang and Indonesian) are sufficiently different from one another to be segregated and confined to regularised situations. A Christian Rotenese, with some education, will deal with government officials (even fellow Rotenese) in Indonesian, will attend church services conducted in Biblical Malay and will rely on Basa Kupang when visiting friends or relatives on Timor. In a sense, the Rotenese have added these new forms of speaking (or writing) to their other conventional forms of speech. As with other forms of speaking, however, there is a strong tendency not to 'mix speech' inappropriately.

These three varieties of Malay are, however, sufficiently similar that the furtherance of one has consequences for the others. On conclusion of the national literacy campaign in the late 1950s, when the island was certified as literate in Indonesian, there was mass conversion to Christianity. Malay had served as a check on conversion and when, by decree, all Rotenese became Malay speakers, this obstacle was removed. Significantly, Biblical Malay is itself seen as a formal ritual language indispensable for Christian rituals. The parallelism that pervades the Old Testament accords well with Rotenese ideas of a ritual language. A church service consists of readings from the Bible with translations in Rotenese, Malay songs and long sermons often in Malay, with long paraphrases in Rotenese, or interspersed Malay and Rotenese, or even a cacophony of two simultaneous sermons, with one preacher speaking Malay and the other translating the Malay into Rotenese.

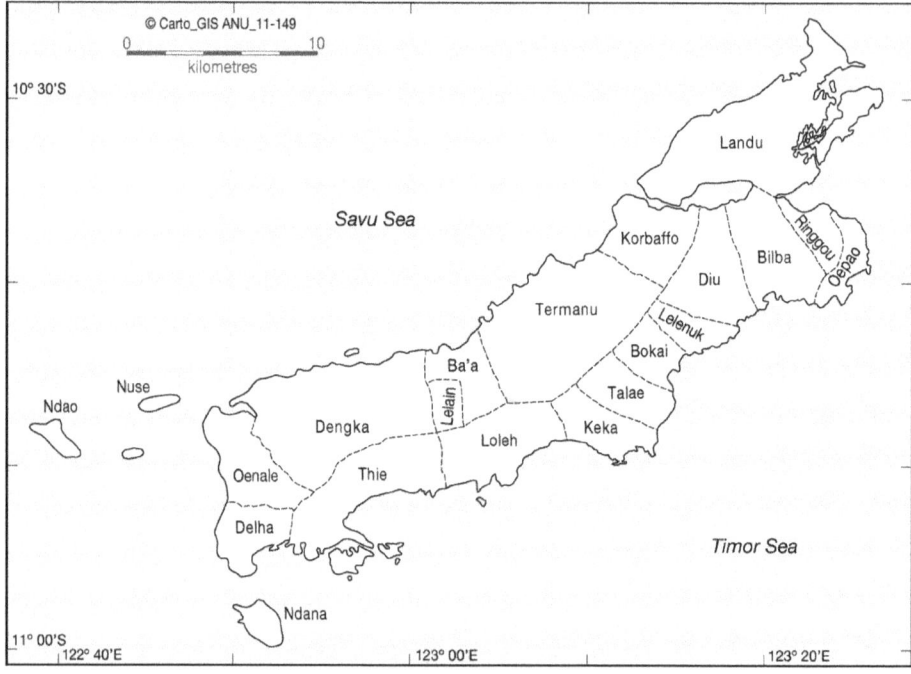

Figure 5.1: Domain Map of the Island of Rote

The dialect communities of Rote

Rotenese is the language of a small, hilly island with no natural barriers to communication. Any village area is within a day's walk or horse ride of any other. Politically, however, the island is divided among 18 native states or domains (*nusak*). Each domain was once ruled by its own lord, who, together with the representative lords of the various clans of that domain, presided at a court and made decisions based on the customary law of the domain. Although borders have always been disputed, the separate existence of these states can be traced, through continuous archival records, over 300 years, to the mid-seventeenth century, when their rulers were first recognised by contracts of trade with the Dutch East India Company. By preventing the expansion of any one state, hampering the fluctuations of men and territory, and by dismembering the largest of these states, the Dutch fostered conditions that maintained separate entities. They froze, in effect, what was a more fluid and flexible situation and created a 'new' tradition of rule. Later, they attempted to counter the effects of their previous policies, but all of these twentieth-century schemes for the amalgamation of states failed. As a consequence, there exist, at present, virtually the same local political domains as existed in 1656 (Fox 1971). For a period after independence, these domains were afforded administrative existence within the bureaucratic structure of the Republic of Indonesia, their lords are acknowledged as administrative officials and their courts allowed to retain jurisdiction over most civil disputes. During Suharto's New Order, the administrative organisation of the island went through a variety of changes and these changes continued into the initial Reformation period. In 2002, however, Rote and Ndao were given local autonomy and since this time, the island's administration has returned recognition to the local domains (Fox 2011).

With its political divisions, local classes, unique clan privileges and subtle social discriminations, its styles of dress and fluctuation of fashion, its variations in the performance of rituals and its differences in customary law, Rotenese culture forms a complex structure by which social groups are distinguished. Rotenese emphasise their minor social peculiarities rather than overall similarities among themselves. In particular, they invest the slight shades of difference between domains with a high degree of significance to denote their separateness from one another. The result is a family of resemblances, traceable throughout the island—a continuous variation along a multitude of non-equivalent scales. Dress—to the outsider, the mark of Rotenese identity—is internally a heraldic display that identifies a person's domain, class, status and, in some instances, court office. Land is the other prime mark of identity. Where no natural, visible barriers occur, the Rotenese have erected political barriers fostered by indirect colonial rule. And most importantly, on the island, there is a proliferation of dialects.

By native account, Rotenese, Dede'a Lote, consists of 18 domain dialects (*dede'a nusak*). The statement is as much political as it is linguistic. The assertion is that every state has its own language. *Nusak*, like *dede'ak*, has multiple levels of meaning. It can refer to the 'domain', the 'resident village' of the lord (*nusak lain*, 'high *nusak*') or, formerly, the 'court' of the domain. The claim to separate *dede'a nusak* implies not only a unique dialect but also unique customary law and, previously, distinctive court procedures for dealing with litigation and other 'affairs' of state.

When qualifications are made to statements about the separateness of domain dialects, the qualifications are also political. The small domains of Keka and Talae achieved Dutch recognition of their independence from their neighbouring state, Termanu, in 1772. By arguments based on a kind of folk etymology in which Rotenese find a particular delight, the people of Talae are said to have 'fled' (*ita lai*, 'we flee') from Termanu. When, in Termanu, it is claimed that Termanu, Keka and Talae have a common dialect, this is recognition of a close linguistic relationship and a tactical assertion of past political claims. It is sometimes said that the small domain of Bokai has 'no language of its own'. Again, this is not a linguistic statement so much as a reference to a well-known myth that relates the curse of the Lord of the Sea on the original inhabitants of this domain. The curse limits the number of these original inhabitants to 30 people and so the domain is said to be composed mainly of outsiders who speak other dialects. The far western domain of Delha, mentioned early in Dutch East India Company records, was the last domain to achieve Dutch recognition of its separation from Oenale, whose dialect it shares. Political factors, especially its long 'non-recognition', have contributed to make Delha a hotbed of resistance to all forms of rule. To other Rotenese, Delha is the backwater area of their island. (People there, it is said, are not Christians, speak no Malay and, before 1965, were 'communist' to a man.) When the Lord of Korbaffo, a domain of eastern Rote, was appointed a government administrative coordinator for the island, he would—as he proudly explained—speak regularly in Oenale but use an interpreter when touring Delha. All Rotenese statements about dialect intelligibility have an important political component.

A subject Rotenese never seem to tire of discussing is domain and dialect differences. The point of reference is the local dialect and comparison is always pair-wise with some other dialect. Evidence is specific, selective and piecemeal. Domains are self-centred to the point that there are relatively few people with a thorough knowledge of another dialect. Except for the high nobility, marriage occurs within the domain. One effect of Dutch rule was to impede the former migration of people among states. Contact with other dialect speakers is frequent but usually temporary. Thus the curious situation exists in which a large number of Rotenese have visited Kupang on Timor while a far smaller number have spent a single night in a domain at one remove from their own. What therefore passes as information on dialect difference, although rarely incorrect, is highly standardised. These selective features are taken up, occasionally in folktales involving strangers, in pseudo-imitation of real differences.

In 1884, D. P. Manafe, a Rotenese schoolteacher from Ba'a, wrote the first account of the Rotenese language. Through the auspices of the Dutch linguist Kern, this article in Malay, 'Akan Bahasa Rotti', was published in a Dutch journal (Manafe 1889:633–48). The article consists almost entirely of a listing of words in the dialects of the island and various verb paradigms in the dialect of Ba'a. Although more extensive and systematic than Rotenese conversational models, the article is itself an excellent native model. After dividing the island into its two divisions, east and west, Manafe presents his own grouping of dialects according to their 'sound'. Although the dialects have different sounds, anyone in the east, he asserts, can, without too much trouble, understand anyone in the west. His list of dialects is as follows.

1. Oepao, Ringgou and Landu

2. Bilba, Diu and Lelenuk

3. Korbaffo

4. Termanu, Keka and Talae

5. Bokai

6. Ba'a and Loleh

7. Dengka and Lelain

8. Thie

9. Oenale and Delha

This list joins several dialects of contiguous domains; the precise criteria for this grouping are not, however, specified and the paradigms that follow illustrate differences in 'sounds' in dialects that are grouped together. The list, however, conforms to Rotenese standards that all valid groupings consist of nine elements, the number of totality. By no means is the list misleading. Intuitively, taking into account language, politics and local geography, it is an accurate representation of perceived domain differences. As a description of dialects, it formed the basis for the dialect study of the Dutch linguist J. C. G. Jonker (1913:531–622).

In discussing dialects, certain sound shifts are particularly noted. Dialects are divided into those that use /l/ and /r/ and those that use /l/ exclusively; those that replace /p/ with /mb/ or those that use /n/ in medial position instead of /nd/. The shift from /ngg/ to /ng/ to /k/ in medial position and the presence or absence of initial /h/ or /k/ are other often-cited distinguishing features. Since a few words, with several of these sound shifts, can be given as evidence of dialect difference, all domains can be shown to have 'a separate language'. While they are thus concerned with linguistic discriminations, Rotenese are not interested in systematic dialectology.

The semantic diversity of dialects is of more significance to Rotenese than any phonological differences. The sound patterns of Rotenese form a continuum, but the occurrence of different words for the same object introduces radical disjunction. Such disjunction can be used to justify social and political separation. In describing themselves, Rotenese readily point out, for example, that the word for 'man' or 'person' in central Rote is *hataholi* (or its cognate, *hatahori*; *atahori*), while in Bilba and Ringgou, it is *dae-hena* (or *dahenda*); that the word for a man's hat is *ti'i-langa* in most eastern areas of Rote, but *so'i-langga* (or *so-langga*) in Ba'a and Thie; or that the word for the annual post-harvest ritual is *hus* in Termanu and eastern Rote but *limba* (or *limpa*) in Thie, Ba'a and western Rote.

This semantic diversity is a resource for ritual language. Some native awareness of this diversity is essential to the continuance of ritual language as an island-wide code. Reflexively, this ritual language provides Rotenese with yet another view of their language and dialect.

Explorations in Semantic Parallelism

Ritual language: A formal speech code

Ritual language is a formal speech code. It consists of speaking in pairs. The semantic elements that form these pairs or dyadic sets are highly determined. Sets are structured in formulaic phrases and their presentation generally consists of compositions of parallel verse. A *bini* can vary in length from two lines to several hundred lines. It includes the genre of 'proverbs' (*bini kekeuk*, 'short *bini*'), 'songs' (*soda bini*, 'to sing *bini*') and 'chants' (*helo bini*, 'to chant *bini*'). Rotenese can qualify the category *bini* in innumerable ways. A taxonomy of these forms would vary on, at the least, two dimensions: one, an enumeration of the various methods of producing *bini*—'singing', 'saying', 'chanting', 'wailing'; the other, a listing of the myriad situations for which *bini* are appropriate—greetings, farewells, petitions, courtship, negotiations and all the ceremonies of Rotenese life. *Bini mamates* ('funeral *bini*'), for example, are further subdivided into a host of *bini* appropriate to categories of deceased people: for a young child, an elder child, a virginal girl, a young noble, a rich man, a widow, and so on. The feature common to all uses of these *bini* is their occurrence in circumstances of formal social interaction. All *bini* are based on the same repertoire of dyadic sets. The same dyadic sets can, therefore, occur in any particular form of *bini*, whether proverb, song or funeral chant. Many forms are equally applicable to a variety of situations. The three *bini* that I quote here can fit any 'situation of succession': the installation of a new lord to continue a line of rule or the replacement of a father with his son or of a lineage member with another lineage member. The imagery is of regeneration and renewal.

Variation (1)

1.	*Oe No Dain bi'in*	The goat of Oe No from Dai
2.	*Na bi'i ma-pau henuk*	The goat has a yellow-necklaced beard
3.	*Ma Kedi Poi Selan manun*	And the cock of Kedi Poi from Sela
4.	*Na manun ma-koa lilol*	The cock has gold-stranded tail feathers.
5.	*De ke heni pau bi'in*	Cut away the goat's beard
6.	*Te hu ela lesu bi'in*	Leaving but the goat's throat
7.	*De se lesun na pau seluk*	That throat will beard again
8.	*Fo na pau henu seluk*	And the beard will be a yellow necklace again
9.	*Ma fe'a heni koa manun*	And pluck out the cock's tail feathers
10.	*Te sadi ela nggoti manun*	Leaving only the cock's rear
11.	*Fo nggotin na koa seluk*	That rear will feather again
12.	*Fo na koa lilo seluk.*	And the tail feathers will be gold strands again.
13.	*Fo bei teman leo makahulun*	Still perfect as before
14.	*Ma tetu leo sososan.*	And ordered as at first.

Commentary (1)

This short *bini* is composed of seven dyadic sets (*bi'i*//*manu*, 'goat'//'cock'; *koa*//*pau*, 'tail feathers'//'beard'; *henu*//*lilo*, 'yellow-bead'//'gold[-strand]'; *fe'a*//*ke* 'pluck'//'cut'...), one redoubled personal name (*Oe No*//*Kedi Poi*), one dyadic placename (*Dai*//*Sela*) and a number of variable connective elements (*ma, fo, ela, de, sel'a*...). *Te hu* (line 6) is generally invariable, but in this composition, the chanter has attempted to cast it in dyadic form: *te hu* is intended to form a couple with *te sadi* (line 10). This is not a required set in ritual language but is the embellishment of a particularly capable chanter. As is evident, parallel lines need not be consecutive or alternating. Sequencing is complex and variable. The parallel lines of this *bini* are: 1/3, 2/4, 5/9, 6/10, 7/11, 8/12 and 12/14. Knowledge of dyadic sets indicates which lines are parallel. Composition is based on these sets, not on whole parallel lines.

Variation (2)

The second variation on the theme of succession uses many of the same sets. It is slightly longer and its imagery more dense. Full explication of its significance would require a diverting discussion of Rotenese cosmological ideas. It is appropriate only to the succession of a high noble or lord and implies his influence over the sea. Like the first, this variation can be used only in situations of male succession. In ritual language, the complex (crossover) formula for a male child is *popi koa*//*lanu manu* ('a rooster's tail feathers'//'a cock's plume').

1. Benga la-fafada	Word is continually told.
2. Ma dasi laka-tutuda:	And voice continually let fall:
3. Manu ma-koa lilok	A cock with gold-stranded tail feathers
4. Do bi'i a-pau henu.	Or a goat with yellow-necklaced beard.
5. Lae: koa lilon loloso	They say: the tail feathers' gold strands flutter
6. Na loloso neu liun	They flutter toward the ocean
7. Fo liun dale laka-tema	The ocean depths are calmed
8. Ma pau henun ngganggape	And the beard's yellow necklace waves
9. Na ngganggape neu sain	It waves toward the sea
10. Fo saini dale la-tetu.	The sea depths are ordered.
11. De besak ia koa lilon na kono	Now the tail feathers' gold strands drop
12. Ma pau bi'in na monu	And the beard's yellow necklace falls
13. Te hu bei ela nggoti manun	Still leaving but the cock's rear
14. Na dei nggotin na koa bai	But that rear feathers once more
15. Fo na koa lilo seluk	And the feathers are gold strands again
16. Ma bei ela lesu bi'in	And still leaving the goat's throat
17. Na dei lesun na pau seluk	That throat beards again

18. Fo na pau henu seluk.	And the beard is a yellow necklace again.
19. Fo leo faik ia	Just like this day
20. Ma deta ledok ia	And as at this time [sun]
21. Boe nggati koa manakonok	A change of tail feathers that were dropped
22. Ma pau manatudak ndia.	And this beard that had fallen.

Commentary (2)

This *bini* introduces eight new sets (*benga*//*dasi*, 'word'//'voice'; *-fada*//*-tuda*, 'to tell'//'to fall'; *loso*//*nggape*, 'to flutter'//'to wave'; *fai*//*ledo*, 'day'//'sun'...) and omits only two sets of the previous *bini* (*fe'a*//*ke, ulu*//*sosa*). Parallel lines are: 1/2, 3/4, 5/8, 6/9, 7/10, 11/12, 13/16, 14/17, 15/18, 19/20 and 21/22. A feature of most invariable elements is that they may be omitted in the second of two parallel lines. Thus, *te hu* (line 13) neither recurs nor is paired with *te sadi* in its corresponding line (line 16). The connective *ma* ('and') is used instead. An interesting embellishment in this composition is the attempt to create a pairing of the morphological elements *la-*//*laka-* (lines 1/2, 7/10). This *bini* also illustrates one of the most crucial features of ritual-language semantics: an element or word may form a pair with more than one other element. Most elements are not confined to a single fixed dyadic set but rather have a variable range of other elements with which they form acceptable sets. In this composition, the element *-tuda* ('to fall') forms a set with *-fada* ('to speak, to tell'); *kono* ('to drop, to tumble down') forms a set with *monu* ('to fall off, to fall from'), but in the final lines, *kono* forms another set with *tuda*. New pairings highlight different aspects of the same semantic element. The linking of elements creates a means of formal inquiry on the semantics of this language.

Variation (3)

This variation is the shortest of the three. Its format closely resembles that of the first *bini*. The imagery of succession has been changed by the use of different sets. Instead of 'goat's beard' and 'cock's tail feathers', renewal is phrased in terms of 'sugarcane sheaths' and 'banana blossoms'. Sugar cane and bananas are, in Rotenese, botanic icons for male persons.

1. Lole faik ia dalen	On this good day
2. Ma lada ledok ia tein na	And at this fine time [sun]
3. Lae: tefu ma-nggona lilok	They say: the sugar cane has sheaths of gold
4. Ma huni ma-lapa losik.	And the banana has blossoms of copper.
5. Tefu olu heni nggonan	The sugar cane sheds its sheath
6. Ma huni kono heni lapan,	And the banana drops its blossom,
7. Te hu bei ela tefu okan	Leaving but the sugarcane's root
8. Ma huni hun bai.	And just the banana's trunk.

9. De dei tefu na nggona seluk	But the sugar cane sheaths again
10. Fo na nggona lilo seluk	The sheaths are gold again
11. Ma dei huni na lapa seluk	And the banana blossoms again
12. Fo na lapa losi seluk.	The blossoms are copper again.

Commentary (3)

This *bini* is based on eight sets. The set *fai//ledo* is the only set retained from the previous variations. *Lilo* ('gold') forms a new set with *losi* ('copper'), while *kono* forms yet another set with *olu* ('to shed'). The linkage that occurs in these short *bini* (*fada//tuda::tuda//kono::kono//monu, kono//olu*) gives an indication of the combinatorial possibilities of elements in ritual language. Underlying all expressions in this language is a stable network of semantic elements whose interrelations can be formally represented in complex graphs.

The network of some of the words for 'speaking' provides a simple example of this kind of graph. The slight differences among the various terms for speaking, questioning, requesting or promising are often difficult to gloss or indicate in translation. These uses are nonetheless crucial and strictly defined. *Fada*, the general verb 'to speak, to say, to tell', is a critical point of articulation (in terms of graph theory), since it may pair with a number of other elements. It forms dyadic sets with *hala*, which occurs as a noun for 'voice' or as a verb 'to voice'; with *nae*, an inflected verbal element for indicating direct quotation; with *noli*, the verb 'to teach, to instruct'; with *nosi*, an element that occurs only in ritual language and is thus interpreted with the same sense as its permitted co-occurrent elements; with *tuda*, the verb 'to fall, to let fall'; and with *tudu* ('to show, to point out'). In turn, most of these elements form sets with other elements. *Hala* forms a set with *dasi*—'the voice or song (of a bird)', 'to sing (of birds)', 'to say something in a pleasing voice'. *Dasi* forms another set with *benga* ('to inform, to explain, to speak when introducing something'). *Nosi* links with various different verbs: 'to question, to ask, to request, to demand.' These include the verbal dyadic set *doko-doe//tai-boni*, which is used, for example, for that special 'gentle demanding' that is supposed to characterise bride-wealth requests. *Tuda* is another articulation point for a series of verbs of falling, with glosses 'to fall off, to tumble, to crumble, to shed, to peel'. The most interesting of these is the verb *olu* ('to shed, to peel'), since it forms a seemingly curious set with *tui*. According to native exegesis, this verb *tui* is identified as the same element as the verb 'to tell a story', as in the partially reduplicated noun *tutuik* ('tale'). In Rotenese, it can be literally said, of trees, that they 'peel bark and tell leaves'. This idiom seems less peculiar when seen in light of those connections in the semantic field of which it forms a part. *(N)ae* pairs with two verbs that occur in the most common formulaic prelude for introducing direct speech, *lole hala//selu dasi*. *Selu* is the verb 'to reply, to alternate, to exchange' and thus also pairs with *tuka* ('to change, to exchange, to barter'). *Selu* is one of the elements that link this network to a larger network of relations. That some of the main verbs for 'speaking' should belong so intimately to the same semantic field as the verbs for 'falling', and also the verbs for 'exchanging', is one of the more interesting discoveries of this form of analysis.

The formal interrelations of all these elements are as follows

(>= forms a set with):

1. *fada*	>	hala, nae/ae, noli, nosi, tuda, tudu
2. *hala*	>	fada, dasi
3. *nac/ae*	>	fada, helu, lole, selu
4. *noli*	>	fada
5. *nosi*	>	fada, tane
6. *tuda*	>	fada, kona, kono, monu, sasi
7. *tudu*	>	feda
8. *dasi*	>	benga
9. *benga*	>	dasi
10. *helu*	>	ae
11. *lole*	>	ae, selu
12. *selu*	>	ae, lole, tuka
13. *tuka*	>	selu
14. *tane*	>	tata, teni
15. *tata*	>	tane, teni
16. *teni*	>	tata, dokodoe
17. *dokodoe*	>	teni, tai-boni
18. *taiboni*	>	doko-doe
19. *kona*	>	tuda
20. *kono*	>	tuda, monu, ngga, olu
21. *monu*	>	tuda, kono
22. *sasi*	>	tuda
23. *ngga*	>	kono
24. *olu*	>	kono, tui
25. *tui*	>	olu

These formal associations account for all uses of these elements within the dialect community of Termanu.

A graphic representation of these interrelations can also be made. It is of interest to note that more general semantic elements are points of articulation while those elements that are idiomatic or have restricted contextual uses are found on the extreme edges of the graph's branching structure.

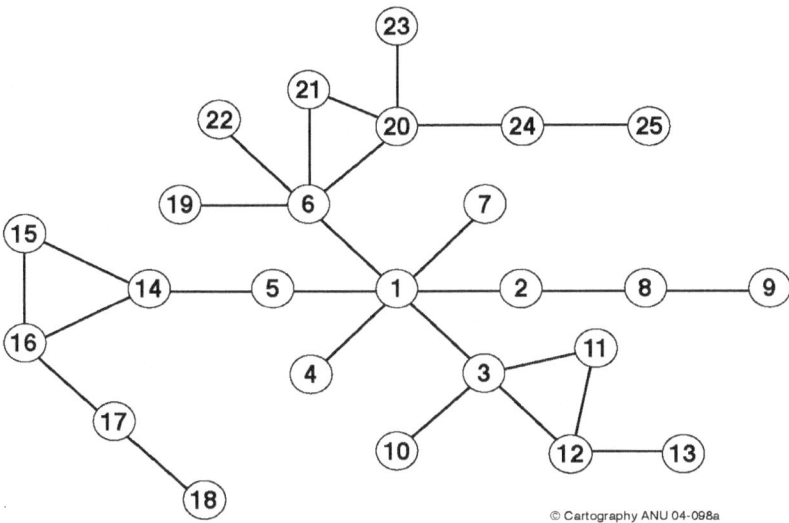

Figure 5.2: Formal Associations of the Verb *Fada:* 'to speak'

While these short *bini* provide some idea of the structure of Rotenese composition, they give no idea of its poetic complexity. Further variations, using similar sets, are unlimited. By describing, for example, only the loss of the 'sugarcane sheath' and 'banana blossom' and by interweaving this with other plant imagery, this *bini* of succession can be transformed into a funeral chant. Most chants continue for hundreds of lines. With elaborations and repetitions, their performance can occupy several hours of an evening. To achieve a minimal fluency and become socially recognised as a promising chanter, an individual must have knowledge of at least 1000 to 1500 dyadic sets.

Communities and resources for performance

One direction of some previous studies on parallelism—those that have followed leads outlined by Lowth (1753, 1778)—has been to distinguish three sorts of parallels: 1) synonymous parallels, 2) antithetic parallels, and 3) synthetic parallels. As a general typology, this approach is somewhat useful, but as a precise analysis of a large lexicon of dyadic sets, it has only limited value. The criteria for synonymy or antithesis are difficult to make precise and the more precise these criteria are made, the more the residual class of synthetic parallels tends to increase. Furthermore, the approach limits analysis to the single relation between elements of a pair and takes no account of an element's range of associations or its location as a node in a network of semantic interrelations.

Using a loose notion of synonymy, however, it is apparent that many pairs have 'similar' meaning. Were these the only class of pairs in ritual language, there would be some justification for reducing parallelism to a mere ritual redundancy. Near synonyms, however, account for only a portion of the lexicon in traditions of pervasive parallelism, and, even between paired elements, differences between these elements cannot be discounted. The general effect is always that of carefully calibrated stereoscopy—a fusion of separate images. A loose notion of synonymy can nonetheless serve as a starting point in the examination of the use of dialect variants in ritual language.

Rotenese bifurcate their island into an eastern division, occasionally known as 'Sunrise', called *Lamak-anan*, and a western division, 'Sunset', called *Henak-anan*. To these divisions, with some justification, Rotenese attribute a host of distinguishing characteristics: economic, political, social and, above all, linguistic. The central domains of Termanu, Keka and Talae straddle the imaginary line that divides the island. There is no consensus on whether these domains belong to the east or west, and they can be assigned by individuals to either division.

In Termanu, it is often explained that in ritual language many synonymous sets are composed of one term from the eastern division and one from the western division. No Rotenese, however, has, nor could have, perfect knowledge of the dialect situation on the island nor do individuals necessarily share the same knowledge of other dialects. In all cases, an individual's knowledge is held in relation to his own local dialect—a specific speech community. The occurrence of a term in any single dialect of one division is sufficient to cast it as the term of that entire division. The situation of individuals literally in the middle—in Termanu, Keka and Talae—is even more complex. For certain pairs, their dialect belongs to the western division and the foreign term comes from the east; for other pairs, theirs is the eastern division and the foreign term comes from the west. Like all native models, the Rotenese view of division dialects is a partial, specific, though not inaccurate, perception that closely partakes of the phenomenon it is intended to describe. Imperfect knowledge is essential to the maintenance of the model.

The simplest illustration of the use of dialect semantics—one that would confirm the native view—is the following list of dyadic sets:

Eastern Rote	Western Rote	Gloss
1. *dae hena [Bilba]*	hataholi [Termanu]	'man, human person'
2. *luak [Korbaffo]*	leak [Termanu]	'cave, grotto'
3. *nafa [Ringgou]*	li [Termanu]	'waves, breakers'
4. *pela [Bilba]*	longe [Termanu]	'to dance in a specific way'
5. *lain [Termanu]*	ata [Dengka]	'heaven, sky; above'
6. *ka [Termanu]*	kiki [Thie, Dengka]	'to bite'
7. *sele [Termanu]*	tane [Loleh]	'to plant'

8. paik [Termanu]	sola [Oenale]	'corner of leaf bucket'
9. -lo [Termanu]	-nggou [Thie, Ba'a]	'to call loudly, to invite'

Examples 4 and 5 illustrate the aspects of borrowing. *Longe* (from *ronggeng*) and *ata* (from *atas*) are probably Malay borrowings. Evidence from Borneo (Hardeland 1858:4–5; Evans 1953:495–6) suggests that the direct borrowing of one term from Malay and the coupling of this term with a term from the native language is a possible, and undoubtedly widespread, means of creating synonymous dyadic sets (compare this with the use of Spanish loan words in the construction of Zinacanteco couplets, as reported by Bricker 1974:379–80). Interestingly, given Rotenese use of Malay, recognisable Malay words in ritual language are surprisingly few. Direct borrowing does not seem to occur. The few Malay words in ritual language are dialect words adopted from Malay in some—but not necessarily all—dialects on the island. Ritual language remains remarkably impermeable to Malay. The same is true of the few Dutch and Portuguese words in ritual language. Instead of being strange foreign words, they are current words in ordinary speech. Two dyadic sets happen, in fact, to combine one Dutch and one Portuguese-derived term. *Kana(k)* ('small table') from Dutch *knaap* forms a set with *kadela* ('chair, stool') from the Portuguese *kadera*; *kuei* ('socks, slippers'), a word compounded of Dutch *kous* and Rotenese *ei(k)* ('foot'), forms a set with *sapeo* ('non-Rotenese hat') from the Portuguese *chapeo*.

10. henu [Termanu]	sofe [Thie]	'full, sufficient'

Example 10 illustrates a further important effect of the use of dialect words. It would be almost impossible to expect dialect terms to be so conveniently segregated in eastern and western areas. The set *henu*//*sofe* is one of the standard sets cited as an example of division dialect segregation. The fact is, however, that *sofe* (or more often *sofe-sofe*) occurs in Termanu dialect. Its sense is altered slightly. Instead of meaning 'full, sufficient', it occurs adverbially to indicate something that is 'too much, overflowing, brimming'. In native exegesis, *sofe*, by its concurrence with *henu*, is taken to have the 'same' meaning and this meaning of *sofe* is, correctly, identified as a dialect usage in Thie. Other examples can be shown:

11. pada [Termanu]	bata [Loleh]	'to forbid'

These words are probably ancient cognates, although /b/→/p/ and /d/→/t/ do not presently operate as dialect sound shifts. *Bata* means 'to forbid' in Loleh, but it also occurs in Termanu with the related sense 'to hinder, to hamper'.

12. tenga [Termanu]	nggama [Ba'a]	'to take up, to grasp'

Tenga is 'to grasp' something in the hand; it forms a set with *nggama*, a verb that in Ba'a has the similar meaning 'to take up' or 'to pick up' something. This verb, when it occurs in Termanu, has quite a different sense: 'to undertake something, to be on the point of doing something'.

> 13. bali *[Termanu]*   se'o *[Ba'a]*   'to mix, to blend'

This set illustrates a minor but common use of dialect words. *Se'o* is recognisably *sedo* in Termanu. Both words have much the same meaning—'to mix non-liquids'—but it is Ba'a's dialect form, not Termanu's ordinary form, that occurs in the ritual language of Termanu. In the third *bini* variation quoted earlier in this chapter (lines 4 and 12), the word *losi(k)* ('copper') occurs with *lilo* ('gold'). The dialect, or other origin, of *losi(k)* is uncertain. The chanter who provided the *bini* noted that *losi(k)* = *liti(k)* ('copper') in Termanu dialect. The sets of ritual language are formulaically fixed. Whether a knowledgeable chanter might legitimately substitute *sedo* for *seö* or *liti* for *losi(k)* is a question I cannot yet determine.

> 14. ndano *[Loleh]*   toko *[Thie]*   'to catch//to throw away'

The use of dialect words is not confined to synonymous sets and these paired elements are not always from either the eastern or the western divisions of the island. This is an antithetical set made up of words from two domains of the western division. *Ndano* is equated with *ndaso* in Termanu since both verbs have a similar sense; *toko* in Termanu has the meaning 'to beat, to knock' rather than 'to throw away'.

> 15. lima *[Termanu]*   kala *[Bilba, Thie]*   'hand//chest'

Lima, the word for 'hand', is used throughout Rote; one element in its range of pairs is *kala* ('chest'). This is equated with the Termanu dialect term *fanak*. *Kala* (or *kara*), however, occurs in eastern dialects and in western dialects but not in Termanu. In areas where *kala* is used, this is not a dialect set. In Termanu, it is; but its distribution does not fit the native dialect model.

> 16. pu *[Termanu]*   oku *[Keka]*   'to scream, to flush out animals with noise'

Pu is found generally through all the dialects; *oku* is apparently specific to Keka. Thus for individuals in Termanu (but not in Ba'a), this set is also at variance with the native model. Dialect use pervades ritual language as a fundamental process in the creation of an elaborate tradition of parallelism. No simple model would be sufficient to explain all its aspects.

Conclusions

The impression of ritual language on its hearers is one of some strangeness—in relation to ordinary speech. The use of dialect variants contributes to this strangeness. Words are used in a variety of ways that make them slightly discrepant from their ordinary usage; but the concurrence of each of these words with another that signals its sense creates a kind of resonant intelligibility—one that varies from individual to individual. This ritual code, in its entirety, is probably beyond the comprehension of any of its individual participants. To these participants, it is an ancestral language that they continue. It is a language into which individuals 'grow' as their acquaintance with proper forms increases. This process should last a lifetime and tales are told of former elders who, as they approached extreme old age, ceased to speak ordinary language and uttered only ritual statements.

As a linguistic proposition, I would suggest that all elaborate forms of parallelism possess dialect variants in their repertoire of poetic words. Language diversification is a process that parallelism exploits. The Hebrew poetry of the Old Testament shares sets in a common tradition with the ancient Canaanite epics. Similarly, the related ritual languages of Borneo utilise dialectal diversity. There is also a good indication that this may hold as well for various Mayan languages. More comparative research is necessary.

In a speculative vein, I would point to the recent neurophysiological research of Pollen et al. (1971) that suggests, rather strongly, that the brain's processing of visual information is of the same form as its processing of auditory information. The analogy of linguistic parallelism with visual stereoscopy—a fusion of separate images—is by no means strained. Nor is parallelism a limited and trivial phenomenon. Systems of pervasive canonical parallelism are extreme (and relatively transparent) elaborations of a principle that appears to underlie much linguistic expression and, as Jakobson has repeatedly argued, most poetry. It is further remarkable that canonical parallelism, in its distribution in the world's oral traditions, is reserved for special situations: scriptures, the utterance of sacred words, ritual relations, curing and communication with spirits. In future studies of semantics, the formal structural systems on which traditions of canonical parallelism are based may provide cases for special study. From these, it could appear that what we refer to as meaning is neither the listing of components nor the accumulation of features but the interval of a function.

Finally, I call attention to the special role of the chanters (*manahelo*) in the maintenance of ritual language as an intelligible code. At present, on Rote, those designated as chanters are a few male elders recognised by a loose popular consensus in each domain. In an earlier account of Rotenese life, however, Heijmering (1843–44:356–7) describes chanters asan elite profession of wandering poets who would journey from domain to domain performing ritual services, particularly at funeral ceremonies. Chanters have now become, or are in competition with, Christian preachers. Almost without exception, the chanters from whom I gathered texts were men of wide experience and capable in their other activities. Those who could provide exegesis on chants had spent some time in one or another domain. My own teacher in ritual language, Stefanus Adulanu, was Head of the Earth (*Dae Langa*) in clan Meno of Termanu; he had lived for a period of his youth in Diu. An old man of near seventy, he was still improving his chant knowledge. In addition to myself, there was another man in his late forties who spent time learning from the old man. After what consisted of more than a year's apprenticeship, I began gathering texts from chanters in other domains. Old Meno was always anxious that I read to him what I had gathered. Those chants that pleased him, he would have me repeat several times until he could render them as his own. When I questioned him on how he had learned all that he knew, he would tell me the same brief story that, as a child, he would lie beside his father at night on a sleeping platform and his father would instruct him. Old Meno is dead now but his line continues.

It is a Rotenese practice, as the final act of the funeral ceremonies a year or more after burial, to erect a raised ring of smooth stones around the base of a large tree to honour a dead man. In alluding to this custom, Meno gave me this further variation on the theme of succession.

Variation (4)

1. *Nggono Ingu Lai lalo*	Nggongo of the Highland dies
2. *Ma Lima Le Dale sapu.*	And Lima of the Riverbed perishes.
3. *Delalo ela Latu Nggongo*	He dies leaving Latu Nggongo
4. *Ma sapu ela Enga Lima.*	And perishes leaving Enga Lima.
5. *Boe te ela batu nangatun*	But he leaves a stone to sit on
6. *Ma lea ai nasalain*	And leaves a tree to lean on.
7. *De koluk Nggongo Ingu Lai*	Plucked is Nggongo from the Highland
8. *Te Latu Nggongo nangatu*	But now Latu Nggongo sits
9. *Ma haik Lima Le Dale*	And scooped is Lima from the Riverbed
10. *Te Enga Lima nasalai.*	But now Enga Lima leans.
11. *Fo lae: Nggongo tutuü batun*	They say: Nggongo's sitting stone
12. *Na tao ela Latu Nggongo*	Was made for Latu Nggongo
13. *Ma Lima lalai ain*	And Lima's leaning tree
14. *Na peda ela Enga Lima.*	Was placed for Enga Lima

6. On binary categories and primary symbols[1]

Introduction[2]

Structural analysis has, in its development, relied exceptionally on the use of dual categories or binary oppositions. Although forms of binary analysis can be traced to Vico in the eighteenth century[3] or to Bachofen in the nineteenth century, it is often argued that some vague analogy with the workings of the computer is primarily responsible for the recent impetus given these studies. Yet despite a vogue that this analogy may have created, binary analysis has its clearer basis in the program for structural linguistics that emanated from Prague in the 1920s, and, although possibly derivative, in the literary studies of Indonesian social structure and mythology developed independently by Leiden anthropologists working in the 1930s. These two 'schools'—Prague and Leiden—have been the chief inspiration for the two varying modes of binary analysis that have been advanced in social anthropology: Claude Levi-Strauss's grand disquisitions on the nature of myth and Rodney Needham's precise two-column analyses of social and symbolic systems. Both contend that their analyses, in some way, tap certain fundamental features of the human mind.

---

1 This chapter first appeared in 1975 in Roy Willis (ed.), *The Interpretation of Symbolism*, ASA Studies Vol. 3, Malaby Press, London. The research on which the original paper was based was originally supported by a US Public Health Service fellowship (MH-23, 148) and grant (MH-10, 161) from the National Institute of Mental Health (NIMH) and was conducted in 1965–66 in Indonesia under the auspices of the Lemabaga Ilmu Pengetahuan Indonesia (LIPI). The continuation of this research was again supported by a NIMH grant (MH-20, 659) and carried out in 1972–73 under the joint sponsorship of LIPI and the University Nusa Cendana in Kupang, Timor. The paper was a product of two specific influences: discussions with Rodney Needham in Oxford in the summer of 1963 as I was preparing for fieldwork on Rote, and later discussions at Harvard with Roman Jakobson after I had returned from Rote and had begun the analysis of the island's ritual system. To both of these scholars, I acknowledge my personal indebtedness. In preparing the final draft of the paper, I benefited from the assistance and comments of Steve Fjellman, Paul Friedrich, David Maybury-Lewis, Rodney Needham, Donald Olivier, David Schneider, John Sodergren and John Whiting. I regret that fieldwork commitments in eastern Indonesia kept me from attending the ASA Decennial Conference for which the original paper was prepared and submitted.
2 When I first published this paper, I included the following quotation from Roland Barthes as a preface to my discussion: 'it is possible to imagine a purely formal lexicon which would provide, instead of the meaning of each word, the set of other words which catalyse it according to possibilities which are of course variable' (Barthes 1967:70). This remark by Barthes offers an image of a formal lexicon whose lexical elements are linked to one another. Something of this sort is an ambition worth considering and is one on which I have embarked. Barthes continues with the added observation that the 'smallest degree of probability would correspond to a "poetic" zone of speech' and then quotes Valle Inclan: 'Woe betide him who does not have the courage to join two words which have never been united.' This conception of poetry as implying undaunted freedom of composition is radically unlike traditions of formulaic oral poetry. Whereas one can imagine a formal lexicon of the sort that Barthes describes and, in fact, begin to construct one, it is my intention in this chapter to indicate that, in the case of this oral poetry, the poetic zone corresponds with the highest, not the smallest, degree of probability.
3 Edmund Leach (1969) has called attention to this aspect of Vico.

Critics of these methods have not infrequently expressed puzzlement in attempting to disengage either mode of analysis from that which, it is argued, is supposed to be inherent in the materials analysed. More searchingly, however, it has been countered that whether or not one accepts the validity of binary categories, the same set of oppositions—male/female, right/left, raw/cooked, Heaven/Earth—recur with such monotonous frequency that they can hardly be expected to provide fresh insights into the ethnographic diversity that anthropologists study.

Those interested in reaching some deeper level of symbolic phenomena regard structural analysis as a poor resort for the problems they face. Thus, although the issue involves scholars of a whole range of differing opinions, it seems, at times, to divide those interested in the discovery of what is deemed to be a limited set of universals or near-universals in human cultures from those who feel themselves committed to the arduous task of recording the contextual richness of these same cultures. More frequently, binary analysis, whether regarded as interesting or trivial, has tended to be accepted with some reservation. Paul Friedrich aptly stated this position:

> The so-called 'principle of binariness', again in phonology and lexicology, may be categorically assumed or carefully guarded and qualified, but most scholars agree that in some form it is a major factor in empirical systems…and that it is often fruitful to assume that it is such a factor. (Friedrich 1975:199-200)

This chapter is intended to consider certain aspects of the use of binary categories. I take, as a starting point, the 'principle of binariness', but my concern is to derive from it a means of going beyond this simple recognition towards a more systematic exploration of the complex use of these categories. In this chapter, I attempt to set forth the initial methods and preliminary results of an analysis of the ritual system of a single society, that of the island of Rote in eastern Indonesia.[4] To generalise, however, from the symbolic system of one of the smaller islands of Indonesia to those of other cultures requires considerable justification. It is, therefore, necessary initially to focus attention on the widespread linguistic phenomenon of parallelism on which my methods of analysis are founded. It is this phenomenon that offers a possibility for the formal comparison of symbol systems.

---

4 The first draft of this analysis was written in Kupang on Timor in 1973 during a respite from fieldwork on the island of Rote. During my stay on the island, I was able to more than double the textual basis for my analysis of the Rotenese ritual system and was, for the first time, invited to perform, with other chanters, a major ritual—in this instance, the final mortuary ceremony for my close friend and instructor in ritual language, the eminent chanter and 'Head of the Earth' in Termanu, S. Adulanu. This analysis is thus based on a combination of fieldwork and close textual analysis of ritual-language materials I have gathered during my fieldwork on the island.

6. On binary categories and primary symbols

The phenomena of semantic parallelism

The term 'parallelism' derives from the researches of Bishop Robert Lowth, who, in the eighteenth century, made the discovery that one of the major principles of composition throughout the Old Testament was a carefully contrived pairing of line, phrase and verse. For this phenomenon, Lowth coined the phrase *parallelismus membrorum*. Since Lowth's time, Biblical scholarship has continued to investigate this phenomenon and has shown that Hebrew oral poetry shared, with Ugaritic and Canaanite traditions, a standardised body of conventionally fixed word pairs (cf. Newman and Popper 1918–23; Gevirtz 1963). It is the required pairing of set terms, according to the canons of the oral tradition, that gives rise to the careful balance of phrase and verse. Modern translations of the Bible often make clearer this parallelism than do the older translations more familiar in English traditions. The prophetic lines of Isaiah (2:2–5) provide an appropriate illustration of this Biblical parallelism:

In days to come,

The mountain of the Lord's house

Shall be established as the highest mountain

And raised above the hills.

All nations shall stream toward it,

Many peoples shall come and say:

'Come, let us climb the Lord's mountain,

To the house of the God of Jacob,

That He may instruct us in His ways,

And we may walk in His paths.'

For from Zion shall go forth instruction

And the word of the Lord from Jerusalem.

He shall judge between nations

And impose terms on many peoples.

They shall beat their swords into ploughshares

And their spears into pruning hooks;

One nation shall not raise the sword against another

Nor shall they train for war again.

O house of Jacob, come,

Let us walk in the light of the Lord!

In these lines, the sets nations//peoples, ways//paths, word//instruction, Zion//Jerusalem, swords//spears give a translated approximation of the word pairs of the original tradition.

The significance of Lowth's researches began to reach well beyond the field of Hebraic studies when it was discovered, at first chiefly by missionary Bible translators, that in many cultures there existed similar traditions of parallelism (cf. van der Veen 1952; Onvlee 1953). There has also gradually accumulated a considerable body of independently motivated research to indicate that parallelism, as a linguistic phenomenon, is of general occurrence among the world's oral literatures. Studies and translations have documented traditions of parallelism in ancient Semitic languages, ancient Egyptian, Chinese, Japanese and early Greek, as well as numerous 'folk' traditions found throughout southern India and most of South-East Asia, in Austronesian languages from Madagascar to Hawai'i, in the various oral literatures of the Ural-Altaic area, in Turkic Mongolian languages, and among American Indian languages, particularly in Middle America, where these traditions reached a flowering in ancient Mayan and Aztec literature.[5]

Thus Isaiah, the *Popul Vuh*, ancient Chinese festival songs, Kachin *Nat* verse and Hawaiian origin chants reflect similar principles in their composition.[6] On this basis, it may not ultimately seem surprising that structural analyses of episodes from Genesis, or of the mythology of Borneo or of highland Burma, or even a portion of American Indian myths, should yield a rich array of binary oppositions, since this may—directly or indirectly—have been their composing principle. Conversely, it would suggest that a comprehending analysis of these forms of elaborate dualism ought to examine this underlying principle of composition.

---

5 Initial bibliographic sources on parallelism can be found in Jakobson (1966) and Fox (Chapter 2, in this volume).
6 I am indebted to a number of scholars who have responded to my first survey of the literature on parallelism (1971) by referring me to further sources: 1) Professor F. Lehman, who has informed me of his own researches on parallelism in Burmese; 2) Professor M. Edmonson, who completed a new verse translation of the *Popol Vuh* (1971); 3) Professor E. Leach, who has referred me to the introduction to the first edition of Hanson's *A Dictionary of the Kachin Language* (1906); 4) Professor P. Voorhoeve, who has directed me to Kern's *Commentaar op de Salasilah van Koetal* (1956); 5) Professor K. Hale, who has written on a Walbiri tradition of antonymy (1971); 6) Professor G. Sankoff, who has been studying the use of lexical pairs in Buang poetry from New Guinea; and 7) Professor W. Davenport, who has referred me to *The Kumulipo* (Beckwith 1951) of the Hawaiians.

On addressing the 'text': A Rotenese myth of culture

Of importance to this discussion is the selection of a 'text'. The problem is somewhat analogous to the one a Rotenese chanter faces in preparation for a performance. The choice of a text is by no means a matter of unrestricted selection. There exists, for major rituals, a recognised repertoire of named chants: chants that each purport, by means of an idealised narrative structure, to 'explain', 'typify' or 'comment' on a ritual situation (cf. Fox 1971:221). These chants resemble the *lakon* of the Javanese *wajang* tradition. Each is a self-contained episode in what appears to have been an epic drama. Close scrutiny of the genealogies that accompany the chants and identify their principal characters provides glimpses of the possible outlines of this epic, but among individual chanters and in the different dialect areas of the island there is a wide variation in the narrative structure of similarly named chants. Nineteenth-century references to bands of wandering poets (Heijmering 1843:356–7), who would appear wherever major rituals were to be performed, suggest that the tradition may once have been more coherent than it is now. For the present, no Rotenese has attempted the Homeric task of resynthesising the island's epic.

For a chanter, therefore, there exists a loose canon of relevant texts. From this canon, he is permitted freedom to adopt, adapt and embellish, within certain limits, the narrative structure that best fits the ritual occasion.[7] Judgments on his chosen text are made in terms of its 'appropriateness' to the situation rather than in terms of some unalterable, abstract standard.

In a similar vein, I have chosen to summarise here a particular Rotenese ritual chant in strict parallelism. It is especially appropriate to a discussion of issues

---

7 To explain some of the factors that this entails, it is best to provide examples. In 1966, two chanters alternated in leading the chorus of the funeral dance for a young, unmarried noble girl in Termanu. Both chanters chose as their text the chant *Meda Manu ma Lilo Losi*, but each, as the evening progressed, developed his own separate version in distinctive ways. Later, I had the chance to ask one chanter about his intentions in the performance. *Meda Manu ma Lilo Losi*, he explained, was the appropriate text for a virginal girl who died 'unripe'. The chant, however, contains no reference to a noble origin, implying in effect that the girl is a commoner. In this situation, the text was not entirely appropriate so what he did was to make Meda Manu and Lilo Losi (chants are usually named after their chief characters) into a noble character. Some time before this funeral, an important male elder of this same noble lineage died. The leading elder of the royal lineage of Termanu, the foremost chanter in the domain at this time, came to honour the deceased. The lineage of the dead man originated as a client line of the royal lineage and as it prospered had given to the royal line a succession of enormous bride-wealth payments to establish its independence and near equality of rank. The text chosen by this royal chanter was *Ndi Loniama ma Laki Elokama*, a chant appropriate for someone who died with great wealth. It is among the most interesting of all Rotenese chants in that it praises the proper use of wealth, honouring the deceased for his generosity and his ability to attract a loyal following. What is more, it places in the mouth of the dying man an admonition to his descendants and heirs to act as he has in life (see Chapter 12). The narrative of the text, however, makes no reference to nobility and the royal chanter in performing added none. Although this could have been taken as a studied insult, it was regarded as appropriate between equals, the royal chanter's presence being sufficient to signify his good intentions.

in structuralism and symbolic analysis because its subject matter appears to be another transformation of the 'mythologic' traditions broached by Lévi-Strauss in *Le Cru et le Cuit* (1964). The chant tells of the hunting of wild pig, of the origin of fire and of cooking and of the obtainment, by exchange, of the material implements of culture. It plays, at times subtly, at times openly, on the connotations of taste and the metaphorical equation of sexual intercourse and eating. And it goes on to explain the breach in the alliance that once ordered the primal powers of the world.

Properly speaking, this chant ought to be designated as the 'myth of the house'. Its chanting is reserved for the ceremonial consecration of a traditional dwelling. Those chanters who have recited this myth for me, and those who have declined to do so, agree in regarding it as the most 'heated' segment of Rotenese esoteric knowledge. It is the only chant, to my knowledge, that is intentionally distorted at its crucial juncture; in this case, to veil the sacrifice that creates the house. Rather than adapt and embellish this chant as a chanter might, I intend instead to excerpt from and alternate between three separate versions of this chant from the domain of Termanu.[8] Together, these versions comprise 677 lines of verse, which makes summary in this context a necessity. My intention is not to do a 'structural analysis', whatever that might entail, but to address these texts as a prelude to a discussion of their underlying symbolic structure.

The Rotenese epic involves the deeds of two opposing families: the descendants of the Sun and Moon (*Ledo do Bulan*) and the descendants of the Lords of the Sea and Ocean (*Liun do Sain*). Many of these deeds occur on Earth and directly involve men on Earth. What gives the epic its social underpinning are claims by various lineages on Rote to direct descent from or ancestral association with figures in the chants. Most of the nobility of Rote, for example, claim descent, by separate lines, from the nine sons of the Moon, while other clan groups identify themselves with ancestors who allied themselves with the Lords of the Sea. Since both families intermarry in the epic, a putative link to one implies a relationship with the other. The significance of this present chant is that it describes the first encounter of these two families—their mutual discovery and its consequences. The setting for the chant is the Earth.

The sons of Sun and Moon, Patola Bulan and Mandeti Ledo, descend to Earth, whistle for their dogs, Pia Dola and Hua Lae, and set out to hunt.

Ala sopu lai basa dae	They hunt throughout the land
Ala fule lai basa oe.	They track throughout the waters.
Leu Ledo lasi nana-papadak	They enter the Sun's forbidden forest

---

8 Complete translations can be found in Fox (1972:I, 98–109; II, 1110–20; III, 156–71). Version one is by the very capable chanter P. Malesi; version two by the chantress L. Keluanan; version three by the former Head of the Earth, S. Adulanu.

Ma Bulan nula nana-babatak	And the Moon's restricted wood
Malala meo dei pana-foe	And catch a pied-nosed cat
Ma kue dei iko-fula,	And a white-tailed civet,
Bulan kue nasa-mao	The Moon's fond civet
Ma Ledo meo naka-boi-na.	And the Sun's tame cat.

Immediately, the Sun and Moon inform them of their error and assign them new regions in which to hunt. The hunt resumes but is unsuccessful.

Asu-la ta fue	The dogs corner nothing
Ma busa-la ta eko.	And the hounds encircle nothing.

They continue to where the land borders the sea and suddenly they encounter the Chief Hunter of the Ocean and the Great Lord of the Sea, Danga Lena Liun and Mane Tua Sain, who have come from the ocean depths with their dogs, Masi Tasi and Deta Dosa. It is essential to an understanding of this and subsequent passages to realise that Rotenese traditions personify the Lords of the Sea as Shark and Crocodile. These creatures can assume glistening human forms when they come up on land. The hunters agree to combine their efforts, as version two makes clear:

Boe ma busa-la laka-bua	The dogs form a pack
Ma asu-la la-esa.	And the hounds join as one.
De ala fule kue	They track civet
Ma ala sopu bafi.	And they hunt pig.
De leo nula Kai Tio dale	Deep in the woods of Kai Tio
Ma lasi Lolo Batu dale	And deep in the forest of Lolo Batu
Boe ma asu-la fua	The dogs corner their prey
Ma busa-la use.	And the hounds give chase.

Here, the hunters catch and kill the pair pig and civet, rather than the forbidden pair, cat and civet. What then follows is an exchange of invitations and a debate about whether to ascend to the heavens or to descend to the sea depths to eat the sacrifice of pig and civet. In the end, it is decided to descend into the sea, where the sons of Sun and Moon discover for the first time the taste of cooked food. Again, the language of version two is clearer:

De leu, de ala fati bafi	They go and they eat the offering of pig
Ma fina kue.	And partake of the sacrifice of civet.
De ala tunu hai bei masu	They roast on a smoking fire
Ma ala nasu oek bei lume	They cook in boiling water
Nai lo heu hai ikon	In a house roofed with ray-fish tails
Ma nai uma sini kea louk.	And in a home decked with turtle shells.

Explorations in Semantic Parallelism

Patola Bulan and Mandeti Ledo secrete a leaf full of this cooked food and carry it off to the Sun and Moon, Bula Kai and Ledo Holo, who, on tasting this morsel, exclaim:

'Ladak ia mai be	'From where is this taste
Ma lolek ia nai be?'	And where is this goodness?'

And they are told:

'Ladak is nai liun	'This taste is in the ocean
Ma lolek ia nai sain.'	And this goodness in the sea.'

Whereupon, in version one, the Lords of the Sea request the daughters of the Sun and Moon; in version two, Sun and Moon propose the marriage of their daughters. These daughters, Fuda Kea Ledo and Tao Senge Bulan, are, however, already married. They must first be divorced before they can be remarried to the Lords of the Sea. Then begins one of the most significant passages in the chant, a passage that is virtually identical in all the versions I have recorded. The Sun and Moon begin to demand bride-wealth payments:

Boe ala doko-doe fae-tena	They demand a payment of livestock
Ma ala tai-boni belfi-batum.	And they claim a bride-wealth of gold.
De ala fe lilo ma-langa menge	They give gold chains with snakes' heads
Ma ala fe kapa ma-ao foek.	And they give buffalo with crocodile-marked bodies.
Te ala bei doko-doe	But still they continue to demand
Ma ala bei tai-boni.	And still they continue to claim.
Besak-ka ala fe bo pa'a-bela	Now they give the bore tool and flat chisel
Ma ala fe taka tala-la.	And they give the axe and the adze.
Ala fe sipa aba-do	They give the plumbline marker
Ma ala fe funu ma-leo.	And they give the turning drill.
Te hu ala bei doko-doe	But they still continue to demand
Ma ala bei tai boni.	And still they continue to claim.
Boe-ma ala fe nesu maka-boka buik	Then they give the mortar whose thudding shakes its base
Ma alu mata-fia tongok.	And the pestle whose thrust blisters the hand.
Te ala bei tai-boni.	And still they continue to claim.
Besak-ka ala fe kutu-ana naü-poin	Then they give the little flint-set with loose tinder grass
Ma una-ana ai-nggeo.	And the little black-sticked fire drill.
Besak-ka ala lae:	Now they say:
'Dai te ta dai	'Whether enough or not enough
O nai ta dai liman	What's in our grip is enough in our hand
Ma nou te ta nou	And whether sufficient or insufficient

O nai kuku nou nen.'	What's in our fingers is sufficient in our grasp.'
Besak-ka lenin neu poin	Now they carry everything to the Heights
Ma lenin neu lain.	And they carry everything to Heaven.

With minor variations and the change of a few names, versions one and two of this chant are remarkably similar. There exists, however, a third version that offers a significantly different interpretation, developing more explicitly, through its play on words, the connection between the eating of cooked food and marriage. Version three follows version two to the point where the hunters enter the sea with the catch of pig and civet and then focuses on the lighting of the cooking fire:

Boe ma ala diu besi no batu	They strike iron on stone
Ma ala una ai no ai.	And they rub stick on stick.
De ala tao kutu na'u poi	They work the tinder-top flint-set
Ma tao una ai nggeo.	And work the black-stick fire-drill.
Boe ala pila nuli neu bafi	And they burn and roast the pig
Ma ala masu ndalu neu kue.	And they smoke and fire the civet.

At this point, the sisters of the Lords of the Sea appear. They are Lole Liuk and Lada Saik—literally 'Ocean Goodness and Sea Tastiness'. Immediately, the chant begins its verbal allusions. Now that the pig and civet have been roasted, the Lords of the Sea ask their sister:

'Te bafi sao no bek	'With what do you marry pig
Ma kue tu no hata?'	And with what do you wed civet?'
Boe te inak-ka Lada Saik	The woman Lada Saik
Ma fetok-ka Lole Liuk nafada nae:	And the girl Lole Liuk speaks, saying:
'Te dengu doli no bafi	'Stamp rice with pig
Ma tutu lutu no kue.'	And pound millet with civet.'

Native exegesis on these lines directly identifies the verb *sao* ('to marry') with the verb *na'a* ('to eat').

The feast proceeds and, at its conclusion, the Lords of the Sea themselves suggest that the sons of Sun and Moon take food to the heavens. On their return journey, they discover the sweet–sour taste of lontar-palm juice, a staple Rotenese food. They remark:

'Seok-ka sain liun lalun-na maladahik:	'Indeed the sea-ocean's beer is tasty:
Kei-kei ma keke'e.	Sweet and sour.
Bulan no Ledo lalun-na so	While the Moon and Sun's beer is
Na namis ma makale'ek-ka.'	Insipid and tart.'

Along with cooked food, therefore, the sons of Sun and Moon return to the heavens with sweet–sour lontar juice. On tasting this food, the Sun and Moon's first response is to wage war on the sea to obtain more:

'Malole ata lea tafa neu sain	'It would be good to extend a sword to the sea
Ma loe dongi neu liun.'	And lower a barbed spear to the ocean.'

The sons reject this proposal as impossible and, instead, propose that they marry the women 'Ocean Goodness and Sea Tastiness'. Sun and Moon react to this by warning their sons that they ought not to attempt to supersede their elders. So Sun and Moon themselves marry the sisters of the Lords of the Sea. This version of the chant thus reverses the relations of the two powers: instead of being wife-giver, the heavens become wife-taker from the sea. In the chant, bride-wealth is left unmentioned while all the cultural goods named as bride-wealth in the other versions are brought by 'Ocean Goodness and Sea Tastiness' as part of their dowry. The same end is achieved but by altering marriage relations.

With the acquisition of tools from the sea, Sun and Moon order the construction of their house. Chanters regard this as the most critical segment of the narrative and those who have recited it for me admit to obscurity at this point. Version two is the clearest.

The trees whose wood is required for the house are the 'two-leaved *keka* tree' (*Ficus* spp.) and 'three-leaved *fuliha'a* tree' (*Vitex* spp.). These are to be made into the *toa*-poles and *sema*-beams—the ridgepoles and support beams of the house. Various builders are called to work on the house but they are unable to erect the main beams. The chant explains:

Te laka-ndolu nai lain	When they work above
Na ana kekeak leo dae mai.	It tilts towards the ground.
Ma laka-ndolu nai dulu	When they work on the east
Na lai leo muli neu.	It leans to the west.
Te laka-ndolu nai muli	But when they work on the west
Na soko leo dulu.	It slants to the east.

The secret of the chant is that the house requires a model for the layout of its beams and poles. Shark and Crocodile, the Lords of the Sea, the original benefactors of the Sun and Moon, are invited from the ocean, killed and their skeletal structures used as a model. The structure of the Rotenese house is thus that of a crocodile, with its head in the east and tail in the west, and its rib cage forming the sloping roof beams. (More than once, some old Rotenese, in the heat of explanation, has bent down on all fours to demonstrate this outstretched layout of the house.) Version two describes this:

6. On binary categories and primary symbols

Touk Danga Lena Liun	The man Danga Lena Liun
Ma ta'ek Man' Tua Sain	And the boy Man' Tua Sain
Ala taon neu uma di'i	They make him into the house posts
Ma ala taon neu eda ai.	And they make him into the ladder tree.
Besak-ka kalu kapa ledo ha'an	Now the sun heats his 'buffalo sinews'
Ma dui manu au te'e-na	And the dew moistens his 'chicken bones'.ᴬ
Alta tao[n] neu sema teluk	They make him into the two sema-beams
Ma taon neu toa duak.	And make him into the two toa-poles.

Note: 'Buffalo sinews//chicken bones' (*kalu kapa//dui manu*) is the standard formula in all rituals for bones disinterred from flesh.

Finally, the true master-builders arrive, a species of spider and a giant stick insect.[9] Laying out the dried bones of the shark and crocodile, they build the house.

Besak-ka Did Bulan mai	Now Moon Stick Insect arrives
Ma Bolau Ledo mai.	And Sun Spider arrives.
De lae: 'Deta ape.	They say: 'Dip spittle.
De deta ape neu be	Where the spittle is dipped
Fo lolo neu ndia.'	There lay the planks.'
Boe te Bolau lolo ape neu be	So wherever Spider lays spittle
Na ala solu limak neu ndia	There they then rest the arms
Ma Didi deta ape neu be	And wherever Stick Insect dips spittle
Na ala fua lolo neu ndia.	There they then place the legs.
Besak-ka sema teluk-kala dadi	Now the three sema-beams are made
Ma toa duak-kala tola.	And the two toa-poles appear.
Besak-ka ala soe sike ikon	They incise a tail design
Ma tati solo-bana langan.	And they cut a head pattern.

And, as version one concludes:

De kue lu'u nai ikon	A civet crouches at the tail
De fani tai nai langan.	Bees nest at the head.

This, I submit, is the kind of myth that structural analysis was developed to elucidate. Similar myths have been searchingly scrutinised. It offers literally

---

9 The *didi* (reduplication of *di*: 'pole') is a species of giant stick insect of the order/suborder *Phasmida*. These insects are at least 20–25 cm long and resemble a mantis in form. They become active only at night and are especially visible in the light of the full moon, hence their association with the moon. The set 'spider//stick insect' (*bolau//didi*) is illustrative of the translation problems one encounters in dealing with ritual language. On my first field trip, I never saw a *didi* and when I asked what this word referred to, I was told by several informants that the *didi* was an insect, 'like the spider'. One night on my second fieldtrip, I discovered the *didi* was really a stick insect: its being 'like a spider' had nothing to do with its shape or appearance, but only its co-occurrence in the same set.

hundreds of binary oppositions to tantalise the analyst and develops a major South-East Asian mythic motif: a primal alliance whose inevitable, creative rupture establishes disorder and imbalance in the world. The myth is intimately connected, as well, with other Rotenese myths that recount the various causes of enmity between men and the Lords of the Sea: how, for example, the shark and crocodile, after forcibly marrying women on Earth, are ambushed as they return to the sea, and their body parts—blood and guts—are strewn out and then copied to become the motifs for Rotenese cloths. The very conventions of the tradition, the use of doubled names and the common (though not always consistent) stylistic alternation of singular and plural forms defy simple, straightforward translation and contribute syntactically to the overriding duality of composition.

The myth is also replete with seemingly minor details for which native exegesis provides no hint: the 'civet cat', for example, occurs first as a pair with 'cat', whose hunting is forbidden, then with 'pig', whose flesh may be eaten, and finally with 'bees', domesticated as a design carved on the ridgepole of the house. Since this myth is a detailed charter, there is a question of how much 'extra' information is needed to inform its analysis. Furthermore, there is the additional problem of the various versions. Version three is a radical departure from versions one and two and it completely avoids mentioning the sacrifice of Shark and Crocodile. When confronted with these alternative interpretations, however, Rotenese with whom I have discussed these matters do not seem disconcerted. Each chanter has his opinion and obviously any of the versions would be adequate for the performance of the consecration of a house. Significance does not seem to reside wholly or even primarily at the message level of the narrative structure.

Considerations of this sort are what lead one to question the usefulness of any single myth analysis or series of analyses. If one takes as axiomatic that myths and their symbols are meaningful as part of a whole, it would seem that any single myth or group of myths is too inadequate and truncated a cultural production to be acceptable on its own. What ought to be a goal of analysis is something far more systematic, and yet at the same time, as has been argued, some principle or set of principles that orders the system.

Ritual language as a cultural code

Among linguists, Professor Roman Jakobson has most frequently drawn attention to the phenomenon of parallelism, noting its 'pervasive' and 'compulsory' qualities and arguing that the existence of a thoroughgoing canonical parallelism provides objective criteria for the study of native correspondences (Jakobson and

Halle 1956:77). A dyadic language of the kind used by Rotenese in their rituals is a formal code comprising the culture's stock of significant binary relations. It is a complex code, not arbitrarily restricted to a particular 'domain' of natural language and it is relatively stable.[10] In appearance, the code gives indication of being an open-ended, focused system of semantic interconnections—what linguists since Trier have designated a semantic field. Furthermore, it is capable of formal study, since it is itself a formal system.

To utilise the terminology I have adopted for the analysis of Rotenese ritual language (Fox 1971, 1974), each dual category or binary opposition is a dyadic set. As such, each dyadic set is a unique semantic grouping that brings into conjunction two separate elements, thereby 'affecting' their individual significance. What is more, an element that forms part of a dyadic set may pair with other elements to create new dyadic sets. Whereas these binary categories can be considered as ordered pairs, they are not exclusive pairs. A ready example is civet cat in the previous chant. Civet forms dyadic sets with 'cat', 'pig' and 'bees', each set signalling an altered significance for its constituent elements. This feature makes possible the study of these relations, as a system, because any element may have a whole range of elements with which it forms a set and these elements, in turn, may pair with still other elements, creating an extensive network of interlinkages. The code for Rotenese ritual language can thus be displayed as a large constellation of complexly interrelated elements but with an array, as well, of elements not necessarily connected to any larger network.

What is more, these interlinkages crosscut conventional grammatical categories, such as verb, adverb, preposition and noun, joining elements instead by what seems to be some other underlying system of semantic values. Tracing relations among these semantic elements—the chains and cycles along edges of what is a symmetric graph—provides a glimpse of the structuring of the cultural code of the Rotenese.

The symbolic analysis of a cultural code

Any form of symbolic analysis must confront the problem of complexity. A prerequisite to this particular analysis is, therefore, the compilation of a relatively large corpus of ritual texts covering an entire range of ceremonial situations. This analysis is based on 25 lengthy chants and a small collection of short chants, the equivalent of just under 5000 lines of verse.

---

10 In 1965, I recited to various Rotenese the untranslated text (Jonker 1911:97–102) of a funeral chant gathered before the turn of the century. On hearing it, those who did not know where I had obtained it assumed it to be one that I had gathered recently. Its structure, pairings of lexical items and formulae are indistinguishable from other chants in my corpus from this dialect area. This point is important since my analysis, in part, relies on the relative stability of ritual language (see Chapter 8).

A dictionary, based on initial texts from the closely related speech communities from Termanu and Ba'a, has been compiled. It includes more than 1000 dyadic sets, but does not yet include names that form a large and important subset of the ritual lexicon. In total, the dictionary comprises more than 1400 entries. In the dictionary, each element or lexical item is translated and has listed for it all other elements with which it forms dyadic sets. The dictionary is thus an initial tabulation of relations among elements in the language.

A number of formal methods involving, for example, graph theory, matrix manipulations or a variety of multidimensional scaling techniques can be usefully employed in studying these relations. A formalisation of these relations would be premature and is, therefore, not intended here. Rather, this analysis is intended primarily to indicate what appears to constitute the present core of this ritual language, to trace certain of its symbolic coordinates and to consider its implications.

To define a core among interrelated elements is a matter of degree. Any 'core' can be as large or as small as one wishes to define it. In this case, I have selected all elements from the dictionary that have a range of five or more sets. There are currently 37 such elements. A range of five, it must be realised, is an arbitrary figure. Choosing a range of six would, for example, decrease the selection of elements from the present dictionary by more than one-third, while the choice of a range of four would nearly double them. A range of five establishes a key group of elements of sufficient size and complexity to illustrate the argument. The total number of links of these key elements to other elements comes to 250. Since many of these links are internal links, we can perform a further selection by eliminating those elements with less than two links to other elements in the key group. Two links is the minimal number necessary to permit cyclical relations.[11] The resultant core forms a semantic network consisting of these elements with a total range of five or more, possessing at least two links in common. Although it could have been defined either more exclusively or more inclusively, and will most likely, by the application of the same criteria, become—as the dictionary develops—a larger and even more saturated network, nevertheless this core locates the area of greatest semantic density and connectivity in the ritual system. The core consists of 21 elements from 1400 possible dictionary entries. The full list of these terms, with glosses and their links to one another, is given in Table 6.1.

---

11 My point is that four, five or six can serve to define an initial selection of elements. A range of seven, however, would define a selection too small to be of particular interest and a range of three one too large to constitute a proper core. In the second-stage selection, two internal links appear to be justified because the application of this reduction proceeds by eliminating elements with only one link to any other element of the key terms. Elimination of this element also eliminates its link, which cannot be counted as one of the required two links for some other element. A rule requiring three internal links would systematically eliminate all the elements of the key group while a rule of one would eliminate only a few terms.

6. On binary categories and primary symbols

Table 6.1 Core Terms

	Element	Glosses	Links
1.	*Ai:*	Plant, tree, stick, wood	*Batu, boa, dae, do(k), na'u, oe, tua*
2.	*Dae:*	Earth, land; below; low, lowly	*Ai, batu, dulu, loe, muli, oe, tua*
3.	*Batu:*	Stone, rock	*Ai, dae, lutu*
4.	*Boa:*	Fruit; counter term for small objects	*Ai, hu(k)*
5.	*Do(k):*	Leaf; counter term for objects in strings	*Ai, hu(k)*
6.	*Na'u:*	Grass, tinder; the quality of being soft, gentle	*Ai, oe*
7.	*Oe:*	Water, semen, juice, liquid	*Ai, dae, naü*
8.	*Tua:*	Lontar palm (Borassus flabellifer), the lontar's products	*Ai, dae*
9.	*Lutu:*	Pile, ring or other arrangement of stones; to pile, erect stones; the quality of being well worked, smooth, refined; ritual name: millet	*Batu, hu(s)*
10.	*Hu(-k, -s):*	Trunk, base, root, origin; counter term for trees; designation for males in the maternal line of affiliation; term for clan origin festival	*Boa, do*
11.	*Ei(k):*	Foot, paw, leg	*Hu(k), langa, lima*
12.	*Lima:*	Hand, arm; five	*Ei(k), langa, tei(k)*
13.	*Tei(k):*	Insides, stomach, womb; lineage	*Langa, lima*
14.	*Langa:*	Head	*Dulu, ei(k), lima, iko, tei(k)*
15.	*Iko:*	Tail	*langa, muli*
16.	*Dulu:*	East	*Dae, langa, muli*
17.	*Muli:*	West; youngest child—that is, last-born	*Dae, dulu, iko*
18.	*Loe:*	To descend, to lower, to be low	*Dae, tai*
19.	*Tai:*	To balance, to cling (to an edge), to border, to be on the edge	*Loe, lu'u, sa'e*
20.	*Lu'u*	To sink or settle down; to lie down (particularly of crocodile and water buffalo half-submerged in water); to brood (of a bird); to request a woman in marriage	*Sa'e, tai*
21.	*Sa'e*	To ride or sit; to perch (of birds); to rise	*Lu'ü, tai*

What this core includes are directional coordinates, the words for 'earth', 'water', 'rock' and 'tree', terms for plants and plant parts, body parts and a peculiar collection of verbs of position involving ideas of balance, ascent and descent. What is significant, however, is not merely the listing of these elements but their relations to one another. A graph of these interconnections is shown in Figure 6.1.

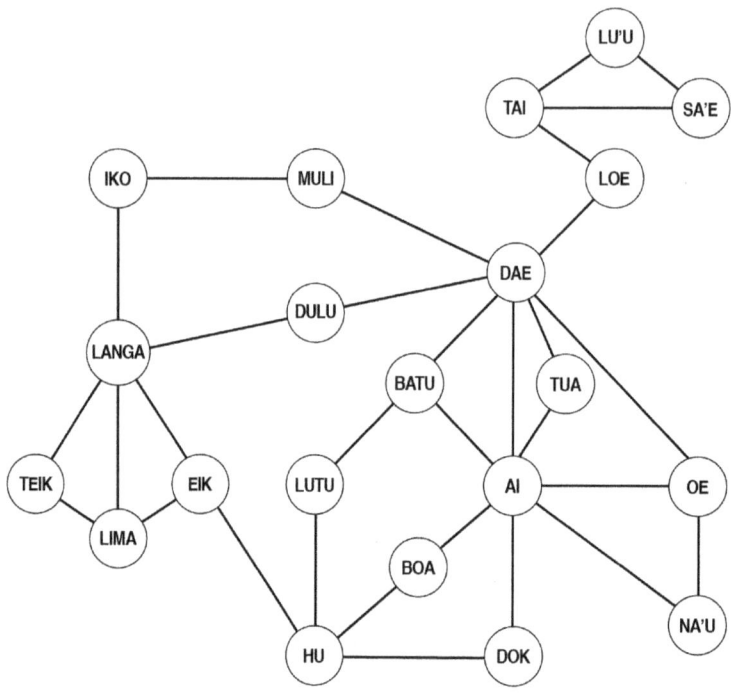

Figure 6.1: Core Terms

Specific interpretation of the ritual core

An interpretation of the significance of these core terms within the ritual system would require lengthy discussion. For my part, this analysis seems to confirm, at a formal level, certain of the far less formal interpretations I have previously made of Rotenese ritual. In an article on 'Sister's child as plant' (Fox 1971), I argue that a major premise of Rotenese rituals is the symbolic equation of man and plant. Rituals are cast in a botanic idiom and specific plants are manipulated as icons to define the precise purpose of each ritual. Their general intent is always life-giving—that is, to provide for the care, cultivation and conduct of a 'plant', even to a point beyond death when, for example, outstanding individuals may be identified with some large hardwood tree, which is then ceremonially surrounded with stones (*lutu*) to form an enduring megalithic monument. The occurrence in the ritual core of 'tree' (*ai*), 'fruit' (*boa*), 'leaf' (*dok*) or 'trunk' (*huk*) is therefore revealing. Simple glosses on these terms, however, can be misleading since they function semantically in a complex way. They serve as counter terms for differently shaped objects and form compound semantic labels for parts of the human body: (*k*)*ai-usuk* ('rib-case'), *use-aik* ('navel cord'), *boa-de'ek* ('kidney'), *langa-dok* ('human hair'), *di'i-dok* ('ears') and *difa-dok* ('lips'). My original argument (1971:240) was that there were a sufficient number of these composite semantic labels to permit native speculative exegesis to create the necessary correspondences between man and plant on which the rituals depend. It would now seem, on the basis of this present analysis, that this native exegesis is itself a secondary elaboration of a more fundamental semantic relation. In this regard, the term *hu* appears to function as a crucial linking node. *Hu*, as 'trunk', is a counter term for trees. *Hus* is the term for the annual clan feast and, via its links with *lutu*, refers to those origin celebrations of 'stone and tree' that are performed around a ring of smooth stone 'seats' at the base of a tree. *Hu* is also the designation for particular individuals of the maternal line of affiliation, *to'o-huk* ('mother's brother') and *ba'i-huk* ('mother's mother's brother'), who are the chief actors in all rituals of the life cycle. Furthermore, *hu*, in its link with *ei*(*k*) ('foot'), serves as a direct semantic bridge between plant parts and body parts.

The inclusion of a single specific plant, the lontar palm (*tua*), is particularly pointed since this tree is the one indispensable source of subsistence for the Rotenese—the virtual 'tree of life'. This large, dioecious palm—the female is marked by clusters of large, hanging fruit, the male by drooping ithyphallic flower stalks—is, I have argued, a focal icon of the Rotenese.

Similarly, in an article on Rotenese symbolic inversions (1973), I suggested that a further premise of Rotenese rituals was an ordering of symbolic space that associated the parts of the body and the directional coordinates. 'East' (*dulu*) is linked with 'head' (*langa*); 'west' (*muli*) is linked with 'tail' (*iko*). The universe, the island of Rote and the Rotenese house are all represented with a 'head' rising to the east and a 'tail' descending to the west. According to different exegeses, this shape is that of the crocodile, a sacrificial water buffalo or even a man. Whatever its specific shape, the essential system is preserved invariant. In accordance with this system, the term *kona* is both 'right' and 'south'; *ki* is 'left' and 'north'. A series of symbolic syllogisms ('The east is as broad as the west, but the Sun comes from the east, therefore, the east is greater than the west', and so on) provides a means of ranking the directions and then, on this basis, there is constructed a host of symbolic associations. For example, native exegesis associates *uluk* ('first-born') with *dulu* (east) in the analogy that *mulik* ('last-born') derives from the root *muli* (west).[12] What this present analysis indicates is that the initial logic of the system is founded on the relations and equations of ritual language. In the graph of the core terms, 'head' (*langa*) serves as a key node linking body-part terms and the directional coordinates.

Close inspection suggests that there could be several discernible foci within the core of the ritual system. Plant terms are linked by *huk* to the words for body parts, which are, in turn, linked by *langa* to the directional coordinates. The root *dae*, as a noun for 'earth', as a directional coordinate 'below' or 'beneath' and as a common adverbial term 'lowly', serves as another crucial connecting node to the chain of positional verbs and to terms for the natural elements 'water', 'rock' and, above all, 'tree' and 'plant'. In terms of their internal links, *ai* ('tree', 'plant'), *dae* ('earth', 'low', 'lowly'), *langa* ('head') and *hu* ('trunk', 'base', 'origin') account for 22 of a possible 31 edges in the graph. The problem is, however, that the elements in this core are highly connected in a complex fashion. In addition, it must be remembered that each element is itself the organising node to an expansive network of semantic elements within the total system. The simple inspection of a reduced graph or the piecemeal examination of various sub-graphs of the system are insufficient, on their own, to provide an understanding of the whole.

Semantic networks and computer classification

The alternative to an intuitive inspection of either a simplified or an enlarged graphic representation of the elements of ritual language must, it seems, be some method of computer classification. The question is not whether to adopt such a strategy—for the complexity of the system leaves little choice—but rather what form of wording strategy to adopt amid the numerous, diverse and ever-increasing number of available methods. For this question, there is no simple answer. Theoretically, it is possible to argue for different methods in terms of the properties of the measures one wishes to consider; pragmatically, it is possible to experiment with several methods to see which provides more 'useful' results. In this regard, there can hardly be a 'true', 'natural' or necessarily 'best' method. The temptation is to mistake these methods for what they are not: to allow the arbitrary to assume the appearance of the natural. The gain in the adoption of any of these methods is one of intelligibility in the face of complexity and, for comparative purposes, the means of a standard procedure for treating different systems.

---

12   I am grateful here to Professor Meyer Fortes, whose studies on the ritual importance of the first-born, presented at a colloquium at Harvard (November 1973), have helped me correct my confusion of the Rotenese distinction between 'first-born'/'last-born' and 'elder'/'younger'.

The core terms—or the relations among any number of elements in ritual language—can be conceived of as a graph and represented by the N x N incidence matrix of that graph. The range of any element—the incidence of that node in a graph—consists of all its positive entries with other elements of the matrix. To determine a measure of similarity among a set of such elements, it is necessary to decide on the properties that constitute the semantics of the system. Several properties would seem to be extremely important: first, every element should be considered not merely in terms of its link with any other element, but in terms of the other pair-wise links it might possess, together with that element, to additional elements in the system. This, in effect, involves considering all dyadic sets and matching elements by the sets they form with each other and via third elements. Second, every element should be considered as a link with itself since this will permit the incorporation of invariant terms—that is, terms in ritual language that have no pairs and functions as a repetition of themselves. In other words, the diagonal of the incidence matrix ought to consist of positive entries. Third, since elements have different ranges of association, some account ought to be taken of the varying total range that any two elements possess. Fourth, the coincidence of all positive matches in the matrix should be counted as more significant than the coincidence of an absence of a match. With these properties in mind, we can adopt, from among the formulae that have been devised to provide a measure of similarity or what is called, in numerical taxonomy, the coefficients of association (Sokal and Sneath 1963:128), a formula that consists, roughly speaking, of the intersection of the range of A and the range of B over the union of the range of A and the range of B. Formally, similarity is defined[13] as follows, where xij = 1 if element i pairs with element j; otherwise 0:

$$Sim\,(i,j) = \frac{\Sigma(2x_{ik} \times x_{jk})}{\Sigma(x_{ik} + x_{jk})}\Big/\Sigma(2x_{ik} + x_{jk})$$

This establishes a first stage—a reasonable measure of pair-to-pair similarity. On this basis, we can derive a new inter-element similarity matrix and, from this matrix, it is possible to devise a variety of inter-group orderings depending on, as always, the measures one adopts. Among the more sophisticated, readily available and economic sorting strategies for such inter-group similarities are the agglomerative or aggregative hierarchical clustering techniques. There is any number of these and their properties vary with the measures utilised (Lance and Williams 1967). Because of the relative economy of these techniques, however, it is possible to develop a program that will, in a single run, submit the same data to a clustering process by a number of different measures of

---

13 The particular application of this formula as an estimator of node similarity has been discussed in Sodergren (1973). I wish to thank Mr Sodergren for his assistance on this section of the chapter.

cluster distance or size. A program of this kind has been developed at Harvard (Olivier 1973). It begins with N single-item clusters and merges pairs of clusters iteratively to form a single N-item cluster. Input is an N x N symmetric matrix of similarity (or dissimilarity) measures for the set of N items. Output is a tree-diagram with an added column of 'values' for each cluster depending on the particular method. Using this program to experiment on the matrix of core terms and studying the clustering obtained by various measures,[14] I concluded that the measure of distance between clusters A and B defined as the mean of the similarities between points A and B gave the closest approximation of my own intuitive understanding of the relations among the core terms. Figure 6.2 is the tree-diagram of the aggregative hierarchical clustering of the core terms by mean distance. It can be compared with the graphic representation of these same terms in Figure 6.1.

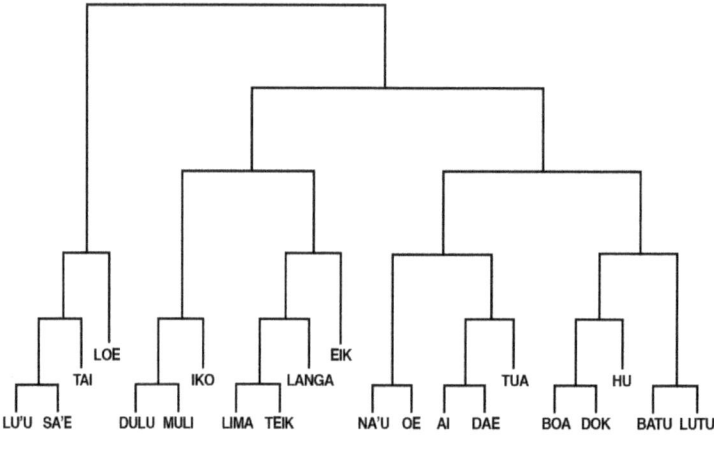

Figure 6.2: Tree Diagram of Aggregative Hierarchical Clustering

The point of this exercise has been to indicate a method that can be used to study the semantic relations of ritual language, noting that, as the complexity of the system increases, it becomes more difficult to decide on criteria for distinguishing among the results of these methods. Implied in this discussion is

---

14 Relying on the Olivier program, I used four measures to cluster the matrix of core terms: the measure of distance between clusters A and B defined as 1) the minimum, 2) the mean, and 3) the maximum of the similarities between points A and points B and also as 4) the increase in total size due to merging A and B into a single new cluster, C (Olivier 1973:3–6). The pair-wise 'similarity' of many terms (*batu///lutu, boa///dok, lima///teik, ai//dae, lu'u//sae*, for example) was consistent for all methods at the lowest level of clustering, whereas differences appeared expectedly at higher levels of ordering. These differences by methods 2 and 4 occurred only at the two highest levels of clustering, and it is therefore worth pointing out that, according to Olivier, these two methods 'give useful results over an especially broad range of applications' (1973:7).

the suggestion that a possible strategy would be to adopt the method that, on a limited scale, gives the best approximation of some intuitive understanding and to assume that, on a larger scale, it will continue to do so. This leaves 'intuition' as a foundation. It is, however, evident that, whatever my intuitions are, they are based on present-day Rotenese practice and the insights and interpretations provided to me by Rotenese elders and chanters. It is also evident, at a theoretical level, that the semantic networks of ritual language are sufficiently complex to permit a variety of practices and, as I have frequently noted in my ethnographic descriptions, alternative interpretations of the same practice. What this seems to imply is that, however one approaches it, ritual language is a lived-in symbolic structure, incapable of exclusive comprehension by any monotypic representation.

This does not, however, mean that the exercise of comprehension is useless. In fact, proceeding from binary oppositions to semantic networks highlights a fundamental aspect of these semantic relations: that certain elements have a range of pairs, that these create networks and that a core, however it is defined, of multi-conjugate nodes within the network acts as primary symbols in the system. This involves consideration of the implications of hierarchy within ritual language.

Hierarchy, taxonomy and polysemy

Structural analysis, of the form we began by considering, is epistemologically a theory of oppositions. For Lévi-Strauss, this analysis consists of the theoretical modelling of the possible combinations and permutations of some defined set of oppositions. Structure is represented as a model that pertains to certain 'strategic' levels of reality and it is the task of the investigator to discover the 'order of orders' that, by transformation, encompasses these separable autonomous levels of structured reality (Lévi-Strauss 1953:528–9, 547–8). Semantically, what this appears to imply is that all binary oppositions are generally autonomous, isomorphic and equal in so far as they are the product of the same ordering logic. Needham, on the other hand, makes the consistent assertion that only certain societies—those of prescriptive alliance—are characterised by a pervasive concordance of complementary oppositions. The ordering of dual categories in all other societies is theoretically an open question. Hence, except in the proposed special test case of prescriptive alliance societies, what is lacking in this epistemology, as critics, particularly Marxist critics (cf. Terray 1972:40), have noted, is any articulated concept of hierarchy. The possibility of transformations between strategic levels is not the same as a hierarchy of levels nor does it seem to involve a hierarchical ordering of elements at any specific level. In any semantic theory, opposition without hierarchy can only lead to endless manipulations.

In contrast, the strength of American ethno-semantics has been in the elucidation of hierarchy via paradigms, taxonomies, tree structures, developmental sequencing and flow-charting. In these investigations, however, lexical 'contrast' has generally involved the notion of 'in-elusions' and has thus resulted in the construction of bounded hierarchic structures ordered horizontally by differentiation and vertically in terms of a subordinating continuum of the particular to the more general. Applying these notions to the construction of folk taxonomies of natural language raises, as the theoreticians of these methods quickly realised, a variety of so-called 'special problems': multiple and interlocking hierarchies, extra-hierarchic relations, synonomy, homonymy and polysemy (cf. Conklin 1969:41–57). It was in response to these hierarchic special problems that Charles Frake first proposed the study of 'interlinkage' (1969:123–37), criticising, in the process, the concept of bounded semantic domains based exclusively on a hierarchy of inclusion:

> [A]ny concept is inter-linked by a variety of relationships to a large number of other concepts, which, in turn, are inter-linked with still other concepts. If a semantic domain is a set of related concepts, then it is clear that there is no one way to separate the conceptual structure of a people into a finite number of discrete, clearly delimited domains. Rather, we have a network of relations whose links enable us to travel along a variety of paths from one concept to another. (Frake 1969:132)

The problem involves the relation of hierarchy and interlinkage and requires a careful and lengthy consideration. Here, only a few remarks can be made. Of its total vocabulary, Rotenese ritual language has a relatively small number of primary symbols that, by their range of linkages, 'organise' other elements, which similarly organise still others to form what appears to be a hierarchy of symbols. If one accepts this understanding of hierarchy, clearly this linguistic hierarchy does not resemble the previous taxonomic structures proposed for the study of folk classification. One can, however, attempt to interpret the higher-level primary symbols in the light of ritual practice; they comprise a seemingly odd and certainly non-obvious collection of lexical items. *Ai* ('plant, tree'), for example, would—in a standard plant taxonomy—appear as the maximal taxon and perhaps again at the next level of contrast, whereas *tua* ('lontar palm') would occur at or near the lowest contrastive level. In ritual language, however, *ai* and *tua* are linked and, because they both possess an equal range of linkages, they have the same hierarchical value. In this hierarchy, it is not taxonomic generality but polysemy—the property of a symbol to relate to a multiple range of other symbols—that becomes the criterion for hierarchical inclusion. To judge from the study of other ritual systems, there seems to be good empirical justification for this kind of criterion. Turner (1967:48–58) has elegantly and subtly argued for a similar criterion. No less than the *mukula* of the Ndembu, the all-important *tua* palm of the Rotenese, can invoke a nexus of symbolic associations.

The implications of this hierarchy for the understanding of change are considerable. Change in a structure conceived of as equal, autonomous dyads can proceed only partially and in piecemeal fashion. Change in a system of hierarchically interrelated combinations of dyads can be appraised only by examination of the point at which this change occurs. Change in this system is a dialectic process but not all change is equally significant. The rupture, resolution or synthetic engagement of elements with a limited range of associations in some peripheral dyad may have little effect on the total system, whereas a similar change among any of the higher-level elements would have immediate and systemic effects throughout the language. The hierarchy of certain symbols—their position within the hierarchy—governs the particular manifestation of the whole.

We need not discuss these notions of change abstractly but can consider what is occurring at present on Rote in terms of ritual language. The majority of Rotenese have comfortably become Protestant Christians without rejecting their former traditions. A small majority is, however, evangelically engaged in a polemic against these traditions, contemptuously referring to the rituals as a 'religion of rock and tree'. They have chosen a key dyad of primary symbols as the focus of their attack. On the other hand, the introduction of the Malay Bible, and particularly the Old Testament with its elaborate tradition of parallel verse, has provided unintended support for Rotenese ritual language. The roles of chanter and preacher are not incompatible, and a modern ritual can interweave chant segments, Psalms or quotations from Isaiah without apparent contradiction. Furthermore, what seems to have begun is a local-level retelling of the Bible in ritual language.

The chanter Peu Malesi, who provided me with version one of the myth of the house, was among the first chanters to offer to recite for me on my return to the island. Now, with the full and unchallenged power of a mature talent, he proposed to tell me what he described as an ancient Rotenese myth about the origin of death. This myth, which he told me before an assembled group of Rotenese, was about the ancestral pair, the man, Teke Telu, and the woman, Koa Hulu, who lived in a walled and forbidden garden at the beginning of time. The woman, Koa Hulu, was tempted by an 'eel and snake' to pluck and eat a 'fruit sweet as lontar syrup and a leaf honeyed as bee's water' and by this act brought into being the tools for 'hewing a coffin and digging a grave'. Thus, according to the standard formulaic phrase, there arose 'the death of the spirits and the decrease of the ghosts'.

This unmistakable Rotenese version of Adam and Eve was delivered in flawless ritual language. As such, it was readily accepted by those who heard it, not as something new, but as something extremely old: a carefully guarded segment of the esoteric knowledge that proves the often-stated Rotenese contention that the Bible is another version of Rotenese tradition. This kind of retelling transforms the seeming challenge of Biblical Christianity into the means of maintaining the essential distinctions of the ritual-language code. It would be foolhardy at this point to predict what changes may occur within the system of ritual language in its encounter with Christianity, but it is possible to appreciate how, in a lived-in system of this complexity, a simple relational change of primary symbols can have far-reaching unintentional effects.

Explorations in ritual language

The initial impetus for the study of the semantic networks of ritual language was comparative: to establish recognisable procedures for the analysis of different ritual systems. Many societies in eastern Indonesia—on Sumba, Timor and Flores—possess traditions of parallelism similar to those of the Rotenese. An adequate corpus of parallel texts already exists for the Atoni of Timor (Middelkoop 1949) and there certainly exist possibilities for doing research on semantic parallelism among other populations on Timor. Comparison of the semantics of the closely related ritual languages of Timor could well become a special field of study. It is also possible to begin this comparative venture by a microanalysis of the different semantic relations between dialect areas of Rote. Beyond eastern Indonesia, large collections of parallel verse exist for Nias, a number of Dayak groups in Borneo and for the Sa'dan Toraja of the Celebes. Gradually, it might be possible to advance comparisons among the semantic networks of these more widely separated languages and from Indonesia to similar systems in South-East Asia and elsewhere.

A further research possibility of semantic networks is to consider their expansion and to trace the formal associations on any selected node within the system. Essentially, the exploration of these networks is the converse operation to that of defining a core. Whereas any element may be chosen as a starting point, it is of particular interest in dealing with verbal and adverbial elements since the referential approaches to the study of semantics are generally inadequate to deal with this vast array of lexical items.[15] In this connection, we can consider the associations of the term *loe* ('to descend, to lower, to be low, lowly'). The chain of associations emanating from *loe*, through *tai*, *sa'e* and *lu'u*, comprises a network of 90 elements, excluding all links to other core terms. To simplify

---

15 See Fox (Chapter 5 in this volume) for a discussion of the network of verbs of 'speaking' in Rotenese.

this large network for the purposes of this discussion, we can exclude all links from *loe* to other core terms, including *tai*, *sa'e* and *lu'u*. This still constitutes a sizeable network of 21 elements. The list of these elements with their glosses and links is set out in Table 6.2.

Table 6.2 Formal Associations of *Loe*

	Element	Glosses	Links
1.	Loe:	To descend, to lower, to be low	(Dae), dilu, le'a, nggolo, peu, sai, sali, (tai), teë
2.	Dilu:	To bend over, to turn down	Loe, sesu
3.	Sesu:	To bend, break, or cut at a joint	Dilu
4.	Le'a:	To stretch, measure, extend, pull, tug, drag; to divine (by stretching spear: Le'a te)	Hela, kani, loe, nole, nuni, tona, tuluk
5.	Hela:	To pull, to tug, to pull out; to divorce (in the compound hela-ketu)	Le'a, nole
6.	Nole:	To carry something so that it hangs down, to drag; to divorce (in the compound nole-ladi)	Hela, le'a
7.	Kani:	To hang down loosely; to divine (by the hanging-stone method: kani batu)	Le'a
8.	Nuni:	To pull, to lead (a horse, for example, by a rope)	Le'a
9.	Tona:	To push forth; to master, to overpower	Le'a
10.	Tuluk:	To shove, to push	Le'a
11.	Nggolo:	To protrude; a protuberance, promontory, snout (of an animal)	Loe
12.	Peu:	To jut forth, to stick out (especially of trees or the branches of trees)	Loe
13.	Sai:	To appear, to arrive, to come upon a place; to fall (of rain)	Loe
14.	Sali:	To pour out, to overflow; overflowing	Doko, loe
15.	Doko:	To hang, to droop, to recede; receding	Benu, sali, (tai)
16.	Benu:	To balance, to be balanced; balanced or balancing	Doko, leo
17.	Leo:	To circle, to go round; circling, surrounding	Benu
18.	Teë:	To rest, to stand still, to place on end; to erect	Hani, loe
19.	Hani:	To wait, to watch over, to tend (animals)	Bafa, hulu, teë
20.	Bafa:	To wait in ambush, to hide	Hani
21.	Hulu:	To draw in; to gather (animals) together	Hani

The graph of their associations appears in Figure 6.3.

Here, *loe* can be seen as a point of articulation for a variety of verbal forms. Some, such as *nggolo, leu* and *sai*, occur in a limited, specific orbit with *loe*. Some, such as *dilu, teë* and *sali*, lead outward in a chain of associations, allowing us to follow, for example, the by no means obvious Rotenese associational logic that one attempts to encapsulate by glosses on descending, pouring out, drooping, balancing and surrounding. Another, *leä*, forms a further point of articulation for a new orbit of associations.

Analysing these networks solves certain problems but raises others—particularly in regard to homonymy. To take one instance, *bafa* in Rotenese has the meanings: 1) 'to wait in ambush, to hide', and 2) 'opening, mouth, beak, gully'. Since these two occurrences of *bafa* sort themselves out in different regions of the semantic network, they can easily be recognised as homonyms. On the other hand, *doko*, although on its own it does not link with *tai*, does so in a compound term: *doko-doe//tai-boni*. This dyadic set is used specifically in the context of bride-wealth negotiations to indicate the persistent prodding or gentle demanding that is supposed to characterise these negotiations. One could formally treat *doko* and *doko-doe* as separate, but associational links of *doko* and *tai* with *loe* suggest that however difficult it can be to divine the association of 'demanding' and 'drooping', there would appear to be some relation.

There is, however, still another major exploratory possibility in the study of ritual language. Jakobson called attention to the investigation of parallelism within the context of an important discussion of what he described, in *Fundamentals of Language* (Jakobson and Halle 1956), as the 'twofold character' of language: selection and combination. Developing distinctions established in linguistics since Saussure, Jakobson identified the associative, the paradigmatic and the selective aspect of language with 'metaphor' and the syntagmatic and the combinative aspect with 'metonym'. (Lévi-Strauss's adaptation of these notions has given them currency in the anthropological literature.) In this terminology, the phenomenon of parallelism relates exclusively to 'metaphor'. In the case of Rotenese ritual language, the delineation of certain of the parameters of metaphor makes it possible to focus attention on metonymic creation.

The issue can also be posed in a different fashion. Rotenese ritual language consists of parallel verse that occurs in grammatically similar lines. In theory, one chanter responds to another by supplying the appropriate second verse to a verse given him by the first chanter. In practice, this is true only of chanters who are acquainted with each other; newly acquainted chanters, in my experience, require a considerable amount of cueing before they begin to respond properly to one another. In theory, the circle of Rotenese dancers is supposed to answer, in chorus, each line of verse initiated by the chanter in its midst. In practice, a chanter sings both verses before the chorus picks up the second verse although this is said not to have been the case formerly. In theory, therefore, when the whole of the ritual-language dictionary has been computerised, it would be an extremely instructive goal—as well as a methodological test—to develop a response program that would answer any line of Rotenese verse with a correspondingly correct line. The problems with this are formidable but grappling with them could elucidate what is involved in metonym.

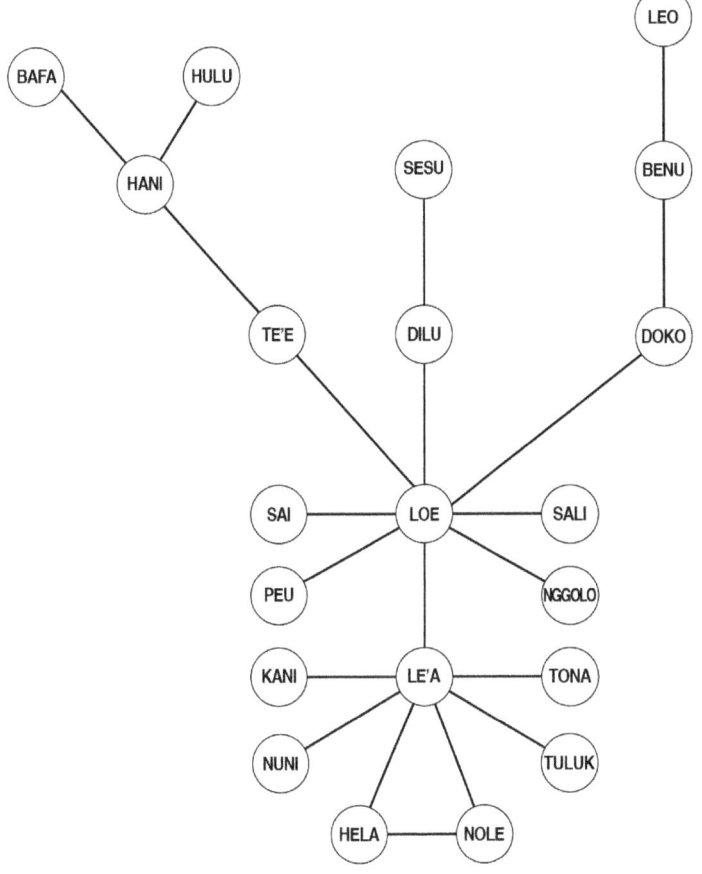

Figure 6.3: Graph of Formal Associations of *Loe*

We can take two lines of verse from the myth of the house as illustration. The first verse presents no problem whatsoever:

1) Ala fe sipa aba-do   They give the plumbline marker

Ala (they) and *fe* (give) are invariant elements so that all that is required is the conjunction *ma* (and) or *do* (or)—either is permissible—and a search in the dictionary for what pairs with *sipa aba-do* (listed as a compound since this is the only way it occurs). The answer is a single link—*funu ma-leo*—so that the only possible correct response is:

> 2) Ala fe funu ma-leo   They give the turning drill

It is apparent, however, that since an element may pair with as many as 10 or more other elements, the permutations and combinations of elements that must be considered to obtain a proper response are potentially enormous. Furthermore, there exists the question of what constitutes a proper response and whether there could be more than one such response. Consider the following line:

> 3) Ala fe lilo ma-langa menge   They give gold chains with snakes' heads

The response to this in the myth is:

> 4) Ala fe kapa ma-ao foek   They give buffalo with crocodile-marked bodies.

There is something strikingly 'mythological' about a correct response that attributes 'crocodile-marked bodies' to water buffalo. One must first comprehend that, according to the mythology, all buffalo originated from the sea as a gift of the Crocodile. One must then realise that in Rotenese *foe* is the word for crocodile and the term used to refer to flecks of white skin pigmentation on men and animals. Etymologically, there is evidence that these two usages of *foe* are derived from different roots, but it is more important to be aware that, in Rotenese folk etymology, they are identical. Other animals can have white markings: the 'cat and civet' mentioned in the first lines of the myth of the house are described as 'pied-nosed and white-tailed'. It is when a buffalo has similar markings, however, that it is considered a throwback that shows evidence of its origin. Folk etymology based on mythology provides the essential means of linking snake-headed chains and crocodile-marked bodies on buffalo.

This 'correct' response appears even more interesting when compared with other possible responses. *Lilo* pairs with seven other elements and *langa* with eight, so that there are altogether 56 possible responses according to the following table:

6. On binary categories and primary symbols

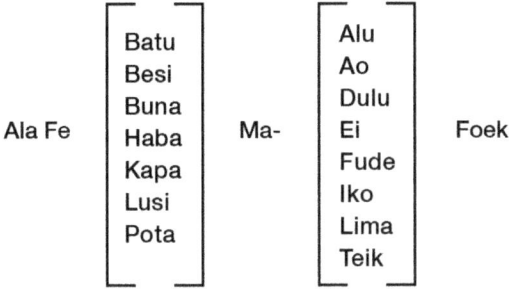

Figure 6.4: Possible responses

The majority of these combinations produce nonsense:

5) *Ala fe besi ma-dulu foek**:	They give iron with crocodile's east
6) *Ala fe buna ma-fude foek**:	They give a flower with crocodile's froth
7) *Ala fe lusi ma-alu foek**:	They give a flower with crocodile's pestle.

The following possible responses, however, raise interesting questions.

8) *Ala fe kapa ma-ei foek**:	They give a buffalo with crocodile feet
9) *Ala fe haba ma-iko foek**:	They give a braided gold with a crocodile's tail
10) *Ala fe batu ma-ao foek**:	They give a rock with a crocodile's body

Line (8) creates confusion in Rotenese classifications. The crocodile, like the monkey, is considered to resemble man in that its forelegs are *lima* (hands, arms) and hind legs are *eik*. A water buffalo, on the other hand, has four *eik*. So a crocodile-footed buffalo would be an anomalous creature.

Line (9) is a plausible response but describes a nonexistent cultural object. For centuries, Ndaonese craftsmen have braided gold strings for the Rotenese and many of these end with reptilian 'heads', but no-one—to my knowledge—has fashioned a corresponding 'tail' to these strings, though this would certainly be within the symbolic conventions of the artistic tradition. The question, however, would remain why its 'tail' rather than its 'head' should identify this object.

Line (10) poses further problems since it describes a common object on Rote. There are numerous rocks of varying sizes that are described as the solidified remains of former crocodiles. The island of Rote, as a whole, is said to be one such enormous rock. The response is perfectly sound, mythologically acceptable, but a rock might be inappropriate as bride-wealth.

As a first-level approximation, what is needed is an understanding of the syntagmatic compound terms, irreversible binomials and ritual formulae, of which there are many, to eliminate the most unlikely and nonsensical combinations. By further reflecting on the networks of ritual language, it might be possible to develop a canon of accordance that would account for still more combinations. This is, however, clearly not the same immense task that the generative linguist sets himself in determining the logical, syntactical, inferential and contextual rules that underlie well-formed, meaningful sentences. For one, the investigation is directed towards a definable segment of possible Rotenese utterances. Second, it is not concerned with generating new sentences but with matching appropriate sentences to already given ones by specific lexical rules. Furthermore, ritual language—although not context free—is a special speech form of formulaic devices whose patterns make change applicable to a variety of ritual situations. Still, however, in the process of this investigation, it is probable that there will occur an abundance of engaging responses that will have to be discussed directly with the chanters of Rote to involve them in the explication of their art.

Comments and conclusions

In this chapter, I have discussed various operations and analyses that can be performed in and on Rotenese ritual language. At this point, I would like to shift perspective and comment briefly on ritual language in relation to the whole of Rotenese verbal culture. It seems evident that a symbol in ritual language—'earth', 'rock', 'tree'—is related to yet differs in its use in, for example, the Rotenese stock of dream omens and consequences, in proverbs, in folktales and genealogical narratives, in the oral codes for legal decisions at Rotenese courts, in ordinary conversation and in baby talk. Each of these usages, speech forms or genres—and more that could be enumerated—I would label a 'language stratum', following Friedrich Waismann in what he announced as 'a programme for the future'. Already in 1946, Waismann was calling on those interested in linguistic analysis to reverse a traditional approach. Instead of defining words by their referents and then analysing referents by their subject matter—material objects, sense data, vague impressions—he urged the examination of linguistic strata to determine their subject matter:

> If we carefully study the texture of the concepts which occur in a given stratum, the logic of its propositions, the meaning of truth, the web of verification, the sense in which a description may be complete or incomplete—if we consider all that, we may thereby characterise the subject matter. We may say, for instance: a material object is something that is describable in a language of such-and-such structure; a sense impression is something which can be described in such-and-such a language; a dream is—, a memory picture is…and so on. (Waismann 1965:246)

In the same discussion, Waismann points to the 'systematic ambiguity' that words take on as they are used in different strata. On this evidence, the propositions of symbolic logic would be, for instance, an inappropriate means for the study of the symbolism of dreams.

Following this lead, I would argue that symbols in Rotenese do indeed change sense—in ways I would be unable to adequately describe—as one proceeds from baby talk or ordinary conversation to the verses of ritual language. I would, however, go further and make explicit what is implicit in my earlier discussion. I would argue that there is a hierarchy of linguistic strata in Rotenese and that this hierarchy involves—to adopt an inadequate metaphor—a 'tightening' of the logic of relations among symbols. I would also see this hierarchy as dependent on a progressive learning process: the gradual comprehension and systematisation of a culture. Ritual language is the recognised culmination of this learning and, for this reason, with the exception of a few gifted individuals, it is the special preserve of the elders. When Bea, the little girl who lived with us, used to refer to the sun as 'moon two', she had embarked on the Rotenese path of learning that, in a few instances, can lead to profound understandings such as those of the Head of the Earth in Termanu, who, before he died, had ceased to be referred to by any other name than that of his clan: Meno.

There is a further social aspect to this argument. When we consider all the situations on Rote in which ritual language may be used—greetings and farewells, petitions, courtship overtures, preludes to negotiations and the ceremonies of the life cycle—they are all moments of formalised interaction that call for a clear statement of shared premises. The social effect of symbols at this level, one can hypothesise, has to do with the clarity of their expression and the density of the semantic network they invoke. The formal simplicity of dichotomous thinking and the continuous partition of all things by two offers the most efficient means to this end.

Comparative evidence, I believe, would lend support to this position. A survey of some of the major instances of pervasive canonical parallelism in its distribution throughout the world's oral traditions suggests that this speech form or language stratum is reserved for special situations: for the preservation of past wisdom, for the utterance of sacred words, for determining ritual relations, for healing and for communication with spirits. The litanies of the priests of Nias, the *Book of Counsel* of the Quiche Maya, the poetry of the Old Testament, the prayer chants of the Hawaiians, the spirit verse of the Kachin, the cosmological speculation of the Ngaju and the epic deeds of gods and men recorded in the *Kalevala* retain, by their parallelism, idealised statements of a specific cultural order.

This has many implications for an understanding of binary categories and for an analysis of them. The curious feature of the dyads in elaborate traditions of parallelism is that they make no distinction between similars and opposites—though commentators on parallelism have attempted to make these distinctions. Complementary, contrary and contradictory terms have in common their *relation* to one another as a pair, so that possibly, at a first-order level, there is a fundamental unity of similars and opposites, a primacy in polarity. Thus the creation of a semantics of relations would be a prerequisite to a semantics of reference. Binary analysis would, therefore, be an essential tool in this investigation, but its field would be more clearly delimited. Jakobson has repeatedly argued that the binary principle appears to underlie much linguistic expression and most poetry. Systems of parallelism are clearly extreme and relatively transparent developments on a binary principle and for this reason are suitable for such analysis. By this same reasoning, however, it would seem unlikely that other aspects of culture would be equally suited for binary analysis.

In advancing the investigation of binary categories, we might be able to broach a speculative question posed by Mauss and Durkheim, implied in Lévi-Strauss's *Mythologiques* and directly formulated by Needham: whether there exist 'certain things in nature [that] seem to exert an effect on the human mind, conducing to symbolic forms of the most general and, even universal, kind' (Needham 1964:147). This is to ask whether certain instruments of the natural world offer themselves as a prevalent means to conceptualisation and thereby form the material basis for the primary symbols of man.

7. Category and complement[1]

There are many forms of dualism. Here I wish to explore the relationship between the dyadic categories encountered in compositions of pervasive parallelism and other binary categories utilised, in Indonesia and elsewhere, to organise dual forms of social organisation. In this regard, it is useful to recall that Lévi-Strauss's 1956 article 'Do Dual Organizations Exist?' was written to honour J. P. B. de Josselin de Jong and that it served as a brief, if somewhat belated, recognition of Dutch research on Indonesian dyadic structures. Lévi-Strauss's intention in the article was to draw a comparison between American-Indian and Indonesian forms of dual organisation, yet the focus of his comparison was curiously incongruent, since it involved a comparative analysis of the specific social structures of the Winnebago and the Bororo on one hand, and a constructed model of an Indonesian-type social structure on the other. This Indonesian-type model, based on five binary oppositions, was characterised by three positive features: non-residential marriage classes, prescribed marriage, and an opposition between the sexes, thus supposedly resulting in a system of moieties distinguished as male and female in association with asymmetric or generalised exchange.

This model is intriguing but its derivation is difficult to fathom. Moieties of a sort occur throughout Indonesia, but they are not invariably designated as male and female and their function is rarely to regulate marriage. In some Indonesian societies, specific categories of men and women are defined as strictly marriageable, but these categories do not constitute marriage classes nor are they coincident with a particular clan structure. Systems of asymmetric prescriptive marriage do indeed occur in Indonesia, but they are by no means universal. Indeed such systems constitute a minority in a region where marriage is overwhelmingly non-prescriptive. In western Indonesia the Toba Batak offer what is considered to be a 'classic' example of asymmetric prescriptive marriage, whereas in eastern Indonesia, societies with similar such systems are found scattered and interspersed among societies with other forms of marriage, primarily on the islands of Flores, Timor and Sumba, and on some of the islands of the Moluccas. Thus, although it is certainly possible to discern the various elements of Lévi-Strauss's model, their combination conforms to no known Indonesian society. Hence it is reasonable to question the relevance of the model for the comparative analysis of dyadic structures in Indonesia. Yet to dismiss this model as irrelevant would be to ignore its relation to (and possible derivation from) the more influential model of eastern Indonesian social structure developed by F. A. E. van Wouden in the doctoral

---

1 In preparing the final draft of the original paper, I benefited in particular from valuable comments from Greg Acciaioli, E. Douglas Lewis and Maureen MacKenzie. The original version of this chapter appeared in D. Maybury-Lewis and U. Almagor (eds), *The Attraction of Opposites: Thought and society in a dualistic mode*, pp. 33–56. Ann Arbor: University of Michigan Press.

dissertation entitled 'Types of social structure in eastern Indonesia', which he wrote under the direct supervision of J. P. B. de Josselin de Jong in 1935 (subsequently translated and published as van Wouden 1968).

Van Wouden, whose work Lévi-Strauss alludes to in his article, attempted to disentangle an accumulation of disparate ethnographic evidence from eastern Indonesia. Like Lévi-Strauss, van Wouden regarded marriage as the 'pivot' for social organisation, whose categories provided the basis for an all-embracing cosmological classification. He also noted that 'ordinary' (MBD/FZD) cross-cousin marriage and 'exclusive' (MBD) cross-cousin marriage represented 'two opposed systems of affinal relationships between groups' (1968:90). Since van Wouden thought that these types of marriage formed the foundation for the dualistic and triadic patterns of classification that were so evidently interwoven in the cosmologies of eastern Indonesia, he was obliged to construct a model that reconciled them. In his model, which was intended to represent the original form of Indonesian social organisation, van Wouden opted for exclusive cross-cousin marriage but in a closed chain of relationships among an even number of clans. By the logic of this model, if the clans are patrilineal there must be an equal number of latent matrilineal groups, resulting in a 'double-unilateral' (or double-unilineal) system. The limiting case required four clans that would ideally produce a four-clan or 'double two-phratry system'. In terms of the model, as van Wouden noted, 'dual organization…is not required by the system, but can very well accompany it' (1968:88).

In retrospect, although it is possible to comprehend both van Wouden's and Lévi-Strauss's models, it is difficult to resuscitate the intellectual ambience that once made these models so compelling. Both models now seem stunningly simplistic. Both are constructed on a simple set of binary oppositions and are thus implicated in a dualism of the sort they are intended to illuminate. Moreover, both models share the same Durkheimian inheritance that ultimately derives classification in general from the categorisation of social forms. As a result, both models focus primarily on the products of classification rather than the processes of classification. For this reason in particular, neither model now offers an appropriate starting point for the study of dyadic structures.

Eastern Indonesia: Three ethnographic cases of dual structures

In eastern Indonesia (and especially in the Lesser Sundas and the Moluccas) comparative research has developed considerably in recent years. When van Wouden wrote his dissertation he had to draw together and attempt to make sense of perhaps a hundred scattered reports of varying lengths and reliability. He had not a single ethnography of note to guide his speculations. Today, however, there are at least a dozen substantial ethnographies on the region and at least another dozen studies now in preparation.[2] The picture that emerges from these studies is somewhat different from the one that van Wouden sketched.

All of these ethnographies, without exception, confirm the prevalence and importance of dyadic structures. Yet the sheer variety and diversity of these structures militate against any conception of a single institution of 'dual organization'. Nor is it simply the variety of these dyadic structures among the many different societies of the region that makes it difficult to apply the classic models of dual organisation; more difficult still is the application of this concept to the diversity of dyadic structures within any single society. To illustrate what I mean by this, I will describe in outline form the dyadic structures of three neighbouring island societies on which I have done fieldwork.

The first case is that of Savu. This island has one of the two societies in eastern Indonesia with a bilineal social organisation that might be considered to resemble van Wouden's double-unilateral model. Together with the tiny offshore island of Raijua, Savu is composed of five ceremonial domains. Each of these domains is, in turn, composed of named, localised, patrilineal clans (*udu*), which are often further divided into lineages (*kerogo*), all of whom recognise the same 'origin' village. Crosscutting the particular allegiances of these localised groups is an island-wide system of ranked matrimoieties: *Hubi Ae* ('The Greater Blossom') and *Hubi Iki* ('The Lesser Blossom'). These moieties, 'The Blossoms', are further subdivided into *Wini* ('Seeds'). On Savu, however, there is neither a terminological nor a systematic rule of marriage governing relationships between patrilineal or matrilineal groups. Instead there is a marked tendency, for reasons of status, for the occurrence of internal marriages within each matrimoiety and intermarriage among high-ranking patrilineal groups.

Each ceremonial domain has its own lunar calendar and a native priesthood to conduct ceremonies in sequence throughout the year. The arrangement of the lunar calendar, the cycle of the ceremonial year, the organisation of the priesthood, and the allocation of ritual duties to specific priests and clans are all based on a series of interrelated dyadic structures. In the domain of Liae (see Fox 1979), the ceremonial year consists in an opposition between the planting season and the lontar-tapping season, the period of ritual silence and the period of gongs and drums, the time when the *Deo Rai* from clan Gopo and his priestly council, *Ratu Mone Telu* ('The Three Male Priests'), preside and the time when the *Apu Lodo* from Napujara and his council, the *Ratu Mone Pidu* ('The Seven Priests'), hold

---

2   The ethnographies of the region include a considerable number of doctoral dissertations that remain unpublished, including Cunningham (1962); Francillon (1967); Fox (1968); Gordon (1975); Traube (1977); Kana (1978); Lazarowitz (1980); Mitchell (1981); Kuipers (1982); Lewis (1982a); Hoskins (1983); and McKinnon (1983). As a result, the remarkable research that is being carried out in this area is not readily accessible to the field of anthropology as a whole.

sway. During the high ceremonial season that marks the transition between these two seasons, in the month of Bangaliwu Gopo, the *Deo Rai* takes precedence; in the following month of Bangaliwu Rame, the *Apu Lodo* takes precedence.

The progress of each lunar month is also conceived in terms of a set of oppositions: waxing and waning, east and west, life and death, above and below. And during each month a complex ritual dialectic assigns lineages and clans as opposing groups with specific ritual functions. Thus, for example, in the great cockfighting ritual of the month of Bangaliwu Rame, one lineage of Napujara, the *Apu Lodo*'s clan, joins Gopo, the clan of the *Deo Rai*, in ceremonial opposition to the clan Nahai, which is joined by an opposing lineage of Napujara. These groups assemble at different village sites, form groups known as *Ada Mone* ('The Male Group') and *Ada Rena* ('The Female Group'), and then position themselves at the 'upper' and 'lower' ends of an enclosure on the top of the hill of Kolarae where they conduct ritual combat with their fighting cocks. Other clans take sides with one or the other group, or divide internally into opposing lineages. The essential point to be made here is that this particular configuration of opposing clans holds only for Bangaliwu Rame; other configurations based on different categories occur in other months of the year. The configuration that I observed and described for Bangaliwu Rame in 1973 is neither fixed nor unchanging but, by common understanding, it is recognised to be, in large part, the result of the internal historical dynamics of the development of the clans of Liae. In effect, on Savu there is no single set of concordant dyadic structures, but rather a proliferation of such structures, each fitted to a particular purpose.

The second case is that of the domain of Thie on the island of Rote. Unlike Savu, Rote has only patrilineal or, more precisely, patronymically ordered descent groups; maternal affiliation, however, is acknowledged for three generations, but this acknowledgment does not form the basis for a coherent matrilineal line of descent. Nor is there any terminologically prescribed rule of marriage.

The island was traditionally divided into 18 domains and, despite administrative consolidation since 1968, these domains retain their role as primary communities of orientation (Fox 1977). For centuries, each domain, under its own separate ruler, developed distinctive traditions and, except for a few royal and high noble inter-domain marriages, each domain has remained largely endogamous, following distinct rules and customary practices. A common set of basic cultural categories is evident throughout the island, but the social application of these categories varies from domain to domain (Fox 1979).

In the domain of Thie (and in one other domain, Loleh) a system of marriage moieties has developed. Of Thie's 26 clans, 14 are assigned to the moiety of Sabarai, of the *Manek* or 'Male Lord', and 12 are assigned to the moiety of Taratu, of the *Fetor* or 'Female Lord'. In his dissertation, van Wouden devoted special attention to Thie, seeing in the domain a phratry system and, on the basis of hints in one source, even a possible eight-class marriage system. When examined in more detail, however, this dual organisation dissolves in a variety of disparate dyadic structures (see Fox 1980). Each moiety is divided into major clans (*leo inak*) and minor clans (*leo anak*), whose status conforms to that of 'noble' and 'commoner' in other domains. The group of noble clans in each moiety is further subdivided into various ancestral groupings with specific political functions, while the minor clans within the moiety of Sabarai form a ritual group associated with the powers and fertility of the earth. These minor clans also form a separate marriage unit that may marry either with Taratu or with the major clans of Sabarai. Thus, at a further level of specification, an apparent dual organisation becomes a triadic structure.[3]

This moiety system dissolves still further, since one clan on each side is exempt from following any moiety rules—in one case because members of the clan originate from an offshore island, and in the other case because the clan's ancestor is said to have arrived late at the ceremonial gathering at which the moiety system was established. These justificatory explanations further highlight an essential conceptual feature of the moieties. They are not conceived as a primordial structure but rather the reverse: as a formal historical ordering of an untidy process of clan formation undertaken at the behest of one of the later rulers of the domain.

As on Savu, in Thie, history is given due recognition. The assignment of groups to a particular dyadic segment is thus considered to be contingent on past events. This becomes clearer when one examines the various ceremonies that were once performed by the moieties. The major clans of both Sabarai and Taratu performed their own origin celebrations. Four minor clans, two from each moiety, also performed individual celebrations; however, the most important ceremonies were performed by the minor, ritually powerful clans of Sabarai. These clans, of which two were associated with the east and three with the west, were obliged to lead an annual ritual combat. At a ritual feast for all the clans, a rice-pounding block would suddenly be tipped over and those who found themselves to the east of the block joined the two clans of the east and those to the west joined the three clans of the west, thus arbitrarily obliterating all other dual structures. Thus, again as on Savu, in Thie there is, despite initial appearances, no single, all-embracing dual organisation, but instead a host of particular dyadic structures.

The third case is that of the Atoni of West Timor. Dualism among the Atoni, based on such categories as male and female, inside and outside, and 'wife-giver'

---

3   The case of Thie bears comparison with the case of the Winnebago cited by Lévi-Strauss. From the point of view of Taratu, the moiety which marries only with Sabarai, the organisation of the whole remains dyadic; whereas from the point of view of Sabarai, the moiety which is subdivided, the organisation of the whole is triadic. Indeed, I have heard sharp arguments among people from Thie as to whether the domain is essentially dyadic or triadic.

and 'wife-taker', has been amply described for the structure of their domains, their descent groups and their houses (Cunningham 1964, 1965, 1966; Schulte Nordholt 1971, 1980). Unlike the Savunese and Rotenese, the Atoni do have a terminological rule of symmetric marriage, though by preference they tend to arrange particular marriages in an asymmetric fashion. Despite this rule, however, the organisation of descent groups defies simple description. In general, domains on the island of Timor are larger than those on Rote or Savu and settlement is more scattered. Moreover, the continual migration of different segments of named descent groups throughout the island has produced a heterogeneous structure within each domain. Thus, a domain whose traditional structure was founded on an idealised set of relationships among certain leading clans actually consists of myriad local relationships among minimal descent groups. Narratives of the wanderings of the ancestors acknowledge these formative processes, all of which create a situation not unlike that on Rote and Savu, where there exist multiple dyadic structures but no classic dual organisation.

Faced with the ethnographic situation in eastern Indonesia, certain conclusions can be drawn. Clearly, the classic models of dual organisation appear inappropriate, for there is no single organisational form for the variety of dyadic structures that is to be found either within any one society or among the numerous different societies of eastern Indonesia. Furthermore, since the variety of dyadic structures implies an absence of a formal concordance between social and symbolic forms, the study of dual classification risks becoming a typological enumeration of dual structures. Hence I would argue that what is needed is a further study not of the products of classification, but of the processes of classification.

Such a study must be undertaken at two levels: first, at a general, abstract level that focuses on the features that seem to underlie processes of dual symbolic classification, and then at a categorical level that focuses on the way in which specific sets of categories form complex systems of symbolic classification. The first level allows comparison with other societies throughout the world, while the second level can only relate to a reasonably defined ethnographic field of study: to historically related societies that share common linguistic categories. Whereas the first level necessarily requires a degree of formalism, close attention to the second level leads ultimately to an intimate examination of related metaphors for living. Since the two levels are related, however, I shall attempt to examine processes of dual classification in relation to the ethnography of eastern Indonesia, focusing on five features of dual symbolic classification systems in eastern Indonesia: 1) parallelism, 2) recursive complementarity, 3) categorical asymmetry, 4) category reversal, and 5) analogical crossover.[4]

---

4 Because at this stage I am primarily interested in describing the classificatory phenomena encountered in eastern Indonesia, I am content to use the term 'feature' rather than 'principle'. Some of these features can occur together, as, for example, 'recursive complementarity' and 'categorical asymmetry'. Furthermore,

The processes of dual classification in eastern Indonesia

Parallelism

Roman Jakobson has argued that the principle of parallelism is implicated in all poetic statements. Jakobson's notion of parallelism is broadly relevant to an understanding of symbolic statements in general (Fox 1977:59–60) and, as I have argued, to ritual performances as well (Fox 1979:169–71). Here, however, I will confine myself to the strict form of parallelism known generally as 'canonical parallelism', since virtually all the societies of eastern Indonesia use some form of canonical parallelism for the expression and transmission of ritual knowledge.[5] Generally this parallelism takes the form of a ritual language in which all or most semantic elements are paired in dyadic sets, structured in formulaic phrases, and expressed as couplets or parallel verses (Fox 1971, 1974, 1975).

As an example of this form of canonical parallelism, I present a brief Rotenese ritual composition by the chanter L. Manoeain of the domain of Ba'a.

1. Sa Lepa-Lai nunun	The Waringin tree of Sa Lepa-Lai
2. Ma Huak Lali-Ha kekan	And the Banyan Tree of Huak Lali-Ha
3. Keka maba'e faluk	The Banyan has eight branches
4. Ma nunun mandana siok.	And the Waringin has nine boughs.
5. De dalak ko sio boe	These are the nine roads
6. Ma enok ko falu boe.	And these are the eight paths.
7. Fo dala sodak nai ndia	The road of wellbeing is there
8. Ma eno mamates nai na.	And the path of death is there.
9. De suli malamumula	Therefore watch with care
10. Ma mete makananae.	And look with attention.
11. Ndanak esa dulu neu	One branch points east,
12. Ma boso musik ndia	But do not follow that
13. Te fiti-ngge ledon dalan ndia	For this is the road of the sun's fiti-ngge
14. Ma telu-ta'e bulan enon ndia.	And the path of the moon's telu-ta'e.
15. De fiti-ngge fiti-fiti	The fiti-ngge thrusts and thrusts
16. Ma telu-tae tati-tati.	And the telu-ta'e chops and chops.
17. De nggelo lesuk nai ndia	The neck breaks there
18. Ma ladi puk nai ndia.	And the thigh snaps there.

'recursion' and 'complementarity' could well be distinguished as analytically separate, though in dual symbolic classification it is precisely their conjunction that is significant. See Needham (1980) for an analytic schema in which 'duality' is itself a principle.

5 See Fox (1988). This volume contains 10 essays on different ritual languages in the region; each essay examines particular uses to which canonical parallelism is put.

19. Ndanak esa muli neu	One branch points west,
20. Boso musik ndanak ndia	Do not follow that branch
21. Te nitu hitu dalan ndia	For this is the road of seven spirits
22. Ma mula falu enon ndia	And this is the path of eight ghosts
23. De mate nituk nai ndia	The death of the spirits is there
24. Ma lalo mulak nai ndia.	And the decease of the ghosts is there.
25. Ndanak esa ki neu	One branch points north,
26. Boso musik ndanak ndia	Do not follow that branch
27. Te pila bii-late dalan ndia.	For this is the road of the red 'goat's grave' spider.
28. Ma modo bolau enon ndia.	And this is the path of the deadly green spider.
29. De peta-aok nai ndia	The swelling of the body is there
30. Ma hina-talek nai na.	And the festering wound is there.
31. Ndanak esa kona neu	One branch points south,
32. Boso musik ndanak ndia	Do not follow that branch
33. Te manufui tela dalan ndia	For this is the road of forest fowl
34. Ma kukuha na'u enon ndia.	And this is the path of four-talon grass bird.
35. De o leno kada telas dale	You only wander within the forest
36. Ma o pela kada na'u dale	And you only turn within the grass.
37. Te ndana esa lido-lido lain neu	But one branch goes forward to Heaven
38. Ma dape-dape ata neu.	And goes straight to the Heights.
39. Na musik ndanak ndia	Then take that branch
40. Te dala sodak nde ndia	For this is the road of wellbeing
41. Ma eno molek nde ndia	And this is the path of peace
42. Fo nini o mu losa kapa sula soda daen	To bring you to the buffalo-horn land of wellbeing
43. Ma mu nduku pa-dui molek oen.	And to the flesh and bone water of peace.
44. Dae sodak nai ndia	The land of wellbeing is there
45. Ma oe molek nai na	And the water of peace is there
46. Fo o hambu soda sio	For you will find the wellbeing of nine
47. Ma o hambu mole falu	And you will find the peace of eight
48. Ma dua lolo ei	And with legs outstretched
49. Ma kala ifa lima	And with arms cradled on the lap
50. Fo ifa limam no limam	Cradle your arms upon your arms
51. Ma lolo eim no eim.	And stretch your legs over your legs.

This composition shows the power of parallelism to create a cosmology, simply and effectively: the world-*waringin* as the tree of life with its branches as paths leading in different directions. The composition is seemingly traditional: the parallelism is impeccable, and standard formulae (as, for example, 'the buffalo-horn land of wellbeing/the flesh-and-bone water of life') are strictly maintained. Moreover, the cosmology created by the imagery of the composition accords with a common tree-of-life cosmology found throughout Indonesia. The fact is, however, that this cosmology does not conform to the standard cultural cosmology of the Rotenese, which, based on imagery of the island as a creature laid out lengthwise, assigns entirely different values to the directions, giving priority to the south and east over the north and west (see Fox 1973:356–8). The blind chanter 'Old Manoeain', who recited this composition for me, was one of the leading Protestant ministers on Rote and was renowned for his use of Rotenese ritual language in his sermons (see Fox 1983). His composition, as far as I can determine, is a personal attempt to create a kind of Christian cosmology. The essential point is that it offers an alternative cosmology—another possible world—using the same dualistic linguistic resources that are regularly used to express and uphold the standard cosmology.

The proper use of these linguistic resources requires a minimal knowledge of at least 1000 dyadic sets. This entails highly specific knowledge of which nouns, verbs, adjectives and prepositional forms may pair to form 'canonical' dyads. Thus, for example, one must know not just that 'north' (*ki*) may pair with 'south' (*kona*), but that *moi*, which functions as either an adjective or a verb meaning 'slick, smooth, to lick', forms a canonical pair with *keni*, 'shiny, glossy, to polish'; or that *nafi*, 'sea-cucumber', only forms a set with *sisik*, 'mollusc'; or that *delas*, the *dedap* tree (*Erythina spp.*) must be paired with *nitas*, the *kelumpang* tree (*Sterculia foetida*); or that *melu*, 'stomach-cramps', only pairs with *langu*, 'headache'; or that *nggio*, which describes the 'creaking or scraping' of tree branches, must be linked to *ke*, which refers to 'annoyance or teasing'; and so on through hundreds of specific dyadic sets.

This pervasive parallelism, however, is entirely neutral. It may contribute to and sustain a thoroughgoing and highly particularised dualistic perception of the symbolic world, but on its own it is insufficient to constitute the kind of ordered dyadic structures associated with dual organisations and dual cosmologies. A dual cosmology—as indeed any dual organisation—is characterised not by a simple pairing of elements but by the analogical concordance of elements within pairs according to some criterion of asymmetry. The rules of parallelism provide no such criterion. Hence dyadic sets are essentially neutral pairs: one element is not superior to another and either element may precede the other in expression. Extra-linguistic criteria are required to transform parallel elements into the elements of a dual organisation or cosmology.

Moreover, systems of canonical parallelism of the kind that are to be found throughout eastern Indonesia are an overly rich resource of dual categories. Most dual organisations rely on a relatively limited number of categories. Only a selection of categories, rather than all the resources of canonical parallelism, would suffice for this function. In short, the canonical parallelism of the ritual languages of eastern Indonesia may account for the elaborateness of dualistic structures in the region, but it cannot explain them. Thus, the argument must be extended further.

Recursive complementarity

Dutch anthropology has long insisted on the importance of complementary dualism to the understanding of societies in Indonesia and elsewhere (see de Josselin de Jong 1977). The complementary categories denoted in these studies are a familiar feature of what is often called two-column analysis—ordered lists of general categories arranged as complementary pairs:

right	left
day	night
sun	moon
east	west
red	black

The possibility of constructing such a table for almost any society and the occurrence of at least some common categories in all such tables limit the usefulness of this kind of analytic exercise. Two-column analysis hardly offers more than a beginning to an understanding of complementary dualism.

In eastern Indonesia the most important and recurrent complementary categories reflect a common Austronesian derivation and a historically shared inheritance of similar metaphors for living. These categories include a variety of directional and spatial coordinates such as north–south, east–west, inside–outside, back–front, right–left and upward–downward. Equally important are colour categories (white–black, red–gold–blue–green), categories for parts of the body (head–tail, or head–buttock), categories for persons and gender (elder–younger, male–female), botanical categories (unripe–ripe, trunk–tip, planted–harvested), and other categories for qualities (cool–hot, bland–bitter). Some of these categories are more than just symbolically associated: they are linguistically synonymous or even identical. Thus, left–right is, in some societies, synonymous with north–south. Similarly, botanical categories that provide the principal metaphors for growth and development may have colour or spatial connotations. The complementary colours green–gold may also be synonymous with the categories unripe–ripe, while the categories of trunk–tip imply a spatial–temporal notion of origin and extension.

7. Category and complement

The major point, however, is that this array of complementary categories represents a relatively small selection from the total resources of all possible canonical pairs furnished by the parallelism of ritual languages. The configuration of this select array of categories varies from one eastern Indonesian society to another, but in each society it constitutes what Needham has described as the set of 'primary factors' in that society's symbolic classification (Needham 1978:12–13). Moreover, and more importantly, these categories serve as the 'operators' of the symbolic system—that is, as organising elements for the classification of other categories and qualities. In this regard, what is significant is the *recursion* of these categories—the way in which they may be applied successively in various contexts and at many levels of signification.

The categories of male–female provide an excellent illustration of recursive complementarity. On Rote, these categories (*mane–feto*) may apply to persons as well as to certain kinds of trees and plants, to political offices, and, in Thie, to opposing moieties; they may also be applied within descent groups to distinguish client lineages, or between descent groups to indicate wife-givers and wife-takers. These categories may also be applied to different gifts exchanged by wife-givers and wife-takers. At yet another level these categories differentiate between the *sirih* or betel catkin, which is always masculine, and the *pinang* or areca nut, which is feminine—objects mutually offered by both sides in ceremonial exchange.

Forth, a recent ethnography on the domain of Rindi in east Sumba indicates how this recursion of male–female categories is extended even further in differentiating articles of bride-wealth given by wife-takers. To begin with, all bride-wealth objects (which consist of horses plus gold, silver, or tin chains and pendants) are classified as masculine in opposition to the dowry goods (textiles, beads and ivory bands) given by wife-givers. Internally, however, 'masculine' goods are distinguished as male and female: horses as a category are male, whereas metal valuables are female. At a further level, horses are distinguished as male and female and should be given as a pair consisting of a stallion and a mare. The metal valuables are also distinguished as male and female: chains are considered masculine and pendants female, and these categorically feminine pendants are still further distinguished according to their decoration as male or female. Similar distinctions can be applied to the 'feminine' goods given by the wife-givers: textiles must include men's cloths and women's skirts, and so on (Forth 1981:360–1).

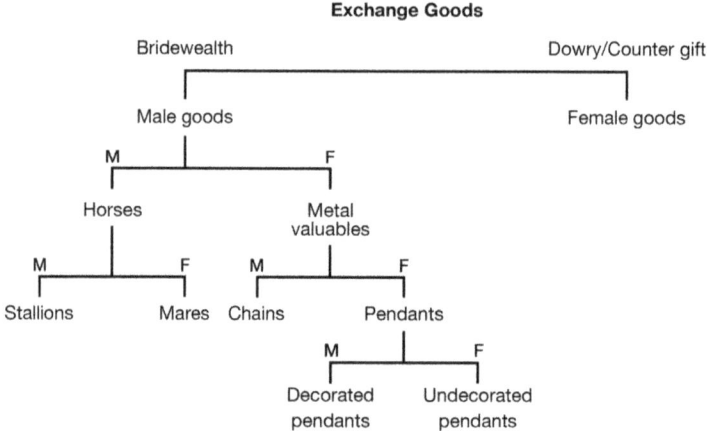

Figure 7.1: Male and Female Exchange Goods

By this principle of recursive complementarity, nothing is exclusively of one category; anything that is categorised according to one component of a complementary pair can *potentially* contain elements of its complement.[6] A great deal of the symbolic elaboration of dualistic structures in eastern Indonesia involves playing with this principle of recursive complementarity: male contains female, female contains male; inside contains outside, and outside, the inside; black, white, and white, black. Similarly, wife-givers are also wife-takers, and a group that is classified as elder to one group may be younger to another.

This principle should not be confused with hierarchy, since it is not wholly systematic and it rarely achieves great taxonomic depth. Other factors affect the application of this principle. Thus it is essential to know in any society in eastern Indonesia which sets of complementary categories apply. In Rote, for example, the categories male–female can be applied to distinguish the two unequal halves of the traditional house. Their application, in this case, is coincident with the categories outside–inside. On the basis of this coincidence, however, to apply male–female categories to the 'Spirits of the Outside' and the 'Spirits of the Inside' would produce a confusion of categories. In effect, no single set of recursive categories is applied systematically throughout the culture.

---

6   This feature of recursive complementarity is not unique to eastern Indonesia. It is the basic idea underlying the ancient Chinese concept of yin and yang. As Maureen MacKenzie has pointed out to me, Joseph Needham (1956:pl. 16) has reproduced a 'segregation table' of the *Book of Changes* deriving from the twelfth century that essentially parallels my diagram of exchange goods on Sumba. As Needham notes: 'Yin and Yang separate, but each contains half of its opposite in a "recessive" state, as is seen when the second division occurs. There is no logical end to the processes but here it is not followed beyond the stage of the 64 hexagrams.'

Categorical asymmetry

Another feature of those recursive complementary pairs that serve as 'operators' for the elaborate dual structures is their asymmetry. In this regard, parallelism is entirely neutral, always consisting of undifferentially paired semantic elements. In Rotenese ritual language, just as there are no criteria to distinguish the verb *ifa* ('to hold on the lap') as, for example, somehow marked in relation to its pair, *ko'o* ('to cradle in the arms or on the hip'), so too one cannot differentiate the directional *dulu* ('east') from its pair, *muli* ('west'). Yet, when east and west are used as recursive complements, east is definitely superior to west. On Rote, where the conflict between traditional and Christian cosmologies has, it seems, prompted a conscious need to justify the traditional, there exist a number of aphorisms that serve as symbolic syllogisms to give 'value' to the directional coordinates. Thus, for example, *Dulu nalu muli, te hu ledo neme dulu mai, de dulu ba'u lena muli*: 'East is as broad as the west, but the sun comes from the east, therefore the east is much greater than the west.' All of the other recursive complements that I have mentioned are similarly distinguished in an asymmetric fashion, although not all are as consciously justified: male is 'superior' to female, inside to outside, head to tail, red–gold to blue–green.

This categorical asymmetry is, in some ways, similar to markedness, but whereas markedness pertains to linguistic levels that are largely arbitrary and unconscious, this asymmetry of complementary categories occurs in socially constructed symbolic systems that can be consciously manipulated. Moreover, the category that is 'marked as superior' functions as the equivalent of the unmarked category. Thus, in those contexts where one component of a complementary pair is required to stand for the whole, it is the category marked as 'superior'. Hence 'male' may stand for the whole in regard to persons, 'inside' for the whole of various bound structures, or 'head' in certain contexts for overall authority or precedence. The very existence of such categorical asymmetry, however, creates the possibility of its inversion.

Category reversal

Category reversal refers to a change in the polarity of any set of complementary categories. This only occurs in special contexts when proper order is subverted and the 'world is turned upside down': outside becomes superior to inside, female to male, west to east, north to south, and so on, in terms of the standard dual asymmetries of the culture.[7]

In eastern Indonesia the contexts for inversion are considered 'extraordinary' even when they occur with annual regularity. On Savu, category reversal appears to be associated with the transition from one calendar year to the next;

---

7   This is similar to what is sometimes referred to in linguistics as 'markedness reversal'.

on Timor, reversal was crucial to headhunting, which invariably occurred in the dry season (McWilliam 1982); on Rote, minor reversals occur at all funerals, but major reversals are associated with the burial of those who have died a bad death (Fox 1973). More generally, however, some Rotenese characterise the whole period of Dutch dominance over the island as a time of partial inversion of the proper cosmic order. In the Rotenese cosmology, south (right), which is the direction of maximal spiritual power, is superior to north (left), which is the direction of sorcery and bad death. During the colonial period, however, the island was under the spell of the Dutch and the proper order was partially inverted. A symbolic syllogism recorded from the domain of Oepao at the turn of the century is reported as follows—*Ona ba'u i boe, te hu Komponi nai i, de i ba'u lena ona*: 'The South (Right) is as great as the North (Left), but the Company (i.e. the Dutch government) is in the North, therefore the North is greater than the South' (Jonker 1913:613). This period, which the Rotenese also describe as a time of native 'ignorance' and 'left-handedness', ended with the achievement of independence and the return of symbolic power to the south.

Analogical crossover

I use the term 'analogical crossover' to refer to another prominent feature of dual symbolic classification in eastern Indonesia. This feature is not an aspect of a single set of dual categories but rather pertains to the potential ordering of complex sets of such categories. It is specifically a property of historically developing systems in particular contexts.

Standard two-column analysis of complementary pairs consists in a simple analogical arrangement based upon the asymmetric valence accorded these categories. The result is an apparent concordance. As I have indicated, it is possible to change the valency of any or all of these categories. In eastern Indonesia this occurs periodically at 'special' intervals and I have termed this change in valency 'category reversal'. But it is also possible to retain standard valencies and instead change the analogical association between sets of complementary categories. It is this that I term 'analogical crossover'.

An illustration of this feature can be taken from the symbolic classification of the Atoni Pah Meto of Timor. As among the Rotenese, the categories male–female (*mone–feto*) form important recursive complements. In most relational contexts, male is superior to female. *Mone*, for example, is used to refer to the wife-giver and, in any local settlement, refers to the *Atoni Amaf*, the 'Father' or 'Father Atoni', who represents the founding lineage segment in the area. Those who have come after this founder and have become wife-takers are designated as *feto*. Similarly, the categories outside–inside form another important set of recursive complements; as a set, inside is considered superior to outside. Thus both inside and male are given a positive valency in relation to their mutual complements, outside and female. There is, however, a further factor that affects the analogical association of these pairs. Timorese folk etymology links the word for 'male' with a similar word meaning 'outside'. The combination of these categories leads to analogical crossover:

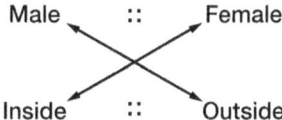

Figure 7.2: Analogical crossover

Male, which is superior in certain contexts, is associated with the outside, which is inferior; and female, which is a subordinate category, is associated with the inside, which is superior. The logic of these categories produces a tension that pervades the traditional classification system of the Atoni, expressing itself in an ideal model of four political units represented as four 'fathers' grouped around a female centre. Like a four-pillared Atoni *lopo*, these male figures 'support' a female centre but remain subordinate by their outside position.

Schulte Nordholt, who has described the Atoni political system at length (1971), has provided another example of this kind of analogical crossover in the various permutations of relationships among the four clans in Bikomi and Miomafo. In their affinal relations, Bana and Senak are male, while Atok and Lahe are female. By one ritual division, Lahe and Senak are inside and hence female, while Atok and Bana are male and outside; but by another internal division, Senak represents the immobile centre, which is female but superior to Lahe, who represents the active male outside (Schulte Nordholt 1980). A similar form of analogical crossover seems once to have formed the basis of the sacred hegemony of the 'matrilineal' Tetun, whose centre was at Wehale (Fox 1983).

The possibility of analogical crossover exists in all systems where a variety of complementary categories is applied to the same groups, persons or objects. The interplay of these categories in different contexts allows the creation of multiple alternative perspectives, or at least marks the contexts where alternative perspectives may apply.

None of the societies of eastern Indonesia appears to have perfectly concordant symbolic systems in which all groups or objects can be classified by categories that define them unequivocally in relation to other groups and objects. The discrepancies between different sets of complementary categories, extended too far for coherence sake, can only lead to evident contradictions. In eastern Indonesian societies, evident contradiction is often avoided by a continual process of mixing metaphors. Instead of allowing any set of complements to be extended to the point of contradiction, other complements are introduced to develop the system.

A brief contrast between Rote and Timor may help to illustrate this point. Rote shares with Timor the same complementary categories of male–female and outside–inside (though in the case of Rote, *mane*, 'male', is not linked explicitly to a word for 'outside'). Nevertheless, the same asymmetries and associations hold true for these categories, and the potential for analogical reversal of the kind that has become elaborated on Timor is evident in Rotenese symbolic classification. The two halves of the Rotenese house, for example, are classified as male–female and outside–inside, the male half being the outside half. On the other hand, in the political realm, the 'Male Lord' (*Manek*), who is the ruler of the domain, occupies the centre or inside and the subordinate 'Female Lord' is relegated to the outside. Among the Rotenese, the inconsistencies and potential contradictions in these realms are muted, but a further problem arises in the classification of spirits which are categorised as belonging to two groups: 'Spirits of the Outside' and 'Spirits of the Inside'. 'Inside' in this case is in reference to the house and, by analogy with other associations within the house, these spirits might conceivably be considered as 'female'. This, however, is not done. Instead, a series of other complementary categories (east–west, firstborn–lastborn) is commonly applied, and by various associations (inside = west = lastborn), the last-born male, who inherits the house, assumes the role of guardian of the 'Spirits of the Inside'.

The point I wish to make is that the possibilities for analogical crossover in these systems are innumerable, but the ones that are given cultural attention may be relatively limited. The Timorese, as well as the Tetun of Wehale, seem to have fashioned one analogical crossover into a mystery on which to found a potent political ideology (Fox 1983).

Conclusions

Before I venture some remarks on the relationship between dualism and hierarchy in eastern Indonesia, it is essential to make clear what is being discussed when these terms are invoked. Dualism, for example, is defined in the *Shorter Oxford English Dictionary* as a 'twofold division' or 'twofold condition'. Since this definition neither specifies the relations that may hold between dual entities nor makes precise the coherence that may pertain within a dyadic division, it does little to elucidate the complex classificatory phenomena that are generally referred to under the rubric of dualism, particularly in the ethnographic literature on eastern Indonesia. The same might be said of the use of the term 'hierarchy', which tends to be used to describe a variety of social phenomena.

Dumont, in his discussion of the Indian caste system, has attempted to give a more precise definition to the term 'hierarchy'. He defines hierarchy as 'the principle by which the elements of a whole are ranked in the relation to the whole', and he goes on to link this 'principle of hierarchy' to a single 'opposition between the pure and the impure' (1970:66). In turn, this opposition is analytically interpreted as a relation between 'that which encompasses and that which is encompassed' (1970:xii).

As useful as this definition of hierarchy may be, an attempt to apply it in eastern Indonesia is problematic for several reasons. The societies of eastern Indonesia do not have the encompassing religious coherence that Dumont has attributed to India; for this reason, hierarchy cannot be described as a single principle nor identified with a specific opposition, such as pure and impure. In eastern Indonesia there is a variety of contending oppositions that are of considerable importance to the definition of hierarchy and it is not one opposition but the interplay among various oppositions that gives rank to elements of a whole in relation to the whole.[8] In these terms, hierarchy is not a principle but an outcome, the result of the application of several principles. By the same token, it is equally problematic to base a conception of hierarchy solely on the analytic distinction between the encompassing and the encompassed. Apart from the fact that the logic of this distinction is, at times, elusive, this is not the only distinction by which 'hierarchy' can be generated.

It is possible, however, to derive another lead from Dumont. In a crucial passage in *Homo Hierarchicus*, Dumont refers to hierarchy as 'an order of precedence' (1970:75). Adapting this phrase for eastern Indonesia, we may consider hierarchy as consisting of various orders of precedence. The issue, then, is to examine the way in which these orders of precedence are categorically structured using prevalent dyadic resources.

The hierarchical use of dual categories depends upon the conjunction of two analytic features: recursive complementarity and categorical asymmetry. With these features, a single set of dual categories can serve as the operator to produce an ordered sequence or graded series. As an example, we may consider the set of dual relative age categories elder–younger, which in eastern Indonesia is generally relied on to define relationships between persons or among groups that are regarded as sharing some aspect of common descent (see Fox 1980:331). Thus, among the Rotenese, Timorese or Tetun, these same-sex categories can be used to distinguish a graded series of status segments within a clan, lineage or birth group. Since a segment in the younger category may be elder to another segment, this series may be represented as follows:

---

8 I take as fundamental Dumont's assertion that judgment must be made in terms of the 'whole', but it is pertinent to note that a 'whole' organised by various interacting principles appears differently to that of a 'whole' organised by a single principle.

```
elder    >    younger
             elder    >    younger
                          elder    >    younger
```

A similar series based on male–female may be used, as among the Timorese, to define an order of precedence between wife-givers and wife-takers:

```
male    >    female
             male    >    female
                          male    >    female
```

In eastern Indonesia the complementary categories used to create ordered series are the same categories that serve as operators for the system as a whole. Besides elder–younger or male–female, such categories as wife-giver–wife-taker, left–right, inside–outside or trunk–tip are particularly prominent. In a remarkable analysis of the ceremonial domain, Wai Brama, of the Ata Tana Ai of central east Flores, E. Douglas Lewis (1982a) has shown how a single line of precedence based on 'origin from the source' constitutes the means for a coherent ordering of all clans and segments of the domain.[9] In a somewhat different context, a single royal descent line serves as the ultimate line of precedence for the hierarchical ordering of lineages and clans in the domain of Termanu on Rote. In this case, however, the ordered series is not structured by a common set of complementary categories but by a precise and rigidly maintained succession of ancestral dyadic names, each of which—after the first name—utilises a component of the preceding name (Fox 1971:42–7).

This leads to the final point I wish to make in this essay. Dualism is a prevalent conceptual resource in eastern Indonesia and as such it may be used either as a major vehicle for the structuring of hierarchy or as a counter to it. In another essay (Fox 1979), I have examined in detail the political and economic differences between the hierarchical structure of the domain of Termanu and the moiety structure of the domain of Thie. In analysing these two domains on Rote, it would be impossible to claim that there was more use of dualism in one domain than in the other. Both domains give evidence of elaborate forms of dualism. In Termanu, however, dual categories are utilised socially to form lines of precedence that foster status rivalry, extend alliance relations, and perpetrate patterns of relative dependence. In contrast, in Thie the primary conceptualisation of the domain is a dichotomy into moieties that are associated as male–female. Thus, for Thie, dualism occurs at the highest order of social

---

9   Lewis's 1982 ANU PhD thesis (now published as People of the Source, 1988b) has a superb discussion of the Ata Tana Ai concept of precedence. I wish to acknowledge my debt to this illuminating discussion that has prompted me to see a variety of ways in which the notion of precedence occurs in the societies of eastern Indonesia. It should be noted, however, that a similar notion of precedence is implied in John Gordon's examination of the 'marriage nexus' among the Manggarai of west Flores (1980:65–7).

classification and, though qualified by other dyadic divisions, this primary dualism has systemic implications for the whole of the domain's system of classification. Any tendency to form lines of precedence always confronts a primary duality that undermines it. As a result, in Thie a systemic dualism serves as a counter to hierarchy.

We may therefore conclude with the observation that it is not dualism per se that defines societies with so-called dual organisation but rather the use of dualism at a general, systemic level, which thus determines the parameters for other forms of classification.

8. Exploring oral formulaic language[1]

Introduction

The study of the use of formulaic language in oral epic poetry—research begun by Milman Parry (1930) and continued by Alfred Lord (1960)—has prompted extensive investigations across a wide spectrum of languages (see Foley 1985). With the enormous proliferation of this research, many different research directions have emerged. For some literary scholars, formulaic language has been used as evidence to argue for an oral tradition underlying the production of ancient literary texts; for others, dealing with living poetic traditions, formulaic language has been seen as a means of sustaining coherent performance, allowing poets considerable oral fluency and a capacity for substantial recall.

As Alan Rumsey (2001) noted in an important recent paper, Parry's original definition of a formula was 'a group of words which is regularly employed under the same metrical conditions to express a given essential idea' (Parry 1930:80). This definition fits only certain forms of oral poetry. The variety of the world's oral poetry defies such simple summary. Not all oral poetry operates under strict 'metrical conditions', but may be subject to other compositional constraints. Hence, as research on 'oral formulaic language' has increased, the definition of what is 'formulaic' has become elusive and needs to be set forth carefully for particular traditions of oral composition. More generally, there is the question as to what precisely is formulaic for a particular poet, or for a particular speech community, or across related speech communities. In this brief chapter, I would like to consider some of these issues by way of illustration.

Since 1965, I have been recording oral poets, known as *manahelo* ('those who chant'), from the island of Rote in eastern Indonesia. These recordings have resulted in a substantial corpus of ritual texts. The island of Rote was once divided into 18 small domains, each of which claimed to be socially and culturally distinctive. Reflecting this social divergence, the language of the island consists of a chain of dialects whose ends are not mutually intelligible. To date, I have recorded mainly

---

[1] This paper was originally written for inclusion in a Festschrift for Andrew Pawley, a colleague and friend. It appeared in the volume edited by John Bowden and Nikolas P. Himmelman entitled *A Journey through Austronesian and Papuan Linguistics and Cultural Space* (Canberra: Pacific Linguistics, 2010, pp. 573–87). My original introduction began with a tribute to Andrew Pawley. I have omitted that peroration to be able to accommodate this paper more appropriately in this volume. Here, however, I wish to reiterate my respect for Pawley's work as a linguist and to thank him for his longstanding commitment to comparative Austronesian research and his support of our mutual friendship.

in the dialect of the central domain of Termanu and the south-western dialect of the domain of Thie, though I am now engaged in recording from dialects across the entire island.

The corpus of the texts I have gathered deals with the origins of the cultural artefacts of the Rotenese: of fire and of cooking, of rice and millet, of the house and its designs, of bride-wealth including water buffalo, and of the tools for building, for weaving, for dyeing and for spinning. The corpus also includes a large number of mortuary chants as well as prayers, sermons and parts of a local Christian liturgy, which is composed in a traditional mode. Over several decades, I have published a considerable number of papers on individual texts, but I have never published comparisons among these compositions. It is only by way of such comparisons that one can appreciate the formulaic aspects of this oral poetry.

In 1965, I began recording a particular chant (*bini*) known as *Suti Solo do Bina Bane*. Over time, I have recorded this chant from numerous oral poets, particularly in the domain of Termanu, where I have done much of my research. Besides recording in the dialect of Termanu, I have recorded this chant in other dialects. I have also been particularly interested in recording the same poet reciting the same chant at different stages in his career. As a consequence, my collection of *Suti Solo do Bina Bane* texts is itself substantial and continues to grow with each new recording session.

In this chapter, I wish to compare the use of oral formulaic language by five different poets, each reciting what can be regarded as the same passage in the chant *Suti Solo do Bina Bane*. For one of these poets, I provide recitations of this passage at an interval of several years to illustrate continuity in personal composition. Four of these poets come from the domain of Termanu; one comes from the domain of Ringgou, whose dialect is substantially different from that of Termanu. This offers an illustration of the use of oral formulaic language across different speech communities.

Suti Solo do Bina Bane as an oral composition

Suti Solo do Bina Bane recounts the journey of two shells cast ashore by the sea. These shells, whose dual name is Suti Solo//Bina Bane, are taken up in the scoop-nets of women fishing along the coast. Once on land, these shells repeatedly voice their feelings of displacement and appeal for permanent companionship. In response, the women urge the shells to shift from one symbolic location to another. They are told, for example, to find their place with the 'Syrup Vat and the Rice Basket', then with the 'Millet's Grain and Ears of Maize', then with the 'Tree's Shade and Lontar's Shadow' or with the 'Forest Cuckoo and River

Watercock'. As each of these sites is vulnerable to change and can only be a temporary resting place, the shells continue to plead for permanence. Their metaphoric journey is a quest for an enduring place of rest.

Originally this chant was recited to reveal and recount the origins of two different kinds of shell: the one used for holding dyes (*suti*) and the other used as the base for the spinning whorl (*bina*). As these rituals for dyeing and weaving have ceased to be performed, however, the chant has been transformed into a mortuary chant for 'orphans and widows'—a category that can be applied to all human beings in conditions of dependency (see Fox 1988). Depending on the intention of the poet, the chant can be given various endings. In Termanu, the shells either are fashioned into implements or return to the sea.

All origin chants may once have formed part of a single narrative structure that recounted relations between the Sun and Moon and the Lords of the Ocean and Sea. Key passages in most versions of *Suti Solo do Bina Bane* that I have recorded betray the connections to this larger epic structure by alluding to events in the realm of the sea that caused the shells to be cast forth on land.

The excerpts that I have selected from each of the poet's compositions vary in length from 13 to 19 lines. Each composition consists of a dialogue between the shells and the women who scooped them up from the sea. The women urge Suti Solo//Bina Bane to find a place with the Rice Basket and Syrup Vat. The pair replies that they will do so, but they worry that when the Rice Basket and Syrup Vat are emptied, they will no longer have a place to remain.

Here, it is important to note that the women who are named in this dialogue as well as the two shells are each conceived of as single dual-named beings. The third-person singular is more generally used than any plural, but third-person plural forms can and do occur in these compositions. Before presenting these various compositions, it is essential to note the conventions of canonical parallelism that apply to them and the research tradition that has developed in the study of this form of poetic composition.

Canonical parallelism in relation to an oral formula

All compositions in Rotenese poetry (or 'ritual language', as I have termed these poetic compositions in many of my publications) are characterised by a strict lexical pairing. Apart from a small number of unpaired forms—pronouns, connectives, 'prepositional' and a few other invariant elements—all lexical terms have at least one pair. Thus, in formal terminology, each semantic element must form part of a 'dyadic set'. In composition, dyadic sets produce parallel lines whose overwhelmingly most common poetic form is the couplet, though other serial arrangements of lines are entirely acceptable and are often considered as evidence of a greater mastery of the language. The elements that compose any particular dyadic set should, in their parallel lines (or occasionally in the two halves of a single line), correspond exactly in position and as far as possible in morphological structure.

The canonical parallelism that occurs in Rotenese is a pervasive feature of much of the world's oral literature. The linguist Roman Jakobson, who contributed greatly to the study of parallelism, described the study of parallelism as opening 'the double door linking the fields of linguistics and anthropology'.

In Jakobson's terminology, the required lexical pairing of semantic elements and the network of associations that underlies this pairing represent a canonical ordering of the paradigmatic or 'metaphoric pole' of language (Jakobson and Halle 1956:76–82). Rotenese ritual language is also remarkably well ordered along the syntagmatic or what Jakobson called the 'metonymic pole' of language. Phrases and lines in these oral compositions are frequently composed of recognisable formulae that, because of the strict requirements of parallelism, become redoubled in parallel formulae. Thus, a considerable portion of Rotenese ritual language consists of couplets and even longer sequences that are formulaic in a paradigmatic and a syntagmatic sense.

Within a large corpus of textual materials, the importance of these formulae becomes increasingly evident. While retaining the required pairing of words, poets add individual grammatical embellishments to distinguish their usage from that of other poets. Individual poets thus develop their own personal 'style' in relation to certain 'standard' forms of their dialect area. The interaction of the formulaic features of ritual language with the rules of parallel composition creates further complexity. One question to be addressed is how these formulae and the pairs underlying them vary among the speech communities of different dialect areas, especially since a high proportion of synonymous dyadic sets are composed of a word from the local dialect and that of some neighbouring dialect.

Suti Solo do Bina Bane: The first poet, Stefanus Adulanu

This first excerpt—the Syrup Vat and Rice Basket sequence—consists of 19 lines from a poem of 297 lines. I recorded this poem from one of the senior poets of the domain of Termanu, Stefanus Adulanu, in 1966. Adulanu was the head of the Meno clan. He was known as 'Old Meno' and held the ritual position of

Head of the Earth (*Dae Langak*). His version of *Suti Solo do Bina Bane* is perhaps the finest and certainly the most extended version of this poem that I have gathered in Termanu.

Apart from personal names (Pedu Hange//Nggeti Seti), which themselves form sets, the poem is composed of 10 dyadic sets: 1) *kokolak//dede'ak* ('to speak'//'to talk'); 2) *inak//fetok* ('woman'//'girl'); 3) *eki//hika* ('to scream'//'to laugh'); 4) *setele//mata-dale* ('shrieking'/'gaily'); 5) *tua bou//neka hade* ('syrup vat'//'rice basket'); 6) *malole//mandak* ('good'//'proper'); 7) *bou//soka* ('vat'//'sack'); 8) *(lama-)kako//(lama-)lua* ('to overflow'//'to run over'); 9) *fude//bafa* ('froth'//'mouth'); 10) *totono//lulunu* (partially reduplicated form of *tono//lunu*) ('to overturn'//'to roll up').

Of interest is the compound set *tua bou//neka hade* ('syrup vat'//'rice basket'). The components of this compound can and do occur on their own in other sets. Here, however, they appear to form a 'personified' set. In a literary sense, they suggest a 'living entity', who can serve as a potential partner of the shells. (Hence, in my translation of the poems, I have capitalised them to suggest their implied personhood.)

Passage: Poem I

'Na Bina au o se	'Then I, Bina, with whom will I be
Ma Suti au o se	And I, Suti, with whom will I be
Fo au kokolak o se	With whom will I talk
Ma au dede'ak o se?'	And with whom will I speak?'
Boe ma inak-ka Nggeti Seti	The woman Nggeti Seti
Ma fetok-ka Pedu Hange nae:	And the girl Pedu Hange says:
'Te eki setele henin	'[If] they scream with a shriek at losing you
Ma hika mata-dale henin na,	And laugh gaily at losing you,
Suti mo Tua Bou	Then Suti, go with Syrup Vat
Ma Bina mo Neka Hade.'	And Bina, go with the Rice Basket.'
Boe ma nae:	Then he says:
'Oo malole-la so	'Oh, these things are good
Ma mandak-kala so.	And these things are proper.
Te leo bou lama-kako fude	But if the vats overflow with froth
Ma soka lama-lua bafa	And the sacks run over at the mouth
Fo bou lo totonon	So that the vats must be overturned
Ma soka no lulunun,	And the sacks must be rolled up,
Na Suti au o se	Then I, Suti, with whom will I be
Ma Bina au o se?'	And I, Bina, with whom will I be?'

This excerpt provides a basis on which to begin the consideration of a succession of other versions of this same passage composed by different oral poets.

Suti Solo do Bina Bane: The second poet, Eli Pellondou

This second excerpt consists of 23 lines from a chant of 210 lines. I recorded it from the poet Eli Pelondou, who was more commonly known by the nickname Seu Ba'i. He was a proud, soft-spoken man of clan Dou Danga and was particularly close to 'Old Meno', Stefanus Adulanu. I first met him on a visit to Old Meno's home in Ola Lain and it appeared to me that he had informally apprenticed himself to the old man. His version of *Suti Solo do Bina Bane* reflects, I believe, this influence.

This excerpt relies on six of the 10 dyadic sets used in Old Meno's composition: 1) *kokolak*//*dede'ak*; 2) *toa bou*//*neka hade*; 3) *malole*//*mandak*; 4) *lulunu*//*totono*; 5) *(lama-)kako*//*(lama-)lua*; 6) *bafa*//*fude*; as well as two other dyadic sets not used in the Meno version: 7) *(nama-)tani*//*(nasa-)kedu* ('to cry'//'to sob'); and 8) *sama*//*deta* ('like'//'as').

In this passage, Seu Ba'i recites one line for which he fails to provide a complement. Were this line to exist, the appropriate complement for the verb *(masa-)lai* ('to rest, lie down') would have been *(manga-)tu* ('to sit').

Pedu Hange//Nggeti Seti is the name of the woman who scoops up the shells. As is clear in the context of the longer poem, she is the speaker in this passage who tells Suti Solo//Bina Bane to 'Go with the Syrup Vat//Go with the Rice Basket'. The woman Lole Holu//Lua Bafa is referred to as the ideal partner, whom Suti Solo//Bina Bane longs to find.

Given that dyadic sets can be treated either as singulars or as plurals, in any single poem, poets can move back and forth from singular to plural. In general, however, they tend to use singular verbs for dual chant characters. For the most part, Pedu Hange//Nggiti Seti or Suti Solo//Bina Bane are treated as single (singular) figures.

Passage: Poem II

Boe te Suti neu nama-tani	But Suti begins to cry
Ma Bina neu nasa-kedu,	And Bina begins to sob,
Nasa-kedu Lole Holu	Sobs for Lole Holu
Ma nama-tani Lua Bafa.	And cries for Lua Bafa.
Boe te ana dede'ak no Suti	So she speaks with Suti

Ma ana kokolak no Bina, lae:	And she talks with Bina, saying:
'Mo tua bou	'Go with the Syrup Vat
Ma mo neka hade	And go with the Rice Basket
Fo masa-lai tua bou.	That you may rest in the Syrup Vat.
[Line missing]	[And that you may sit in the Rice Basket.]'
Boe te Bina neu kokolak	But Bina begins to talk
Ma Suti neu dede'ak, nae:	And Suti begins to speak, saying:
'Au u o tua bou	'I will go with the Syrup Vat
Ma au [u] o neka hade.	And I will go with the Rice Basket.
De malole ndia so	This is good
Do mandak ndia so.	Or this is proper.
Te neka lamakako bafa	But if the baskets overflow at the mouth
Fo soka lo lulunun	So that the sacks must be rolled up
Ma tua lamalua fude	And the syrup runs over with froth
Fo bou lo totonon,	So that the vats must be overturned,
Au dede'ak o se	With whom can I speak
Ma au kokolak o se?	And with whom can I talk?
Sama leo Lua Bafa	Just as with Lua Bafa
Ma deta leo Lole Holu?'	And exactly as with Lole Holu?'

It is particularly interesting to note that despite the fact that Seu Ba'i's passage relies on many of the same dyadic sets as Old Meno's passage, only two lines in these passages are the same. It is instructive to compare the way in which each poet expresses what might be considered the same 'formulaic' lines.

Old Meno gives the following two lines:

'Oo malole-la so	'Oh, these things are good
Ma mandak-kala so.'	And these things are proper.'

Seu Ba'i, on the other hand, renders this same formula as follows:

De malole ndia so'	'This is good
Do mandak ndia so.'	Or this is proper.'

Old Meno then goes on to recite the following lines:

'Te leo bou lamakako fude	'But if the vat overflows with froth
Ma soka lamalua bafa	And the sack runs over at the mouth
Fo bou lo totonon	So that the vat must be overturned
Ma soka no lulunun...'	And the sack must be rolled up...'

In the last two of these four lines, Old Meno does what expert poets do frequently (to the maddening frustration of the translator): he creates a kind of contrastive dyadic set by coupling a plural form (*lo*) with a singular form (*no*).

Seu Ba'i renders these lines in a slightly different fashion. Where vat//sack (*bou*//*soka*) form a set in relation to the verbs (*lama-kako*//*lama-lua*) in Old Meno's composition, Seu Ba'i uses the set basket//syrup (*neka*//*tua*) with these verbs. He does, however, maintain a plural agreement throughout.

'*Te neka lama-kako bafa*	'But if the basket overflows at the mouth
Fo soka lo lulunun	So that the sack must be rolled up
Ma tua lama-lua fude	And the syrup runs over with froth
Fo bou lo totonon...'	So that the vat must be overturned...'

Technically, *soka lo lulunun*//*bou lo totonon* are the only lines that both poets share, yet even this seemingly shared similarity has been altered by Old Meno's use of a singular and a plural form.

Suti Solo do Bina Bane: The third poet, Mikael Pellondou

In 1985, on a brief trip to Rote, I was told of the death of Seu Ba'i. Among the group who came to tell me of his death was a clan cousin of his from Dou Danga, Mikael Pellondou. As far as I have been able to determine, the two men had the same great-grandfather. They had lived in close proximity to one another and referred to each other as 'elder' and 'younger'. On hearing of Seu Ba'i's death, I expressed my sadness and praised him for his abilities as a master poet. In response, others in the group quickly informed me that Mikael was also an able poet, and to demonstrate his ability, Mikael agreed to record for me his version of *Suti Solo do Bina Bane*. This passage is taken from that version.

This is an excerpt of 15 lines from a composition that runs to only 101 lines. Although shorter than the two previous excerpts, it contains many of the same sets. Mikael Pellondou uses: 1) *kokolak*//*dede'ak*; 2) *inak*//*fetok*; 3) *toa bou*//*neka hade*; and 4) *fude*//*bafo*; but instead of (*lama-*) *kako*//(*lama-*) *lua*, he uses: 5) (*lama-*)*kako*//(*lama-*)*solo*, which has much the same meaning. The only new set is a commonly used set: 6) (*na-*)*tane*//(*na-*)*nosi* ('to ask'//'to request'). Also in Mikael's composition, the name Pedu Hange//Nggeti Seti is given as Pedu Hange//Suti Seti. Although this seems only a minor difference, it is over the names of chant characters that poets have their greatest arguments.

Passage: Poem III

Boe te na-tane ma na-nosi.	But he still asks and requests.
'*Bina dede'ak no se*	'With whom will Bina speak
Ma Suti kokolak no se?'	And with whom will Suti talk?'

Boe te inak leo Pedu Hange	So the woman like Pedu Hange
Ma fetok leo Suti Seti, nae:	And the girl like Suti Seti, says:
'Dede'ak mo neka hade	'Speak with the Rice Basket
Ma kokolak mo tua bou.'	And talk with the Syrup Vat.'
Boe te Suti na-tane	But Suti asks
Ma Bina na-nosi, de nae:	And Bina requests, saying:
'Au dede'ak o tua bou	'I speak with the Syrup Vat
Ma au kokolak o neka hade	And I talk with the Rice Basket
Te neka lama-kako bafo,	But if the basket overflows at the mouth,
Na au dede'ak o se	Then with whom will I speak
Ma tua lama-solo fude,	And if the syrup runs over with froth,
Na au kokolak o se?'	Then with whom will I speak?'

Suti Solo do Bina Bane: The fourth poet, Petrus (Pe'u) Malesi

Of all the poets of Termanu, Pe'u Malesi was the one from whom I recorded the most material. He was a frequent visitor to my home at Ufa Len and probably the most willing of all poets in Termanu to seek to have his compositions recorded.[2]

Like Seu Ba'i, Malesi was a member of clan Dou Danga, but the two men were rivals. Seu Ba'i, in particular, would challenge Malesi's knowledge of the names of chant characters and, in fact, as is evident in Malesi's telling of *Suti Solo do Bina Bane*, the names of the key women who scoop the shells from the sea are entirely different.

Due to the closeness of our relationship, I had the opportunity to record various versions of *Suti Solo do Bina Bane* as recited by Malesi. Here, I include two such versions, one recorded in 1973 and the other in 1977. These short excerpts, which are remarkably similar, can be compared with one another and with the excerpts of the other poets of Termanu, Old Meno and Seu Ba'i.

Malesi's first version of the Syrup Vat and Rice Basket passage consists of only 14 lines from a composition of 222 lines.

One immediately obvious difference in Malesi's version is the name of the woman chant character who carries on the dialogue with Suti Solo//Bina Bane. In place of Pedu Hange//Nggeti Seti, Malesi names this woman Sama Dai//Kuku Nou. Another notable difference is that Malesi reverses the order of the

---

[2] Malesi is the 'poet' in the film *The Water of Words* (Fox et al. 1983) and appears as well in the film *Spear and Sword* (Fox et al. 1988).

compound phrase *Tua Bou ma Neka Hade*. He recites this as *Bou Tua ma Neka Hade*. In terms of the ordering of dyadic sets, this would seem to be a preferable order: *bou* (vat) thus forms a set with *neka* (basket) and *tua* (lontar syrup) with *hade* (rice). Whereas this would appear to make logical sense and would not be rejected in performance, Malesi may in fact be tampering with an established idiom. The evidence for this is the final passage I quote from the poet Ande Ruy, from the relatively distant dialect region of Ringgou. Ande Ruy uses both forms—that used by Old Meno and Seu Ba'i and the form used by Malesi.

Malesi's passage shares several common dyadic sets with the versions by Old Meno or Seu Ba'i: 1) *inak//fetok*; 2) *kokolak//dedea'ak*; 3) *malole//mandak*; 4) *tono//lunu*. He also uses the dyadic set: 5) *(anga-)tu//(asa-)lai* ('sit'//'lie down'), a set that Seu Ba'i left incomplete in his composition. Malesi also uses another common set: 6) *lole halan//selu dasin*, which is a frequently used expression meaning 'to speak, to reply', and embellishes this with the set *lele//doko-doe* ('encouragingly'//'coaxingly').

Passage: Poem IV

Inak kia Sama Dai	The woman Sama Dai
Ma fetok kia Kuku Nou	And the girl Kuku Nou
Ana lole lele halan	She lifts her words encouragingly
Ma selu doko-doe dasin, nae:	And raises her voice coaxingly, saying:
'Mu no bou tua	'Go with the Syrup Vat
Ma mu mo neka hade.'	And go with the Rice Basket.'
Bina Bane kokolak	Bina Bane speaks
Ma Suti Solo dede'ak ma nae:	And Suti Solo replies and says:
'Malole la so	'That would be good
Ma mandak kala so.	And that would be proper.
Bou tua na tono	[But if] the Syrup Vat is overturned
Ma neka hade lulunu	And the Rice Basket is rolled up
Na au asa-lai o se	Then with whom will I rest
Ma au anga-tu o se?'	And with whom will I sit?'

This next excerpt, which consists of 16 lines, was recorded in 1977—roughly four years after the earlier passage—but is remarkably similar to that passage. There are only a few differences. For example, the set *lele//doko-doe* is not used with *lole halan//selu dasin* and instead of the *tono//lunu* set, Malesi uses another set with a similar sense: *heok//keko* ('to turn'//'to shift'). He concludes with a refrain that uses the set *(nama-)tani//(nasa-)kedu* ('to cry'//'to sob'), which was used by Seu Ba'i in his composition. Malesi also pairs another verb for speaking, *na-fada*, with the term *kokolak*, which normally forms a set with *dede'ak*. In performance terms, this would be considered acceptable but nonetheless a flaw in composition.

8. Exploring oral formulaic language

Figure 8.1: The poet, Eli Pellondou, known as Seu Ba'i, prepares to recite by first partaking of the 'water of words'

Explorations in Semantic Parallelism

Passage: Poem V

Boe ma inaka Kuku No'u	So the woman Kuku No'u
Ma fetoka Sama Dai	And the girl Sama Dai
Lole halana neu	Raises her voice
Ma selu dasi na neu ma nae:	And lifts her speech and says:
'Meu mo neka hade	'Go with the Rice Basket
Ma meu mo bou tuana.'	And go with the Syrup Vat.'
Boe ma Suti Solo nafada	Then Suti Solo talks
Ma Bina Bane kokolak ma nae:	And Bina Bane speaks and says:
'Ah, malole la so	'Ah, that would be good
Ma mandakala so.	And that would be proper.
[Te] bou tua la heok	But if the Syrup Vats turn
Ma neka hade la keko	And if the Rice Baskets shift
Na au asalai o se	Then with whom shall I rest
Ma au angatu'u o se?'	And with whom shall I sit?'
Suti bei nama-tani,	Suti continues to cry,
Ma Bina bei nasa-kedu.	Bina continues to sob.

In short, all of the sets in this particular passage can be considered to form part of a shared linguistic heritage with speakers of the Termanu dialect.

Suti Solo do Bina Bane: The fifth poet, Ande Ruy from Ringgou

The final example in this series consists of a passage of 20 lines from a composition of 184 lines by the poet Ande Ruy from the eastern Rotenese domain of Ringgou, which has its own distinct dialect of Rotenese—a dialect that is different from that of Termanu but close enough to be intelligible. Some of the sound changes evident in this passage are:

Termanu		Ringgou
ng	>	k
medial k	>	—
l/nd	>	r

Despite these differences, it is possible to recognise the shared inheritance of common dyadic sets. Ruy uses five sets that also occur in the passages of the poets from Termanu. These sets are: 1) *inak//fetok*; 2) *lole hara//selu dasi*; 3) *dasi//hala*; 4) *nea hade//bou tua* or *nea hade//tua bou*; and 5) *hade//tua*. Ruy also uses a number of other sets that are common in the speech community of Termanu: 6) *fai//ledo* ('day'//'sun'); 7) *na//ria* ('there'//'at that place'); 8) *iku//leo* ('land'//'clan'); 9) *rui//sau* ('to scoop'//'scrape'); 10) *tama//tesa* ('to be together'//'to be one'); 11) *te'i//dale* ('stomach'//'inside'). Although I have not recorded the set *sasau//kokola* (the reduplicated form of the verbs *sau//kola*), it would appear to be an acceptable variant of the more commonly used set *ndui//sau* in Termanu (or *rui//sau*, as it occurs in this excerpt). It also is worth noting that the compound form *tesa te'i//tama dale* (literally, 'stomachs as one'//'hearts together'), as used by Ruy, is not an expression that I have recorded in Termanu. Although not common in Termanu, however, it was immediately recognisable by Termanu speakers who heard Ruy, and was considered poetically attractive.

Passage: Poem VI

Boe ma ina Oli Masi	Then the woman Oli Masi
Ma feto a Bisa Oli	And the girl Bisa Oli
Nadasi neu Suti Solo	Spoke to Suti Solo
Ma nahara neu Bina Bane:	And said to Bina Bane:
'Iku fo mo nea hade ma	'Your place is with the Rice Basket
Ma leo fo mo bou tua.'	And your clan is with the Syrup Vat.'
Tehu Suti Solo lole haran	But Suti Solo raised his words
Ma Bina Bane selu dasin:	And Bina Bane lifted his words:
'Ami iku fo mo nea hade	'Our place is with the Rice Basket
Ma ami leo fo mo tua bou, tebe!	And our clan is with the Syrup Vat, indeed!
Tehu fai esa nai na	But on some day
Ma ledo esa nai ria,	And at some time,
Nea sasau hade,	They continually scrape out rice,
Sau heni nea hade	They will scrape the Rice Basket clean
Ma rui kokola tuan	And they continually scoop syrup
Rui heni bou tua.	They will scoop the Syrup Vat clean.
Na ami iku fo mo be a	Then with whom will our place be
Ma ami leo fo mo be a?	And with whom will our clan be?
Te [bei] ta tesa tei	This does not make us one
Ma bei ta tama dale.'	And not yet join us together.'

The dyadic resources of the five poets

Table 8.1 lists all the dyadic sets used by the five poets. The excerpts from the poets of Termanu are similar enough in composition to share many sets together; Ruy's composition introduces seven sets not used by the Termanu poets. All of these sets are, however, of common occurrence in Termanu. If a larger comparison were made, the seeming differences in Ruy's composition—at least in the use of these particular sets—would diminish, if not disappear.

Table 8.1 Dyadic Sets Used in all Poems

	Dyadic sets	I	II	III	IV	V	VI
1	kokola//dede'ak	x	x	x	x	x	
2	ina//feto	x	x	x	x	x	x
3	eki//hika	x					
4	setele//mata-dale	x					
5	tua bou//neka hade	x	x	x			x
6	bou tua//neka hade				x	x	x
7	malole//manda	x	x	x	x	x	
8	bou//soka	x	x				
9	lama-kako//lama-lua	x	x				
10	lama-kako//lama-solo			x			
11	fude//bafa (bafo)	x	x				
12	totono//lulunu	x	x				
13	sama//deta		x				
14	nama-tani//nama-kesu		x				
15	nama-tani//na-nosi			x			
16	lole-lele//doko-doe				x		
17	hala//dasi				x	x	x
18	nasa-lai//na-tu		(x)		x	x	x
19	lole//selu					x	x
20	na-fada//kokolak					x	
21	heo//keko					x	x
22	fai//ledo						x
23	ria//na						x
24	iku//leo						x
25	lui//sau						x
26	sau//kola						x
27	tesa//tama						x
28	te'i//dale						x

In earlier publications, I have argued that Rotenese ritual language surmounts dialect differences and is broadly intelligible across the entire island of Rote. One way in which this is done is by the use of variant dialect terms to form synonymous sets. Certainly, the comparison of this passage from Ruy with the excerpts by other poets from Termanu would appear to support this argument. While accurate in showing similarities between these speech communities, however, Ruy's excerpted passage is too short to illustrate some of the differences that do indeed occur. Providing a more precise indication of the differences in ritual language across dialect boundaries involves work that is currently in progress to record a reasonably large corpus of materials from these different dialects.

Conclusion

In his pioneering study, Parry was able to identify a particular 'technique of oral verse-making'. His initial research has given rise, as Pawley has noted, to a distinct but particularly important research tradition. In this tradition, 'formulas may show special word order, enabling a word sequence to be adapted to the metrical requirements of a half line of verse' (Pawley 2007:6). This kind of formula is, as Pawley has recognised, a 'substitution system'. He defines this substitution system as 'a group of formulas which show lexical substitutions expressing the same basic structure and idea, or which express the same basic idea with a varying number of syllables, enabling the poet to meet a range of different metric conditions' (Pawley 2007:6).

Strict canonical parallelism offers techniques of oral composition different from those based on regular metrical strictures. These techniques, strictly speaking, do not involve substitution as in Parry's epic tradition nor are they constrained by metric requirements. Instead, any line of verse calls forth its complement. All lexical elements in one line should pair with partner elements in a complementary line. Such compositions are ideally suited for chorus performance, in which a poet annunciates an initial line and the complementary line is provided by collective response—a mode of ritual performance that was once common on Rote, as elsewhere in eastern Indonesia. To be effective, the knowledge of paired terms—what I call dyadic sets—must be shared widely within a speech community.

This chapter provides an illustration of just how widely these dyadic sets are shared, not just among poets within a particular speech community but also across different speech communities. This illustration gives a sense of the stability and continuity of this ritual language as a distinctive cultural heritage among the Rotenese—and its potential effectiveness in maintaining continuing oral-based memory.

The Traditional Oral Canon

9. Genealogies of the Sun and Moon[1]

Introductory comment

The poetic imagination of the Rotenese reaches from the heavens to the seas. Their ritual narratives variously recount the encounters of the sons and daughters of the Sun and Moon with the Lords of the Ocean and Sea. My intention here is to consider whether these oral narratives once formed part of a longer literary work of epic proportions.

To do this, I begin with an examination of the oral tradition as it now exists on the island. Once I have outlined the essential features of this oral tradition, I go on to consider the evidence that would link various important narratives within a larger structure. Although this evidence cannot be considered conclusive, the examination of the possible linkages among these different oral narratives does provide some understanding of Rotenese mythology.

The Rotenese oral tradition: *Bini*

At present, the Rotenese possess no long oral epic. They possess, instead, a variety of specifically named oral compositions in ritual language, the performance of which is or was appropriate to particular occasions. These occasional compositions were of two kinds: mortuary compositions and origin compositions. A growing number of compositions based on Biblical knowledge have been added to this repertoire and these are currently used in prayers and sermons. Although the occasions for traditional performances were ostensibly quite different, the compositions themselves follow basically the same structural format. In Rotenese, these chants are all referred to simply as *bini*.

---

1   This chapter was first published in 1997 as 'Genealogies of the Sun and Moon: interpreting the canon of Rotenese ritual chants', in E. K. M. Masinambow (ed.), *Koentjaraningrat dan Antropologi di Indonesia*, Assosiasi Antropologi Indonesia/Yayasan Obor, Jakarta, pp. 321–30. It was dedicated to Professor Dr Koentjaraningrat as a personal acknowledgment of my deep gratitude to him for his continuing support of my research. Professor Koentjaraningrat was the official sponsor of my initial doctoral research, which I carried out on the island of Rote in 1965–66, and he continued, for more than 30 years, as a friend and colleague, to maintain his interest in my research efforts. He took note of my work in his *Sejarah Teori Antropologi* (1980) and he invited me to contribute a paper describing my Rotenese researches for a volume he was editing on the human aspects of social research (Koentjaraningrat and Emmerson 1982). He also did me the great honour of writing the '*Pengantar*' (foreword) to the Indonesian translation of my book on Rote and Savu, which appeared under the title *Panen Lontar* in 1996. In offering this chapter on the Rotenese poetic imagination, I endeavoured to call attention to the notable fact that Professor Koentjaraningrat, in his life's work, was a research scholar and a gifted artist. It is thus appropriate that the foundations of the anthropology of Indonesia, which he so carefully set in place, should combine research and scholarship directed towards an understanding of all the creative possibilities of the human spirit.

Both kinds of compositions are identified according to their principal chant character and each composition consists of a narrative that recounts various episodes or events relating to the principal chant character. Since these compositions are recited in strict parallel form, all chant characters have dual names.[2] These dual names must be interpreted as references to a single character, otherwise the compositions appear nonsensical.

The performance of a mortuary chant was once required—before reliance on Christian rituals began to eliminate this need—at all funeral ceremonies. The deceased was likened to the principal chant character of the chosen chant and the episodes of the chant were intended as a figurative exemplification of the life course of the dead person.

The mortuary chants are structured to encompass diverse categories of Rotenese society. There are specific chants for nobles and for commoners, for wealthy non-nobles, for the young and for the old, for young girls who died 'unripe' and for boys who died in their love-making years. There were also a number of all-purpose 'orphan and widow' chants that could, if necessary, be used to cover most other categories of person. Chanters were also able to alter and embellish a standard composition, to a certain extent, to adapt it to the occasion of a particular funeral.

Recitations of origin chants, on the other hand, were considered essential to establish the 'origin' of—and the 'precedence' for—aspects of Rotenese culture. In Rotenese terms, such recitation was needed to consecrate or 'to make whole' (*naka-tetema*) particular activities or objects.

The single most important origin composition recounts the origin of the house. Its importance lies in the fact that it accounts, not just for the house, but also for the foundations of Rotenese culture. Besides this chant, other chants account for the origin of rice and millet, for the origin of weaving and for the patterns used in the tie-dyeing process and, quite separately, for certain seashells associated with dyeing and spinning. In addition, there is a variety of other origin chants: chants, for example, that recount the origin of specific, ritually important rock formations, the origin of the particular ritual performances and even chants that recount the origin of gold and silversmithing and of the playing of the distinctive Rotenese musical instrument, the *sesandu*.

The spread of Christianity throughout Rote has curtailed the opportunities for performance of many of these origin chants. Previously, each of the domains of the island carried out a series of post-harvest origin ceremonies, which were

---

2   As a consequence of this use of dual names, it is difficult, when writing in English, to decide whether to refer to chant characters in the singular or in the plural. This difficulty is often compounded by the fact that some chanters create further parallelism by alternating between singular and plural pronouns in reference to these characters. In this chapter, for the sake of consistency, I shall refer to all double-named chant characters in the singular.

known collectively as *hus* (from the root *hu*, meaning 'origin, base, cause'). In some areas of west Rote, these *hus* ceremonies were performed until the 1950s; in one small area, they continue to be performed to this day. Elsewhere, however, these ceremonies had all but ceased by the 1930s. The demise of these ceremonies has made it impossible to recover all of the specific chants performed at these festivities. What chants remain are fragments of cultural knowledge that exist without the appropriate occasion for their performance.

Domains, dialects and ritual-language variation

Chants are intended to convey something of the Rotenese conception of an idealised order of knowledge. A chant, in this sense, is identified by the name of its principal chant character. Thus in the domain of Termanu the chant of the origin of rice and millet is known by the double-named chant character *Doli Mo ma Lutu Mala* (or, sometimes, simply *Doli do Lutu*); similarly, the chant of the origin of the patterns used in making textiles is known by the name(s) *Pata Iuk ma Dula Foek*. In this same way, particular mortuary chants are referred to, for example, by names such as *Pau Balo ma Bola Lungi* or *Ndi Loniama ma Laki Elokama*.

All such named chants are intended to reflect a common understanding, which a chanter attempts either to express or, if the need arises, to alter for a particular purpose. Chanters often disagree among themselves over key elements of a chant, but generally insist that their particular version reflects a valid ancestral inheritance. Despite this personal insistence on a particular version, there is a tact recognition and subtle tolerance of variation, within limits, in compositions. As a consequence, there can be as many versions of a chant as there are performances. Versions of a chant are considered the personal—always imperfect—efforts of the chanter who performs them. (This conception accords well with Rotenese insistence that perfection is a heavenly quality that can never be attained on Earth.) The authority of the chanter and the coherence of his chant are invariably considered in evaluating the merits of a particular composition.

There are 18 domains on the island of Rote and all but one, Bokai, are said to have their own separate dialect or language (*dede'ak*). The idea of a single named version of a chant extends, however, beyond the limits of the speech community of the domain. This means, in effect, that the same—or nearly the same—names occur for the designation of many chants throughout Rote.[3]

---

3 One project that I have undertaken is to gather as many versions of the text named *Suti Solo ma Bina Bane* as I can. This collection includes almost two dozen compositions from most of the main speech communities on Rote. I have also recorded the same chanter on different occasions and at different stages of his career. My aim is to publish this compilation with analysis and commentary to give an idea of variation in composition and performance.

This is, in itself, significant because so much else of Rotenese cultural life is circumscribed by domain boundaries. For example, the recitation of socially significant genealogies is confined to relationships within the domain, and all oral historical narratives—the hallmark of which is their distinct *dede'ak*—trace precedence only among the clans within the domain.

Ritual language utilises dialect differences as one of its resources for the creation of its dyadic sets or paired terms. Although ritual language can be used, and understood, in formal communication among domains, it does not constitute a common linguistic register for the entire island. The patterning of ordinary speech is evident in the ritual speech of each domain.

Reports from the first half of the nineteenth century indicate that some chanters would travel from area to area to compete with one another in ritual performances, particularly at funerals. (The indication is that chanters moved from domain to domain but how extensive the wanderings of these chanters were is, in fact, impossible to ascertain.) Formerly, the rulers of domains would sponsor chanting 'contests' that would draw chanters from different domains.

Several of the chanters I have recorded had lived for some time in another domain or on Timor and had learned a portion of their repertoire from chanters outside their own area. It is also still quite common for chanters to come from neighbouring areas, even neighbouring domains, to take part in large funeral ceremonies. All of these factors, past and present, have undoubtedly contributed to the sharing of the knowledge of chants in ritual language. Variations in versions of different chants, as well as the commonalities of the tradition, can be shown to have a historical and a sociological basis.

In the course of my research on Rote, I gathered an extensive collection of chants in two domains: Termanu and Thie.[4] Termanu is on the north central coast, whereas Thie is located on the south-western coast of the island. Other domains separate these domains from one another. Their dialects are quite distinct, as is their political and social organisation. For much of the past 300 years, these two domains have been in opposition to one another but their rulers have also concluded mutual marriage alliances (see Fox 1979).

If there were some underlying structure to the diverse chants that make up the repertoire for the performance of rituals on Rote, this structure would have to be evident in domains as different from one another as Termanu and Thie.

---

4   I have also a considerable collection of texts from the domain of Talae, which were gathered from chanters of this domain in Kupang. Talae once formed part of the realm of Termanu and its dialect is very close to that of Termanu. Because chants from Talae are closely related to those of Termanu, they are not as suitable as those from Thie for the purposes of the comparison I undertake in this chapter.

9. Genealogies of the Sun and Moon

Tracing chant genealogies: Termanu and Thie

Chants from Termanu and Thie have much the same format. This format comprises similar oral formulae, including the formula of the 'genealogical introduction'—a kind of prologue that serves to identify the principal chant character and to give an account of the connubial relations that led to his or her birth. The correct identification of important chant characters is critical to the recitation of most ritual chants. Since the recitation of long genealogies as a means of establishing relations of precedence is an essential aspect of Rotenese social life, it is in no way surprising that this same method should be utilised as part of the narrative structure of chants.

There are, however, differences in the way in which genealogies are traced in Termanu and in Thie and these differences would seem to have their counterpart in the structuring of ritual chants in the two domains.

The main genealogy of Termanu is the dynastic genealogy of the royal clan of Termanu. For the most part, the genealogies of the other clans have separate origins and thus no necessary connection to the genealogy of the royal clan. As a result, there is no overarching genealogy to link all of the clans of the domain. Most of the clans of Termanu have been united within the domain either through alliance with, or through conquest by, the royal clan (see Fox 1971).

In contrast, in Thie, there is a single branching genealogy that purports to embrace all of the clans of the domain. In addition, the clans of Thie are organised in a basic moiety structure. A combination of genealogy and moiety unites the domain of Thie (see Fox 1979).

Although genealogy is equally important in both domains, the way it is used is significantly different. Correspondingly, in Termanu, no chanter whom I recorded ever attempted to draw genealogical connections from one text to another. Like the clans of Termanu, each chant constituted a separate entity. Only in Thie did I encounter the claim that there were genealogical connections between the chant characters of all major ritual texts. In Thie, therefore, there exists something of the idea of an epic, even though the parts of this epic are—as in Termanu—segregated to different ritual occasions.

In Thie, the idea of an epic is more than an assertion. Genealogical introductions for important chant characters, whose names are known in Termanu and Thie, are 'extended' in Thie to connect these characters to one another. A good example of this genealogical elaboration is the case of the chant character known in Termanu as Manu Kama ma Tepa Nilu and in Thie (following 'n' > 'l' and 'l' > 'r' sound shifts) as Malu Kama ma Tepa Niru. The first eight lines of the genealogical introduction to the chant of this same name from Termanu is as follows:

Manu Kama ma Tepa Nilu

Soku-lala Silu Lilo	They lift Silu Lilo
Ma lali-lala Huka Besi.	And they carry Huka Besi.
Lelete neu sao	She bridges the path to marry
Do fifino neu tu	Or joins the way to wed
Sao Kama Lai Ledo	To marry Kama Lai of the Sun
Do tu Nilu Neo Bulan.	Or to wed Nilu Neo of the Moon.
De bongi-nala Tepa Nilu	She gives birth to Tepa Nilu
Ma lae-nala Manu Kama.	And she brings forth Manu Kama.

The equivalent, but far longer, genealogical introduction of this same chant character in Thie is as follows:

Malu Kama ma Tepa Niru

Hida bei na fan	Still at an earlier time
Dalu bei na don	Still in a previous period
Dote Dai Lenak anan,	Dote Dai Lenak's child,
Soku ina Dila Dote	They lift the woman Dila Dote
Neu tu touk Bula Kai	To go to marry the man Bula Kai
Leo na, Teti So Resik anan,	Similarly, Teti So Resik's child,
Lali fetok Fafo Teti	They carry the girl Fafo Teti
Neu sao taek Ledo Horo.	To go to wed the boy Ledo Horo.
Bonggi heni touk,	She gives birth to the man,
Niru Neo Bulan	Niru Neo of the Moon
Ma rae heni taek,	And she brings forth the boy,
Kama Lae Ledo.	Kama Lae of the Sun.
Hu na de ara lali rala	After that, they carry
Besi Nggeo Liun anan,	Besi Nggeo of the Sea's child,
Inak kia Hu'a Besi	The woman Hu'a Besi
Soku rala	And they lift
Lilo Modo Sain anan,	Lilo Modo of the Ocean's child,
Fetok kia Silu Lilo.	The girl Silu Lilo.
Leu tu Niru Neo Bulan	They go to marry Niru Neo of the Moon
Ma ana sao Kama Lae Ledo.	And she weds Kama Lae of the Sun.
Ana bonggi heni Malu Kama	She gives birth to Malu Kama
Ma rae heni Tepa Niru	And she brings forth Tepa Niru
Bei ruma Timu Dulu	Still in Timu in the east
Ma Sepe Langga.	And still in Sepe at the head.

The names cited in Rotenese genealogies follow a clear order. Each name has two parts: the first part is an ancestral (or heavenly) name determined by divination; the second part is the first name of the father, if bride-wealth has been paid, or the first name of the mother, if bride-wealth has not been paid. The names of the chant characters follow the same order but in a double construction.

In the lines from the Termanu chant, only two generations are recorded and only one marriage is cited. In the passage from the chant from Thie, three generations are recorded and two marriages cited. In fact, elsewhere in the chant, Malu Kama//Tepa Niru's marriage is also recorded. The genealogy of this chant character therefore encompasses four generations in the male line and recognises three different marriages, in each of which her chant names and those of her father identify the bride.

The genealogies and marriage relations cited in the two chants are as follows.

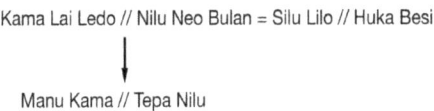

Figure 9.1: A Two-Generation Genealogy of the Sun and Moon from Termanu

Figure 9.2: A Four-Generation Genealogy of the Sun and Moon from Thie (with the identification of spouses by father's name)

Explorations in Semantic Parallelism

The genealogy in the chant from Thie is of particular interest because it extends, in a single composition, for four successive generations from Ledo Horo//Bula Kai to Mata Malu//Idu Tepa, the son of Malu Kama//Tepu Niru. It identifies the father of a woman who marries a man in each generation within the male line.

The genealogy of the Sun and Moon

In Thie and in Termanu, the chants that account for the origin of cultural objects and practices recount the exploits of chant characters who belong to one of two groups: those of the Sun and Moon (*Ledo do Bulan*) and those of the Ocean and Sea (*Liun do Sain*). In Thie, in particular, it is the genealogy of the Sun and Moon that provides the structure that connects ritual chants with one another. This genealogy begins with the figure Kai Mangaresi//Horo Mangaru. The whole of the genealogy, however, is difficult to piece together because of the numerous marriages of the key chant character, Bula Kai//Ledo Horo. The genealogy of Malu Kama//Tepa Niru, for example, derives from one such marriage by Bula Kai//Ledo Horo.

The following is a portion of this genealogy, as told to me by the chanter S. Ndun. It refers to another marriage by Bula Kai//Ledo Horo. From this marriage, there were four offspring, all of whose double names bear, as their last names, the initial names of their father (Bulan//Ledo: 'Moon//Sun') (Figure 9.3).

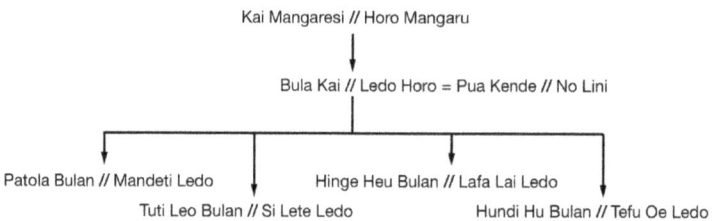

Figure 9.3: A Genealogy of the Grandchildren of the Sun and Moon

The crucial figure in this group of children is the chant character Patola Bulan//Mandeti Ledo, who gives his name to the single most important ritual text in Rotenese, the text that recounts the 'origin' of the house.

According to this text, while hunting pig and civet cat on Earth, Patola Bulan//Mandeti Ledo encounters the Lord of the Ocean and Sea and descends with him to his 'house roofed with ray-fish tails' and his 'home decked with turtle shells'. There, Patola Bulan//Mandeti Ledo discovers the cooking fire and the taste of roasted meat as well as rice, millet and the utensils for building and for pounding rice. The litany of these objects includes the 'bore tool and flat chisel', the 'axe and adze', the 'plumbline and turning drill', the 'rice mortar and pestle' and the 'flint set and fire-drill'. Marriage is concluded between the Sun and Moon and the Ocean and Sea and in the exchanges that result from this marriage these objects pass from the Sea to the Heavens.

Patola Bulan//Mandeti Ledo is recognised as a chant character in Thie and in Termanu but there are divergent views about the women who are given in marriage in the chants. In one version from Termanu, Patola Bulan//Mandeti Ledo's sister, Tao Senge Bulan//Kudu Kea Ledo, is given in marriage to the Lord of the Sea, Danga Lena Liun//Mane Tua Sain. In another version from Termanu, Bula Kai//Ledo Holo marries a woman of the sea, Lole Liuk//Lada Saik. In Thie, it is another child of the Sun and Moon, Sao Ledo//Mani Bulan, who marries not the Lord of the Sea but his son, Tio Danga//Ruse Mane.

Similar problems arise in relation to other chants. In Termanu, one version of the origin of weaving mentions the heavenly figure Henge Ne Ledo//Feo Futu, who gives the first shuttle and loom to her counterpart in the sea. In Thie, the candidate for the role of Henge Ne Leo//Feo Futu Bulan is the woman (mentioned in the previously cited genealogy) Hinge Heu Bulan//Lafa Lai Ledo.

The structure of the canon of Rotenese ritual chants

If there was once a greater coherence to the ritual chants and if this coherence was once sufficient to constitute some kind of epic then the narrative structure of this epic told of relationships between the realms of Heaven and Sea. By their names, the creatures of Heaven are identified with the Sun and Moon, stars, rainbow, lightning and other similar heavenly phenomena. The Lord of the Sea is identified with the shark and crocodile and his retinue includes specific creatures such as turtle and sea cow, ray-fish and dolphin as well as numerous smaller (and more difficult to identify) kinds of fish and crustaceans. Earth serves as the meeting place for members of these two realms, and human beings on Earth are the ultimate beneficiaries of intercourse between these realms.

In most instances, the cultural wealth named in the chants, such as the seeds of rice and millet or the special shells associated with spinning and dyeing, come from the sea. Women searching for the offspring of Heaven and Sea scoop up these objects in their fish-nets. Women also make offerings to attract objects to remain and to grow and prosper in their locality. Significantly, the women who perform these actions bear chant names that personify places on Rote and it is through these personified placenames that the ritual chants are specifically 'grounded' in a recognisable landscape.

Placenames thus provide yet another critical dimension to the structure of the chants. These names create a ritual geography of their own, quite apart from the everyday geography of the island. Rote and all of its domains have special ritual names. Similarly, all of the surrounding islands have ritual names; and there are also ritual names for places beyond the confines of ordinary geography—realms to the east and west and beyond the horizon.

Equally important are the specific ritual names of virtually every locality on the island. It is at the level of these localities that placenames are, depending on context, personified. Such names, like all ritual names, are doubled; and, like the names of chant characters, these double names can be based on limited genealogies. Some chants consist largely of a recitation of placenames, personified as women, who transfer objects and the knowledge of their cult from place to place on Rote.

Conclusion

If the chants in ritual language were to be considered as a single, long literary work, this epic creation would indeed have a cosmic scope. It would have no single hero but rather two families whose members each have a special role to play. As a work shaped to ritual occasions, 'naming' would be one of the critical literary features of this work. It would not necessarily provide political authority to support the rule of any particular dynasty on the island but it could be used to enhance and uphold the idea of a noble order. In a genuine sense, this grand composition would have to be considered as a religious, rather than a political, work of art.

10. Manu Kama's road, Tepa Nilu's path[1]

The ritual chant *Manu Kama ma Tepa Nilu*, a poem of more than 330 lines in strict canonical parallelism, is the oldest recorded chant in Rotenese ritual language. It offers a glimpse of a world created through the cultural imagination of the Rotenese. Here I wish to examine the underlying assumptions, conventional expressions and complex philosophy of life that give coherence to this poetic world.

My intention is to examine this text, selectively, at various levels, from its metaphysical allegory to the minutiae of the formulae embodied in it. As such, this reading, I hope, may provide something of an introduction to the literary possibilities of Rotenese poetry.

Introduction to the historical text

In 1911, the renowned Dutch linguist J. C. G. Jonker published the text of a long Rotenese ritual chant. He added this single chant to his collection of Rotenese texts as an 'example of poetic style' that he recognised was characterised by 'sustained parallelism'. Instead of translating the chant, however, which he implied was 'obscure', he merely provided a series of notes to it with a translation of an ordinary-language paraphrase that accompanied the text (Jonker 1911:97–102, 130–5).[2] In 1913, Jonker published another collection of texts in a variety of Rotenese dialects and, in 1915, his massive Rotenese grammar, but he never again gave further consideration to the chant, so it remained the only untranslated portion of his vast corpus of Rotenese material.

---

1   This chapter was first published in 1988 as '"Manu Kama's road, Tepa Nilu's path": theme, narrative and formula in Rotenese ritual language', in J. J. Fox (ed.), *To Speak in Pairs: Essays on the ritual languages of eastern Indonesia*, Cambridge University Press, Cambridge, pp. 161–201. The research on which the original paper was based spanned a considerable period. It involved extensive fieldwork on Rote in 1965–66 and again in 1972–73, as well as brief visits in 1977 and 1978. This research was supported by grants from the US National Institute of Mental Health (MH-10, 161; MH-20, 659), the US National Science Foundation (2NS-7808149 A01) and The Australian National University. In Indonesia, all research was conducted under the auspices of the Lembaga Ilmu Pengetahuan Indonesia and in cooperation with the University of Nusa Cendana in Kupang.
2   Jonker published the original text in double columns with unnumbered lines. I have numbered the lines for identification and made a number of minor corrections: line 43, *lelena* for *lelea*; line 103, *Lide* for *Lede*; line 131, *Doli* for *Dali*. In lines 163 and 164, *do* should probably be read as *o*, which would be grammatically correct. In lines 218 and 220, the same *do* appears again but is less easily interpretable. Only one line in the entire text made little or no sense—this was line 232, which originally appeared as '*lope lea de neu*' and was corrected, on Rotenese advice, to '*lelo afe de lope*', which is the correct formulaic parallel to line 231, '*fo'a fanu de la'o*' (see lines 155–6). In addition, in lines 123, 126, 166 and 200, I have shifted the word *nae* ('to say, to speak') from the next line. Nothing is changed except line length, which is variable; the shift facilitates, however, overall phrasing. I have also simplified Jonker's transcription of Rotenese words.

Far from being 'obscure', this untranslated text, entitled *Ana-Ma Manu Kama ma Falu-Ina Tepa Nilu*, is a clear, superbly structured example of Rotenese ritual language. It is a funeral chant that belongs to the broad class of chants for *ana-mak ma falu-ina* ('orphans and widows'). In all probability, it was gathered in 1900 when Jonker visited the Timor area, or shortly thereafter, when he had returned to Makassar but continued to correspond with and receive written textual material from various local Rotenese informants.[3] This makes the *Manu Kama ma Tepa Nilu* chant the oldest full ritual text available for comparison with present forms of ritual language.

My first purpose in this chapter is to provide a translation of the *Manu Kama ma Tepa Nilu* text. Rather than simply translate the words of the text, however, I would like to offer some explanation of the basic ideas expressed in it, since these ideas embody concepts that are fundamental to a Rotenese philosophy of life. At a more technical level, I wish to make comparisons between forms in this chant and those in current use in Rote, and thereby begin to explicate how the conventions of canonical parallelism interact with the syntactic requirements of an oral poetry to produce stylised phrases and formulae.

This chapter comprises three parts. I begin, in part one, with a personal preface to the text, describing its importance to my own field research on ritual language. I then examine the fundamental idea in the text—the concept of 'orphan and widow'—and, with this as a background, give an outline summary and brief exegesis of the text itself. In part two, I discuss the formal structure of Rotenese ritual language and, to illustrate continuity in the language, I compare examples from the text with excerpts from compositions by contemporary oral poets, focusing specifically on formulae used to mark episodes and advance chant narration.[4] I conclude this discussion with various remarks on oral intercommunication, narrative structure and verbal authority in Rotenese poetry. Finally, in part three, I provide a complete translation of the *Manu Kama ma Tepa Nilu* text. The translation of this text effectively completes the Jonker corpus of Rotenese texts, and is offered in homage to a Leiden scholar of great stature on whose work I have relied from the beginning of my research on eastern Indonesia.

---

3 Jonker does not identify the chanter from whom he obtained the *Manu Kama ma Tepa Nilu* text. In his preface to *Rottineesche Teksten* (1911), Jonker thanks D. A. Johannes, a native religious instructor in Keka, for his assistance in the gathering of the written texts, and J. Fanggidaej, the head of the native school at Babau, for checking and correcting the manuscripts.
4 With the exception of one short excerpt from the chant *Sua Lai ma Batu Hu*, all of the contemporary material I quote in this paper is taken from Fox (1972).

Preface to the text

On my first trip to Rote in 1965, I took with me a copy of Jonker's *Rottineesche Teksten* (1911), which contains the untranslated text of *Manu Kama ma Tepa Nilu*. In the early stages of my fieldwork, as I was attempting to formulate a direction to my research, I was assisted by two poets: Peu Malesi, who would visit me occasionally in the hamlet of Ufa Len where I lived; and Stefanus Adulanu, 'Old Meno' as he was called, the ritual 'Head of the Earth' in Termanu, whom I visited in the nearby hamlet of Ola Lain.

Peu Malesi was the first poet from whom I was able to record a lengthy chant, and it took me several weeks of intermittent work to manage to transcribe, translate and comprehend what he had recited for me. A schoolteacher, J. Pello, assisted me with the transcription, while Meno and two elders from Ufa Len, Mias Kiuk and Nggi Muloko, helped in the slow, line-by-line translation and exegesis of the transcribed text. At the time, I had virtually no grasp of the Rotenese language, no idea of the structure of ritual language and no clear sense of what I was doing other than responding to what the Rotenese themselves insisted was the most important thing for me to do. During this period, Meno willingly answered my questions and allowed me to accompany him when he attended the local court, where he and other clan elders heard and judged disputes, but at no time, despite several promises, did he recite for me a chant of his own. As he explained to me later, he was uncertain of my intentions and seriousness and he was waiting to see how I proceeded.

When, eventually, I reached the point of understanding the Malesi chant and had begun to make sense of its structure, I realised that the *Manu Kama ma Tepa Nilu* text had much the same structure and, from the little that I could make out, was obviously of ritual importance. I therefore resolved to translate it. As a start, without any prior explanation of its origin, I simply read it, as carefully I could, to Kiuk and Muloko. They were indeed impressed but, to my surprise, they assumed it was another chant that I had recorded from Malesi. The language of the text was such that, without being alerted, their assumption was that it was a contemporary specimen of ritual language. Only when I explained the background to the text were they able to point to expressions that they felt were no longer commonly used by chanters.

After working on the text for some time, I offered to read it to Meno, but he instead proposed that I read it before all the assembled elders at the end of a court session. Without my fully realising it, he was arranging my first public performance as a chanter. With a suitable preface about how I was bringing back to Rote a chant that had been taken down and safeguarded in Holland for generations, my performance, even though it only involved reading a text, was sufficient to establish some credibility to my endeavours and allow me to enter into an exchange of chants among the poets of Termanu. From then on, Meno and other poets were willing and indeed eager to allow me to record them.

The *Manu Kama ma Tepa Nilu* chant initiated a dialogue in another sense. Chanters regularly respond to other chanters by interpolating passages in their performances that allude to previous performances. In my case, even after having translated *Manu Kama ma Tepa Nilu*, its meaning remained elusive. On Rote, there are mortuary chants intended to fit all appropriate social categories of the deceased—nobles or commoners, rich or poor, those who die old or those who die unmarried—but the most general of all are 'orphan and widow' chants, of which there are many, which can be adapted to suit almost any mortuary occasion. *Manu Kama ma Tepa Nilu* belongs to this general class of chants. One of my difficulties, however, in discussions with Meno, was in understanding the significance the Rotenese attached to the concept of 'orphan and widow'. It was in answer to my questioning on this subject, months later, that Meno interpolated a passage in his recitation of the chant *Lilo Tola ma Koli Lusi* that alluded to my queries about *Manu Kama ma Tepa Nilu*. This passage was the first of many dialogue exchanges conducted in ritual language as part of the process of my learning the language and its significance.

As in all skilful interpolations, it is difficult—and to some extent arbitrary—to designate where in the *Lilo Tola ma Koli Lusi* chant the interpolated passage begins or ends. Here, I quote 16 lines that are clearly the most pertinent part of Meno's reply:

Se ana-mak?	Who is an orphan?
Na basang-ngita ana-mak	All of us are orphans.
Ma se falu-ina?	And who is a widow?
Na basang-ngita falu-ina.	All of us are widows.
Fo la-fada lae	They speak of
Manu Kama dala Dain	Manu Kama's road to Dain
Ma Tepa Nilu eno Selan.	And Tepa Nilu's path to Selan.
Na basang-ngita ta enon	All of us have not his path
Ma basang-ngita ta dalan.	And all of us have not his road.
Sosoa-na nai dae bafak kia nde, bena	This means that on this Earth, then,
Ana-mak mesan-mesan	Each person is an orphan
Ma falu-ina mesan-mesan.	And each person is a widow.
De mana-sapeo nggeok	Those who wear black hats
Do mana-kuei modak ko,	Or those who wear green slippers,
Se ana-ma sila boe	They will be orphans too
Ma falu-ina sila boe.	And they will be widows too.

Meno's reply contains three elements that point to an understanding of the *Manu Kama ma Tepa Nilu* text and its underlying philosophy. First, Meno makes explicit the basic Rotenese conception of widowhood and orphanhood as a metaphor symbolising a universal human condition. Then, in alluding to 'Manu Kama's road to Dain//Tepa Nilu's path to Selan', he refers to various courses of human life, all of which imply mortality. From this follows his third point that since mortality is the fundamental cause of the condition of widowhood and orphanhood, it is at the same time the obliterator of all social distinctions of class or origin. The phrase 'Those who wear black hats//Those who wear green slippers' is an old formulaic designation for the Dutch. (This phrase probably dates from the period of the Dutch East India Company, 'black' and 'green' being the symbolic colours of the north and west quadrants from which the company was considered to have originated.) Powerful Europeans, like all others, are reduced to widowhood and orphanhood. Hence, despite differences in life course and origin, there are ultimately no differences in the human condition. Meno's reply is thus a highly condensed statement of various closely related notions. From the several points he makes can be derived other notions that are equally important to an understanding of the concept of widow and orphan, and these notions are what I propose to examine in greater detail as a prelude to a consideration of the *Manu Kama ma Tepa Nilu* text.

The concept of widow and orphan

The concept of widow and orphan is a multiplex notion whose basis is to be found in the context of the funeral ceremony. On Rote, death's disruption is regarded as affecting primarily the close relatives of the deceased, particularly brothers and sisters, parents, descendants and spouse. These relatives are the 'bereaved' (*mana-faluk*). They are responsible for providing the funeral feast, but must themselves fast until after the burial. Women among the bereaved are expected to bewail the deceased. Maternal relatives who are invited to the feast, on the other hand, are paid to perform ritual services at the funeral. They are supposed to cleanse the bereaved on the day after the burial and provide the foods that break their fast.

In ritual language, the bereaved are referred to as 'orphans and widows' (*ana-mak ma falu-inak*) and their condition is described as *ma-salak ma ma-singok*. The full formula for the bereaved is *ana mak ma-salak ma faluina ma-singak*. The Rotenese word *sala(k)* embraces many of the related senses of its Indonesian cognate *salah* ('error, mistake, fault, guilt, wrong') and has become, for Christian Rotenese, the word for 'sin'. *Sala(k)* may refer, however, to actions that were done intentionally and those that occurred by accident, and in many contexts merely implies that something is 'out of place' or simply 'displaced'. *Singo(k)*, the term with which *sala(k)* is paired, has a similar sense. It refers to something that is 'off course, deviant or divergent'—something that has missed its target or strayed from its set path. Since the Rotenese conceive of an ideal order that is manifest only in the heavenly spheres, all of human life is condemned to disorder and imperfection. Death is merely the most prominent occasion at which the human condition is made evident.

Given this understanding, the metaphor of widow and orphan can be used in numerous contexts. In situations of dependency, and particularly in making requests for assistance, the subordinate party identifies his position as that of orphan and widow. Such a position is one of distress and requires compassion:

Te au ana-ma ma-salak	I am an orphan displaced
Ma au falu-ina ma-singak,	And I am a widow astray,
De au ana mak loe-loe	I am a humble orphan
Ma au falu inak dae-dae.	And I am a lowly widow.

The hope is expressed that the superior party will be generous and unstinting:

Fo ela neka lama-koko bafa	Let the rice basket overflow its brim
Na dai ana-ma tee,	To be enough for a clan of orphans,
Ma bou lama-lua fude	And let the lontar jar froth over
Na ndule falu-ina ingu.	To be sufficient for a lineage of widows.

Previously, the orphan and widow metaphor was used to characterise the relationship of all subjects to the lord of their domain. The same metaphor can still be used to describe the relationship of dependants to patrons within their clan or lineage. This short petition given to me by Meno is a good example of the imagery used in making requests. The images are characteristically Rotenese: the cooking of lontar-palm syrup and the cutting of leaves and leafstalks from the palm. The concluding image of a dense forest with branches touching one another is a common botanic metaphor for order and harmony in society.

Lena-lena ngala lemin,	All you great ones,
Lesi-lesi ngala lemin,	All you superior ones,
Sadi mafandendelek,	Do remember this,
Sadi rnasanenedak:	Do bear this in mind:
Fo ana-ma tua fude	Save the froth of the cooking syrup for the orphans
Ma falu-ina beba langa la	And the heads of the palm leafstalks for the widows
Tua fude dua kako na,	When the froth spills over twice,
Kako kao mala sila,	Scoop it up for them,
Ma beba langa telu te na,	And when the stalk's head droops thrice,
Te tenga mala sila,	Lop it off for them,
Fo ela-ana-ma bei tema	So the orphans may remain intact

Ma falu-ina bei tetu,	And the widows stand upright,
Fo leo tema toe-ao lasin na,	Intact like a dense forest,
Teman losa don na,	Intact for a course of time,
Ma tetu lelei nulan na,	And upright like a thick wood,
Tetun nduku nete na.	Upright for an age.

Using more elaborate metaphors, a patron may be compared with a shepherd who tends a 'herd' of orphans and a 'flock' of widows, or with a great tree around which orphans gather and widows circle. Two examples of this kind of imagery—both taken from the same chant, *Ndi Lonama ma Laki Elokama*, which I recorded from the poet Stefanus Amalo in 1966—may serve as illustration. The first utilises the image of the herdsman:

Te hu touk Ndi Lonama,	The man Ndi Lonama,
Ma ta'ek Laki Elokama,	And the boy Laki Elokama,
Tou ma-bote bilk	Is a man with flocks of goats
Ma ta'e ma-tena kapak.	And is a boy with herds of water buffalo.
De basa fai-kala	On all days
Ada nou ledo-kala	And every sunrise
Ana tada mamao bote	He separates the flock in groups
Ma ana lilo bobongo tena	And forms the herd in circles
Na neni te tada tenan	Bringing his herd-separating spear
Ma neni tafa lilo bote-na,	And bringing his flock-forming sword,
Fo te nade Kafe Sari	His spear named Kafe Lasi
Ma tafa nade Seu Nula.	And his sword named Seu Nula.
Fo ana toe tafa neu be na,	Where he lowers his sword,
Bote hae neu ndia,	The flock stops there,
Ma te'e te neu be na,	And where he rests his spear,
Tena lu'u neu ndia.	The herd lies down at that place.
Fo tena ta neu lu'u	It is not the herd that lies down
Ma bote ta neu hae,	And not the flock that stops,
Te ana-mak-kala hae	But it is orphans who stop
Ma falu-ina-la lu'u.	And widows who lie down.

The second example is contained in the instructions of the dying Ndi Lonama//Laki Elokama. (Because of the rules of parallelism, all chant characters—as indeed all places—have double names. By convention, I refer to these characters in the singular but by their double name.) Ndi Lonama//Laki Elokama thus instructs his family to continue his practice of caring for orphans and widows:

De tati mala bau ndanan,	Cut and take a branch from the Bau-tree,
Ma aso mala tui baen	Slice and take a limb from the Tui-tree
Fo tane neu dano Hela	To plant at the lake Hela

Ma sele neu le Kosi	And to sow at the river Kosi
Fo ela okan-na lalae	That its roots may creep forth
Ma samun-na ndondolo	And its tendrils may twine
Fo ela poek-kala leu lain	For shrimp to cling to
Ma nik-kala leu feon;	And crabs to circle round;
Fo poek ta leu lain	It is not shrimp that cling there
Te ana-mak leu tain,	But orphans who cling there,
Ma nik ta leu feon	And it is not crabs that circle round
Te falu-ina leu feon.	But widows who circle round.

In virtually all widow and orphan chants, emphasis is placed on the wanderings of the orphan and widow: the quest of the displaced for sustenance, support and a proper abode. For example, in a chant by Meno that relates the death of the chant character Lusi Topo Lani//Tola Tae Ama, his widow, Bisa Oli//Ole Masi, is left to care for his orphan, Lilo Tola//Koli Lusi. Much of this chant is taken up with the search by the widow for food to raise her orphan child. Her need prompts her to seek 'the early millet harvest//the first lontar yields' in the domain of Medi do Ndule, and her request, as she journeys, is as follows:

Na kedi fe au dok	Cut for me a leaf
Ma dui fe au bifak,	And strip for me a leafstalk,
Fo au ane neu lapa eik	That I may plait sandals for [my] feet
Ma au sika neu sidi su'uk,	And I may open out a cover for [my] breast,
Fo au la'o unik ledo Medi	For I walk toward Medi's sun
Ma au lope unik fai Ndule.	And I head for Ndule's day.

In the Christian reinterpretation of traditional cultural themes, this quest is regarded as a kind of pilgrim's progress—mankind's journey to a heavenly home. The general structure of orphan and widow chants, as will be evident from the *Manu Kama ma Tepa Nilu* chant, lends itself to a variety of similar allegorical interpretations. There is a commonality between the narrative structure of these chants and the Rotenese conception of the course of human life.

Outline of the *Manu Kama ma Tepa Nilu* text

The text of *Manu Kama ma Tepa Nilu* runs to 334 lines and can be divided into five main episodes. Episode one (lines 1–34) begins with the marriage of the woman Silu Lilo//Huka Besi with the man Kama Lai Ledo//Nilu Neo Bulan, and the birth and early childhood of Manu Kama//Tepa Nilu (henceforth MK//TN). All chant characters have dual names and MK//TN takes the second portion of his name (Kama//Nilu) from that of his father, Kama Lai Ledo//Nilu Neo Bulan. His father's name includes the names Ledo//Bulan ('Sun'//'Moon'), which signify a high heavenly origin. Recognition of this origin is essential to appreciate what happens in later episodes when MK//TN is not given the respect he deserves.

Episode one continues in describing first the death of MK//TN's father and then of his mother. This leaves MK//TN as an orphan and widow. Since in ritual language 'father' pairs with 'mother's brother' and 'mother' pairs with 'father's sister', being an orphan and widow is described as lacking these important relatives. The episode ends, as do subsequent episodes, leaving MK//TN with tears streaming from his eyes and snot running from his nose. This is portrayed with elaborate botanic imagery:

31. *De lu ko boa na'u,*	Tears like bidara-fruit in the grass,
32. *Ma pinu kaitio telan*	Snot like kaitio-[leaves] in the underbrush
33. *Lama-noma oba-tula*	They pour like juice from a tapped gewang
34. *Do lama-titi ate lasi.*	And flow like sap from an old ate.

Episode two (lines 35–98) describes MK//TN's encounter with the woman Bula Pe//Mapo Tena, who finds him weeping and takes him in as his mother and aunt:

45. *Bo ana-ma Manu Kama,*	Oh, orphan Manu Kama,
46. *Do bo falu-ina Tepa Nilu,*	Oh, widow Tepa Nilu,
47. *Mai, te Silu Lilok nde au*	Come, Silu Lilok am I
48. *Do Huka Besik nde au.*	Or Huka Besik am I.
49. *Boe ma ta nae Bula Pe*	So do not say Bula Pe
50. *Te nae Silu Lilok,*	But say Silu Lilok,
51. *Ma ta nae Mapo Tena*	And do not say Mapo Tena
52. *Te nae Huka Besik.*	But say Huka Besik.

Then one day at dawn, MK//TN hears the 'soft voices and gentle songs' of 'friarbirds and green parrots' (*koa//nggia*). In Rotenese poetry, the set friarbird and parrot is the conventional metaphor for a young attractive girl, and, as these honeybirds and parrots approach MK//TN:

61. *Boe ma ala kako dodoe hala-nala*	They sing with soft voices
62. *Ma ala hele memese dasi-nala.*	And they warble with gentle songs.
63. *De ala kako-lala Manu Kama dalen*	They sing to Manu Kama's heart
64. *Ma hele-lala Tepa Nilu tein.*	And warble to Tepa Nilu's inner being.

At this, MK//TN wakes Bula Pe//Mapo Tena and asks her:

77. *Muasa fe-ng-au koa halak*	Go buy for me the friarbird's voice
78. *Do tadi fe-ng-au nggia dasik*	Or get for me the green parrot's whistle
79. *Fo eta au a-hala nggia halak*	So that I may reply to the green parrot's voice
80. *Ma au a-dasi koa dasik.*	And I may sing to the friarbird's song
81. *Fo sama leo inang boe*	So that you may be just like my mother
82. *Do deta lea te'ong boe.*	Or that you may be similar to my aunt.

In the conventions of the poetry, this is a request that Bula Pe//Mapo Tena provide the bride-wealth, consisting of water buffalo and gold, to allow MK//TN to marry. In reply, Bula Pe//Mapo Tena says that she has nothing of value except her person, which she offers in the place of proper bride-wealth.

83. Mu bola inam leo kapa,	Go, tie your mother like a water buffalo,
84. Fo leo-leo leo kapa;	Circling round like a water buffalo;
85. Ma mu tai te'om leo lilo,	And go weigh your aunt like gold,
86. Fo benu-benu leo lilo,	Balanced gently like gold,
87. Te au ina ndeli-lima-ku'u-tak	For I am a woman without a ring on her finger
88. Ma au feto liti-ei-tak	And I am a girl without copper on her legs.

On hearing this answer, MK//TN feels the 'heart's regret of an orphan and the inner grief of a widow'. He takes up his father's bow and his uncle's blowpipe and he leaves, with tears running down his cheeks and snot falling from his nose. 'Bow and blowpipe'—material objects that have long since disappeared from use on Rote—are significant in poetry as the principal objects with which young men 'hunt' honeybirds and green parrots.

Episode three (lines 99–176) repeats and elaborates similar events to those in episode two. This time, MK//TN meets the woman Lide Muda//Adi Sole, to whom he reveals his plight and elaborates on his sorry condition:

111. Au ana-ma Manu Kama	I am the orphan Manu Kama
112. Ma au falu-ina Tepa Nilu	And I am the widow Tepa Nilu,
113. Au a -ina ingu inan,	I have, as mother, the land of my mother
114. Ma au ate'o leo te'on.	And I have, as aunt, the clan of my aunt.
115. Ala hopo kedok Manu Kama,	Gruffly, they mix lontar syrup for Manu Kama,
116. Ma ala sode odak Tepa Nilu,	Sourly, they serve rice to Tepa Nilu,
117. Ala lo tuluk Tepa Nilu	They offer things with a shove to Tepa Nilu
118. Ma ala sipo le'ak Manu Kama	And they take things with a tug from Manu Kama.
119. Au ana-ma dai-lena-ng,	My orphaned state is increased,
120. De au ana-ma-ng boe mai,	I am more an orphan than ever,
121. Ma au falu-ina tolesi-ng,	My widowed state is made greater,
122. Au falu-ina-ng bee mai.	I am more a widow than ever.

Lide Muda//Adi Sole offers to take him in, saying:

124. Bo Manu Kama-e,	Oh, Manu Kama,
125. Mai uma-t-ala uma leon,	Come to our house,
126. Ma fetok ia Adi Sole nae:	And the girl Adi Sole says:
127. Bo Tepa Nilu-e,	Oh, Tepa Nilu,
128. Mai lo-t-ala lo leon,	Come to our home,

129. Te au lea inam Silu Lilo boe,	For I will be like your mother, Silu Lilo,
130. Ma au leo te'om Huka Besik boe!	And I will be like your aunt, Huka Besik!

MK/TN settles in and is properly served rice and millet. He calls Lide Muda//Adi Sole 'his mother of birth and his true aunt'.

Again, however, at dawn, come the soft voices and gentle songs of the honeybirds and parrots, and again he wakes his newly found mother and aunt and requests bride-wealth with which to marry:

153. Bo ina-ng-o-ne,	Oh, my mother,
154. Do bo te'o-ng-o-ne,	Oh, my aunt,
155. Fo'a fanu mapa-deik,	Wake and stand up,
156. Ma lelo afe manga-tuk!	Come awake and sit up!
157. Te siluk nai dulu so	Morning is in the east
158. Ma hu'ak nai langa so.	And dawn is at the head.
159. Buluk-a bei Manu Kama inan	If you are Manu Kama's mother
160. Do buluk-a bei Tepa Nilo te'on,	Or if you are Tepa Nilu's aunt,
161. Mu asa fe-ng-au koa	Go buy for me a friarbird
162. Ma mu tadi fe-ng-au nggia!	And go get for me a green parrot!
163. Te au ae-[d]o Silu Lilok	So I may call you Silu Lilok
164. Ma au ae [d]o Huka Besik	And I may call you Huka Besik

Lide Mudak//Adi Sole, however, replies in the same way as Bula Pe//Mapo Tena:

167. Au ina ndeli-lima (-ku'u)-tak	I am a woman without a ring on her finger
168. Ma au feto liti-ei-tak.	And I am a girl without copper on her legs.

So, once more, with snot and tears, MK//TN sets off on his quest:

169. Boe ma ana-ma Manu Kama	So the orphan Manu Kama
170. Le'a-na kou-koa-n	Grabs his friarbird-hunting bow
171. Ma falu-ina Tepa Nilu	And the widow Tepa Nilu
172. Nole-na fupu-nggia-n.	Snatches his parrot-hunting blowpipe.
173. De neu tunga sanga ina bongin	He goes in search of a mother of birth
174. Ma neu afi sanga te'o te'en	And goes to look for a true aunt
175. Na te lu dua tunga enok	Two tears fall along the path
176. Ma pinu telu tunga dalak.	And three drops of snot fall along the road.

Episode four (lines 177–232) describes MK//TN's next encounter, with the woman Lo Luli//Kala Palu, who offers to adopt him. This time, late at night, MK//TN hears the sound of drum and gongs, 'the resounding buffalo-skin drum and the booming goat-skin beat', and he is told that the Sun and Moon are giving a feast at Rainbow Crossing and Thunder Round. MK//TN asks Lo Luli// Kala Palu to lead him to the celebration and there he is recognised by the Sun and Moon. Instead of being served properly, however, MK//TN is insulted.

215. *Boe ma la-lelak Manu Kama*	They recognise Manu Kama
216. *Ma la-lelak Tepa Nilu,*	And they recognise Tepa Nilu,
217. *De ala ko'o fe Manu Kama nesuk*	They pick up a rice pestle for Manu Kama
218. *De lae [do] kana,*	And they call it a small table,
219. *Ma ala keko fe Tepa Nilu batu*	And they push over a rock for Tepa Nilu
220. *De lae [do] kandela.*	And they call it a chair.
221. *De malole-a so*	This was good
222. *Do mandak-a so.*	And this was proper.
223. *Te boe ma ala ke te'i*	But then they cut and divide the meat
224. *Ma ala sode ndui,*	And they spoon and scoop food,
225. *De ala fe Tepa Nilu betek*	They give Tepa Nilu millet
226. *Ma ala fe-n neu lu'ak,*	And they give it to him in a rice basket,
227. *Ma fe Manu Kama bak*	They give Manu Kama lung
228. *Ma ala fe-n neu lokak.*	And they give it to him in a meat bowl.
229. *Boe ma Manu Kama nasa-kedu*	So Manu Kama begins to sob
230. *Ma Tepa Nilu nama-tani.*	And Tepa Nilu begins to cry.
231. *Boe ma ana fo'a fanu de la'o*	He gets up and leaves
232. *Ma ana lelo afe de lope.*	And he stands up and goes.

This puts an end to this episode and MK//TN continues his search.

Episode five (lines 233–334), with which the chant concludes, is the longest and most complex segment of the poem. This time, MK//TN meets the woman Kona Kek//Leli Deak and together they go to live in Lini Oe//Kene Mo. MK//TN, who has by this time become an able-bodied young man, begins to do work for his new mother and aunt, tapping lontar palms and working in the fields:

245. *Ana pale mane fe inan*	He taps male lontars for his mother
246. *Ma lenu feto fe te'on,*	And saps female lontars for his aunt,
247. *Fe te'on Kona Kek*	To give to his aunt, Kona Kek,
248. *Ma fe inan Leli Deak.*	And give to his mother, Leli Deak.
249. *Neu lele bina fe inan*	He goes to clear a field for his mother
250. *Ma seku ndenu fe te'on*	And he prepares a garden for his aunt

While MK//TN is working in a distant field, a ship appears and Kona Kek//Leli Deak, who sees it, goes to ask:

261. *Baluk se balu-n-o?*	This ship, whose ship is it?
262. *Ma tonak se tona-n-o?*	And this perahu, whose perahu is it?
263. *Salem fua loba Selak,*	[If] your ship carries loba-bark from Selak,

264. Tonam ifa lani Daik,	[If] your perahu bears lani-herbs from Daik,
265. Na au asa ala fa dei	Then, I'll buy a little
266. Do au tadi ala fa dei!	And I'll get a little!

The perahu's captain, Bui Kume//Lo Lengo, invites Kona Kek//Leli Deak on board, saying:

267. Au Buik balun-na ia	I, Buik, own this ship
268. Do au Lok tona-na ia.	Or I, Lok, own this perahu.
269. Lolek sio lai lain	Nine fine things are on board
270. Ma ladak falu lai ata.	And eight delightful things are on top.
271. Laba kae mai lain,	Mount and climb, come on board,
272. Ma tinga hene mai ata.	And step and ascend, come on top.
273. Fo dale be na asa,	What pleases you, buy it,
274. Ma pela be na peda-n!	And what displeases you, put it back!

While Kona Kek//Leli Deak is on board and is busy rummaging through the goods on the ship, Bui Kume//Lo Lengu sets sail for Sela//Dai. When MK//TN returns home at the end of the day, he is told that his mother and aunt have been carried away and are now on Sela//Dai. On hearing this, MK//TN climbs into a 'pig's feeding trough and giant clam shell' and sets off in search of his mother and aunt on Sela Sule//Dai Laka:

307. Boe ma ana-ma Manu Kama	So the orphan Manu Kama
308. Ma falu-ina Tepa Nilu	And the widow Tepa Nilu
309. Hela hako hani bafin	Pulls a pig's feeding trough
310. Ma le'a kima lou metin.	And tugs the tide's giant clamshell.
311. Ana sa'e kima lou metin	He perches upon the tide's clamshell
312. Ma ana tai hako hani bafin.	And nestles in the pig's feeding trough.
313. De ana tunga inan Kona Kek,	He searches for his mother, Kona Kek,
314. Ma ana afi te'on Leli Deak,	And he looks for his aunt, Leli Deak,
315. De leo Sela Sule neu	And goes to Sela Sule
316. Ma leo Dai Laka neu,	And goes to Dai Laka,
317. Neu de nita inan Kona Kek,	Goes and sees his mother, Kona Kek,
318. Ma nita te'on Leli Deak,	And sees his aunt, Leli Deak,
319. Nai Sela Sule	On Sela Sule
320. Do nai Dai Laka.	Or on Dai Laka.

After having reached Sela//Dai, MK//TN rests for a while and then tells Bui Kume//Lo Lengu to take a message back to the lords and headmen of Lini Oe//Kene Mo from whence he has come. It is with this message that the chant ends:

323. Bo Bui Kume-e,	Oh, Bui Kume,
324. Do ho Lo Lengu-e,	Oh, Lo Lengu,

325. Mai leo Lini Oe mu	When you go back to Lini Oe
326. Do leo Kene Mo mu,	Or go back to Kene Mo,
327. Mu ma-fada lena Lini-la	Go and tell the lords of Lini
328. Do ma-fada lesi Kene-la,	Or tell the headmen of Kene,
329. Mae: 'Sek-o make-nilu neo-la	Say: 'Come and see me
330. Tasi-oe pepesi-la.	Where the water of the sea strikes the land.
331. Dae lai Dain boe	There is land on Dain too
332. Ma oe lai Selam boe.	And there iswater on Selan too.
333. De au lo-ai kada Selan	My tomb-house will be on Selan
334. Ma au late-dae kada Dain.'	And my earthen-grave will be on Dain.'

This final message announces an end to the quest. As in other chants, the orphan and widow find a home, but this home is 'a tomb-house and earthen-grave'. The message confirms the deep allegorical sense in which the chant is intended to be taken and reinforces its appropriateness to a funeral setting.

In Rotenese mortuary rituals, the coffin is described as a 'ship' and burial involves the launching of this ship of the dead on its voyage to the other world. Meno, in his response to my questions about this chant, referred to 'Manu Kama's road to Dain//Tepa Nilu's path to Selan'.[5] The context of this reference makes it clear that he interprets MK//TN's journey as a passage to the grave. Although each person's journey is different, the end is the same for all. This is the Rotenese equivalent of the medieval *memento mori*—the ultimate qualification on all human endeavour.

A formal description of Rotenese ritual language

Rotenese ritual language is based on a variety of cultural conventions. To understand the language and to facilitate comparisons with other languages that utilise some form of parallelism, it is essential to specify these cultural conventions as precisely as possible. For this reason, in previous publications, I have attempted to fashion a formal terminology to describe the language. Here, I wish to review briefly my description of ritual language and indicate how far my present studies have carried me.

Rotenese ritual language is characterised by a strict canonical parallelism. This means, in effect, that apart from a small number of unpaired forms—pronouns,

---

5 In ritual language, *Sela(n) do Dai(n)* or *Sela Sule do Dai Laka* refers to a distant, unspecified land. Some Rotenese, however, claim that this placename refers to the island of origin of the Rotenese people, though this is in itself somewhat dubious since Rotenese disagree about their origins. The argument is based on sound similarity: *Sela(n)* is sometimes identified with the island of Ceram in the Moluccas and sometimes with the island of Ceylon (Sri Lanka). In the text, no such association is hinted at and Meno suggested no such exegesis.

connectives, 'prepositional' and a few other invariant elements—all elements must be paired. In formal terminology, each individual element must form part of a 'dyadic set'. In composition, dyadic sets produce parallel lines, whose overwhelmingly most common poetic form is the couplet, though other serial arrangements of lines are entirely acceptable and are often considered evidence of a greater mastery of the language. The elements that compose any particular dyadic set should, in their parallel lines (or occasionally in the two halves of a single line), correspond exactly in position and as far as possible in morphological structure. Paired elements often have the same number of syllables but, as far as I can determine, this is not a requirement. Parallel lines may thus be, and frequently are, of different syllable lengths. Lines may vary from seven to 11 syllables, with the majority hovering around the eight or nine-syllable mark.

On the basis of a systematic study of the lexicon of Rotenese ritual language comprising approximately one-third of my present corpus of texts (Fox 1972), it is possible to specify in some detail the linkages among elements of the language. Any element that forms a dyadic set with another element is said to be 'linked' to that element, and the number of an element's links constitutes its 'range'. An element that forms a set with only one other element has a 'range of one', whereas an element that forms sets with various other elements has a range equal to the number of its links.[6] For example, on the basis of all the texts that I have so far translated and analysed, the word *nade*(*k*), the generic word for 'name', forms a set only with the specific word for 'ancestral name', *tamo*(*k*). Because of this single link, its range is one. Similarly, the word *nafi*(*k*) ('sea cucumber') forms a set only with *sisi*(*k*) ('mollusc'); its range is therefore also one. In contrast, the word *dae*, meaning 'earth, land, low, below', has links with 11 other elements, as do *ai* (meaning 'plant, tree, wood') and *tua* (the word for the lontar palm and its products). All these elements have a range of 11.

From this point of view, linkages (and the semantic associations they imply) are more important than the dyadic sets themselves, since, on their own, individual dyadic sets tend to obscure more complex interrelations. It is critical to focus on linkages because the elements that form any one dyadic set may have a very different range of linkages. Thus, for example, the word *meo* ('cat') has a range of one since it links only with *kue* ('civet cat'), whereas *kue* has a range of four, linking not only with *meo* but with *kode* ('monkey'), *bafi* ('pig') and *fani* ('bee'). Similarly, *asu*, the word for 'dog' that occurs only in ritual language, links with

---

6   Formally, it is possible to define repetition as the linkage of an element with itself. By this convention, all elements would have a potential range of one. Repetition, though it occurs, is not an admired feature of ritual language and, since it would be difficult to differentiate between the potential for repetition and the real repetition of certain words, I have chosen not to adopt this convention.

busa, the ordinary-language word for 'dog'; *busa*, in turn, links as well with *manu* ('chicken') and with other elements that form compound or complex dyadic expressions.

In the present dictionary of ritual language (Fox 1972), which consists of just under 1400 lexical elements, every element can be identified precisely in terms of its specific linkages. By conservative enumeration, that disregards all names and compound forms—46 per cent of all elements link with only one other element. If compounds were treated as single forms, this percentage would rise considerably, to well more than 60 per cent of the lexicon. In practice, this means that a Rotenese poet must know in remarkable detail exactly which words form obligatory sets: that *kedu* ('to sob') can pair only with *tani* ('to cry'); or that *nitu* ('spirit') can pair only with *mula* ('ghost'). On the other hand, a substantial portion of the lexicon has a range greater than one, allowing the poet some flexibility in composition. Only a small proportion of these elements, however—33 in the present dictionary—has a range greater than five. These multiple-linkage elements, which include various words for directional orientation, words for 'earth', 'water', 'rock' and 'tree', plant parts, body parts and verbs for expressing position or balance, may be considered to form a core of primary symbols in the ritual language.

Graph procedures are eminently suited to represent the formal semantic associations among elements with multiple linkages and it is possible to speculate that as the dictionary of ritual language develops it may yield one or two large networks that would encompass as much as half of the lexicon, leaving perhaps the other half as a particularistic array of single-linked elements. This would provide a more precise understanding of one aspect of the canonical structure of Rotenese ritual language.

Rotenese ritual language is, however, 'canonical' in another sense. In the terminology of Roman Jakobson, who devoted considerable attention to the study of parallelism, the required lexical pairing of semantic elements and the network of associations that underlies this pairing represent a canonical ordering of the paradigmatic or 'metaphoric pole' of language (Jakobson and Halle 1956:76–82). Strictly speaking, parallelism refers to this patterning based on 'positional similarity'. Rotenese ritual language, however, is also remarkably well ordered along the syntagmatic, or what Jakobson called the 'metonymic pole' of language. In other words, phrases and lines in ritual language are frequently composed of recognisable formulae, which, because of the strict requirements of parallelism, become redoubled in parallel formulae. Thus a considerable portion of Rotenese ritual language consists of couplets and even longer sequences that are formulaic in a paradigmatic and a syntagmatic sense.

Within a large corpus of textual materials, the importance of these formulae becomes increasingly evident. Most poets—indeed all poets from whom I have been able to elicit a sufficient corpus on which to base a judgment—rely on what could be called, somewhat redundantly, 'standard' formulae, to which they might add some minor individual embellishment to distinguish their usage from that of other poets.[7] Individual poets thus develop their own personal 'style' in relation to certain 'standard' forms of their dialect area. Variations in formulae occur because personal style is regarded as important; yet within the general radius of any particular dialect area rival poets are expected to gather on ritual occasions to take turns in leading a chorus of fellow chanters. This requires poets to 'attune' themselves to one another and to 'play' with variations on their personal patterns of expression.

The interaction of the formulaic features of ritual language with the rules of parallel composition creates further complexity. Since approximately 50 per cent of the lexicon consists of elements that may pair with more than one other element, it is possible and indeed common for a formulaic line to couple with two (or more) variant, yet equally formulaic, lines. Individual poets on their own tend to settle on a single pattern for their couplets, but, in the company of other poets, they can alter their set patterns to suit the occasion.

To define and demonstrate what is in fact 'formulaic' in Rotenese ritual language is a difficult task requiring a large and varied corpus and, equally importantly, a historical perspective. It is in this respect that the Jonker text is crucial, since it can be reasonably considered to represent the standard pattern of ritual language at the turn of the century. I therefore propose to examine selected formulae in the text and compare them with formulae from various chants I have gathered since 1965.

The continuity of formulae in ritual language

In some sense, all ritual language is formulaic. Certain formulae, however, occur repeatedly not simply as couplets but as a patterned sequence of lines. Invariably, these sequences mark the beginning of a chant and episodes within it. More exactly, they punctuate a narrative sequence, which, though strictly patterned, could have recourse to less obvious formulaic devices. Elsewhere, I have referred to these formulae as 'formulaic chains' and developed a simple notation that could be used to generate a beginning for any mortuary chant.

---

7   The linguistic situation on Rote is one of diversity. Each of the 18 former domains on the island claims to have its own 'language'. In turn, these domain 'languages' can be sorted into roughly six dialect areas. Although ritual language varies less than ordinary language across these dialect areas and, in fact, uses words from different dialects to form synonymous pairs, there are nonetheless noticeable differences in ritual language. Within each dialect area there are standard forms that affect the way specific formulae are phrased.

Because of the patterning of ritual language, it would be a relatively simple exercise to develop similar notational schemes for other formulaic chains—as indeed it is possible to devise a notational description for any sequence in ritual language. To indulge in such exercises, however, would be to overlook a crucial feature of ritual-language composition—namely, that certain sequences occur frequently and are, as it were, the basic stock-in-trade of all poets in a particular dialect area. These sequences—to adopt another metaphor—are the reliable subroutines of a poet's program, whereas other sequences can be highly individual in their compositional phrasing.

A crucial step toward understanding the 'formulaic' is to recognise the degree of difference in composition among the various sequences of a chant. This can be done only by the comparison of a large body of texts from different contemporary poets or by the comparison of historical texts with contemporary ones. Each procedure provides its own view of the nature of composition. Since *Manu Kama ma Tepa Nilu* is the only text that offers the possibility of substantial historical comparison, I would like to devote my attention to a careful examination of some of the formulaic sequences whose continuity with contemporary forms makes them of particular interest. Specifically, I consider five examples of formulaic sequences in the text, some of which occur more than once. Comparisons—internally as well as with contemporary examples—are intended to highlight the way in which these sequences serve as recognisable, narrative markers.

Genealogical introduction

The first 24 lines of *Manu Kama ma Tepa Nilu* are composed entirely of common formulae. Many mortuary chants rely on an opening sequence that provides the genealogical and connubial affiliations of the chief chant character. In some chants, this can cover two or more generations. For purposes of identification, this might be called a 'genealogical introduction' sequence. Ostensibly, this sequence describes the marriage and birth of the chief chant character. What is critical, however, to a Rotenese audience is the information conveyed about this character by the succession of names. In MK//TN's case, his heavenly origins are revealed by the addition of the words for sun and moon as part of his father's name. As comparative illustration, the first eight lines of the text can be compared with the first eight lines of the chant *Ndi Lonama ma Laki Elokama* by Stefanus Amalo (Fox 1972:34–43).

Manu Kama ma Tepa Nilu

1. *Soku-lala Silu Lilo*	They lift Silu Lilo
2. *Ma lali-lala Huka Besi.*	And they carry Huka Besi.
3. *Lelete neu sao*	She bridges the path to marry
4. *Do fifino neu tu,*	Or joins the way to wed,

5. Sao Karna Lai Ledo	To marry Kama Lai of the Sun
6. Do tu Nilu Neo Bulan.	Or to wed Nilu Neo of the Moon.
7. De bongi-nala Tepa Nilu	She gives birth to Tepa Nilu
8. Ma lae-nala Manu Kama.	And brings forth Manu Kama.

Ndi Lonama ma Laki Elokama

Soku Lisu Lasu Lonak	They lift Lisu Lasu Lonak
Ma lali Dela Musu Asuk.	And they transfer Dela Musu Asuk.
De lelete neu sao	She bridges the path to marry
Ma fifinoneu tu.	And she joins the way to wed.
De ana tu Ndi Lonama.	She weds Ndi Lonama.
Ma sao Laki Elokama.	And she marries Laki Elokama.
Boe ma ana bongi-na Solu Ndi	She gives birth to Solu Ndi
Ma ana lae-na Luli Laki.	And she brings forth Luli Laki.

A trivial difference is in the use of verbal suffixes that indicate whether the subject and/or object of the verb are singular or plural. In ritual language, this distinction is regarded as irrelevant since, as Rotenese explain, 'singulars' are always phrased as 'duals'. Another minor difference is in the sequencing of the verbs 'to marry': *sao//tu*. The *Manu Kama ma Tepa Nilu* text first uses *sao*, then *tu*, whereas Amalo reverses this order, using *tu*, then *sao*. Both, however, use the same formulae: *lelete neu sao//fifino neu tu*. This appears to be a relatively stable formula in that *tu* and *sao* are not reversed (*lelete neu tu//fifino neu sao**), though there is nothing in the rules of the language, except common usage, to exclude such a phrasing. Nor is this the only formula that relies on the dyadic set of *lelete//fifino*. For example, the chanter Seu Ba'i (Eli Pellondou) in the origin chant for a rock formation in Termanu entitled *Sua Lai ma Batu Hu* uses the following formula:

Ana tao lelete batu	He makes a stone bridge
Ma ana tao fifino dae.	And he makes an earthen path.
De ana tu inak-ka Soe Leli,	Then he weds the woman Soe Leli,
Ma sao fetok-ka Pinga Pasa.	And marries the girl Pinga Pasa.

It is also worth noting that there are less elaborate opening sequences. Meno, for example, commonly used a simpler sequence that substituted the verb *ifa*, which means 'to carry by cradling', for the verb *lali*, which has the sense of 'shifting' or 'transferring'. Both verbs can be used to refer to the bridal procession by which a woman is physically carried or led (see the photograph in Fox 1980:103) to her husband's house. An example of this is taken from the chant *Lilo Tola ma Koli Lusi* by Meno (Fox 1972:85–97):

Ala soku-la Ole Masi	They lift Ole Masi
Ma ala ifa-la Bisa Oli.	And they cradle Bisa Oli.

De ana tu Lusi Topu Lani	She marries Lusi Topu Lani
Ma ana sao Tola Tae Ama.	And she weds Tola Tae Ama.
De bongi-na Lilo Tola	She gives birth to Lilo Tola
Ma ana lae-na Koli Lusi.	And she brings forth Koli Lusi.

Death and abandonment

What might be termed a 'death and abandonment' sequence occurs twice in the text. Lines 13–16 recount the death of MK//TN's father and lines 21–4 repeat this sequence, with only a slight variation, in reporting the death of MK//TN's mother. As an episode ending, this sequence occurs in virtually all mortuary chants. As an example, it is possible to compare lines from *Manu Kama ma Tepa Nilu* with those from the chant *Lilo Tola ma Koli Lusi*, in which Meno has given a slightly different embellishment to this formula.

Manu Kama ma Tepa Nilu

13. *Te hu Kama Lai Ledo lalo*	But Kama Lai of the Sun dies
14. *Ma Nilu Leo Bulan sapu.*	And Nilu Neo of the Moon perishes.
15. *De sapu ela Manu Kama*	He dies leaving Manu Kama
16. *Ma lalo ela Tepa Nilu.*	And he perishes leaving Tepa Nilu.
17. *Ela Tepa File no inan*	Leaving Tepa Nilu with his mother
18. *Ma ela Manu Kama no te'on.*	And leaving Manu Kama with his aunt.

Lilo Tola ma Koli Lusi

Boe ma Lusi Topu Lani sapu	So Lusi Topu Lani dies
Ma Tola Tae Ama lalo.	And Tola Tae Ama perishes.
Ana sapu ela Koli Lusi	He dies leaving Koli Lusi
Nanga-tu no te'on	To sit with his aunt
Ma lalo ela Lilo Tola	And he perishes leaving Lilo
Nasa-lai no inan.	To lean upon his mother.

The first 24 lines of the *Manu Kama ma Tepa Nilu* text are remarkable for their sustained and repeated use of common formulae. Two death and abandonment sequences are deftly linked to a genealogical introduction by the use of what is probably the single most common episode-ending formula in ritual language: the couplet *De malole-a so//Do mandak-a so* ('This was good or this was proper'), which occurs in lines 11 and 12 and again in lines 19 and 20. Between the genealogical introduction and the death of MK//TN's father, only a single formulaic couplet is inserted as reference to MK//TN's childhood. In many mortuary chants, this can be a subject for considerable elaboration.

The composition of these first 24 lines can be analysed in terms of the following formulae: 1) genealogical introduction (lines 1–8); 2) childhood couplet (lines

9–10); 3) good-and-proper couplet (lines 11–12); 4) death and abandonment sequence (lines 13–18); 5) good-and-proper couplet (lines 19–20); and 6) death and abandonment sequence (lines 21–4). The theme of 'orphan and widow' is then announced and the chant proceeds to a set of formulae that initiates the second episode in MK//TN's life journey.

Grief and the tearful encounter

Various expressions of grief mark transitions in the *Manu Kama ma Tepa Nilu* text. At six different junctures in the text, MK//TN is described as crying, usually with tears and snot running down his face (lines 31–4, 40–2, 97–8, 175–6, 183–6, 229–30). By the conventions of parallelism, *lu* ('tears') and *pinu* ('snot') form an obligatory dyadic set, whereas *idu* ('nose') may form a set with either *mata* ('eye') or *nasu* ('cheek'). Similarly, the verbs *-sasi//-tuda* ('to overflow, pour down, drop down') and the verbs *-kedu//-tani* ('to cry, weep, sob') also form pairs. All of the various descriptions of crying in the text use one or more of these sets, yet each is different and each expression varies.

The first of these expressions, which I have already noted, involves elaborate botanic comparisons with a number of sap and juice-yielding plants. Others of these expressions, however, conform with recognisable formulae. For example, when MK//TN leaves the woman Silu Lilo//Huka Besi, the following lines occur embedded in a set of other formulae:

97. Nate lu lama-sasi nasu	But tears pour down his cheeks
98. Ma pinu lama-tuda idu.	And snot falls from his nose.

These lines can be compared, for example, with lines in any of a number of compositions: *Suti Solo no Bina Bane* by the blind chanter of Ba'a, Lasaar Manoeain, or *Meda Manu ma Lilo Losi* by Meno.

Suti Solo no Bina Bane

Ala mai nda Bina Bane no Suti Solo,	They meet Bina Bane and Suti Solo,
Pinu lama-tuda idu	Snot falls from his nose
Ma lu lama-sasi mata.	And tears pour from his eyes.

Meda Manu ma Lilo Losi

De inan leo Ona Ba'a,	Her mother like Ona Ba'a,
Pinu lama-tuda idu,	Snot falls from her nose,
Ma te'on leo Lusi Lele,	And her aunt like Lusi Lele,
Lu lama-sasi mata,	Tears pour from her eyes.

The only difference in the contemporary examples is the use of eye (*mata*) instead of cheek (*nasu*).

Similar comparisons can be made in regard to the formula for sobbing and crying. Thus, when MK//TN is served meat improperly at the heavenly feast, the following lines occur as MK//TN prepares to leave:

229. Boe ma Manu Kama nasa-kedu	So Manu Kama begins to sob
230. Ma Tepa Nilu nama-tani.	And Tepa Nilu begins to cry.

In the version of *Suti Solo ma Bina Bane* by Meno, similar lines occur at different junctures:

Suti Solo ma Bina Bane I
Te hu Suti bei nama-tane	But Suti continues to cry
Ma Bina bei nasa-kedu.	And Bina continues to sob.

Suti Solo ma Bina Bane II
Bina boe nasa-kedu	Bina thus begins to sob
Ma Suti boe nama-tani.	And Suti thus begins to weep.

Again, in a chant, *Doli Mo ma Lutu Mala*, that reveals the origin of rice and millet, Meno has utilised the same formula, repeating in an entirely different context the theme of the quest in *Manu Kama ma Tepa Nilu*:

Doli Mo ma Lutu Mala
Doli Mo nasa-kedu	Doli Mo begins to sob
Ma Lutu Mala nama-tani,	And Lutu Mala begins to weep,
Fo nasa-kedu sanga inan	Sobbing for his mother
Ma nama-tani sanga te'on.	And crying for his aunt.

These various expressions of crying and weeping do not, on their own, qualify as full formulaic sequences. At most, they involve the use of only a couple of dyadic sets; yet they invariably serve as transitional markers indicating the end of an episode or event and the beginning of another. In the chant *Suti Solo ma Bina Bane*, they mark each stage of an extended dialogue; in *Doli Mo ma Lutu Mala*, they mark the first encounter with the seeds of rice and millet. In these and other chants, including *Manu Kama ma Tepa Nilu*, they are themselves only part of a longer formulaic sequence. One version of this sequence could be described as the 'tearful encounter' sequence. It is possible to compare three examples of this in *Manu Kama ma Tepa Nilu*.

Tearful encounter I
97. Nate lu lama-sasi nasu	But tears pour down his cheeks
98. Ma pinu lama-tuda idu.	And snot falls from his nose.
99. Boe ma lima leu la-nda	Then arms go to meet
100. Do langa leu la-tongo	Or heads go to encounter
101. Inak dua esa nade Lide Muda	Two women, one named Lide Muda

102. Ma esa nade Adi Sole.	And one named Adi Sole.
Tearful encounter II	
175. Nate lu dua tunga enok	Two tears fall along the path
176. Ma pinu telu tunga dalak,	And three drops of snot fall along the road,
177. Boe ma langa leu la-tongo	Then heads go to encounter
178. Ma lima leu la-nda	And arms go to meet
179. Inak esa nade Lo Luli	A woman named Lo Luli
180. Ma fetok esa nade Kala Palu.	And a girl named Kala Palu.
Tearful encounter III	
229. Boe ma Manu Kama nasa-kedu	So Manu Kama begins to sob
230. Ma Tepa Nilu nama-tani,	And Tepa Nilu begins to cry,
...	...
233. Boe ma lima leu la-nda	Then arms go to meet
234. Ma langa leu la-tongo,	And heads go to encounter,
235. Mai tongo Leli Deak	Come to encounter Leli Deak
236. Do mai nda Kona Kek.	Or come to meet Kona Kek.

In these tearful encounters, the women who meet MK//TN are able to strike up a dialogue and inquire about his condition and destination. These sequences can be compared with the extended sequence in *Suti Solo no Bina Bane* by Lasaar Manoeain in which Suti Solo//Bina Bane encounters the women of Timor:

Boe ma ina Helok-ka mai nda duas	The Helok woman comes to meet the two
Ma fetok Sonobai mai tongo duas-sa	And the Sonobai girl comes to encounter the two
Lu la-sasi mata,	Tears pour from their eyes,
Ma pinu la-tuda idu	Snot falls from their nose
Boe ma lae:	So they say:
Sala hata leo hata	What wrong like this
Ma singo hata leo hatak,	And what mistake like this,
De ei pinu idu	This snot from your nose
Ma lu mate?	And these tears from your eyes?

As always, the tearful encounter dramatically refocuses on the condition of the orphan and widow.

Desire and the dawn encounter

Besides these tearful encounters, however, there is another set of 'encounters' in *Manu Kama ma Tepa Nilu*. We can call these 'dawn encounters'. In these encounters (lines 53–60, 137–46), green parrots and honeybirds come to sing to MK//TN. In the conventions of Rotenese poetry, these birds are the iconic representation of sexually attractive women, and their most alluring songs are always heard at dawn.

The two encounters are virtually identical (lines 53–4 = 137–8, 55–60 = 141–50); the only difference is the addition of two lines describing the colour of the dawn in the second encounter (lines 39–40). The shorter of these two passages is as follows:

53. Boe ma faik esa ma-uni	Then on one certain day
54. Ma ledek dua ma-te'e	And at a particular time
55. Siluk ana mai dulu	Morning comes to the east
56. Ma huak ana mai langa.	And dawn comes to the head.
57. Boe ma koa bei timu dulu-la,	Friarbirds are still in the dawning east,
58. Ala meli ei de ala mai.	They lift their legs, they come.
59. Ma nggia bei sepe langa-la,	And the green parrots are still at the reddening head,
60. Ala la lida de ala mai.	They flap their wings, they come.

These lines merely set the scene for the birds' songs. They are of interest, however, because they consist of common formulaic sequences and express crucial symbolic conventions about space and time. The first two lines, for example, contain one of the most recurrent episode-initiating formulae in Rotenese poetry. The following literal translation gives an idea of the specific dyadic sets that make up this formula:

Boe ma faik esa ma-uni	Then day one certain
Ma ledo dua ma-te'e	And sun two true

The sequence links the words for 'day' and 'sun', the numerals 'one' and 'two' and terms that assert 'specificity' and 'truth'. With some variation, the formula is a recognisable part of the repertoire of all the poets I have recorded. For example, Amalo and the poetess Lisbet Adulilo use the following variant: *Faik esa ma-nunin ma ledo dua ma-teben* (*manunin* is an alternative form for *ma-unin* and *mate'e* for *ma-teben*). This usage is generally accepted as standard. On the other hand, Meno and Seu Bai, who learned from him, use the variant *Faik esa ma-nunin ma ledok esa mateben*. The repetition of the numeral *esa* (meaning 'one') is an obvious imperfect parallelism and, as far as I can determine, is used specifically by these two poets as a distinctive key signature to their compositions.

The second formula in these lines can be translated literally as follows:

Siluk ana mai dulu,	Morning, it comes east,
Ma hu'ak ana ma langa.	And dawn, it comes head.

The dyadic set *dulu//langa*, which links 'east' and 'head', is one of several dyadic coordinates that structures Rotenese symbolic space. Other sets link 'west' and 'tail', 'north' and 'left' and 'south' and right', thus representing the island in the image of an outstretched creature that is variously conceived of as a crocodile, a buffalo or a man (see Fox 1973:356–8). In this symbolic structure, the east, as the source of the dawn and of the renewal of life, constitutes a privileged direction, and dawn encounters are potentially auspicious in contrast with midnight encounters, which are generally dangerous and inauspicious. Dawn encounters and midnight encounters are both standard poetic situations.[8] There is even what might be called the 'false dawn encounter' in which a chant character misjudges the time by mistaking the dead of night for the early morning and so rises to meet his or her doom. Thus in the poem *Meda Manuma Lilo Losi* by Meno (Fox 1972:44–51), two chant characters enter into a dialogue about the dawn. Meda Manu//Lilo Losi says:

Te busa-a na-hou	For the dog has barked
De siluk lai dulu so,	So daylight is in the east,
Ma manu-a kokoa	And the cock has crowed
De hu'ak lai langa so.	So dawn is at the head.

Her mother, Lusi Lele//Ona Ba'a, replies:

Te siluk bei ta dulu	Daylight is not yet in the east
Ma hu'ak bei ta langa.	And dawn is not yet at the head.
Besak-ka bolo-do neu dua	Now night is at its height
Ma fati-lada neu telu.	And dark is at its peak.

In the end, Meda Manu//Lilo Losi disregards her mother's advice and leaves the house, only to be attacked by wandering spirits.

Tomb guarding and planting

As a final example of the use of formulae to mark transitions in narrative structure, we can consider the way in which the *Manu Kama ma Tepa Nilu* text concludes. Unlike the elaborate formulaic sequences that were strung together at the beginning, the chant ends with a simple couplet:

| 333. *De au lo-ai kada Selan,* | My tomb-house will be on Selan, |
| 334. *Ma au late-dae kada Dain.* | And my earthen-grave will be on Dain. |

---

8   In lines 57 and 59, I have translated the double-dyadic set *timu dulu//sepe langa* as 'dawning east'//'reddening head'. I have done so because these terms are followed by a pluralising marker, *-la*, which reflects back to the subject, the frairbirds//green parrots: *ala mai* ('they come'). In other poems, this set might be better interpreted as a placename designating some region in the east. As a placename, this set can also be taken up as a personal name. This occurs, for example, in the poem *Kea Lenga ma Lona Bala* by Seu Bai. An auspicious pair of bats is referred to as Soi Ana Sepe Langa//Bau Ana Timu Dulu ('Tiny Bat of Dawning East'//'Flying Fox of Reddening Head'), and they form part of a family with Timu Tongo Batu//Sepe Ama Li ('Dawn Tongo Batu'//'Reddening Ama Li') and his daughter, Buna Sepe//Boa Timu ('Flower Reddening'//'Fruit Dawning').

The reference here is to the wooden structure resembling a house that Rotenese once commonly built over the grave to form a kind of tomb. This ending is thus appropriate to a mortuary chant, but the use of this single couplet, on its own, gives no indication of the fact that in other mortuary chants similar couplets are generally part of longer, more elaborate formulaic sequences. At best, this couplet can be considered as a truncated evocation of these other sequences.

Two variant sequences, both commonly employed in mortuary chants, can be distinguished. One might be called the 'tomb-guarding' variant; the other, the 'tomb-planting' variant. A short example of 'tomb guarding' can be taken from the poem *Pau Balo ma Bola Lungi* (Fox 1972:192–211) by Stefanus Amalo. In this poem, a bereaved daughter, Liu Pota//Menge Solu, watches over the tomb of her father:

Pota Popo sapu	Pota Popo perished
Ma Solu Oebau lalo.	And Solu Oebau died.
De au anga-tu late-dae	Thus I sit upon an earthen-grave
Ma au asa-lai lo-ai.	And I lean upon a tomb-house.

In this way, Liu Pota//Menge Solu is able to refuse Pau Balo and Bola Lungi's overtures and he must go off in search of another woman. As an example of 'tomb planting', the final sequence of the poem *Kea Lenga ma Lona Bala* (Fox 1972:142–55) by Seu Ba'i can be cited. The Ndaonese chant character Kea Lenga//Lona Bala, whose wife has died while he is away, sends a coconut and areca nut back to Ndao to be planted at his wife's grave. The poem concludes with these words:

Fo ela na la-boa langan	Let the coconut grow fruit at her head
Ma ela pua la-nggi ein,	And let the areca nut sprout stalks at her feet,
Fo ela au falik leo Ndao u	So that when I return to Ndao
Na au lelu u late-dae	I may go to look upon her earthen-grave
Ma au tulek leo Folo u	And when I go back to Folo
Na au lipe u lo-ai.	I may stare upon her tomb-house.

Concluding remarks

I proposed this chapter as an introduction to the possibilities of Rotenese poetry. Only in analysing a long poem do various of these possibilities become evident. Although I have focused on a single text, I have tried to indicate some of the strategic levels at which this poetry can be read. In conclusion, I would like to comment on the text in terms of three features of the poetry. These relate to oral intercommunication, narrative structure and verbal authority.

The fact that the *Manu Kama ma Tepa Nilu* text was originally gathered at the beginning of the twentieth century did not prevent it from being taken up immediately as part of a continuing dialogue among contemporary poet-chanters in Termanu. Meno responded to my public rendering and to my questions about the text by inserting comments in his own compositions. This is how chanters communicate with one another. Any chant can, and often does, relate to a variety of other chants—sometimes by the briefest of passing allusions (the change of a single word, for example, to imitate another chanter's style) and, at other times, by taking up a theme and elaborating on it. All of this is part of a dense web of oral intercommunication, much of which is so specific that it is difficult to recover outside the immediate context of a particular performance. Ritual gatherings were—and to a lesser extent still are—the occasions at which chanters would gather to vie with one another in performance. This basic aspect of social life provides the means of maintaining oral intercommunication and collective textual elaboration.

The formulaic structures of *Manu Kama ma Tepa Nilu* serve to facilitate this oral intercommunication. Although Rotenese poetry is virtually all 'formulaic', certain formulaic sequences are distinguishable as markers at the beginnings and ends of episodes. These routine sequences are remarkably similar among poets and they stand out as such in contrast to the subtler composition of other lines. The fact that the *Manu Kama ma Tepa Nilu* text was mistaken for a contemporary chant by several Rotenese was due in large part, I suspect, to the prominence of these formulaic markers throughout its narrative structure.

The narrative structure of *Manu Kama ma Tepa Nilu* is similar in form to the structures that articulate virtually all long Rotenese chants. These chants invariably recount a tale of some sort and a high proportion of them feature a journey. Here, there is a coincidence between a formal narrative order and an image of the course of life. In the predominant Rotenese view, enhanced as it is with ideas from Christianity, life is conceived of as a successive movement, consisting of a series of transformations, leading to an eventual end. This progressive development from an initial base—a process that can be represented by various botanic metaphors—is not conceived of as turning back on itself or as ending in a cyclical return. Instead, it is articulated as an ordered sequence with a clear beginning and a definite end. Such sequences are a common occurrence throughout Rotenese culture and constitute what I would argue are a privileged image in the overall structuring of Rotenese cultural conceptions.[9]

---

9   Hints of an earlier view of life as a process ending in ultimate return can still be detected in Rotenese ritual, but these are now muted or reinterpreted to conform to contemporary views. In the late 1950s and early 1960s, a congregational rupture occurred in the Timorese Protestant Church (Gereja Masehi Injili Timor, GMIT). The split was largely Rotenese inspired and Rotenese based and the new group that was formed at the time called itself the Gereja Musafir ('The Pilgrim Church'). The label 'pilgrim' typifies what has now become the traditional view that the Rotenese have of themselves.

This privileged status of the ordered sequence contributes to the authority with which certain texts are endowed. Although ritual language can be used in any situation of formal interaction, there are only two occasions for which there exist established canonical poems: celebrations of origin and celebrations of conclusion. Similarly, there are only two kinds of canonical poems: origin chants and mortuary chants. Origin chants bless the beginnings of specific activities. They recount the founding of these activities and the acquisition of the essential objects with which they are associated: the origin of fire and of tools, and the building of the first house; the origin of the first seeds of rice and millet and their transmission and planting; the origin of coloured dyes, of weaving and the creation of cloth. In contrast, mortuary chants recount the demise of an individual, but do so by comparing the individual with a character whose life course follows a definite pattern.

The formulaic utterances of ritual language are regarded as ancestral wisdom. A chanter is thus the medium of an authoritative cultural voice, which speaks decisively at the beginnings and ends of sequences that define an order to life itself.

Reference text

Ana-Ma Manu Kama ma Falu-Ina Tepa Nilu

1. *Soku-lala Silu Lilo*	They lift Silu Lilo
2. *Ma lali-lala Huka Besi.*	And they carry Huka Besi.
3. *Lelete neu sao*	She bridges the path to marry
4. *Do fifino neu tu,*	Or joins the way to wed,
5. *Sao Kama Lai Ledo*	To marry Kama Lai of the Sun
6. *Do tu Nilu Neo Bulan.*	Or to wed Nilu Neo of the Moon.
7. *De bongi-nala Tepa Nilu*	She gives birth to Tepa Nilu
8. *Ma lae-nala Manu Kama.*	And brings forth Manu Kama.
9. *De na-lelak fiti fulik*	He learns to play with fulik-marbles
10. *Ma na-lelak selo so'ek.*	And learns to spear the coconut shell.
11. *De malole-a so*	This was good
12. *Do mandak-a so*	Or this was proper.
13. *Te hu Kama Lai Ledo lalo*	But Kama Lai of the Sun dies
14. *Ma Nilu Neo Bulan sapu.*	And Nilu Neo of the Moon perishes.
15. *De sapu ela Manu Kama*	He dies leaving Manu Kama
16. *Ma lalo ela Tepa Nilu,*	And he perishes leaving Tepa Nilu,
17. *Ela Tepa Nilu no inan*	Leaving Tepa Nilu with hismother
18. *Ma ela Manu Kama no te'on*	And leaving Manu Kama with his aunt
19. *De malole-a so*	This was good

20. *Do mandak-a so.*	Or this was proper.
21. *Te hu neu ma Silu Lilo ana lalo,*	But then Silu Lilo, she dies,
22. *Ma Huka Besi ana sapu.*	And Huka Besi, she perishes.
23. *De sapu ela Manu Kama*	She dies leaving Manu Kama
24. *Ma lalo ela Tepa Nilu.*	And she perishes leaving Tepa Nilu.
25. *De ana-ma Manu Kama*	An orphan is Manu Kama
26. *Ma falu-ina Tepa Nilu.*	And a widow is Tepa Nilu.
27. *Ana sala ama-na bai,*	He lacks a father too,
28. *Ma singo ina-na bai,*	He misses a mother too,
29. *Sala to'o-na bai,*	Lacks a mother's brother too,
30. *Ma singo te'o-na bai.*	And misses a father's sister too.
31. *De lu ko boa na'u,*	Tears like bidara-fruit in the grass,
32. *Ma pinu kaitio telan,*	Snot like kaitio-[leaves] in the underbrush,
33. *Lama-noma oba-tula*	They pour like juice from a tapped gewang
34. *Do lama-titi ate lasi.*	And flow like sap from an old ate.
35. *Boe ma inak ia Bula Pe*	Then the woman Bula Pe
36. *Ma fetok ia Mapo Tena*	And the girl Mapo Tena
37. *Lelu naka-nae nita-n,*	Looks and stares at him,
38. *Ma lipe nala-mula nita-n,*	Gazes and inspects him,
39. *De ana-ma Manu Kama,*	The orphan Manu Kama,
40. *Lu dua-o dua,*	Tears falling two by two,
41. *Ma falu-ina Tepa Nilu,*	The widow Tepa Nilu,
42. *Pinu telu-o telu.*	Snot running three by three.
43. *Boe ma na-le lelena*	So she calls out loudly
44. *Mana-nggou ngganggali.*	And she shouts out clearly.
45. *Nae: 'Bo ana-ma Manu Kama,*	She says: 'Oh, orphan Manu Kama,
46. *Do bo falu-ina Tepa Nilu,*	Oh, widow Tepa Nilu,
47. *Mai, te Silu Lilok nde au*	Come, Silu Lilok am I
48. *Do Huka Besik nde au.*	Or Huka Besik am I.
49. *Boe ma ta nae Bula Pe*	Do not say Bula Pe
50. *Te nae Silu Lilok,*	But say Silu Lilok,
51. *Ma ta nae Mapo Tena*	And do not say Mapo Tena
52. *Te nae Huka Besik.'*	But say Huka Besik.'
53. *Boe ma faik esa ma-uni*	Then on one certain day
54. *Ma ledok dua ma-tee*	And at a particular time
55. *Siluk ana mai Mu*	Morning comes to the east
56. *Ma hu'ak ana mat langa.*	And dawn comes to the head.
57. *Boe ma koa bet timu dulu-la,*	Friarbirds are still in the dawning east,
58. *Ala meli ei de ala mai.*	They lift their legs, they come.
59. *Ma nggia bei sepe langa-la,*	And the green parrots are still at the reddening head,
60. *Ala la lida de ala mai.*	They flap their wings, they come.

Explorations in Semantic Parallelism

61.	*Mai boe ma ala kako dodoe hala-n-ala*	Then, they sing with soft voices
62.	*Ma ala hele memese dasi-n-ala.*	And they warble with gentle songs.
63.	*De ala kako-lala Manu Kama dalen*	They sing to Manu Kama's heart
64.	*Ma hele-lala Tepa Nilu tein.*	And warble to Tepa Nilu's inner being.
65.	*Boe ma ana-ma Manu Kama*	The orphan Manu Kama
66.	*Ma falu-ina Tepa Nilu,*	And the widow Tepa Nilu,
67.	*Ana fafae neu inan*	He wakes his mother
68.	*Ala o'ofe neu te'on,*	And shakes his aunt,
69.	*Ma nae: 'Bo ina-ng-o-ne,*	And says: 'Oh, my mother,
70.	*Do bo te'o-ng-o-ne,*	Oh, my aunt,
71.	*Fo'a fanu mapa-deik,*	Wake and stand up,
72.	*De lelo afe manga-tuk,*	Come awake and sit up,
73.	*Te siluk nai dulu so*	Morning is in the east
74.	*Ma hu'ak nai langa so.*	And dawn is at the head.
75.	*Buluk-a ma-dalek nai o*	Now have a heart
76.	*Do ma-teik nai o.*	And be concerned.
77.	*Mu asa fe-ng-au koa halak*	Go buy for me the friarbird's voice
78.	*Do tadi fe-ng-au nggia dasik*	Or get for me the green parrot's whistle
79.	*Fo ela au a-hala nggia halak*	So that I may give voice to the friarbird's voice
80.	*Ma au a-dasi koa dasik*	And I may sing to the green parrot's song
81.	*Fo sama leo inang boe*	That you may be just like my mother
82.	*Do deta lee te'ong boe.'*	Or that you may be similar to my aunt.'
83.	*Boe ma nae: 'Mu bola inam leo kapa*	Then she says: 'Go, tie yourmother like a water buffalo
84.	*Fo leo-leo leo kapa;*	Circling round like a water buffalo;
85.	*Ma mu tai te'om leo lilo,*	And go weigh your aunt like gold,
86.	*Fo benu-benu leo lilo,*	Balanced gently like gold,
87.	*Te au ina ndeli-lima-ku'u-tak*	For I am a woman without a ring on her finger
88.	*Ma au feto liti-ei-tak.'*	And I am a girl without copper on her legs.'
89.	*Boe ma ana-ma Manu Kama*	So the orphan Manu Kama
90.	*Ma falu-ina Tepa Nilu*	And the widow Tepa Nilu
91.	*Ana sale dale-ana-ma-na*	He has the heart's regret of an orphan
92.	*Ma ana tuka tei falu-ina-na*	And has the inner grief of a widow.
93.	*Besak-a le'a-na aman kou-na*	Now he grabs his father's bow
94.	*Ma nole-na to'om fupa-na*	And snatches his uncle's blowpipe
95.	*De ana lope no hu'a-langak,*	He goes, swinging his arms, with dawn at the head,
96.	*Ma ana la'o no silu-duluk,*	And he goes, lifting his legs, with morning in the east,
97.	*Nate lu lama-sasi nasu*	But tears pour down his cheeks
98.	*Ma pinu lama-tuda idu.*	And snot falls from his nose.

10. Manu Kama's road, Tepa Nilu's path

99. *Boe ma lima leu la-nda*	Then arms go to meet
100. *Do langa leu la-tongo*	Or heads go to encounter
101. *Inak dua esa nade Lide Muda*	Two women, one named Lide Muda
102. *Ma esa nade Adi Sole.*	And one named Adi Sole.
103. *De lide Mudak na-nggou.*	Lide Muda shouts out.
104. *Nae: 'Bo manu Kama-e,*	She says: 'Oh, Manu Kama,
105. *Leo dae be mu?'*	To what land are you going?'
106. *Ma Adi sole na-lo*	And Adi Sole calls out
107. *Nae: 'Bo tepa nilu-e,*	She says: 'Oh, Tepa Nihu,
108. *Leo oe be mu?'*	To what water are you going?'
109. *Ma nae: 'Aue! Lide Mudak*	And he says: 'Aue! Oh, Lide Mudak
110. *Do o Adi Sole!*	Oh, Adi Sole!
111. *Au ana-ma Manu Kama*	I am the orphan Manu Kama
112. *Ma au falu-ina Tepa Nilu*	And I am the widow Tepa Nilu.
113. *Iau a-ina ingu inan*	I have, as mother, the land of my mother
114. *Ma au ate'o leo te'on.*	And I have, as aunt, the clan of my aunt.
115. *Ala hopo kedok Manu Kama*	Gruffly, they mix syrup for Manu Kama,
116. *Ma ala sode odak Tepa Nilu*	Sourly, they serve rice to Tepa Nilu,
117. *Ala lo tuluk Tepa Nilu*	They offer things with a shove to Tepa Nilu
118. *Ma ala sipo le'ak Manu Kama.*	And they take things with a tug to Manu Kama.
119. *Au ana-ma dai-lena-ng,*	My orphaned state is increased,
120. *De au ana-ma-ng boe mai,*	I am more an orphan than ever,
121. *Ma au falu-ina tolesi-ng,*	My widowed state is made greater,
122. *Au falu-ina-ng boe mai.'*	I am more a widow than ever.'
123. *Boe ma inak ia Lide Muak nae:*	So this woman Lide Mudak says:
124. *'Bo Manu Kama-e,*	'Oh, Manu Kama,
125. *Mai uma-t-ala uma leon',*	Come to our house',
126. *Ma fetok ia Adi Sole nae:*	And the girl Adi Sole says:
127. *'Bo Tepa Nilu-e,*	'Oh, Tepa Nilu,
128. *Mai lo-t-ala lo leon,*	Come to our home,
129. *Te au lea inam Silu Lilo boe,*	For I will be like your mother, Silu Lilo,
130. *Ma au leo te'om Huka Besik boe!'*	And I will be like your aunt, Huka Besik!'
131. *Hu ndia de ala dengu doli Manu Kama*	So they pound rice for Manu Kama
132. *De ala hao hade Manu Kama*	And they serve rice to Manu Kama.
133. *Hu ndia de ala tutu lutu Tepa Nilu*	And they offer millet to Tepa Nilu
134. *De ala fati bete Tepa Nilu.*	And they prepare millet for Tepa Nilu.
135. *Boe ma nae do ina bongin*	So he calls her his mother of birth
136. *Ma nae do te'on teen.*	And he calls her his true aunt.
137. *Boe ma faik esa ma-uni*	Then on one definite day

138. Ma ledok dua ma-tee,	And at a certain time,
139. Pila poe-oe-na-n	Red as a shrimp in water
140. Ma modo masala-na-n,	And yet still green,
141. Siluk ana mai dulu,	Morning comes to the east,
142. Ma hu'ak ana mai langa	Dawn comes to the head
143. Boe ma koa bei timu-dulu-la,	Friarbirds are still in the dawning east,
144. Ala meli ei de ala mai.	The lift their legs, they come.
145. Ma nggia bei sepe-langa-la,	And green parrots are still at the reddening head,
146. Ala la lida de ala mai.	They flap their wings, they come.
147. Mai boe ma ala kako dodoe hala-n-ala	There, they sing with soft voices
148. Ma ala hele memese dasi-n-ala	And they warble with gentle songs,
149. De ala kako-lala Manu Kama dalen,	They sing to Manu Kama's heart,
150. Ma Hele-lala Tepa Nilu Tein.	They warble to Tepa Nilu's inner being.
151. Boe ma Manu Kama Fafae Lide Mudak	Then Manu Kama wakes LideMudak
152. Ma Tepa Nilu o'ofe Adi Sole.	And Tepa Nilu shakes Adi Sole.
153. Nae: 'Bo ina-ng-o-ne,	He says: 'Oh, my mother,
154. Do bo te'o-ng-o-ne,	Oh, my aunt,
155. Fo'a fanu mapa-deik,	Wake and stand up,
156. Ma leli afe manga-tuk!	Come awake and sit up!
157. Te Siluk nai dulu so	Morning is in the east
158. Ma hu'ak nai langa so.	And dawn is at the head.
159. Buluk-a bei Manu Kama inan	If you are Manu Kama's mother
160. Do buluk-a bei Tepa Nilu te'on,	Or if you are Tepa Nilu's aunt,
161. Mu asa fe-ng-au koa	Go buy for me a friarbird
162. Ma mu tadi fe-ng-au nggia,	And go get for me a green parrot,
163. Te au ae: o Silu Lilok,	So I may call you Silu Lilok,
164. Ma au ae: [o Huka Besik.'	And I may call you Huka Besik.'
165. Boe ma inak ia Lide Mudak	So this woman, Lide Mudak,
166. Ma fetok ia Adi Sole nata ma nae:	And this girl, Adi Sole, answersand says:
167. 'Au ina ndeli-lima [-ku'u]-tak	'I am a woman without a ring on her finger
168. Ma au fete liti-ei-tak.'	And I am a girl without copper on her legs.'
169. Boe ma ana-ma Manu Mama	So the orphan Manu Kama
170. Le'a-na kou-koa-n	Grabs his friarbird-hunting bow
171. Ma falu-ina Tepa Nilu	And the widow Tepa Nilu
172. Nole-na fupu-nggia-n.	Snatches his parrot-hunting blowpipe.
173. De neu tunga sanga ina Bongin	He goes in search of a mother of birth
174. Ma neu ad sanga te'o te'en.	And goes to look for a true aunt.

175. *Na te lu dua tunga enok*	Two tears fall along the path
176. *Ma pinu telu tunga dalak.*	And three drops of snot fall along the road.
177. *Boe ma langa leu la-tongo*	Then heads go to encounter
178. *Ma lima leu la-nda*	And arms go to meet
179. *Inak esa nade Lo Luli*	A woman named Lo Lull
180. *Ma fetok esa nade Kala Palu.*	And a girl named Kala Palu.
181. *Nae: 'Bo Manu Kama-e,*	She says: 'Oh, Manu Kama,
182. *Do bo Tepa Nilu-e,*	Oh, Tepa Nilu,
183. *O lu-mata leo hatik*	Why the tears from your eyes
184. *Do o pinu-idu leo hatak?'*	Or why the snot from your nose?'
185. *Boe ma nae: 'Au lu mata-sanga inang*	So he says: 'The tears in my eyes seek my mother
186. *Ma au pinu idu afi te'ong,*	And the snot of my nose looks for my aunt,
187. *Sanga inang Silu Lilok*	Seeks my mother, Silu Lilok,
188. *Ma aft te'ong Huka Besik,'*	And looks for my aunt, Huka Besik.'
189. *Ma nae: 'Ata uma-t-ala uma leon*	And she says: 'Our home, come to our home
190. *Ma ala lo-t-ala lo leon!*	And our house, come to our house!
191. *Te au sama lee inam boe*	For I will be like your mother
192. *Ma deta lea te'om boe.'*	And I will be similar to your aunt.'
193. *Bolok-ala tao do,*	Late in the evening,
194. *Ma fatik-ala tao lada,*	In the middle of the night,
195. *Boe ma lama-nene lololo,*	They constantly listen to,
196. *Ma lama-nia ndanda,*	They continually hear,
197. *Labu kapa behoe*	The resounding buffalo-skin drum
198. *Ma dele bi'i bendena.*	And the booming goat-skin beat.
199. *Boe ma na-tane neu inan*	So he asks his mother
200. *Ma teteni neu te'on nae:*	And questions his aunt, saying:
201. *'Labu sila leme be mai*	'Where do the drums come from
202. *Ma meko sila leme he mai?'*	And where do the gongs come from?'
203. *Ma nae: 'Leme Elu Ladi mai*	And she says: 'From Rainbow Crossing
204. *Do leme Tata Feo mai,*	Or from Thundering Round,
205. *Te.Bulan ana tati hani*	For the Moon kills animals
206. *Ma Ledo ana soe usu.'*	And the Sun slaughters stock.'
207. *Nae: 'Na la'o le'a au dei,*	He says: 'Lift your legs, carry me then,
208. *Ma lope nuni au dei.*	And move your arms, lead me then.
209. *Fo meko teu taka-neni*	Let us go and see the gongs
210. *Ma labu teu ta-nilu.'*	And let us go and observe the drums.'
211. *Boe ma leo Elu Ladi leu*	So they go to Rainbow Crossing
212. *Ma leo Tata Feo leu.*	And they go to Thundering Round.
213. *Leu te Bulan ana tao feta*	They go, for the Moon gives a feast
214. *Ma Ledo ana tao dote.*	And the Sun has a celebration.

215. Boe ma la-lelak Manu Kama	They recognise Manu Kama
216. Ma la-lelak Tepa Nilu.	And they recognise Tepa Nilu.
217. De ala ko'o fe Manu Kama nesuk	They pick up a rice mortar for Manu Kama
218. De lae [do] kana	And they call it a small table
219. Ma ala keko fe Tepa Nilu batu	And they push over a rock for Tepa Nilu
220. De lae [do] kandela.	And they call it a chair.
221. De malole-a so,	This was good,
222. Do mandak-a so.	And this was proper.
223. Te boe Ma ala ke te'i	But then they cut and divide the meat
224. Ida ala sode ndui.	And they spoon and scoop food.
225. De ala fe Tepa Nilu betek	They give Tepa Nilu millet
226. Ma ala fe-n neu lu'ak,	And they give it to him in a rice basket,
227. Ma fe Manu Kama bak	They give Manu Kama lung
228. Ma ala fe-n neu lokok.	And they give it to him in a meat bowl.
229. Boe ma Manu Kama nasa-kedu	So Manu Kama begins to sob
230. Ma Tepa Nilu nama-tani.	And Tepa Nilu begins to cry.
231. Boe ma ana fo'a fanu de la'o	He gets up and leaves
232. Ma ana lelo afe de lope.	And he stands up and goes.
233. Boe ma lima leu la-nda	Arms go to meet
234. Ma langa leu la-tongo.	And heads go to encounter.
235. Mai tongo Leli Deak	Come to encounter Leli Deak
236. Do mai nda Kona Kek.	Or come to meet Kona Kek.
237. De na-ina Leli Deak	Then he has a mother, Leli Deak,
238. Ma na-te'o Kona Kek.	And he has an aunt, Kona Kek.
239. De noke nae Silu Lilok	She asks to call her Silu Lilok
240. Ma hule nae Huka Besik,	And she requests to call her Huka Besik,
241. Te bei Lini Oe bobongin	For she is still in Lini Oe's birth group
242. Ma bei Kene Mo lalaen.	And she is still in Kene Mo's descent group.
243. Boe ma ala leo Lini Oe leu	So they go to Lini Oe
244. Do leo Kene Mo leu.	Or they go to Kene Mo.
245. Ana pale mane fe inan	He taps male lontars for his mother
246. Ma lenu feto fe te'on,	And saps female lontars for his aunt,
247. Fe te'on Kona Rek	To give to his aunt, Kona Kek,
248. Ma fe inan Leli Deak.	And give to his mother, Leli Deak.
249. Neu lele bina fe inan	He goes to clear dry fields for his mother
250. Ma seku ndenu fe te'on.	And he prepares gardens for his aunt.
251. Ana-ma Manu Kama	The orphan Manu Kama
252. Falu-ina Tepa Nilu	And the widow Tepa Nilu
253. Nala neu lele bina	Goes to clear dry fields
254. Ma nita neu seku ndenu	And goes to prepare gardens
255. Nai tadu-hade dea	At a distant rice village

256. Ma nai nggolo-bete dea.	And a distant millet spot.
257. Boe ma Buik tona-na toda	Then Buik's ship appears
258. Ma Lok balu-na sou	And Lok's perahu becomes visible.
259. De Leli Deak lipe nita-n	Leli Deak looks and sees it
260. Ma Kona Kek leli' hapu-n.	And Kona Kek stares and discovers it.
261. Boe ma nae: 'Baluk se balu-n-o?	She says: 'This ship, whose ship is it?
262. Ma tonak se tona-n-o?	And this perahu, whose perahu is it?
263. Balum faa loba Selak,	[If] your ship carries loba-bark from Selak,
264. Tonam ifa lani Diak	[If] your perahu bears lani-medicine from Daik
265. Na au asa ala fa dei	Then, I'll buy a little
266. Do au tadi ala fa dei!'	And I'll get a little!'
267. Nae: 'Au Buik balu-na ia	He says: 'I, Buik, own this ship
268. Do au Lok tona-na ia.	Or I, Lok, own this perahu.
269. Lolek sio lai lain	Nine fine things are on board
270. Ma ladak falu lai ala.	And eight delightful things are on top.
271. Laba kae mat lain,	Mount and climb, come on board,
272. Ma tinge gene mat ata.	And step and ascend, come on top.
273. Fo dale be na asa,	What pleases you, buy it,
274. Ma pela be na peda-n!'	And what displeases you, put it back!'
275. De inak ia Kona Kek	The woman Kona Kek
276. Ma fetok ia Leli Deak	And the girl, Leli Deak
277. Tinga hene neu lain,	Steps and ascends on board,
278. Do laba kae neu ata.	Mounts and climbs on top.
279. Mai de peda esa nggao esa,	There, she puts one thing back, takes another,
280. Ma hoi esa nggali esa.	And picks up one thing, throws another back.
281. Sek-o inak ia Bui Kume	Indeed, this woman is for Bui Kume
282. Ma fetok ia Lo Lengu,	And this girl is for Lo Lengu,
283. Ina malei selak	A woman to increase the cargo
284. Alla fete ma tale banak.	And a girl to add to the load.
285. Bee ma ala kale kola dua-dua,	So they shake the oar-rings two by two,
286. De ala la'o,	They leave,
287. Ma ala hela tuku telu-telu,	And they pull the oars three by three,
288. De ala leu,	They go,
289. Leko la Selan leu	Turning the sail toward Sela
290. Do pale uli Dain leu.	Or guiding the rudder toward Dai.
291. Boe te ana-ma Manu Kama	So the orphan Manu Kama
292. Ma falu-ina Tepa Nilu	And the widow Tepa Nilu
293. Ledo neu hula manun	At the time of the sun for gathering chicken
294. Ma fai neu hani bafin,	And at the time of the day for feeding pigs,
295. Ma ana seku ndenu lolo-fali	He returns from preparing gardens
296. Ma ana lele bina diku-dua.	And he comes back from clearing fields.

297. De uma nala uma mai	He reaches his home
298. Malo nala lo mai.	And reaches his house.
299. Mai boe ma inak-a Lide Mudak	There, the woman Lide Mudak
300. Do fetok-ia Adi Sole nafada nae:	Or the girl Adi Sole speaks, saying:
301. 'Inam nai Selan so	'Your mother is on Sela
302. Do te'om nai Dain so,	And your aunt is on Dai,
303. Sela mana-babi boa-la	Sela concealed behind great boa-trees
304. Ma Dai mana-hapa piko-la.	And Dai covered by great piko-trees.
305. Fua leni-n ana so	They have carried her away
306. Ma ifa leni-n ana so.'	And have cradled her away.'
307. Boe falu-ina Tepa Nilu	So the orphan Manu Kama
308. Ma falu-ina Tepa Nilu	And the widow Tepa Nilu
309. Hela hako hani bafin	Pulls a pig's feeding trough
310. Ma le'a kima lou metin.	And tugs the tide's giant clamshell.
311. Ana sa'e kima lou metin	He perches upon the tide's clamshell
312. Ma ana tai hako hani bafin.	And perches in the pig's feeding trough.
313. De ana tunga inan Kona Kek	He searches for his mother, Kona Kek,
314. Ma ana afi te'on Leli Deak	And he looks for his aunt, Leli Deak,
315. De leo Sela Sule neu	And goes to Sela Sule
316. Ma leo Dai Laka neu,	And goes to Dai Laka,
317. Neu de nita inan Kona Kek	Goes and sees his mother, Kona Kek,
318. Ma nita te'on Leli Deak	And sees his aunt, Leli Deak,
319. Nai Sela Sule	On Sela Sule
320. Do nai Dai Laka.	Or on Dai Laka.
321. Ana sungu Dain fai dua	He sleeps on Dai for two days
322. Do ana pe'uk Selan ledak telu.	And he rests on Sela for three days.
323. Boe ma nae: 'Bo Bui Kume-e,	Then he says: 'Oh, Bui Kume,
324. Do bo Lo Lengu-e,	Oh, Lo Lengu,
325. Mai leo Lini Oe mu	When you go back to Lini Oe
326. Do leo Kene Mo mu.	Or go back to Keno Mo.
327. Mu ma-fada lena Lini-la	Go and tell the lords of Lini
328. Do ma-fada lesi Kene-la,	Or tell the headmen of Kene,
329. Mae: "Sek-o maka-nilu neo-la	Say: "Come and see me
330. Tasi-oe pepesi-la.	Where the water of the sea strikes the land.
331. Dae lai Dain boe	There is a homeland on Dain too
332. Ma oe lai Selan boe.	And there is native water on Selan too.
333. De au lo-ai kada Selan	My tomb-house will be on Selan
334. Ma au late-dae kada Dain."'	And my earthen-grave will be on Dain."'

11. Genealogy and topogeny

Introduction

Initially, I wish to introduce the notion of 'topogeny'. By 'topogeny', I refer to an ordered succession of placenames. I see the recitation of a topogeny as analogous to the recitation of a genealogy. Both consist of an ordered succession of names that establish precedence in relation to a particular starting point—a point of origin. In the case of a genealogy, this is a succession of personal names; in the case of a topogeny, this is a succession of placenames. Whereas considerable attention has been directed to the study of the significant genealogies, little attention has been given to the study of the recitation of placenames. In eastern Indonesia, and among Austronesian-speaking populations in general, topogenies are as common as genealogies. Generally these topogenies assume the form of a journey: that of an ancestor, an origin group or an object. Often, however, it is difficult to distinguish placenames from personal names and both cohere to form a combination of genealogy and topogeny.

Certain Austronesian societies give preference to topogeny over genealogy. Other Austronesians rely on both such ordering structures but confine themselves to different contexts. Too often, however, topogenies are disregarded as all but unintelligible prefaces to narratives. The variety of forms such topogenies assume is largely overlooked as are the contexts in which such topogenies are given. Indeed one of the critical comparative questions is in what cultural contexts genealogies are cited (as opposed to topogenies) as specific narrative devices among different Austronesian populations. This chapter explores some of these issues as they apply to the Rotenese of eastern Indonesia. At the same time, it provides some explication of the use of placenames in a particular form of Rotenese topogeny.

On Rote, personhood cannot be explicated without reference to place. Places may take on the attributes of persons, and persons the attributes of place. The interconnection is basic and thus placenames can provide a useful starting point for the study of proper names.

The complexity that such names pose necessitates approaches from several directions. In this chapter, I examine aspects of the ethnography of Rotenese proper names by focusing on the use of placenames in ritual language. Although this examination may appear tangential to the issue of personal names, it is in fact crucial to an ethnography of Rotenese naming.

The Rotenese context

The Rotenese have developed both elaborate genealogies and elaborate topogenies. Each of the 18 domains (*nusak*) on the island has its own genealogy, which is centred on the dynastic line of that domain's ruler. This genealogy could be expanded to embrace the high nobles of the domain and, in some areas, to provide links to the founders of the domain's constituent clans. Such genealogies can extend to 36 or more generations and, as far as can be documented in the case of the domain rulers, were preserved orally with remarkable accuracy (see Fox 1971). Generally, for members of commoner clans, genealogies were of less importance and were not greatly elaborated. The dynastic genealogies of each domain provided the structure for extensive political narratives that recounted the origin and development of the domain. This genre of oral narrative is told exclusively in the dialect of the particular domain.

In contrast, the elaboration of topogenies among the Rotenese occurs only in ritual-language accounts of the origin of particular culturally important objects. These are 'origin accounts', like virtually all other ritual-language chants, but their purpose is also to account for the spread of particular objects. Hence they consist of a recitation of the placenames of the island. Thus, unlike genealogies that are generally concentrated, even in ritual-language performances, at the beginning of a recitation, recounting of topogenies may require an entire recitation.

All topogenies must conform to the requirements of ritual language. Thus all places referred to in ritual language must have double names. Knowing the ordinary name of a place may provide a clue to its dyadic ritual name, but often the connection between the two is minimal. Ritual names, however, are not secret names. Such names are generally common knowledge and provide a further dimension to the knowledge about particular places. Knowledge of the ritual names of numerous sites is a specialisation, confined to chanters who pride themselves on their ability to recite long ritual-language narratives.

Names and the cosmology of place

The cosmology of the compositions in ritual language consists of three worlds. There is first a heavenly world, which is referred to as Poin do Lain, or occasionally as Ata do Lain ('The Heavens and the Heights'). This is the world presided over by the Sun and Moon. In opposition to this world is the world beneath the sea, which is referred to as Liun do Sain ('The Ocean and the Sea'). This world is the realm of the Mane Tua Sain ma Danga Lena Liun ('The Great Lord of the Ocean and the Chief Hunter of the Sea'), whose personification is the Shark and Crocodile. Between these worlds is the Earth, referred to as Dae Bafak ma Batu Poin (literally 'The Earth's Mouth and the Rock's Point').

The identity of characters in these three worlds is often revealed in their names. Heavenly creatures have names that include the terms for the Sun, Moon, stars or heavenly phenomena such as a rainbow or lightning. Thus there are names such as Patola Bulan ma Mendeti Ledo or Fudu Kea Ledo ma Tao Senge Bulan. By linking different chants, it is possible to detect a genealogical structure linking some of the descendants of the Sun and Moon (Fox 1997).

Creatures of the sea are identified by the terms 'sea' and 'ocean' in their names or simply as 'Creatures of the Sea', and they form the retinue of the Lord of the Sea. Thus there are characters in the chants with names such as Lada Liuk ma Lole Saik ('Ocean Goodness and Sea Tastiness') or names such as Pata Iuk ma Dula Foek ('Figure Shark and Pattern Crocodile').

Creatures of the Earth are far more numerous and their names far more complex. Many names include the terms for earth, rock, river and water—all of which serve as markers for specific places. Thus personal names are specifically linked to place.

The names of Rote and the symbolic coordinates of place

A place may have more than one ritual name and such names may have a simple and a more elaborate form. Thus, for example, the most common ritual name for the island of Rote (Lote in Termanu dialect) is Lote do Kale; however, this name may be elaborated as Lote Lolo Ei ma Kale Ifa Lima ('Lote of the Outstretched Legs and Kale of the Folded Arms'). The image is one of rest: legs stretched out and arms folded in the lap. Another name for the island that invokes a similar sense is Lino do Ne ('Quiet and Peace'). Yet another name for Rote, which was once current but is now rejected as inappropriate, is Ingu Manasongo Nitu ma Nusa Manatangu Mula ('The Land that Offers to the Spirits and the Island that Sacrifices to the Ghosts'). Rote's population is now almost entirely Christian and hence this name is no longer considered suitable. It is a name from the past.

The island of Rote is conceived of as having a 'head' (*langa*) and a 'tail' (*iko*), a 'right' side (*kona*) and a 'left' side (*ki*). The 'head' of the island is in the east (*dulu*), its 'tail' in the west (*muli*). The 'right' side of the island is to the south, the 'left' side to the north. Reflecting on these coordinates, some Rotenese contend that their island is like an immense crocodile resting in the sea with its head raised slightly higher than its tail.

These coordinates are regularly used to identify places on and beyond the island. A few examples of placenames composed of these coordinates may illustrate the underlying system. The island of Savu to the west of the island of Rote figures in

Rotenese ritual chants. Because it is to the west, it is referred to as Seba Iko ma Safu Muli ('Seba of the Tail and Savu of the West'). The same categories (west//tail) are applied to the westernmost domain on Rote, the domain of Delha, which is referred to, in ritual language, as Dela Muli ma Ana Iko ('Dela of the West and Child of the Tail'). In contrast, one of the ritual names of the domain of Diu is Diu Dulu ma Kana Langa ('Diu of the East and Kana of the Head'). One of the names of Thie, a domain in the southern central part of the island, is Tada Muli ma Lene Kona ('West Tada and South Kona').

The ritual names of the domain of Termanu

Currently the most common name for Termanu is Koli do Buna. The following six-line parallel poem aptly illustrates the use of this name:

Koli nai talada	Koli at the centre
Buna nai use boson	Buna at the navel
Te'o nai tutulin	An aunt at the halting place
Ina nai laladin	A mother at the place to pause
De lope tuli te'o dae	As you go, halt at your aunt earth
Ma lao ladi ina dae.	And, as you pass, pause at your mother earth.

Koli do Buna can also form part of a more complex set of names. Thus, Koli do Buna can become Koli Dale do Buna Dale ('Inside Koli or Inside Buna') or Lima Koli do Ei Buna ('The Arms of Koli or Legs of Buna'). Koli do Buna is, however, only the latest in a succession of names.

One of the most interesting features of ritual names is their historical dimension. Certain important sites may have a series of names that form a historical succession. Each name may thus be commemorative of a particular period or event. The ritual names of the domain of Termanu provide a good illustration of this historical succession of names.

Termanu has had at least five earlier ritual names, each commemorating a stage in the extension of the domain and its prosperity

1. Sina Seo ma Mau Daka
2. Ngginu Ia ma Ngganu Pa
3. Pesa Nesu ma Te Alu
4. Pinga Dale ma Nggusi Bui
5. Pada Kode do So Meo.

Each one of these names carries a great weight of local exegesis. Thus the first, Sina Seo ma Mau Daka, refers to the warlike exploits of certain clans in the initial expansion of the domain. The second, Ngginu Ia ma Ngganu Pa, refers to containers for fish and meat, and alludes to a kind of rich, pre-agricultural period in the domain's early history. The name defines a specific phase in the development of the domain that coincides with the deeds of particular ancestors. Similarly, the third name, Pesa Nesu ma Te Alu, refers to the pounding of rice, thus alluding to the opening of new sources of irrigation in the south and east of the domain. Pinga Dale ma Nggusi Bui alludes to the incorporation of irrigated rice areas in the region south of Fea Popi, the centre of the domain, while Pada Kode do So Meo ('Monkey-Pada or Cat-Oath') alludes to the period following Termanu's bitterest dynastic dispute.

In short, ritual placenames can succeed each other, almost as personal names in a genealogy do.

Narrative topogeny: The chant of the origin of rice and millet

Some ritual chants consist almost entirely of topogenies. They provide an opportunity for the successive recitation of placenames throughout the island. The most important of these topogeny chants recounts the origin of rice and millet. The chant is identified by the names Doli do Lutu or Doli Mo ma Lutu Mala, which are the ritual names for rice and millet, or alternatively by the names of the creatures of the sea that become rice and millet, Bole Sou ma Asa Nao. The background explanation for the arrival of these creatures on Rote (in the two versions of the chant I have gathered) is so brief and tantalisingly cryptic that it is difficult to provide extensive exegesis. In one version, the explanation of the 'origin' of rice and millet forms a kind of preface of some 18 lines out of a total of more than 280 lines.[1] The chant is as follows:

1. Touk leo Bole Sou	The man like Bole Sou
2. Ma taek leo Asa Nao	And the boy like Asa Nao
3. Ala ke bibia iu	They cut and hack the shark
4. Ma ala tati momola foe.	And they slash and slice the crocodile.

---

1   The first version of this chant, which I refer to throughout the chapter, was recorded in Termanu during fieldwork in 1965–66. It was given to me by S. Adulanu. At the time I was helped in transcribing and interpreting this chant by P. Malesi, from whom I later recorded a second version, in 1977, while involved in filming on the island. Tim Asch filmed the recording of P. Malesi reciting the second version of this topogeny (See Appendix). The text of the first chant can be found in Fox (1971:172–87). This chapter was published in in J. J. Fox (ed.) *The Poetic Power of Place: Comparative perspectives on Austronesian ideas of locality*, pp. 91–102. Canberra: Research School of Pacific and Asian Studies, The Australian National University.

5. Boe ma iu neu namanasa	Then the shark grows angry
6. Ma foe ana nggenggele.	And the crocodile becomes furious.
7. Hu ndia de tasi lu Asa Nao	At this the sea rises with Asa Nao
8. Ma oli lama Bole Sou.	And the estuary lifts Bole Sou.
9. Boe te lu neni Doli Mo	So the tide carries Doli Mo
10. Ma lama neni Lutu Mala.	And the flow carries Lutu Mala.
11. De nenin neu Mae Oe	It carries him to Mae Oe
12. Ma nenin neu Tena Lai	And carries him to Tena Lai
13. Fo Mae Oe Loek lutun	To the fish-catch at Mae Oe Loek
14. Ma Tena Lai Laok dean.	And to the seawall at Tena Lai Laok.
15. Besak-ka nupu non na dadi	Now the coconut shoots begin to grow
16. Ma sadu puan na tola	And the pinang shoots begin to appear
17. De li lakadodofun	The waves cover him
18. Ma nafa lapopolin.	And the surf soaks him.

Both the Rotenese exegesis on this version of the chant and lines in a subsequently recorded version identified Bole Sou and Asa Nao as a 'small shrimp and tiny crab' (*poe-ana ma ni'i-ana*). They are described as biting and pinching a coconut and areca nut that carry them bobbing in the sea to the shores of Rote at a place called Tena Lai ma Mae Oe. This ritual site is located in the domain of Landu at the far eastern end of the island.

From Tena Lai ma Mae Oe, the topogeny begins and proceeds in an anticlockwise cycle around the island: first towards the western end of the island, along the north coast and then back to the east along the south coast, returning finally to Tena Lai ma Mae Oe. This cycle is conducted by some women who successively pick up Doli do Lutu and carry them to a new field and plant them. Thus each name cited in the topogeny is supposed to be the name of a rice and a millet field.

The versions of this chant that I have gathered come from the domain of Termanu. For Termanu, each name cited is indeed a rice-field complex known as a *lala*. The names of other sites in more distant domains are in fact the most widely known names of these domains. In some cases, these names are not specific names of fields but general designations of the domains; however, in terms of the topogeny, all such names are described as they referred to rice or millet fields.

The chant is highly repetitious since each successive movement of the rice and millet follows a similar formulaic phrasing. A crucial feature of the chant is the close identification of women with specific fields. In some cases, women's names are a variant of the field name; in other cases, the identity of woman and field is assumed to the extent that only the women's names are cited. References to particular fields are implied.

Initially in the chant, the planted rice and millet do not grow. The first woman to encounter Doli do Lutu (Bole Sou ma Asa Nao) bears the dual name Masu Pasu ma He Hai. She carries the rice and millet from Tena Lai ma Mai Oe to a field in the domain of Korbaffo, which takes its ritual name from its large bay, Tunga Oli ma Namo Ina ('Follow the Inlet and Mother Harbour'). These lines of the chant follow:

19. Faik esa ma-nunin	On one certain day
20. Ma ledo esa ma-teben	And at a particular time
21. Tasi la huka papa	The sea opens its planks
22. Ma meti la si unu.	And the tide tears wide its slats.
23. Boe te inak-ka Masu Pasu	So the woman Masu Pasu
24. Ma fetok-ka He Hai	And the girl He Hai
25. Neu nafadama lutu limak	Goes to probe the arms of the fish-catch
26. Ma nafaloe dea eik.	And goes to grope at the foot of the seawall.
27. Boe to neu nda lilima	There they encounter [Doli Mo]
28. Ma neu tongo lololo.	And there they meet [Lutu Mala].
29. Doli Mo nasakedu	Doli Mo is sobbing
30. Ma Lutu Mala namatani	And Lutu Mala is crying
31. Fo nasakedu sanga inan	Sobbing for his mother
32. Ma namatani sanga teon,	And crying for his aunt,
33. Te hu inan nai Asa Nao	A mother to Asa Nao
34. Ma teon nai Bole Sou.	And an aunt to Bole Sou.
35. Besak-ka inak-ka, Masu Pasu	Then the woman Masu Pasu
36. Ma fetok-ka, He Hai neu.	And the girl He Hai goes [there].
37. Ifa neni falik Doli	Returns carrying Doli in her lap
38. Ma ko'o neni tulek Lutu	And comes back cradling Lutu in her arms
39. De tulek Asa Nao	She brings back Asa Nao
40. Ma falik Bole Sou.	And returns Bole Sou.
41. Mai bei nai Tunga Oli ma Namo Ina.	She arrives at Tunga Oli and Namo Ina.
42. De sele lakaboboin	They plant him with care
43. Ma tane lasamamaon	And they sow him with attention
44. Te hu bokon ta dadi	But the bending stalk does not grow
45. Ma do belan ta tola.	And the heavy leaves do not appear.

It is at this stage that the rice and millet are carried to Termanu by the woman Fi Bau ma Seda Kola, and planted in the field Bau Peda Dele ma Kola Sifi Ndai, the first of a series of rice fields where initially rice and millet do not grow. This segment of the chant is as follows:

46. Besak-ka inak-ka Fi Bau	Now the woman Fi Bau
47. Ma fetok-ka Seda Kola	And the girl Seda Kola
48. Ko'o do ifa nenin.	Cradles or carries him away.
49. De sele nakaboboin	She plants him with care
50. Ma tane nasamamaon	And sows him with attention
51. Nai Bau Peda Dele fuan	In the field at Bau Peda Dele
52. Ma Kola Sifi Ndai mon,	And in the plain at Kola Sifi Ndai,
53. Te do belan ta dadi	But the heavy leaves do not grow
54. Ma hu bokon ta tola.	And the bending stalk does not appear.

A succession of women—Kada Ufa ma Dila Latu, Hau Hala ma Kae Kopa, Leli Onge ma Fula Fopo and Soe Leli ma Pinga Pasa—each of whom can be identified with the site of a particular field complex on Termanu's north coast, comes forward, takes the rice and millet, and plants them; they do not succeed in getting them to grow. It is only when the woman Lole Bako ma Fiti Nggoli carries them with full ceremony and plants them in the field named Bako Bau Dale ma Nggoli Kai Tio that the rice and millet finally sprout and grow. This sequence of the chant is as follows:

83. Besak-ka inak-ka Fiti Nggoli	Now the woman Fiti Nggoli
84. Ma fetok-ka Lole Bako	And the girl Lole Bako
85. Ana tolo mu sasali	She comes running
86. Ma nalai lelena.	And she comes dashing.
87. De neni pua lisu lasi boak	She brings an areca nut round as a bowed cotton ball
88. Ma malu boa dongi aik	And a betel fruit long as a barbed spear shaft
89. Pou leu pana-daik	A sarong with pana-daik bands
90. Ma sidi soti tola-teek.	And a ritual cloth with the tola-teek stitches.
91. Mai de ana ifa so ko'o nenin.	Coming, she carries or cradles him away.
92. De neu tane nasamamaon	She goes to sow him with attention
93. Do sele nakaboboin	And plant him with care
94. Neu Bako Bau Dale mon	In the plain of Bako Bau Dale
95. Ma neu Nggoli Kai Tio fuan	And in the field of Nggoli Kai Tio
96. Ma ana mole sepe do fua oli.	And she celebrates the sepe-basket and lays the oli-basket [rituals].
97. Besak-ka kalen-na didiku	Now his kernel bends over
98. Ma pulen-na loloso.	And his buds creep upward.
99. Boe ma besak-ka oku-bolu ma do-se'ek	Now they yell and make noise [to drive away the birds]
100. Nai Bako Bau Dale mon	In the plain of Bako Bau Dale
101. Do Nggoli Kai Tio fuan.	And in the field of Nggoli Kai Tio.

After this success, two more women from Termanu, Dulu Kilik ma Leo Lasuk and Pinga Peto ma Lu'a Lela, take the rice and millet and sow them in the field complexes of Ki Lama ma Le Ina and Peto Lesi Ama ma Lela Bala Fia. Again the grains sprout and grow.

This is the last of the sequence of named rice fields in Termanu. After this, the chant proceeds to describe the transference of the seeds and their planting in a circuit through the Rote domains. A brief segment for the domain of Loleh is sufficient to illustrate the repeated formula of the chant. Here the chant refers to Loleh by its two most commonly known ritual names, Ninga Ladi ma Heu Hena and Teke Dua ma Finga Telu.

174. *Boe ma inak bei Ninga Ladi*	The woman of Ninga Ladi
175. *Ma fetok bei Heu Hena*	And the girl of Heu Hena
176. *Inak bei Teke Dua*	The woman of Teke Dua
177. *Ma fetok bei Finga Telu*	And the girl of Finga Telu
178. *Inak-ka Tui Beba*	The woman Tui Beba
179. *Do fetok-ka Oe Ange*	Or the girl Oe Ange
180. *Ana if a do ko'o nenin.*	She carries or cradles him away.
181. *De ana sele do tane*	She plants or sows
182. *Neu Ninga Ladi do Heu Hena.*	In Ninga Ladi or Heu Hena.
183. *De oku boluk ma do-se'ek.*	They yell and make noise.

Finally, after completing a circuit of the island, Doli and Lutu are returned to the Tena Lai ma Mae Oe where they began by a woman identified with the domain of Landu. The chant concludes with the lines:

275. *Boe ma feto bei Soti Mori*	A girl of Soti Mori
276. *Ma ina bei Bola Tena*	And a woman of Bola Tena
277. *Inak-ka Liti Lifu*	The woman Liti Lifu
278. *Do fetok-ka Henu Helok*	Or the girl Henu Helok
279. *De ifa do ko'o nenin*	She carries or cradles him away
280. *Ko'o mangananaun*	Cradles him gently in her arms
281. *Ma ifa tapandondoen.*	And carries him tenderly on her lap.
282. *De ana tane do sele*	She sows or plants
283. *Neu Tena Lai do Mae Oe.*	At Tena Lai or Mae Oe.
284. *Te fuak ta Tena Lai*	But there is no field at Tena Lai
285. *Ma mok ta Mae Oe.*	And there is no plain at Mae Oe.
286. *Boe ma ana tulek leo liun neu*	Then he goes back to the ocean
287. *Ma falik leo sain neu.*	And returns to the sea.

Explorations in Semantic Parallelism

Mapping the path of rice and millet onto the body of the island

Topogenies take various forms, defining different paths. The path of Doli do Lutu, for example, differs from that of the path of the great rocks of Sua Lai and Batu Hun that stand as the coastal landmarks of the domain of Termanu. These topogenies differ in their points of origin and of termination and, even more significantly, in the trajectories of their individual paths. The topogeny of Sua Lai and Batu Hun has its origin in Termanu; the trajectory of the path it narrates proceeds eastward to the island of Timor where a transformation occurs that directs the journey of the two rocks back westward to a point—Pao Kala ma Peni Kea—at the south-eastern end of Rote. From there, the path of the rocks follows a clockwise movement along Rote's south coast and eventually back to the rocks' 'ancestral harbour' in Termanu on Rote's north coast. In contrast, the topogeny of Doli do Lutu begins at Tena Lai ma Mae Oe—at the eastern end of Rote. The path of rice and millet involves an anticlockwise circumambulation of the island from the 'head' to the 'tail', with a return to the place of origin at the head.

Just as any topogeny can be defined by its point of origin and termination, it can also be defined by the named places that mark the path between origin and termination. The topogeny of Doli do Lutu in this chapter consists of a recitation of 32 ritual placenames, all of which can be mapped onto the body of the island.

Ritual place names in the topogeny of rice and millet

1. Tena Lai ma Mae Oe
2. Tunga Oli ma Namo Ina
3. Bau Peda Dele ma Kola Sifi Ndai
4. Bako Bau Dale ma Nggoli Kai Tio
5. Ki Lama ma Le Ina
6. Peto Lesi Ama ma Lela Bala Fia
7. Tanga Loi ma Oe Mau
8. Pena Pua ma Maka Lama
9. Dae Mea ma Tete Lifu
10. Nele Dene ma Nada Dano [Ni Le ma Lada Dano]
11. Dela Muli ma Ana Iko
12. Tada Muli ma Lene Kona
13. Tuda Meda ma Do Lasi
14. Ninga Ladi ma Heu Hena
15. Tufa Laba ma Ne'e Feo
16. Pila Sue ma Nggeo Deta
17. Longa Fa ma Feo Ne
18. Sosolo Lean ma Batu Tanga
19. Ko Solo ma Nilu Foi
20. Keko Nesu ma Te Alu
21. Medi Daen ma Ndule Oen
22. Lenu Peto ma Safe Solo
23. Diu Dulu ma Kana Langa
24. Pele Pou ma Nggafu Lafa
25. Sapan Daen Oe Utuk ma Seun Oen Fi Bolo
26. Feni Fi ma Tane Bau
27. Londa Lusi ma Batu Bela
28. Saba Lai ma Dele Bui
29. Tua Nae ma Lele Beba
30. Fai Fua ma Ledo Sou
31. Lifa Lama ma Lutu Oen
32. Soti Mori ma Bola Tena

Each individual recitation of a topogeny invariably reflects the knowledge and interests of its narrator. The topogeny examined in this chapter was told by a narrator, S. Adulanu, from Termanu and it therefore gives greater attention to places within this domain. For other parts of the island, one or another of the ritual names of that domain is invoked to stand for its rice fields. Thus, in effect, the recitation relies on a general knowledge of the ritual names of the domains of Rote.

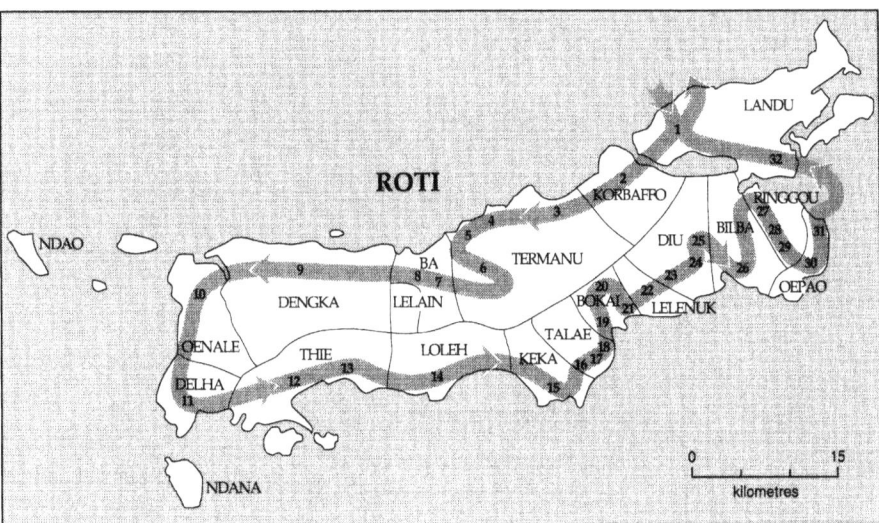

Map 11.1: The Path of Rice and Millet

Map 11.1 shows the domains of the island of Rote with numbers to mark and identify the ordered sequence of places named in this particular topogeny. Since many of these placenames represent domains, the map also shows these domains.

The creation of ritual space

There exist only two ways of establishing succession: in time or in space. Genealogy functions to establish a succession in time. Topogeny functions to establish a succession in space. Genealogy relies on personal names, topogeny on placenames. In both, points of origin and termination are critical. Topogenies have the advantage that they may form cycles by returning to an initial point of departure. Topogenies can be traced, relived, revisited. Genealogy may be more abstract but is often structured in a spatial mode—in Austronesian societies as some form of botanic icon like an immense tree, a clump of bamboo, or a twisting vine. And the contours of these icons can be traced. For topogeny, it is the metaphor of the journey that is important. In the ritual chant I have examined, this journey traces the path of rice and millet. The specifics of the journey are part of the revelation of the chant.

The version of this journey of Doli do Lutu comes from Termanu and it is in relation to Termanu that it must be primarily interpreted. From this perspective, it establishes a relationship between Tena Lai ma Mae Oe and the principal rice fields of Termanu. Within Termanu, it establishes a relationship between Bako Bau Dale ma Nggoli Kae Tio, as the premier rice field of the domain, and all other rice fields. It goes beyond this and testifies to the importance of three fields on the western side of the domain (of which Bau Dale, Peto and Lela are of great popular, historical significance): Bako Bau Dale ma Nggoli Kae Tio, Ki Lama ma Le Ina and Peto Lesi Ama ma Lela Bala Fia.

For Termanu, the chant creates a ritual space of specific localities. For the rest of the island, it is a recitation of political entities. It produces by way of placenames what a genealogy does by means of personal names. Termanu is not the first of the domains; it is the navel and the centre of these domains.

12. Blood-red millet: An origin narrative[1]

Introduction

The short narrative *Lakimola Bulan Ma Kaibake Ledo* tells of the origin of a variety of millet. Composed in formulaic canonical parallelism, it provides an illustration of a Rotenese 'origin chant'. Such chants recount the origins of a great variety of critical cultural items ranging from the tools for building a traditional house and the implements for weaving and dyeing to the key sources of the Rotenese livelihood. This composition comes from the domain of Termanu on the island of Rote. It is remarkable for its brevity and for the fact that it provides an account of the origin of a specific kind of millet. This account, though linked to the larger encompassing narrative of the children of the Sun and Moon, offers a separate origin for millet to that of a long narrative that accounts for the origin and spread of rice and millet on the island.

Narratives of the Sun and Moon

In Rotenese ritual language, the complementary pair *Ledo//Bulan* ('Sun'//'Moon') represents the heavenly powers. Although no longer recognised as a unified whole, the overwhelming majority of Rotenese origin narratives appear to form part of a single interconnected narrative—a kind of epic contest—in which the Sun and Moon and their heavenly descendants encounter, dispute and intermarry with the rival powers who rule over the sea (*Liun//Sain*) and are represented as Shark and Crocodile. The Earth is the meeting place for these encounters and it is from them that the Rotenese trace the origins of their cultural goods and institutions.

The principal character in this narrative on the origin of millet is Lakimola Bulan//Kaibake Ledo. This dual name identifies these personages as children of the Sun and Moon and links their actions to the larger narrative. The narrative hints at a ruptured relationship and recounts the rejection by the Sun and Moon of a request for seed. This, in turn, prompts the actions of Lakimola Bulan//Kaibake Ledo.

---

1 This paper was initially written in English, but it was published in German in a festschrift in honour of Karl-Heinz Kohl (Fox 2008:401–9).

In the overarching narrative of the Sun and Moon, rice and millet derive from the sea. The opening lines of the various versions of this narrative, which I have recorded, are as cryptic as the key passages in the Lakimola Bulan//Kaibake Ledo narrative. An altercation in the sea drives the two creatures Bole Sou//Asa Nao, identified as a tiny crab and shrimp, into a stone weir at a site at the eastern end of Rote known as Mai Oe//Tena Lai, where they are fished forth and become the seeds of rice and millet, thereafter referred to as Doli Mo//Lutu Mala. These seeds are then taken and planted in an ordered succession of fields around the island of Rote until they arrive back at Mai Oe//Tena Lai and return to the sea.

The Lakimola Bulan//Kaibake Ledo narrative bears no resemblance to the Doli Mo//Lutu Mala narrative. On the other hand, it does bear resemblance to another origin narrative associated, in Termanu, with another of the heavenly children of the Sun and Moon, Patola Bulan//Mandeti Ledo. This narrative is perhaps the single most important, ritually charged narrative in the Rotenese origin corpus. It recounts the first encounter of the son(s) of the Sun and Moon with the Lords of the Sea, the discovery of fire in the sea, the strategic marriage between Heaven and Sea intended to obtain this cooking fire and other cultural goods from the sea and then the construction of the Rotenese house.[2] Embedded in this narrative is the allusion to the sacrifice of the crocodile to obtain a schematic pattern for the house. According to elders, origin narratives touch on actions of such cosmic portent that they can never be voiced but only hinted at.

The Lakimola Bulan//Kaibake Ledo narrative begins in a similar way to that of Patola Bulan//Mandeti Ledo. Lakimola Bulan//Kaibake Ledo descends to the Earth and begins to hunt with dogs whose names are specified. The hunt is for 'pig//civet cat'. To this point and only to this point, the narratives are similar. The Lakimola Bulan//Kaibake Ledo composition then leaps to the preparation of a garden and a request for seeds from the Sun and Moon. When this request is refused, Lakimola Bulan//Kaibake Ledo cuts a little finger of the right hand and a little toe of the left foot to draw blood and then stomps through the cleared field, dripping blood that grows into blood-red millet.

Lakimola Bulan Ma Kaibake Ledo

A. Amalo

Lae:	**They say:**
1. Hida hatan ma data don na,	In a former period and a past time,
2. Touk Lakimola Bulan	The man Lakimola Bulan
3. Ma ta'ek Kaibake Ledo	And the boy Kaibake Ledo
4. Ala lona ue leme poin mai	They come down from the Heights
5. Ma felo fa leme lain mai	And they swing down from Heaven

---

2 See Fox (1975) for a version of this narrative.

12. Blood-red millet: An origin narrative

6. *De ala tena mai dae bafok*	They land upon the Earth
7. *Ma tuda mai batu poi*	They fall to the ground
8. *De ala mai mamanak esa*	They arrive at a place
9. *Nade Pokodanon [Korbaffo].*	Called Poko Danon [in Korbaffo].
10. *Nde be na, ala lona lo busan telu*	And they come down with three dogs
11. *De esa nade Solu Ndan*	One is named Solu Ndan
12. *Esa nade Lau Masin*	One is named Lau Masin
13. *Ma esa nade Deta Dosa.*	And one is named Deta Dosa.
14. *De ala kati kofio busa*	They whistle for their dogs
15. *Ma fu tolesi asu*	And they call for their hounds
16. *De leu Nula Tati Bafi daen*	And they go to the land of Nula Tati Bafi
17. *Ma leu Seda Solo Mako oen.*	And they go to the water of Seda Solo Mako.
18. *De ala sopu bafi leme ndia*	They hunt pig there
19. *Ma fule kue leme ndia*	And they pursue civet cat there
20. *Boe ma ala tao osi leme ndia*	Then they make a dry garden there
21. *Ma ala tao tina leme ndia*	And they make a dry field there
22. *Boe ma leu loke bini no ngges*	And they go to ask for seed and grain
23. *Lai poin do lain*	From the Heights and Heaven
24. *Fo Bulan uman ma Ledo lon.*	The Moon's house and the Sun's home.
25. *Te hu aman Bulan do Ledo ta fe fan*	But their father, Sun or Moon, would give none
26. *Nenik ani'i-ana sila late'a henis.*	Because their children had separated themselves.
27. *De hu ndia de ala lona leo*	Therefore they descend to
28. *Dae bafa batu poi a mai.*	The Earth and the world.
29. *De ala fali ma'is*	When they return
30. *Boe ma ha'i la felas sa ma dope a leon*	They take up their machete and knife
31. *De ala paun neu lima ku'u dao konan na*	And they stab the little finger of their right hand
32. *Ma paun neu ei ku'u dao kin na.*	And they stab the little toe of their left foot
33. *Boe ma ala lao feo*	They walk around
34. *Osi a no tina a dalen na leon.*	Within the dry garden and the dry field
35. *De dan na nesik be*	Wherever their blood falls
36. *Na ana moli te betek ma pela*	It grows up as millet and maize
37. *Fo loke lae bete pila lai doli*	They call the red quick-maturing millet
38. *Ma [pela] pila pa dak*	And the red flesh and blood [maize]
39. *Losa faik ia*	To this day and
40. *Ma nduku besak ia.*	Until this present time.
41. *Basan nde ndia so.*	This is the end.

Compositional flaws: An internal critique

Rotenese ritual language is canonical in the sense that it is composed using recognised pairs: formal dyadic sets. Because of this semantic structure, it is possible to evaluate any composition as to how well it makes use of conventionally required pairs. Rotenese origin narratives are also canonical in another sense. They belong to a corpus of compositions that relate to each other. The compositions embody what Rotenese consider to be the most basic foundational knowledge they possess.

The oral poets of Rote are not simply performers: they are the custodians of fundamental knowledge. Hence there is often fierce debate among them over particular chant character names and about the sequences within particular compositions. Based on some of these criteria, it is also possible to assess the quality of this particular composition.

Clearly, this composition has links to the overarching origin narrative whose different episodes are encountered throughout the island. Although the poet who provided this narrative came from the domain of Termanu, his recitation refers to a particular field in the neighbouring domain of Korbaffo, identified as Poko Danon. It is therefore possible that because the narrative relates to the special local knowledge of another domain, the poet regarded his composition as one that could be told succinctly.

The dual chant character names Lakimola Bulan//Kaibake Ledo suggest this relationship to the overall narrative. These chant characters are children of the Sun and Moon. Elsewhere on Rote, however, the name Lakimola would more likely appear as Lakamola. Lakamola is the name of a distinctive outcrop in the domain of Bilba in east Rote associated with the origin of what the Rotenese refer to as the nine seeds (*pule sio*).

The names of their dogs cited in this composition would also likely be the subject of criticism. Three names are given, which is unusual since one would expect one pair or two pairs of names. The assumption would have to be that the name that should partner with Solu Nda has been omitted. The other dogs' names, Lau Masin and Deta Dosa, are the same as, or similar to, the names of the dogs associated with the Lords of the Sea; hence, they would be unlikely as the hunting dogs of the sons of the Sun and Moon.

The pervasive dualism of ritual language often presents a problem of translation. Singular and plural, which are grammatically critical in English, for example, are ambiguous in ritual language. Whether a dual chant character name identifies one or two characters is indeterminate and largely irrelevant. Some gifted poets actually treat the singular and plural third-person pronouns as a dyadic set, leaving the translation to alternate between a 'he' and a 'they'. In this composition, however, the third-person plural forms are used consistently except in reference to the Sun and Moon where a third-person singular is used.

In terms of composition, lines 8, 9 and 10 as well as lines 25, 26, 27 and 29 plus lines 33 and 35 are not in strict parallelism. They advance the narrative but not through properly composed verses. This, too, is an internal deficiency that lessens the quality of the composition.

In short, this composition is flawed; it is revealing but frustratingly elusive. It was recorded in 1965 from a Rotenese chanter who, during a brief encounter, could have been interested principally in hearing his voice played back to him on what was, at the time, the first tape recorder on the island. At best, the composition is a tantalising fragment rather than a full account—a small piece in a large jigsaw puzzle that I am still struggling to assemble.

Conclusion

A substantial proportion of the population of eastern Indonesia, particularly in the province of Nusa Tenggara Timur, are committed Christians. In his notable ethnography *Der Tod der Reisjungfrau* (1998), Karl-Heinz Kohl has provided a well-structured investigation of a particular local community: that of the Belogili in the domain of Lewolema in eastern Flores. The people of Lewolema among whom Kohl did his fieldwork are Catholics, while the Rotenese are, for the most part, Protestants. Like the Rotenese, the people of Lewolema retain the knowledge of their origin narratives, but continue to reformulate the bases of this ancestral knowledge within a Christian conceptual framework.

Most Lewolema origin narratives are composed in strict canonical parallelism and Kohl provided translations of these narratives that are remarkable for their literal clarity. His work therefore has considerable value for the comparative study of traditions of parallelism in eastern Indonesia. The title of the volume, 'The Death of the Rice Maiden', refers to the charter narrative for the origin of dry rice: the ritual killing of the maiden Tonu Wujo by her youngest brother. The body of Tonu Wujo, sacrificed in a field prepared for interment, gives rise to the first crop of rice. Nearly one-third of Kohl's ethnography is devoted to the careful translation of this text, which is combined with exegesis and linked to local ritual practice.[3]

In his conclusion, Kohl quotes at length the words of one of his key informants, Bene, who endeavoured to interpret for him the relationship between Catholicism

---

[3] Kohl's work follows a tradition begun by Adolf Jensen, whose study *Hainwele*, published in 1939, initiated the study of this botanical theme among the Wemale of the Seram in eastern Indonesia.

and traditional beliefs. As a good Catholic, Bene explained that Christ offered Himself for the salvation of the souls of mankind while Tonu Wujo—the rice maiden—offered herself for humankind's physical wellbeing. One sacrifice was intended for the care of the spirit, the other for the care of the body. Both sacrifices were necessary and thus complementary rather than contradictory.

Like the people of Lewolema, the Rotenese, as one of the oldest Christian populations in the region, have for some time been involved in interpreting the relationship between their traditional knowledge and Christianity. Recently, Lintje H. Pellu, a Rotenese student at The Australian National University, who has carried out fieldwork in the domain of Landu on Rote—one of the last remaining areas where millet is still a prominent crop—encountered a local interpretation of the origin of blood-red millet that echoes the interpretation of Kohl's informant.

According to the account she was told, the first millet, referred to as white millet (*bete fulas*), came from God. It was given to Ibrahim, who, in turn, gave it to his wife, Masa Rai (Sara), and his daughter, Dati Lenu Tasi. They passed the seeds to Masi Mai in the sea from whence these seeds came to land at Tena Lai and Mae Oe—the place of origin of rice and millet acknowledged widely throughout Rote. When this white millet proved insufficient, a man, who is not identified in Landu, pierced his ankle and allowed his blood to soak the white millet, turning it into fast-growing blood-red millet. Christians of Landu see an analogy between this blood sacrifice that created the new millet—purifying the seeds and making them whole—and Christ's sacrifice of His blood to purify humankind of its sins. On this basis, the various stages in the preparation of millet fields in Landu, each with their required traditional sacrifices, have a Christian equivalent with appropriate prayers that allow the continuation of ancestral procedures with new spiritual underpinnings (see Pellu 2008:189–93).

Karl-Heinz Kohl would certainly recognise this intellectual transformation since he has, in his own research in eastern Indonesia, documented a similar intellectual effort at reinterpreting traditional knowledge.

13. Admonitions of the ancestors: Giving voice to the deceased[1]

Introduction

Rotenese mortuary chants are compositions whose intention is to invoke deep emotions, particularly when they are recited, at night, among a gathering of mourners. Here I wish to examine a particular chant of exceptional power and poignancy. My concern is with the 'voice' that emerges in this chant. In the chant, the recently deceased, represented as a particular 'chant character', is given voice. The deceased speaks to the living and offers admonition and instruction to his immediate family. The power of this performance derives from the fact that the chant gives voice to the deceased as part of his burial ceremonies.

This chant is one among various possible forms of Rotenese mortuary recitations. The question, however, that I wish to pose is whether its use of voice is unique or whether—as I suspect—such use of voice can be found in the rituals and poetry of other Austronesian-speaking populations. This chapter thus poses a comparative question and calls for other examples of this kind of singular use of voice.

Among the Iban, for example, the deceased is given voice to speak to the living. An excellent illustration of this use of voice can be found in Clifford Sather's *Seeds of Play, Words of Power* (2001). In the 'rite to sever the flower' (*pelian beserara' bunga*), a ritual in which the spirits of the dead take leave from the world of the living, the dead person speaks through a *manang* or shaman chanter and addresses members of the surviving family:

> Although I have died and gone to the other world,
>
> From there I will continue to watch over you,
>
> My precious child, in this world,

---

[1] This chapter was first published in 2003 as 'Admonitions of the ancestors: giving voice to the deceased in Rotenese mortuary rituals', in Peter J. M. Nas, Gerard Persoon and Rivke Jaffe (eds), *Framing Indonesian Realities: Essays in symbolic anthropology in honour of Reimar Schefold*, Leiden: KITLV Press, pp. 15–26. As appropriate, I originally began this study with a recognition of Reimar Schefold's work: 'The Austronesian-speaking world offers a rich field for ethnographic inquiry. Within this field, Reimar Schefold has distinguished himself as one of the great contemporary explorers. His meticulous study of the social and ritual activities of the Sakuddei of Siberut is a truly remarkable contribution to our understanding of the possibilities of Austronesian living. His entire corpus on the Sakuddei—but in particular his masterwork, *Lia: Das grosse Ritual auf den Mentawai-Inseln* (1988), with its accompanying photographs—is a work of subtle artistry linked to ethnographic acumen. In his most recent writing, Schefold has begun an exploration of the patterns of ritual blessing in a number of different Indonesian societies. In the spirit of this new exploration and in recognition of Reimar's nuanced attention to individual ritual performance, I dedicate this particular exploration.'

To help you become rich and successful, so that your name is known far and wide. (Sather 2001:95)

Another example of this use of voice can be found in a remarkable poem, *Kasaksian Bapak Saijah*, by the Indonesian poet Rendra. By way of comparison in this chapter, once I have considered the Rotenese text in which the deceased speaks to the living, I would like to discuss Rendra's use of the voice of the dead in his poem.

I begin with an examination of the Rotenese chant *Ndi Lonama ma Laki Elokama*.

The text: *Ndi Lonama ma Laki Elokama*

I recorded the text of *Ndi Lonama ma Laki Elokama* from the eminent chanter (*manahelo*) Stefanus Amalo in 1965. At the time, Amalo had already reached a distinguished old age and was regarded as a poet at the height of his powers. He was a member of the royal line of Termanu and one of the few noble chanters in the domain. During the time of my first fieldwork in 1965–66, the two most respected chanters in Termanu were Stefanus Amalo and Stefanus Adulanu, the Head of the Earth, who was known as 'Old Meno' (Meno Tua). Old Meno was my principal instructor in ritual language and he assisted me with the transcription and initial translation of this text. To some extent, therefore, this text, as presented here, is a product of a joint collaboration of these two remarkable men.

Each mortuary chant in the Rotenese repertoire is identified by the name of a specific chant character. Each chant character's life course is associated with a social category: noble, commoner, rich man or young man or woman who has died young or unmarried. There also exist a number of all-purpose 'orphan and widow' chants that can be adapted to fit most funeral situations. The selection of a specific mortuary chant is intended to fit the social status of the deceased and to provide a general representation of his or her life.

In the present text, Ndi Lonama and Laki Elokama form the double name of a single chant character. Since the text is in strict canonical parallelism, all lines are paired and all personal names and placenames must therefore have a double form. *Ndi Lonama ma Laki Elokama* is the chant appropriate for a rich man who dies with most of his wealth intact, leaving behind a family to continue his house.

Mortuary chants generally follow a standard format beginning with a stylised genealogical recitation. The chant then recounts the life of the chant character, focusing on the occasion of his or her death. After the death of the character, most chants soon come to an end.

13. Admonitions of the ancestors

The chant *Ndi Lonama ma Laki Elokama* is unusual in its overall structure: more than half of the chant consists of the admonition on the verge of the chant character's death. It is at this point that Ndi Lonama//Laki Elokama begins to counsel his family, telling them what to do with his wealth but also describing his forthcoming journey to the afterworld.

The chant begins not with Ndi Lonama//Laki Elokama's genealogy but with his marriage to the woman Lisu Lasu Lonak//Dela Musu Asuk. The chant briefly describes her marriage transfer as follows:

Soku Lisu Lasu Lonak	They lift Lisu Lasu Lonak
Ma lali Dela Musu Asuk.	And they transfer Dela Musu Asuk.
De lelete neu sao	She bridges the path to marry
Ma fifino neu tu.	And she joins the way to wed.
De ana tu Ndi Lonama	She weds Ndi Lonama
Ma sao Laki Elokama.	And she marries Laki Elokama.

The chant then describes the birth of Ndi Lonama//Laki Elokama's children, first a boy, Solu Ndi//Luli Laki, who is metaphorically identified as 'a cock's tail'//'a rooster's plume', and then a girl, Henu Ndi//Lilo Laki. The names of these children have subtle connotations. For the boy, Solu implies that he is a commoner rather than a noble; Luli that he is potentially a 'stormy' character. For the girl, Henu refers to valued *mutisalak* beads and Lilo to 'gold', suggesting that she is her parents' treasure.

Boe ma ana bongi-na Solu Ndi	She gives birth to Solu Ndi
Ma ana lae-na Luli Laki	And she brings forth Luli Laki
Fo popi koak Solu-Ndi	A cock's tail feathers, Solu Ndi
Ma lano manuk Luli Laki.	And a rooster's plume, Luli Laki.
Boe te ana bei boe bongi	But she still continues to give birth
Ma bei boe lae.	And still continues to bring forth.
Lae-nala Henu Ndi.	She brings forth Henu Ndi.
De ke fetok;	She is a girl child;
Ma lae-nala Lilo Laki,	And she brings forth Lilo Laki,
De tai inak.	She is a woman child.

At this point, the chant proclaims:

De malole-la so	These things are good
Ma mandak-kala so.	And these things are proper.

Ndi Lonama//Laki Elokama's particular regard for his daughter is emphasised in the chant when he tells his wife to have another girl child who will be a help to the household. Instead of recounting the birth of another child, the chant proceeds immediately to create a portrait of the character Ndi Lonama//Laki Elokama. His defining identification is his wealth of goats and water buffalo:

Te hu touk Ndi Lonama	The man Ndi Lonama
Ma ta'ek Laki Elokama	And the boy Laki Elokama
Tou ma-bote biik	Is a man with flocks of goats
Ma tae ma-tena kapak.	And is a boy with herds of buffalo.

Some lines later, the extent of this wealth is emphasised:

Fo bote-la dai lena	The flock is great
Ma tena-la to lesi.	And the herd is extensive.

Ndi Lonama//Laki Elokama's other defining characteristic is his generosity. The chant's portrayal of this generosity is coded in a distinctive Rotenese poetic fashion, relying on the key metaphor of 'orphan and widow'. The metaphor has a wide range of meanings.[2] At its core, the metaphor of 'orphan and widow' implies a state of dependency. As such, whoever is dependent as 'orphan and widow' is defined in relation to a benefactor, who can be a ruler in relation to his subjects or a rich man in relation to those whom he supports. In this chant, Ndi Lonama//Laki Elokama is portrayed as a rich man who supports a large number of dependants. The herd that he tends—the basis of his wealth—is itself likened to the flock of orphans and widows whom he supports. This equivalence is expressed in the following lines that metaphorically link his daily routine with his social obligations:

De basa fai-kala	On all the days
Ma nou ledo-kala	And every sunrise
Ana tada mamao bote	He separates the flock in groups
Ma ana lilo bobongo	And forms the herd in circles
Na neni te tada tenan	Bringing his herd-separating spear
Ma neni tafa lilo bote-na	And bringing his flock-forming sword
Fo te nade Kafe Lasi	His spear named Kafe Lasi
Ma tafa nade Seu Nula.	And his sword named Seu Nula.
Fo ana loe tafa neu be na	For where he lowers his sword
Bote hae neu ndia	The flock stops there
Ma te'e to neu be na	And where he rests his spear
Tena lu'u neu ndia,	The herd lies down at that place,
Fo tena ta neu lu'u	But it is not the herd that lies down
Ma bote ta neu hae	And not the flock that stops
Te ana-mak-kala hae	But it is orphans who stop
Ma falu-ina-la lu'u.	And widows who lie down.

---

[2] See Fox (1988:165–9) for an extensive discussion of this metaphor.

Having thus succinctly defined Ndi Lonama//Laki Elokama's character, the chant proceeds to recount the sickness that strikes him.

Te hu faik esa manunin	But one certain day
Ma ledok dua mateben	And on a second particular time [sun]
Boe ma touk Ndi Lonama	The man Ndi Lonama
Ma ta'ek Laki Elokama	And the boy Laki Elokama
Ana mela tei neu tein	He feels stomach cramps in his stomach
Ma ana langu langa neu langan.	And he feels head dizziness in his head.
Boe te mela tein sanga hene	The stomach cramps begin to rise
Ma langu langan sanga kae.	And the head dizziness begins to mount.

At this point, he addresses his son, Solu Ndi//Luli Laki:

'Au mela teing ta lui	'My stomach cramps do not subside
Ma au langu langang to hai	And my head dizziness does not heal
De fai-a neu fai	From day to day
Ma ledo-a neu ledo.	And sun to sun.
Te se au sapu nitu	So it is my spirit is about to die
Ma se au lalo mula...'	And my ghost is about to perish...'

Ndi Lonama//Laki Elokama then begins his admonition. When this chant is recited on the night of a funeral ceremony, it is the voice of the deceased instructing his family.

Te sadi mafa-ndendelek	But do remember
Ma sadi masa-nenedak	And do keep in mind
Mala mu tada tena	When you go to separate the herd
Do mala mu lilo bote	And you go to form the flock
Na muni au te tatada tena-nga	Take my herd-separating spear
Ma au tafa lililo bote-nga	And my flock-forming sword
Fo ela o te'e te neu be	Go where you rest the spear
Ma oe tafa neu be na,	And where you lower the sword,
Ela tena lu'u leu ndia	This lets the herd lay down
Ma bote hae leu na;	And the flock stop at that place;
Fo tena ta leu lu'u	It is not the herd that lies down
Ma bote ta leu hae	And not the flock that stops
Te ela ana-mak leu luu	But orphans who lie down
Ma falu-ina leu hae	And widows who stop
Fo leo tetun esa boe	As is right
Ma leo teman esa boe.	And as is fitting.

The admonition to care for 'orphans and widows' is continued. Solu Ndi//Luli Laki is told that in guiding the herd back to its corral, he should not throw a flock-herding stone or stick so as to strike any of those who depend on him, thus causing them to weep. Instead, Ndi Lonama//Laki Elokama speaks to his son in the first person, advising him to rely on his herd dogs and to do as he did when he was alive:

Ma sadi mafa-ndendelek	And do remember
Ma sadi masa-nenedak	And only do keep in mind
Au teng nade Kafe Lasi	My spear's name is Kafe Lasi
Ma au tafang nade Seu Nula	And my sword's name is Seu Nula
Ma au busang nade Lepa Lae	And my dog's name is Lepa Lae
Ma asung nade Doi Soi;	And my hound's name is Doi Soi;
Fo au ala u tada tena	When I go to separate the herd
Na au o Doi Soi	Then I go with Doi Soi
Ma au ala u lilo bote	And when I go to form the flock
Na au o Lepa Lae	Then I go with Lepa Lae
Fo makuma na-hala lai dua	And if he barks twice
Na au tati ai dua	Then I cut two sticks
Ma na-dasi lai telu	And if he howls thrice
Na au ndalu longik telu boe.	Then I trim three vines.

Some of the elusiveness of these lines depends on an understanding of Ndi Lonama//Laki Elokama's dog's name, Doi Soi//Lepa Lae. Ritual names are particularly elusive because they cannot be directly translated. Often, however, they consist of words whose meaning in ordinary language is generally clear. In the context of ritual language, these words coalesce to imply a sense for these names. Thus, Doi//Lepa are verbs for 'carrying'; *lepa* as a noun can also refer to 'provisions'—that which is carried on a journey. The dyadic soi//lae, in this context, suggests 'affection', a willingness to clear things up, make things right. Thus the dog's name signals a willingness to assist others and help in removing obstacles and encumbrances. Hence, when the dog barks, Ndi Lonama//Laki Elokama acts accordingly and advises his son to do the same.

He then goes on to instruct his son in what his daughter should do:

Ma ma-fada ke fetok Henu Ndi	And say to the girl child Henu Ndi
Te o dudi-no ma-lolem	Your good near-relative
Ma ma-fada tai inak Lilo Laki	And say to the woman child Lilo Laki
Te o tola-tunga ma-ndam	Your proper close-kin
Fo ela leo be na	In this way that
So'e sasau neka	She should scoop and scrape from the rice basket
Na so'e sau no inan	Scoop and scrape with her mother
Fo inak Lisu Lasu Lonak	Her mother, Lisu Lasu Lonak,

13. Admonitions of the ancestors

Ma kola ndundui tua	And draw and serve from the lontar-syrup jar
Na kola ndui no te'on	Draw and serve with her aunt
Fo te'on Dela Musu Asuk.	Her aunt, Dela Musu Asuk.
Fo ela neka lama kako bafa	Let the rice basket overflow at the mouth
Na dai ana-ma leo	To be enough for a clan of orphans
Ma bou lama lua fude	And the syrup jar run over with froth
Na ndule falu-ina ingu.	To be sufficient for a band of widows.

This passage is the most explicit in its urgings to support 'orphans and widows' from the wealth of the family. Having thus repeatedly instructed his family to provide for all of his dependants, Ndi Lonama//Laki Elokama foreshadows his journey to the afterlife in a series of striking images. These images of being carried by perahu to the west, of seeking his 'mother and aunt' and of marriage with the Earth as spouse follow one another in succession, ending with the refrain that this is the fate of all who die.

Te au touk Ndi Lonama	For I am the man Ndi Lonama
Ma au ta'ek Laki Elokama	And I am the boy Laki Elokama
Na au tonang sanga sosokun	My boat is about to lift
Ma au balung sanga sasa'en	And my perahu is about to rise
Fo au ala a tunga inang	For I am going to search for my mother
Ma ala u afi te'ong	And I am going to seek my aunt
Nai muli loloe	In the receding west
Ma iko tatai,	And at the tail's edge,
Fo au leo Dela Muli u	For I go to Dela in the west
Ma leo Ana Iko u.	And I go to Ana at the tail.
De se au tonang ta diku-dua	My boat will not turn back
Ma au balung ta lolo-fali,	And my perahu will not return,
Te dae sa'on doko-doe	The earth demands a spouse
Ma batu tun tai-boni.	And the rocks require a mate.
De se mana-sapuk mesan-mesan	Those who die, this includes everyone
Mana-lalok basa-basan.	Those who perish, this includes all.

The chant continues in the first person, describing this passage to the underworld:

De neuk-o fai a neu fai	As day follows day
Ma ledo a neu ledo.	And sun follows sun
Te au dilu Ana Iko len	I turn down to the river of Ana Iko
Ma au loe Dela Muli olin.	I descend to the estuary of Dela Muli.
Nde be na iu sio lai dalek	There are nine sharks down below
Ma foe falu lai dalek.	And eight crocodiles down below.
De ala silu dope lai dalek	They bare their knife teeth down below

Ma ala dali noli lai dalek.	And they sharpen their fangs down below.
De neuk-o se au balung to diku-dua	Now my boat will not turn back
Ma au tonang ta lolo-fali.	And my perahu will not return.

The chant concludes with a final admonition to care for 'orphans and widows', this time invoking a botanic metaphor of the tree that offers shelter and protection. In a special mortuary ritual for noted individuals in Rotenese society, a large tree is selected and ringed with smooth river stones to form a wide, rounded platform defined by the shade of the tree's branches. This monument of remembrance is known as a *tutus* and the ceremony to celebrate the establishment of a *tutus* is possibly the single largest ritual celebration performed by the Rotenese. This passage appears to allude to this practice but is remarkable in that Ndi Lonama// Laki Elokama's instruction is first to plant and then care for the tree (*Tui*//*Bau*), allowing its roots to grow into water to provide a sanctuary for shrimp and crabs, who are taken to represent 'orphans and widows'.

Te sadi mafa-ndendelek	But do remember
Ma sadi masa-nenedak	And do keep in mind
Heo Ingu-Fao baun	The Bau-tree at Heo Ingu-Fao
Ma Dolo Sala-Poi tuin na	And the Tui-tree at Dolo Sala-Poi
Bau naka-boboik	A Bau-tree to care for
Ma tui nasa-mamaok.	And a Tui-tree to watch over.
De tati mala bau ndanan	Cut and take a branch of the Bau-tree
Ma aso mala tui ba'en	Slice and take a limb from the Tui-tree
Fo tane neu dano Hela	To plant at the lake Hela
Ma sele neu le Kosi	And to sow at the river Kosi
Fo ela okan-na lalae	That its roots may creep forth
Ma samun-na ndondolo	And its tendrils may twine
Fo ela poek-kala leu tain	For shrimp to cling to
Ma nik-kala leu feon,	And crabs to circle round,
Fo poek ta leu tain	For it is not for shrimp to cling to
Te ana-mak leu tain	But for orphans to cling to
Ma nik ta leu feon	And not for crabs to circle round
Te falu-ina leu feon.	But for widows to circle round.

The use of voice in this chant—the singular 'I' who admonishes—is a literary device that is used to powerful effect because the 'I' in this case is the deceased and his words, after his death and just before his burial, thus take on immediate and poignant significance.

The comparative question

To initiate the comparison that I have called for in this chapter, I would like to consider briefly one striking instance of a similar use of voice in the poem *Kasaksian Bapak Saijah* by the poet Rendra, which he has included in the volume entitled *Orang Orang Rangkas Bitung* (1993). *Kasaksian Bapak Saijah* is a poem of 67 lines, from which I have selected a few illustrative stanzas. The poem was composed in Depok in 1991 and is ostensibly a poem of protest set in the colonial period. Clearly, however, at the time of its writing during the New Order period in Indonesia, it was intended to be interpreted with wider implications. Admonition, in the Rotenese case, becomes, in Rendra's poem, testimony (*kesaksian*)—a statement of profound protest. Although there is no formal ritual context for its recitation, its performance, as I have heard Rendra give it, is highly charged and, in this sense, fully ritualised. As a comparative example drawn from the Austronesian-speaking world, it is thus well worth noting.

I have selected and translated five stanzas taken from different parts of the poem. These stanzas include the beginning and the end of the poem plus several illustrative sections that provide a good indication of Rendra's use of the voice of the dead—in this case, a poor, murdered peasant.

Ketika mereka bacok leherku	When they slashed my neck
dan parang menghunjam ke tubuhku	and the machete pierced my body
berulang kali,	repeatedly,
kemudian mereka rampas kerbauku,	and as they sold my water buffalo,
aku agak heran	I was somewhat surprised
bahwa tubuhku mengucurkan darah.	that my body gushed blood.
Sebetulnya sebelum mereka bunuh	For long before they killed me
sudah lama aku mati...	I was already dead...
Sekarang setelah mati	Now that I am dead,
baru aku menyadari	I have become aware
bahwa ketakutan membantu penindasan,	that fear serves oppression,
dan sikap tidak berdaya	and feelings of hopelessness
menyuburkan ketidakadilan...	bury injustice...
Baru sekarang setelah mati	Only now that I am dead
aku sadar ingin bicara	I am aware of the desire to speak
memberikan kesaksian.	and give testimony.
O, gunung dan lembah tanah Jawa!	O you mountains and valleys of Java!

Apakah kamu surga atau kuburan raya?	Are you heaven or a grandiose graveyard?
O tanah Jawa,	O Java,
bunda yang bunting senantiasa	ever pregnant mother
ternyata para putramu	it is evident that your children
tak mampu membeliamu.	are unable to protect you.
Kesaksianku ini	This testimony is
kesaksian orang mati,	the testimony of a dead man,
yang terlambat diucapkan.	uttered too late.
Hendaknya ia menjadi batu nisan	My hope is this will be the gravestone
bagi mayatku yang dianggap hilang,	for my corpse, considered lost,
karena ditendang ke dalam jurang.	cast down into a deep chasm.

The effect of these lines—with their use of a singular 'I' in the defiance of death and injustice—is indeed rhetorically powerful. It is a superlative use of a literary device. The audience to whom it is addressed, however, is aware that Bapak Saijah is a fictional creation, the representative of an oppressed class of peasants.

In contrast, in the Iban case (Sather 2001:92–7), the voice rendered by the *manang* in his ritual can be that of a particular dead individual who addresses his immediate family. Instead of defiance, however, there is an element of deep sadness on the part of the deceased:

How reluctant I am to be severed by Nyara…

For I still wish to seek riches in this world.

The power of this voice is concentrated by the capacity of the *manang* to access the spirit world and thus speak the words of the dead.

In fact, however, the Iban ritual of 'severing the flower' involves a complex dialogue, which is reflected in the different voices in the chant. The dead can speak through the *manang* but the *manang* may speak on behalf of various other spirits whom he impersonates; or he may speak on his own behalf as performer of the ritual, or as the guide and conductor of the spirits of the dead on their journey by boat to Sebayan, the land of the dead. The dead can also speak to the *manang* and the *manang* can reply on behalf of the living to answer the words of the dead. Indeed, there is even a giving of gifts between the living and the dead.

The Rotenese case is different again. Ndi Lonama//Laki Elokama is the name of a chant character in a recognised recitation that can be used for any number of wealthy individuals. In this sense, it is a literary vehicle. On the other hand, when this chant is performed, it is performed for a particular individual at his funeral and is usually embellished with additional lines that allude to this individual. The chanter (*manahelo*) who leads the chant, however, is not credited with powers of accessing the spirit world but the deceased's spirit is believed to be present. The power of the chant is in the beauty of its language, in the insistence of the long monologue and in the immediacy of its message directed explicitly to the bereaved family.

Concluding remarks

Reimar Schefold has called for the comparative study of blessings. In a recent article (2001), he compared the modalities of blessings in a variety of societies from the Vazimba of Madagascar and the Sakuddei of Siberut to the Ata Tana Ai of Flores and the Laboya of Sumba, linking these modalities with the concept of precedence and the power of the ancestors. This contribution, intended as a complement to Schefold's comparative explorations, is a call for more explicit attention to be paid to the 'voices' of the ancestors in their communication with the living.

14. To the aroma of the name: The celebration of a ritual of rock and tree

Introduction

The Rotenese are indifferent ritualists. As I have portrayed them, the Rotenese 'can talk a good ceremony, but they are rarely concerned with actually performing one' (Fox 1979:148). In what passes as ritual performance, the Rotenese do not 'preserve' routinised traditions; rather they continually recreate and reformulate their traditions through elaborate forms of oration. The order of any performance follows a simple set of 'verbal frames' that gives the ritual a 'textual' underpinning but only hints at how such frames are to be enacted (Fox 1988). Thus paradoxically no two rituals are the same, though they follow the same formulae.

This chapter describes the creation of a new ritual in an old guise. It is an account of my involvement in Rotenese ritual and requires, at the outset, an explanation of this involvement. In recounting my participation in this specific ritual, I propose to examine some of the basic Rotenese ideas about ritual.

Personal preface

During my first fieldwork on the island of Rote in 1965–66, my closest confidant, teacher and advisor on all matters Rotenese was the Head of the Earth in Termanu, Stefanus Adulanu of clan Meno. An old man, severely hobbled by arthritis, 'Old Meno', as he was generally referred to, kept to his house in the settlement of Ola Lain.

Since his youth, Meno had served as scribe to the court of Termanu. When the Lord Manek of Termanu, Ernst Amalo, was appointed as district officer (*camat*) of central Rote and was obliged to reside in the town of Ba'a, Old Meno continued to guide the domain. He and Amalo's deputy, the Wakil Manek of Termanu, Frans Biredoko, would preside at court gatherings to judge disputes on behalf of the Lord Manek. In deference to Meno, these court gatherings were generally held in Ola Lain rather than in the centre of the domain, Feo Popi.

The figures of Manek (Lord) and Dae Langak (Head of the Earth) represent the polarity on which the domain of Termanu was founded. Together as ruler and ritual authority, the 'Wakil Manek' and 'Old Meno' possessed sufficient personal presence to maintain, for a time, the fiction that the traditions of Termanu remained intact, in spite of the past encroachments of the Dutch colonial government and the continuing bureaucratic intrusions of the Indonesian State.

Ernst Amalo, as Lord of Termanu, had granted me permission to conduct my research in his domain and had declared me his 'sister's child', an act that made him personally responsible for my physical welfare. To enable me to learn the traditions of Termanu, he entrusted me to Old Meno. Meno, however, took months to decide whether to take me and my work seriously. When he did, he adopted me as a 'son'. Thus I was curiously situated with the Lord Manek as my 'mother's brother' and the Head of the Earth as my 'father'. My social situation was particularly curious, in terms of Rotenese social conventions, since the Lord Manek represented the pinnacle of royal status from which all nobility was derived whereas the Head of the Earth, in formal contrast, embodied a primordial commoner status.

To complicate matters, Ernst Amalo arranged residence for me and my wife in the village of Ufa Len, near where his deputy, Frans Biredoko, resided. I lived in the house of another man, Mias Kiuk, of the commoner clan Ingu Beuk, whose wife had come from the noble Biredoko line. In time, Kiuk also accepted me as a 'son' and this acceptance provided me with another network of social relationships. Here, too, I had a 'father' of commoner origin and a 'mother's brother' of high noble status.

Ola Lain, where Meno lived, was about 4 or 5 km from where I lived in Ufa Len. At least once or twice a week, I would journey to Meno's residence to see him and to attend court sessions. Through the whole of my stay on Rote, even after I had moved to reside in other domains, I would return to Ola Lain to see Old Meno and to continue our discussions.

When I finished my field research and returned to Oxford to write my dissertation, I would, on occasion, write to Meno and he would usually reply. On one occasion, I wrote to announce the impending birth of my first child and he wrote to propose a Rotenese name for my son. This name eventually formed the basis for the teknonym by which I came to be addressed in Termanu.

As Meno's son later recounted to me, the old man grew increasingly frail and, on 30 March 1970, he died. By one reckoning, he was eighty-eight. By my estimation, based on his memories of past events, old Meno must have been well into his seventies when he died.

Two years later, in September 1972, I returned to Rote and once more took up residence in Ufa Len. Immediately on my arrival, as Meno's returning 'son', I proposed to hold a concluding mortuary ritual in his honour. I discussed my proposal first with Meno's Rotenese son, my 'elder brother' Ayub, and, with his concurrence, I publicly announced an intention to erect a *tutus* and to carry out the ceremonies associated with it.

Tutus as ritual of rock and tree

A *tutus* is the union of rock and tree. It consists of a ring of smooth stones set on a foundation of loose rock extending around the base of a large tree. This forms a broad stone seating platform that serves as a monument to the dead, a representation erected only to prominent individuals as the final, optional stage in a succession of mortuary rituals.

Figure 14.1: Erecting the *Tutus* in Honour of 'Old Meno'

All Rotenese rituals of the life cycle are phrased in a botanic idiom that draws multiple metaphoric analogies between human life and the growth of specific plants. Thus a single idiom encompasses both human and agricultural rituals.

For example, the marriage overtures to a potential wife-giver are spoken of as 'a search for seed'. In the dyadic language of ritual, young unmarried women are likened to 'coconut//areca nut palms', and the marriage ceremony, in its traditional form, is performed so 'that the shoot of the coconut may grow and that the germ of the areca nut may sprout'.

The mother's brother, as the representative of the wife-giving maternal relatives, is referred to as 'mother's brother of origin' (*to'o-huk*), using the term *huk*, which designates the 'base, trunk or stem' of a tree.[1] The mother's brother, in turn, refers to his sister's children as his 'plants' (*selek*).

Maternal relatives represented by the mother's brother perform the rituals that sustain the life and growth of those whom they have 'planted'. All rituals from the pre-birth ceremonies that 'open' the womb for 'the eldest sprout//the first fruit' to the final ceremonies that conduct the deceased to the grave require the participation of maternal relatives. Specific symbolic payments are provided for each of these maternal rituals by those who share most intimately in the 'name' (*nadek*) of the person for whom they are performed. This is generally a group that considers itself a single 'house'.

All Rotenese possess what is called a *nade balakaik* (a 'hard, firm or strong name').[2] This name is given shortly after birth and remains unchanged throughout life. Unlike a variety of endearing 'soft or tender names' (*nade mangana'uk*) by which an individual may be addressed at different stages in life, a person's hard name should not be spoken except in a ritual context. Various devices exist to hint at the ancestral basis of this hard name, which is not secret, but because of its intimate connection with the person, nonetheless ought not to be uttered.

A person's hard name is his or her genealogical name and links that person to a succession of ancestral predecessors. Generally, this succession of ancestral names comprises a line of male predecessors. Female predecessors, however, for whom no bride-wealth was received, can and do provide links in this succession and often constitute critical junctures in lineage formation .

These genealogical names trace another form of 'origin' (*huk*). Unlike the origin traced through the maternal relatives that focuses on a person's corporeal substance, the line of origin traced through names is identified with the 'spirits' (*nitu*) of those who are named. This origin is also intimately associated with the 'renown' (*bo-nadek*: literally, 'the aroma of the name') of one's group. In this notion, aspects of spirit, name and renown merge as a single concern.

As a consequence of this distinction, when the burial has occurred and the members of the maternal line have been honoured and compensated for their ritual services, their role ends. Thereafter, the remaining mortuary rituals are the exclusive concern of those who share most closely the names of the

---

1   In Termanu, this same term, *huk*, is also applied to designate the prior generation in a line of maternal derivation represented by the *ba'i-huk*, the 'mother's mother's brother of origin', while in east Rote (in the domains of Bilba, for example), the term *huk* is extended even further to a third generation of maternal derivation represented by the *solo-huk*, the 'mother's mother's mother's brother of origin', which in this case denotes a male descendant within this line of origin.
2   Names are a subject of considerable cultural elaboration among the Rotenese. Here, I discuss only the *nade balakaik*, a person's 'hard name'.

deceased. For the most part, these are the direct lineal successors of the dead person who have legitimised their rights of succession by their formal payments to the maternal relatives.

Subsequent mortuary rituals on the third, ninth, fortieth and sometimes the hundredth day after burial are directed to the spirit (*nitu*) of the deceased, who is known by his or her hard name. For the overwhelming majority of Rotenese, the celebration on the fortieth or hundredth day after burial marks the conclusion of these rituals.

For a few prominent individuals, a further *tutus* ceremony may be performed. In the Rotenese botanic idiom, such individuals may be likened to tall hardwood trees. Like their 'hard names', these individuals continue as prominent figures even after death.[3] Thus, the chant lines:

Pota Popo lalo	Pota Popo has died
Ma Solu Oebau sapu.	And Solu Oebau has perished.
De late batu kakoli na	His stony grave is like a kokoli tree
Ma lo ai tangatean na.	And his wooden tomb like a tangatean tree.

As described in Rotenese chants, these trees provide shade for lowly 'orphans and widows', a metaphoric phrase that refers to the bereaved as well as to all those in a dependent status. Thus a prominent image of the ideal society—strong, erect and enduring—is that of a 'dense forest or a thick wood' (*toe-ao lasin//lelei nulan*).

Meno's tutus chant

On my first fieldtrip, Meno himself provided me with one short example of a chant that pertains specifically to the ceremony of the *tutus*. The chant focuses on the process of replacement, which is succinctly expressed by a succession of genealogical names (in this case, a double succession of names, as required by the poetic rules of parallel composition). Thus in the chant, Nggongo Ingu Lai ('Nggongo of the Highlands') is replaced with his successor, Latu Nggongo, and Lima Le Dale ('Lima of the Riverbed') is replaced with Enga Lima.

This short chant is as follows:

Nggongo Ingu Lai lalo	Nggongo Ingu Lai dies
Ma Lima Le Dale sapu	And Lima Le Dale perishes
De lalo ela Latu Nggongo	He dies leaving Latu Nggongo

---

3 It is possible to speculate that the Rotenese term *balakaik* (meaning 'hard, stiff, strong') is in fact a metaphoric expression based on the root (*kaik/ai*) for 'tree'. Saying that something *is bala-kaik* implies that it is 'tree-like'.

Ma sapu ela Enga Lima.	And perishes leaving Enga Lima.
Boe te ela batu nangaitun	But he leaves a stone to sit on
Ma ela ai nasalain.	And he leaves a tree to lean on.
De koluk Nggongo Ingu Lai	Plucked is Nggongo Ingu Lai
Te Latu Nggongo nangatu	But Latu Nggongo sits
Ma haik Lima Le Dale	And taken is Lima Le Dale
Te Enga Lima nasalai.	But Enga Lima leans.
Fo lae: Nggongo tutu'u batun	They say: Nggongo's sitting stone
Na tao ela Latu Nggongo	Was made for Latu Nggongo
Ma Lima lalai ain	And Lima's leaning tree
Na peda Enga Lima.	Was set for Enga Lima.

A *tutus* is concerned with succession and with the remembrance of names. The term '*tutus*' is derived from the root *tu*, '(to) sit'; *nanga-tu* is the verb 'to sit'; *tutuk* is 'a seat' (Jonker 1908:646). A *tutus* is, however, a special kind of 'seat': a ring of raised stones set around a large tree. Formerly, *tutus* were used as ceremonial points for the performance of clan 'origin rituals' known as *hus* (a term, like *huk*, derived from the root *hu*, meaning the 'base' or 'stem' of a tree, 'origin' or 'cause'). It was at these annual origin ceremonies that the full list of genealogical names of the group was recited, beginning from the 'origin' (*hu*) of the group and continuing, in proper succession, to the generation of the living. The earliest clan *tutus* were monuments to the origin of the clan and the *tutus* itself was the locus of the names that derived from this origin. It was a fundamental point of genealogical reckoning.

In Termanu, *hus* ceremonies ceased to be performed in the 1920s or early 1930s. For many Rotenese of the present generation, however, the association of *hus* and *tutus* is so strong that these two distinct celebrations have come to be regarded as if they were a single ritual. Indeed, for Rotenese Christians in 1972, a *tutus* ceremony was, like the *hus*, a relic of the past.

The Christian polemic against hus and tutus ceremonies

Already in the nineteenth century, *tutus* and *hus* ceremonies were denigrated in Christian preaching. Both ceremonies were viewed with suspicion because they involved contact with the spirits of the dead, who, in Christian eyes, were designated as *setan*. An example of this association can be seen in the brief text recorded by the Dutch linguist J. C. G. Jonker from the local Rotenese 'religious teacher' D. A. Johannes at the turn of the century. In this text, Johannes rejects any association of *tutus*-building with Biblical practice or with Dutch custom. Instead, by linking the *tutus* with offerings to the spirits, Johannes insinuates that such ceremonies are opposed to proper Christian practice:

> For particular individuals, a *tutus* is erected. Some say that the purpose of the *tutus* is the same as in the Bible where it is said that the Jews erected stone monuments of honour, and some say it is the same as Dutch plastered graves. But the Rotenese do not erect *tutus* on graves, but at the base of trees set apart from the graves of the dead. When they erect a *tutus*, they make a feast at the base of the tree and they beat gongs, race horses, and dance. Some say that the purpose of the *tutus* is to recall and remember the one who has died. This could be but I think not. Those who erect a *tutus*, whenever they pass it, leave betel and areca nut at the *tutus* and then go on. What is the purpose of that? I think that this comes close to the truth and I suspect that the betel and areca nut is left so that the dead may partake of it and this is the purpose of the *tutus*: for the spirits of those who have died and who wander around and are tired, that they may rest at the *tutus*. (Jonker 1911:84, 112)

Eventually, this kind of polemic had its effect and *tutus* and *hus* ceremonies were effectively ended in Termanu.[4] Thus, at the time of my precipitous announcement that I would erect a *tutus* in Meno's honour, there had been no *tutus* ceremony held in Termanu for several decades—perhaps for as long as 50 years. Precisely what this ceremony would involve was therefore by no means clear.

No-one questioned the suitability of performing such a ritual for Meno since he was an esteemed figure in the domain, nor did anyone reject my claim of an obligation to sponsor such a performance. If, however, it is true that Rotenese prefer to 'talk' a good ceremony rather than actually perform one, my proposal provided potential for an ideal ritual. Meno died on 30 March 1970 and, based on Rotenese ritual requirements for sequences of multiple threes, a minimum of three years had to elapse before a *tutus* ceremony could be performed. At the time of my announcement of the ceremony in September, it was clear that there would have to be six months before the ceremony could be performed.

As an initiator of the ceremony, it might be presumed that I held a privileged position to be able to direct its performance. In fact, my chief task was getting various participants to cooperate. Preparation and organisation were paramount. The ceremony was a topic of endless conversation but most of the talk focused on practical matters: how much rice, how much palm gin, how many horses would race, what gifts would be given to the horsemen and to the chanters? That there would be a great feast, horseracing and chanting was clear but what

---

4 Elsewhere on Rote, these ceremonies continued for much longer. Now the celebration of the *hus* is confined to ceremonies in one area of west Rote.

the 'ceremony' would consist of was never discussed in any detail. To a great extent, the 'performance' was left to an uncertain number of 'performers' at the time of the ceremony.

At the time of the ceremony, my responsibility in attending to the demands of an improvised organisation, the requirement of having to perform a specific role (rather than being able to move more freely as an observer) and the need to respond to contingencies during the celebration limited my ability to study what I was sponsoring. In the end, several thousand people attended the celebration and most of the work involved in it was either delegated or simply assumed by the appropriate individuals. In so far as I succeeded in carrying out my expected role, I was unable to observe all that went on. Much of what occurred I learned only after the fact, when those delegated with particular tasks informed me of what had happened.

This chapter is by no means a complete record of all the events that followed my announcement of the proposed ceremony; it is not a detailed account of all the activities involved in erecting the *tutus*; and it is not an analysis of all the chants spoken in celebrating its construction.

Instead, in this chapter, I wish to offer comment on Rotenese ritual as a creative process—on how 'tradition', defined in its broadest sense to include the full cultural resources of a community, can be called on to create an appropriate performance. The *tutus* ceremony, which I proposed for enactment, was performed, after a long hiatus, by a wholly Christian population. This critical factor, my peculiar involvement in the ceremony and a complex set of changes that had been imposed on the domain of Termanu all prompted a substantial restructuring of the social and symbolic underpinnings of the ritual. The ceremony that eventuated, however, satisfied the expectations of a Rotenese ritual and, to judge from general comments after the ceremony, was regarded as 'traditional'.

Preparation for the tutus ceremony

Between the time of my first fieldtrip and my second trip, the domain of Termanu ceased to be recognised as an official unit within the Indonesian governmental structure. The domains of Termanu, Keka and Talae were joined to form a single district (*kecamatan*) and 'village areas' consisting of a number of scattered settlements were designated as *desa* ('villages'). To emphasise this transformation, all *desa* were accorded new names. Although the domain remained the popular focus of social and personal identities, these changes formally ended the role of the Manek as Lord of the Domain and the Dae Langak as Head of the Earth. Moreover, these changes introduced divisions within the domain.

The settlement of Ufa Len, where I had resided on my first trip, had become part of Desa Nggodi Meda, while Meno's settlement at Ola Lain had become part of Desa Ono Tali. The new names for these villages were explicitly chosen to express a complementarity. Nggodi Meda and Ono Tali allude to wealth measured in gold and water buffalo. They are dyadic names taken from a short poem that is quoted widely in various versions:[5]

Lilo ta dai oma	If the gold is not enough to make an oma's weight
Nggodi meda fo dai oma.	Smelter a bit to make an oma.
Kapa ta dai fadi	If the buffalo is not old enough to have a sibling
Ono tali fo dai fadi.	Draw a rope to add a sibling.

The poetic allusion here is to a supportive mutuality that completes what is lacking in the other, and the names Nggodi Meda ('Smelter a bit') and Ono Tali ('Draw a Rope') signify this mutuality.

A further complementarity between the villages was established in the choice of their 'new' headmen. Frans Biredoko, the former Wakil Manek, became the village headman of Desa Nggodi Meda and Ayub Adulanu, who had succeeded his father, became the village headman of Desa Ono Tali. Together they recreated the fundamental opposition (between the Lord and the Head of the Earth) that structured the domain, but in this case as the leaders of separate units at the same level in a new bureaucratic structure. It was within this new framework that the ordering of the *tutus* ritual had to be accommodated.

The first issue that had to be settled was where along the road joining the two villages the *tutus* was to be located. Old Meno's grave was at Ola Lain in Desa Ono Tali. A *tutus*, however, must always be erected at a distance from the grave. There was a good site with an excellent tall tree near the border between Ono Tali and Nggodi Meda but definitely on the Nggodi Meda side of the 'border'. This location, my involvement and the insistence of Frans Biredoko on having the *tutus* in Nggodi Meda were persuasive but the issue had to be deliberated at length and alternative possibilities considered. Ultimately, an argument based on symbolic complementarity prevailed. Since Old Meno's grave was in Ono Tali, where it was the primary responsibility of his elder son, Ayub, it was considered appropriate that his *tutus* should be in Nggodi Meda, where I as the 'younger son' was to have principal responsibility. In concurring on the matter of location, Ayub himself articulated this formulation of responsibility. Other factors—for example, that the largest and wealthiest branch of clan Meno resided within the boundaries of Nggodi Meda—were clearly relevant but not alluded to in discussions.

---

5   For another version of this poem, which refers to the two main rivers of the domain of Ba'a, see Fox (1980:58).

A major obstacle to the performance of the ceremony centred on this branch of clan Meno. One of Biredoko's sons wanted to marry a woman from this branch of the Meno clan. The woman's family was agreeable since this offered a marriage of high status; but perhaps for the converse reason, Frans Biredoko opposed the marriage. As a result, Ayub, as the head of Meno, was placed in a position of opposition to Frans, although personally the two men were close friends. For more than six months, the position remained deadlocked and, for this period, no planning could proceed for the *tutus*.

Most of the community at Ufa Len was in favour of the marriage, including the boy's mother. In terms of my adopted kinship position, Fran's son was my 'father's sister's son'. Thus I was called on to intervene. This, however, was hardly necessary. Everyone, including Frans Biredoko, realised that I had only limited time on Rote. My evident need to get on with preparations for the ceremony was thus used by others as one of the arguments to persuade Frans to relent in his opposition. In the end, he did relent and negotiated bride-wealth for the marriage. This cleared the way to resume preparations.

Once the way was cleared, my next task was to acquire the animals that would be needed for the feast. My other task was to dispel worries that the ceremony—however it was to be performed—was going to be conducted without Christian blessing. To resolve this problem, I was able to barter a watch for a large pig owned by the Christian preacher and local chanter Esau Pono. On agreeing to provide an animal for the ceremony, he also agreed to preside at the ceremonies on the day of the feast.

All feasts require a calculation of needs. These calculations are reckoned more in terms of meat than in rice since an invitation to a feast is phrased, in Rotenese, as an invitation 'to eat meat'. Since feasts are generally open affairs, one can never be certain how many people will come. It was assumed that a majority of the two villages would come and it was considered likely others would come from further away. Since the *tutus* involved a single feast and there were to be no meat distributions, which often double the number of animals slaughtered, I was advised to acquire one large water buffalo, five good-sized pigs and a goat for any Muslims who might attend the celebration. If more animals were needed on the day of the feast, it would always be possible to conclude a quick deal, generally at a higher than normal price, to acquire the necessary animals from stocks at hand in the village.

Besides the expectation of rice, which is brought as a contribution to a feast, there was the possibility that there would be an additional contribution of animals. Uncertainty, however, about the nature of social obligations for this kind of ceremony made calculations difficult. In this context, however, village Nggodi Meda was considered the 'feast-giver'.

In the end, members of Nggodi Meda contributed more than 400 kg of unhusked rice to the feast, with prominent members of clan Meno from Nggodi Meda contributing rice and animals. At dawn on the day of the feast, H. Tupuama, the head of the branch of clan Meno in Nggodi Meda, whose daughter was to marry Fran's son, brought a large water buffalo, which he slaughtered as his personal contribution to the ceremony.[6]

Another major task was to acquire sufficient palm gin for the feast and for the night's celebration that was to precede it. As Mias Kiuk assured me, 'If there is enough gin, people don't even remember if they have eaten'. Securing a sufficient supply meant contracting an entire week's production from the main licensed stills in Termanu and in the neighbouring domain of Ba'a. This production came to more than 100 L of palm gin. Besides the gin, I had to acquire a substantial supply of tobacco, betel and areca nuts, coffee, sugar, spices, kerosene and *spiritus* for pressure lamps as well as a variety of 'gifts' to bestow on the chanters and horse riders who would take part in the performance. Additional rice and animals were required to feed the men who erected the *tutus* and the women who pounded rice in preparation for the main feast.

Erecting and naming the tutus

A *tutus* is a model of construction simplicity. It is an enduring structure built to accommodate the tree it surrounds. There is enough loose rock around the tree to allow for years of growth without any disturbance to the general structure. Erecting the *tutus* entailed no special ceremony and work was organised by Frans Biredoko as a collective village effort. The only heavy labour required was in carrying flat river rocks from the nearby riverbed. At one stage, village schoolchildren were given several hours' free time to join in the carrying of smaller rocks to place around the tree. These loose rocks formed the inner core of the construction on which and around which the heavier flat river rocks were set. Once erected, the *tutus* had to be named. Mias Kiuk assembled the elders and ritual chanters of Nggodi Meda and Ono Tali for a special meeting. The Indonesian word *sidang*, associated with a special church gathering, was used to underline the seriousness of the discussion. Only in retrospect did I realise that this 'naming' was the single most important step in all the preparations for the

---

6   The only exception to this pattern of contributions was Ayub Adulanu, who contributed a large quantity of rice although he was not from Nggodi Meda. A tally was kept of all individual contributions and was given to me after the feast as a record. Members of Nggodi Meda also contributed all the cooking equipment and other utensils that were used for the feast. A record was kept of these contributions as well. As for animals, as far as I was able to ascertain after the feast, two water buffalo, five pigs and two goats were slaughtered to feed the assembled guests. Although I acquired most of these animals, the slaughtering was delegated. To this day, I am uncertain whether one of my five pigs was slaughtered for the *sidang* to decide the name of the *tutus* or whether this was an animal that Mias Kiuk supplied himself.

ceremony. Mias Kiuk slaughtered a pig and provided the rice for the evening's gathering at which various individuals proposed different names and everyone argued about the significance and merits of these names.

In the end, the name 'Dale Sue' was agreed on. This name, like all of the names proposed, consists of half of a complementary set. In ritual language, Dale Sue pairs with Tei Lae. *Dale//Tei* forms a dyadic set meaning 'inside, stomach' and *Sue//Lae* another set meaning 'affection, love, empathy'. Thus one possible translation of Dale Sue would be 'inner affection'. Although I did not enter into the debate about the choice of the name, the debate was carried out in my presence and for my benefit since the 'inner affection' alluded to in the name was my affection for Meno that prompted the *tutus* celebration.

Finally, when the name had been set, a formal announcement of the ceremony could be made. Informally, everyone over a wide area had long been aware of the target date that had been set for the celebration: Saturday, 30 June 1973. Nevertheless, an announcement had to be sent to the relevant government officials: the Camat and the Wakil Bupati. A special document was prepared in proper, formal Indonesian with the heading *Berita Hus/Tutus Dale Sue* ('Announcement of the *Hus/Tutus* Dale Sue'). In providing a brief summary of Meno's life and work as grounds for holding the ceremony, this document explicitly identified the ceremony to be performed as a composite of a *hus* and a *tutus* ceremony—thus combining two distinct and separate rituals. At this point, after the *Berita* was sent, the stage was set for the celebration itself.

The celebration of Hus/Tutus 'Dale Sue'

The night before the feast was devoted to a major part of the ceremony: the inauguration of the *tutus* by ritual chanting accompanied by the beating of a drum or gong (*bapa*). The chants for this kind of occasion are known as *hahate bini*. They recount a eulogised origin. Verbal invitations had gone out to chanters in the surrounding area and five prominent chanters came forward to vie with one another: Mesak Bedak and Johannes Bauanan from the domain of Korbaffo and Ta'e Dau, Peu Malesi and Set Apulungi from Termanu. (Other capable chanters were present but chose not to take an active part in the chanting.) Each of these chanters took turns reciting and responding to the other, each recounting a version of an origin that would often take its lead from another chanter's poetic imagery.

The chanter Peu Malesi, who was a participant in the debate about the name of the *tutus*, represented the village of Nggodi Meda. Since he was aware of local ideas about the intention of the performance, his initial chanting set the direction for the other chanters. The young chanter Set Apulungi, a Ndaonese resident from Mok Dae in Ono Tali village, turned out to be particularly fluent. There was a strong alternation between these two, which left the other chanters to draw their themes from these two contenders. From time to time, one or another chanter, especially the two from Korbaffo, would withdraw to lead the circle-dancing that went on simultaneously with the reciting on the *tutus* around the tree.

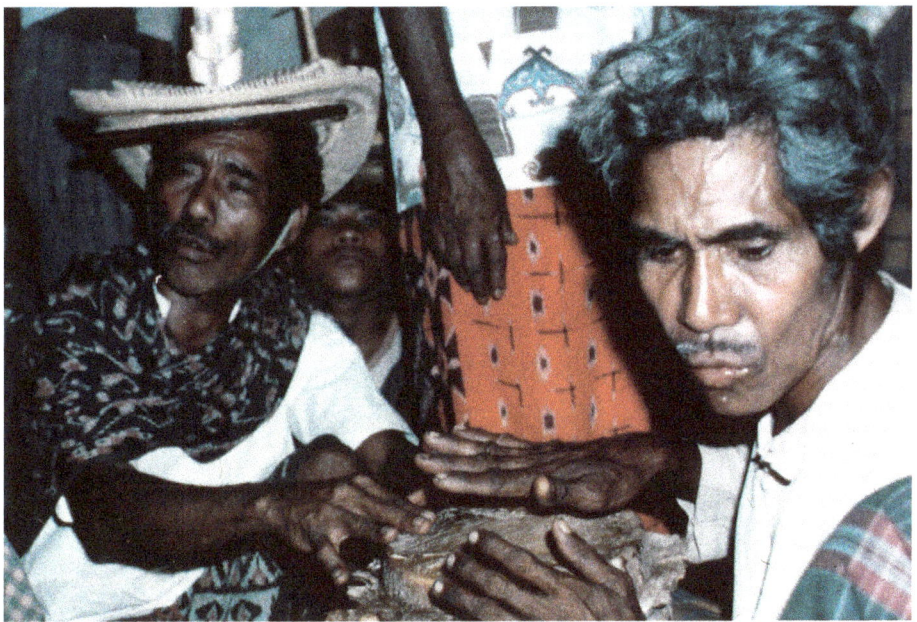

Figure 14.2: Peu Malesi leading the chanting on the night before the *Tutus* Celebration

Those chants that I was able to record amid other activities ran to hundreds of lines. They form a small corpus with an internal structure of its own, collectively shaped by the way particular chanters responded to each other's language. Here I will refer only to Malesi's chanting, which guided the rest. This chanting was consciously worked in advance to express the intentions of the ceremony as it was conceived by the Nggodi Meda community. Malesi took various turns. Each successive turn, however, rephrased the same constructed narrative. Following the Rotenese convention of naming chants after their principal chant character, the narrative fashioned to fit the occasion was named *Funu Feo ma Tepa Doki*. The chant told of Funu Feo//Tepa Doki's journey to Rote, his encounter with Sio Meda//Lepa Lifu, their 'sharing of thoughts', Funu Feo//Tepa Doki's departure for his own land, Sio Meda//Lepa Lifu's death, Funu Feo//Tepa Doki's return and his decision to erect a *tutus* in honour of Sio Meda//Lepa Lifu. Essentially, it was a straightforward narrative, in ritual-language form, of my relationship with Meno from the time of my first visit and thus of the origin of the *tutus* itself.

Explorations in Semantic Parallelism

Bini Hahate: *Funu Feo ma Tepa Doki*

Malesi's narrative begins with a formulaic opening that places events in a specific symbolic setting in the ritual past. In Rotenese rituals, the symbolic coordinates of north//west are opposed to those of south//east. To identify my place of origin, Malesi created the new dyadic set, *Amerika//Olana* (America//Holland).[7]

Hida bei leo fana	In a former period
Do data bei dona	Or at a past time
Touk leo Funu Feo	The man like Funu Feo
Ma ta'ek leo Tepa Doki	And the boy like Tepa Doki [was]
Bei nai Ki Dae	Still in the North Land
De Ki Amerika Daen	The North America Land
Ma nai Muli Oe	And [was] still at West Water
De Muli Olana Oen...	The West Dutch Water...

Funu Feo//Tepa Doki speaks, saying:

Kale lai dame do	Kale is far away
Au afi taon na le'e	I must think of how
Ma Lote nai sei sala	And Lote is at a distance
Na au dua tao na le'e	I must ponder how
Fo dadi neu tola-tungak	To become a kinsman
Ada moli neu dudi-nok	And grow to be a relative
Fo inak esa bobongin	As if born of one woman
Ma leo touk esa lalaen	And as if begotten of one man.

At one point of his chanting, Malesi inserted an explanation for the different peoples of the world based on a common Rotenese interpretation of the Biblical tale of Noah. In Rotenese, Noah has become Nok Bulan (literally, 'Coconut of the Moon') and his three sons, Ham Nok, Sem Nok and Jafe Nok. The Rotenese claim to derive from Sem Nok, whereas the Dutch and others are said to derive from Jafe Nok. As a descendant of Jafe Nok, living in America//Holland, Funu Feo//Tepa Doki sets out in his boat to sail to Rote (Lote do Kale), passing the dangerous straits of Puku Afu that separate the island from Timor.

Ana pale uli titidi	He guides the splashing rudder
Ma leko la kukulu	And charms the rippling sail [through]
Enok telu Puku Afu	The three paths of Puku Afu
Ma dalak sio Use Bou...	And the nine paths of Use Bou...

---

7   In the domain of Thie, in southern Rote, another chanter faced with the need to identify my place of origin created the poetically pleasing new dyadic set, *Amerika//Afrika* (America//Africa).

Eventually, Funu Feo//Tepa Doki reaches Termanu (Buna Dale ma Koli Dale) and anchors at a site on the northern coast, Oe No ma Kedi Poi. There, Funu Feo//Tepa Doki meets two characters who stand watch and are likened to Frans Biredoko and Mias Kiuk. In various origin chants—as, for example, that for the origin of rice and millet—personified objects are washed ashore where they are then picked up and carefully carried around the island. Malesi uses a similar imagery, but in a figurative fashion, to emphasise the desire for knowledge that brought me to Ufa Len:

Ko'o manganana'un	They cradle him softly
Ma ifa tapandondoen...	And they lift him gently...
Ko'o lo ndolu ingu	Cradling with knowledge of the land
Ma ifa lo lela leo.	And lifting with wisdom of the clans
Mai Ufa Lai Ama	Coming to Ufa Lai Ama [Ufa Len]
Ma mat Latuk Oe No...	And coming to Latuk Oe No...

There, in Ufa Len, Funu Feo//Tepa Doki explains his purpose for coming. Here, the Rotenese metaphors are particularly dense and elusive. To share one's thoughts is said to make the 'head of gold grow tall and the tail of iron grow wide'. This sharing of thoughts is associated with the sharing of 'blood or fluid', a relationship that is likened figuratively to the dripping of lontar juice into a single bucket. All of these images are compressed in Funu Feo//Tepa Doki's statement:

Au mai sanga dudu'ak falu	I come to seek eight views
Ma sanga a'afik sio	And to seek nine thoughts
Fo ela au tao neu besi ikok	That I may make an iron tail
Ma au tao neu lilo langak	And I may make a gold head
Fo lilo langan nama-tua	That the gold head may grow tall
Ma besi ikon nama-nalu.	And the iron tail may grow wide.
Boso ladi lilo langan	Don't snap the gold head
Ma boso ketu besi ikon.	And don't break the iron tail.
Boso ketu titi-nonosin	Don't break the dripping juice of relations
Boso ladi da-fa	Don't snap the flow of blood
Bei nai Kale daen	While still in the Land of Kale
Ma bei nai Lote oen...	And still in the Water of Lote...

In response to this request, Funu Feo//Tepa Doki is directed to meet Sio Meda//Lepa Lifu, with whom he becomes a 'friend and companion' (sena//tia), who shares with him 'eight views and nine thoughts'. These thoughts Funu Feo//Tepa Doki takes with him when he returns to the North Land and West Water.

In 1973, according to Malesi's chanting, Funu Feo//Tepa Doki returns and searches for his friend and companion, but the 'Heights have requested and Heaven has demanded, requested his friend and demanded his companion', Sio Meda//Lepa Lifu. On learning this, Funu Feo//Tepa Doki responds, saying:

Au afi taon na le'e	I am thinking about what to do
Ma au dua taon na le'e	And I am pondering about what to do
Tianga sapu nitu	My friend has died a spirit death
Do senanga lalo mula.	Or my companion has met a ghostly demise.
Ma leo au idung nai ia	Yet my nose is here
Ma au matang nai ia	And my eyes are here
Fo au sue fo to lesi	For I have great affection
Ma au lae fo dai lena.	And I have overwhelming love.

Funu Feo//Tepa Doki thinks for a while and then says:

Au daeng nai dame do	My land is far away
Te tao-tao au ela ho kuen	But what if I leave the odour of the civet
Ma oeng lai sei sala	And my waters are at a distance
Te tao-tao au ela piu moka.	But what if I leave the smell of the moka-fish.
De lane ai mai dalak	Set a tree along the road
Ma tutu batu mai enok	And pile rocks along the path
Tao neu koni-keak	To serve as a remembrance
Ma tao neu hate-haik.	And to serve as a memory.

Here, strong odours—those of the civet cat and of a particularly pungent-smelling fish—signify remembrance. Both creatures mark their passing with powerful smells. In this case, the implication is that the lingering odour is that of Funu Feo//Tepa Doki rather than that of Sio Meda//Lepa Lifu.

At another point in his chanting, Malesi used an entirely different set of metaphors comparing the *tutus* with the burial cloths given by the mother's brother to wrap the sister's child. In the process, he was able to signal the name given to the *tutus*:

Dale sue Sio Meda boe	Inner affection for Sio Meda
Ma tei lae Lepa Lifu boe	And heart's love for Lepa Lifu
Tehu dae lai dame do	Although the lands are far away
De palu pita ta losa	The winding sheet does not reach
Ma oe lai sei salak	And the waters are at a distance
De la soni ta losa...	The burial cloth does not reach...
De ala lane ai mai dalak	So they set a tree along the road
Ma tutu batu nai enok	And pile rocks on the path
Fo tao neu palu pita	To make a winding sheet
Ma tao neu la soni.	And make a burial cloth.

Finally, having erected the *tutus*, Funu Feo//Tepa Doki boards his boat and returns to his land in the north-west. Thus, according to the chant, my primary reason for returning to Rote was to perform the *tutus* ceremony and when I had done this, I could depart.

Rain, sometime after midnight, interrupted the chanting, which would otherwise have continued until dawn, and eventually everyone dispersed to await the next day's activities. For their efforts, four chanters received fancy pocketknives and Malesi received a large hunting knife.

In comparison, the next day's formal ceremonies were brief, modern and Christian. Someone, at great effort, brought several woven-plastic chairs and set them on top of the *tutus* for honoured guests. The preacher, Esau Pono, led a prayer and then spoke eloquently but briefly. Ayub's eldest daughter, with a fluency learned mainly from her grandfather, spoke on behalf of clan Meno. I then spoke briefly.[8] My simple chant harkened back to the links between Nggodi Meda and Ono Tali, evoking some of the same images that Malesi had used the night before:

Faik ia dalen	On this day
Ma ledo ia tein	And at this time
Ita takabua	We have gathered together
Ma ita taesa	And we have come as one
Fo peda batu neu batu	To lay stone on stone
Ma fua dae neu dae	And to place earth on earth
Fo Meno tutus a dadi	So that Meno's tutus would occur
Ma Adulanu lutun na tola	And Adulanu's stone pile would appear
Nai nitas ia	At this nitas-tree
Ma nai delas ia.	And at this delas-tree.
Meno tutus ia Sio Meda	Meno's tutus here is Sio Meda
Ma Adulanu lutun ia Lifu Lepa	And Adulanu's stone pile is Lepa Lifu
Te sadi mafa-ndendele	Remember, do remember
Ma sadi masa-neneda	And recall, do recall
Batu nangatu nai Koli Dale	The stone to sit upon in Koli
Ma ai nasalai nai Buna Dale	And the tree to lean upon in Buna
Nai Nggodi Meda	Is in Nggodi Meda
Ma nai Ono Tali.	And in Ono Tali.
Lao ladi ia	As you walk past, stop here
Ma lope tuli ia.	And as you swing past, rest here.

---

8   I have briefly described my involvement in this *tutus* ritual in an earlier paper published in Indonesia (Fox 1982).

After my short chant, the ceremony concluded. For the main participants, traditional costume was required and all speeches were in ritual language. None of these speeches followed the narrative format of the night before. Instead, they focused on the *tutus* as a form of remembrance and monument of succession (thus, much like the poem that Meno had provided to me for such a *tutus* ceremony).

Thereafter, most of the day's attention was directed to feasting and to the running of the horses. This racing originated from a ritual circumambulation on horseback that was the equivalent during the day of circle-dancing at night. Since for the feast people sat scattered around the *tutus*, there was too little room to race the horses in a circle around the tree. It was therefore decided to hold the races along a straightway on the road near the *tutus*. This gave everyone the opportunity of a good view of the racing.

There were two categories of racing: 1) *lala'ok*, a dignified trotting style of race in which the horse carries its tail high and may not break its stepping gait; and 2) *kukuak*—what Rotenese call 'dog running'—an exciting but undignified outright gallop. *Lalaok* requires skill in handling and usually the owner rides his own horse; for *kukuak*, young boys ride most of the horses with an abandoned recklessness. There were at least 12 horses in each category, including horses from the domains of Ba'a and Korbaffo, and a succession of races were run at intervals, leading to the final race in each category in late afternoon as the day's activities were coming to an end. Almost as if to complete the complementarity that had characterised all of the stages of the *tutus*, the horse of a schoolteacher from the village of Ono Tali took first place in the *lala'ok* category and a horse from the village of Nggodi Meda took first place in the *kukuak* category. With the final race and the giving of the prizes—different-quality sarongs, dishes or cigarette lighters for the top four winners in each category—the day's festivities ended.

Conclusion: Constructing ritual in retrospect

A ritual on Rote does not end with its performance. It is, as it were, 're-performed' in discussions afterwards and often in this re-performance it is given a more ordered representation.

My initial reaction after the ceremony was simply one of relief in having been able to carry out my proposal in spite of initial obstacles and continuing uncertainties about what would happen. Local attitudes, however, were more positive. The *hus/tutus* ceremony was judged a major success. The chanting and dancing of the preceding night and the morning's brief ritual speaking were considered the mark of tradition. It was seen as important that no-one had used Indonesian, which is a permissible, though non-traditional, ritual register for ceremonial gatherings. Furthermore, contributions to the feast were substantial and numerous. This was clear evidence of widespread local support and an assurance of sufficient food for the feast. The quantity of gin that I had provided satisfied the 'elders' and added a glow to guests' perceptions of the proceedings. Enough horses had come for the racing and the racing was seen as exciting. Everyone seemed satisfied by the outcome of the races and with the gifts that had been awarded. Also, quite importantly, Ernst Amalo, the 'retired' Lord Manek of the domain, had come and pronounced his satisfaction with the day's activities.

In retrospect, the symbolic duality of the proceedings was re-emphasised. The complementarity between the villages of Nggodi Meda and Ono Tali was confirmed in a series of oppositions: Ono Tali::Nggodi Meda, elder brother::younger brother, grave::*tutus*.

The fact that complementarity is a modality of argumentation and that these oppositions were arrived at to settle a disagreement about the location of the *tutus* did not lessen their validity once they had been agreed on. These oppositions had become part of a dual symbolic order. Even the outcome of the horseracing could be viewed as an appropriate confirmation of this order.

The chief resource for the creation of this order is a rich and varied poetic tradition based on canonical parallelism. With this resource, it is possible to vest any set of complementary oppositions with a full panoply of dyadic representations.

Once this has been accomplished, the whole system can be alluded to in terms of its parts. The 'Dale Sue' would be sufficient, in the local context, to invoke the *hus/tutus* ceremony and the relationships that went into producing it. In pointing to this power of invocation, one approaches an understanding of the creativity of Rotenese ritual.

Several years after the *tutus* ceremony, in 1977, I returned once more to Termanu, this time with the filmmaker Timothy Asch. By this time, the *tutus* had become an integral part of the local landscape, so that when a site was required to film Peu Malesi reciting the origin of his ancestor's discovery of lontar juice, the *tutus* was chosen as the appropriate location.

The beginning and the end of the film, *The Water of Words*, focuses on the *tutus*, with Malesi, Ayub Adulanu, Frans Biredoko and Mias Kiuk sitting on it: 'Nggongo's sitting stone//Lima's leaning tree.' The aroma of the name lingered.

The Christian Oral Canon

15. The appropriation of Biblical knowledge in the creation of new narratives of origin

Introduction

The ancestral knowledge of origins is a fundamental feature of the epistemology of the Rotenese. The knowledge of origins and the formal recitation of this knowledge are considered necessary to account for persons, places and most objects of cultural significance. Thus the origins of fire for cooking, the sourcing of seeds for planting, the first tools for house-building, for weaving and for dyeing as well as the initial colours and design patterns for cloth, the specific derivation of persons and the naming of places—all have their recitations of origin; each is told in a ritual format requiring the pairing of terms in a strict canonical parallelism.

The Rotenese have adopted a similar epistemological stance in relation to Christianity. This stance has resulted in an appropriation of Biblical knowledge and the development of a variety of formal narratives. One of the most important of these narratives recounts conversion to Christianity as an active and eventually successful quest for new knowledge and wisdom. Equally important, however, is the retelling of Genesis in a variety of versions. Here I propose to examine these Christian narratives of origin as distinctive linguistic creations. To do so, however, requires some examination of the conversion of the Rotenese to Christianity.

Although the first royal conversion was made in the early eighteenth century, the subsequent conversion to Christianity of the population of the island was a gradual process that occurred over more than two centuries. The fact that this process was initiated a full hundred years before the first Dutch missionary attempted to establish residence on the island and was propagated predominantly by the Rotenese themselves is what distinguishes contemporary Christian adherence.

The most significant aspect of this process was the linguistic transformation that took place in the transmission of Christianity. Initially and for more than a century thereafter, there was an almost exclusive insistence on the use of Malay as the only appropriate vehicle for the transmission of Biblical knowledge. The appropriation of this knowledge and its assimilation to a Rotenese ritual canon were a singular historical achievement that is now taken for granted among present-day Rotenese. It is this underlying achievement that needs to be highlighted to appreciate Rotenese creativity in their use of ritual language.

In this chapter, I want to try to identify when ritual language began to be used on Rote not to replace Malay but to enhance its use in the preaching of Christianity. I then want to examine some of the special dyadic lexicon that was developed for this purpose, and finally, but most importantly, I want to present the ritual narrative of origin that recounts the beginnings of Christianity and thereafter compare two ritual-language versions of Genesis. Recitations of this kind are now a critical component of Rotenese oral traditions. As recourse to the traditional canon in ritual language begins to decline, the use of ritual language to convey the Christian canon continues to increase. The origins of these changes can be traced to the Rotenese encounter with the Dutch beginning in the seventeenth century.

Local dynastic politics, schooling and the use of Malay on Rote

Soon after the Dutch East India Company had established itself at Kupang in 1653, Company officers made contact with various Rotenese rulers and became immediately embroiled in local disputes purportedly to strengthen their 'allies' against their 'enemies' (see Fox 1977:95). In 1662, the first of a succession of contracts was signed between the Company and Rotenese rulers to whom the Company gave official recognition. Among these rulers, the ruler of Termanu, whose domain was strategically located on the north central coast of the island, came to be regarded as the Company's most loyal ally. In 1677, a fortified enclosure (*pagar*) was built at a site near Namo Dale in Termanu and two soldiers were stationed there as representatives of the Company. In this same year, the Dutch took the young ruler of Termanu to Kupang to learn Malay (see Fox 2011). This was the beginning of the Rotenese use of Malay as a means of elite communication. This use of Malay expanded when the Company created a Council of Rulers that was convened in Kupang as the forum for hearing local disputes among all the rulers allied with the Dutch in the Timor area.

In 1729, one of the rulers of Rote, Pura Messa, from the domain of Thie, in the south-west of the island, managed, without the knowledge or permission of the Company, to have himself and his family baptised by a *dominee*/predicant named Da Fonseca. Precisely how this was managed and with what motivation is difficult to determine. Shortly after his baptism, Pura Messa and two of his sons died in a smallpox epidemic that swept the island. Pura Messa's son, Benjamin Messa, was installed as Radja.

Conversion to Christianity at this juncture transformed the politics of the island. At the time, Thie and a number of neighbouring domains were under pressure from an expanding domain, Termanu, where the Company had located its fortification and exercised its influence.

Benjamin Messa immediately claimed to be accorded the rights of a 'Christian king' among the island's pagan rulers. He formed an alliance with the rulers of several other domains who clamoured to become Christian. By 1741, the Church Council in Batavia had received requests for baptism from almost 900 Rotenese from among this alliance of domains.

More significantly, Benjamin Messa requested that a schoolmaster be sent to his domain to teach Malay—and, in particular, the Malay Bible. The initial call for schools by the alliance of Christian rulers set off a wave of requests from all of the rulers of the island who were determined to have a school of their own as a mark of their status and sovereignty. The Company complied with these requests but at a price that eventually could only be afforded by the larger domains.

By 1754, the six largest domains, none of whose rulers was Christian, had their own schools. Over 3000 children were reported to be enrolled in these schools. The smaller domains, mostly Christian, could not afford the Company's demands. In response, the Company reduced the payments it demanded for schoolmasters. Eventually the high costs of schools ushered in a further phase in local education. The smaller Christian domains were among the first to take responsibility for instruction in Malay, replacing outside teachers with knowledgeable Rotenese. By 1769, a local Rotenese school system had begun to take shape and payments to the Company declined.

As a result of this process, Malay became the vehicle that provided access to new forms of knowledge—to a Dutch world as represented by the company, and above all, the knowledge of Christianity.

Christianity proceeded in tandem with schooling and the knowledge of Malay. To know Malay, to speak Malay, was in effect to become a Christian and a sign of elite status. In their schools, the Rotenese taught themselves and began the process of assimilating Biblical knowledge. Schoolmasters were also responsible for preaching in local churches—all of this before the arrival of the first Dutch missionaries.

The first mission efforts on Rote

The first missionary delegated by the Netherlands Mission Society (Nederlandsche Zendeling-Genootschap)[1] arrived in Kupang in 1819. This missionary, Dr R. Le Bruijn, remained stationed on Timor but he made an effort to reinvigorate the Rotenese school system. With his assistance, by 1825, there were eight domain schools on Rote, all staffed by local Rotenese. In 1827—nearly one hundred years after the first royal conversion—Rote received its first missionary: a young Dutchman by the name of J. K. ter Linden. Although he had married a high-ranking Rotenese woman from Termanu, within a year, he had become so disillusioned with the 'shameful and godless conduct' of the Rotenese schoolteachers that he closed all the schools that Le Bruijn had opened. He himself retreated to Kupang. Some years later, Le Bruijn's successor, G. Heijmering, once more set about reopening the Rotenese schools. Heijmering was also responsible for baptising the first ruler of the royal line of Termanu to become a Christian.

After Heijmering's re-establishment of Rotenese schools, no-one attempted to close them. Although several Dutch missionaries were sent to Rote, none lasted for more than a year. In 1847, the Mission Society appointed a Rotenese from Termanu to supervise the schools on the island. Even as mission support declined, Rotenese rulers—whether Christian or not—continued to give strong support to their domain schools whose activities included a Sunday church service. In fact, the number of schools on the island increased; however, with the withdrawal of the Nederlandsche Zendeling-Genootschap in 1851, schooling on Rote went into a temporary decline.

In 1857, the Dutch Colonial government assumed responsibility for funding one school in each of the 18 domains of Rote. In some domains, however, additional village schools were established with contributions from the local population. By 1871, this number of schools had increased to 34 with a school population of more than 3275. Formal instruction was in Malay.[2] In the nineteenth century, schoolmasters were respectfully designated as *mese malai* ('Malay masters'). Mastery of High Biblical Malay, with the religious authority it conveyed, conferred upon these Malay masters an elite status. Even after the colonial

---

[1] The Netherlandsche Zendeling-Genootschap was founded in 1797 on the model of the London Mission Society. Its mission was to preach and instil the Calvinist traditions of the Dutch Reformed Church (Nederlandsche Hervormde Kerk), which is today constituted on Rote as the Protestant Evangelical Church of Timor (Gereja Masehi Injili di Timor, GMIT). Peter van Rooden (1996) has provided a useful sketch of the foundation of this missionary organisation. An extended account of nineteenth-century Dutch mission activities in the Timor Residency can be found in Coolsma (1901:823–62).

[2] J. A. van der Chrijs (1879) has provided a detailed account of schooling on Rote as he found it in 1871. This account, filled with amusing anecdotes, also includes a list of school locations, their enrolments, and a listing of the Malay texts used for instruction at this time. Van der Chrijs notes that the teachers in all these schools were themselves Rotenese.

government took over most schooling on Rote, schoolmasters were still obliged to teach catechism on Saturdays and to lead church services on Sundays. Thus the tasks of teaching and preaching in Malay remained intimately intertwined.

In the second half of the nineteenth century, however, the preaching of Christianity began to take a new turn. This change was largely the work of two missionaries, August Jackstein and G. J. H. Le Grand, both of whom resided on Rote for more than a decade and, as a result of this long residence, acquired a considerable knowledge of the Rotenese language and of local traditions. The first of these missionaries, August Jackstein, was a German, originally a member of the Gossner Mission Society, who lived on Rote—with only a brief interlude in Kupang—from 1860 until just before his death in 1875. One hundred years after his death, he was still remembered for the fact that although he became blind, he continued to preach as he was led on horseback from village to village. The second of these missionaries, G. J. H. Le Grand, who lived on Rote between 1890 and 1907,[3] had an even greater influence on the preaching of Christianity

The Le Grand inheritance

In published correspondence with his mission society, Le Grand notably articulated the critical changes that he was involved in effecting on the island. He recognised clearly that Malay had become the 'vehicle of Christian thought' on Rote but he questioned its use as an exclusive means for the transmission of Christian ideas. According to his account, after a period of more than 170 years, only one-fifth of the Rotenese population were baptised Christians and, during his 10 years, these numbers had grown by only about 35 baptisms a year.

Although visitors to the island remarked on the evidence of Christian influence on the island, Le Grand's personal assessment of this influence was frank and to the point: 'If you ask me what my total impression of Rotenese Christians is, I would answer: for many, Christianity is nothing more than Sunday apparel, which they wear at certain times, while their household undergarment is made of heathen material and woven with heathen patterns' (Le Grand 1900:373).

With this view of the realities of conversion, Le Grand set out during his time on the island to promote the use of Rotenese, in opposition to some of his predecessors. He was the first missionary to oversee a translation of a portion of the Bible into Rotenese. This was the Gospel of Luke: *Manetualain*

---

[3] Le Grand took leave to visit the Netherlands in 1899 but he returned to Rote to resume his duties in 1901. In 1905, he became, for a period, the minister (predicant) for Kupang, but returned to Rote again in 1907 before being transferred in 1908 to Minahassa. In 1912, he again returned to Kupang and in 1912 was transferred to Batavia.

Dede'a-Kokola Maneni Soda-Molen-a Lukas, translated by J. Fanggidaej into the central dialect of Termanu, Talae and Keka and published by the Nederlandsch Bijbelgenootschap in 1895.

As Le Grand admitted to his mission society, however, this translation was not the success that he had expected. He attributed this lack of success to the fact that reading of Rotenese was not part of the school curriculum. Both reading and writing were confined exclusively to Malay. What Le Grand, however, appears not to have appreciated was the diversity of the island and the political-linguistic rivalry among the different domains that prevented the acceptance of the Gospel in Termanu dialect in most other domains.

It is evident that Le Grand gained some grasp of the Rotenese language and even managed to acquire some knowledge of Rotenese ritual language. In his letter to his mission society, he included a short excerpt from a Rotenese death chant for which he provided a general paraphrase rather than a precise translation. His stated purpose was to contrast the Rotenese view of death with that of the Christian message. Although the Dutch linguist J. C. G. Jonker may have gathered his single example of Rotenese ritual language—the superlative *Manu Kama ma Tepa Nilu* text—about the same time as Le Grand, his text was not published until 1911. Le Grand's 28 lines of ritual language therefore represent the earliest (published) illustration of the Rotenese ritual-language register and are therefore worth translating.

Le Grand's orthography for the Rotenese is recognisable but idiosyncratic; it does not resemble the far more appropriate orthography used by J. Fanggidaej in his translation of the Gospel of Luke. (To what extent Le Grand's published text was a product of the mission society editors who worked from Le Grand's letters cannot be determined.) There are other puzzling features: while most of the text and its formulaic idioms are predominantly those of the central dialect of Rote, several dyadic sets are dialectically anomalous, suggesting that Le Grand's grasp of Rotenese was a personal mixture of Rotenese dialects. Although there are two lines of Le Grand's text (1900:363) that I cannot understand, most of the text is composed of dyadic sets and formulae that have continued to the present.

1. *Pata Dai ao lilo*	Pata Dai with golden body
2. *Te Solo Soeti ao engë kala*	Solo Suti with leaden body
3. *Ma tene besi*	And iron chest
4. *Langa saä kala.*	Hardened head.
5. *Sila sapoe boï*	They, too, die
6. *Ma lalo boï*	And they, too, perish
7. *Lalo kela soeki bete nala*	Perish, leaving their food and wealth
8. *Ma lalo kela lole lada*	And perish, leaving their tasty goods
9. *Ma sapoe kela dula doki*	And die, leaving their patterned cloths

10. Malole do malaä.	This is good or proper.
11. Lalo kela bou toewa la bengoewa	Die leaving lontar vats...
12. Ma neka hade la batole	And rice baskets...
13. Ma sapoe kela iko mana fifiu	And die, leaving tail-waving flocks
14. Ma soela mana mamasuk kala.	And horn-lifting herds.
15. Sama lèo fai ia	As on this day
16. Ma deta lèo ledo ia	And at this time
17. Ita tolo non ia boï.	We, relatives, here too
18. Lèo late dae a neu	Are heading for an earthen grave
19. Fo dai holun ma batu lunin.	For the earth embraces and rock crushes.
20. De ita boï o	Oh, we, too,
21. Mana-sapoe ma mana-lalo.	Are the ones who die and who perish.
22. De dai holoe, ita boï	The earth embraces us too
23. Ma batu luni, ita boï.	And the rock crushes us too.
24. De teman ta dae bafo do batu poi.	Order is not of the earth or the world
25. Tebe leo na tebe,	Truly it is true:
26. Tetu lele lasi	Order...
27. Ma tema toi ao nula	And perfection...
28. Teman ta dae bafo	Perfection is not of the earth
29. Ma tetu ta batu poi.	And order is not of the world.

Hence though he set about to encourage the use of Rotenese for the preaching of Christianity and can be credited with encouraging a local cultural foundation to the understanding of Christianity, the blossoming of this use of Rotenese occurred at a local level in the different dialects of Rotenese, making Rotenese Christianity an even more multifaceted creation.

Le Grand's most significant contribution to the grounding of a traditional church on Rote was his role in training an entire generation of Rotenese schoolteachers (*Inlandsch leeraar*) imbued with his views of preaching Christianity. From the time he arrived on Rote, he began a program of training to produce a cohort of teachers who were versatile in their capacities to become preachers and ministers but also to be certified to teach in government schools. (On Rote, Le Grand served as the secretary of the School Commission for both government and church schools.) In 1902, he was instrumental in transforming his personal teaching efforts into a formal teachers' training school (School tot Opleiding van Inlandse Leraren: STOVIL), which, for two decades, was strategically located on Rote. Although this school was open to students from the region, the overwhelming majority of its intake was from Rote. Its graduates, many of them drawn from the noble families of Rote, became leading figures on the island and among them were some of the notable preacher-chanters who contributed to the creation of a Christian canon in ritual language.

In 1965, there was one surviving member of Le Grand's cohort: Laazar Manoeain, who was considered at that time to be one of the master poets of the island. By then, he was blind, which only increased his reputation for oral performance, and living quietly in a house outside the town of Ba'a. His cosmological poem in Christian mode offers a prime example of the infusion of Christian ideas in a traditional format. Although this poem relies heavily on traditional formulae and might be mistaken for part of an ancestral oral canon, the key metaphors at its conclusion that offer the promise of heavenly rest are recognisably part of a lexicon fashioned for the preaching of Christianity (see Chapter 7 for the whole of this poem and a further discussion of its significance).

The poem begins with the lines:

Sa Lepa-Lai nunun	The Waringin tree of Sa Lepa-Lai
Ma Huak Lali-Ha kekan	And the Banyan Tree of Huak Lali-Ha
Keka maba'e faluk	The Banyan has eight branches
Ma nunun mandana siok.	And the Waringin has nine boughs.
De dalak ko sio boe	These are the nine roads
Ma enok ko falu boe	And these are the eight paths
Fo dala sodak nai ndia	The road of wellbeing is there
Ma eno mamates nai na	And the path of death is there…

The poem expounds on the threats offered along each of the branching paths leading in a different direction. The path leading west is described with the lines:

Ndanak esa muli neu	One branch points west
Boso musik ndanak ndia	Do not follow that branch
Te nitu hitu dalan ndia	For this is the road of seven spirits
Ma mula falu enon ndia	And this is the path of eight ghosts
De mate nituk nai ndia	The death of the spirits is there
Ma lalo mulak nai ndia	And the decease of the ghosts is there

After detailing these different threats, the poem describes the one path—the path of life and road of wellbeing (*eno molek//dala soda*)—that leads to Heaven and the Heights (*ata//lain*) where there is eternal rest and salvation (*soda sio//mole falu*). The use of the numerals eight and nine (*falu//sio*) to indicate an eternal completion, as indeed the use of the even more striking (and difficult to translate) description of Heaven as the 'buffalo-horn land of wellbeing and the flesh and bone water of life' (*kapa sula soda daen//pa duik mole oen*), is part of a new interpretative coding of older dyadic metaphors.

Te ndana esa lido-lido lain neu	But one branch goes toward Heaven
Ma dape-dape ata neu	And goes straight to the Heights
Na musik ndanak ndia	Then take that branch
Te dala sodak nde ndia	For this is the road of wellbeing
Ma eno molek nde ndia	And this is the path of life
Na musik ndanak ndia	Then take that branch
Te dala sodak nde ndia	For this is the road of wellbeing
Ma eno molek nde ndia	And this is the path of life
Fo nini o mu losa kapa sula soda daen	To bring you to the buffalo-horn land of wellbeing
Ma mu nduku pa-dui molek oen.	And to the flesh and bone water of life.
Dae sodak nai ndia	The land of wellbeing is there
Ma oe molek nai na	And the water of life is there
Fo o hambu soda sio	For you will find the wellbeing of nine
Ma o hambu mole falu	And you will find the life of eight
Ma dua lolo ei	And with legs outstretched
Ma kala ifa lima	And with arms cradled on the lap
Fo ifa limam no limam	Cradle your arms upon your arms
Ma lolo eim no eim.	And stretch your legs over your legs.

The role of the *utusan* as messenger, preacher and cultural interpreter

When the role of the schoolteacher became circumscribed within a more formal system of colonial education, teachers themselves became differentiated. By 1871, the Dutch recognised three classes of teachers on Rote, each of whom was at a different payment scale (van der Chrijs 1879:14). When in 1857 the colonial government took over the schooling system, it allowed only one school in each of Rote's 18 domains. In the larger and more populous domains, there was a demand for additional schools. Initially when these village schools were established, teachers in them were supported by the local populations. Eventually, however, all of the teachers received government support, but a hierarchy was set in place: first-class teachers were those who taught in the domain school. The records for 1871 show that 12 of Rote's 18 domains had more than one school; eight of these domains—Dengka, Oenale, Thie, Loleh, Termanu, Korbaffo, Bilba and Ringgou—had two village schools in addition to their main domain school. As a result there were almost as many village schools (16) as domain schools (18) on the island. In the years that followed, as school numbers continued to increase, the expansion of the system was in village schools with lesser-ranked teachers.

As the knowledge of Malay increased as a result of schooling, the role of the lay preacher—the *utusan* who was educated in the Bible and with considerable fluency in Malay—came to the fore. Teachers could be *utusan* and many were, but the position of *utusan* was not exclusively the prerogative of such teachers. In the later part of the nineteenth century through to the 1960s, the preaching of Christianity was carried forward by these *utusan* as evangelical 'messengers' and local church leaders. Although they had limited theological training, these *utusan* were often accorded the title of 'minister' (*pendeta*) by their church congregations. Since preaching required considerable fluency, individuals with impressive speaking capacities were attracted to becoming *utusan*. Often this speaking ability included a command of the Rotenese ritual language. The role of ritual leader could merge with that of the preacher. Among the *utusan* as well as among schoolteachers high Biblical Malay was appropriated, adapted and translated into the Rotenese ritual-language register. This process was facilitated by the fact that much of the Old Testament was based on similar formal features of parallelism—the duplication of expression in a dyadic format.

The creation of a dyadic lexicon for conveying the Christian canon

The translation of Biblical knowledge into the Rotenese ritual register called for the creation of a new vocabulary in dyadic form. This involved not simply the creation of new concepts but also the creative refashioning of existing idioms to convey new meaning.

Because this translation process took place in different dialect areas and in different congregations at different times, the theological lexicon created to convey Biblical knowledge varies from one dialect area to another but is still generally recognisable throughout the island.

Thus, for example, in the domain of Landu, God the Father as Creator can be referred to as

Tou Mana-Sura Poi a	The Inscriber of the Heights
Ma Tate Mana-Adu Lai a	And the Creator of the Heavens

while in the nearby domain of Ringgou, God the Creator is referred to as

Tate Mana-Sura Bula	The Inscriber of the Moon
Do Tou Mana-Adu Ledo	Or the Creator of the Sun.

Throughout most of Rote, metaphoric terms that allude to the tie-dye patterning of cloth are used to describe the Holy Spirit; however, the specific dyeing terms used in the different dialects vary. In Termanu, the Holy Spirit is referred to as the *Dula Dalek ma Le'u Teik* ('Patterner of the Spirit and Marker of the Heart'), while in Ringgou, this expression is *Dula Dale//Malala Funa* ('The Patterner of the Spirit and the Shaper of the (Woven) Core').

For Christ, there are many designations, most of which draw on traditional metaphoric phrases and imagery. In Termanu, for example, Christ can be described simply as the *Tou Mana Soi ma Ta'e Mana Tefa* (Redeemer and Ransomer: literally, 'The Man who redeems and the Boy who ransoms'), but Christ can also be referred to, using another common metaphor, as a healer and repairer of injury:

Touk Mana-So Sidak	The Man who sews what is torn
Ta'ek Mana-Seu Saik	The Boy who stitches what is ripped
Seu naka tema saik	He stitches to make whole what is ripped
Ma so naka tetu sidak.	And sews to make complete what is torn.

Heaven, in this dyadic lexicon, is:

Nusa Soda ma Ingu Tema	Domain of wellbeing and land of fullness
Bate Falu ma Tema Sio.	Eightfold abundance and ninefold fullness.

The Rotenese narrative of the coming of Christianity

The Rotenese trace the beginnings of Christianity on their island to the conversion of the rulers of three domains in the central south of the island. Primacy in this process is generally attributed to the ruler of the domain of Thie but just as often all three rulers are given credit together. The rulers referred to in this narrative—Foe Mbura from Thie, Ndi'i Hua from Loleh, and Tou Denga Lilo from Ba'a—are all historically identifiable individuals whose names appear in Dutch archival records for the 1720s.

A version of this narrative was first recorded in the nineteenth century from Rotenese schoolteachers living in Timor by the Dutch linguist J. C. G. Jonker, and was published with a Dutch translation in a collection of texts in 1905. Since this time, this particular tale has been used in schools and churches and has been accorded an almost canonical status. The original version was a locally embedded text—what would normally be described as a 'standing-tale' (Fox 1979)—told in the distinctive dialect of central Rote. Today this narrative has become the only 'standing-tale' that has island-wide recognition and is recounted in all dialects on the island. Even more significantly, this tale has been taken up and rendered into ritual language and actually used as part of church liturgy.

This radical shift to another speech genre gives this tale a form like that of the origin narratives of the island. It requires the strict use of parallelism but also the adaptation of a variety of traditional metaphors in a new context, imbuing these metaphors with new Christian meaning.

In the nineteenth-century telling of this narrative, the three rulers set sail for Batavia where they meet the Dutch Governor-General and obtain from him, in return for the payment of 30 slaves, the knowledge of Christianity. At the same time, they also obtain the knowledge of gin distilling, which has become for the Rotenese an indispensable feature of social interaction. In some dialects of Rotenese, the word for God, *Allah*, resembles the word for distilled gin, *ala* (from Malay, *arak*), thus allowing them to claim, by a play on words, that the journey of the rulers to Batavia resulted in the acquisition of two Al(l)ah. This double gain is made symbolically appropriate by long-established tradition, whereby locally distilled gin is dyed a reddish colour and used in the communion service.

In the narrative, each of the rulers is given a staff of office and, as a result of their journey, Dutch East India Company rule is installed on the island, protecting the rulers of the small domains at the south-western end of Rote against the expanding domain of Termanu. In the ritual telling of this tale as an origin narrative, much of this political dimension is elided to concentrate on the spiritual quest for Christianity.

To illustrate the ritual telling of this narrative of origin of Christianity, I have selected passages from the liturgy prepared for the 'Yubileum' ceremony of the Protestant Evangelical Church of Timor, which was held at Fiulain in the village of Danoheo in the domain of Thie on 1 October 1997.[4] This ritual passage can be divided into three segments: 1) an introductory passage that focuses on the pre-Christian period on Rote; 2) the passage that describes the journey of the rulers of Rote to Batavia and their return with the knowledge of Christianity; and 3) the progressive 'planting' of Christianity throughout the island. The chant is given the dual chant name *Sanga Ndolu ma Tunga Lela* ('To Seek Counsel and to Stalk Wisdom'). In this passage, as in other versions that I have recorded, the knowledge of Christianity is represented as two species of tree: the *Tui*-tree and the *Bau*-tree—both large trees that grow in close proximity to water.[5] These trees representing Christianity are what are then 'planted' from place to place on the island. Each part of the island is designated by its dual ritual name, and the 'planting' of Christianity follows, in form, the origin chant for the dissemination of the seeds of rice and millet on Rote. As an ordered recitation of placenames, the spread of Christianity from one domain to the next is recounted as a Rotenese topogeny (see Chapter 10).

---

4   This text in Termanu dialect (with others in different dialects) was published in a four-page supplement in the newspaper *Pos Kupang* on 30 September 1997.
5   The *Bau*-tree is known as a *waru* in Indonesian (*Hibiscus tiliaceus*); the *Tui*-tree remains unidentified.

15. The appropriation of Biblical knowledge in the creation of new narratives of origin

To provide a sense of how traditional metaphors and imagery are adapted, I quote several lines from the mortuary chant *Ndi Loniama ma Laki Elokama*. In this mortuary chant, the deceased is given voice to advise his living descendants before he sets sail on his voyage to the west (see Chapter 13 for an extended discussion of this mortuary chant and its significance). He speaks as follows:

1.	'De neuk-o se au balung ta diku-dua	'Now my boat will not turn back
2.	Ma au tonang ta lolo-fali.	And my perahu will not return.
3.	Te sadi mafa-ndendelek	But do remember
4.	Ma sadi masa-nenedak	And do keep in mind
5.	Heo Ingu-fao baun	The Bau-tree at Heo Ingu-fao
6.	Ma Dolo Sala-Poi tuin na,	And the Tui-tree at Dolo Sala-Poi,
7.	Bau naka-boboik	A Bau-tree to care for
8.	Ma tui nasa-mamaok.	And a Tui-tree to watch over.
9.	De tati mala bau ndanan	Cut and take a branch of the Bau-tree
10.	Ma aso mala tui baen	Slice and take a limb from the Tui-tree
11.	Fo tane neu dano Hela	To plant at the Lake Hela
12.	Ma sele neu le Kosi	And to sow at the River Kosi
13.	Fo ela okan-na lalae	That its roots may creep forth
14.	Ma samun-na ndondolo	And its tendrils may twine
15.	Fo ela poek-kala leu tain	For shrimp to cling to
16.	Ma nik-kala leu feon,	And crabs to circle round,
17.	Fo poek ta leu tain	For it is not for shrimp to cling to
18.	Te ana-mak leu tain	But for orphans to cling to
19.	Ma nik ta leu feon	And not for crabs to circle round
20.	Te falu-ina leu feon.'	But for widows to circle round.'

Prominent also in these lines is reference to the image of 'orphans and widows', a recurrent theme in virtually all Rotenese mortuary compositions. At one level, at a funeral, 'orphans and widows' refer to the family of the deceased, but more often this notion is generalised: all humans are 'widows and orphans'—a condition of loss and separation that is the basic state of humankind.

The introductory section of this chant describes Rote in its pre-Christian period when offerings were made to the spirits and ghosts and there were only weeping and sadness. Then the Holy Spirit—in Rotenese: the *Dula Dalek//Le'u Teik* ('The Patterner of the Spirit and the Marker of the Heart')—appears in order to effect a change upon the island. The Holy Spirit speaks to announce a new pathway for a life of peace and wellbeing of life.

Explorations in Semantic Parallelism

I

Sanga Ndolu ma Tunga Lela

1.	Hida bei fan	At a time in the past
2.	Ma data bei don	And a period long ago
3.	Ingu manasongo nitu	The land offering to spirits
4.	Ma nusa manatangu mula	And the domains sacrificing to ghosts
5.	Soda ta nai daen	Wellbeing was not in that land
6.	Ma tema ta nai oen.	And harmony was not in those waters.
7.	De falu-ina lasakedu	The widows cry
8.	Ala lasakedu bedopo	They cry continually
9.	Ma ana-mak lamatani	And the orphans sob
10.	Ala lamatani balu-balu.	They sob steadily.
11.	Nai Lino daen	In the land of Silence
12.	Do Ne Oen.	Or the waters of Quiet.
13.	Benga nafafada,	The Word is spoken,
14.	Benga neme Dula Dalek	Word from the Patterner of the Spirit
15.	Ma dasi natutuda,	And the voice falls down
16.	Dasi neme Le'u Teik:	The voice from the Marker of the Heart:
17.	'Soda dae nai ata	'The land of wellbeing is on High
18.	Ma mole oen nai lain.	And the waters of life are in Heaven
19.	Sanga dala soda	Seek the road of wellbeing
20.	Ma tunga eno molek	And follow the path of life
21.	Fo hapu soda sio	To gain the wellbeing of nine
22.	Ma hapu mole faluk	And gain the peace of eight
23.	Nai Lote daen	In the land of Rote
24.	Ma Kale oen.'	And the waters of Kale.'

In this second section, the rulers from three small domains are inspired by the Holy Spirit to build a perahu and sail it to Batavia. In the first section, the Holy Spirit speaks; in this next section, the rulers speak, explaining their mission: 'to seek Counsel and stalk Wisdom'. This—the wisdom of Christianity—is represented as two species of trees: the *Tui*-tree of Wellbeing and the *Bau*-tree of Life, which the Rotenese rulers bring back to the island.

II

The Journey in Quest of Christianity

1.	Faik esa manunin	On one particular day
2.	Ma ledo dua mateben	And on a second certain time
3.	Mane dua lakabua	Two rulers gathered together
4.	Ma boko telu laesa	And three lords gathered as one
5.	Lakabua fo lamanene	Gathered together to listen

15. The appropriation of Biblical knowledge in the creation of new narratives of origin

6. Ma laesa fo lamania	And gathered as one to hear
7. Benga neme Dula Dalek	Word of the Patterner of the Spirit
8. Ma dasi neme Le'u Teik.	And the voice of the Marker of the Heart.
9. Ita lakabua sanga ndolu	We gather together to seek knowledge
10. Ma ita laesa tunga lela	And we gather as one to seek wisdom
11. Nai Batafia ma Matabi.	In Batavia and Matabi.
12. Mane dua ma boko telu	The two rulers and three lords
13. Neme Tada Muli ma Lene Kona	From Tada Muli and Lene Kona
14. Neme Ninga Lada ma Heu Hena	From Ninga Lada and Heu Hena
15. Neme Pena Bua ma Maka Lama	From Pena Bua and Maka Lama
16. Boe ma ala lakandolu tona ofan	They conceive of a sailing boat
17. Ma ala lalela balu paun.	And they fashion a sailing perahu.
18. Tehu latane:	But they ask:
19. 'Ita fe tona nade hata?	'What name will we give the boat?
20. Ma ita fe balu tamo be?'	And what designation will we give the perahu?'
21. De ala fe nade Sanga Ndolu	They give the name: 'To Seek Counsel'
22. Ma ala fe tamo Tunga Lela.	And they give the designation: 'To Stalk Wisdom'.
23. De malole nai Lote	It was good on Rote
24. Ma mandak nai Kale.	And proper on Kale.
25. Faik esa matetuk	On one determined day
26. Ma ledo esa matemak	And at one appropriate time
27. De ala laba lala tona ofa	They climb upon the boat
28. Ma ala tinga lala balu paun	And they board the perahu.
29. Ala hela tuku telu-telu	They pull the oars three-by-three
30. Ma ala kale kola dua-dua.	And shake the oar-rings two-by-two.
31. Ala pale uli titidi	They guide the splashing rudder
32. De leu	They go
33. Ma ala la kukulu	And they manoeuvre the flapping sail
34. De leu	They go
35. Fo sanga ndolu sio	To seek thorough counsel [counsel of nine]
36. Ma tunga lela falu	And to stalk full wisdom [wisdom of eight]
37. Nai Batafia daen	In Batavia's land
38. Ma Matabi oen.	And Matabi's water.
39. Losa meti Batafia daen	Arriving at the tidal waters of Batavia's land
40. Ma nduku tasi Matabi oen	And reaching the sea of Matabi's water
41. Ala leu tongo lololo	They go to meet
42. Ma ala leu nda lilima	And they go to encounter
43. Lena-lena nai ndia	The great figures there

44. Ma lesi-lesi nai na, lae:	And the superior ones there, saying:
45. 'Ami mai neme Lote Daen	'We come from Lote's Land
46. Ma ami mai neme Kale Oen	And we come from Kale's Waters
47. Sanga Tui Sodak fo tane	Seeking the Tui-tree of Wellbeing to plant
48. Ma tunga Bau Molek fo sele	And stalking the Bau-tree of Life to sow
49. Nai Lote Daen ma Kale Oen.'	On Lote's Land and Kale's Waters.'
50. Hapu Tui Sodak ma Bau Molek	They gain the Tui of Wellbeing and Bau of Life.
51. Ala lolo-fali leu Sepe Langak	They return to Reddening Head
52. Ma diku-dua leu Timu Dulu	And go back to the Dawning East
53. For tane Tui lakaboboin	To plant the Tui-tree with care
54. Ma sele Bau lasamamaon.	And sow the Bau-tree with attention.

The next section of this liturgy consists of a topogeny: an ordered succession of dyadic placenames that identify different domains on the island of Rote. Christianity is first planted in the domain of Thie (Tuda Meda ma Do Lasi), and then in Loleh (Teke Dua ma Finga Telu) and then in Ba'a (Tanga Loi ma Oe Mau). The trees of the knowledge of Christianity spread their roots and tendrils in the centre of Thie at Dano Hela ma Le Kosi and the inhabitants of other domains come and take these trees and plant them in their domains. What follows is a further topogeny that proceeds east along the southern coast of Rote and then from the furthest eastern domain tracks back along the north coast of the island and on to the offshore island of Ndao. An excerpt from this topogeny is as follows.

III

The Topogeny of the Planting of Christianity on Rote

1. Tane leu Tuda Meda	They plant at Tuda Meda
2. Ma sele leu Do Lasi	And they sow at Do Lasi
3. Tane leu Teke Dua	They plant at Teke Dua
4. Ma sele leu Finga Telu	And they sow at Finga Telu
5. Tane leu Tanga Loi	They plant at Tanga Loi
6. Ma sele leu Oe Mau.	And they sow at Oe Mau.
7. Tui Sodak nai Dano Hela	The Tui of Wellbeing at Dano Hela
8. Okan na lalae	Its roots spread out
9. Ma Bau Molek nai Le Kosi	And the Bau of Life at Le Kosi
10. Samun na ndondolo.	Its tendrils spread forth.
11. Boe ma hataholi neme basa daen	People from all the lands
12. Ma dahena neme basa oen	And inhabitants from all the waters
13. Tati lala Bau ndanan	Cut the Bau-tree's branches
14. Ma aso lala Tui ba'en	And slice the Tui-tree's boughs
15. Fo tane nai Lote ingu	To plant in Lote's domains

16. *Ma sele nai Kale leo.*	And sow among Kale's clans.
17. *Tane leu Pila Sue*	They plant at Pila Sue
18. *Ma sele leu Nggeo Deta*	And they sow at Nggeo Deta
19. *Tane leu Tufa Laba*	They plant at Tufa Laba
20. *Ma sele leu Ne'e Feo*	And they sow at Ne'e Feo
21. *Tane leu Meda*	They plant at Meda
22. *Ma sele leu Ndule*	And they sow at Ndule
23. *Tane leu Soti Mori*	They plant at Soti Mori
24. *Ma sele leu Bola Tena*	And they sow at Bola Tena
25. *Tane leu Tunga Oli*	They plant at Tunga Oli
26. *Ma sele leu Namo Ina*	And they sow at Namo Ina
27. *Tane leu Koli*	They plant at Koli
28. *Ma sele leu Buna*	And sow at Buna
29. *Tane leu Tefu Buna*	They plant at Tefu Buna
30. *Ma sele leu Nggafu Huni*	And they sow at Nggafu Huni
31. *Tane leu Dae Mea*	They plant at Dae Mea
32. *Ma sele leu Tete Lifu*	And they sow at Tete Lifu
33. *Tane leu Tasi Puak*	They plant at Tasi Puak
34. *Ma sele leu Li Sona*	And sow at Li Sona
35. *Tane leu Dela Muri*	They plant at Dela Muri
36. *Ma sele leu Anda Iko*	And sow at Anda Iko
37. *Tane leu Ndao Nusan*	They plant at Ndao Nusa
38. *Ma sele leu Folo Manu.*	And sow at Folo Manu.
39. *Tui Soda na dadi*	The Tui-tree of Wellbeing comes forth
40. *Ma Bau Mole na tola*	And the Bau-tree of Life appears
41. *Boe ma ana-mak leu tai*	The orphans gather round
42. *Ma falu-ina leo feon*	And the orphans encircle it
43. *Fo hapu soda sio*	To obtain complete wellbeing
44. *Ma hapu mole falu*	And obtain full life
45. *Tao neu nakababanik*	To create great promise
46. *Ma tao neu namahenak*	And to create great hope
47. *Losa faik ia dale*	Up to this day
48. *Ma nduku ledo ia tein*	And until this time
49. *Nai Lote do nai Kale.*	On Rote and on Kale.

The retelling of Genesis as a Rotenese origin narrative

Although ritual language is commonly used in Christian liturgical contexts in Termanu, there is a tendency to keep traditional origin narratives distinct from Christian narratives. In contrast, in some eastern domains of Rote, particularly in Ringgou and Landu, there is a greater fusion of ritual-language genres. As in

Explorations in Semantic Parallelism

any oral genre, there are no fixed texts but a variety of compositions purporting to convey the same message. As such, it is useful to contrast two versions of Genesis, the one from Landu and the other from Ringgou, that differ in the degree to which they appropriate Biblical texts and fuse—or perhaps, more accurately, infuse—them with traditional ideas and metaphors.

To illustrate the first of these compositions, I quote a succession of passages from the Genesis chant of the poet Julius Iu, who is himself a lay preacher in the Protestant Evangelical Church of Timor (Gereja Masehi Injili di Timor: GMIT).[6] His chant begins with the initial creation of the world.

I

Initial Creation of the World

Au tui ia nana, nae:	I tell of
Tui dae ina dadadi	The creation of the world
Masosa na le maulu a	Its beginning and commencement.
Tou Mana Sura Poi a	The Inscriber of the Heights
Ma Tate Mana Adu Lai a	And the Creator of the Heavens
Adu neme lalai no dae ina.	Created Heaven and Earth.
Boema adu do tao nalan	Then He created and made them
Tehu bei kiu-kiu kima rou	But still there was darkness like the inside of a shell
Ma bei hatu-hatu do tafeo	And still there was gloom all round
Bei nafaroe dea ei	As if still groping in the legs of a fish weir
Bei nafadama lutu lima	Still fumbling in the arms of a fish trap.
Basa boema adu nala malua a	When He created the brightness
Ma riti ndala makaledo a	And generated daylight
De malua nala dulu	The sun rose in the east
Ma makaledo nala laka.	And the daylight appeared at the head.

II

The Command from God not to Eat of the Tree in the Garden

Boe ma Tou Mana Adu Lai a	The Creator of the Heavens
Ma Tate Mana Sura Poi a	And the Inscriber of the Heights
Ana hara no heke nè	He spoke with binding command
Ma dasi no bara tada:	And He gave voice to a prohibition:
'De basa-basa hata	'All things growing there
Nai oka ma nai dea dale ia	In that garden and in that precinct

---

6   This chant was recorded in 2007 and its translation is a joint effort by myself and Dr Lintje Pellu, who did her research in Landu. The chant is a particularly long and interesting text that Dr Pellu and I hope to examine in greater detail in a future publication.

Bole upa ma tesa tei a	You can eat to your full
Ma minu a tama dale a	And drink to your satisfaction
Te noi ai esa nai oka talada	But there is a tree in the middle of the garden
Nai ia nade ai pala keka	Its name is the Keka-tree of prohibition
Ma batu ndilu ndao.	And the Ndao-stone of regulation.
Boso tai lima	Do not lay your hand
Ma ei na neu.	Nor your foot upon it.
De fai bea o tai lima ma neu	On the day you put your hand on it
Ho dua kemi upa sama-sama	For if the two of you drink together
Ma mia sama-sama	And eat together
Sono neu ko fai esa na ndia	Then on that day
Ma ledo dua nai na	And at that time
Te lu mata mori	Then tears will grow
Ma pinu idu a dadi neu ko emi dua	And mucus will originate for both of you
Dadi neu tu'e tei	Becoming a heart's regret
Ma mori neu sale dale.'	And growing into inner disappointment.'

III

The Snake's Dialogue with Eve

Tehu no nitu a duduku na	But with the devil's seduction
Ma no mula a o'oti na	And with the ghost's persuasion
Na neu no naneta no Hawa	He came and met Hawa
Lima nda lima pua	Hand met hand like an areca nut
Ma laka toko laka no	And head touched head like a coconut
Selu dasi na neu	Raised his voice
Ma lole hara na neu	And brought forth his words
Neu Hawa nae:	Saying to Hawa:
'Hu ubea tao	'What was the reason
Ma sala ubea	And what was wrong
Ma siko ubea	And what was the matter
De ndi na basa-basa hata fo rai oka	That all things in this garden
Ma dea dale ia	And inside this precinct
Emi dua bole mi'a ma minu	You two may eat and drink
Hu ai nai oka a talada	But the tree in the middle of the garden
Emi dua ta mia?'	You two may not eat?'
Boema Hawa nae	Then Hawa said:
'Kalau hara heke ne ara mori	'The words of binding command have been given
Ma dasi bara tada ara dadi	And the voice of prohibition has been raised
Nae kalau ami dua upa ma mia minu	That if we two eat and drink
Sono meu ko ami dua	Then for both of us

Lalu mula a mori	The spirit death will appear
Ma sapu nitu a dadi.'	And deathly demise occur.'
Boe ma meke ana selu dasi a neu	Then the snake raises its voice
Ma lole hara na neu:	And brings forth its words:
'Nai kalau emi dua mia	'If both of you eat
Sono neu ko dadi matafali ao	Then you will transform
Ma masadua ao	And you will change
Dadi neu Tou Mana Sura Poi	To become the Inscriber of the Heights
Ma Tate Mana Adu Lai...'	And the Creator of the Heaven...'

IV

God's Dialogue with Adam

Tou Mana Adu Lai a	The Creator of the Heaven
Ma Tate Mana Sura Poi a	And the Inscriber of the Heights
Mai teteni ma mai natane	Come to see and come to ask
Seluk dasi a neu	Again raising His voice
Ma lole hara a neu:	And bringing forth His words:
'Adam-Adam, te o nai bea?'	'Adam-Adam, where are you?'
Adam seluk dadae dasi	Adam replies in a humble voice
Ma lole mamale hara nae:	And speaks with weakened words:
'Ami dua nai ia.	'Both of us are here.
Tehu ami dadi nai masala	But we have become guilty
De oli bui masala	In a wide estuary of guilt
Ma ami mori nai masiko	And we have grown sinful
De le tende masiko	In a wide river of sin
De ami dua lao soro funi ao	Both of us walk hiding our bodies
Ma amii dua hae bubui ao	And we two rest covering ourselves
De ami dua nai bea na	For the two of us are in this situation
Bina do ta palu paun	Bina-leaves cannot wrap the thighs
Ma ta palu ami dua paun	And cannot wrap both our thighs
Ma kode-ke ta ndule kere	And kode-ke-bark cannot cover the loins
Te ta ndule mai dua keren.'	Nor can it cover round both our loins.'

Julius Iu's composition follows, in recognisable fashion, the Genesis narrative. Another composition, this one by Ande Ruy from the domain of Ringgou, offers a narrative of creation that has a more specific traditional content. Ande Ruy is a well-known ritual-language performer who is steeped in the traditions of his domain. Unlike Julius Iu, he is not a lay preacher and his version of Genesis is more idiosyncratically his own.

Figure 15.1: The poets Yulius Iu from Landu and Ande Ruy from Ringgou

Another telling of a Rotenese Genesis

Of particular note are the specific acts of creation and the way in which God the Creator speaks and calls forth the creation of particular animals: 'You, *Moka Holu* fish, come forth//You, *Dusu Lake* fish, appear…Lizard of the Sun come forth//Gecko of the Moon, appear…Swallows of the Sun come forth//Kestrels of the Moon appear.'

The following are excerpts from this composition by Ande Ruy.

I

Initial Creation: Darkness to light

Hida bei leo hata na	At a time long ago
Ma data bei leo dona	At a time since past
Bei iu-iu kima lou	Still dark as the inside of a clam
Ma bei hatu-hatu data feo.	Still gloom wrapped all round.
Ma lua bei taa	Sunlight was not yet
Ma makaledo bei taa	Daylight was not yet

Ma bei pela oe leleu	Still surface water throughout
Bei tasi oe lala.	Still the water of the sea surrounding.
Ma tate mana sura bula	The Inscriber of the Moon
Fo nai Tema Sio	In the Fullness of Nine
Do tou mana adu ledo	Or the Creator of the Sun
Fo nai Bate Falu	In the Abundance of Eight
Bei ise-ise leo apa	Still isolated as a buffalo
Ma bei mesa-mesa leo manu	Still lonely as a chicken
Bei iku nonoi.	Still in the heights.
Dula Dale namaleu	The Patterner of the Heart comes
Bei malalao	Still hovering above
Do Malala Funa bei leu-leu	Or the Shaper of the Core still comes
Do bei lala-lala rae	Or still hovering over the Earth
Pela oe leleu	Moving over the water
Do tasi oe lalama.	The waters of the sea extending.
Ma Tate mana sura bula	The Inscriber of the Moon
Do Tou mana adu ledo	Or the Creator of the Sun
Lole hara na neu	Raises forth His voice
Fo hara eke na neu	The leaden voice comes forth
Ma selu dasi na neu	Lifts forth His words
Fo dasi lilo na neu, nae:	Golden words go forth, saying:
'Makaledo a dadi ma	'Let there be sunlight
Ma malua a mori.'	And let daylight appear.'

II

Creation of the Earth

Selu dasi na neu	He lifts forth His words
Ma lole hara na neu	And raises forth His voice
Fo hara eke na neu	The leaden voice comes forth
'Dadi mai Batu Poi a.'	'Let there be the Rock's Point.'
Ma dasi lilo na neu:	And the golden words come forth:
'Mori mai Dae Bafo a.'	'Let there appear the Earth's surface.'
Boe ma mana mori, ara mori	What appears, appears
Ma mana dadi, ara dadi.	And what comes forth, comes forth.
Fo biti ne ara dadi do mori	Plants come forth or appear
Fo mori reni hu ana	Appear with tiny trunks
Ma dadi reni hu ina.	And come forth with large trunks.
Boe ma feli nade neu	So He gives them their name
Ma beka bon, rae:	And their aroma, saying:
Hu mana rerebi do	Trunks that grow thick
Do mana sasape ara	Leaves that hang down

15. The appropriation of Biblical knowledge in the creation of new narratives of origin

Fo rabuna bitala	That flower bud forth
Ma raboa bebeku	And that fruit droop
Fo buna nara, mafa modo	Flowers of half-ripe green
Ma boa nara, latu lai	And fruit of over-ripe yellow
Fo ono rule Dae Bafo a	Coming down on to the Earth
Ma refa feo Batu Poi a.	And descending round the world.

III

Continuation of Creation: The sea and the creatures of the sea

Selu dasin neu Sain	His voice goes to the sea
Ma lole haran neu Liun	And His words go to the ocean
Fo ela rai tasi a dadi	So that the sea comes forth
Ma seko meti a mori.	And the ocean appears.
Boe ma nahara neu sain, nae:	He speaks to the sea, saying:
'Moka Holu o dadi	'You, Moka Holu fish, come forth
Na dadi mo tia tasim	Come forth with sea oysters
Fo ela tia tasi mai tai	That the sea oysters may cling
Ma Dusu Lake o mori	And you Dusu Lake fish, appear
Na mori mo Lopu Le	Appear with the River Lopu
Fo ela Lopu Le mai feo	That the River Lopu may come round
Nai sai makeon	In the darkened sea
Do nai liu ma momodo na	Or the deep green ocean
Fo ela oli seu meu esa	So that in the estuary, you go as one
Ma nase te meu esa	And like small Nase fish, you go as one
Ma nai nura meu esa	And in the forest, you go as one
Fo ode rane meu esa.'	So as playful monkeys, you go as one.'

IV

Further Creation: Specific creatures of the Earth

Boe ma lole hara na neu	His word goes forth
Ma selu dasi na neu,	And His voice goes forward
Nadasi neu dae bafo a	The voice directed to the Earth
Ma hara mai batu poi a, nae:	And words directed to the world, saying:
'Korofao ledo o dadi	'Lizard of the Sun, come forth
Dadi mai dae bafo a	Come forth upon the Earth
Dadi mo basa tia dedena mara	Come forth with all your friends
Ma teke labo bula o mori	And gecko of the Moon, appear
Mori mo basa sena mara	Appear with all your companions
Fo dadi meu mana tui dasi	To come forth with those who give voice
Do mori meu mana malosa hara.'	Or appear with those who give word.'

Ma hara neu poin	And the word goes to Heaven
Ma dasi neu lain, nae:	And the voice goes to the sky, saying:
'Li Lao Ledo a dadi	'Swallows of the Sun come forth
Dadi mu mana fako ani	Come forth with those who follow the wind
Dadi mo soi ana timu dulu ra	Come forth with the small bats of the east
Ma Selu Pela Bula o mori	And kestrels of the Moon appear
Mori mu mana relu saku	Appear with those who see the storms
Mori mo bau ana sepe laka ra...'	Appear with the tiny flying foxes of the dawn...'
Boe ma lole hara na neu	His word goes forth
Ma selu dasi na neu:	And His voice goes forth:
'Iko mana fefelo o dadi	'Swaying tails come forward
Ma sura mana mamasu o mori	And lifting horns appear
Mori mu lete a	Appear to go upon the hills
Ma dadi mu mo a.'	And come forth to go upon the fields.'
Fo hule rae	So He calls, saying:
'Sura mana mamasu	'Horns that lift
Do iko mana fefelo ara.'	Or tails that sway.'
Fo ela beka rae:	And He announces, saying:
'Bulan bote bibi nara	'The Moon's flock of goats
Ma Ledo tena apa nara.	And the Sun's herd of water buffalo.
Rai lete bote bibi	On the hills are flocks of goats
Do mo tena apa a.	Or on the fields herds of water buffalo.
Boe ma bote bibi ra dadi	So flocks of goats come forth
Ma tena apa ra mori.'	And herds of water buffalo appear.'

In this version of Genesis, God is involved in the creation of a Rotenese world: monkeys and geckos, swallows and kestrels, goats and water buffalo appear at the beginning of creation. This is less a theological retelling of Genesis than a personal synthesis of elements of two canons, fusing ancestral knowledge in a Christian format.

Conclusions

The Rotenese adopted the Malay Bible as a critical cultural text and as the means of establishing themselves as a literate and educated Christian people. In time, as Christianity took hold on the island, they engaged in the retelling of this prime text as an oral narrative. Genesis, in particular, offered the opportunity to add to the all-important knowledge of origins. The ancestral canon, which recounts a host of origins, had no account of the physical creation of the world but only an account of the first meeting upon the Earth of the children of the Sun and

Moon with the Lords of the Sea and Ocean. For this reason, it would seem Genesis as a narrative was readily incorporated within a corpus of traditional origin narratives. This account as an iconic beginning, in conjunction with the appropriation of Biblical knowledge in general, is central to present-day Rotenese identity.

16. Adam and Eve on the island of Rote[1]

The Rotenese are a Christian people. In their oral histories, they assert that they sought and obtained the Christian religion before there were Dutch missionaries to preach it. They are therefore confident n their tacit clam to be the oldest and foremost Protestant Christians of the Timor area. This early establishment of Christianity, which can be traced in the archival records of the Dutch East India Company beginning in the eighteenth century, has given the Rotenese the grace of time to assimilate Biblical knowledge with their own culture, creating in the process a distinctive local tradition. In the past 250 years, this local Christian tradition has developed deep roots on the island.

A feature of this tradition is its aristocratic origins. The formal establishment of Christianity began with the conversion of the ruling families of several small domains in southern central Rote (Fox 1977:101–12), and the new religion was taught via a school system that was originally sponsored and supported by the rulers of these domains. Because the schools taught Malay and, in particular, the Malay Bible, Christianity became intimately and inextricably associated with education and literacy in Malay. While Malay came to be the vehicle of Christianity, the Rotenese language, in its various forms, continued to provide for the oral preservation of older indigenous traditions.

The progress of Christianity was gradual. It spread generally from nobles to commoners in most domains, yet in several there were rulers who personally rejected the new religion and refused conversion, even though members of their own families and fellow clansmen adopted Christianity. This chequered combination of acceptance and rejection persisted throughout the nineteenth century and into the first half of the twentieth century. After independence, however, as a result of a mass literacy campaign, an insistence on compulsory primary education for all children, apprehension engendered by the events of the 1965 communist coup and the recent introduction of a variety of competing forms of Christianity—Catholic, Pentecostal and Adventist—the conversion of Christianity was now complete. The process of accommodating Christianity and traditional wisdom, however, continues in a complexity of oral and written guises. The following is a brief vignette that attempts to describe aspects of this process.

---

1 This chapter is a revised version of a paper originally presented at a conference on Transmission in Oral and Written Traditions held at the Humanities Research Centre of The Australian National University, 24–28 August 1981. The principal research on which this chapter is based was conducted in Indonesia in 1965–66 and 1972–73 under the auspices of various US Public Health Service grants (MH-23, 148; MH-10, 161 and MH-20, 659). Continuing research since 1975 has been supported by The Australian National University.

Introduction to the recitation

On my return to the island of Rote in 1972, the oral poet Peu Malesi promised to recite for me a chant that I had never heard before. This chant, he explained, recounted the origin of death and contained knowledge of the past that was rarely revealed. The promise was made in the course of a long evening's discussion of a number of narrative texts, some of which I had gathered during my previous stay on Rote in 1965–66. The clan lord, Mias Kiuk, with whom I was living, had specifically asked that I read to him the texts of variou tales relating to his clan, Ingu-Beuk, which I had originally gathered from the former Head of the Earth, Stefanus Adulanu. This man, 'Old Meno' or simply 'Meno', as he was generally called, had died in the interval between my visits. Already in 1965, however, because of his ritual position, his age and his personal knowledge, Meno was regarded as the most knowledgeable elder in the domain of Termanu, and after his death his reputation continued to grow. My reading of Meno's texts was an occasion of special importance and Malesi—Meno's junior in age and status—had come expressly to hear the texts and to judge them. Most of the evening focused on a discussion of 'historical narratives' (*tutui-teteëk*), which, in the cultural traditions of Rote, is an oral genre distinct in form and subject matter from the formulaic ritual chants (*bini*) that preserve knowledge of primal origins (Fox 1979, 1980). (In the narratives, however, occasional lines and phrases from the chants occur.) At one point during the evening, I took the opportunity of Malesi's presence to ask the assembled elders about the meaning of a cryptic paired phrase in a narrative I had recorded from Malesi. The narrative in question concerned the coming of the first royal ancestors to Termanu and therefore, in the Rotenese time perspective, related to a period 16 generations in the past when the history of the domain began to unfold. The lines, in formal parallelism, were simply:

| *Ala ta fua beu* | They did not burden the beu-tree |
| *Ma ala ta ndae ka* | And they did not drape the ka-tree |

As I expected from past experience, Malesi said little or nothing, since his invariable approach to questions of exegesis was to recite other lines in the poetry itself. On the other hand, Kiuk, himself no poet, but a superb, patient and knowledgeable commentator on the intricacies of ritual speech, was able to explain these lines as a reference to the former practice of tree burial, which preceded the present custom of earthen burial. Prompted by these lines and, I suspect, by the desire to be seen as Meno's successor, Malesi offered to recite the chant of the origin of death. In three days, he said dramatically, he would return and recite this chant. Kiuk accepted his offer on my behalf and agreed to make the arrangements for the gathering. Word of the occasion spread in the Ufa

Len area and, on the agreed night, quite a number of people assembled to hear Malesi, who, having been given a good meal and sufficient palm gin to induce a 'flow of words', recited the following chant:

Teke Telu ma Koa Hulu: Text and translation

1.	*Hida dodo bei leo fan*	Once long ago
2.	*Sapu nitu bei ta*	There was no spirit death
3.	*Datu bei leo don*	Once in a bygone time
4.	*Lalo mula bei ta.*	There was no ghostly demise
5.	*Poin bei fua beuk*	Heaven still burdened the beu-tree
6.	*Lain bei ndae kak.*	The Heights still draped the ka-tree.
7.	*Ma Lesik Lain Lelebe*	The Lord of the Exalted Heights
8.	*Ma Manek Ata Malua*	And Ruler of the Heavens Above
9.	*Nafada Koa Hulu*	Told Koa Hulu
10.	*Ma nafada Teke Telu*	And told Teke Telu
11.	*Nafada ita bain*	Told our male ancestor
12.	*Ma nafada ita bein*	And told our female ancestor
13.	*Nanea lutu kiu*	To guard the surrounding stone wall
14.	*Ma lutu kiu fani oe*	The wall surrounding the honey tree
15.	*Ma nanea pa'a feo*	And to guard the encircling fence
16.	*De pa'a feo tua nasu.*	The fence encircling the syrup tree.
17.	*Siluk ka soi dulu*	Sunrise opened the east
18.	*Do huak mai langa.*	Dawn arrived at the head.
19.	*Inak Koa Hulu*	The woman Koa Hulu
20.	*Neu fetu lae Menge Batu*	Went and stepped on Rock Snake
21.	*Ma hange lae Tuna Buta.*	And trod on Eel Serpent.
22.	*Tuna Buta natane*	Eel Serpent asked
23.	*Ma Menge Batu natane:*	And Rock Snake asked:
24.	*'Singo-na nai be*	'Where is the error
25.	*Ma salan nai bei*	Where is the wrong
26.	*De ta ketu do tua nasu*	To pluck a leaf of the syrup tree
27.	*Ma seu boa fani oen?'*	And to pick a fruit of the honey tree?'
28.	*Boe ma inak leo Koa Hulu*	So the woman Koa Hulu
29.	*Lole halana*	Raised her voice
30.	*Na selu dasin na neu:*	And elevated her speech, saying:
31.	*'Lesik leo poin*	'The Lord of Heaven
32.	*Ma Manek leo lain*	And the Ruler in the Heights
33.	*Ma ana henge ne*	He bound us
34.	*Ma ana bala taa, nae:*	And tied us, saying:
35.	*'Boso ketu do fani oen*	'Do not pluck the leaf of the honey tree
36.	*Ma seu boa tua nasu.*	And do not pick the fruit of the syrup tree.
37.	*Tee o seu boa tua nasu*	If you pick the fruit of the syrup tree

Explorations in Semantic Parallelism

38. *Do o ketu do fani oen*	Or if you pluck the leaf of the honey tree
39. *Makaheduk nai ndia*	There is sourness there
40. *De sapu nitu nai ndia*	A spirit death lies there
41. *Makes nai ndia.*	There is bitterness there.
42. *De lalo mula nai ndia.'*	A ghostly demise lies there.'
43. *Boe ma Menge Batu kokolak*	So Rock Snake spoke
44. *Ma Tuna Buta dede'ak, nae:*	And the Eel Serpent conversed, saying:
45. *'Seu boak tua nasu na*	'Pick the fruit of the syrup tree
46. *Mandak nai ndia*	For that is proper
47. *Ma ketu do fani oe na*	And pluck the leaf of the honey tree
48. *Malole nai ndia.'*	For that is good.'
49. *Boe ma inak leo Koa Hulu*	So the woman like Koa Hulu
50. *Seu boak tua nasu*	Picked the fruit of the syrup tree
51. *Ketu do fani eo*	Plucked the leaf of the honey tree
52. *De neni fe Teke Telu.*	She took and gave it to Teke Telu.
53. *De leu laa boa tua nasu*	Then they ate the fruit of the syrup tree
54. *Ma do fani oe.*	And the leaf of the honey tree.
55. *Boe ma Lesik Lain Lelebe*	The Lord of the Exalted Heights
56. *Manek Ata Malua*	The Ruler of the Heavens Above
57. *Tolamu sasali*	Came rushing
58. *Ma nalai lelena.*	And came hurrying.
59. *Lesik Lain Lelebe*	The Lord of the Exalted Heights
60. *Ma Manek Ata Malue*	And the Ruler of the Heavens Above
61. *Ma naggo Koa Hulu*	Called Koa Hulu
62. *Ma nalo Teke Telu.*	And shouted to Teke Telu.
63. *Teke Telu nahala*	Teke Telu spoke
64. *Ma Koa Hulu nahala ma nae:*	And Koa Hulu spoke, saying:
65. *'Ami die dongo nai ia*	'We wait right here
66. *Ma nene fino nai ia.*	And we stand right here.
67. *Ami malelak ndolu ingu*	We know the rules of the land
68. *Ma malelak lela leo.'*	We know the wisdom of the clan.'
69. *Boe ma inak Koa Hulu*	So the woman Koa Hulu
70. *Nahala nasosi nae:*	Spoke and replied, saying:
71. *'Au fetu lae Menge Batu*	'I stepped on Rock Snake
72. *Ma hange lae Tuna Buta,*	And I trod on Eel Serpent,
73. *Tuna manatunga salak*	The eel who misleads
74. *Ma Menge manasanga singok.*	The snake who misdirects.
75. *De au seu boa tuna nasu*	Then I picked the fruit of the syrup tree
76. *Ma au ketu do fani oe.'*	And I plucked the leaf of the honey tree.'
77. *Boe ma nae:*	So he said:
78. *'Kalau leo ndiak sona*	'If this is so that

79. *O seu boak tua nasu*	You picked the fruit of the syrup tree
80. *Ma o ketu do fani oe*	And you plucked the leaf of the honey tree
81. *Na au henge ne neu o*	Then I bind you
82. *Ma bala ta neu emi*	And I tie you
83. *Loe mo late-dae*	To descend in the earth's grave
84. *Ma dilu mo kopa-tua.'*	And to go down in a lontar coffin.'
85. *Fai esa manuni*	On that day
86. *Ma ledok dua mateben*	And at that time
87. *Boe ma touk leo Teke Telu*	The man like Teke Telu
88. *Ma inak leo Koa Hulu*	And the woman like Koa Hulu
89. *Ana sapu tolomumu*	He died instantly
90. *Ma lalo solo bebe.*	And she perished suddenly.
91. *Boe ma besak ka fifilo langa*	So they felled the coffin head
92. *Ma tati nonoli dulu*	And they cut the casket top
93. *De ala tao neu kopa tua*	And they made them into a lontar coffin
94. *Ma ala tao neu bolo dae.*	And they made them into an earthen hole.
95. *Pisa [hu] hulu dae la*	The baskets for digging the earth
96. *Boe ma ala dadi.*	They originated then.
97. *Boe ma taka huhuma tua*	And the axes for cutting the lontar
98. *Boe ala tola.*	They appeared then.
99. *Boe soe huhulu dae la*	Coconut shells for scooping the earth
100. *Beo ala dadi.*	They originated then.
101. *Boe ma besi kakali dae la*	And the iron sticks for digging the earth
102. *Boe ala dadi.*	They originated then.
103. *Hu touk-ka Teke Telu,*	So the man Teke Telu,
104. *Ana sapu*	He died
105. *Ma inak ka Koa Hulu,*	And the woman Koa Hulu,
106. *Ana lalo.*	She perished.
107. *Besak ka pisak huhulu dae la*	Thus the baskets for scooping the earth
108. *Ala dadi*	They originated
109. *Ma taka huhuma tua la*	And the axes for cutting the lontar
110. *Ala tola.*	They appeared.
111. *Nduku faik kia boe*	To this very day
112. *Ma losa ledok kia boe.*	And to this very time.
113. *Hu ala molo tunga momolok*	So it is that all men walk in their footsteps
114. *Ma ala tabu tunga tatabuk*	And all men tread their path
115. *Leo faik ia dalen*	As on this day
116. *Ma nduku ledok ia tein.*	And at this time.

Reaction to the recitation

When Malesi had finished his recitation, the reaction of those present was unanimous. Without exception, the presentation was accepted approvingly as precisely what it had been declared to be: the revelation of a crucial portion of indigenous esoteric wisdom. Everyone seemed to appreciate the chant for its beauty and for its unusualness. The fact that no-one could remember having heard it before seemed only to confirm the rarity of the revelation. Since I had tape-recorded it, I was asked to replay my tape that night and on numerous subsequent occasions.

The recitation began to gain some local notoriety and eventually the poet Seu Ba'i, Malesi's fellow clansman and rival, came from Namo Dale to Mias Kiuk's house especially to hear the recording. His reaction to the text was quite different from that of others who heard the chant, for he immediately rejected it as false. His grounds, however, were thoroughly traditional: the almost predictable reaction of an accomplished chanter. 'Teke Telu' and 'Koa Hulu' were not proper chant names and the text therefore belonged to none of Rote's established ritual canons. Only one person—a schoolteacher—from among all those to whom I played the tape recognised the chant as a reworking in oral tradition of the Genesis story of Adam and Eve.

The text and its relation to the Rotenese canon

Since 1965, I have been systematically studying the way in which oral poetry is produced on the island of Rote. This has meant recording as large a corpus of texts as possible, but, even more importantly, gathering numerous versions of the 'same' chant from different poets as well as, on subsequent return visits, the 'same' chant as told by the same poet. From this research, it is clear that the chief feature of all Rotenese poetry is a thoroughgoing parallelism dependent on a rigorous pairing of semantic elements. Knowledge of these permissible semantic pairs or dyadic sets is the requisite of proper poetic composition. An accomplished poet must know the canons of his tradition. Specific chants within this canon are linked to and identified with a body of chant names, each of which is itself a compound pair. The exploits or exemplary life features of these named characters and their interrelations are the subjects of the chants.

Broadly speaking, these chants belong to two classes: one tells of the complex, complementary deeds of beings of the heavens and of the sea, whose interactions gave rise to the cultural objects and institutions of the Rotenese. These chants could once have formed part of a single epic, now told only in fragments, as the ritual prelude (or conclusion) to the use of the specific 'objects' in question (as, for example, the tools for building a home, the implements for weaving, the containers used for dyeing or the objects for bride-wealth exchange). The other class of chants comprises a large and diverse collection of mortuary compositions that are elaborated to cover all possible categories of deceased people (nobles or commoners, rich or poor, widows or orphans, young or old). Following the format common to these chants, the deceased is compared with a specific chant character and then the stereotyped genealogy and life course of this character is told, often allowing the character to explain the reasons for his or her death and to admonish the living on what they must do. The recitation of these chants is confined to funerals.

Figure 16.1: The poet, Peu Malesi, who recounted *Teke Telu ma Koa Hulu*

Although these two broad canonical classes do not exhaust the possibilities of ritual languages, which the Rotenese insist can be used for any purpose, they do identify the major components of the traditional canon. It is from this vantage point that one can judge Malesi's presentation of *Teke Telu ma Koa Hulu* and the reaction to it.

From the point of view of Rotenese tradition, several features of Malesi's composition make it unusual, if not unique. The first is that it assumes neither the format of an origin chant nor that of a mortuary chant but instead attempts to merge these two formats. As an origin chant, it purports to explain the inception of earthen burial as opposed to tree burial, a change hinted at in other contexts; more specifically, it explains the origin of a group of objects associated with the preparation of the coffin and the grave: 'baskets for digging the earth and axes for cutting the lontar', 'coconut shells for scooping the earth and iron sticks for digging the earth'. The format and phraseology of this section of the chant are precisely those of an origin chant and are made the more plausible by the existence of other origin chants that explain the origin of similar objects, such as axes and adzes. The key feature of the chant, however, is its explanation of the origin of death: 'Thus all men walk in their footsteps and all men tread their path.' This is achieved by providing an explanation of the cause of the death of the first ancestors, following the common format of a mortuary chant: 'So the man Teke Telu, he died and the woman Koa Hulu, she perished…as on this day and at this time.' The cogency of this explanation hinges on specific cultural associations. The poetic reference to 'honey tree' and 'syrup tree' is to the lontar or *Borassus* palm that provides the basis of the Rotenese economy. The tree (*tua*) is identified by the honey-sweet syrup that is produced from juice that is regularly extracted from its crown. The fact that most Rotenese are buried in coffins made from this same tree provides the critical link in the underlying cultural argument: the tree in the garden—the tree of life—becomes the tree of death. Tree burial gives way to earthen burial as the *beu*-tree and the *ka*-tree are replaced with felling the honey tree and the syrup tree. Only in dealing with the subject of death and by relying on specific cultural associations is it possible to combine the formats of origin and mortuary chant so felicitously.

Similarly—except for one structural flaw—the chant is rendered in technically perfect, indeed exquisite, parallelism, for Malesi is a master of poetic composition. The flaw, however, is the one that Seu Ba'i recognised in rejecting the chant and is directly related to its non-traditional derivation. Seu Ba'i objected not to the names Teke Telu and Koa Hulu, but to the possibility of such names. By the very rules of composition, the double names of chant characters must be either masculine or feminine; they cannot be hermaphroditic names of the sort that Malesi has created. Given the need to transform an Adam and Eve pair into a Rotenese equivalent, Malesi has had to decompose his chant character into separate parts. For example, since only the woman Koa Hulu steps on the snake, line 19 has no parallel line to accompany it. Similarly, lines 28, 49, 52, 53 and 69 lack parallel lines and are therefore improperly composed. At one point, in fact, Koa Hulu gives 'fruit and leaf' to Teke Telu, which is perfectly intelligible but formally unacceptable according to the rules of the naming system in ritual speech.

Nonetheless, for the majority of Rotenese who heard Malesi's chant, these formal flaws do not seem to have detracted from the power and beauty of the composition, nor were the chant's partial parallels with Biblical events worthy of note or objection. This chant is, however, exceptional for the fact that it draws on Rote's other tradition: a 250-year-old literary tradition based on the Malay Bible.

Two traditions of transmission

In 1679, one of Rote's local rulers was taken to Kupang on Timor to study Malay at the behest of the Dutch East India Company. By 1729, the first of these rulers had converted to Christianity and, within a few years, had succeeded in establishing a Malay school in his domain. Three other local rulers followed this precedent and, by 1754, there were six Malay schools on the island. By 1765, these schools—staffed with Rotenese teachers—had become nearly self-sustaining and remained so through the first half of the nineteenth century, with occasional assistance from the Netherlands Missionary Society. The purpose of these schools from the beginning was to teach Malay, and their major text and resource was the Malay Bible. After 1857, Rotenese schools were given direct colonial government support, and their numbers increased rapidly. Rotenese government schools were then obliged to follow a standard curriculum. By 1871, there were no less than 34 local schools on the island. As Malay was the basis for Indonesian, the Rotenese made an effortless transition to the use of the national language in their schools.[2]

The Rotenese have therefore had long exposure to a written tradition and are, in fact, among the paramount exponents of its use in the Timor area. What is remarkable, however—and requires explanation—is the relative disjunction of Rotenese oral and written traditions, each with its distinct source of inspiration. This disjunction is itself reflected in a social etiquette that insists on separate linguistic genres and, until recently, showed a marked aversion to language mixing. The lack of a single standard form of spoken Rotenese and the reliance on a variety of dialects to convey local traditions have also contributed to a situation in which Malay alone is deemed appropriate for written communication and either dialect or ritual language for oral traditions. (When I arrived on Rote

---

2   For a fuller discussion of this linguistic situation and its history, see Fox (1974; 1977:61–195).

in 1965, there was as yet no significant effort to record oral traditions in a written form of Rotenese.) Furthermore, as longstanding Christians, most Rotenese do not see their traditions as being at variance with those of Christianity and indeed often see in their origin myths and chants evidence of a kind of ancestral perception of Biblical occurrences. Finally, from a social point of view, it is evident that a fully functional literacy was, in the past, confined largely to the upper strata of Rotenese society and began to affect the whole of society only after independence.

Despite the possession of a written tradition, it is an oral tradition that remains dominant on Rote. The Rotenese place great stress on speaking well and value verbal abilities above all others. Hence, in any social interaction, the written word is almost always transmuted into strikingly different verbal forms. This process is most evident, for example, in church services that are supposedly based on the written word.

In the past (as missionary letters reveal), Rote's popular preachers were themselves oral poets and they, it seems, were principally responsible for the development and elaboration of a 'new' theological vocabulary and a set of conventions in ritual language for rendering the Scriptures in an appropriate oral mode. The canonical parallelism in much of the Old Testament—itself of comparative significance—seems to have encouraged this process of translation among the Rotenese.

Thus the borrowing of established dyadic sets and the common use of a botanic idiom carry sermons in ritual language well beyond the original written text. Christ, for example, is compared with 'a banana with copper blossom and a sugar cane with golden sheath' and His death and resurrection are metaphorically likened to the growth cycle of 'yam and taro'. In this way, a text becomes the 'pretext' for a new form of speaking.

Comment and conclusion

This chapter has taken as its starting point the recitation of an unusual chant in the ritual language of the Rotenese and has attempted to indicate how a crucial Christian religious text has been transformed in the Rotenese oral tradition. I would argue that this forms part of a general process by which Christianity has been assimilated by the traditional culture. In this process, an oral mode of transmission has managed to predominate, despite the existence of an established tradition of writing. Ultimately, this predominance of the spoken word rests on the authority and ability of people and the value accorded to speaking.

One final point deserves noting. This study would not have been possible, in its present form, were it not for the existence of yet another form of transmission—namely, that of the tape-recording. In 1965, I brought the first tape recorder to the villages of Rote and its effect was dramatically evident among the poets of the island. My 'voice catcher' (*penangkap suara*), as it was immediately named, provided the means of recording spontaneously and permanently the spoken word of particular individuals. From the Rotenese point of view, this exceeded by far anything that could be achieved by writing. It represented the triumph of oral transmission.

Since my first visit to Rote in 1965, tape-recording has become a ubiquitous feature of everyday life. What this suggests is that oral cultures of this and other parts of the world now have a technological means for their own preservation, which oral cultures in past ages did not. On Rote, a new phase of oral presentation has begun and with it has come new modes of religious accommodation.

17. The Rotenese sermon as a linguistic performance[1]

The increasing use of Rotenese and the special use of Rotenese ritual language to convey the knowledge of Christianity have led to the creation of hybrid forms of linguistic performance where Rotenese is combined with Malay. A prime occasion for this linguistic virtuosity is the sermon.

The sermon or *chotbah* is a form of elevated speech that occurs in a well-defined context for an audience who, though largely silent, is attentive to the stylistic nuances of the performance. It is supposed to be provocative, persuasive and exhortatory. It invariably derives its inspiration from a scriptural theme that serves as its source and it is thus frequently interspersed with references to other exemplary linguistic forms that require commentary and explanation.

In an Austronesian context, as its name implies, the *chotbah* is a derived, rather than a traditional, speech form. In Islamic and Christian regions of Indonesia, the *chotbah* has now become a highly valued form of speaking worthy of careful comparative examination.

In this chapter, I wish to examine briefly the Rotenese *chotbah* as a linguistic performance. Because of the variety of linguistic resources on which it draws, the *chotbah* can be considered one of the most complex forms of speaking among Rotenese today. For this reason, and because there is considerable variation in their performance, *chotbah* cannot be described simply or briefly. Furthermore, a *chotbah* is merely the high point of a religious service and to be fully comprehended must be considered in this wider context. For the purposes of this chapter, I shall therefore concentrate my analysis and draw my examples from a single performance. This is a performance that was filmed and recorded in its entirety during a period of ethnographic film research on the island of Rote in 1978. Although I shall be focusing on the verbal aspects of this performance, a fuller analysis will eventually include examination of crucial nonverbal aspects as well.

---

1   This chapter first appeared in 1982 in A. Halim, L. Carrington and S. A. Wurm (eds), *Papers from the Third International Conference on Austronesian Linguistics. Volume 3: Accent on variety*, Canberra: Pacific Linguistics C-76, pp. 311–18.

The linguistic situation: Resources for the performance

Most Rotenese are conversant in two languages: Rotenese and Malay. This, in itself, is not of great significance. What are significant are the various registers of these two languages that are utilised in speaking. In both languages, there are 'high' and 'low' registers, and their use parallels one another.

Figure 17.1: Esau Pono preaching in the GMIT Church in Nggodi Meda

The Rotenese language refers not to a single undifferentiated language but to a number of related dialects. The Dutch linguist J. C. G. Jonker, in his dictionary (1908:ix–x), distinguished nine dialects of Rotenese but failed to take account of the dialect of Delha on which he had no information. A list of 10 dialects, however, would not do justice to the sociolinguistic reality on the island, for the Rotenese themselves invariably insist that each of the 18 former political domains (*nusak*) possesses its own dialect (*dede'a nusak*). The evidence cited for this claim derives from a conglomeration of phonological, grammatical and semantic differences between neighbouring domains, yet it is clear that since the mid-seventeenth century speakers of Rotenese dialects have attempted to distinguish themselves further from one another to justify political recognition and autonomy (Fox 1971; 1977:81–3). Thus even today, every Rotenese speaks a specific dialect that serves as a sign of local identity or origin. This is equally true of Rotenese who live in villages on Timor that have been settled for more than 100 years. Although somewhat attenuated, Rotenese dialects on Timor still reflect *nusak* origins on Rote.

In addition to a local dialect that is the register for everyday speech, most Rotenese understand a high register of Rotenese. This is a poetic form of speech—a ritual language. Although there are distinct phonological as well as semantic differences in its use, ritual language is broadly intelligible throughout the island. This is in part due to the fact that ritual language incorporates synonymous or equivalent terms from different dialects to create many of its canonical pairs or dyadic sets. It thus exploits semantic differences among dialects to foster intelligibility that extends beyond the boundaries of any one speech community. As the vehicle for proverbs, poetry, songs and chants, ritual language is used in situations of formal interaction whenever an elevated form of Rotenese is deemed necessary.

Malay

Like Rotenese, Malay has high and low registers. In the Timor area, the lowest of these registers is Basa Kupang, a dialect of Malay that has been developing in Kupang since the mid-seventeenth century. Basa Kupang is related to other eastern Indonesian dialects of Malay (Larantuke, Ambon, Minahasa) but includes a considerable number of Rotenese loan words, since the Rotenese have long been the dominant population of the Kupang area. The following sentence is a simple illustration:

1) *Beta su pi ma lu sonde ada.*

Saya sudah pergi tapi kamu tidak ada.

The pronouns *beta* and *lu* are typical of Malay dialects in eastern Indonesia, as is the tendency to drop final syllables in the case of *su* from *sudah* (and in contrast with Jakarté, where initial syllables are dropped); whereas *ma* is a possible conflation of the Rotenese conjunction *ma*, with an abridged form of the Dutch conjunction *maar*, and *sonde* is the curious negative (possibly from the Dutch *zonder*) that is distinctive of Basa Kupang. This register is the everyday language of the market, of intimate interaction among members of distant *nusak* and among school friends and acquaintances from other islands.

Another register of Malay is standard Indonesian (Bahasa Indonesia). This is of increasing importance because it is taught in all schools and is used in all official and public situations. It is important to note that Rotenese pride themselves on speaking a proper Indonesian and on not mixing the registers of Basa Kupang and standard Indonesian.

Yet another register—the highest of all—is 'Biblical Malay', a form of Malay based originally on the early translations of the Bible. Since Rote has a tradition of local schools dating from the 1730s, and since one of the principal goals of these schools was to teach the language of the Malay Bible, this register is deeply embedded in Rotenese culture and its forms of speaking. Although in recent years a more modern translation of the Bible has been promoted and used in Protestant churches throughout the island, it is still common to hear quotations from the 'old' translation (much as in the English-speaking world, recourse is still made, on formal occasions, to the King James translation).

In this there occurs a significant cross-cultural coincidence of linguistic forms. The highest Rotenese register coincides with the highest Malay register in its reliance on parallelism. In particular, the Book of Job, the Psalms, Proverbs, Song of Songs, the Book of Isaiah and much of Jeremiah are expressed in a parallelism that is hardly mistakable in the Malay Bible. A simple juxtaposition of a few lines from the Song of Songs in the *Alkitab* used on Rote (*Sjiru'l-Asjar Solaiman* 2:1–3) with English translation from the King James version and a few lines from a popular Rotenese poem give a clear idea of the similar, traditional use of parallelism.

2) *Malay:*

Akulah bunga air-mawar dari Sjaron	I am the rose of Shar'on
Dan bunga bakung dari lembah.	And the lily of the valleys.
Seperti bunga bakung diantara duri-duri,	As the lily among thorns
Demikianlah adinda diantara segala anak-dara	So is my love among the daughters
Seperti pokok djeruk diantara segala pohon kaju hutan	As the apple tree among the trees of the wood
Demikianlah kekasihku diantara segala anak-teruna.	So is my beloved among the sons.[A]

3) *Rotenese:*

Te leo mafo ai-la hiluk	But if the trees' shade moves
Ma sao tua-la keko	And the lontars' shadow shifts
Na, Suti, au o se	Then I, Suti, with whom will I be
Ma, Bina, au o se	And I, Bina, with whom will I be
Fo au kokolak o se	With whom will I talk
Ma au dede'ak o se	And with whom will I speak
Tao neu nakabanik	To be my hope
Ma tao neu namahenak?	And my reliance?

Note A: Note the difference in translation of the same Hebrew passage in the Malay Alkitab and the King James Bible as, for example, 'djeruk' ('a kind of orange') in the Malay translation and 'apple' in the English translation.

Coincidence is, however, not identity and there are also differences between these two 'high' registers. Rotenese ritual language may be used only for the production of parallel utterances, whereas Biblical Malay, though used to express similar parallel verses, has many other uses as well. (It is the medium for translating an original Hebrew that, like Rotenese, distinguished between poetic and ordinary discourse.) Thus the use of these two registers does not result in the expression of parallel statements in one and then the other medium, but rather encourages the rendering of Biblical statements in canonical Rotenese forms.

This has far-reaching implications for understanding the processes of linguistic creativity. To render Biblical ideas into Rotenese ritual language, equivalent parallel terms must be created. Some of these are understood and accepted throughout the island; others seem to be confined to a particular dialect area and others idiosyncratic to specific preachers. Some commonly recognised terms are as follows:

4)	(a)	Heaven:	*Nusa Sodak//Ingu Temak*	Domain of Wellbeing//Land of Fullness
	(b)	The Holy Spirit:	*Dula Dalek//Le'u Teik*	Patterner of the Heart//Marker of the Inner Self
	(c)	To repent:	*Sale Dalek//Tuka Teik*	To turn the heart// To change the inner self
	(d)	Golgotha:	*Lete Langaduik//Puku Pakulimak*	Hill of the Skull// Mount of the Nailed Hands
	(e)	To redeem:	*Soi//Tefa [Tifa]*	To free//To pay
	(f)	The Redeemer:	*Mana-soi//Mana-tefa*	The One who freed//The One who paid

These terms are relatively simple compared with the majority that are highly metaphoric and often theologically dense and difficult to translate. Christ, for example, is referred to as Maleo Lain Pua-na//Masafali Poin Tua-na, which implies that Christ is the transformer of God's mercy (Maleo Lain//Masafali Poin, indicating this heavenly transformation).

As in so much ritual language, many metaphors are based on a botanic idiom. *Tale//fia* (taro//yam) are botanic icons for the (male) person. Christ's crucifixion is thus referred to as *lona fia//male tale*, which implies a withering or temporary death of these plants. Similarly, using an entirely traditional ritual expression, Christ can be referred to as:

(5)	*Huni ma-lapa litik//Tefu ma-nggona liliok*	The banana with copper blossom//The sugar cane with golden sheath

This accounts for another—perhaps the most important—rhetorical feature of Rotenese sermons. Since Rotenese and Malay are both intelligible, there is seemingly no need for both languages to be used in a sermon. The chief rhetorical feature of sermons is, however, that both languages are used in a complex way. This duality is explicable not as a translation of one language into another, but as another form of parallelism in which similar statements are expressed, in elevated form, as pairs. The rest of this chapter will be devoted to an examination of this kind of linguistic performance.

A Rotenese chotbah: The performance

A preacher, like an oral poet, is expected to warm up and become 'hot' during the course of his sermon. Thus sermons begin slowly using a combination of ordinary Rotenese and Malay, work up to a crescendo and then gradually taper off. Ideally, the crescendo is marked by the use of Rotenese ritual language. The sermon that I wish to analyse here follows precisely this format. The theme of the sermon as announced at the very beginning is taken from the gospel reading Luke 19:1–10. (As Jesus enters Jericho, a rich tax collector, Zacchaeus, climbs a tree to see Him. Jesus looks up and tells him to come down quickly from the tree because He intends to spend the night at his house.) The preacher, Esau M. Pono of Termanu, gives particular emphasis to Christ's order to Zacchaeus to come down immediately from the tree. This becomes a major metaphor that he develops at length.

The sermon begins slowly in Rotenese with a simple restatement of the gospel story. The medium is ordinary Rotenese marked by numerous parallel phrases. The gospel, for example, is:

6)	(a)	*Lamatuaka dede'a-kokolan fo nan'detak do nan'sulak*	The Lord's speech//talk that is marked or written
	(b)	*Tunga faik ma tunga ledok ita basa tama-nene*	Each day and each sun we all listen
	(c)	*Ita basa-basa tala-pakak ita di'i-don, buka ita dalen*	We all open our ears, open our hearts

Only once in the initial part of the sermon is Malay used and this single sentence is also marked by a parallel phrase:

7)	*Dengarlah firman Allah hari ini, apa artinya dan tujuannya buat hidup kita.*	Listen to the word of God today, what is its meaning and purpose for our lives.

The next time Malay occurs it is used in parallel with the same statement in Rotenese.

8)	(R)	*Kona lai-lai te faik ia boe o au menumpang nai o uman dale.*	Hurry down because I am going to stay in your house today.
	(M)	*Segera turun karena aku menumpang didalam rumahmu hari ini.*	

This 'double-language parallelism', once begun, continues throughout the sermon. In fact, once introduced, each new rhetorical device becomes part of an ever more complex repertoire. Simple repetition is another such feature.

9)	*Lai esuk seluk afada...*	Once again I say...
	Zakeos! Segera turun karena hari ini aku menumpang didalam rumahmu Zakeos! Lai-lai kona faik ia au menumpang nai o uman dale.	Zakeos! Hurry down because today I am going to stay in your house.

Yet another subtle form of parallelism is to make a statement in one language but to use a single word or expression from the other language—particularly at the beginning or end—for the purposes of emphasis. This cross-language parallelism can work either way.

10)	(a)	*Malay with the emphasis on a single Rotenese word:*	
		*Bukan begitu banyak Tuhan panggil, tapi satu kali:, **kona**!*	God does not call many times, but just once: **descend**!
	(b)	*Rotenese with the emphasis on a single Malay word (in this case, the Malay terms themselves form a contrastive pair):*	
		***Bukan** ana sanga hataholi ndos*	**Not that** he seeks a man who is true
		***Tapi** ana sanga hataholi manamopok*	**But rather** he seeks a man who is lost

Intermixed with all of these rhetorical devices—Rotenese parallelism, double-language parallelism, cross-language parallelism and simple repetition—the sermon is highlighted with quotations from the old translation of the Malay Bible:

11)	*Kalau menurut terjemahan lama:*	So according to the old translation:
	'Berbahagialah segala orang yang rendah hatinya,	'Happy are all those with a humble heart
	karena mereka itu yang empunya keradjaan sorga.'	For they will possess the kingdom of heaven.'

It is at this stage, the crescendo, that the preacher switches to an extended use of Rotenese ritual language with only an occasional word or phrase in Malay.

12)	*Maleo Lain pua-na,*	The Heavenly Lord's son [lit. areca palm]
	Ana moli pengo naleon	He underwent a change
	Ma Masafali Poin tua-na	And High God's son [lit. lontar palm]
	An' dadi hilu nasafalin	He was transformed

Sehingga an'dadi neu huni malapa litik	So that He became the banana tree with copper blossom
Ma an' dadi neu tefu manggona lilok	And He became the sugar cane with golden sheath
De lapa litin fifiu	The copper blossom sways
Ma nggona lilon ngganggape	And the golden sheath waves
De ana ngape leli Hela Dulu	He waves toward Hela Dulu
Ma fiu feo Kosi Kona,	And sways toward Kosi Kona,
Fo ana-ma Hela Dulu	The orphan Hela Dulu
Boe o nanasuluka la, boe-ma	As it is written, so
Falu-ina Kosi Kona	The widow Kosi Kona
Lo nanahapak,	As is mentioned,
Sesuai no kokoa-kiok	In the praise-song [lit. crowing-peeping]
Neme ita tolano kor-museik.	From our choir.
Ana-ma Binga Lete la	The orphans Binga Lete
Ala lamatani	They cry
Ma falu-ina Kade Seli la	And the widows Kade Sali
Lasa-kedu bedopo	They sob sadly
Ma lama-tani balu-balu	And they cry pathetically
Ala doko-doe se?	Whom do they request?
Ala doko-doe hanya	They request only
Touk Dali Asa Koli	The man Dali Asa Koli [Christ]
Do Ta'ek Lolo Mata Sina,	Or the Boy Lolo Mata Sina [Christ],
Tou manaso sidak	The man who sews what is ripped
Ma Taëk manaseu saik.	And the boy who stitches what is torn.
Inilah Zakeos!	This, then, is Zacchaeus!
Ana doko-doe se?	Whom does he request?
Ana doko-doe kada Kristus mesakana	He requests only Christ alone
Adalah Tou manaso sidak	Here is the man who sews what is ripped.
Ma Ta'e manaseu saik.	And the boy who stitches what is torn.

Here in the heat of the sermon, the preacher calls forth an array of powerful images and metaphors. All of these are essentially traditional. The comparison of Christ with the 'Banana tree with copper blossom//Sugar cane with golden sheath' involves the extension of traditional botanic icons to a new context.[2] The Rotenese recognise a large corpus of canonical chants, each of which is identified by the name of the chief chant character. To invoke the name of this character is to recall the appropriate chant and the message it conveys. This brief passage contains several of these oral literary allusions. Hela Dulu// Kosi Kona and Binga Lete//Kade, for example, are separate chant-character

---

2 For the use of these same icons in a traditional context, compare with Fox (1971:242–4).

names that call to mind specific chants. (Hela Dulu//Kosi Kona are also evoked in a ritual-language song sung by the choir earlier in the service.) What these characters have in common is that they are 'widows and orphans'. This then forms the underlying metaphor for the passage. In the Rotenese view, man's dependence in an imperfect world is likened to being an orphan and a widow. This is also Zacchaeus's condition. What all these 'orphans and widows' have in common is their need for Christ, who, in this passage, is referred to in three different ways: 1) as Banana tree//Sugar cane; 2) by the chant name Touk Dali Asa Koli//Ta'ek Lolo Mata Sina; and 3) as the Man who sews what is torn//the Boy who stitches what is ripped.

Of linguistic significance is the fact that several lines that should be paired are, in fact, incomplete. This is the case in particular with the lines that contain the verb *doko-doe* ('to request'). *Doko-doe*, however, is a word that occurs almost exclusively in ritual language and its normal pair, *tai-boni*, is well known and unequivocal. A network analysis of the verbs for speaking shows clearly and graphically the position of *doko-doe//tai-boni* in this semantic field. It can be argued therefore that the more specific the terms of a set parallel phrase are, the more likely it is that its counterpart phrase can be left unstated but understood in a real performance.

The passage I have just analysed is one of three in this particular sermon. Each is marked by a brief statement or statements in a mix of Malay and ordinary Rotenese. Thus the crescendo of the sermon consists of peaks and troughs, after which there is a return to the rhetorical style that preceded these high points. It is in this style that the sermon ends.

Conclusion

For anyone who understands the registers of the languages involved, a sermon is an exhilarating experience. A good preacher can always draw an audience from beyond his local parish. As a performance, a sermon is, however, unlike a traditional chanting ceremony. Sermons are relatively short and consist of a series of dramatic bursts, whereas a traditional chanting ceremony is a steady rhythmic continuum that can occupy an entire evening. The goal of traditional chanting is to preserve continuity with the ancestral wisdom of the past. In sermons, by the use of involved and sometimes convoluted metaphors, preachers push ritual language in new directions for their own spiritual purposes.

It should not be imagined that sermons of the kind I have discussed are a recent phenomenon. Hints in the missionary literature indicate that the use of traditional parallelism in sermons was already in use by the end of the nineteenth century and certainly these usages flourished in the prewar period of the twentieth century. Ironically, 'traditional' sermons could be in more danger of disappearing than the older forms of chanting. The Protestant Church of Timor (GMIT) has trained a new generation of young Rotenese ministers (*pendeta*) in theological schools in Kupang and Jakarta, and these ministers are not as well attuned to local forms of speaking as the old *utusan injil*. What the next generation holds for the development of speaking on Rote remains to be seen.[3]

---

3   The research on which this chapter is based was conducted on various trips to the island of Rote since 1965. It was supported by grants from the US Public Health Service (NIMH), the National Science Foundation and The Australian National University. This research was done under the auspices of the Lembaga Ilmu Pengetahuan Indonesia and with the sponsorship of the Universities of Nusa Cendana in Kupang and Satya Wecana in Sala Tiga. I express my thanks to all of these institutions, and to Timothy Asch, who accompanied me to Rote in 1977 and 1978 to film the performance of sermons as one aspect of a program for the ethnographic film documentation of Rotenese culture.

18. Present and future research

These essays represent paths I have taken in the study of semantic parallelism. My explorations were initiated during my first period of fieldwork on Rote in 1965–66 and, as particular pieces of research, these essays began to appear in print in the early 1970s. Each was originally intended to examine a specific aspect of parallelism. I continued in this fashion, over a period of more than 40 years, to the present.

A characteristic of exploratory paths is that they open onto new paths and hint at other directions for further research. Rather than conclude this volume with an attempted summation, I will discuss some of the new work that I am currently involved in and consider the implications of this work for the continuing study of semantic parallelism.

Over the years, I have done my research on parallelism in bursts punctuated by quiet periods when I have turned my attention to other research interests. These quiet periods, however, seemed to have revived my interests and directed them to new avenues for exploration. I now feel that I am well into another burst of research.

The research I am presently pursuing was initiated at about the time of my formal retirement in 2006. Until that time, most of my work of recording, translating and analysing Rotenese parallel compositions was focused on a single dialect: that of the domain of Termanu. This concentrated focus on a single speech community offered both advantages and disadvantages for the study of parallelism. Over time, it led to a reasonably comprehensive understanding of the repertoire of Termanu's traditional corpus of ritual compositions, but by the same token, it left me with relatively little knowledge of the ritual-language traditions of the rest of the island. During fieldwork in 1966 and again in 1973, I had managed to record a substantial corpus of recitations from two remarkably able poets in the southern domain of Thie, but this second point of reference provided only a hint of the diversity of styles and traditions of parallel recitation on Rote.

The 'Rotenese' language consists of a dialect chain that extends across the island. As a consequence the linguistic diversity on Rote is considerable. This diversity consists of more than just phonological and grammatical differences. There are significant semantic differences across the speech communities of the island. Speech communities in neighbouring areas on the island can understand each other but intelligibility declines between more distant areas to the extent that speakers of Rotenese at the eastern end of the island find it difficult to comprehend speakers of Rotenese at the western end of the island.

Underlying these differences is a social and political dynamic that continues to operate to the present. Rote comprises some 18 traditional domains, each of which is named and claims to have its own social and cultural identity. Traditionally each of these domains (or *nusak*) once had its own ruler and celebrated its distinctive ritual traditions. Each domain also claimed to have its own 'language' (*de'deak*). In a variety of my other writings, I have documented the historical existence of these domains and their formal recognition by the Dutch East India Company (VOC) dating back to the middle of the seventeenth century. An initial group of domains—Termanu, Dengka, Korbaffo and Bilba—was first recognised in a treaty with the Dutch in 1662. Another group of domains—Thie, Oenale, Landu, Loleh, Ringgou, Oepao, Bokai and Lelain—was given treaty recognition in 1690, while yet other domains were accorded recognition in stages throughout the eighteenth century. Although in the twentieth century, the Dutch attempted to amalgamate these domains, the domains remain to this day the basic units of social identity for all Rotenese and many of these domains have re-emerged in the twenty-first century as official subdistricts (*kecamatan*) of the island (see Fox 2011:143–8). In short, there is an enormous historical diversity of traditions on Rote and this diversity is reflected in and, as I would argue, utilised in the parallel traditions of the island.

Master poets, ritual masters project

Having concentrated my research on the domain of Termanu, my decision to try to record and analyse the parallel traditions of the other domains was a major undertaking and, as I became engaged in this effort, I came to realise just how large an undertaking this was. I was fortunate in being able to obtain an Australian Research Council (ARC) Discovery Grant, which provided me with initial funding for three years to begin this research. My ARC grant was entitled 'The Semantics of Canonical Parallelism: An Analysis of the Bases of Oral Composition among the Poets of the Island of Roti in Eastern Indonesia', but was gradually recast with a good parallel name, 'The Master Poets, The Ritual Masters Project'. From the outset, among other things, I proposed to record, transcribe, translate and eventually archive the ritual-language compositions of leading oral poets from different dialect areas of the island. The project was enormously ambitious and hopelessly overoptimistic in estimating the time that the research would take. I was able to stretch my ARC funding to an additional two years and thereafter had to find other funding to continue the work. At present, after more than seven years of recording, transcribing and translating, the project is still taking shape.

It was impossible in the field, particularly in Termanu, to set out to record recitations systematically. Virtually all recordings I made relied on local events, were recorded on ritual occasions, or offered to me unexpectedly, often after repeated requests, and frequently given in a revelatory mode not to me but to my tape recorder. In 1965, I brought to Rote the first tape recorder—as the Rotenese called it, the first 'voice-catcher' (*penangkap suara*) to reach the island.

Figure 18.1: The Gathering of Master Poets in Bali on 10 October 2009: Back Row: Markus Bolla, Lifinus Penu, Henrik Foeh, Frans Lau, Esau Pono, Efrain Ndeo, Lintje Pellu and James Fox. Front Row: Julius Kele, Anderias Ruy, Jakobis Ndun, Esau Nale and Kornalius Medah

A key feature of my proposed new research was to overcome the ritual restrictions and social hindrances that allowed me only opportunistic local recording of parallel compositions. I proposed to remove Rote's master poets from their local communities and to bring them to Bali, where I hoped and suspected local social constraints would tend to diminish. Moreover, the idea was to bring several master poets together from different dialect areas to demonstrate their abilities on behalf of their domain. Historically, rivalry among poets has always been a feature of public recitation.

Bringing the Rotenese poets to Bali proved successful. Most of the poets were elderly, some had never left the island, and the airplane journey—'above the clouds'—served my purposes. On separate occasions, one or another elderly poet confided in me that their experience in the plane was like travelling to heaven. Bali was considered as a place removed to which they gave the dual name *Bali Dae ma Nusa Dewata*: 'Land of Bali and Island of the Gods'. In Bali, the poets were both willing and eager to recite—especially in the company of other poets whose knowledge and ability rivalled their own.

When I began this new research, I had two tasks: the first was to achieve a basic coverage of the dialect diversity on Rote and the second was to identify who were the master poets of Rote. Only in the course of my research was I able, slowly, to succeed in these tasks.

I began in Termanu by inviting my oldest living informant, Esau Pono, who, over the years that I have known him since 1965, had become one of Termanu's leading poets. Through him, I was able to recruit two more notable poets from Termanu. But I also travelled to the domain of Ringgou to contact another poet, Ande Ruy, whose reputation as a poet and singer was known throughout Rote. The first trial recording session (29 June to 12 July 2006) on Bali included only four poets and was heavily weighted to voices from Termanu but it set the stage for subsequent recording sessions. Reports of this first session spread on Rote and the two poets, Esau Pono and Ande Ruy, helped recruit poets from other domains. They also joined all subsequent recording sessions.

The second recording session (14 to 21 October 2007) included poets from Landu and Bilba; the third session (26 October to 2 November 2008) brought three poets from Dengka and a poet from Talae. It also included an able schoolteacher to help with transcriptions of the dialect of Dengka. The fourth session (7 to 14 June 2009) concentrated on the dialect of Thie, bringing four poets from that domain plus one of the poets who had previously come from Dengka. In addition to Pak Pono and Pak Ruy, the fifth session (4 to 11 October 2009) included poets who had previously come from Thie and Dengka plus four new poets from Bilba, a couple of poets from Korbaffo and one from Oenale. As these recording groups grew larger, the coverage of dialects expanded, but also critically, it became clearer which poets were genuine master poets.

Five years into this research, I ventured my first tentative demarcation of the dialect geography of Rote. While the poets would each maintain the distinctiveness of the dialect of their domain, they would also recognise similarities among neighbouring areas. As a consequence, I distinguished six 'dialect areas' on Rote. In drawing up this demarcation, I took into account previous research (Manafe 1889; and Jonker 1913) as well as historical developments including subsequent cross-domain migration, but above all I tried to base this delineation on the semantics of the ritual-language compositions that I had recorded. I grouped Ringgou and Oepao (and one part of Landu) as part of Dialect Area I, even though there are notable differences among these domains; I then grouped the rest of eastern Rote—Bilba, Diu, Korbaffo and Lelenuk (with another part of Landu)—together as Dialect Area II; the central domains of Termanu, Bokai, Talae, Keka with Ba'a and Lelain as Dialect Area III; the southern domains of Thie and Loleh as Dialect Area IV; Dengka as Dialect Area V; and Oenale and Delha as Dialect Area VI. There are ambiguities in this demarcation. For example, the domain of Landu was ruthlessly depopulated in 1756 on orders of the Dutch East India Company and has slowly repopulated with speakers of other domains (Pellu 2008). At the other end of the island, although I have grouped Oenale and Delha together, Oenale shares much with Dengka just as Delha shares features with Thie.

I have assumed that, as recording continues, it will be possible to further refine this dialect map. There were various domains for which I continue to search for a master poet to record. After five years of recording sessions on Bali, I felt that I had only begun to fathom the diversity of Rote's parallel traditions.

Session six (21 May to 2 June 2010) was an experiment. I brought to Bali a number of poets from Bilba along with other Rotenese poets whose families had migrated from Bilba to live on the neighbouring island of Semau. In addition, I invited two Helong-speaking poets from Semau, hoping perhaps to see some 'blending' of ritual-language traditions as a consequence of close social interaction and co-residence over a period of more than 100 years. The recordings were prolific: the Rotenese poets from Semau capably maintained the ritual-language traditions of Bilba while the Helong poets retained their own distinct traditions. It was difficult to discover anything in common between the two language traditions.

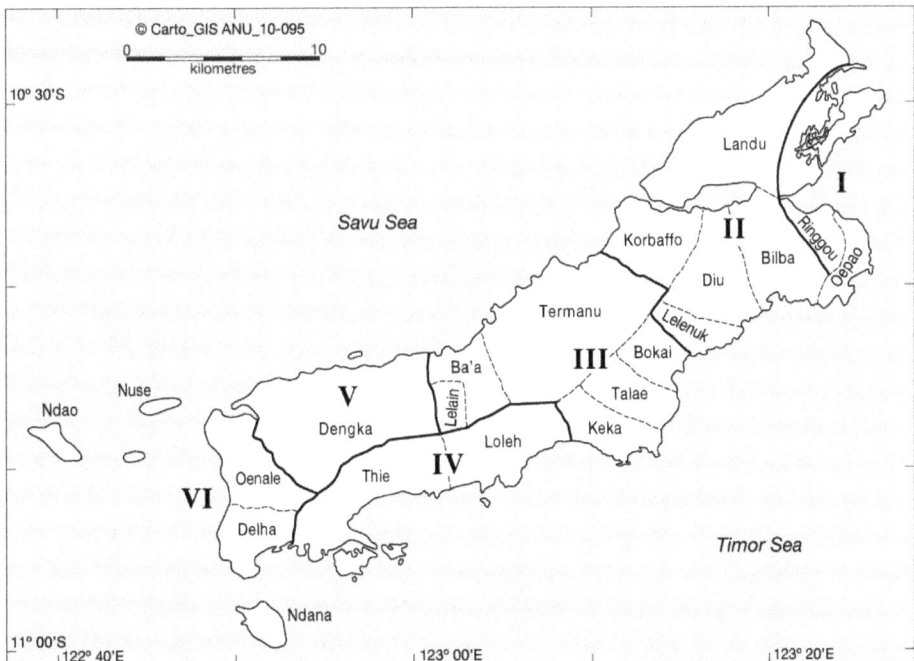

Figure 18.2: Dialect Map of Rote

Session seven (23 to 30 October 2011) returned to an exclusively Rotenese focus. I brought together poets who, on the basis of previous sessions, were the most knowledgeable and capable poet-chanters from their respective domains: from Landu, Ringgou, Bilba, Termanu, Thie and Oenale plus a new poet from the domain of Oepao. The session lacked a master poet from Dengka. One remarkable poet from Dengka, who joined the group in 2007, had died and another poet who had accompanied him in 2007 declined to join the group because he was ill. As a recording session, the gathering was enormously productive. Had Dengka been represented, it would have encompassed almost the full range of the dialect areas on Rote.

Session eight (6 to 14 April 2013) took yet another turn. It included most of the master poets who had joined session seven—from Landu, Ringgou, Bilba, Termanu and Thie—but no poets from Dengka and Oenale. In addition, this session included two remarkably able poets from the Tetun ritual centre of Wehali on Timor. A well-known Rotenese folk tradition insists that the ancestors of eastern Rotenese, particularly those in Bilba, came from the Tetun-speaking area of Belu on Timor. As a consequence, the Rotenese poets treated the poets from Wehali with great respect and quickly began comparing similar ritual-language expressions with one another, which, for the assembled group, satisfactorily established their relatedness. Linguistically, this session opened yet another path for the study of parallelism.

The organisation and logistics of these eight recording sessions over seven years were a substantial but productive undertaking that provided many new insights into the nature of parallel composition. Each session was intensive. Recordings would begin early in the morning by nine o'clock and continue for at least a couple of hours, usually with another recording session in the afternoon and often another in the evening. Following Rotenese custom, most poets would take a drink of gin before their recitation and another at its conclusion and would generally be joined in this drinking by several other poets. Hence there was a need to break for lunch and dinner to continue the flow of words. Many of the best poets were specifically reinvited to join the group for two or more visits to Bali. Thus, after the first two years of recording, a good deal of time was devoted to correcting, deciphering and discussing the interpretation of previous recitations with their poet composers and with the other poets as well.

Two recordings were made of each recitation: one a digital recording, the other a tape recording. Someone in the group, generally one or another of the local schoolteachers who were invited to join the group, was assigned to do the initial transcription. For the first four sessions until his death, my student and colleague Tom Therik joined the group, having from the beginning helped with the logistics of getting the poets from Rote to Kupang and on to Bali; during the fourth session and for each subsequent session, this task was taken up by another of my students, Lintje Pellu. Born in Termanu, Lintje wrote her ANU PhD thesis on Landu in the east of Rote and, during her fieldwork, gained a reasonable command of the dialects of Landu and Ringgou. She eventually took charge of transcriptions from these dialects.

Every session was a learning experience. At the most general level, Rote shares broad cultural traditions. Each of the poets would offer recognised compositions drawn from this shared canon, but these versions would differ from domain to domain. Many poets would also provide compositions that belonged to the rituals of their particular domain. A majority of recitations followed the chanting pattern of Termanu but occasionally a poet would recite or sing in a different style. The poet Ande Ruy was a master of various such styles. On his first visit to Bali, he brought a drum to accompany his chanting, and on other visits he improvised to chant in this drumming (*bapa*: 'beating') style. Occasionally he would perform the same chant both in normal chant style and in drumming style. In both versions, the semantics of the chant would remain the same. Dramatic emphasis would be created in the drumming style by the statement of the first two words of each line to the beat of the drum followed by the complete line.

This drumming style can be illustrated with a few lines taken from Ande Ruy's recitation of the narrative of the first Rotenese rulers' journey to Batavia in search of Christianity:

Hene ralahene rala balu lain	They climb, they climb aboard the boat
Tika rala, tika rala tonda lain	They step, they step aboard the perahu
Balu nade, balu nade Saka Rolu	The boat named, the boat named Saka Rolu
Ma ofa nadeofa nade Tungga Lela a.	And the vessel named, the vessel named Tungga Lela.
Fai na pale uli, pale uli fo reu ma	That day, they guide the steering board, they guide the steering board forward
Leko la, leko la fo reu o	They set the sail, they set the sail to go forward
Tati nafa, tati nafa dua-dua	They cut the waves, they cut the waves two-by-two
Ma lena ri'i, lena ri'i telu-telu fo.	And they mount the crests, they mount the crests three-by-three.

Termanu has a wide variety of funeral chants (see Chapters 4, 10, 13 and 14) that are intended to cover all manner of social positions and possibilities: there exist specific chants for elders, or widows and orphans, for men rich with livestock, for nobles or commoners and even for young girls who die prematurely before they marry. The deceased is likened to the chief character in these chants and thus the life, death and journey of the deceased to the other world can be recounted. Similar chants are found throughout most of Rote. Ande Ruy, however, provided a variety of funeral chants that were a variant on this theme. Each was shaped to fit a different category of person whose life could be described but a key feature of these chants was the way they were directly addressed to the deceased and guided the deceased through all stages of Rotenese mortuary rituals. These chants gave the impression of an older tradition that may have been the basis for Termanu's more 'literary' funeral compositions.

Perhaps, for me, most striking was the discovery of just how widespread the use of ritual language was, particularly in eastern Rote, in retelling the Scriptures. I had recorded one chant in Termanu that retold the story of Adam and Eve in ritual language (Chapter 16), but I was struck by just how this ritual-language rendering of the Scriptures was taking shape as the dominant mode of parallel composition in some parts of Rote. For one of the most able of the poets from Landu, who was himself a lay preacher, this was his principal focus. He was able to take almost any passage from Scripture and retell it in beautiful parallelism. Many of the poets also had their own repertoire of scriptural compositions. My addition of Chapter 15 to this volume represents my attempt to document the development of the use of parallelism for such religious purposes. Although as far as can be determined, this tradition may only have begun a little more than 100 years ago, it is likely in the future that this use of parallelism will come to predominate throughout Rote.

Although in the end I was able to record 26 Rotenese poets from 10 different domains/speech communities on Rote, my coverage of the island as a whole remains incomplete. The recording of material from Dengka began well and gave hints of a rich tradition with many interesting and possibly distinctive aspects, but it ended abruptly. Similarly, the quality of recordings from Oenale was excellent but these recordings, too, hinted at much more. I made reasonably representative recordings from Landu, Ringgou, Bilba, Termanu and Thie but as of now, none from Loleh—situated between Termanu and Thie—nor any from the small domains, particularly on the south coast of the island. Inevitably, as long as it is possible, this research needs to be continued.

Suti Solo do Bina Bane project

Soon after I arrived on Rote in 1965, I met 'Jap' Amalo, the elder brother of Ernst Amalo, who was both the district head (*camat*) of Rote and the ruler (*manek*) of Termanu. In preparing for my fieldwork, I had seen Dutch Government documents that indicated that 'Jap' would have been appointed 'Radja Rote' had it not been for his nationalist, anticolonial political views. By 1965, Jap had retired and was, after decades away from Rote, rediscovering Rotenese culture. He knew that his younger brother was about to take me to Termanu to meet an assembly of the elders of Termanu. Ernst's idea was to introduce me and my wife, to give his formal support to our plans to live in the domain and to declare that I was to become the historian of the domain. Jap's advice to me was different to that of his brother. History was important but even more important were the ritual language and poetry of Termanu. It was this poetry that he told me he was himself just beginning to appreciate. His advice was in fact quite specific. There was one particular ritual composition—a composition called *Suti Solo do Bina Bane*—which he considered the most beautiful of Rotenese chants. He urged me to record this chant and use it to understand ritual language.

As a consequence of this advice and without further knowledge of what I was asking, I was able to declare, on my first meeting with Termanu's elders in Feapopi, that I wanted to record *Suti Solo do Bina Bane*. In response, one of my very first recordings was indeed that of *Suti Solo do Bina Bane*, recited by Stefanus Adulanu, the Head of the Earth (*dae langak*) in Termanu.

Unwittingly my declaration in Feapopi became the starting point of a recording project that has continued for more than 45 years. To date, I have recorded 21 separate versions of this chant from Termanu and seven other domains on Rote. Initially most of my recordings were from Termanu but when I began to gather poets in Bali from different domains, I was able to expand my repertoire of recordings across the dialects of Rote.

Although *Suti Solo do Bina Bane* is well known by name throughout most of Rote, its narrative content varies from area to area. In most domains, *Suti Solo do Bina Bane* is considered an origin chant and therefore belongs to the cycle of origin chants. Everywhere on Rote, these origin chants tell of the encounter and creative involvement of the Sun and Moon and their heavenly descendants with the Lords of the Sea, represented as Shark and Crocodile, and their realm of sea creatures. In this regard, *Suti Solo do Bina Bane* refers to a pair of shells: Suti is a nautilus shell and Bina a baler shell. How these shells fit within a narrative of origins, however, varies. In Termanu, for example, Suti becomes the shell container for indigo dye while Bina becomes the shell that forms the base for winding cotton into thread; by contrast, in the domain of Ringgou, both Suti and Bina become a pair of clappers for warding off birds from planted fields.

Despite these different endings, almost all versions of *Suti Solo do Bina Bane* are concerned with the journey of these shells from the sea across the land, and in some versions, back to the sea again. The journey of the shells involves their 'emplacement' in different symbolic niches. Thus the chant can be and indeed is regarded as an allegorical search for appropriate companionship. In the course of the search for this companionship, Suti and Bina continually refer to themselves as 'orphan and widow'—an expression that serves as a metaphor for the human condition (see Chapter 10). As a consequence, *Suti Solo do Bina Bane* as a chant can be excerpted from its moorings in the cycle of origin chants and recited as a funeral chant.

I am now preparing a monograph on all my recorded versions of *Suti Solo do Bina Bane*. In these different versions, I analyse, in detail, similarities in the use of canonical pairs and formulaic phrasing as well as differences including distinctive usages that arise in particular speech communities. Among these versions are recordings I obtained from the same master poet at different times as well as recordings by related poets within the same community. At a fine-grained level, it thus becomes possible to discern different local traditions as well as individual styles of recitation. Chapter 8 in this volume provides an indication of this analysis. It examines a single short passage from five separate versions of *Suti Solo do Bina Bane*, four of which are from Termanu. Most versions of *Suti Solo do Bina Bane* are more than 100 lines and many of the most elaborate of these versions range from more than 200 to 400 poetic lines. The monograph is well advanced; comparison among the texts is a formidable task but this kind of analysis provides a unique opportunity to examine the use of formulaic expression over a period of almost half a century and across the range of local traditions and dialects that form the basis of Rotenese ritual language.

The semantics of dialect concatenation

Early in my research on Rotenese ritual language (see Chapter 5), I noted the consistent use of terms from different dialects to form synonymous dyadic sets. In traditions of canonical parallelism, this is by no means unique. Various scholars have similarly commented on and/or documented the particular use of lexical elements from different dialects or even different languages in the formation of canonical pairs (see, for example, Prentice 1981 for Murut; Mannheim 1986 for Quechua; Holm 2003 for Zhuang; and Hull 2012 for a variety of Mayan languages). All of these studies cite selected examples to identify the phenomenon. To date, no extended study has yet been undertaken on the use of such pairs within any tradition of parallelism. Such an examination could well provide a further perspective on canonical parallelism. It shifts focus from the perspective of a single speech community to that of possible clusters of intercommunicating speech communities and, perhaps more significantly, to other related speech communities that have ceased to communicate with one another. The ritual language of Rote with its significant dialect variation offers the possibilities for such an examination.

It was only when I began recording recitations from poets from different dialects that I began to appreciate the significance of this use of dialect terms as a pervasive linguistic feature of ritual language. I coined the term 'dialect concatenation' to describe the complex intertwining of dialect expressions involved in this usage.

The dialects of Rote have diverged from one another and are certainly semantically more divergent than I had originally imagined from my time in the domain of Termanu. The capacity to understand one another among non-contiguous speech communities and particularly those at either end of the island's dialect chain is often limited. Yet the ritual language of each of these communities retains a considerable semantic reservoir of terms and expressions that remain current in other dialects but have fallen out of use in ordinary everyday speech of that particular community. This reservoir of largely synonymous terms allows greater intelligibility when speakers of different communities utilise ritual language in formal gatherings. As one elderly poet remarked: 'Ritual language is our international language' (*bahasa internasional*)!

The first step in this research has been to recognise the intricacies of dialect concatenation. In my earlier discussion of this phenomenon, I was only able to represent it from the perspective of Termanu. The following examples illustrate this phenomenon from the perspective of seven different speech communities across the island.

An Illustration of Dialect Concatenation among the Ritual Languages of Rote

	'Human being'	'Name'	'Dry field'	'To divide'
Landu	*hataholi//lahenda*	*nade//bo'o*	*oka//tine*	*pala//bati*
Ringgou	*hataholi//laihena*	*nade//bo'o*	*oka//tine*	*pala//bati*
Bilba	*hataholi//dahena*	*nade//bo'o*	*oka//tine*	*pala//bati*
Termanu	*hataholi//daehena*	*nade//tamo*	*tina//osi*	*tada//ba'e*
Thie	*hatahori//andiana*	*nade//bo'o*	*lane//tine*	*ba'e//bati*
Dengka	*hataholi//andiana*	*nade//tola*	*osi//mamen*	*pala//ndu*
Oenale	*hatahori//andiana*	*nade//nara*	*tine//osi*	*banggi//ba'e*

Although this illustration provides only a few examples, it does give some hint of the complexity of the phenomenon. The domains of Landu, Ringgou and Bilba share related dialects. Lexical differences appear less than might be the case if other examples had been chosen. Termanu in central Rote, Thie in southern Rote, Dengka in the west and Oenale at the far western end of the island all show a variety of lexical differences in the composition of these dyadic sets.

If one takes the example of the word for 'name' (*nade*), 'name' is linked to the word for 'aroma' or 'smell'. In Rotenese understanding, the memory of personal names lives on after death and this memory is commonly referred to as 'the aroma of the name'. The domains of eastern Rote—Landu, Ringgou and Bilba—share this dyadic set with the domain of Thie in southern Rote. Termanu links the word for 'name' with another word for name, *tamo*—one's genealogical name, formerly determined by divination from a stock of ancestral names. Whether speakers in the domains of eastern Rote still remember this tradition is unclear, hence in this case, Termanu stands out in preserving an old tradition. Similarly, Dengka's use of the term *tola* as synonymous with *nade* evokes the term *tola-no*—used in Termanu and other domains—as a word for 'relative'. By contrast, Oenale at the western end of Rote links *nade* with *nara*. *Nara* is not a term known in eastern, central or southern Rote but this form is retained as the term for 'name' in other languages on Timor, such as Tetun. In fact, *nade* and *nara* are both cognate forms of the Proto-Malayo-Polynesian (PMP) term for 'name', *ŋajan.

A speaker in a particular speech community may vary in his knowledge of the lexical elements in the pairs he uses in ritual language. He will know one of the lexical elements in a pair depending on the community in which he lives and will assume from this pair the meaning of the other lexical element. It may be a term that exists in his dialect but is not in frequent use, or it may be a term from another dialect. It could also be a term whose metaphoric meaning is based on local tradition. While he may only know one of the two lexical items, it is also possible, given his experience, that he may know the meaning of both terms of a particular pair. He might even, in some cases, recognise that one such term derives from another dialect. But knowledge of the origin of such terms is not necessary for proper local recitation.

This dialect concatenation becomes more complex in many formulaic expressions that are used in ritual language. A couple of examples may illustrate this further complexity.

	'Stop, wait//stand, listen'	'Strong legs//powerful arms'
Landu	*niku pu mahani//nene fino tata*	*pu huk tere//lima boa neke*
Ringgou	*ni'a fo tata//manene mahani*	*pu huk tere//lima boa neke*
Bilba	*mapadeik//mahani* [stand//wait]	*biti boa makapi//lima boa balakai*
Termanu	*dei-dongo//nene-fino*	*biti boa manu tola//lima boa balakai*
Thie	*ni'a fo nenene//tak fo mahani*	*biti boa manu tola//lima boa nefeo*

In Landu, a common formulaic expression links the activity of 'tapping a lontar palm' with 'working a dry field'. The expression for 'tapping a lontar' is *pei tua*. Other domains also use the same or a similar expression (in Ringgou, the expresson is *peu tua*). Focusing on *pei tua*, it is possible to trace various formulaic expressions associated with this expression in different dialects as far as Termanu:

Pei tua as constant:

Domain	Dual expression	Gloss
Landu	Pei tua//se'u tine	'Tap the lontar palm'//'work a dry field'
Ringgou	Peu tua//so'a dae	'Tap the lontar palm'//'turn the earth'
Bilba	Pei tua//soka dae	'Tap the lontar palm'//'turn the earth'
Termanu	Pei tua//papa dae	'Tap the lontar palm'//'upturn the earth'

In Landu, however, the expression *pei tua* can also be linked with the expression for 'working (in) a rice field', *rele hade*. A similar pairing occurs in Ringgou but in Termanu there is a different pairing.

Rele [Lele] Hade as constant:

Domain	Dual expression	Gloss
Landu	Rele hade//pei tua	'Work a rice field'//'tap a lontar palm'
Ringgou	Lele hade//peu tua	'Work a rice field'//'tap a lontar palm'
Termanu	Lele hade//o'oko bete	'Work the rice field'//'harvest a millet field'

As these examples indicate, the interrelation between forms and expressions in the distinct 'ritual languages' of the separate speech communities of Rote is deeply intertwined. Rotenese ritual language as a whole consists of all these distinct but interrelated versions of ritual speech. The lexical resources of Rotenese ritual language embrace the whole of the island, but the particular expression of these resources varies. Their use allows ritual language to be understood across ever diverging dialects of Rote. This divergence may already be at the point at which it could be said that Rotenese ritual language is actually communicating across different languages.

This situation points to another fundamental feature of ritual language. A distinction can be made between lexical pairing and semantic pairing. Rotenese ritual language retains some of its basic semantic pairings even as lexical pairing continues to diverge. Semantic pairing is category pairing; lexical pairing is the constituent aspect of semantic pairing. The canonical pairs in Rotenese are categorically based semantic pairings made up of various, often different, lexical pairs. This distinction is fundamental to an understanding of the continuing traditions of canonical parallelism. Here one can draw a comparison between the traditions of Rotenese parallelism and that of the Mayans.

In an examination of the opening stanzas of the Mayan 'Book of Counsel' (*The Popul Vuh*), Munro Edmonson (1973) attempted to assign the canonical pairs that begin this composition to a categorical continuum from universal to particular. Some pairs he classified as 'widespread categories' and thus common to many but not all cultures. Many of the canonical pairs in *The Popul Vuh* were, in his view however, distinctive to the traditions of Middle America while others were more specifically categories pertinent to the culture of the Quiche

Maya of the sixteenth century. In a similar fashion, Kerry Hull has traced the continuity—or what he calls the 'poetic tenacity'—of various general Mayan canonical pairs from the now deciphered early Mayan hieroglyphic inscriptions through texts preserved in the colonial period to present-day Mayan ritual performances. Although the lexical items that make up these canonical pairs may vary, the continuity of these general Mayan categories provides evidence for a tradition of shared parallel categorisation that extends over more than a millennium (Hull 2012:73–132).

A similar exercise can be done with the canonical pairs in Rotenese ritual language. For many canonical pairs, the semantic pairing could be considered universal: 'sun'//'moon', 'head'//'tail', 'rock'//'tree' or 'trunk'//'root'. The numerical pairs 'seven'//'eight' or 'eight'//'nine' could be considered as general categories, though most traditions of parallelism rely on only a few possible numerical pairs. In other cases, this categorisation is less general but certainly widespread and thus could be common to many cultures: 'pestle'//'mortar', 'drum'//'gong', 'spear'//'sword', 'betel'//'areca nut' or 'orphan'//'widow'. For many other canonical pairs, however, pairing is more specific. Thus, for example, 'shame' forms a pair with 'fear', 'lung' forms a pair with 'liver', while a great number of specific plants and animals form specific (and highly symbolic) pairs: 'banana'//'sugar cane', 'yam'//'taro', 'friarbird'//'parrot', 'turtle'//'dugong', or *'dedap'*//*'kelumpang'* trees. This list of specific pairs could be substantially extended to particular Rotenese verbs, adverbial terms and many other nouns.

Many of the more general pairs are shared by all the dialects of Rote, but they may have different lexical constituents. Many of these same canonical pairs are also found in other languages of the Timor region. Rote's tradition of canonical parallelism is thus part of a larger regional tradition. As evidence of this wider regional tradition, I provide here a short, select list of shared canonical pairs in Rotenese (Termanu dialect), Tetun (Lia Tetun) and Atoni (Uab Meto). These canonical pairs contain many shared lexical cognates since both Lia Tetun and Uab Meto are languages related to Rotenese.

Rotenese, Tetun and Atoni Canonical Pairs

	Dede'a Lote	Lia Tetun	Uab Meto
1. sun//moon	*ledo//bulan*	*loro//fulan*	*manse//funan*
2. rock//tree	*batu//ai*	*fatu//ai*	*fatu//hau*
3. trunk//root	*hu//oka*	*hun//abut*	*uf//baaf*
4. areca//betel	*pua//manus*	*bua//fuik*	*puah//manus*
5. seven//eight	*hitu//walu*	*hitu//walu*	*hitu//faon*
6. eight//nine	*walu//sio*	*walu//sio*	*faon//siwi*
7. pestle//mortar	*alu//nesu*	*alu//nesung*	*alu//esu*
8. shame//fear	*mae//tau*	*moe//tauk*	*mae//mtaus*

9. banana//sugar cane	*huni//tefu*	*hudi//tohu*	*uki//tefu*
10. tuber//tales	*ufi//talas*	*fehuk//talas*	*laku//nali*
11. lung//liver	*ba//ate*	*afak//aten*	*ansao//ate*
12. thigh//navel	*pu//puse*	*kelen//husar*	*pusun//usan*
13. turtle//dugong	*kea//lui*	*kea//lenuk*	*ke//kunfui*
14. friarbird//parrot	*koa//nggia*	*kawa//birus*	*kol ao//kit neno*
15. orphan//widow	*ana ma//falu ina*	*oa kiak//balu*	*an manat//ban banu*
16. dedap//kelumpang	*delas//nitas*	*dik//nitas*	*ensa//nitas*
17. waringin//banyan	*keka//nunu*	*hali//hedan*	*nunuh//lete*
18. spear//sword	*te//tafa*	*diman//surit*	*auni//suni*
19. drum//gong	*labu//meko*	*bidu//tala*	*kee//sene*
20. head//tail	*langa//iku*	*ulun//ikun*	*nakan//ikon*

This kind of comparative evidence points to a shared tradition that goes beyond—but also links—the speech communities of the Timor area and eastern Indonesia in general.

Network analysis of the lexicon of Rotenese dyadic language

From the beginnings of my work on Rotenese ritual language, I have argued that the semantics of canonical parallelism could and should be viewed not simply in terms of the dyads that constitute its constituent elements but also within a network framework: tracing the way particular semantic elements link to a range of other semantic elements. As such, canonical parallelism offers the opportunity to consider meaning within definable, potentially large and relatively stable semantic fields. Thus in an early paper, published in 1974 (Chapter 5), I examined the semantic network formed among 21 verbs for forms of speaking: 'stating', 'asserting', 'revealing', 'requesting', 'cajoling' and 'questioning'. Similarly in another paper, published the following year, in 1975 (Chapter 6), I tried to set out the semantic network that appeared to be at the core of Rotenese language. Formally this core consists of those semantic elements that have the greatest number of linkages with each other and with other semantic elements in ritual language.

The exploration of these analytic possibilities is based on the occurrence of semantic relations that extend beyond the pairing of particular terms. In my terminology, I refer to the set pairing of 'particular terms' or 'semantic elements'—I have been prone to use these two phrases interchangeably— as 'dyadic sets'. A majority of semantic elements are not confined to a single dyadic set. Thus term A may form a set with terms B, C and D; similarly, in addition to the set it forms with A, B may form a dyadic set with terms F, G, H and so on. The number of other terms with which any one semantic element forms a dyadic set constitutes the 'range' of its semantic linkages. Some semantic elements in ritual language have an extended range of linkages; others have a more limited range and others have a range that is restricted to a single dyadic set. Documenting linkages between semantic elements provides an insight into the overall semantic fields entailed in the use of canonical parallelism. If one charts the interrelation among the semantic elements of ritual language, it is possible to trace a complex network of relations.

The semantic networks that I first constructed and analysed were based on the compositions that I had gathered during my first fieldwork on Rote in 1965–66. I prepared a so-called *Dictionary of Rotinese Formal Dyadic Language* (1972) to accompany a volume of *Rotinese Ritual Language: Texts and Translations* (1972) during my time at the Center for Advanced Study in the Behavioral Sciences in 1971–72 prior to a second trip to Rote and before the recording of yet another body of ritual-language recitations. This dictionary, which was exclusively based on Termanu dialect, was hardly a full or proper dictionary. Although it had more than 1300 entries, many of these entries could technically be considered duplicates because I entered complex sets (two-part formulaic pairs with special meanings) as entries in their own right while also providing separate entries for their constituent elements. Thus, for example, the dictionary had separate entries for the complex set *ina-lenak*, which forms a pair with *feto lesik*, as well as entries for *ina* and *feto* plus *lena(k)* and *lesi(k)*. The critical aspect of the dictionary was to document the linkages between semantic elements. Hence every entry included all of the other elements with which that particular element paired.

The dictionary was keyed to the Termanu texts in my volume of *Rotenese Ritual Texts* and each entry contained a reference to a specific text in which that particular entry or set occurred. The dictionary provided an English gloss for each term but only occasionally offered notes on a term's cultural usage and significance. Finally, wherever possible, an entry included a specific reference to where that term was to be found in J. C. G. Jonker's *Rottineesch-Hollandsche woordenboek* (1908).

For many years, this dictionary remained a working reference document; however, I was eventually persuaded and assisted by Charles Grimes to transfer the dictionary to an electronic format using Tool-Box. The basic focus of the dictionary—namely, its attention to semantic linkages—was retained, but in the new format, it became easier to edit and correct previous entries, add notes, distinguish complex sets from their constituent elements, create a special subset of the dictionary for dual personal names and placenames and, most importantly, to expand the dictionary by adding new semantic elements.

When I undertook to refocus my research on the various dialects of Rote, I also determined to continue my research on the dialect of Termanu. From the beginning, my close friend and collaborator Esau Pono joined the gathering of poets as a key participant and he was often accompanied by other poets from Termanu. This has meant that my corpus of compositions in Termanu dialect has continued to expand, and with a steady addition of new compositions, I have been able to continue to expand my *Dyadic Dictionary* based on the Termanu dialect. The dictionary remains a working document but its expansion has made possible a more extended analysis of the semantic networks in Rotenese ritual language.

Complex network analysis: Work in progress

From my first attempts at network analysis, I was convinced that this kind of analysis would provide insights into the semantic structure underlying Rotenese ritual language. My first illustrative analyses on the verb for speaking and on a symbolic core offered promising insights. Even with simple pencil-and-paper analysis, I could trace the emergence of several large semantic clusters. As a result, I became interested in the research on small-world/scale-free networks and realised that this research opened up the possibilities for the application of new forms of analysis to these semantic networks (Watts 1999, 2003; Barabási 2002). Scale-free networks, unlike random networks, are characterised by multi-linked nodes ('hubs') with a distribution of linkages that follows a decreasing function. These seemed to be precisely the features that characterised the semantic networks that I was trying to trace for Rotenese ritual language. On a brief visit to the Santa Fé Institute in 2004, where I presented some of my ideas on parallelism, I was alerted to the existence of *Pajek: Program for Large Network Analysis* as an analysis program, and given a demonstration, with a small set of my data, on how useful it might be to my needs.

Pajek offered everything one might wish for in a network analysis program but it was not the easiest of programs to learn and to use properly. A more serious challenge to my grand ambitions, however, was the fact that my *Dyadic Dictionary* was only a work in progress. Network analysis based on an incomplete set of data, though interesting, was not what I was aiming for.

At the beginning of my research, I speculated on just how many dyadic sets a poet would need to know to begin to recite and how many more dyadic sets that poet would then have to comprehend to be recognised as a 'man of knowledge' (*hataholi malelak*), a true master of ritual language. I guessed that 1000 dyadic sets would provide an initial competence. The first version of my *Formal Dyadic Dictionary*, with its 1300 or so entries, had in fact just more than 1000 dyadic sets and was therefore, to my mind, a good start. On the basis of my current work on existing compositions in Termanu dialect, I consider it probable that the dictionary will double: 2500 to 2700 entries—or approximately 2000 dyadic sets—is the point at which a proper network analysis would make sense. This would certainly provide a relatively comprehensive representation of the parallel semantics of ritual language and would, I speculate, see the formation of a single large semantic network from what now appear to be various independent semantic clusters.

As a start towards a more comprehensive analysis and with the assistance of David Butterfield, who had just finished his PhD thesis at the University of Melbourne (Butterworth 2008), dealing with a tradition of parallelism among the Krowé population of Flores, I was able to make a preliminary attempt at using *Pajek* to analyse Rotenese semantic networks. This exploration was based on just less than 1600 entries in the dictionary, constituting just more than 1200 dyadic sets: in *Pajek* network terminology—1595 vertices and 1211 lines. The results gave some indication of what a more extended analysis might reveal. Unsurprisingly the analysis highlighted the 'symbolic core' I had previously noted: this consisted of such terms as *tua* ('lontar palm'), *ai* ('tree'), *dae* ('earth'), *batu* ('rock') and *oe* ('water') plus plant parts such as *boa* ('fruit'), *dok* ('leaf') and *huk* ('trunk'), body parts such as *lima* ('hand') and *langa* ('head'), *te'i* ('stomach') and *eik* ('leg'), all of which are linked to—paired with—one another and to numerous other terms (see Chapter 6: Figure 6.1).

Using *Pajek*, it was possible to identify several large semantic clusters; however, there remained also numerous smaller clusters as well as an array of 336 'isolated' dyadic sets. These dyadic sets stood on their own as specific dyadic sets, neither of whose constituent elements is connected to any other terms. The high proportion of these dyadic sets would, it seems, militate against any possible all-embracing semantic network.

The existence of these numerous dyadic sets, as indicated in the *Pajek* analysis, prompts consideration of these dyadic sets as a distinct semantic class. Perhaps in a language register that is so emphatically dyadic, the presence of these fixed paired terms should not seem surprising. On inspection, they include an array of highly specific pairings of plant names, animal (including bird, fish, even insect) names as well as a considerable number of synonymous pairs in which one of the terms is derived from another dialect. Whereas a poet has some flexibility in pairing terms like 'tree', 'earth', 'rock' or 'water' that have multiple combinatorial possibilities, learning highly specific pairs and being able to use them appropriately are the real marks of a master poet.

18. Present and future research

Perhaps one of the great values of *Pajek* is its capacity to produce impressive graphic visualisations of different network clusters that can then be carefully considered. As an example, the following *Pajek* visualisation shows a semantic cluster with some 470 connected vertices.

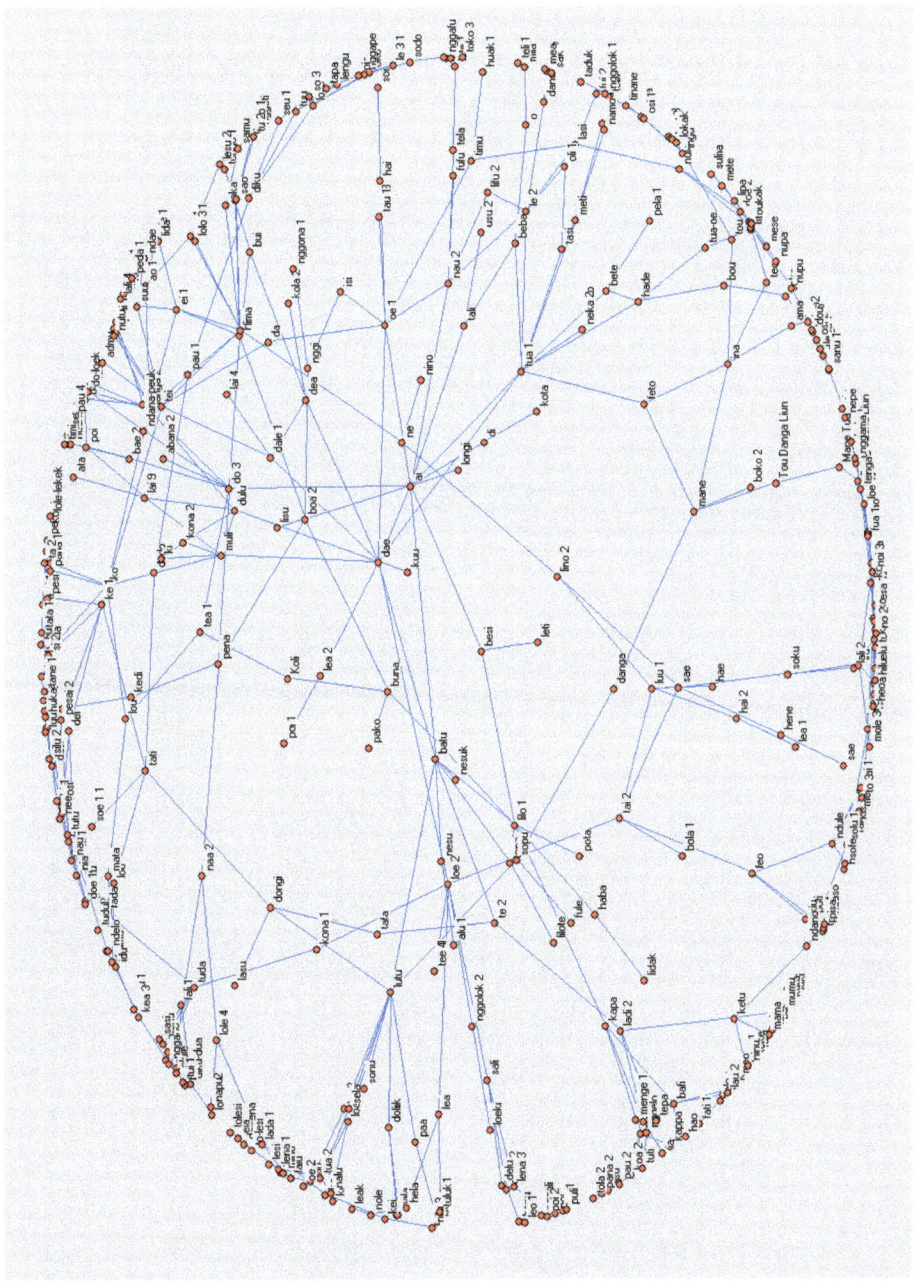

Figure 18.3: Semantic Cluster with 470 Vertices

New and continuing research: Rotenese within the parallel traditions of Timor

I have been fortunate to have had many good students. Most of those who have done their research in eastern Indonesia were able to focus significant attention on other regional traditions of canonical parallelism. Their contribution to the comparative study of parallelism has been considerable. Three of my students—Eriko Aoki, E. Douglas Lewis and Satoshi Nakagawa—doing research on Flores contributed to the volume *To Speak in Pairs* (1988). Eriko Aoki studied parallelism among a Lio-speaking population, Satoshi Nakagawa parallelism among the neighbouring Endenese. Besides his paper in the 1988 volume, Douglas Lewis has written extensively on the traditions of parallelism of the populations of Tana 'Ai and of Sikka. His ethnography *People of the Source: The social and ceremonial order of Tana Wai Brama on Flores* (1988b) draws extensively on Tana 'Ai canonical parallelism and his study *The Stranger-Kings of Sikka* (2010) includes a number of parallel texts in Sikkanese. Two other students of mine, Penelope Graham and Michael Vischer, have written masterfully on other traditions of parallelism in Flores. Penelope Graham's thesis, 'To Follow the Blood: The path of life in a domain of eastern Flores' (1991), is an ethnography of the Lamaholot-speaking domain of Lewo Tala in eastern Flores, while Michael Vischer's thesis, 'Children of the Black Patola Stone: Origin structures in a domain on Palu'e Island' (1992), is an ethnography of the small island of Palué off the northern coast of Flores. Similarly Philipus Tule's study of Christian–Muslim relations among the Kéo of central Flores, *Longing for the House, Dwelling in the House of the Ancestors* (2004), has a substantial selection of Kéo prayers and ritual narratives in canonical parallelism.

Just as in Flores, those students of mine who have done research on Timor have also written on the parallelism and ritual traditions of the island. Elizabeth Traube's classic study *Cosmology and Social Life: Ritual Exchange among the Mambai of East Timor* (1986) provides a brilliant representation of the Mambai of Aileu from a perspective phrased in the formulaic parallelism of their origin narratives. Andrew McWilliam's ethnography of the Atoni Pah Meto, *Paths of Origin: Gates of Life: A study of place and precedence in southwest Timor* (2002), with its focus on the domain of Nabuasa in west Timor, makes extensive use of the parallelism from the south-western dialect of Meto. The narrative of the expansion of Nabuasa clan is an extended topogeny, in parallelism, that recounts the walk of the Nabuasa name through Timor (see also McWilliam 1997). In his book *We Seek Our Roots: Oral tradition in Biboki, West Timor* (2011), Gregor Neobasu offers a study of the diverse oral traditions of the domain of Biboki. As something of a Meto poet, Gregor Neobasu gives great attention to various Meto genres of Biboki that utilise canonical parallelism. Yet another important work highlighting the importance of the ritual use of parallelism on Timor is Tom Therik's *Wehali, the Female Land: Traditions of a Timorese ritual centre* (2004). Working with the elders in the 'female centre and source' of the Tetun-speaking population of Timor, Therik's work opened up new vistas for the study of a rich and extensive tradition of parallelism.

Tom Therik's family—the Therik lineage—originates from the domain of Bilba, but Tom himself was raised in Atambua on Timor and his first language was Tetun. His book on Wehali is a study of the ritual traditions of Wehali. Tom grounds his ethnography in the interpretation of parallel recitations he recorded, quoting excerpts from these compositions throughout his book. To support this ethnography, however, he also includes some 40 pages of the narratives and recitations in parallelism that he recorded during fieldwork—the largest collection of its kind of Tetun parallelism.

Tom Therik joined me for the first three gatherings of Rotenese poets on Bali. Tom had the idea that our gatherings would eventually include master poets from Wehali and he would in fact tease the various Rotenese poets by claiming that they would certainly be bested in any poetic competition with the ritual masters of Wehali. Unfortunately Tom became ill and died in Kupang before he could see his ambition carried out, but several of the Rotenese remembered the challenge that he had put to them.

As the gatherings of the poets continued and as attention to dialect concatenation emerged as a research focus, it became theoretically compelling to consider Rotenese ritual language in a chain of ritual languages extending across Timor. To the extent that Tetun is closely related to Rotenese, a study of Tetun ritual language can be regarded as a good strategic step in understanding the traditions of parallelism across Timor. Like Rotenese, Tetun is divided into a variety of dialects whose contours are barely understood (see van Klinken 1999). These dialects extend in a broken pattern along the southern half of Timor-Leste as far as the once great domain of Luca in the district of Viqueque. If dialect concatenation is a critical feature of Rotenese ritual language then a study of dialect concatenation among Tetun dialects would offer a valuable comparative perspective on this phenomenon. Finally, and perhaps most significantly, the Tetun populations of Timor, even as far as Luca, still acknowledge Wehali as their 'source' of origin. To bring the various long-separated Tetun-speaking populations back into dialogue with Wehali would in itself be a major achievement. In a Tetun cultural idiom, this would require Wehali as 'mother' to call upon her 'children' to return.

It was with these ideas in mind that in April 2013, I invited two master poets, Ferdy Seran and Piet Tahu Makoan from Wehali, to join the gathering of poets on Bali. That April gathering included a select group of master poets from different dialect areas of Rote. The two Tetun poets were comfortable in joining their Rotenese counterparts. Both poets knew Tom Therik well and they were accompanied by Gabriel Bria, another of Tom's close Tetun colleagues. The gathering went brilliantly.

The Wehali poets provided numerous recitations and frequently engaged the Rotenese poets in specific poetic comparisons. They embraced the idea of inviting other Tetun poets from Timor-Leste to future gatherings and were particularly intent on determining who from among the Tetun-speaking populations of Timor-Leste would need to be invited to represent Wehali's conception of its departed children. By the end of a week's recitation, the two poets had produced an enormous outpouring—what amounted to more than 40 pages of texts, which Gabriel Bria managed to transcribe.

As a result, the call had gone out from Wehali and, with it, a new phase in the exploration of comparative forms of canonical parallelism has, I hope, begun.

Bibliography

Adriani, N. 1932a. *De Toradjasche vrouw als priesteres. Verzamelde Geschriften*, vol. II, pp. 190–2125. Haarlem: De Erven F. Bohn N. V.

Adriani, N. 1932b. *Indonesische priestertaal. Verzamelde Geschriften*, vol. III, pp. 1–21. Haarlem: De Erven F. Bohn N. V.

Adriani, N. 1932c. *Magische Sprache. Verzamelde Geschriften*, vol. III, pp. 167–75. Haarlem: De Erven F. Bohn N. V.

Adriani, N. 1932d. *Verzamelde Geschriften*, 3 vols. Haarlem: De Erven F. Bohn N. V.

Ahlqvist, A. 1863. *Suomalainen runousoppi kielelliseltä kannalta* [*Finnish Poetry from a Linguistic Standpoint*]. Helsinki.

Allen, N. J., 1978. 'Sewala Puja Bintila Puja: Notes on Thulung ritual language' *Kailash* 6(4):237-56.

Anderson, L. B. 2012. 'Understanding discourse: beyond couplets and calendrics first', in K. M. Hull and M. D. Carrasco (eds) *Parallel Worlds: Genre, discourse, and poetics in contemporary, colonial, and classical Maya literature*, pp. 161–80. Boulder: University of Colorado Press.

Anttonen, P. 1994. 'Ethnopoetic analysis and Finnish oral verse', in A. L. Siikala and S. Vakimo (eds) *Songs Beyond the Kalevala: Transformations of oral poetry*, pp. 113–37. Studia Fennica Folkloristica 2. Helsinki: Suomalaisen Kirjallisuuden Seura.

Aoki, E. 1988. 'The case of the purloined statutes: the power of words among the Lionese', in J. J. Fox (ed.) *To Speak in Pairs: Essays on the ritual languages of eastern Indonesia*, pp. 202–27. Cambridge: Cambridge University Press.

Arndt, P. 1933. *Gesellschaftliche Verhältnisse im Sikagebiet(östl. Mittelflores)*. Ende: Arnoldus-Druckerel.

Alters, R., 1985. *The Art of Biblical Poetry*. New York: Basic Books.

Austerlitz, R. 1958. *Ob-Ugric metrics*, F. F. Communications No. 174. Helsinki.

Baier, M., Hardeland, A. and Schärer, H. 1987. *Wörterbuch der Priestersprache der Ngaju-Dayak*. Verhandelingen van het Koninklijk Instituut voor Taal-, Land- en Volkenkunde 128. Dordrecht: Fortis Publications.

Barabási, A-L., 2002. *Linked: The New Science of Networks*. Cambridge: Perseus Pub.

Barwick, L. 1989. 'Creative (ir)regularities: the intermeshing of text and melody in performance of Central Australian song', *Australian Aboriginal Studies* 1989/1:12–29.

Barthes, R. 1967. *Elements of Semiology*. London: Jonathan Cape.

Beckwith, M. W. 1951. *The Kumulipo*. Chicago: University of Chicago Press.

Berlin, A. 1979. *Enmerkar and Ensuhkešdanna*. Philadelphia: The University Museum.

Berlin, A. 1985. *The Dynamics of Biblical Parallelism*. Bloomington: Indiana University Press.

Bernot, D. and Pemaungtin, B. 1966. 'Le vocabulaire concret du birman et les notions abstraites', *Revue de l'École Nationale des Langues Orientale* 3:1–18.

Berthe, L. 1972. *Bei Gua: Itineraire des Ancêstres*. Paris: Editions du Centre National de la Recherche Scientifique.

Bloomfield, M. 1916. *Rig-Veda Repetitions*, 2 vols. Cambridge, Mass.: Harvard University Press.

Boas, F. 1927. *Primitive Art*. Reprint [1955]. New York: Dover Press.

Boling, R. G. 1960. 'Synonymous parallelism in the Psalms', *Journal of Semitic Studies* V:221–55.

Boodberg, P. A. 1954–55a. 'On crypto-parallelism in Chinese poetry' (#001–540701), in *Cedules from a Berkeley Workshop in Asiatic Philology*. Berkeley, Calif.

Boodberg, P. A. 1954–55b. 'Syntactical metaplasia in stereoscopic parallelism' (#017–541210), in *Cedules from a Berkeley Workshop in Asiatic Philology*. Berkeley, Calif.

Boodberg, P. A. 1954–55c. '"T"/"M" parallelism once more' (#030–550420), in *Cedules from a Berkeley Workshop in Asiatic Philology*. Berkeley, Calif.

Boster, J. 1973. K'ekchi Maya curing practices in British Honduras, Unpublished AB thesis, Harvard University, Cambridge, Mass.

Bricker, V. R. 1974. 'The ethnographic context of some traditional Mayan speech genre', in R. Bauman and J. Sherzer (eds) *Explorations in the Ethnography of Speaking*, pp. 368–88. Cambridge: Cambridge University Press.

Bright, W. 1990. 'With one lip, with two lips: parallelism in Nahuatl', *Language* 66(3):437–52.

Brinton, D. 1887–89. 'American aboriginal poetry', *Proceedings of the Numismatic and Antiquarian Society of Philadelphia*.

Butterworth, D. 2008. Lessons of the ancestors: ritual, education and the ecology of mind in an Indonesian community, Unpublished PhD thesis, University of Melbourne, Melbourne.

Cajanus, E. 1697. Linguarum ebraeae et finnicae convenientia, Dissertation, Åbo Faculty of Theology, Lund.

Cassuto, U. 1971. *The Goddess Anath: Canaanite epics of the patriarchal age.* Jerusalem: The Magnes Press, Hebrew University.

Cauquelin, J. 2008. *Ritual Texts of the Last Traditional Practitioners of Nanwang Puyuma.* Taipei: Institute of Linguistics, Academia Sinica.

Chrijs, J. A. van der 1879. 'Het Inlandsch onderwijs in de Residentie Timor in 1871', *Tijdschrift voor Indische Taal-, Land- en Volkenkunde* 25:1–51.

Christenson, A. J. 2012. 'The use of chiasmus in the ancient K'iche Maya', in K. M. Hull and M. D. Carrasco (eds) *Parallel Worlds: Genre, discourse, and poetics in contemporary, colonial, and classical Maya literature,* pp. 311–38. Boulder: University of Colorado Press.

Clementi, C. 1904. *Cantonese Love Songs.* Oxford: The Clarendon Press.

Coe, M. 1992. *Breaking the Maya Code.* New York: Thames & Hudson.

Colop, L. E. S. 2012. 'Poetics in the Popul Vuh', in K. M. Hull and M. D. Carrasco (eds) *Parallel Worlds: Genre, discourse, and poetics in contemporary, colonial, and classical Maya literature,* pp. 281–310. Boulder: University of Colorado Press.

Conklin, H. C. 1969. 'Lexicographical treatment of folk taxonomies', in S. Tyler (ed.) *Cognitive Anthropology,* pp. 41–59. New York: Holt, Rinehart & Winston.

Coolhaas, W. P. 1971. *Generale Missiven van Gouverneurs-Generaalen Raden aan Heren XVII der Verenigde Oostindische Compagie,* vol. IV, pp. 1675–85. The Hague.

Coolsma, S. 1901. *De Zendingseeuw voor Nederlandsch Oost-Indië.* Utrecht: C. H. E. Breijer.

Corte-Real, B. d. A. 1999. Mambai and its verbal art genre: a cultural reflection of Suru-Ainaro, East Timor, Unpublished PhD thesis, Macquarie University, Sydney.

Corte-Real, B. d. A. 2000. 'Social order and linguistic symmetry: the case of the Mambai, Suru-Ainaro', in *Studies in Languages and Cultures of East Timor,* vol. 3, pp. 31–56. Sydney: Academy of East Timor Studies, University of Western Sydney.

Culley, R. C. 1967. *Oral Formulaic Language in the Biblical Psalms*. Toronto: University of Toronto Press.

Cunningham, C. E. 1962. People of the dry land: a study of the social organization of an Indonesian people, Unpublished DPhil thesis, Oxford University, Oxford.

Cunningham, C. E. 1964. 'Order in the Atoni house', *Bijdragen tot de Taal-, Land- en Volkenkunde* 120:34–68.

Cunningham, C. E. 1965. 'Order and change in an Atoni diarchy', *Southwestern Journal of Anthropology* 21:359–83.

Cunningham, C. E. 1966. 'Categories of descent groups in a Timorese village', *Oceania* 37:13–21.

Cruz de Abeles, H. 2009. Persuasive speeches of San Juan Quiahije governmental authorities: A comprehensive analysis of poetic, rhetorical, and linguistic structure of traditional Chatino oratory, Unpublished MA thesis, University of Texas at Austin.

Dahood, M. 1974. 'Chiasmus in Job: a text-critical and philological criterion', in H. N. Bream, R. D. Heim and C. A. Moore (eds) *Old Testament Studies in Honor of Jacob M. Myers*, pp. 119–30.

Dahood, M. 1975. 'Ugaritic–Hebrew parallel pairs' and 'Ugaritic–Hebrew parallel pairs supplement', in L. R. Fisher (ed.) *Ras Shamra Parallels: The texts from Ugarit and the Hebrew Bible*, vol. II, pp. 1–33, 34–9. Rome: Pontificium Institutum Biblicum.

Dahood, M. 1981. 'Ugaritic–Hebrew parallel pairs' and 'Ugaritic–Hebrew parallel pairs supplement', in S. Rummel (ed.) *Ras Shamra Parallels: The texts from Ugarit and the Hebrew Bible*, vol. III, pp. 1–179, 178–206. Rome: Pontificium Institutum Biblicum.

Dahood, M. and Penar, T. 1970. 'The grammar of the Psalter', in *The Anchor Bible, Psalms III 101–150*. Garden City, NY: Doubleday.

Dahood, M. and Penar, T. 1972. 'Ugaritic–Hebrew parallel pairs', in L. R. Fisher (ed.) *Ras Shamra Parallels: The texts from Ugarit and the Hebrew Bible*, vol. I, pp. 71–95. Rome: Pontificium Institutum Biblicum.

Davis, J. F. 1830. 'On the poetry of the Chinese', *Transactions of the Royal Asiatic Society of Great Britain and Ireland* 2:393–461.

Dearnley, M. 1968. *The Poetry of Christopher Smart*. London: Routledge & Kegan Paul.

Dumont, L. 1970. *Homo Hierarchicus: The caste system and its implications*, trans. M. Sainsbury. Chicago: University of Chicago Press.

Dunnebier, W. 1938. 'De plechtigheid "waterscheppen" in Bolaang Mongondow', *Tijdschrift voor Indische Taal-, Land- en Volkenkunde, uitgegeven door het Bataviaas Genootschap* 78:1–56.

Dunnebier, W. 1953. *Bolaang Mongondowse Teksten*, Koninklijk Instituut voor Taal-, Land- en Volkenkunde. 's-Gravenhage: Nijhoff.

Dunselman, D. 1949. 'Bijdrage tot de kennis van de taal en adat der Kendajan Dajaks van West-Borneo', *Bijdragen tot de Taal-, Land- en Volkenkunde* 105: 59–105, 147–218.

Dunselman, D. 1950a. 'Over de huwelijksadat der Moealang-Dajaks van West-Borneo', *Bijdragen tot de Taal-, Land- en Volkenkunde* 106:1–45.

Dunselman, D. 1950b. 'Bijdrage tot de kennis can de taal en adat der Kendajan-Dajaks van West-Borneo II', *Bijdragen tot de Taal-, Land- en Volkenkunde* 106:321–73.

Dunselman, D. 1954. 'Kana Sera of Zang der Zangerschap', *Bijdragen tot de Taal-, Land- en Volkenkunde* 110:52–63.

Dunselman, D. 1955. *Kana Sera*, Verhandelingen van het Koninklijk Instituut voor Taal-, Land- en Volkenkunde 17. 's-Gravenhage: Nijhoff.

Dunselman, D. 1959a. 'Gezangen behorend tot het huwelijksceremonieel der Mualang-Dajaks', *Anthropos* 54:460–74.

Dunselman, D. 1959b. *Uit de literatuur der Mualang-Dajaks*. 's-Gravenhage: Nijhoff.

Dunselman, D. 1961. 'Ngebau tadjau, een Kosmogonie der Mualang-Dajaks', *Anthropos* 56:409–37.

Eaton, M. R. 1994. Word-pairs and continuity in translation in the ancient Near East, Unpublished PhD thesis, University of Otago, Dunedin.

Edmonson, M. S. 1968. 'Metofora Maya en literature y en arte', *Verhandlungen des XXXVIII. Internationalen Amerikanistenkongresses. (Stuttgart-München, 12 bis 18 August 1968)*, vol. 11, pp. 37–50.

Edmonson, M. S. 1970. 'Notes on a new translation of the *Popol Vuh*', *Alcheringa* I:14–23.

Edmonson, M. S. 1971. *The Book of Counsel: The Popol Vuh of the Quiche Maya of Guatemala*, Middle American Research Institute Publication 35. New Orleans: Tulane University.

Edmonson, M. S. 1973. 'Semantic universals and particulars in Quiche', in M. S. Edmonson (ed.) *Meaning in Mayan Languages: Ethnolinguistic studies*. The Hague: Mouton.

Edmonson, M. S. 2008. *Heaven Born Merida and its Destiny: The Book of Chilam Balam of Chumayel*. Austin: University of Texas.

Emeneau, M. B. 1937. 'The songs of the Toda', *Proceedings of the American Philosophical Society* 77:543–60.

Emeneau, M. B. 1951. *Studies in Vietnamese (Annamese) Grammar*. Berkeley: University of California Press.

Emeneau, M. B. 1974. 'Ritual structure and language structure of the Toda', *Transactions of the American Philosophical Society* [NS] 64(6).

Engelenhoven, A. van, 1997. *'Words and expressions: Notes on parallelism in Leti'*, Cakalele 8:1–25.

Engelenhoven, A. van, 2010. 'The war of words: lexical parallelism in Fataluku discourse' in Sarmento, C. (ed), From here to diversity: Globalization and intercultural dialogues, pp 241-253. Newcastle upon Tyne: Cambridge Scholars Publishing.

Evans, I. H. N. 1953. *The Religion of the Tempasuk Dusun of North Borneo*. Cambridge: The University Press.

Fanggidaej, J. 1895. *Manetualain Dede'a-Kokola Maneni Soda-Molen-a Lukas (Het Evangelie van Lukas vertaald in het Rottineesch)*. Amsterdam: Nederlandsch Bijbelgenootschap.

Field, D. Z. 1975. With a flower, with a candle, with a prayer, Unpublished AB thesis, Harvard University, Cambridge, Mass.

Field, M. and T. Blackhorse, Jr., 2002 'The dual role of metonymy in Navajo Prayer' *Anthropological Linguistics* 44(3):217-230.

Florey, M. J. 1998. 'Alune incantations: continuity or discontinuity in verbal art?' *Journal of Sociolinguistics* 2(2):205–31.

Florey, M. J. and Wolff, X. Y. 1998. 'Incantations and herbal medicines: Alune ethnomedical knowledge in a context of change', *Journal of Ethnobiology* 18:39–67.

Foley, J. M. 1985. *Oral-Formulaic Theory and Research: An introduction and annotated bibliography*. New York: Garland Publishing.

Forth, G. 1988. 'Fashioned speech, full communication: aspects of eastern Sumbanese ritual language', in J. J. Fox (ed.) *To Speak in Pairs: Essays on the ritual languages of eastern Indonesia*, pp. 129–60. Cambridge: Cambridge University Press.

Forth, G. 1996. 'To chat in pairs: lexical pairing as a pervasive feature of Nage mundane speech', *Canberra Anthropology* 19:31–51.

Forth, G. L. 1981. *Rindi: an ethnographic study of a traditional domain in eastern Sumba*, Verhandelingen van het Koninklijk Instituut voor Taal-, Land- en Volkenkunde No. 93. The Hague: Martinus Nijhoff.

Fox, J. J. n.d. The oldest topogeny: the lament for Ur, Unpublished ms.

Fox, J. J. 1968. The Rotinese: a study of the social organization of an eastern Indonesian people, Unpublished DPhil thesis, Institute of Social Anthropology, Oxford University, Oxford.

Fox, J. J. 1971. 'A Rotinese dynastic genealogy: structure and event', in T. O. Beidelman (ed.) *The Translation of Culture*, pp. 37–77. London: Tavistock.

Fox, J. J. 1971. Rotenese ritual language: texts and translations, Unpublished ms, Palo Alto, Calif.

Fox, J. J. 1971. 'Semantic parallelism in Rotinese ritual language', *Bijdragen tot de Taal-, Land- en Volkenkunde* 127:215–55.

Fox, J. J. 1971. 'Sister's child as plant: metaphors in an idiom of consanguinity', in R. Needham (ed.) *Rethinking Kinship and Marriage*, pp. 219–52. London: Tavistock.

Fox, J. J. 1972. Dictionary of Rotinese formal dyadic language, Unpublished ms, Palo Alto, Calif.

Fox, J. J. 1972. Rotinese ritual language: texts and translations, Unpublished ms, Palo Alto, Calif.

Fox, J. J. 1972. 'The Helong', in F. Lebar (ed.) *Ethnic Groups of Insular Southeast Asia*, vol. 1, p. 105. New Haven, Conn.: Human Relations Area Files.

Fox, J. J. 1972. 'The Rotinese', in F. Lebar (ed.) *Ethnic Groups of Insular Southeast Asia*, vol. 1, pp. 106–8. New Haven, Conn.: Human Relations Area Files.

Fox, J. J. 1972. 'The Ndaonese', in F. Lebar (ed.) *Ethnic Groups of Insular Southeast Asia*, vol. 1, p. 109. New Haven, Conn.: Human Relations Area Files.

Fox, J. J. 1973. 'On bad death and the left hand: a study of Rotinese symbolic inversions', in R. Needham (ed.) *Right and Left: Essays on dual symbolic classification*, pp. 342–68. Chicago: University of Chicago Press.

Fox, J. J. 1974. '"Our ancestors spoke in pairs": Rotinese views of language, dialect and code', in R. Bauman and J. Sherzer (eds) *Explorations in the Ethnography of Speaking*, pp. 65–85. Cambridge: Cambridge University Press.

Fox, J. J. 1975. 'On binary categories and primary symbols: some Rotinese perspectives', in R. Willis (ed.) *The Interpretation of Symbolism*, ASA Studies 2, pp. 99–132. London: Malaby Press.

Fox, J. J. 1977. *Harvest of the Palm: Ecological change in eastern Indonesia*. Cambridge, Mass.: Harvard University Press.

Fox, J. J. 1977. 'Roman Jakobson and the comparative study of parallelism', in C. H. van Schooneveld and D. Armstrong (eds) *Roman Jakobson: Echoes of his scholarship*, pp. 59–90. Lisse: Peter de Ridder Press.

Fox, J. J. 1979. 'A tale of two states: ecology and the political economy of inequality on the island of Roti', in P. Burnham and R. F. Ellen (eds) *Social and Ecological Systems*, ASA Monograph 18, pp. 19–42. London: Academic Press.

Fox, J. J. 1979. 'Standing in time and place: the structure of Rotinese historical narratives', in A. Reid and D. Marr (eds) *Perceptions of the Past in Southeast Asia*, no. 4, pp. 10–25. Kuala Lumpur: Heinemann Educational Books (Asia).

Fox, J. J. 1980. 'Figure shark and pattern crocodile: the foundations of the textile traditions of Roti and Ndao', in M. Gittinger (ed.) *Indonesian Textiles*, pp. 39–55. Washington, DC: Textile Museum [Irene Emery Roundtable on Museum Textiles, 1979 Proceedings].

Fox, J. J. 1980. 'Obligation and alliance: state structure and moiety organization in Thie, Roti', in J. J. Fox (ed.) *The Flow of Life: Essays on eastern Indonesia*, pp. 98–133. Cambridge, Mass.: Harvard University Press.

Fox, J. J. 1980. 'Models and metaphors: comparative research in eastern Indonesia', in J. J. Fox (ed.) *The Flow of Life: Essays on eastern Indonesia*, pp. 327–33. Cambridge, Mass.: Harvard University Press.

Fox, J. J. 1980. 'Retelling the past: the communicative structure of a Rotinese historical narrative', *Canberra Anthropology* 3(1):56–66.

Fox, J. J. (ed.) 1980. *The Flow of Life: Essays on eastern Indonesia*. Cambridge, Mass.: Harvard University Press.

Fox, J. J. 1982. 'Dimensi waktu dalam penelitian sosial: Suata studi kasus di Pulau Roti', in Koentjaraningrat and D. K. Emmerson (eds) *Aspek Manusia Dalam Penelitian Masyarakat*, pp. 116–39. Jakarta: P. T. Gramedia/Yayasan Obor Indonesia.

Fox, J. J. 1983. 'Adam and Eve on the island of Roti: a conflation of oral and written traditions', *Indonesia* 36:15–23.

Fox, J. J. 1983. 'The Great Lord rests at the centre: the paradox of powerlessness in European–Timorese relations', *Canberra Anthropology* 5(2): 22–33.

Fox, J. J. 1983. 'The Rotinese *chotbah* as a linguistic performance', in A. Halim, L. Carrington and S. A. Wurm (eds) *Papers from the Third International Conference on Austronesian Linguistics. Volume 3:Accent on Variety*, pp. 311–18. Canberra: Pacific Linguistics.

Fox, J. J. 1988. '"Chicken bones and buffalo sinews": verbal frames and the organization of Rotinese mortuary performances', in D. S. Moyer and H. J. M. Claessen (eds) *Time Past, Time Present, Time Future: Essays in honour of P. E. de Josselin de Jong*, pp. 178–94. [KITLV, Verhandelingen No. 131.] Dordrecht: Foris Publications.

Fox, J. J. 1988. 'Introduction', in J. J. Fox (ed.) *To Speak in Pairs: Essays on the ritual languages of eastern Indonesia*, pp. 1–28. Cambridge: Cambridge University Press.

Fox, J. J. 1988. '"Manu Kama's road, Tepa Nilu's path": theme, narrative and formula in Rotinese ritual language', in J. J. Fox (ed.) *To Speak in Pairs: Essays on the ritual languages of eastern Indonesia*, pp. 161–201. Cambridge: Cambridge University Press.

Fox, J. J. 1988. *To Speak in Pairs: Essays on the ritual languages of eastern Indonesia*. Cambridge: Cambridge University Press.

Fox, J. J. 1989. 'Category and complement: binary ideologies and the organization of dualism in eastern Indonesia', in D. Maybury-Lewis and U. Almagor (eds) *The Attraction of Opposites: Thought and society in a dualistic mode*, pp. 33–56. Ann Arbor: University of Michigan Press.

Fox, J. J. 1989. 'To the aroma of the name: the celebration of a Rotinese ritual of rock and tree', *Bijdragen tot de Taal-, Land- en Volkenkunde* 145:520–38.

Fox, J. J. 1991. 'The heritage of traditional agriculture in eastern Indonesia: lexical evidence and the indication of rituals from the outer arc of the Lesser Sundas', *Indo-Pacific Journal10/Indo-Pacific Prehistory 1990*, vol. I, pp. 248–62. Canberra: Indo-Pacific Prehistory Association. [Also published in J. J. Fox (ed.) *The Heritage of Traditional Agriculture among the Western Austronesians*, 1992, pp. 67–88. Canberra: Occasional Paper, Department of Anthropology, The Australian National University.]

Fox, J. J. 1992. '"Bound to the core, held locked in all our hearts": prayers and invocations among the Rotinese', *Canberra Anthropology* 14(2):30–48.

Fox, J. J. 1993. 'Memories of ridgepoles and crossbeams: the categorical foundations of a Rotinese cultural design', in J. J. Fox (ed.) *Inside Austronesian Houses: Perspectives on domestic designs for living*, pp. 140–79. Canberra: Department of Anthropology, Research School of Pacific and Asian Studies, The Australian National University.

Fox, J. J. 1996. *Panen Lontar: Perubahan Ekologi dalam Kehidupan Masyarakat Pulau Rote dan Sawu*. Jakarta: Pusaka Sinar Harapan.

Fox, J. J. 1997. 'Genealogies of the sun and moon: interpreting the canon of Rotinese ritual chants', in E. K. M. Masinambow (ed.) *Koentjaraningrat dan Antropologi di Indonesia*, pp. 321–30. Jakarta: Assosiasi Antropologi Indonesia/Yayasan Obor.

Fox, J. J. 1997. 'Genealogies of the Sun and Moon: interpreting the canon of Rotenese ritual chants', in *Festschrift for Professor Koentjaraningrat*. Jakarta: Asosiasi Antropologi Indonesia.

Fox, J. J. 1997. 'Genealogy and topogeny: toward an ethnography of Rotinese ritual place names', in J. J. Fox (ed.) *The Poetic Power of Place: Comparative perspectives on Austronesian ideas of locality*, pp. 91–102. Canberra: Research School of Pacific and Asian Studies, The Australian National University.

Fox, J. J. 1997. 'Place and landscape in comparative Austronesian perspective', in J. J. Fox (ed.) *The Poetic Power of Place: Comparative perspectives on Austronesian ideas of locality*, pp. 1–21. Canberra: Research School of Pacific and Asian Studies, The Australian National University.

Fox, J. J. 2003. 'Admonitions of the ancestors: giving voice to the deceased in Rotinese mortuary rituals', in P. J. M. Nas, G. Persoon and R. Jaffe (eds) *Framing Indonesian Realities*, pp. 87–109. Leiden: KITLV Press.

Fox, J. J. 2005. 'Ritual languages, special registers and speech decorum in Austronesian languages', in A. Adelaar and N. Himmelman (eds) *The Austronesian Languages of Asia and Madagascar*, pp. 87–109. London: Routledge Curzon Press.

Fox, J. J. 2008. 'Blutrote Hirse. Eine locale Ursprungserzählung von der Insel Roti', in V. Gottowik, H. Jebens and E. Platte (eds) *Zwischen Aneignung und Verfremdung: Ethnologische Gratwanderung*, pp. 401–9. Frankfurt: Campus.

Fox, J. J. 2010. 'Exploring oral formulaic language: a five poet analysis', in J. Bowden and N. P. Himmelman (eds) *A Journey through Austronesian and Papuan Linguistics and Cultural Space*, pp. 573–87. Canberra: Pacific Linguistics.

Fox, J J., 2011.'Re-Considering Eastern Indonesia' in *Asian Journal of Social Science* 39:131-149.Fox, J. J. 2011. 'Assertion and silence: evidence and entertainment from the past in Rotenese oral dynastic narratives', in H. Hägerdal (ed.) *Tradition, Identity and History-Making in Eastern Indonesia*, pp. 11–25. Växjö, Kalmar: Linneaus University Press.

Fox, J. J., Asch, T. and Asch, P. 1983. *The Water of Words: A cultural ecology of an Eastern Indonesian Island*. [16 mm colour film. 30 mins.] Watertown, Mass.: Documentary Educational Resources.

Fox, J. J., Asch, T. and Asch, P. 1988. *Spear and Sword: A payment of bridewealth*. [16 mm colour film. 25 mins.] Watertown, Mass.: Documentary Educational Resources.

Frake, C. 'Notes on Queries in ethnography' in Tyler, S.A. (ed), Cognitive Anthropology, pp. 123-137. New York: Holt, Rinehart and Winston, Inc.

Francillon, G. 1967. Some matriarchic aspects of the social structure of the Tetun of middle Timor, Unpublished PhD thesis, The Australian National University, Canberra.Freedman, D. N. 1972. 'Prolegomenon to *The Forms of Hebrew Poetry* by G. B. Gray.' Reprint. New York: KTAV Publishing House.

Friedrich, P. 1975. 'The lexical symbol and its non-arbitrariness', in M. Dale Kinkade, K. L. Hale and O. Werner (eds) *Linguistics and Anthropology: In honor of C. F. Voegelin*, pp. 199–247. Lisse: Peter de Ritter Press.

Friedrich, P. 1991. 'Polytropy', in J. Fernandes (ed.) *Beyond Metaphor: A theory of tropes in anthropology*, pp. 17–55. Stanford: Stanford University Press.

Frog and Stepanova, E. 2011. 'Alliteration in (Balto-)Finnic languages', in J. Roper (eds) *Alliteration and Culture*, pp. 195–218. Houndmills, UK: Palgrave Macmillan.

Gaenszle, M., B. Bickel, G. Banjade, E. Lieven, N. Paudyal, I. Rai, N. Kishor and S. Stoll, 2005. 'Worshipping the king god: a preliminary analysis of Chintang ritual language in the invocation of Rajdeu' in Yadava, Y., G. Bhattarai, R. R. Lohani, B. Prasain and K. Parajuli (eds) *Contemporary Issues in Nepalese Linguistics*. Kathmandu: Linguistic Society of Nepal.

Gaenszle, M., B. Bickel, N. P. Sharma, J. Pettigrew, A. Rai, S. K. Rai, and D. Schacow, 2011. 'Binomials and the noun-to-verb ratio in Puma Rai ritual speech' *Anthropological Linguistics* 53:365-381.

Gabelentz, H. C. von der, 1837. 'Einiges über mongolische Poesie', *Zeitschrift für die Kunde des Morgenlandes* I:2–37.

Garibay, A. M. 1953. *Historia de la Literatura Nahuatl*, 2 vols. Mexico: Biblioteca Porrua.

Geirnaert-Martin, D. C. 1992. *The Woven Land of Laboya: Socio-cosmic ideas and values in West Sumba, eastern Indonesia*. Leiden: Centre of Non-Western Studies, University of Leiden.

Gevirtz, S. 1963. *Patterns in the Early Poetry of Israel*, Studies in Ancient Oriental Civilization No. 32. Chicago: Chicago University Press.

Gill, S. 1980. *Sacred Words: A study of Navajo religion and prayer*. Westport, Conn.: Greenwood Press.

Ginsberg, H. L. 1935. 'The victory of the Land-God over the Sea God', *Journal of the Palestine Oriental Society* 15:327.

Gonda, J. 1959. 'Stylistic repetition in the Veda', *Verhandelingen der Koninklijke Nederlandsche Akademie van Wetenschappen, Afd. Letterkunde, Nieuwe Reeks* 65(3).

Gordon, J. L. 1975. The Manggarai: economic and social transformation in an eastern Indonesian society, Unpublished PhD thesis, Harvard University, Cambridge, Mass.

Gordon, J. L. 1980. 'The marriage nexus among the Manggarai of west Flores', in J. J. Fox (ed.) *To Speak in Pairs: Essays on eastern Indonesia*, pp. 48–67. Cambridge, Mass.: Cambridge University Press.

Gossen, G. H. 1970. Time and space in Chamula oral tradition, Unpublished PhD thesis, Harvard University, Cambridge, Mass.

Gossen, G. H. 1974a. *Chamulas in the World of the Sun*. Cambridge, Mass.: Harvard University Press.

Gossen, G. H. 1974b. 'To speak with a heated heart: Chamula canons of style and good performance', in R. Bauman and J. Sherzer (eds) *Explorations in the Ethnography of Speaking*, pp. 389–413. Cambridge: Cambridge University Press.

Gossen, G. H. 2002. *Four Creations: An epic story of the Chiapas Mayas*. Norman: University of Oklahoma Press.

Graham, P. 1991. To follow the blood: the path of life in a domain of eastern Flores, Unpublished PhD thesis, The Australian National University, Canberra.

Granet, M. 1919. *Fêtes et Chansons Anciennes de la Chine* [translated as *Festivals and Songs of Ancient China*, 1932]. Paris: Editions Ernest Leraux.

Gray, G. B. 1972 [1915]. *The Forms of Hebrew Poetry*. New York: KTAV Publishing House.

Gunawan, I. 2000. *Hierarchy and Balance: A study of Wanokaka social organization*. Canberra: Research School of Pacific and Asian Studies, The Australian National University.

Hale, K. 1971. 'A note on a Walbiri tradition of antonymy', in D. D. Steinberg and L. A. Jakobovits (eds) *Semantics*, pp. 472–82. Cambridge: Cambridge University Press.

Hamonic, G. 1987. *Le Langage des Dieux: Cultes et Pouvoirs Pré-Islamic en Pays Bugis Célèbes-Sud Indonésie*. Paris: Editions du CNRS.

Hanson, O. 1906. *A Dictionary of the Kachin Language*. Rangoon.

Hardeland, A. 1858. *Versuch einer Grammatik der Dajackschen Sprache*. Amsterdam.

Hardeland, A. 1859. *Dajacksch-Deutsches Wörterbuch*. Amsterdam.

Harrison, T. 1966. 'Borneo writing and related matters', *Sarawak Museum Journal, Special Monograph No. 1*.

Heijmering, G. 1843-44. 'Zeden en Gewoonten op het Eiland Rottie', *Tijdschrift voor Nederlandsche-Indië* 6:81–98, 353–67.

Herder, J. G. 1782. *Vom Geist der ebräischen Poesie* [translated as *The Spirit of Hebrew Poetry*, 1833]. Dessau.

Hervey-Saint-Denys, M. J. L. 1862. *Poésies de l'Époque des Thang*. Paris.

Hightower, J. R. 1959. 'Some characteristics of parallel prose', in *Studia Serica Bernhard Karlgren*, pp. 60–91. Copenhagen: Ejnar Munksgaard.

Hightower, J. R. 1966. *Topics in Chinese Literature*. Cambridge, Mass.: Harvard University Press.

Hofling, C. A. 2012. 'A comparison of narrative style in Mopan and Itzaj Mayan', in K. M. Hull and M. D. Carrasco (eds) *Parallel Worlds: Genre, discourse, and poetics in contemporary, colonial, and classical Maya literature*. Boulder: University of Colorado Press.

Holm, D. 2001. 'Aspects of funeral among the Zhuang—the Horse Play', in C.-K. Wang, Y.-C. Chuang and C.-M. Chen (eds) *Proceedings of the Conference on Society, Ethnicity and Cultural Performance*, pp. 215–60. Taipei: Center for Chinese Studies.

Holm, D. 2001. 'The ancient song of Doengving: a Zhuang funeral text from Donglan, Guangxi', *Monumenta Serica, Journal of Oriental Studies* 49:71–140.

Holm, D. 2003. *Killing a Buffalo for the Ancestors: A Zhuang cosmological text from southwest China*, Monograph Series on Southeast Asia No. 5. De Kalb: Northern Illinois University.

Holm, D. 2004. *Recalling Lost Souls: The Baeu Rodo scriptures, Tai cosmological texts from Guangxi in southern China*. Bangkok: White Lotus Press.

Hopkins, G. M. 1959. 'Poetic diction', in H. House and G. Storey (eds) *The Journals and Papers of Gerard Manley Hopkins*. London: Oxford University Press.

Hoskins, J. 1983. Spirit worship and feasting in Kodi, West Sumba: paths to riches and renown, Unpublished PhD thesis, Harvard University, Cambridge, Mass.

Hoskins, J. 1988. 'Etiquette in Kodi spirit communication: the lips told to pronounce, the mouths told to speak', in J. J. Fox (ed.) *To Speak in Pairs: Essays on the ritual languages of eastern Indonesia*, pp. 29–63. Cambridge: Cambridge University Press.

Hoskins, J. 1993. *The Play of Time: Kodi perspectives on calendars, history and exchange*. Berkeley: University of California Press.

Hull, K. M. 2003. Verbal art and performance in Ch'orti' and Maya hieroglyphic writing, Unpublished PhD thesis, The University of Texas at Austin.

Hull, K. M. 2012. 'Poetic tenacity: a diachronic study of kennings in Mayan languages', in K. M. Hull and M. D. Carrasco (eds) *Parallel Worlds: Genre, discourse, and poetics in contemporary, colonial, and classical Maya literature*, pp. 73–122. Boulder: University of Colorado Press.

Hull, K. M. and Carrasco, M. D. (eds) 2012. *Parallel Worlds: Genre, discourse, and poetics in contemporary, colonial, and classical Maya literature*. Boulder: University of Colorado Press.

Huynh Sanh Thong 1973. *The Tale of Kieu* [translation of Nguyen Du's *Truyen Kieu*]. New York: Random House.

Hymes, D. 1980. 'Particle, pause, and pattern in American Indian narrative verse', *American Indian Culture and Research Journal* 4(4):7–51.

Jablonski, W. 1935. 'Les Siao-ha (i-eu) l-yu de Pekin: un essai sur la poésie populaire en Chine'. Cracow.Jacobsen, T. 1987. *The Harps That Once...: Sumerian poetry in translation*. New Haven, Conn.: Yale University Press.

Jakobson, R. 1960. 'Concluding statement: linguistics and poetics', in T. A. Sebeok (ed.) *Style in Language*. Cambridge, Mass.: MIT Press.

Jakobson, R. 1966. 'Grammatical parallelism and its Russian facet', *Language* 42:398–429.

Jakobson, R. 1968. 'Poetry of grammar and grammar of poetry', *Lingua* 21:597–609.

Jakobson, R. 1969. 'The modular design of Chinese regulated verse', in I. Pouillon and P. Maranda (eds) *Échanges ct Communications: Mélanges Offerts à Claude Lévi Strauss*. The Hague: Mouton.

Jakobson, R. 1970. 'Subliminal verbal patterning in poetry', in R. Jakobson and S. Kawamoto (eds) *Studies in General and Oriental Linguistics*, pp. 302–8. Tokyo: TEC Company Limited.

Jakobson, R. 1973. *Questions de Poétique*. Paris: Editions du Seuil.

Jakobson, R. 1977. 'A few remarks on Peirce, pathfinder in the science of language', *MLN* 92:1026–32.

Jakobson, R. and Halle, M. 1956. *Fundamentals of Language*. 's-Gravenhage: Mouton.

Jardner, H. W. 1999. *Die Kuan-Fatu-Chronik*. Berlin: Dietrich Reimer Verlag.

Jensen, A. E. 1939. *Hainwele: Volkserzählungen von der Molukken-Insel Ceram*. Frankfurt-am-Mainz.

Jonker, J. C. G. 1908. *Rottineesch-Hollandsche woordenboek*. Leiden: E. J. Brill.

Jonker, J. C. G. 1911. *Rottineesch Teksten*. Leiden: E. J. Brill.

Jonker, J. C. G. 1913. 'Bijdragen tot de kennis der Rottineesche tongvallen', *Bijdragen tot de Taal-, Land- en Volkenkunde* 58:521–622.

Josselin de Jong, J. P. B. de, 1941. 'Oost-Indonesische Poezie', *Bijdragen tot de Taal-, Land- en Volkenkunde* 100:235–54.

Josselin de Jong, P. E. de (ed.) 1977. *Structural Anthropology in the Netherlands*, Koninklijk Instituut voor Taal-, Land- en Volkenkunde Translation Series. The Hague: Martinus Nijhoff.

Jousse, M. 1925. *Études de psychologie linguistique: Le style oral rythmique et mnémotechnique chez les verbo-moteurs*. Paris.

Juslenius, D. 1728. *Oratio de convenientia lingua Fennicae cum Hebraea et Graeca Schwedische Bibliothec*. Stockholm: Ben. Joh. Henr. Russtworm.

Kaartinen, T. 1998. 'Voices of the other: authenticity and consciousness of language in an eastern Indonesian song tradition', *Akademika* 53:87–112.

Kailasapathy, K. 1968. *Tamil Heroic Poetry*. Oxford: The Clarendon Press.

Kana, N. L. 1978. Dunia Orang Sawu: Satu lukisan analitis tentang azas-azas penataan dalam kebudayaan Orang Mahara di Sawu, Unpublished PhD thesis, Universitas Indonesia, Nusa Tenggara Timur.

Kate, H. F. C. ten 1894. 'Verslag eener Reis in de Timorgroep en Polynesië', in *Tijdschrift van het Koninklijk Nederlandsch Aardrijkskundig Genootschap* [2nd series] 11:195–246, 333–90, 541–638, 659–700.

Keane, W. 1997. *Signs of Recognition: Powers and hazards of representation in an Indonesian society*. Berkeley: University of California Press.

Kemmer, E. 1903. *Die polare Ausdrucksweise in der griechischen Literatur*. Würzburg.

Kern, W. 1956. *Commentaar op de Salisilah van Koetai*, Verhandelingen van het Koninklijk Instituut voor Taal-, Land-, en Volkenkunde Vol. 19. 's-Gravenhage: Martinus Nijhoff.

Kiparsky, P. 1974. 'The role of linguistics in a theory of poetry', in E. Haugen and M. Bloomfield (eds) *Language as a Human Problem*, pp. 233–46. New York: W. W. Norton & Company.

Klinken, Catharina Lumien van. 1999. *A Grammar of the Fehan Dialect of Tetun: An Austronesian Language of West Timor*. Pacific Linguistic C-155. Canberra: Research School of Pacific and Asian Studies.

Koentjaraningrat 1980. *Sejarah Teori Antropologi*. Jakarta: Universitas Indonesia Press.

Koentjaraningrat 1996. *'Pengantar' to Panen Lontar*. Jakarta: Pusaka Sinar Harapan.

Koentjaraningrat and Emmerson, D. K. (eds) 1982. *Aspek Manusia Dalam Penelitian Masyarakat*. Jakarta: Yayasan Obor Indonesia.

Kohl, K.-H. 1998. *Der Tod der Reisjungfrau: Mythen, Kulte un Allianzen in einer ostindischischen Lokalkultur*. Stuttgart: Kohlhammer Verlag.

Kowalski, T. 1921. 'Ze studjów nad forma. poezji ludów tureckich', *Mémoires de la Commission orientale de l'Academie polonaise des sciences et des lettres*, no. 5. Cracow.

Kramer, F. W. 1970. *Literature among the Cuna Indians*, Ethnologiska Studier No. 30. Göteborg.

Kramer, S. N. 1979. *From the Poetry of Sumer: Creation, glorification, adoration*. Berkeley: University of California Press.

Kugel, J. J. 1981. *The Idea of Biblical Poetry: Parallelism and its history*. New Haven, Conn.: Yale University Press.

Kuipers, J. C. 1982. Weyewa ritual speech: a study of language and ceremonial interaction in eastern Indonesia, Unpublished PhD thesis, Yale University, New Haven, Conn.

Kuipers, J. C. 1988. 'The pattern of prayer in Weyéwa', in J. J. Fox (ed.) *To Speak in Pairs: Essays on the ritual languages of eastern Indonesia*, pp. 104–28. Cambridge: Cambridge University Press.

Kuipers, J. C. 1990. *Power in Performance: The creation of textual authority in Weyewa ritual speech*. Philadelphia: University of Pennsylvania Press.

Kuipers, J. C. 1998. *Language, Identity and Marginality in Indonesia: The changing nature of ritual speech on the island of Sumba*. Cambridge: Cambridge University Press.

Kunene, D. P. 1971. *Heroic Poetry of the Basotho*. Oxford: The Clarendon Press.

Lagemann, H. 1893. 'Das Niassische Mädchen', *Tijdschrift voor Indische Taal-, Land- en Volkenkunde, uitgegeven door het Bataviaas Genootschap* 36:296–324.

Lagemann, H. 1906. 'Ein Heldensong der Niasser', *Tijdschrift voor Indische Taal-, Land- en Volkenkunde, uitgegeven door het Bataviaas Genootschap* 48:341–407.

Lang, E. 1987. 'Parallelismus als universelles Prinzip sekundärer Strukturbildung' in Lang, E. and G. Sauer (eds), *Parallelissmus und Etymologie: Studien zu Ehren von Wolfgang Steinitz*, pp. 1-54. Berlin: Akademie der Wissenshaften der DDR Zentralistitut für Sprachwissenshaft.

Lang, E. and G. Sauer (eds), 1987. *Parallelissmus und Etymologie: Studien zu Ehren von Wolfgang Steinitz*. Berlin: Akademie der Wissenshaften der DDR Zentralistitut für Sprachwissenshaft.

Lambooij, P. J. 1932. 'Evangelie-Prediking in Oosterschen Vorm', *De Macedoniër* 36:134–44.

Lance, G. N. and Williams, W. T. 1967. 'A general theory of classificatory sorting strategies: 1, hierarchical systems', *Computer Journal* 9:373–9.

Lau, D. C. and Ames, R. T. 1998. *Yuan Dao: Tracing Dao to its source*, Classics of Ancient China. New York: Ballantine Books.

Law, D. 2012. 'Appropriating sacred speech: aesthetics and authority in colonial Ch'olti'', in K. M. Hull and M. D. Carrasco (eds) *Parallel Worlds: Genre, discourse, and poetics in contemporary, colonial, and classical Maya literature*, pp. 171–282. Boulder: University of Colorado Press.

Lazarowitz, T. F. 1980. The Makassai: complementary dualism in Timor, Unpublished PhD thesis, State University of New York at Stony Brook.

Leach, E. 1969. 'Vico and Lévi-Strauss on the origins of humanity', in G. Tagliacozzo and H. White (eds) *Giambattista Vico*, pp. 309–18. Baltimore: Johns Hopkins Press.

Le Grande, G. J. H. 1900. 'De zending op Roti', *Mededeelingen van wege het Nederlandsch Zendinggenootschap* 44:361–77.

Leino, P. 1986. *Language and Metre: Metrics and the metrical system of Finnish*, trans. A. Chesterman, Studia Fennica 31. Helsinki: Suomalaisen Kirjallisuuden Seura.

Lekkerkerker, C. 1910. 'Mededeeling over het Keblai der Rotineezen', *Bijdragen tot de Taal-, Land- en Volkenkunde, uitgegeven door het Koninklijk Instituut* 63:111–14.

Lemoine, J., 1972. 'L'Initiation du mort chez les Hmong' *L'Homme* 12(1): 105-134; 12(2) 85-125; and 12(3) 84-110.

Leon-Portilla, M. 1969. *Pre-Columbian Literature of Mexico*. Norman: University of Oklahoma Press.

León-Portilla M., (ed), 1986. *Coloquios y doctrina cristiana, con que los doce frailes de San Francisco, enviados por el papa Adriano VI y por el emperador Carlos V, convirtierona los indios de la Nueva Espana. En lengua mexicana y española*. Edición facsimilar, introducción, paleografia, versión del náhuatl y notas. Instituto de Investigaciones Históricas, México: Universidad Nacional Autónoma de México.

Lévi-Strauss, C. 1953. 'Social structure', in A. L. Kroeber (ed.) *Anthropology Today*, pp. 524–53. Chicago: University of Chicago Press.

Lévi-Strauss, C. 1956. 'Les organisations dualistes, existent-elles?' *Bijdragen tot de Taal-, Land- en Volkenkunde* 112:99–128.

Lévi-Strauss, C., 1964. *Le Cru et Le Cuit. Mythologiques: I*. Paris: Plon.

Lewis, E. D. 1982a. Tana Wai Brama: a study of the social organization of an eastern Florenese domain, Unpublished PhD thesis, The Australian National University, Canberra.

Lewis, E. D. 1982b. 'The metaphorical expression of gender and dual classification in Tana Ai ritual language', *Canberra Anthropology* 5(1):47–59.

Lewis, E. D. 1988a. 'A quest for the source: the ontogenesis of a creation myth of the Ata Tana Ai', in J. J. Fox (ed.) *To Speak in Pairs: Essays on the ritual languages of eastern Indonesia*, pp. 246–81. Cambridge: Cambridge University Press.

Lewis, E. D. 1988b. *People of the Source: The social and ceremonial order of the Tana Wai Brama on Flores*, Verhandelingen 135. Dordrecht: Foris Publications.

Lewis, E. Douglas. 2010. *The Stranger-Kings of Sikka*. Verhandelingen 257. Leiden: KITLV Press.

Lichtheim, M., 1973. *Ancient Egyptian literature: a book of readings Vol 1: The old and middle kingdoms*. Berkeley: University of California Press.

Liu, D. J. 1983. 'Parallel structures in the canon of Chinese poetry', *Poetics Today* 4(4):639–53.

Liu, J. J. Y. 1962. *The Art of Chinese Poetry*. London: Routledge & Kegan Paul.

Lloyd, G. E. R. 1966. *Polarity and Analogy*. Cambridge: Cambridge University Press.

Longfellow, H. W. 1855. *The Song of Hiawatha*. Boston: Ticknor & Fields.

Longfellow, S. 1893. *The Life of Henry Wadsworth Longfellow*. Boston.

Lönnrot, E. 1835–36. *Kalewala taikka wanhoja Karjalan runoja Suomen kansan muinosista ajoista* [*The Old Kalevala*], vols I and II. J. C. Frenckellin ja Poika.

Lönnrot, E. 1849. *Kalewala* [*The New Kalevala*]. *Suomalaisen Kirjallisuuden Seura*.

Lönnrot, E. 1888. *The Kalevala: The epic poem of Finland*, trans. J. M. Crawford. University Park, Pa: Penn State Electronic Classics Publication, <http://www2.hn.psu.edu/faculty/jmanis/kalevala/kalevala-crawford.pdf>

Lönnrot, E. 1963. *The Kalevala: Poems of the Kaleva district*, trans. F. P. Magoun, jr. Cambridge, Mass.: Harvard University Press.

Lord, A. 1960. *The Singer of Tales*. Cambridge. Mass.: Harvard University Press.

Lotz, J. 1954. 'Kamassian verse', *Journal of American Folklore* 67:369–77.

Lounsbury, F. G. 1989. 'The ancient writing of Middle America', in W. N. Senner (ed.) *The Origins of Writing*, pp. 203–37. Lincoln: University of Nebraska Press.

Lowth, R. 1753. *De Sacra Poesia Hebraeorum Praelectiones Academicae* [translated as *Lectures on the Sacred Poetry of the Hebrews*, Boston, 1829].

Lowth, R. 1778. *Isaiah X–XI* [translated as *Isaiah*, Boston, 1834].

Lundström, H., 2010. *I will send my song: Kammu vocal genre in the singing of Kam Raw*. Copenhagen: NIAS Press.

Lundström, H. and K. R. Tayanin, 2006. *Kammu songs: The songs of Kam Raw*. Copenhagen: NIAS Press.

McKinnon, S. M. 1983. Hierarchy, alliance and exchange in the Tanimbar islands, Unpublished PhD thesis, University of Chicago, Chicago.

McWilliam, A. 1982. Harvest of the Nakaf: a study of head-hunting among the Atoni of west Timor, Unpublished BLitt thesis, The Australian National University, Canberra.

McWilliam, A. 1991. 'Prayers of the sacred stone and tree: aspects of invocation in West Timor', *Canberra Anthropology* 14:49–59.

McWilliam, A. 1997. 'Mapping with metaphor: cultural topographies in West Timor', in J. J. Fox (ed.) *The Poetic Power of Place: Comparative perspectives on Austronesian ideas of locality*, pp. 103–15. Canberra: Research School of Pacific and Asian Studies, The Australian National University.

McWilliam, A. 2002. *Paths of Origin, Gates of Life: A study of place and precedence in southwest Timor*. Leiden: KITLV Press.

Malkiel, Y. 1959. 'Studies in irreversible binomials', *Lingua* 8:113–60.

Manafe, D. P. 1889. 'Akan Bahasa Rotti', *Bijdragen tot de Taal-, Land- en Volkenkunde* 38:634–48.

Mannheim, B. 1986. 'Poetic form in Guaman Poma's *Warigsa Arawi*', *Amerindia* 11:41–59.

Mannheim, B. 1986. 'Popular song and popular grammar: poetry and metalanguage', *Word* 37(1–2):45–75.

Mannheim, B. 1987. 'Couplets and oblique contexts: the social organization of a folksong', *Text* 7(3):265–88.

Marmier, X. 1842. 'De la poésie finlandaise', *Revue des Deux Mondes* 32:68–96.

Masing, J. 1997. *The Coming of the Gods: An Iban invocatory chant (Timang Gawai Amat) of the Baleh region, Sarawak*. Canberra: Research School of Pacific and Asian Studies, The Australian National University.

Matthes, B. F. 1872. *Over de Bissoe's of Heidensche Priesters en Priesteressen der Boeginezen*. Amsterdam.

Metcalf, P. 1989. *Where are You, Spirits: Style and theme in Berawan prayer*. Washington, DC: Smithsonian Press.

Metcalf, P. 1994. '"Voilà ce que je dis": la projection de la parole dans la prière berawan", *L'Homme* XXXIV(4):59–76.

Meyer, R. M. 1889. *Die altgermanische Poésie nach ihren formelhaften Elementen beschreiben*. Berlin.

Middelkoop, P. 1949. 'Een Studie van het Timoreesche Doodenritueel', *Verhandelingen van het Bataviaasch Genootschap van Kunsten en Wetenschappen*, vol. 76. Bandoeng: A. C. Nix & Co.

Mitchell, D. 1988. 'Method in the metaphor: the ritual language of Wanukaka', in J. J. Fox (ed.) *To Speak in Pairs: Essays on the ritual languages of eastern Indonesia*, pp. 64–86. Cambridge: Cambridge University Press.

Mitchell, I. G. 1981. Hierarchy and balance: a study of Wanukaka social organization, Unpublished PhD thesis, Monash University, Melbourne.

Morey, S. n.d. 'Poetic forms in Nocte, Singpho, Tai and Tangsa' Paper produced in connection with the project, *The Traditional Songs and Poetry of Upper Assam* (htpp://www.mpi.nl/DoBeS).

Mottin, J. 1980. *55 Chant D'Amour Hong Blanc*. Bangkok: Siam Society.

Nakagawa, S. 1988. 'The journey of the bridegroom: idioms of marriage among the Endenese', in J. J. Fox (ed.) *To Speak in Pairs: Essays on the ritual languages of eastern Indonesia*, pp. 228–45. Cambridge: Cambridge University Press.

Needham, J. 1956. *Science and Civilization in China: History of scientific thought*, vol. 2. Cambridge: Cambridge University Press.

Needham, R. 1964. 'Blood, thunder and the mockery of animals', *Sociologus* 14:136–49.

Needham, R. 1967. 'Percussion and transition', *Man* 2:606–14.

Needham, R. (ed.) 1973. *Right and Left: Essays on dual symbolic classification*. Chicago: University of Chicago Press.

Needham, R. 1978. *Primordial Characters*. Charlottesville: University Press of Virginia.

Needham, R. 1980. 'Principles and variations in the structure of Sumbanese society', in J. J. Fox (ed.) *The Flow of Life: Essays on eastern Indonesia*, pp. 21–47. Cambridge: Cambridge University Press.

Neonbasu, G. 2011. *We Seek Our Roots: Oral tradition in Biboki, West Timor*, Studia Instituti Anthropos 53. Fribourg: Academic Press Fribourg Switzerland.

Newman, L. I. and Popper, W. 1918–23. *Studies in Biblical Parallelism. Part I: Parallelism in Amos* [Newman]; *Part II: Parallelism in Isaiah, Chapters 1–10* [Popper]; *Parallelism in Isaiah, Chapters 11–35* [Popper], vol. 1. Berkeley: University of California Publications in Semitic Philology.

Nguyen Dinh Hoà 1955. 'Double puns in Vietnamese: a case of "linguistic play"', *Word* 11:237–44.

Nguyen Dinh Hoà 1965. 'Parallel construction in Vietnamese', *Lingua* 15:125–39.

Nguyen Van Huyen 1933. *Les Chants Alternes des Garçons et des Filles en Annam*. Paris: Librairie Paul Geuthner.

Oinas, F. J. 1976. 'Negative parallelism in Karelian-Finnish folklore', *Studia Fennica* 20:222–9.

Oinas, F. J. 1985. *Studies in Finnish Folklore: Homage to the Kalevala*. Helsinki: Suomalaisen Kirjallisuuden Seuran Toimituksia.

Olivier, D. 1973. Aggregative hierarchical clustering program, Unpublished ms, Department of Psychology and Social Relations, Harvard University, Cambridge, Mass.

Onvlee, L. 1934. 'Voorbereidend werk', *De Macedoniër* 38:385–98.

Onvlee, L. 1953. 'Van Zang en psalm', *De Heerbaan* 6:16–23.

Oras, J. 2012. 'Musical manifestations of text patterning in Estonian *regilaul*', *Journal of Ethnology and Folkloristics* 4(2):55–68.

Parry, M. 1930. 'Studies in the epic technique of oral verse-making, vol. 1. Homer and the Homeric style', *Harvard Studies in Classical Philology* 41:73–147.

Paulhan, J. 1913. *Les Hain-Teny Merinas*. Paris: Librairie Paul Geuthner.

Pawley, A. 1985. 'On speech formulas and linguistic competence', *Lenguas Modernas* [Chile] 12:84–104.

Pawley, A. 2007. 'Developments in the study of formulaic language since 1970: a personal view', in P. Skandera (ed.) *Phraseology and Culture in English*, pp. 3–45. Berlin: Mouton de Gruyter.

Pellu, L., 2008. A Domain United, A Domain Divided: An Ethnographic Study of Social Relations and Social Change among the People of Landu, East Rote, Eastern Indonesia. Unpublished PhD Thesis, Canberra: The Australian National University

Petersen, D. L. and Richards, K. H. 1992. *Interpreting Hebrew Poetry*. Minneapolis: Fortress Press.

Peukert, H. 1961. *Serbokroatische und makedonische Volkslyrik*. Berlin: Akademie-Verlag.

Phillips, N. 1981. *Sijobang: Sung narrative poetry of West Sumatra*. Cambridge: Cambridge University Press.

Poe, E. A. 1902. *The Complete Works of Edgar Allan Poe*, ed. J. A. Harrison. New York.

Pollen, D. A., Lee, J. R. and Taylor, J. 1971. 'How does the striate cortex begin the reconstruction of the visual world?' *Science* 173:74–7.

Poppe, N. 1955. *Mongolische Volksdichtung, Sprüche, Lieder, Märchen und Heldensagen*. Wiesbaden.

Poppe, N. 1958. 'Der Parallelismus in der epischen Dichtung der Mongolen', *Ural-Altaische Jahrbücher* 30:195–228.

Porthan, H. G. 1766. *Dissertationis de Poesi Fennica*. Åbo: Joh. Christoph. Frenckell.

Prentice, D. J. 1981. 'The minstrel-priestess: a Timugon Murut exorcism ceremony and its liturgy', in N. Phillips and Khaidir Anwar (eds) *Papers on Indonesian Languages and Literatures*, pp. 121–44. London: Indonesian Etymology Project, SOAS, University of London.

Proschan, F. 1984. Love dialogues in Southeast Asia: highland and lowland, vocal and instrumental, Unpublished paper presented at the American Folklore Society Meetings.

Proschan, F. 1989. Khmhu verbal art in America: the poetics of Khmhu verse, Unpublished PhD thesis, The University of Texas at Austin.

Proschan, F. 1992. 'Poetic parallelism in Khmhu verbal arts: from texts to performances', in A. Catlin and T. Mahoney (eds) *Text, Context and Performance in Cambodia, Laos and Vietnam*, Selected Reports in Ethnomusicology Vol. 9, pp. 1–32. Los Angeles: University of California.

Quack, A. 1981. *Das Wort der Alten: Erzählungen zur Geschichte der Pujuma von Katipol (Taiwan)*, Collectanea Instituti Anthropos Vol. 12. St Augustin: Anthropos-Institute.

Quack, A. 1985. *Priesterinnen, Heilerinnen, Schamaninnen?: Die po'ringao der Puyuma von Katipol (Taiwan)*, Collectanea Instituti Anthropos Vol. 32. Berlin: Reimar.

Rappoport, D., 2013 'Speech and Songs in the Toraja Highlands' in Revel, Nicole (ed), 2013. *Songs of Memory in Islands of Southeast Asia*, pp 73-104 Cambridge: New Castle on Tyne: Cambridge Scholars Publishing.

Reichard, G. A. 1944. *Prayer: The compulsive word*, Monographs of the American Ethnological Society Vol. 7. Seattle: University of Washington Press.

Renard-Clamagirand, B. 1988. 'Li'i marapu: speech and ritual among the Wewewa of West Sumba', in J. J. Fox (ed.) *To Speak in Pairs: Essays on the ritual languages of eastern Indonesia*, pp. 87–103. Cambridge: Cambridge University Press.

Rendra, 1993. *Orang orang Rangkas Bitung* . Yogyakarta : Bentang.

Revel, N., 2013 'Vivid and Virtual Memory' in Revel, Nicole (ed), 2013. *Songs of Memory in Islands of Southeast Asia*, pp. 27-58. Cambridge: New Castle on Tyne: Cambridge Scholars Publishing.

Ridder, R. de, 1989. The poetic *Popul Vuh*: an anthropological study, Proefschrift, Leiden University, Leiden.

Rooden, P. van, 1996. 'Nineteenth-century representations of missionary conversion and the transformation of Western Christianity', in P. van der Veer (ed.) *Conversion to Modernities: The globalization of Christianity*, pp. 65–87. London: Routledge.

Rosner, V. 1961. 'The Bhak Katek ritual in use among the Sadars of Jashpur, Madhya Pradesh (India)', *Anthropos* 56:77–113.

Rothe, E. 2004. Wulla Poddu: Bitterer Monat, Monat der Tabus, Monat des Heiligen, Monat des Neuen Jahres in Loli, Unpublished PhD thesis, Ludwig-Maximilians-Universität, München.

Rumsey, A. 1995. 'Pairing and parallelism in the New Guinea Highlands', in P. Silverman and J. D. Loftlin (eds) *SALSA II*. Austin: University of Texas.

Rumsey, A. 2001. 'Tom Yaya Kange: a metrical narrative genre from the New Guinea Highlands', *Journal of Linguistic Anthropology* 11(2):193–239.

Rumsey, A. 2002. 'Aspects of Ku Wara Ethnosyntax and social life', N. J. Enfield (ed.) *Ethnosyntax: Explorations in grammar and culture*, pp. 259–85. Oxford: Oxford University Press.

Rumsey, A. 2010. 'Musical, poetic and linguistic form in "Tom Yaya" song from Papua New Guinea', *Anthropological Linguistics* 19(3–4):235–82.

Sabatier, L. 1933. 'La Chanson de Damsan', *Bulletin de l'École Française d'Extrême-Orient* 33:143–302.

Šafranov, S. N. 1878–79. 'O sklade narodno-russkoj posennoj reči, rassmatrivaemoj v svjazi s *napevami*', *Žurnal Ministerstva narodnogo prosveščenija* (2):199–205.

Salomon, G. 1919. *Die Entstehung und Entwicklung deutschen Zwillingsformeln*. Göttingen.

Sandin, B. 1977. *Gawai Burong: The chants and celebrations of the Iban Bird Festival*, ed. and intro. C. A. Sather. Pulau Pinang: Penerbit Universiti Sains Malaysia.

Sankoff, G. [n.d.] Sini: poetry of the Buang of Papua New Guinea, Unpublished paper.

Sankoff, G. 1977. 'Le parallélisme dans la poésie Buang', *Anthropolgica* [NS] XIX(1):27–48.

Sather, C. 2001. *Seeds of Play, Words of Power: An ethnographic study of Iban shamanic chants*, Borneo Classic Series Vol. 5. Tun Jugah Foundation & Borneo Research Council.

Scarborough, W. 1875. *A Collection of Chinese Proverbs*. Shanghai: American Presbyterian Mission Press.

Schärer, H. 1966. *Der Totenkult der Ngadju Dajak in Süd-Borneo*, Verhandelingen van het Koninklijk Instituut voor Taal-, Land- en Volkenkunde Vol. 51, parts I and II. 's-Gravenhage: Nijhoff.

Schefold, R., 2001. 'Three sources of ritual blessings in traditional Indonesian societies' *Bijdragen tot de Taal, Land en Volkenku*nde 157: 359-381.

Schirmunski, V. 1965. 'Syntaktischer Parallelismus und rhythmische Bindung im alttürkischen epischen Vers', in *Beiträge zur Sprachwissenschaft, Volkskunde und Literaturforschung*. Berlin: Akademie-Verlag.

Schlegel, G. 1896. *La loi du parallelisme en style chinois démonstée par la preface du 'Si-yu-ki'*. Leiden.

Schoolcraft, H. R. 1839. *Algic Researches*, 2 vols. New York.

Schröder, D. and Quack, A. 1979. *Kopfjagdriten der Puyuma von Katipol (Taiwan)*, Collectanea Instituti Anthropos Vol. 11. St Augustin: Anthropos-Institute.

Schulte Nordholt, H. G. 1971. *The Political System of the Atoni of Timor*, Verhandelingen van het Koninklijk Instituut voor Taal-, Land- en Volkenkunde 60. The Hague: Martinus Nijhoff.

Schulte Nordholt, H. G. 1980. 'The symbolic classification of the Atoni of Timor', in J. J. Fox (ed.) *The Flow of Life: Essays on eastern Indonesia*, pp. 231–47. Cambridge: Cambridge University Press.

Schultze, B. 1982. Der Wordparallelismus als Stilmittel der ostjakischen Volksdichtung, Dissertation, Akademie der Wissenschafften der DDR, Berlin.

Sherzer, D. and Sherzer, J. 1972. 'Literature in San Blas: discovering the Cuna Ikala', *Semiotica* 4:182–99.

Sherzer, J. 1974a. 'Namakke, Sunmakke, Kormakke: three types of Cuna speech event', in R. Bauman and J. Sherzer (eds) *Explorations in the Ethnography of Speaking*, pp. 263–82. Cambridge: Cambridge University Press.

Sherzer, J. 1974b. *Semantic systems, discourse, structure and the ecology of language*, Working Papers in Sociolinguistics No. 17. Austin, Tex.: Southwest Educational Development Laboratory.

Sherzer, J. 1983. *Kuna Ways of Speaking: An ethnographic perspective*. Austin: University of Texas.

Sherzer, J. 1990. *Verbal Art in San Blas: Kuna culture through its discourse*. Cambridge: Cambridge University Press.

Shih, V. Y. C. 1959. *The Literary Mind and the Carving of Dragons* [translation of Liu Hsieh's *Wen-hsing Tiao-lung*]. New York: Columbia University Press.

Sibree, J. 1880. *Madagascar: The Great African Island*. London.

Siikala, A.-L. and Vakimo, S. (eds) 1994. *Songs Beyond the Kalevala: Transformations of oral poetry*, Studia Fennica Folkloristica 2. Helsinki: Suomalaisen Kirjallisuuden Seura.

Siskel, S. 1974. With the spirit of a jaguar: a study of shamanism in Zincinton, Chamula, Unpublished AB thesis, Harvard University, Cambridge, Mass.

Smart, C. 1950. *The Collected Poems of Christopher Smart*, ed. N. Callan. Cambridge, Mass.: Harvard University Press.

Smith, A. H. 1902. *Proverbs and Common Sayings from the Chinese*. Shanghai: American Presbyterian Mission Press.

Smith, C. A. 1894. *Repetition and Parallelism in English Verse*. New York.

Sodergren, J. 1973. Matching coefficients as estimators of node similarity in symmetric and non-symmetric graphs, Typescript, Department of Anthropology, Harvard University, Cambridge, Mass.

Sokal, R. and Sneath, P. 1963. *Principles of Numerical Taxonomy*. London: W. H. Freeman.

Sri Kuhnt-Saptodewo, J. 1993. *Zum Seelengeleit bei den Ngaju am Kahayan. Auswertung eines Sakraltextes zur Manarung-Zeremonie beim Totenfest*. München: Akademischer Verlag.

Sri Kuhnt-Saptodewo, J. 1999. 'A bridge to the upper world: sacred language of the Ngaju', *Borneo Research Bulletin* 30:13–27.

Steinhart, W. L. 1934. 'Niassche teksten met Ned. Vertaling en aanteekeningen', *Tijdschrift voor Taal-, Land- en Volkenkunde* 74:326–75, 391–440.

Steinhart, W. L. 1937a. 'De Evangelie-prediker en zijn houding ten opzichte van de Inheemsche cultuur', *Zendingstijdschrift De Opwekker* 82(4):147–60.

Steinhart, W. L. 1937b. *Niassche Teksten*, Verhandelingen van het Bataviaasch Genootschap Vol. 73. Bandoeng: A. C. Nix & Co.

Steinhart, W. L. 1938. *Niassche Priesterlitanieën*, Verhandelingen van het Bataviaasch Genootschap Vol. 74. Bandoeng: A. C. Nix & Co.

Steinhart, W. L. 1950. 'Niasse teksten met Ned. vertaling en aantekeningen', *Tijdschrift voor Taal-, Land- en Volkenkunde* 84:33–109.

Steinhart, W. L. 1954. *Niassche Teksten*, Koninklijk Instituut voor Taal-, Land- en Volkenkunde. 's-Gravenhage: Nijhoff.

Steinitz, W. 1934. *Der Parallelismus in der finnisch-karelischen Volksdichtung*, F. F. Communications No. 115. Helsinki.

Steinitz, W. 1939–41. *Ostjakische Volksdichtung und Erzählungen aus zwei Dialekten*. Tartu and Stockholm. [Reprint, Vol. I: 1975, Budapest: Akademiai Kiado; Vols II–IV: 1976, Berlin: Akademie-Verlag.]

Strauss, H. 1990. *The Mi-Culture of the Mount Hagen People, Papua New Guinea*, trans. B. Shields, eds G. Stürzenhofecker and A. J. Strathern, Ethnographic

Monographs No. 13. Pittsburg: University of Pittsburg. [Originally published in 1963 as *Die Mi-Kultur der Hagenberg-Stämme im Östlichen Zentral-Neuguinea*. Hamburg: De Gruyter & Co.]

Strehlow, T. G. H. 1971. *Songs of Central Australia*. Sydney: Angus & Robertson.

Sundermann, H. 1905. 'Niassische Texte mit Deutscher Obersetzung', *Bijdragen tot de Taal-, Land- en Volkenkunde, uitgegeven door het Koninklijk Instituut* 58:1–72.

Tchang Tcheng-Ming, B. S. J. 1937. *Le Paralllisme dans les vers du Cheu King*, Variétés Sinologiques No. 65. Paris: Paul Geuthner.

Tedlock, D. 1985. *Popul Vuh: The Mayan book of the dawn of life*. New York: Simon & Schuster. Revised and Expanded Edition: 1996.

Tedlock, D. 1987. 'Hearing a voice in an ancient text: Quiché Maya poetics', in J. Sherzer and A. C. Woodbury (eds) *Native American Discourse: Poetics and rhetoric*, pp. 140–75. Cambridge: Cambridge University Press.

Tedlock, D. 2003. *Rabinal Achi: A Mayan drama of war and sacrifice*. Oxford: Oxford University Press.

Tedlock, D. 2012. 'Drawing and designing with words', in K. M. Hull and M. D. Carrasco (eds) *Parallel Worlds: Genre, discourse, and poetics in contemporary, colonial, and classical Maya literature*, pp. 181–94. Boulder: University of Colorado Press.

Telban, B. 2008. 'The poetics of the crocodile: changing cultural perspectives in Ambonwari', *Oceania* 78:217–35.

Terray, E. 1972. *Marxism and 'Primitive' Societies*. New York: Monthly Review Press.

Therik, G. T. 2004. *Wehali, the Female Land: Traditions of a Timorese ritual centre*. Canberra: Research School of Pacific and Asian Studies & Pandanus Books.

Thompson, J. E. S. 1950. *Maya Hieroglyphic Writing: Introduction*, Publication 589. Washington, DC: Carnegie Institution of Washington.

Toner, P. G. 2001. When the echoes are gone: a Yolngu musical anthropology, Unpublished PhD thesis, The Australian National University, Canberra.

Traube, E. 1980. 'Mambai rituals of black and white', in J. J. Fox (ed.) *The Flow of Life: Essays on eastern Indonesia*, pp. 290–314. Cambridge: Cambridge University Press.

Traube, E. 1986. *Cosmology and Social Life: Ritual exchange among the Mambai of East Timor*. Chicago: University of Chicago Press.

Traube, E. G. 1977. Ritual exchange among the Mambai of East Timor: gifts of life and death, Unpublished PhD thesis, Harvard University, Cambridge, Mass.

T'sou, B. K. 1967. Studies in linguistic parallelism and poetic diction, Unpublished MA thesis, Harvard University, Cambridge, Mass.

T'sou, B. K. 1968. 'Some aspects of linguistic parallelism and Chinese versification', in C. E. Gribble (ed.) *Studies Presented to Roman Jakobson by His Students*. Cambridge, Mass.: Slavica Publishers.

Tule, P., 2004. *Longing for the House of God, Dwelling in the House of the Ancestors*. Studia Instituti Anthropos No 50. Academic Press Fribourg Switzerland.

Turner, V. 1967. 'Ritual symbolism, morality and social structure among the Ndembu', in *The Forest of Symbols*, pp. 48–58. Ithaca, NY: Cornell University Press.

Turpin, M. 2007. 'The poetics of Central Australian song', *Australian Aboriginal Studies* 2:100–15.

Tuuk, H. N. van der 1864–67. *Tobasche Spraakkunst*. Amsterdam.

Vandermeersch, L. 1989. 'Les origines divinatoires de la tradition chinoise du parallélisme littéraire', *Extrême-Orient—Extrême-Occident* 11:11–33.

Veen, H. van der, 1929. 'Een wichel-litanie der Sa'dan-Toradja's', *Feestbundel uitgegeven door het Koninklijk Bataviaasch Genootschap van Kunsten en Wetenschappen bij gelegenheid van zijn 150 Jarig Bestaan 1778–1928*, vol. II, pp. 396–411. Weltevreden: G. Kolff & Co.

Veen, H. van der, 1940. *Tae'-Nederlandsch woordenboek met register Nederlandsch-Tae*, Koninklijk Instituut voor Taal-, Land- en Volkendunde. 's-Gravenhage: Nijhoff.

Veen, H. van der, 1950. 'De Samenspraak der beide priesters, de woordvoerders van bruid en bruidegom bij de huwelijksplechtigheid der Sa'dan-Toradja's', in *Bingkisam Budi (Een Bundel Opstellen aangeboden aan Dr. Philippus Samuel van Ronkel)*. Leiden: Sijthoff.

Veen, H. van der 1952. 'Gebruik van literaire of dichtertaal bij de vertaling van poëtische gedeelten van de Bijbel in de Indonesische taal', *De Heerbaan* 5: 211–40.

Veen, H. van der, 1965. *The Merok Feast of the Sa'dan-Toradja*. 's-Gravenhage: Nijhoff.

Veen, H. 1966. van der, *The Sa'dan-Toradja Chant for the Deceased*. 's-Gravenhage: Nijhoff.

van Ooy, F. 1994. Ritual language of Sawu Dimu, eastern Indonesia, Paper presented at the 7th International Conference on Austronesian Linguistics, Leiden.

Vischer, M. 1992. Children of the black Patola stone: origin structures in a domain on Palu'e Island, Unpublished PhD thesis, The Australian National University, Canberra.

Vroklage, B. A. G. 1952. *Ethnographic der Belu in Zentral-Timor*, 3 vols. Leiden: E. J. Brill.

Waismann, F. 1965. 'Language strata', in A. Flew (ed.) *Logic and Language*, pp. 226–47. New York: Doubleday.

Walker, A., 1972. 'Blessing Feasts and Ancestor Propitiation among the Lahu Nyi (Red Lahu) in *Journal of the Siam Society* 60:345-375.

Walsh, M. 2010. 'A polytropical approach to the "Floating Pelican" song: an exercise in rich interpretation of a Murriny Patha (northern Australia) song', *Australian Journal of Linguistics* 30(1):117–30.

Wang, C. H. 1974. *The Bell and the Drum: Shih Ching as formulaic poetry in an oral tradition*. Berkeley: University of California Press.

Watson, B. 1971. *Chinese Rhyme-Prose*. New York: Columbia University Press.

Watson, W. G. E. 1980. 'Gender-matched parallelism in the Old Testament', *Journal of Biblical Literature* [Philadelphia] 99(3):321–41.

Watson, W. G. E. 1984. *Classical Hebrew Poetry: A guide to its techniques*. Sheffield: JSOT Press, University of Sheffield.

Watts, Duncan J. 1999. Small Worlds: The Dynamics of Networks between Order and Randomness. Princeton: Princeton University Press.

Watts, Duncan J. 2003. Six Degrees: The Science of a Connected Age. New York:W.W. Norton and Co.

Waugh, L. 1980. 'The poetic function and the nature of language', *Poetics Today* 2(Ia):57–82.

Webster, A. K., 2008. 'Running again, roasting again, touching again: On repetition, heightened affective expressivity, and the utility of the notion of linguaculture in Navajo and beyong.' *Journal of American Folklore* 121: 441-472.

Weiner, J. F., 1991. *The empty place: poetry, space, and being among the Foi of Papua New Guinea*. Bloomington: Indiana University Press.

Wetering, F. H. van de, 1925. 'Het Huwelijk op Rote', *Tijdschrift voor Indische Taal-, Land- en Volkenkunde, uitgegeven door het Bataviaas Genootschap* 65:1–36, 589–667.

Whallon, W., 1963. 'Formulaic poetry in the Old Testament' *Comparative Literature*:1-14.

White, K., 1982. *Kr'ue Ke (Showing the way): A Hmong Initiation of the Dead*. Bangkok: Pandora.

Wigglesworth, Hazel J., 1980. 'Rhetorical devices distinguishing the genre of folktale (fiction) from that of oral history (fact) in Ilianen Manobo narrative discourse', *Philippine Journal of Linguistics* Vol 11 (1):45-80.

Witherspoon, G., 1977. *Language and Art in the Navajo Universe*. Ann Arbor: University of Michigan Press.

Wolkstein, D. and Kramer, S. N. 1983. *Inanna, Queen of Heaven and Earth: Her stories and hymns from Sumer*. New York: Harper & Row.

Wouden, F. A. E. von, 1968. *Types of Social Structure in Eastern Indonesia*, trans. R. Needham, Koninklijk Instituut voor Taal-, Land- en Volkenkunde Translation Series Vol. 2. The Hague: Martinus Nijhoff.

Wu, H. L., 1988. 'The concept of parallelism: Shengtan's Critical Discourse on The Water Margin' Doleželová-Velingerová, M. (ed) *Poetics: East and West*. Victoria College, University of Toronto: Toronto Semiotic Circle.

Yoder, P. B., 1971. 'A-B Pairs and Oral Composition in Hebrew Poetry' in *Vetus Testamentum* 21:470-489.

'Yubileum' 1997. *Pos Kupang* (Supplement), 30 September.

Appendix: Petrus Malesi's Recitation Of 'The Coming Of Rice'

Petrus Malesi

In 1973, the filmmaker Tim Asch recorded a recitation by the poet, Petrus Malesi which he entitled 'The Coming of Rice'. This is a version of the Origin of Rice (and Millet) that I originally recorded from him during my first fieldwork in 1965-66. At the time, I was still struggling to understand ritual language, so I brought this chant to Stefanus Adulanu ('Old Meno') for help in transcription and understanding. Stefanus Adulanu offered his help and in the process also added to the recitation. The Malesi-Adulanu version. which bears the chant name, *Doli Mo ma Lutu Mala*. was the focus of my paper, 'Genealogy and Topogeny', Chapter 11 in this volume. This recitation by Malesi in 1973 is quite similar to the earlier version. The following is a complete transcription and translation of Petrus Malesi's filmed recitation and is intend to accompany Malesi's recitation.

The video of this recitation is available on the ANU Press website.

Hade Mamai-Na

Petrus Malesi

1.	Fetok Tai Oli Moli	The girl Tai Oli Moli
2.	Do inak Fo Fai Foe	Or the woman Fo Fai Foe
3.	Ana tuü heni nupu no-na	She throws away the coconut shoot
4.	Ma ana nggali heni sadu pua-na.	And she tosses away the areca nut sprout.
5.	Ana bonu boa basa namo-la	It bobs about in all the harbours
6.	Ma ana ele piko basa meti-la,	And it floats on all the tides,
7.	De meti leo Tena Lai-la	A tidal shore like Tena Lai
8.	Ma namo leo Mae Oe-la.	And a harbour like Mae Oe
9.	Boe ma ala neka nita lai ndia	They feel attachment to things there
10.	Ma ala lili dela lai ndia.	And they are attracted to things there.
11.	Faik esa manuni-na	Then on a certain day
12.	Ma ledok esa matebe-na	And at a particular time

13.	*Inak-a Masu Pasu*	The woman, Masu Pasu
14.	*Do fetok-a He Hai*	Or the girl, He Hai
15.	*Ana ene dolu nai liun*	She lowers a fish line in the ocean
16.	*Ma ana nafu kafa nai sain;*	And she sets a hook in the sea;
17.	*Neu tongo lololo*	It happens to meet
18.	*Ma nda lilima*	And happens to encounter
19.	*Nupu nok bonu boa*	The bobbing coconut shoot
20.	*Ma sadu puak ele piko*	And the floating areca nut sprout.
21.	*Boe ma ana ifa-na nupu non*	So she cradles the coconut shoot
22.	*Ma ko'o-na sadu puan*	And she embraces the areca nut sprout.
23.	*Ala mai meti leo Bola Sou-la*	They come to a tide point like Bola Sou
24.	*Ma tasi leo Asa Nao-la.*	And to a sea area like Asa Nao.
25.	*Mai te Danga Lena Liun uma-na*	There at the home of Danga Lena Liun
26.	*Ma Mane Tua sain lo-na*	And at the home of Mane Tua Sain
27.	*Eki-kala beke-doto*	There is joyful shouting
28.	*Ma hema-kala bekao.*	And there is great clamour.
29.	*Boe ma inak-a Masu Pasu*	So the woman, Masu Pasu
30.	*Do fetok-a He Hai*	Or the girl, He Hai
31.	*Ana leno sosodo ei-na*	She shuffles her feet in the dance
32.	*Ma ana pena nggangape lima-na*	And she sways her arms with the music
33.	*Nggenge te meti nala Bola Sou*	Startlingly the tide rushes in on Bola Sou
34.	*Ma tasi nala Asa Nao.*	And the sea floods Asa Nao.
35.	*Boe ma poe-ana Asa Nao*	A small shrimp at Asa Nao
36.	*Ma nii-ana Bola Sou*	And a tiny crab from Bola Sou
37.	*Ala ngge'e leni nupu-non*	They pinch and carry away the coconut shoot
38.	*Ma ka'a leni sadu pua-na.*	And bite and carry away the areca nut sprout.
39.	*Mai te inak Manu Leo Oli*	Then comes the woman, Manu Leo Oli
40.	*Ma fetok Enga Lutu Namo*	And the girl, Enga Lutu Namo
41.	*Ana dei dongo*	She stands and waits
42.	*Ma ana nene fino*	And she stops and listens
43.	*De ana ifa-na nupu nok*	She cradles the coconut shoot
44.	*Do ana ko'o-na sadu puak.*	Or she embraces the areca nut sprout.
45.	*Ana lutu kiun*	She places stones around them
46.	*Ma ana pa'a feon*	And she fences them all round.
47.	*Ana toli oen*	She pours water on them

48.	Ma ana fu'a daen	And she covers them with earth.
49.	Te do belan ta dadi	But no heavy leaves arise
50.	Do hu bokon ta tola	And no bending stalks appear
51.	Pule duan ta lesu	No two grains come forth
52.	Ma kale telum ta dadi.	And no three kernels appear.
53.	Fai esa manuni-na	Then on a certain day
54.	Do ledo esa manda-na	Or at a particular time
55.	Inak-a Dela Kola	The woman, Dela Kola
56.	Ma fetok-a Dila Latu	And the girl, Dila Latu
57.	Ana tolomu sasali	She comes running
58.	Ma nalai lelena	And she comes hurrying
59.	De ifa neni nupu nok	She cradles and carries away the coconut shoot
60.	De ko'o neni sadu puak.	She embraces and carries away the areca sprout.
61.	Ana mai de ana tane nasamamaon	She comes and she plants them tenderly
62.	Ma ana sele nakaboboin	And she sows them with care
63.	Te hu bokon ta tola	But no bending stalk appears
64.	Ma do belan ta dadi	And no heavy leaves arise
65.	Ma kale duan ta lesu	And no two kernels come forth
66.	Ma pule telun ta dadi.	And no three grains arise.
67.	Inak-a Fi Bau	The woman, Fi Bau
68.	Do fetok-a Kade Ufa neu	Or the girl, Kade Ufa, she goes
69..	De ana ifa do ko'o neni	She embraces them and cradles them away
70.	De ana tane nasamamaon	Then she plants them tenderly
71.	Ma ana sele nakaboboin	And she sows them with care
72.	Boe o hu bokon ta tola	But no bending stalks appear
73.	Ma do belan ta dadi.	And no heavy leaves arise.
74.	Fai esa manuni-na	Then on a certain day
75.	Ma ledo esa manda-na	And at a particular time
76.	Inak-a Fula Fopo	The woman Fula Fopo
77.	De ana ifa neni nupu no-na	She cradles and carries away the coconut shoot
78.	[Missing Line]	
79.	Ma ana ko'o neni sadu pua-na	And she embraces and carries away the areca nut sprout
80.	Neu de tane nasamamaon	She goes and plants then tenderly
81.	Ma sele nakaboboin	And she sows them with care
82.	Te hu bokon ta dadi	But no bending stalks arise
83.	Ma do belan ta lesu	And no heavy leaves come forth.
84.	Boe ma pule duan ta tola	No two grains appear

85.	*Ma kale telun ta dadi.*	And no three kernels arise.
86.	*Boe ma inak-a Pinga Pasa*	Then the woman, Pinga Pasa
87.	*Ma fetok-a Soe Leli, ana mai*	And the girl, Soe Leli, she comes
88.	*Ana ifa neni nupu non*	She cradles and carries away the coconut shoot
89.	*Ma ko'o neni sadu puan*	And she embraces and carries away the areca nut sprout
90.	*Neu de ana tane nasamamaon*	She goes and she plants them tenderly
91.	*Nai Leli Ko Eko mon*	In the plain at Leli Ko Eko
92.	*Ma sele nakaboboin*	And she sows them with care
93.	*Nai Pase Bo Boi fuän.*	In the field at Pase Bo Boi.
94.	*Te hu bokon ta dadi*	But no bending stalks arise
95.	*Ma do belan ta moli*	And no heavy leaves appear
96.	*Ma kale duan te lesu*	And no two kernels come forth
97.	*Ma pule telun ta dadi.*	And no three grains arise.
98.	*Fai esa manuni-na*	Then on a certain day
99.	*Ma ledok esa manda-na*	And at a particular time
100.	*Inak bei Bau Dale*	The woman at Bau Dale
101.	*Ma fetok bei Bau Dale [Kai Tio]*	And the girl at Bau Dale
102.	*Inak-a Fiti Nggoli*	The woman, Fiti Nggoli
103.	*Ma fetok-a Lole Bako*	And the girl, Lole Bako
104.	*Ana ndae pou neu alun*	She drapes a sarong upon her shoulder
105.	*Ma ana su sidi neu langa,*	And she sets a cloth upon her head
106.	*Pou dula tolo-teik*	A sarong with a tola-teik pattern
107.	*Ma sidi leü pan' daik*	And a cloth with a panadaik design
108.	*Boe ma pua lisu lasu boak*	Brings areca as round as a tuft of cotton
109.	*Ma malu boa dongi aik.*	And betel fruit as long as a barbed spear.
110.	*Boe ma ana ifa-na nupu non*	She cradles the coconut shoot
111.	*Ma ana ko'o-na sadu puan*	And she embraces the areca nut sprout
112.	*Nai Leli Ko Eko mon*	In the plain at Leli Ko Eko
113.	*Ma Pase Bo Boi fuän*	And the field at Pase Bo Boi
114.	*Neu de ana sele nakaboboin*	She goes and she sows them with care
115.	*Ma ana tane nasamamaon*	And she plants them tenderly
116.	*Nai Bako Bau Dale fu'an*	In the field at Bako Bau Dale
117.	*Do Nggoli Kai Tio mon.*	Or in the plain at Nggoli Kai Tio.
118.	*Boe ma pule-na fafaku*	Then the grains come forth
119.	*Ma kale-na loloso*	And the kernels come out
120.	*Ma do bela-na dadi*	The heavy leaves arise

121.	*Ma hu boko-na tola.*	And the bending stalks appear.
122.	*Eki-kala beke-doto*	There is joyful shouting
123.	*Ma hema-kala bekao.*	And there is great clamour.
124.	*Boe ma inak-a Leo Lasu*	Then the woman, Leo Lasu
125.	*Do fetok-a Nuli Kili, ana mai*	Or the girl, Nuli Kili, she comes
126.	*De ana ifa neni(n)*	She cradles and carries them
127.	*Do ana ko'o nenin*	Or she embraces and carries them
128.	*Neu de ana tane new Ki Lama*	She goes and plants them at Ki Lama
129.	*Ma ana sele neu Le Ina.*	And she sows them at Le Ina.
130.	*Kale dua-na tola*	The two kernels appear
131.	*Ma pule telu-na dadi*	And the three grains arise
132.	*Do bela-na lesu*	The heavy leaves come forth
133.	*Ma hu boko-na moli.*	And the bending stalks appear.
134.	*Eki-kala beke-doto*	There is joyful shouting
135.	*Ma hema-kala bekao*	And there is great clamour.
136.	*Boe ma besak-a fetok leo Lesi Ama la*	Now the girls of Lesi Ama
137.	*Do inak-a [leo] Bala Fia la*	Or the women of Bala Fia
138.	*Ala tolomu sasali*	They come running
139.	*Ma lalai lelena*	And they come hurrying.
140.	*Mai de ifa do ko'o leni*	There they cradle or they embrace them, carrying them away.
141.	*De ala tane neu Peto Lesi Ama mon*	They plant them in the plain of Peto Lesi Ama
142.	*Do Lela Bala Fia fu'an*	Or in the field at Lela Bala Fia.
143.	*Hu boko-na tola*	The bending stalks appear
144.	*Ma do bela-na dadi*	And the heavy leaves arise
145.	*Ma kale dua-na lesu*	The two kernels come forth
146.	*Ma kale [pule] telu-na tola.*	And three kernels [grain] appear.
147.	*Eki-kala beke-doto*	There is joyful shouting
148.	*Ma hema-kala bekao.*	And there is great clamour.
149.	*Boe ma fai esa manuni-na*	Then on a certain day
150.	*Ma ledo esa manda-na*	And at a particular time
151.	*Ina bei Pena Pua la*	The women who are still at Pena Pau
152.	*Do fetok bei Maka Lama*	Or the girls still at Maka Lama
153.	*Ina bei Oe Mau la*	The women still at Oe Mau
154.	*Do fetok bei Tanga Loi la*	Or the girls still at Tanga Loi
155.	*Ala tolomu sasali*	They come running
156.	*Ma lalai lelena*	And they come hurrying
157.	*Mai de ala ifa leni Doli Mo*	There they cradle and carry away Doli Mo

158.	*Do ko'o leni Lutu Mala,*	Or they embrace and carry away Lutu Mala,
159.	*Leni neu Oe Mau*	Carrying them to Oe Mau
160.	*Do leni neu Tanga Loi*	Or carrying them to Tanga Loi
161.	*Leni neu Pena Pua*	Carrying them to Pena Pua
162.	*Do leni neu Maka Lama*	Or carrying them to Maka Lama
163.	*Ala tane lasamamaon*	They plant them tenderly
164.	*Ma ala sele lakaboboin*	And they sow them with care
165.	*Hu boko-na tola*	The bending stalks appear
166.	*Ma do bela-na dadi*	And the heavy leaves arise
167.	*Ma kale dua-na lesu*	And the two kernels come forth
168.	*Ma pule telu-na tola.*	And the three grains appear.
169.	*Eki-kala beke-doto*	There is joyful shouting
170.	*Ma hema-kala bekao.*	And there is great clamour.
171.	*Fetok bei Tete Lesi la*	The girls still at Tete Lesi
172.	*Ma inak bei Dae Mea la*	And the women still at Dae Hea
173.	*Ina bei Dau Dolu la*	The women still at Dau Dolu
174.	*Do fetok bei Pau Biti la*	Or the girls still at Pau Biti
175.	*Ina Dae Mea Iko*	The woman, Dae Mea Iko
176.	*Ma Fetok Oe Ana Muli, ala mai*	And the girl, Oe Ana Muli, they come
177.	*De ala ifa leni Doli Mo*	They cradle and carry away Doli Mo
178.	*Ma ko'o leni Lutu Mala*	And they embrace and carry away Lutu Mala
179.	*Tane nasamamaon*	Planting them tenderly
180.	*Ma sele nakaboboin*	And sowing them with care
181.	*Do bela-na tola*	The heavy leaves appear
182.	*Ma hu boko-na dadi*	And the bending stalks arise
183.	*Do pule dua-na lesu*	Or the two grains come forth
184.	*Ma kale telu-na dadi*	And the three kernels arise
185.	*Eki-kala beke-doto*	There is joyful shouting
186.	*Ma hema-kala bekao.*	And there is great clamour.
187.	*Boe ma besaka fetok bei Dela Muli-la*	Now the girls still at Dela Muli
188.	*Do ina bei Ania Iko-la*	Or the women still at Ana Iko
189.	*Inak-a Tasi Puka*	The women, Tasi Puka
190.	*Ma fetok Li Solu, ana mai*	And the girl, Li Solu, she comes
191.	*De ana ifa do ko'o nenin*	She cradles or embraces and carries them away
192.	*De neni neu Dela Muli*	She carries them to Dela Muli
193.	*Ma neni neu Dela Milu [Ania Iko]*	And she carries them to Dela Muli [Ana Iko]
194.	*Neni neu Laba Kola*	Carries them to Laba Kola
195.	*Do neni neu Sio Meko*	Or she carries them to Sio Meko

196.	*Tane nasamamaon*	Planting them tenderly
197.	*Ma sele nakaboboin*	And sowing them with care
198.	*Boe ma hu boko-na tola*	Then the bending stalks appear
199.	*Do bela-na dadi*	And the heavy leaves occur
200.	*Ma kale dua-na lesu*	And the two kernals come forth
201.	*Ma pule telu-na dadi*	And the three grains arise
202.	*Eki-kala beke-doto*	There is joyful shouting
203.	*Ma hema-kala bekao.*	And there is great clamour.
204.	*Boe ma fetok bei Bebe Dela*	Then the girls still at Bebe Dela
205.	*Do inak bei Ango Beu la*	Or the women still at Ango Beu
206.	*Tolomu sasali*	They come running
207.	*Do lalai lelena*	Or they come hurrying
208.	*Mai-a ifa leni Doli Mo*	There they cradle and carry away Doli Mo
209.	*Ma ko'o leni Lutu Mala*	And they embrace and carry away Lutu Mala
210.	*De ala tane neu Ni Le*	They plant them at Ni Le
211.	*Ma ala sele neu Lada Dano*	And they sow them at Lada Dano
212.	*Do bela-na tola*	The heavy leaves appear
213.	*Ma hu boko-na dadi*	And the bending stalks arise
214.	*Ma kale dua-na lesu*	The two kernels come forth
215.	*Ma pule telu-na tola.*	And the three grains appear.
216.	*Eki-kala beke-doto*	There is joyful shouting
217.	*Ma hema-kal bekao.*	And there is great clamour.
218.	*Boe ma besaka fetok leo Tada Muli la*	Now the girls like Tada Muli
219.	*Do inak-a Lene Kona la*	Or the women like Lene Kona
220.	*Inak-a Putu Koe*	The woman, Putu Koe
221.	*Ma fetok ka Le Mako*	And the girl, Le Mako
222.	*Ana tolomu sasali*	She comes running
223.	*Ma nalai lelena*	She come hurrying
224.	*Mai de ifa neni Doli Mo*	There she cradles and carries away Doli Mo
225.	*Ma ko'o neni Lutu Mala.*	And she embraces and carries away Lutu Mala.
226.	*Neu de ana tane nasamamaon*	She goes and she plants them tenderly
227.	*Ma ana sele nakaboboin.*	And she shows them with care.
228.	*Do belan-na dadi*	The heavy leaves occur
229.	*Ma hu boko-na tola*	And the bending stalks appear
230.	*Kale dua-na lesu*	The two kernels come forth
231.	*Ma pula telu-na dadi*	And the three grains arise
232.	*Eki-kala beke-doto*	There is joyful shouting
233.	*Ma hema-kala bekao.*	And a great clamour.

234.	*Besaka fetok bei Ninga Ladi la*	Now the girls still at Ninga Ladi
235.	*Inak-a bei Hengu Hena la*	And the women still at Hengu Hena
236.	*Inak bei Tena Dua la*	The women still at Tena Dua
237.	*Do fetok bei Bote Telu la*	Or the girls still at Bote Telu
238.	*Inak-a Pua Kene*	The women, Pua Kene
239.	*Ma fetok-a No Kene*	And the girl, No Kene
240.	*Ana tolomu sasali*	She comes running
241.	*Ma nalai lelena*	And she come hurrying
242.	*Mai de ana ifa neni Lutu Mo*	There she cradles and carries away Lutu Mo
243.	*Ma ko'o neni Lutu Mala*	And embraces and carries away Lutu Mala
244.	*Neu de ana tane nasamamaon*	She goes and plans them tenderly
245.	*Ma ana sele nakaboboin*	And she sows them with care
246.	*De do belan-na lesu*	The heavy leaves come forth
247.	*Ma hu boko-na dadi*	The bending stalks arise
248.	*Kale dua-na tola*	The two kernels appear
249.	*Ma pule telu-na lesu*	And the three grains come forth
250.	*Eki-kala beke-doto*	There is joyful shouting
251.	*Ma hema-kala bekao*	And there is great clamour.
252.	*Boe ma fetok bei Tufa Laba*	The girls still at Tufa Laba
253.	*Ma inak bei Nëe Feo La*	And the women still at Nëe Feo
254.	*Ina bei Koa Ma'e la*	The women still a Koa Maë
255.	*Ma fetok bei Dae Dulu la*	And the girls still at Dae Dulu
256.	*Inak-a Hulu Nggela*	The woman, Hulu Nggela
257.	*Ma fetok-a Seu Lopo*	And the girl, Seu Lopo
258.	*Ana Tolomu sasali*	She comes running
259.	*Ma a la [lalai] lelena*	And she comes hurrying
260.	*Mai de ana ifa neni Doli Mo*	There she cradles and carries away Doli Mo
261.	*Ma ana ko'o neni Lutu Mala*	And she embraces and carries away Lutu Mala
262.	*De neu tane nasamamaon*	She goes and plants them tenderly
263.	*Ma sele nakaboboin*	And she sows them with care
264.	*De hu boko-na tola*	The bending stalks appear
265.	*Ma do bela-na dadi*	The heavy leaves arise
266.	*Ma kale dua-na lesu*	The two kernels come forth
267.	*Ma pule telu-na dadi*	And the three grains arise
268.	*Eki-kala beke-doto*	There is joyful shouting
269.	*Ma hema-kala bekao*	And there is great clamour
270.	*Boe ma besaka feto bei Pia Ketu la*	Now the girls still at Pia Ketu
271.	*Do inak bei Faka Ladi la*	Or the women still at Faka Ladi

272.	*Inak bei Pila Sue la*	The women still at Pila Sue
273.	*Do fetok bei Nggeo Deta la*	Or the girls still at Nggeo Deta
274.	*Inak bei Lona Fa la*	The women still at Lona Fa
275.	*Ma fetok bei Feo Ue la*	And the girls still at Feo Ue
276.	*Fetok-a Latu Lope*	The girl, Latu Lope
277.	*Do inak-a Meni Holo*	Or the woman, Meni Holo
278.	*Ana tolomu sasali*	She comes running
279.	*Do nalai lelena*	Or she comes hurrying
280.	*De ana mai de ana ifa neni Doli Mo*	She cradles and carries away Doli Mo
281.	*Ma ana ko'o neni Lutu Mala*	And she embraces and carries away Lutu Mala
282.	*De ana tane nasamamaon*	She plants them tenderly
283.	*Me sele nakaboboin*	And she sows them with care
284.	*De do bela-na dadi*	The heavy leaves arise
285.	*Ma hu boko-na lesu*	The bending stalks come forth
286.	*Ma pule dua-na dadi*	The two grains arise
287.	*Ma kale telu-na tola*	And the three kernels appear
288.	*Eki-kala beke-doto*	There is joyful shouting
289.	*Ma hema-kala bekao*	And there is great clamour.
290.	*Boe ma besak-a feto bei Ndule Oe la*	Now the girls still at Ndule Oe
291.	*Ma ina bei Medi Dae la*	And the women still at Medi Dae
292.	*Ala tolomu sasali*	They come running
293.	*Ma lalai lelena*	And they come hurrying
294.	*De ala ifa leni Doli Mo*	They cradle and carry away Doli Mo
295.	*Ma ko'o leni Lutu Mala*	And they embrace and carry away Lutu Mala
296.	*Leu de tane nasamamaon*	They go and they plant them tenderly
297.	*Ma sele lakaboboin*	And they sow them with care
298.	*De inak-a Le Feko*	The woman, Le Feko
299.	*Ma fetok-a Tuni Dae*	And the girl, Tuni Dae
300.	*Ifa do ko'o nenin*	Cradles and embraces them away
301.	*De neu de ana tane*	She goes and she plants
302.	*Do ana selen*	Or she sows them
303.	*De do bela-na tola*	The heavy leaves appear
304.	*Ma hu boko-na dadi*	And the bending stalks arise
305.	*Ma kale dua-na lesu*	And the two kernels come forth
306.	*Ma pule telu-na dadi*	And the three grains arise
307.	*Eki-kala beke-doto*	There is joyful shouting
308.	*Ma hema-kala bekao*	And there is great clamour
309.	*Fai esa manuni-na*	On a certain day

310.	*Ma ledo esa matebe-na*	And at a particular time
311.	*Inak bei Lenu Petu*	The woman still at Lenu Petu
312.	*Do fetok bei Safe Solo*	Or the girl still at Safe Solo
313.	*Fetok bei Soni Manu*	The girl still at Soni Manu
314.	*Ma inak bei Koko Te*	And the woman still at Koko Te
315.	*Inak bei Di Bolo la*	The women still at Di Bolo
316.	*[Missing Line]*	
317.	*Ma fetok Fua Mengo la*	And the girl Fue Mengo
318.	*Ma inaka Koko Meti mai*	And the woman, Koko Meti, comes
319.	*De ana ifa do ko'o neni*	She cradles and embraces away
320.	*Doli Mo ma Lutu Mala*	Doli Mo and Lutu Mala
321.	*Neu de ana tane nasamamaon*	She goes and she plants them tenderly
322.	*Ma ana sele nakaboboin*	And she sows them with care
323.	*Bei nai Lenu Petu*	Still at Lenu Petu
324.	*Ma bei nai Safe Solo*	And still at Safe Solo
325.	*Hu boko-na dadi*	The bending stalks arise
326.	*Ma kale dua-na tola*	And the two kernals appear
327.	*Ma pule telu-na dadi*	The three grains arise
328.	*Ma do bela-na moli*	And the heavy leaves appear
329.	*Eki-kala beke-doto*	There is joyful shouting
330.	*Ma hema-kala bekao*	And there is great clamour
331.	*Besak-a fetok bei Diu Dulu la*	Now the girls still at Diu Dulu
332.	*Do inak bei Kana Langa*	Or the women still at Kana Langa
333.	*Inak bei Pinga Dai*	The women still at Pinga Dai
334.	*Do fetok bei Lata Nae la*	Or the girls still at Lata Nae
335.	*Inak bei Oli Henu la*	The woman still at Oli Henu
336.	*Ma fetok bei Le Lilo la*	And the girl still at Le Lilo
337.	*Do inak bei Keka Mali la*	Or the woman still at Keka Mali
338.	*Ma fetok bei Dano Hela*	Or the girl still at Dano Hela
339.	*Fetok bei Pele Pou la*	The girls still at Pele Pou
340.	*Ma nak bei Nggafu Lafa la*	Or the women still at Nggafu Lafa
341.	*De inak-a Leo Lata*	The women, Leo Lata
342.	*Ma fetok-a Adu Pinga*	And the girl, Adu-Pinga
343.	*Ana tolomu sasali*	She comes running
344.	*Ma nalai lelena*	And she comes hurrying
345.	*Mai de ana ifa neni Doli Mo*	She comes and she cradles and carries away Doli Mo
346.	*Ma ana ko'o neni Lutu Mala*	And she embraces and carries away Lutu Mala
347.	*De tane neu Diu Dulu*	She plants them at Diu Dulu
348.	*Ma sele neu Kana Langa*	And she sows them at Kana Langa

349.	*Sele neu Pele Pou*	She sows them at Pele Pou
350.	*Ma tane neu Nggafu Lafa*	And she plants them at Nggafu Lafa
351.	*Do belna-na dadi*	The heavy leaves arise
352.	*Ma hu boko-na tola*	The bending stalks appear
353.	*Ma kale dua-na lesu*	The two kernels come forth
354.	*Ma pule telu-na dadi*	And the three grains arise
355.	*Eki-kala beke-doto*	There is joyful shouting
356.	*Ma hema-kala bekao*	And there is great clamour
357.	*Boe ma besak-a fetok bei Pengo Dua la*	Now the girls still at Pengo Dua
358.	*Ma inak bei Hilu Telu la*	And the women still at Hilu Telu
359.	*Inak bei Nggia Lu'u la*	The women still at Nggia Lu'u
360.	*Ma fetok bei Koa Sa'e*	And the girls still at Koa Sa'e
361.	*Fetok bei Fetu Fi la*	The girls still at Fetu Fi
362.	*Do inak bei Tane Bau la*	Or the women still at Tane Bau
363.	*Inak-a Pila Bengu*	The woman, Pila Bengu
364.	*Ma fetok-a Nggeo Laö*	And the girl, Nggeo Laö
365.	*Ana mai de ana ifa neni Doli Mo*	She comes and she cradles and carries away Doli Mo
366.	*Ma ko'o neni Lutu Mala*	She embraces and carries away Lutu Mala
367.	*Boe ma ana tane nasamamaon*	She plants them tenderly
368.	*Ma ana sele nakaboboin*	She sows them with care
369.	*De bela-na dadi*	The heavy leaves arise
370.	*Ma hu boko-na tola*	The bending stalks appear
371.	*Pule dua-na lesu*	The two grains come forth
372.	*Ma kale telu-na dadi.*	And the three kernels arise.
373.	*Eki-kala beke-doto*	There is joyful shouting
374.	*Ma hema-kala bekao.*	And there is great clamour.
375.	*Boe ma besak-a fetok bei Londa Lusi la*	Now the girls still at Londa Lusi
376.	*Ma inak-a bei Batu Bela la*	And the women still at Batu Bela
377.	*Inak bei Tua Nae la*	The women still at Tua Nae
378.	*Ma fetok bei Selu Beba la*	And the girls still at Selu Beba
379.	*Fetok bei Huni Hopo la*	The girls still at Huni Hopo
380.	*Inak bei Tefu Mafo la*	The women still at Tefu Mafo
381.	*Ala tolomu sasali*	They come running
382.	*Ma lalai lelena.*	And they come hurrying.
383.	*Inak-a Oko Meti*	The woman, Oko Meti
384.	*Do fetok-a Tui Beba*	Or the girl, Tui Beba
385.	*Mai ifa neni Doli Mo*	She cradles and carries away Doli Mo
386.	*Ma ko'o neni Lutu Mala*	And she embraces and carries away Lutu Mala

387.	*De neni neu Londa Lusi*	She carries them to Londa Lusi
388.	*Ma neni neu Batu Bela*	She carries them to Batu Bela
389.	*Ma neni neu Tua Nae*	She carries them to Tua Nae
390.	*Ma neni neu Sula Beba*	She carries them to Selu Beba
391.	*Neni neu Huni Hopo*	She carries them to Huni Hopo
392.	*Do neni neu Tefu Ma'o [Mafo]*	Or she carries them to Tefu Ma'o
393.	*Tane nasamamaon*	She plants them tenderly
394.	*Ma sele nakaboboin*	She sows them with care
395.	*De hu boko-na tola*	The bending stalks appear
396.	*Ma do bela-na dadi*	And the heavy leaves arise
397.	*Ma kale dua-na lesu*	The two kernels come forth
398.	*Ma pule telu-na dadi*	And the three grains arise
399.	*Eki-kala beke-doto*	There is joyful shouting
400.	*Ma hema-kala bekao.*	And there is great clamour.
401.	*Boe ma feto bei Fai Fua la*	The girls still at Fai Fua
402.	*Do ina bei Do Ina [?]*	Or the women still at Do Ina
403.	*Bei Ledo Sou la*	Still at Ledo Sou
404.	*Inak-a Meda Afe*	The woman, Meda Afe
405.	*Ma fetok-a Tai Nggenge*	And the girl, Tai Nggenge
406.	*Leni neu Ledo Sou*	They carry them to Ledo Sou
407.	*Ma leni neu Fai Fua*	And carry them to Fai Fua
408.	*Ma leni neu Oe Manu*	And carry them to Oe Manu
409.	*Ma leni neu Fi Iko*	And carry them to Fi Iko
410.	*Tane nasamamaon*	They plant them tenderly
411.	*Ma sele nakaboboin*	And sow them with care
412.	*De hu boko-na tola*	The bending stalks appear
413.	*Ma do bela-na dadi*	And the heavy leaves arise
414.	*Kale dua-na lesu*	The two kernels come forth
415.	*Ma pule telu-na moli*	And the three grains appear
416.	*Boe ma eki-kala beke-doto*	There is joyful shouting
417.	*Ma hema-kala bekao.*	There is great clamour
418.	*Boe ma fetok bei Bolo Tenda la*	The girls still at Bolo Tenda
419.	*Do inak bei Soti Mori la*	Or the women still at Soti Mori
420.	*Inak bei Tena Lai la*	The women still at Tena Lai
421.	*Do fetok bei Mae Oe la*	Or the girls still at Mae Oe
422.	*Tolomu sasali*	They come running
423.	*Ma lalai lelena*	And they come hurrying
424.	*Mai de ifa leni Doli Mo*	They come and cradle and carry away Doli Mo
425.	*Ma ko'o leni Lutu Mala*	And embrace and carry away Lutu Mala

426.	*Leu de ala tane neu Mae Oe*	They go and they plant them at Mae Oe
427.	*Ma sele neu Tena Lai*	And they sow them at Tena Lai
428.	*Te fu'ak ta Mae Oe*	But there is no plain at Mae Oe
429.	*Ma mok ta Tena Lai*	And there is no field at Tena Lai
430.	*De Doli ta dadi*	So Doli does not rise
431.	*Ma Lutu ta moli*	And Lutu does not appear
432.	*Nduku faik ia*	To this day
433.	*Ma losa ledok ia.*	To this time.

The person who has told this history is Petrus Malesi.

Index

Adulanu, Ayub 297, 303, 304, 305n.6, 311, 313
Adulanu, Stefanus (Old Meno) xi, 6, 10, 13, 14, 15, 91n.2, 94n.7, 148, 150n.4, 154n.8, 204–10, 231–4, 236, 242, 247–50, 252, 253, 255, 269n.1, 275, 284, 295–7, 299–301, 303–7, 311, 312, 344, 373, 419
Amalo, Ernst 295, 296, 313, 372
Amalo, Stefanus 15, 235, 246, 247, 252, 254, 284
ancestors 73, 84, 95, 105, 154, 185, 186, 265, 269, 293, 313, 344, 345, 350, 370, 384
anthropology 3, 7, 20, 23, 29, 149, 150, 174, 183n.2, 190, 204, 219n.1
asymmetry 40, 120, 186, 189, 193, 197
  see also symmetry

Ba'a 38, 96, 137, 146, 162, 187, 249, 295, 303n.5, 305, 312, 324, 327, 332, 368
Bible 22, 24n.7, 38, 42, 46, 47, 69, 76, 92, 94n.6, 133, 151, 152, 171, 172, 301, 321, 326, 358
  Malay 10, 319, 340, 343, 351, 358, 361
  Scriptures 10, 352, 372
Biblical 4, 5, 8, 11, 25, 33, 42–8, 54, 59, 91, 95n.8, 133, 151, 172, 219, 301, 308, 317–41, 343, 351, 352, 358, 359
Bilba 136, 137, 144, 146, 280, 298n.1, 325, 366, 368, 369, 370, 372, 375, 376, 377, 385
bini (named chants) 91, 95, 96, 97, 105, 109, 131, 138, 139, 140, 141, 143, 146, 202, 219, 306, 308, 344
  see also chants, individual chant names
Bokai 135, 137, 221, 366, 368

chants
  mortuary 10, 13, 14, 59, 82, 202, 203, 219, 220, 221, 232, 245, 246, 248, 254, 256, 283, 284, 329, 349, 350
  origin 10, 12, 14, 15, 17, 115, 152, 154, 203, 219–21, 226, 227, 247, 250, 256, 266, 269–73, 277–82, 309, 313–41, 344, 350, 352, 356, 373, 374, 384
  see also *bini*, individual chant names
chotbah 355, 360
  see also sermon
Christianity 10, 67, 69, 75, 130, 133, 172, 255, 282, 317–19, 321, 323, 324, 326, 327–33, 340, 343, 352, 355, 371
  conversion to 12, 132, 317, 319, 351
  spread of 94n.6, 220
church 15, 19, 133, 305, 319, 320, 321, 323, 326, 327, 352
  see also Islam, religion

Dela Koli ma Seko Bunak 6, 13, 14, 99, 106–19
Delha 98, 102, 103, 115, 126, 136, 137, 268, 356, 369
Dengka 137, 144, 325, 366, 368, 369, 370, 372, 375, 376
dialects 70, 78, 79, 88, 133, 171, 184, 384, 385
  areas 6n.3, 11, 15, 153, 161n.10, 172, 201, 204, 245, 246, 266, 326, 359, 366, 367, 369, 370, 386
  Rotenese 9, 17, 18, 45, 59, 87, 95, 108, 109, 129, 131, 134–7, 144–7, 201–2, 204, 212, 214–15, 221–2, 229, 322, 323, 327, 328, 351, 356, 357, 368, 371–9, 381, 385
  see also Termanu—dialect, Thie—dialect
Doli Mo ma Lutu Mala 221, 250, 269, 419
domains, see *nusak*, individual names
Dutch East India Company 129, 131–4, 136, 233, 318, 319, 328, 343, 351, 366, 369

education 133, 319, 325, 343
  see also schools
ethnography 9, 22, 75, 80, 81, 93, 95, 98, 129, 150, 169, 182, 183, 186, 191, 196, 265, 283n.1, 355, 364n.3, 384, 385

formulaic 24, 52, 77, 85, 91–3, 98, 105, 109, 113, 141, 146, 149n.2, 178,

433

201–15, 233, 244, 245, 248, 256, 308, 322, 344, 380
  chains 105, 116, 117, 246
  expressions 9, 47, 374, 376
  parallelism 74, 229n.2, 277, 384
  phrases 138, 171, 187, 270, 374
  sequence 250, 252, 253, 254, 255
  structure 82

genealogy 10, 13, 52, 71, 95, 96, 114–18, 153, 178, 222–8, 246–8, 265–7, 269, 276, 284, 285, 298–300, 349, 376

Helong 131, 132, 369
Hopkins, Gerard, Manley 3, 19, 20, 28

Islam 80, 304, 355, 384
Iu, Yulius 337

Jakobson, Roman 3, 4, 6–8, 19–40, 41, 42, 47, 48, 72, 86, 91, 92, 147, 149n.1, 160, 174, 180, 187, 204, 244

Kea Lenga ma Lona Balo 253n.8, 254
Keka 135, 137, 144, 146, 230n.3, 302, 322, 368
Korbaffo 136, 144, 271, 279, 280, 306, 307, 312, 325, 366, 368
Kramer, Samuel Noah 4, 5n.1, 29, 33, 49, 50, 51
Kupang 132, 133, 136, 149n.1, 150n.4, 222n.4, 229n.1, 318, 320, 321, 351, 357, 364

Landu 136, 270, 273, 282, 326, 333, 334, 337, 366, 368–72, 375, 376, 377
Lelenuk 136, 368
Loleh 137, 144, 145, 146, 184, 273, 325, 327, 332, 366, 369, 372
Lowth, Robert 4, 5, 20, 21, 22, 25, 27, 31, 32, 42, 47, 71, 89, 91, 121, 143, 151, 152

Malay 9, 10, 12, 79, 131, 132, 133, 136, 317–22, 326, 343, 351, 355, 356, 357–60, 361, 363
  schools 17, 18
  words 78, 109n.17, 145, 328
  see also Bible—Malay
Malayo-Polynesian 24, 376
Malesi, Petrus (Peu) ix, 14, 15, 17, 154n.8, 171, 209–10, 231, 269n.1, 306–11, 313, 344, 345, 348–51, 419, 425–31
Manu Kama do Tepa Nilu 224, 229, 230–56, 322
Maya 4, 7, 29, 34, 38, 60, 63, 64, 65, 66, 67, 68, 69, 85, 86, 87, 88, 92, 130, 147, 152, 179, 374, 377, 378
Meda Manu ma Lilo Losi 153n.7, 249, 253
mortuary chants, *see* chants—mortuary
Muslim, *see* Islam

named chants, *see bini*, individual chant names
Ndao 131, 132, 135, 177, 254, 306, 332, 333
Ndi Loniama ma Laki Elokama 153n.7, 221, 329
network analysis 9, 39, 48, 87, 88, 119, 141–3, 161, 162, 166, 169, 170, 172, 173, 178, 179, 204, 244, 296, 363, 379–83
nusak (domain) 134, 135, 266, 356, 357, 366
  see also individual domain names

Oenale 96n.9, 136, 137, 145, 325, 366, 368, 369, 370, 372, 375, 376
Oepao 131, 136, 194, 366, 368, 370
origin chants, *see* chants—origin, individual chant names

Pau Balo ma Bola Lungi 15, 221, 254
Peirce, Charles Sanders 7
Pellondou, Eli (Seu Ba'i) 206, 211, 247
Pellondou, Mikael 208
Pono, Esau (Pak Pono) ix, 15, 16, 17, 304, 311, 356, 360, 367, 368, 381

religion 63, 75, 171, 343
  Catholic 75, 80, 281, 282, 343
  Protestant 171, 189, 255n.9, 281, 320n.1, 328, 334, 343, 356, 358, 364
  see also church, Islam

religious 27, 67, 79, 120, 197, 228, 230n.3, 300, 320, 352, 353, 355, 372
    language 23, 30, 80, 96
Ringgou 17, 136, 137, 144, 202, 210, 212, 325–7, 333, 334, 336, 337, 366, 368, 370–3, 375, 376, 377
Rotenese dialects, *see* dialects—Rotenese
Ruy, Ande (Pak Ande) 17, 210, 212, 213, 214, 336, 337, 367, 368, 371, 372

schools 10, 17, 18, 80, 95n.8, 130, 132, 133, 318–19, 320–3, 325–7, 343, 351, 357, 364
    see also education
sermon 11, 129, 133, 189, 202, 219, 355–64
    see also chotbah
Suti Solo do Bina Bane 9, 15, 202, 203, 204–13, 221n.3, 249, 250, 251, 372–4
symmetry 27
    see also asymmetry

Talae 135, 137, 144, 222n.4, 302, 322, 368
Teke Telu ma Koa Hulu 345, 349, 350
Termanu 6, 14, 15, 96n.9, 97, 108, 109, 115, 126, 137, 145, 153n.7, 162, 179, 198, 202–5, 221–7, 247, 268–76, 277–8, 295, 296, 300–2, 305, 309, 313, 318, 319, 320, 327, 328, 333, 344, 360, 365, 366, 372–6
    dialect 9, 38, 107, 142, 145, 146, 162, 202, 212, 213, 267, 298n.1, 322, 327, 377–82
    poets 6, 14, 15, 91n.2, 148, 150n.4, 204, 209, 214, 231, 232, 255, 280, 284, 295, 306, 360, 368, 370, 371
Thie 15, 94n.7, 184, 185, 191, 198, 199, 202, 222–7, 268, 308n.7, 318, 319, 325, 327, 328, 332, 365, 366, 369, 372, 394
    dialect 38, 94, 137, 144–6, 368, 375
    poets 14, 368, 370

Water of Words' (lontar gin) 91, 97, 211

www.ingramcontent.com/pod-product-compliance
Lightning Source LLC
Chambersburg PA
CBHW040934240426
43670CB00033B/2970